The Global Commercial Aviation Industry

This book provides a state-of-the-art overview of the changes and development of the civil international aircraft/aviation industry. It offers a fully up-to-date account of the international developments and structure in the aircraft and aviation industries from a number of perspectives, which include economic, geographical, political and technological points of view.

The aircraft industry is characterized by very complex, high-technology products produced in relatively small quantities. The high-technology requirements necessitate a high level of R&D. There exist few other industries with a higher level of inter-dependence and cross-fertilization of advanced technology. Consequently, most of the world's large aircraft companies and technology leaders have been located in Europe and North America. During the last few decades many developing countries have tried to build up an internationally competitive aircraft industry.

The authors study a number of important issues, including the political economy of the aircraft industry, globalization in this industry, innovation, newly industrializing economies and the aircraft industry. This book also explores regional and large aircraft, transformation of the aviation industry in Central and Eastern Europe, including engines, airlines, airports and airline safety. It will be of great value to students and to researchers seeking information on the aircraft industry and its development in different regions.

Sören Eriksson is Professor of Economic Geography at JIBS, Sweden.

Harm-Jan Steenhuis is Professor of Management, International Business at the College of Business, Hawaii Pacific University, USA.

Routledge studies in the modern world economy

1 **Interest Rates and Budget Deficits**
A study of the advanced economies
Kanhaya L. Gupta and Bakhtiar Moazzami

2 **World Trade after the Uruguay Round**
Prospects and policy options for the twenty-first century
Edited by Harald Sander and András Inotai

3 **The Flow Analysis of Labour Markets**
Edited by Ronald Schettkat

4 **Inflation and Unemployment**
Contributions to a new macroeconomic approach
Edited by Alvaro Cencini and Mauro Baranzini

5 **Macroeconomic Dimensions of Public Finance**
Essays in honour of Vito Tanzi
Edited by Mario I. Blejer and Teresa M. Ter-Minassian

6 **Fiscal Policy and Economic Reforms**
Essays in honour of Vito Tanzi
Edited by Mario I. Blejer and Teresa M. Ter-Minassian

7 **Competition Policy in the Global Economy**
Modalities for co-operation
Edited by Leonard Waverman, William S. Comanor and Akira Goto

8 **Working in the Macro Economy**
A study of the US labor market
Martin F.J. Prachowny

9 **How Does Privatization Work?**
Edited by Anthony Bennett

10 **The Economics and Politics of International Trade**
Freedom and trade: volume II
Edited by Gary Cook

11 **The Legal and Moral Aspects of International Trade**
Freedom and trade: volume III
Edited by Asif Qureshi, Hillel Steiner and Geraint Parry

12 **Capital Markets and Corporate Governance in Japan, Germany and the United States**
Organizational response to market inefficiencies
Helmut M. Dietl

13 **Competition and Trade Policies**
Coherence or conflict
Edited by Einar Hope

14 **Rice**
The primary commodity
A.J.H. Latham

15 **Trade, Theory and Econometrics**
Essays in honour of John S. Chipman
Edited by James C. Moore, Raymond Riezman and James R. Melvin

16 **Who Benefits from Privatisation?**
Edited by Moazzem Hossain and Justin Malbon

17 **Towards a Fair Global Labour Market**
Avoiding the new slave trade
Ozay Mehmet, Errol Mendes and Robert Sinding

18 **Models of Futures Markets**
Edited by Barry Goss

19 **Venture Capital Investment**
An agency analysis of UK practice
Gavin C. Reid

20 **Macroeconomic Forecasting**
A sociological appraisal
Robert Evans

21 **Multimedia and Regional Economic Restructuring**
Edited by Hans-Joachim Braczyk, Gerhard Fuchs and Hans-Georg Wolf

22 **The New Industrial Geography**
Regions, regulation and institutions
Edited by Trevor J. Barnes and Meric S. Gertler

23 **The Employment Impact of Innovation**
Evidence and policy
Edited by Marco Vivarelli and Mario Pianta

24 **International Health Care Reform**
A legal, economic and political analysis
Colleen Flood

25 **Competition Policy Analysis**
Edited by Einar Hope

26 **Culture and Enterprise**
The development, representation and morality of business
Don Lavoie and Emily Chamlee-Wright

27 **Global Financial Crises and Reforms**
Cases and caveats
B.N. Ghosh

28 **Geography of Production and Economic Integration**
Miroslav N. Jovanović

29 **Technology, Trade and Growth in OECD Countries**
Does specialisation matter?
Valentina Meliciani

30 **Post-Industrial Labour Markets**
Profiles of North America and Scandinavia
Edited by Thomas P. Boje and Bengt Furaker

31 Capital Flows without Crisis
Reconciling capital mobility and economic stability
Edited by Dipak Dasgupta, Marc Uzan and Dominic Wilson

32 International Trade and National Welfare
Murray C. Kemp

33 Global Trading Systems at Crossroads
A post-Seattle perspective
Dilip K. Das

34 The Economics and Management of Technological Diversification
Edited by John Cantwell, Alfonso Gambardella and Ove Granstrand

35 Before and Beyond EMU
Historical lessons and future prospects
Edited by Patrick Crowley

36 Fiscal Decentralization
Ehtisham Ahmad and Vito Tanzi

37 Regionalisation of Globalised Innovation
Locations for advanced industrial development and disparities in participation
Edited by Ulrich Hilpert

38 Gold and the Modern World Economy
Edited by MoonJoong Tcha

39 Global Economic Institutions
Willem Molle

40 Global Governance and Financial Crises
Edited by Meghnad Desai and Yahia Said

41 Linking Local and Global Economies
The ties that bind
Edited by Carlo Pietrobelli and Arni Sverrisson

42 Tax Systems and Tax Reforms in Europe
Edited by Luigi Bernardi and Paola Profeta

43 Trade Liberalization and APEC
Edited by Jiro Okamoto

44 Fiscal Deficits in the Pacific Region
Edited by Akira Kohsaka

45 Financial Globalization and the Emerging Market Economies
Dilip K. Das

46 International Labor Mobility
Unemployment and increasing returns to scale
Bharati Basu

47 Good Governance in the Era of Global Neoliberalism
Conflict and depolitization in Latin America, Eastern Europe, Asia and Africa
Edited by Jolle Demmers, Alex E. Fernández Jilberto and Barbara Hogenboom

48 The International Trade System
Alice Landau

49 **International Perspectives on Temporary Work and Workers**
Edited by John Burgess and Julia Connell

50 **Working Time and Workers' Preferences in Industrialized Countries**
Finding the balance
Edited by Jon C. Messenger

51 **Tax Systems and Tax Reforms in New EU Members**
Edited by Luigi Bernardi, Mark Chandler and Luca Gandullia

52 **Globalization and the Nation State**
The impact of the IMF and the World Bank
Edited by Gustav Ranis, James Vreeland and Stephen Kosak

53 **Macroeconomic Policies and Poverty Reduction**
Edited by Ashoka Mody and Catherine Pattillo

54 **Regional Monetary Policy**
Carlos J. Rodríguez-Fuentez

55 **Trade and Migration in the Modern World**
Carl Mosk

56 **Globalisation and the Labour Market**
Trade, technology and less-skilled workers in Europe and the United States
Edited by Robert Anderton, Paul Brenton and John Whalley

57 **Financial Crises**
Socio-economic causes and institutional context
Brenda Spotton Visano

58 **Globalization and Self Determination**
Is the nation-state under siege?
Edited by David R. Cameron, Gustav Ranis and Annalisa Zinn

59 **Developing Countries and the Doha Development Round of the WTO**
Edited by Pitou van Dijck and Gerrit Faber

60 **Immigrant Enterprise in Europe and the USA**
Prodromos Panayiotopoulos

61 **Solving the Riddle of Globalization and Development**
Edited by Manuel Agosín, David Bloom, George Chapelier and Jagdish Saigal

62 **Foreign Direct Investment and the World Economy**
Ashoka Mody

63 **The World Economy**
A global analysis
Horst Siebert

64 **Production Organizations in Japanese Economic Development**
Edited by Tetsuji Okazaki

65 **The Economics of Language**
International analyses
Edited by Barry R. Chiswick and Paul W. Miller

66 Street Entrepreneurs
People, place and politics in local and global perspective
Edited by John Cross and Alfonso Morales

67 Global Challenges and Local Responses
The East Asian experience
Edited by Jang-Sup Shin

68 Globalization and Regional Integration
The origins, development and impact of the single European aviation market
Alan Dobson

69 Russia Moves into the Global Economy
Breaking out
John M. Letiche

70 The European Economy in an American Mirror
Barry Eichengreen, Michael Landesmann and Dieter Stiefel

71 Working Time Around the World
Trends in working hours, laws, and policies in a global comparative perspective
Jon C. Messenger, Sangheon Lee and Deidre McCann

72 International Water Treaties
Negotiation and cooperation along transboundary rivers
Shlomi Dinar

73 Economic Integration in the Americas
Edited by Joseph A. McKinney and H. Stephen Gardner

74 Expanding Frontiers of Global Trade Rules
The political economy dynamics of the international trading system
Nitya Nanda

75 The Macroeconomics of Global Imbalances
European and Asian perspectives
Edited by Marc Uzan

76 China and Asia
Economic and financial interactions
Edited by Yin-Wong Cheung and Kar-Yiu Wong

77 Regional Inequality in China
Trends, explanations and policy responses
Edited by Shenggen Fan, Ravi Kanbur and Xiaobo Zhang

78 Governing Rapid Growth in China
Equity and institutions
Edited by Ravi Kanbur and Xiaobo Zhang

79 The Indonesian Labour Market
Shafiq Dhanani, Iyanatul Islam and Anis Chowdhury

80 Cost–Benefit Analysis in Multi-level Government in Europe and the USA
The case of EU cohesion policy and of US federal investment policies
Alessandro Ferrara

81 The Economic Geography of Air Transportation
Space, time, and the freedom of the sky
John Bowen

82 **Cartelization, Antitrust and Globalization in the US and Europe**
Mark LeClair

83 **The Political Economy of Integration**
Jeffrey Cason

84 **Critical Issues in Air Transport Economics and Business**
Rosario Macario and Eddy Van de Voorde

85 **Financial Liberalisation and Economic Performance**
Luiz Fernando de Paula

86 **A General Theory of Institutional Change**
Shiping Tang

87 **The Dynamics of Asian Financial Integration**
Edited by Michael Devereux, Philip Lane, Park Cyn-young and Wei Shang-jin

88 **Innovative Fiscal Policy and Economic Development in Transition Economies**
Aleksandr Gevorkyan

89 **Foreign Direct Investments in Asia**
Edited by Chalongphob Sussangkarn, Yung Chul Park and Sung Jin Kang

90 **Time Zones, Communications Networks, and International Trade**
Toru Kikuchi

91 **Miraculous Growth and Stagnation in Post-War Japan**
Edited by Koichi Hamada, Keijiro Otsuka, Gustav Ranis, and Ken Togo

92 **Multilateralism and Regionalism in Global Economic Governance**
Trade, investment and finance
Edited by Junji Nakagawa

93 **Economic Growth and Income Inequality in China, India and Singapore**
Trends and policy implications
Pundarik Mukhopadhaya, G. Shantakumar and Bhanoji Rao

94 **Foreign Direct Investment in China**
Spillover effects on domestic enterprises
Deng Ziliang

95 **Enterprise Forms and Economic Efficiency**
Capitalist, cooperative and government firms
Kazuhiko Mikami

96 **Diversity and Transformations of Asian Capitalism**
Edited by R. Boyer, H. Uemura and A. Isogai

97 **Knowledge Transfer in the Automobile Industry**
Global–local production networks
Dessy Irawati

98 **Exchange Rates and Foreign Direct Investment in Emerging Asia**
Selected issues and policy options
Ramkishen S. Rajan

99 **Singapore, the Energy Economy**
From the first refinery to the end of cheap oil, 1960–2010
Ng Weng Hoong

100 **China–India Economics**
Challenges, competition and collaboration
Amitendu Palit

101 **Case Studies on Chinese Enterprises**
Edited by Donglin Xia

102 **Argentina's Economic Growth and Recovery**
Michael Cohen

103 **The Korean Labour Market After the 1997 Economic Crisis**
Edited by Joonmo Cho, Richard B. Freeman, Jaeho Keum and Sunwoong Kim

104 **China and India**
The quest for energy resources in the 21st century
Zhao Hong

105 **Beyond the Global Crisis**
Structural adjustments and regional integration in Europe and Latin America
Edited by Lionello Punzo, Carmen Aparecida Feio and Martin Putchet Anyui

106 **The Global Economic Crisis in Latin America**
Impacts and responses
Edited by Michael Cohen

107 **The Processes and Practices of Fair Trade**
Trust, ethics and governance
Edited by Brigitte Granville and Janet Dine

108 **Regional Development through Ecological Business**
Unique cases in Japanese rural regions
Makoto Hirano

109 **Aging and Economic Growth Potentials in the Pacific Region**
Edited by Akira Kohsaka

110 **Crises of Global Economy and the Future of Capitalism**
An insight into the Marx's crisis theory
Edited by Kiichiro Yagi, Nobuharu Yokokawa, Shinjiro Hagiwara and Gary A. Dymski

111 **The Financial History of the Bank for International Settlements**
Kazuhiko Yago

112 **Freight Transport and the Modern Economy**
Michel Savy and June Burnham

113 **Thoughts on Economic Development in China**
Edited by Ma Ying and Hans-Michael Trautwein

114 **China's Ethnic Minorities**
Social and economic indicators
Rongxing Guo

115 **Globalization, Outsourcing and Labour Development in ASEAN**
Shandre Thangavelu and Aekapol Chongvilaivan

116 **The Role of Informal Economies in the Post-Soviet World**
The end of transition?
Colin C. Williams, John Round and Peter Rodgers

117 **Demystifying the Chinese Economy Miracle**
The rise and future of relational capitalism
Yongqin Wang

118 **Globalism and Regional Economy**
Edited by Susumu Egashira

119 **Russia's Changing Economic and Political Regimes**
The Putin years and afterwards
Andrey Makarychev and André Mommen

120 **Innovation and Regional Development in China**
Edited by Ingo Liefner and Yehua Dennis Wei

121 **International Trade Negotiations and Domestic Politics**
The intermestic politics of trade liberalization
Edited by Oluf Langhelle

122 **Emerging Knowledge Economies in Asia**
Current trends in ASEAN 5
Edited by Dessy Irawati and Roel Rutten

123 **The Internationalization of the Renminbi**
International Monetary Institute, Renmin University of China

124 **Financial Globalization and Regionalism in East Asia**
Edited by Takuji Kinkyo, Yoichi Matsubayashi and Shigeyuki Hamori

125 **Successful Business Dealings and Management with China Oil, Gas and Chemical Giants**
EurIng. Henry K.H. Wang

126 **State Building and Development**
Edited by Keijiro Otsuka and Takashi Shiraishi

127 **International Economic Development**
Leading issues and challenges
Edited by Fu Lai Tony Yu, Wai Kee Yuen and Diana S. Kwan

128 **Innovation, Globalization and Firm Dynamics**
Lessons for enterprise policy
Edited by Anna Ferragina, Erol Taymoz and Kamil Yilmaz

129 **International Remittance Payments and the Global Economy**
Bharati Basu with James T. Bang

130 **The Open Society and its Enemies in East Asia**
The relevance of the Popperian framework
Edited by Gregory C.G. Moore

131 **The Economics of Knowledge Generation and Distribution**
The role of interactions in the system dynamics of innovation and growth
Edited by Pier Paolo Patrucco

132 **Japan's Aid**
Lessons for economic growth, development and political economy
Edward M. Feasel

133 **The Geographical Transformation of China**
Edited by Michael Dunford and Weidong Lui

134 **The Economics of Cooperative Education**
A practitioners' guide to the theoretical framework and empirical assessment of cooperative education
Yasushi Tanaka

135 **Comparing Post War Japanese and Finnish Economies and Societies**
Edited by Yasushi Tanaka, Toshiaki Tamaki, Jari Ojala and Jari Eloranta

136 **Measuring National Income in the Centrally Planned Economies**
Why the west underestimated the transition to capitalism
William Jefferies

137 **Crises in Europe in the Transatlantic Context**
Economic and political appraisals
Edited by Bruno Dallago and John McGowan

138 **The International Monetary System, Energy and Sustainable Development**
Edited by Sung Jin Kang and Yung Chul Park

139 **Capitalism and the World Economy**
The light and shadow of globalization
Edited by Toshiaki Hirai

140 **Irish Economic Development**
High-performing EU state or serial under-achiever?
Eoin O'Leary

141 **Banking on Equality**
Women, work and employment in the banking sector in India
Supriti Bezbaruah

142 **Poverty, Inequality and Growth in Developing Countries**
Theoretical and empirical approaches
Edited by Atsushi Maki

143 **Decentralization and Infrastructure in the Global Economy**
From gaps to solutions
Edited by Jonas Frank and Jorge Martínez-Vázquez

144 **The Global Commercial Aviation Industry**
Edited by Sören Eriksson and Harm-Jan Steenhuis

The Global Commercial Aviation Industry

Edited by Sören Eriksson and Harm-Jan Steenhuis

Routledge
Taylor & Francis Group
LONDON AND NEW YORK

First published 2016
by Routledge
2 Park Square, Milton Park, Abingdon, Oxon OX14 4RN

by Routledge
711 Third Avenue, New York, NY 10017

Routledge is an imprint of the Taylor & Francis Group, an informa business

British Library Cataloguing in Publication Data
A catalogue record for this book is available from the British Library

Library of Congress Cataloging-in-Publication Data
The global commercial aviation industry / edited by Sören Eriksson, Harm-jan Steenhuis.
pages cm. – (Routledge studies in the modern world economy)
1. Aircraft industry. 2. Aeronautics, Commercial. I. Eriksson, Sören, editor. II. Steenhuis, Harm-jan, editor.
HD9711.A2G66 2015
338.4'762913334–dc23 2015003276

ISBN: 978-0-415-81821-6 (hbk)
ISBN: 978-0-203-58202-2 (ebk)

Typeset in Times New Roman
by Wearset Ltd, Boldon, Tyne and Wear

Printed and bound in the United States of America by Publishers Graphics, LLC on sustainably sourced paper.

Contents

Figures

Tables

Contributors

Hamad Al-kaabi undertook his PhD as a member of the Logistics Systems Dynamics Group at Cardiff University. His research focused mainly on the aviation supply chain, aviation maintenance and airlines logistics configurations. Hamad is now a Lecturer in Supply Chain Management and Operation Management at universities in Bahrain. He started his career as an aircraft engineer in the Bahrain Air Force, and later specialized in logistics. He has managed many projects in aviation, supply chains and healthcare.

Zbigniew Bochniarz is Affiliated Professor at the Evans School of Public Affairs, University of Washington in Seattle, United States. His teaching and research focus on strategies for sustainable development, competitiveness and clustering, particularly in the aerospace industry, as well as economic, environmental, institutional and social aspects of sustainability of the transformation processes in Central and Eastern Europe.

Isabelle Dostaler is Associate Professor in the Management Department at the John Molson School of Business, Concordia University, Montreal, Canada. Her research interests include airlines competitive strategies, the management of global aerospace supply chains as well as the management of aerospace product development.

Sören Eriksson is Professor of Economic Geography at Jönköping International Business School, Sweden. His teaching and research focus on global economic and industrial changes, East and Southeast Asia's economic and technology development, and regional development, including clusters and logistics issues. A main research interest is the aerospace industry. He has lectured, delivered seminars and has been appointed as a member of doctoral dissertation committees at a number of foreign universities and research establishments.

John Fiset is Assistant Professor-Lecturer in the Management Department at the John Molson School of Business, Concordia University, Montreal, Canada. His research interests include how leaders influence intragroup workplace dynamics, organizational ambidexterity, workplace ostracism and multilingualism at work.

Hans Heerkens has an MSc in Public Administration and a PhD in Decision Theory. His research is in importance of assessment processes, focusing on the aviation industry. He runs a course aimed at improving importance assessment processes for actors involved in strategic organizational decision processes. Hans teaches on research and design methodology at the University of Twente (Netherlands) and at several business schools, and does consultancy work on the aviation industry for the Dutch Ministry of Economic Affairs and others, focusing on the interplay between technological, economic and management issues in decision processes. He has made a large number of contributions on decision making and the aviation industry in national and international journals. He is chairman of the Platform Unmanned Cargo Aircraft.

Zbyněk Hruška is Executive Director of the Association of Aerospace Manufacturers of the Czech Republic, Prague. Within the scope of the association, Zbyněk is personally involved in promotion and protection of aerospace industry interests. Zbyněk is a member of the Czech Confederation of Industry Members Council and a Czech aircraft history enthusiast.

Alma Lozano is a consultant, trainer and coach specialized in strategic organizational effectiveness and progression. Alma holds a PhD in Strategic Studies from the Nanyang Technological University (Singapore) and works with high-performing organizations in a variety of industrial sectors around the world.

James Maquire received his MBA from Eastern Washington University, United States.

Mohamed Naim is the Deputy Dean at Cardiff Business School, Cardiff University. He is also a co-director of the Logistics Systems Dynamics Group and the Centre for Advanced Manufacturing Systems at Cardiff. He is currently the Cardiff lead on the £27m Welsh European Funding Office part-funded project Advanced Sustainable Manufacturing Technologies (ASTUTE). His current research interests may be summarized as the development of novel business systems engineering approaches to establish resilient supply chains. This encompasses sustainable supply chains and the role of flexibility in lean, agile and leagile systems.

Grzegorz Pisarczyk is a PhD candidate, researcher and Project Manager at Rzeszow School of Business, Poland. His teaching and research activities focus on management, group process facilitation, competitiveness and clustering, especially in the aerospace industry.

Andrew Potter is a reader in Transport and Logistics at Cardiff University. Much of his research has particularly focused on how freight transport can become more integrated within supply chains. However, he also has an interest in the aviation industry, through both research and teaching. Andrew is a Member of the Chartered Institute of Logistics and Transport (UK) and, as chair of the Cymru-Wales region in the UK, often provides commentary to the media on transport-related issues. He is a member of the Editorial Board of the *European Management Journal* and *International Journal of Logistics Management*.

Marie-Josée Roy is Full Professor at the Faculty of Business Administration of Université Laval, Canada. Roy teaches strategic management and her research interests include corporate social responsibility and corporate governance. She has written several articles on these topics, focusing on implementation issues and performance measurement.

Emilia Barbara Sienko-Kulakowska, PhD, is a researcher at Rzeszow School of Business, Poland. Her teaching and research activities focus on finance, management, competitiveness and clustering, especially in the aerospace industry.

Harm-Jan Steenhuis is Professor of Management, International Business at Hawaii Pacific University, United States. He has taught international operations; operations strategy; strategy, competitiveness and economic development; and operations and supply chain management. His main research interests include technological and economic development, international business, technology transfer, and the aerospace industry.

Daniel Todd was Professor of Geography at the University of Winnipeg, Canada before his retirement. His area of expertise is economic geography, specializing in transportation and transport-equipment industries.

Dániel Vértesy is a post-doc researcher at the Joint Research Centre of the European Commission in Ispra, Italy. His areas of expertise cover the evolution of the aerospace industry, sectorial innovation system dynamics, and measuring research and innovation performance. He graduated in international studies at the Corvinus University of Budapest, and obtained his PhD at UNU-MERIT/Maastricht University, where he conducted research on latecomer aircraft industries in emerging economies, with in-depth field visits to China and Brazil.

Josef Zbořil is a member of the European Economic and Social Committee, Brussels, Belgium, and resident of the Czech Republic. He is focused on industrial and transport affairs and change, sustainability and strategic planning, and competitiveness of industries in general. Josef was personally involved in the Czech industry transformation in the 1990s and is an honorary member of the Czech Confederation of Industry. He is an aircraft history and manufacturing enthusiast.

Preface

Sören Eriksson and Harm-Jan Steenhuis

After both of us met at Jönköping International School in February 2011, we started a discussion to develop a book about the aviation industry that included various facets of the industry. The main goal of the book is to provide a comprehensive overview of the global commercial aviation industry that partly includes a geographical element – that is, to look at where activities take place. This implies that several parts of the book deal with global economic and industrial changes within the aviation industry. Due to the enormous size, variations and different subsectors of the aviation industry, we are not able to deal with all parts of this multidimensional industry. For instance, we have excluded air traffic management, pure engineering, financing, etc. Within the aircraft manufacturing industry we have, among other things, excluded the manufacturers of large aircraft and the developments in that segment because a lot of literature already covers Airbus and Boeing, and we wouldn't be contributing much.

With those things in mind we decided to focus on some important and interesting topics, with the aim to present new and interesting dimensions. We invited experts and scholars with a common research interest in aviation, who together offer a rich and varied description of the global commercial aviation industry.

Chapter 1, 'The contours of global commercial aircraft manufacturing industry' by Dániel Vértesy, provides a starting point for the discussion. The chapter provides interesting statistical data on the global industry and its developments, most notably the second wave of internationalization. A main conclusion is that the global commercial aircraft industry is undergoing major transformation.

The next five chapters deal with different segments of the aviation industry. In Chapter 2, 'Regional aircraft' by Harm-Jan Steenhuis, the developments in the manufacturing of regional aircraft are analysed from 1980 onwards. These analyses show that the manufacturers in developing countries are becoming more prominent. Chapter 3, 'Airline companies: strategies and trends' by Isabelle Dostaler and John Fiset, looks at the users of aircraft, that is, the airlines. Their analysis delves into the consequences of deregulation, the trends in numbers of airlines and the formation of three major alliances. They conclude that airlines that survived the changing competitive landscape have either successfully seized the opportunities to create new business models or managed to thwart the threats posed by deregulation. Chapter 4, 'Engines' by Daniel Todd and Sören Eriksson, delves into a major component in aviation – the engine. The chapter describes the evolution of engine technologies and different placement options on the aircraft. It then proceeds with an analysis of global cooperation and concludes that the engine segment is still dominated by a few companies in industrialized nations. Another important part of the industry is covered in Chapter 5, on airports, by Dan Todd, James Maquire and Harm-Jan Steenhuis. This chapter describes the different types of airports and their classifications, and includes an analysis of airport growth. In terms of the busiest airports in the world, it demonstrates that high growth is occurring in the developing countries and that, for example, the representation of the United States in the top-30 of the world's busiest airports is declining. The final chapter in this context is Chapter 6, 'Aircraft maintenance, repair and overhaul' by Andrew Potter, Hamad Al-Kaabi and Mohamed Naim. This chapter shows that outsourcing of MRO has grown significantly, but that key activities such as line maintenance remain within control of the airline.

We then move to a different but very important aspect of aviation – safety. Chapter 7, 'Safety in commercial aviation' by Hans Heerkens, provides an extensive discussion of factors that influence aviation safety. Several recent aviation accidents are discussed. It is concluded that across the world aviation safety has improved, but one critical element seems to be the human–technology interface.

The next three chapters take a geographical perspective and focus on particular areas of the world. Chapter 8, 'Newly industrializing economies and the aircraft industry: economic and industrial policy views in Asia' by Sören Eriksson, looks at Asia's newly industrializing countries and the aircraft manufacturing industry. The number of countries that have tried to foster an aircraft industry in 'the shadow' of the leading aerospace nations have steadily increased. This is especially true for Asia, where the aircraft industries frequently have been used as a target and tool for economic and industrial development. These policies show varying degree of success and failure.

This is followed by Chapter 9, 'The commercial aircraft industry in Russia and Ukraine: strategic transformation and prospects' by Alma Lozano and Sören Eriksson. This chapter describes how the end of the Cold War has affected the former Soviet Union aviation industry. The two most important aviation countries that emerged were Russia and Ukraine. This chapter discusses modernization strategies and policy reforms, as well as the surviving aircraft and engine manufacturers and their products. The geographical regional focus ends with Chapter 10, 'Transformation of the aviation industry in Central and Eastern Europe: Czech Republic and Poland' by Zgibniew Bochniarz, Zbyněk Hruška, Emilia Barbara Sieńko-Kułakowska, Grzegorz Pisarczyk and Josef Zbořil. This chapter provides additional insight into countries that were part of the Soviet Bloc and how the end of the Cold War impacted them. Manufacturers in the Czech Republic and Poland have undergone radical changes after the disappearance of the military, which was the major historical driver of the industry. Working with market forces instead of the planned economy proved to be a formidable obstacle, but nevertheless these industries have shown resilience and prospects for growth.

The book would not be complete without some attention on the environment. Chapter 11, 'Governance and environmental performance: an airlines perspective' by Marie-Josée Roy, Isabelle Dostaler and John Fiset, discusses the impact of airlines on the environment. It shows that corporate airline boards are increasingly being asked to play a bigger role in environmental performance goals. Several airlines and their environmental approaches and achievements are discussed.

We would like to acknowledge our sincere gratitude to all authors who have contributed their knowledge, time and support to this book. We also offer our sincere appreciation to managers and staff in companies and organizations who contributed information.

1 The contours of the global commercial aircraft manufacturing industry

Dániel Vértesy

Introduction

The capacity to design and produce an airplane is very much distributed around the world today. If we board a plane flown by any major airline today, we will find that it is made of advanced parts and components produced in American, European and Asian countries. It has not been this way throughout the history of commercial aircraft manufacturing. Even during the 1960s, aircraft design and engineering, manufacturing and product support activities were typically conducted in the same country, and in all these activities the dominance of US producers was overwhelming.

Events affecting the international developments of the aircraft industry often feature in news headlines. Not only new technologies, but also changes in markets and global shifts in the industry garner public interest. For example, news on the new Chinese aircraft manufacturer Comac starting to establish risk-sharing partnerships to develop its C-919 mid-range jet that would make it a direct competitor of Boeing and Airbus, on Embraer and Airbus opening aircraft assembly lines in China, or Bombardier establishing a component manufacturing centre in Mexico[1] attract heated debate. Many argue that the potential impact of such international redistribution of technological capabilities and production is worrisome for traditional industry players. For instance, MacPherson and Pritchard (2003) link the increased use of global suppliers to a significant reduction in the number of aerospace jobs in the United States and fear the effect on future competitiveness. Others see this high-tech industry as an instrument for moving up the value chain and a way of breaking out of the middle-income trap (Wade 2010). In addition to being a source of prestige and national security, commercial aircraft manufacturing is an important economic activity that can generate significant export revenues and demand for highly skilled employment.

Regardless of its impact, the international expansion of the aircraft industry is not a new phenomenon. This chapter argues that what is new is the direction of internationalization and its driving mechanisms. International trade in aircraft has intensified, and the reliance on global supply chains is a reality in today's commercial aircraft industry. However, it is easy to overestimate its scale without assessing relevant statistical evidence.

This chapter investigates the changing global patterns of production and trade in civil aircraft, and aims to paint with broad strokes the contours and the major underlying dynamics that define that. This being said, it is about commercial aircraft manufacturing rather than military,[2] and is about the producers or large aircraft-making companies rather than their user, the airlines; also, its main focus is on dynamics at the country level. The questions that guide our investigation are:

- In what way is the current wave of internationalization different from previous ones?
- What is the size of the global commercial aircraft industry and how has it evolved over the past five decades?
- What are the main producer and exporter countries?
- How has globalization shaped the industry? Can we observe any patterns in the internationalization of commercial aircraft manufacturing?

This chapter will provide an empirical overview of the evolution of the global aircraft industry from an economic point of view and identify changing patterns in its geographical distribution.

Two waves of internationalization

The process of internationalization of the aircraft industry has been studied for some time. Mowery and Rosenberg (1989) explained how the process took off at the end of the 1970s due to a confluence of changes in policies, market conditions and technology. Deregulation in the US air transport services sector, the erosion of the government's funding of (primarily military) research and development (R&D) which was essential for establishing US dominance in the industry, the decline in the commonality of military and commercial technology, the increasing technological complexity and the increasing development costs all contributed to increased financial risks for companies. Furthermore, the market share of the United States in new aircraft started to decline, making foreign sales crucial for financial success of US producers, spurring international collaboration. By the 1990s, as Golich (1992) pointed out, collaboration of former national champion enterprises had become the only means of survival in an industry characterized by high risks and costs associated with R&D and production, long investment cycles which had increased 2–3-fold to 10–15 years since the end of World War II, and features of the market it served, in which – apart from a product's price, performance and on-time delivery – politics played a key role for competitiveness.

Eriksson (1995) surveyed the sector in a number of newly industrialized economies and emphasized the increased importance of East and Southeast Asia in the global aircraft industry. Niosi and Zhegu (2005) highlighted that the main steps in the internationalization process following the initial period of the United States' supremacy were Europe's catching up in the 1970s and 1980s and the emergence of the duopolistic war between Airbus and Boeing, and eventually the worldwide diffusion of the industry.

The industry today is characterized by concentration, competition and also collaboration in R&D, while new countries are becoming part of the international aircraft supply chain. Esposito (2004) showed that the evolution and intensification of international collaboration in commercial and military aircraft and engines has been a gradual process which began with collaboration agreements initiated by engine makers, and continued through the creation of the European Airbus consortia, which was building on lessons from the *Concorde* project, evolving into a complex web of global cooperation. Hagedoorn (2002) offered further evidence that international R&D partnering in the aerospace and defense industry increased substantially by the 1990s, in contrast with that of the previous three decades, and in that decade in particular, also in contrast with other high-tech industries. With regards to the more recent trends, authors point out that new countries beyond the US–Europe core are entering the industry through the supply chain; e.g., China emerged as an international parts and components supplier, applying its strong bargaining power to offer market access (Eriksson 1995; Goldstein 2006; Eriksson 2011).

From another point of view, the internationalization of the industry in the past half a century happened in two waves. What began with the intensification of collaboration between producers that vertically integrated the capacity to design and produce aircraft, internationalization through joint ventures for R&D collaboration, company spin-offs, mergers and acquisitions, reshaped the industry in such a way that today's producers are mostly specialized in a few activities along the supply chain. In the multi-tier structured industry, the largest aerospace (and defense) producers may be competitors at some level in certain products, while collaborating in others – for instance, as risk-sharing partners in components and subsystems. Even for the United States, where many of the collaborating partners are domestic, the trend observed by Craypo and Wilkinson (2011) on Boeing jetliners is rather telling: while only 2 percent of the B-707, a product of the 1960s, was produced outside the United States, this share was 30 percent for the B-777 of the 1990s; we now see that around 65 percent of the latest B-787 *Dreamliner* airframe relies on foreign suppliers.[3]

This first wave of internationalization, which began in the 1960s and ended with a major shakeout and consolidation in the 1990s, typically occurred between incumbent countries and firms of the North America–Europe–Japan triad. More recently, a second wave of aerospace internationalization has emerged, distinguishing itself from the first wave. Whereas the first wave saw the set of aerospace-producing countries largely unchanged, this new wave sees a global expansion of the industry. This expansion has many underlying reasons – structural, political and economic. The new structure of the industry had crystallized by the end of the 1990s and is more favorable for new entrants. By comparison, those latecomers that attempted to join the industry after World War II often faced insurmountable technological and capital barriers when they tried to launch mega-projects and establish (copying incumbents) the entire vertical spectrum of aerospace production. It is hardly surprising that many of these attempts – from Argentina to Indonesia, and even China – failed to deliver the ultimate goal, the serial production of indigenous aircraft; or, if successful, were short-lived (Eriksson 1995; Vertesy 2011).[4] Yet both the technological and capital barriers of entry are significantly lower when a new entrant climbs gradually along the supply chain. From Mexico to China and South East Asia, we see new producers that specialize in supplying high-quality, high-tech components for major system assemblers such as Boeing and Airbus. They produce and innovate, as observed in many other high-tech industries (Kim 1997; Amsden 2001; Hobday 1995). This results in less visible, large-scale projects, but is probably economically more sustainable.[5]

After the end of the Cold War the world order was multipolar, in the economic and political sense (Wade 2011). Establishing aerospace production (and innovation) capabilities is seen in this context as a contributing factor for high-tech competitiveness, and a strategic aim for many emerging economies (BRIC countries, as well as others) that aim at increasing their regional or global influence. Given that airlines in these countries are often in state hands, they can strategically trade market access in exchange for access to technology, often in the form of offset agreements. On the one hand, high economic growth and demand for transportation go hand in hand, thus the growing demand for new aircraft gives strong leverage for emerging economies. On the other hand, incumbent parts and component suppliers also see potential in capitalizing on the growth outside their home territories, and are ready to invest even if it takes longer to recover their investments, and even if they are forced to enter joint ventures in partnership with receiving governments.

The second wave of internationalization is driven by transnational corporations, which integrate design and engineering, manufacturing, distribution and after-sales support activities in multiple locations around the world (Aerostrategy 2009). On the receiving end, governments increasingly compete to attract firms in the supply chain by establishing aerospace business parks, providing tax breaks and even supporting R&D.

In search of statistical evidence

Despite considerable public interest in the aviation industry, there is surprisingly little consistent statistical data available to compare the industry performance of aircraft-producing countries around the world. Without comparable production and export statistics, it is very easy to exaggerate any threat to established structures posed by new entrants to the industry, or overestimate the success of an industry that achieved the maiden flight of a new model but failed to sell to airlines. Why is it so difficult to find publicly available, comparable data? In general, this is due to the particularities of the industry. Aerospace producers are typically large firms, often without significant domestic competition, and often dual producers of commercial as well as defense products, which makes confidentiality a key issue. Of course, the reasons for limited data availability differ from country to country, but there are a few common patterns. For most of the industrialized economies (members of the OECD) data are available from 1970 onwards, but for earlier years it is mostly published as part of the more aggregated transport equipment manufacturing branch. Former socialist countries (from Central Eastern Europe to China) carefully limited access to information during the Cold War years, since all of the sector's products were considered strategic assets for national security. Even the otherwise highly insightful estimates in declassified CIA reports (Maddison 1998) do not offer data on this industry in the USSR. (Spy agencies appear to have only been interested in aerospace as a source of military capabilities and less as a source of wealth creation.) Even today, the Russian Federation does not publish sectoral value added or sales figures, thus impeding historical extrapolations.

The high degree of concentration of industrial activity is another major difficulty, especially in newly industrializing economies. Often, there is only a single enterprise. In order to not jeopardize the respondents' anonymity in industrial surveys, statistical offices are forced to publish branch-level aggregate figures when the industry consists of only a handful of firms. In other cases the manufacturing activity in the sector was simply too low to be measured separately. But even if domestic aircraft-manufacturing activities were measurable, they were short-lived (i.e. some Latin American countries) or could not be differentiated from maintenance, repair and overhaul activities. In sum, it is not surprising that no comparative study was ever published on the growth of aerospace manufacturing. Yet, in a sector with a low number of producers and highly visible products, at least the commercial data unavailable in national statistical publications can be obtained from company reports or secondary sources.

How to measure country performance?

The most commonly used indicator to measure the size and changing geography of the global commercial aircraft industry has been the relatively available export statistics and company sales data. The main advantage of export statistics is their global coverage and the systematic collection and publication of data from both trading partners. At the same time, export data do not distinguish trade in new or used products, so it is only a second-best indicator of successful foreign sales of domestically produced aircraft, if figures are biased by the foreign sales of used wide-body aircraft in the million-dollar price range. This makes it particularly difficult to compute indicators of international specialization and comparative advantage of countries. Company sales data offer better insight into the performance of actual products; however, not all aerospace companies are publicly traded or are forced to publish their detailed results. More aggregate national statistics for the aircraft industry on sales and value added are therefore better indicators of actual aircraft production activities; however, as will be discussed below, such figures may be too aggregated and make it difficult to distinguish commercial from military production.

Given these considerations, this chapter primarily relies on a combination of data on exports, production (value added) to draw the contours of the commercial aircraft industry and the latest developments in its internationalization.

About the sources

The statistics described here offer a historical overview of the growth of the aerospace industry since the 1970s in 45 countries. The core dataset originates from national statistical data, obtained directly from national accounts data in yearbooks, data from manufacturing surveys, but also from UNIDO, OECD, Eurostat and other international statistical databases, or compiled datasets of the Groningen Growth and Development Center (GGDC). In some cases, data were augmented by data from company reports. These datasets have been scrutinized and adjusted for purposes of cross-country comparisons; values in national currencies were converted with industry-of-origin unit value ratios in all possible cases. Detailed information on data sources and extrapolation methods used for each country are provided in Vertesy (2011).

The aim was to provide data that were as reliable as possible for the overall time span, and covering as many countries as possible for the last 25 years on value added, gross output (sales), employment and exports. Unfortunately, investment figures (such as gross capital formation, R&D investment) were unavailable on a yearly basis and incidental figures are meaningless in this context where project success depends on investment accumulated over decades. Yet it remains our hope that transparency in the sector will increase (at least in the archives) so that future research will be able to fill this gap.

Disentangling the definitions and numbers

The term "commercial aircraft industry" is unknown to official statistics. On the one hand, the production of commercial aircraft is part of the manufacturing industry as "aerospace products and parts manufacturing"; on the other hand, the airline industry forms part of the service industry as "air transport services." This chapter deals with the manufacturing industry only, which is still very complex. "Aerospace" itself covers aircraft, spacecraft, their parts and components (including engines and propulsion systems). First, it is extremely difficult to distinguish industrial activities based on their purpose: commercial or military, due to the fact that all the large producers are active in both market segments and many of the products and components are of dual use. Commercial aircraft development directly benefits from defense-oriented R&D subsidies and military orders received by the same company. Second, it is somewhat easier to disentangle aircraft and space vehicles manufacturing, although not all statistical agencies provide such disaggregated information and not for all years. The 2010 *Annual Survey of Manufactures* provides an example from the United States (see Table 1.1): the first three sectors within aerospace product and parts manufacturing are responsible for aircraft, engines, their parts and auxiliary equipment

Table 1.1 The elements of aerospace manufacturing in the US Annual Survey of Manufactures (2010)

NAICS 2007 Code and description		*Subsector's share in ...*	
		employment (%)	*value added (%)*
3364	Aerospace product and parts manufacturing	100	100
336411	Aircraft manufacturing	38	49
336412	Aircraft engine and engine parts manufacturing	17	15
336413	Other aircraft parts and auxiliary equipment manufacturing	27	21
336414	Guided missile and space vehicle manufacturing	12	11
336415	Guided missile and space vehicle propulsion unit and propulsion unit parts manufacturing	4	3
336419	Other guided missile and space vehicle parts and auxiliary equipment manufacturing	2	1

Source: United States Census Bureau.

(336411 to 336413) that constitute 85 percent of the industry in terms of value added, and 82 percent in terms of employment. The rest of the industry is related to the manufacturing of guided missiles and space vehicles. Official Chinese statistics for the few years where a distinction is available provide a similar share of about 15 percent for the space industry, but this proportion is unknown for most other Western producer countries. In these cases it is fair to estimate that the share is lower, given their more limited space activities.

Next to overall data availability, these issues present an additional challenge for monitoring the evolution of the commercial aircraft industry. Our choice in this chapter was to tackle the first challenge that is overall data availability, and present the evolution of the industry in broad strokes. The aggregate statistics on the evolution of the aerospace industry allows us to chart the contours of the industry by presenting the main trends, which is interesting as it has never been published in a book. At the same time, we emphasize that the size of commercial aircraft manufacturing is smaller than manufacturing statistics show, but we have no means to provide exact figures.

At the same time, trade statistics make the distinction between commercial and military as well as between air and space activities possible. Whenever we present export and import data, we focus on the commercial aircraft segment only.

The state of commercial aircraft manufacturing and its main development trends

Before turning to a discussion of the changing patterns of production and trade in aircraft, we first look at how demand for aircraft has changed over the past decades. Air transport growth is the key commercial driver of new aircraft sales, a major "pull factor" for growth of aircraft manufacturing.

The changing landscape of demand for new aircraft

World air traffic has been growing rapidly over the last four decades. The number of air passengers has grown more than eight-fold between 1970 and 2010. To better understand the volume growth at the global scale, let us suppose that every air passenger flies only once per year. While only every twelfth person could have flown in 1970, about every third citizen of the world could have experienced this fastest means of travel in 2010. In reality, of course, access to air travel depends on income, and until as recently as the year 2000, some 90 percent of the world's air passengers came from high- or upper-middle-income countries. Yet as new economic powerhouses emerge in East Asia, so changes the geographical distribution of demand for air transport services. According to World Development Indicators of the World Bank, three-quarters of air traffic was concentrated in Western Europe and North America in 1970; this share had fallen to half in 2010. Over the same period, Latin America and the Caribbean region maintained a flat 7 percent while the East Asia and Pacific region doubled its share to nearly one-third by 2010. This latter region has, for the first time, overtaken the European Union in terms of number of passengers carried.

For a long time, the aviation market was very limited in many of the emerging economies, despite their large territories. China was one of the best examples of an "earthbound" country. Even in 1980 it showed passenger-kilometer levels similar to those of European countries before the jet age. The number of air passengers in China in 1990 was similar to that of South Korea. The passenger levels of 2006 are still lower than US levels of 1970. Nevertheless, the growth of air traffic within and outside of the country exceeded that of many countries with the largest air transport markets. Annual average growth in China between 1990 and 2007 was nearly 15.8 percent, while it was only 6.7 percent in the UK and 3.1 percent in the United States. It was only China that managed to sustain high growth rates – due in part to the very low initial levels of air transport. Still, there is great potential for further growth by further opening up airspace for commercial traffic, improving air traffic control infrastructure and overcoming pilot shortage.

The growth of global air transportation has clearly gained speed after 1980. A major reason for this was the 1978 deregulation in the United States, resulting in the entry of new airlines and the expansion of services. Similar deregulation took place in Europe in the 1990s, but many of the emerging air transport markets remain highly regulated even today. To a large extent, the growth is constrained by infrastructural limitations and airport and air traffic management capacities. Nevertheless, many of the Asian emerging economies have made large investments into tackling these issues and have nurtured the largest airport development projects in recent decades.

Another way to measure the volume of air traffic is by looking at the sheer number of commercial departures. In emerging economies air traffic has been expanding at a much faster rate than in industrialized economies. The average rate for the period 1973–1990 was 4.5 percent for emerging and only 2 percent for industrialized economies. For the period 1990–2007 it was 5.8 percent and 3.8 percent, respectively. The most rapid growth in traffic in this last period was observable in China and Korea. Changes in air traffic are closely linked to changes in economic growth, and the above-average GDP growth in Asia explains the above-average growth in traffic. Put into historical perspective, the number of airline departures in China in 2007 (1.75 million) was still lower than that in Western Europe (1.85 million) in 1973, not to mention the United States (7.93 million).[6]

The efforts to bring aircraft manufacturing to Asia are reasonable in light of the economic growth predictions (Maddison 2007) and (related to these predictions) new aircraft delivery forecast of the world's four largest manufacturers (see Table 1.2). The Asia-Pacific region is expected to take up about one-third of all new aircraft deliveries, becoming the largest buyer. Calculating in 2009 dollars, aircraft sales to Asia will be in the range of a trillion US dollars over the next two decades. According to all major manufacturers, China alone is expected to receive 11–14 percent of all aircraft deliveries in the same period. North America and Europe remain neck-and-neck in the total forecast of both large commercial aircraft manufacturers, accounting for about one-quarter of global demand. North America will remain the largest market for regional aircraft (including both jets and turboprops), but predictions on the shares differ significantly (between 35 and 47 percent). According to three of the producers, around one in every four new regional aircraft will land in Asia; only Airbus predicts a somewhat lower share.

If the various predictions are correct, every percentage point of market share translates into 3.1–3.6 billion dollars of aircraft acquisition over the upcoming two decades. Such a growth is a clear indication of increased demand for aircraft and parts in countries of this group, considering also the additional demand for maintenance, repair and overhaul services. All these present strong incentives for a further globalization of aircraft manufacturing capabilities, and offer strong leverage potential for countries such as China to strategically define the terms of attracting foreign producers to manufacture at least some parts and components locally.

Business cycles in the aircraft manufacturing industry

Let us now look at aircraft manufacturing from the suppliers' perspective. The evolution of the global aerospace industry closely reflects major macroeconomic,

Table 1.2 Demand forecast for new aircraft by major manufacturers

Company	*Boeing*		*Embraer*		*Airbus*		*Bombardier*	
Outlook Period	*2009–2029*		*2010–2029*		*2009–2028*		*2010–2029*	
A. Regional aircraft								
Seating capacity definition:	<90 seats		30–120 seats		<100 seats		20–99 seats	
Market value (USD billion)	60		200		n.a.		~239	
Regional market size	*Total*	*Share*	*Total*	*Share*	*Total*	*Share*	*Total*	*Share*
New deliveries next 20 years	1,920	100%	6,875	100%	8,321	100%	6,100	100%
North America	800	42%	2,400	35%	2,899	35%	2,860	47%
Latin America	20	1%	575	8%	661	8%	350	6%
Europe	310	16%	1,510	22%	2,160	26%	(incl. CIS) 950	16%
Asia-Pacific	470	24%	575	22%	1,374	17%	1,580	26%
Of which P.R. China	*280*	*15%*	*950*	*14%*	*n.a.*	*n.a.*	*860*	*14%*
Russia/CIS	200	10%	405	6%	467	6%	n.a.	0%
Middle East	70	4%	240	3%	154	2%	(incl. Afr.) 360	6%
Africa	50	3%	220	3%	506	6%	n.a.	
B. Total commercial aircraft market								
Total Market value (USD bln)	3,590		n.a.		3,100		n.a.	
All new deliveries next 20 years	30,900	100%			30,175	100%		
North America	7,200	23%			7,675	25%		
Latin America	2,180	7%			2,090	7%		
Europe	7,190	23%			7,585	25%		
Asia-Pacific	10,320	33%			8,726	29%		
Of which P.R. China	*4,330*	*14%*			*3,272*	*11%*		
Russia/CIS	960	3%			1,332	4%		
Middle East	2,340	8%			1,497	5%		
Africa	710	2%			1,270	4%		

Sources: Boeing Current Market Outlook 2009–2029; Embraer Market Outlook 2010–2029; Airbus Global Market Forecast 2009–2028; Bombardier Commercial Aircraft Market Forecast 2010–2029.

technological and political events. The rapid expansion of air transportation was made possible by the diffusion of technological innovations such as the jet engine after World War II and the emergence of a dominant design of airliners, and was fueled by growth of the global economy. Continuous technological improvements in the civilian aircraft industry benefited from military research and development activities in the aircraft and spacecraft segments, particularly in the context of the Cold War.

Accepting the limitation of official statistics discussed above, that for most countries it is not possible to disentangle air and space, and civilian from military production, it is still very informative to chart the trends of the aerospace industry. Even if the scale may differ, the cyclical trends are very similar for the largest segment – commercial aircraft. Table 1.3 provides an overview of the evolution of the global aerospace industry between 1960 and 2010. Over these

Table 1.3 Key indicators on the evolution of the aerospace industry, 1960–2010

	1960	*1973*	*1985*	*1990*	*1995*	*2000*	*2005*	*2010*
Total value of output (GO)	78,350	108,516	164,700	213,034	159,924	221,769	257,029	300,110
Gross value added (VA)	38,586	56,568	75,846	91,878	61,593	77,716	100,359	136,612
Total employees (thousands)	953	1,075	1,680	1,839	1,669	1,531	1,357	1,324
No. of countries in GO sample	15	20	27	33	38	40	40	39
Missing data for significant producers[a]	*6*	*6*	*7*	*5*	*1*	*0*	*0*	*0*
No. of countries in VA sample	16	23	31	34	40	42	43	43
Missing data for significant producers[a]	*3*	*4*	*4*	*3*	*0*	*0*	*0*	*0*

Source: Vertesy (2011).

Notes

Data cover all aerospace producer countries, with the exception of the Russian Federation.

a Countries in the sample with missing data most likely exceeding 100 million USD and value added exceeding 50 million USD.

five decades value added increased by a factor 3.5 to 136.6 billion USD; gross output increased four-fold to over 300 billion USD. The growth of the industry was not linear. Figure 1.1 shows a cyclical growth pattern with peaks in 1973–1974, 1980–1981 and 1991, followed by periods of decline. The most rapid growth in value added took place from 1995 to 2007 (annual average of 6.8 percent), the largest of the drops occurred in the years following the end of the Cold War (average 7.7 percent annually between 1990 and 1995). Currently, aerospace globally accounts for over 1.4 million jobs, which is already lower by 23 percent than at its peak in 1990. Between 1990 and 2007 more than 400,000 aerospace jobs were lost around the world.

This production landscape is shaped by periods of economic expansion and recession in the major producers, such as the expansion periods of the late 1970s, the second half of the 1980s or the late 1990s, or the recessions following the oil crisis (1973–1975), during the early 1980s, the early 1990s and after 2008. Our consistent time series on aerospace producers ends in 2010, which prevents us from observing whether a full recovery from this latest crisis has happened yet. Recently published US and European data for 2012 show that aerospace manufacturing, in terms of value added in real terms, has just recovered to pre-crisis levels.

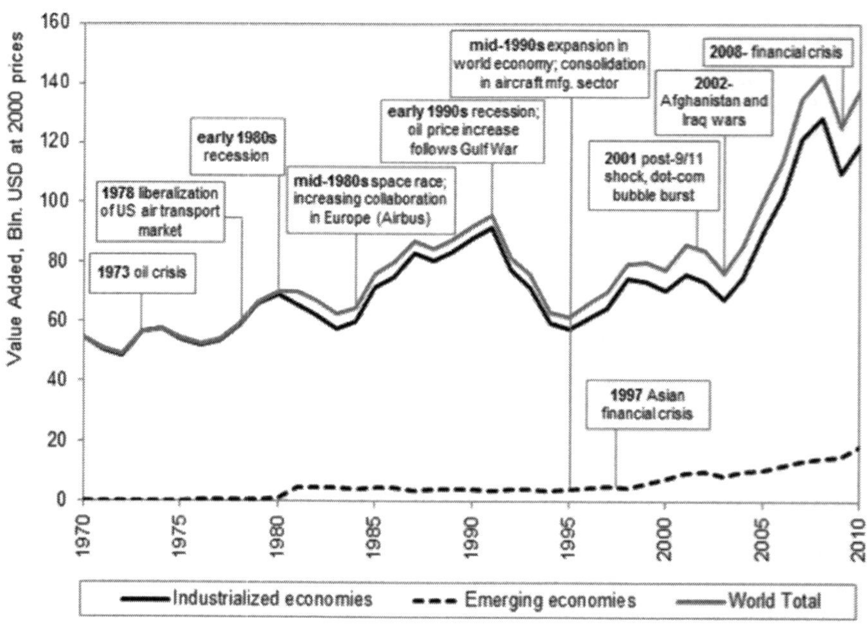

Figure 1.1 Evolution of the aerospace industry, 1970–2010 (source: own calculations based on official national and international business statistics).

Note
Includes commercial, military and space segments.

During the four decades of the Cold War, the industry benefited greatly from high defense expenditures and from the fact that national security considerations often overrode economic considerations. However, it is noteworthy that the growth resulting from the increasing commercial sales during the post-Cold War era was more rapid than ever before. Global production in terms of value added increased 2.2-fold over only 12 years between 1995 and 2007. To put this expansion in perspective, it took 30 years to achieve a 2.4-fold increase between 1960 and 1990.

The aggregate figures presented here provide a comprehensive overview of the industry in the most advanced as well as emerging economies. Nevertheless, there are a few countries that are not included in the sample which have an impact on the total figures. As already mentioned, the Russian Federation (and the former Soviet Union) has not published comparable output value figures for the industry. We estimate that Russian output may have matched US levels during the Cold War in military production, but commercial production was significantly lower given the more limited air transport industry in former communist countries. It is impossible to estimate how the inclusion of the Russia and the Soviet Union would influence global aggregate figures.[7]

Table 1.3 also indicates a growing sample size, which reveals the diffusion of the industry rather than missing data. Although times series data were incomplete for a few producers, this has only limited impact on the global aggregate. Countries missing from the early sample are China, the former socialist countries of Central Eastern Europe and Israel. China is the main source of inconsistencies over time, because our time series data begin in 1981.[8] However, it has a more limited effect on the global aggregates. In 1981 China was responsible for 4.7 percent of global production, in 1985 this was 3.9 percent. The exact volume of production is unknown because most of the aircraft produced in China have not left the borders of the country. Secondary sources suggest that military aircraft production (by far the largest share of total output) started to increase in the mid-1960s and peaked around 1980. We estimate that the inclusion of China would only increase the 1960 levels by 1–2 percent and the 1973 values by 2–4 percent. Other countries excluded from the earlier periods of the value added series include Israel (with no data before 1990) and Central and Eastern European producers (Czechoslovakia, Poland, Romania, with no data before 1995) responsible for a significant amount of fighter and trainer production. At this point we cannot estimate their significance, but it is reasonable to believe that their aggregate would be lower than that of China in 1973 but higher in 1960. In sum, the margin of error for the value output estimates could be 5–8 percent for the years before 1981.

Similarly to value added, it is also very difficult to quantify the number of persons employed in commercial aircraft manufacturing. Even if the entire aerospace industry is considered, the aggregate figures not only hide the civilian/military distinction, but also the qualitative change in labor in the industry. Some signs can be read from the trends. Cycles are similarly observable as in the value added series, and employment does not deviate from these latter figures until the mid-1990s. Since then, however, value added increased while employment decreased. In fact, aerospace manufacturing (once again, assuming the broad statistical definition) employment peaked in 1990, at around 1.8 million persons employed; over 500,000 jobs were lost worldwide by 2010. This is the outcome of a combination of factors, including declining military expenditure after the Cold War, the consolidation of the industry through mergers and acquisitions or outsourcing activities, and the diffusion of information and communication technologies in all areas of design, production, maintenance or management. For instance, advances in computational fluid dynamics and computer aided design virtually replaced wind tunnel tests and the need for model construction; the three recent decades also represent the most significant qualitative change in aerospace employment. It is also interesting to look at the geographical breakdown of the reduction in jobs: aerospace employment in the United States decreased by 400,000 jobs, and about 100,000 in Europe and China. Surprising as it may sound, in fact aerospace conglomerates were consolidated by reducing secondary non-aerospace activities of these firms (which were previously also included in the statistics). This global reorganization will be revisited in the section on internationalization; we conclude here that the overall industry (including the commercial segment) experienced significant efficiency gains but lost experienced human resources.

The largest industrial players

High market concentration characterizes the aircraft industry not only globally, but also within countries. The largest American and European aerospace and defense companies match and even exceed the size of entire countries' aerospace industries, both in terms of turnover as well as in terms of labor force. Boeing or EADS, with all their activities in the aeronautics (commercial and military) and space segments around the world combined, generate more annual sales and employ more persons than entire important aerospace producer countries such as France, Germany or the UK. This degree of concentration is the result of a consolidation process of several decades, ending in the late 1990s, through which the global industry underwent dramatic mergers and acquisitions and the formation of vast transnational corporations that integrate a large variety of aerospace and defense production activities and services.

Company size is important in the sector because only the largest players can raise sufficient capital (often in joint ventures) to finance the development of new projects with new technology.

Among the largest aerospace producing companies (Figure 1.2) one finds not only those whose main activity is to design, manufacture or sell aircraft, such as Boeing, EADS, Lockheed Martin, Bombardier or Embraer, but also engine producers such as United Technologies Corporation, General Electric, Safran or Rolls-Royce, or avionics and other component and system suppliers, such as Honeywell or Thales. Many firms have heterogeneous activities, acting both as system integrators and parts designers; some are active in both the fixed wing and the rotary wing markets. Much of the sales of the top 20 companies are military oriented; a few of the top companies (Lockheed Martin, General Dynamics or Northrop Grumman) are not active at all in the civilian aircraft market. For other companies, the share of commercial sales (at least for those that report it) varies hugely, from about one-quarter or less (BAe Systems or Finmeccanica) to around two-thirds (Boeing, EADS, Dassault) to 100 percent (as in the case of Bombardier Aerospace). In fact, the top ten companies change significantly if producers are ranked based on their commercial sales (this alternative rank is shown by the number in square brackets preceding company names in Figure 1.2). In terms of geographical distribution, most of the companies have their headquarters in the United States (Boeing, Lockheed Martin, General Dynamics, Northrop Grumman, United Technologies, Raytheon, General Electric, to mention a few) or in Europe (e.g. EADS, BAe Systems, Finmeccanica, Thales, Safran); however, a growing share of their activities are more globally spread. At the same time, it is very telling for the type of internationalization of

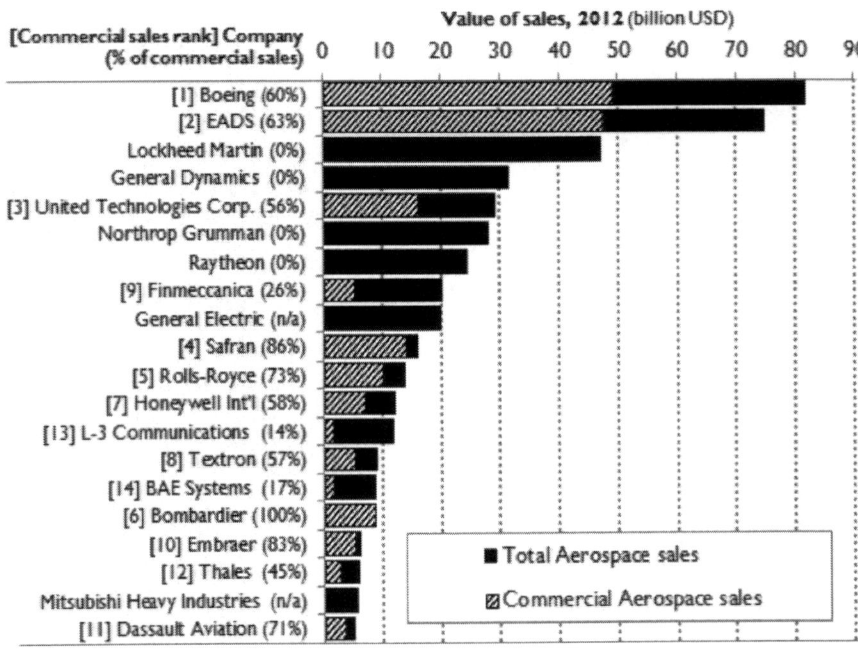

Figure 1.2 Total and commercial segment sales for the global top 20 aerospace producers, 2012 (sources: "Aerospace and Defence Top 100 Special Report" in *Flight International*, 24–30 September 2013, and the 2012 Annual Reports of the respective companies).

Note
Total sales value of companies excludes non-aerospace market segments companies, but includes sales at the defense market by the company together with all its subsidies around the world. Commercial includes all civilian sales, including the executive market. A commercial/defense breakdown was not available ("n/a") in the financial statements of a few companies.

the global aerospace industry that Embraer, the fourth largest commercial aircraft producer, represents the only company in the list with its headquarters located in an emerging economy. In a more extensive list of the global top 100 aerospace companies, there are a few more companies originating from outside Europe or North America, including AVIC of China, Hindustan Aerospace (HAL) of India, ST Aero of Singapore and Korean Aerospace Industries (KAI).[9] These companies are parts and components suppliers as well as producers of defense products for local air forces, with the exception of ST Aero. This company, part of the ST Engineering group, has gained competitive advantage in the maintenance, repair and overhaul (MRO) and upgrade segments, offering a further example of the heterogeneity of what the broad definition of aerospace manufacturing entails. It is also the most internationalized among these latter.

How significant is the aircraft industry with respect to the national economy?

In the leading industrialized economies that produce commercial aircraft, the size of the industry directly accounts for around 0.2–0.4 percent of GDP. Even larger shares can be observed in Singapore (over 1.5 percent) and the United States (around 0.8 percent). The indirect impact of the aircraft industry is estimated to be as much as three times its direct size, considering its linkages with other sectors of the economy. The United States shows a declining share of the industry with respect to its GDP following 1990, which is due to the declining defense and space activities after the end of the Cold War. An opposite trend is observable for most other producer countries, including Europe, Canada and China, where the relative size of the industry has been increasing since the 1990s.

The aircraft industry is one of the most important positive contributors to the trade balance of countries, including the United States, France, the United Kingdom, Israel, Ukraine, Canada, Italy and Spain. With the shift of many industrial activities to cheaper locations, advanced economies have experienced increased global competition even in high-tech industries. As we have seen, aerospace has so far remained one of the last industrial resources of "the West," which is also apparent in their export figures. These leading producer countries show a revealed comparative advantage in aircraft trade,[10] while only two emerging countries join them: Brazil in aircraft and Singapore in the export of parts and components.

General patterns of internationalization

It is a striking feature of the globalized world economy that the commercial aircraft industry, which was an important driver of the globalization process, has continued to be concentrated in the North Atlantic region over the past 50 years. The majority of the planes flown around the world today are sold by Boeing or Airbus, and the majority of their parts have been produced in the United States or in Europe. While the emergence of low-, medium- and high-tech production capabilities have boosted the overall export performance of newly industrializing countries of Asia and of the Southern Hemisphere, so much that their share in total world merchandise exports has increased from 10 percent in 1970 to one-third in 2010, the global share of these countries in aircraft exports still hardly exceeds 10 percent today.[11] These figures are especially striking if contrasted with another transport manufacturing sector which is both capital and technology intensive, such as the automobile industry, which is much more evenly spread around the world, with every second car or truck being produced in Asia, more than one-fifth in China alone.[12]

The world's growing appetite for aircraft is well reflected in the evolution of imports.[13] In the 1960s, the average volume of aircraft imports was around 8 billion US dollars (at 2005 prices); this increased to 18 billion USD in the 1970s, and doubled over the 1980s as well as the 1990s, surpassing 100 billion USD by 1999 and topping at nearly 160 billion USD in 2013. Countries of Europe have always been the largest importers throughout these years, accounting for 53 percent of it in the 1960s, 35 percent in the 1990s as a consequence both of the short recession and of the large civil aircraft production picking up speed. In subsequent years, imports increased once again due to intensive internal collaboration, reaching 65 percent of global imports in the 2010–2012 period. Even if internal trade is excluded, the EU accounts for over 30 percent of global aircraft imports today. North America, a primary producer, is less of an important importer, responsible for less than one-quarter of world aircraft imports both in the 1960s as well as during the 2000s (23 percent), with a brief decline in the 1990s.

The region that experienced the biggest growth in aircraft imports was East Asia/Pacific. If we exclude here the OECD countries, we see that the region which, on average, accounted for merely 1.5 percent of global imports in the 1960s (hardly over 100 million USD, less than Latin America), began a strong growth period in the 1980s. As the economies of the region's countries started to grow rapidly, the region's global share in aircraft imports increased to 9.5 percent in the 1990s, and further to 24 percent by 2010–2012 – or, with OECD countries included (and the EU considered as a bloc), to 31 percent. An eight-fold increase between 1986 and 1996 brought the region to the center of attention. After the 1997 financial crisis, which had an impact until 2000, the region's import growth regained momentum, reaching 35 billion USD in 2012, surpassing even that of the EU (not counting intra-EU trade).

Latin America, which was responsible for 7 percent of global aircraft imports in the 1960s, experienced a growth period in the 1970s with import volume doubling, but remaining flat at around 1 billion USD in the following two decades. After the relatively weak decade of the 1990s, when the region accounted for less than 2 percent of global imports, the 2000s saw a rapid growth to 7.4 billion in 2011, and the region's share reached around 5 percent in the 2000s.

Exporters and producers

The global evolution of commercial aircraft exports is punctuated by similar growth spurts and down-cycles that were observed in the case of production. As portrayed in Figure 1.3, North American and European exporters have benefited most significantly from growing demand abroad. Considering only the period between 1980 and 2012, their combined exports have more than quadrupled in real terms. Aircraft export figures have an important drawback, because they can include the sales of second-hand planes, which can be substantial considering that their prices can range between a few million to over 100 million USD. Nevertheless, looking at the 50-year trend shows interesting patterns on the slow regional redistribution of exports.

One notable trend is the gradual loss of market share by North American producers. In the 1960s and 1970s, 61 percent of commercial aircraft exports (of capitalist countries) came from North America, with more than half of it from the United States alone. By 2012, only 38 percent was originating from North America and one-third from the United States. Most of this lost market share was taken by Europe, which increased its global share in the 1980s and 1990s in particular, from 38 percent in the 1960s to 48 percent by the 1990s – and leveled off since (it was observed at 49 percent in 2012). Much of the gain is due to the increased collaboration between European countries in the framework of the Airbus project. In fact, if we considered extra-EU exports only, Europe and the United States are neck-and-neck, accounting for around 40 percent of global

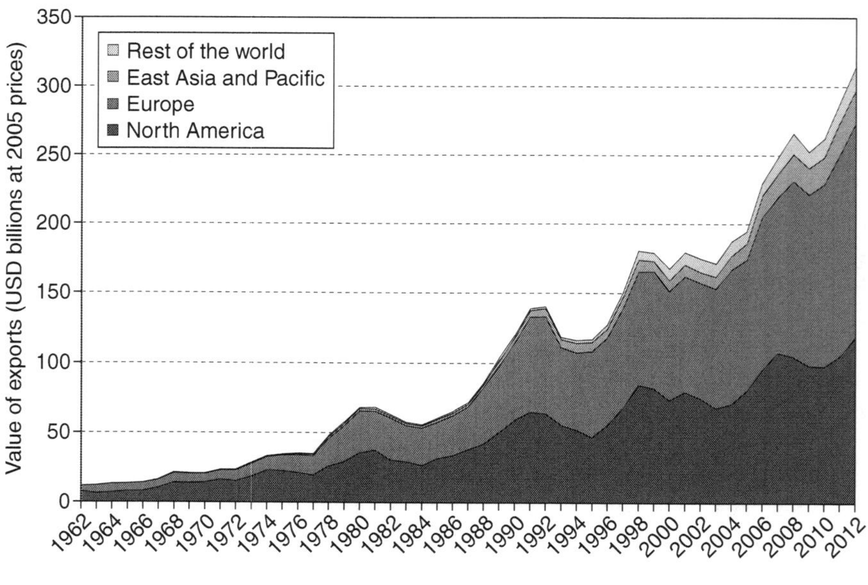

Figure 1.3 Evolution of commercial aircraft exports by regions (source: UN Comtrade).

Note
Aircraft exports defined by ISIC Rev.3 codes 792 (excl. 7925), 7131, 714 and 87411.

commercial aircraft exports. As Figure 1.4 shows, the top five exporter countries that account for 77 percent of world exports – the United States, France, Germany, the UK and Canada – have remained among the top five since 1980.

Considering the global growth trends since 1990, we see that the aircraft export of industrialized economies (mostly OECD countries) on total increased on average by around 3 percent per year, while that of emerging economies – due to their relatively smaller initial scale – grew by 12.5 percent. This owes much to the success of Brazil as an aircraft exporter, and Asian countries as parts and components exporters. Looking at emerging economies, we see that commercial aircraft exports experienced an eastward global shift, but not a southward shift: Latin America, despite the success of Embraer in Brazil and the growth of Mexican aerospace clusters, has a marginal export share. From half a percent in the 1970s, the region increased its global commercial aircraft exports share to 2.6 percent by 2012. In contrast, commercial aircraft exports from the East Asia and Pacific region have grown about twice as fast as the world average over the period of 1962–2012 (around 13 percent annual average growth in real terms), reaching a global share of about 8 percent. The three main engines of the region's growth have been Japan since the mid-1980s, Singapore since the late 1990s and, most recently, China. Other East Asian aerospace producers, such as South Korea or Indonesia, have achieved more moderate export growth since the 1990s.

Zooming in to the country level, comparing the list of the top ten exporters (Figure 1.4) and the top ten producers (Figure 1.5) offers interesting insights into the competitiveness of countries. The United States is a leader both in terms of exports and value added. Four European countries – France, Germany, the UK

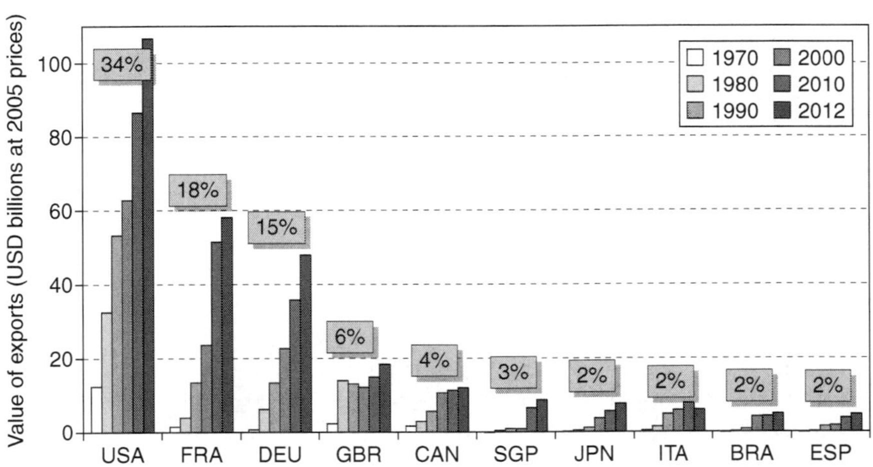

Figure 1.4 The ten largest aircraft exporters (1970–2012) and their market share (in 2012, %) (source: UN Comtrade).

Note
Aircraft industry defined by ISIC Rev.3 codes 792 (excl. 7925), 7131, 714 and 87411.

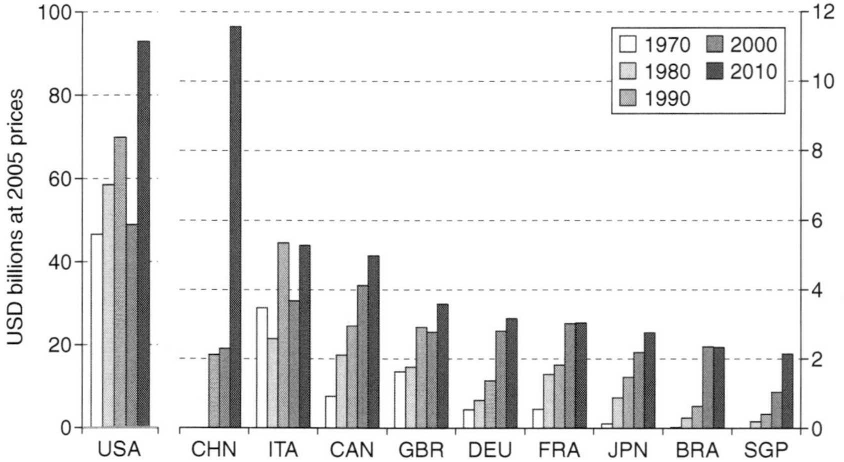

Figure 1.5 The ten largest aerospace producer countries by value added, 1970–2010 (sources: OECD, EUKLEMS, Eurostat, UNIDO, national statistical offices).

Note
Aerospace includes aircraft and spacecraft manufacturing.

and Italy – feature among the top exporters as well as top producers, but their rank changes significantly if we consider value added rather than export value, which is affected by the strategy of internal collaboration and the pricing of intermediate and final products. Most striking is the second position of China among the top producers. Here, we have to note that these figures may be exaggerated due to counting Chinese company's outputs based on their main industrial activity, and also including military production. Nevertheless, most of these products are for domestic use; China is yet to establish itself as a major aircraft exporter. The other countries appearing on both top list – Canada, Brazil, Japan and Singapore – each have a competitive edge in some segments of the industry. Canada owes this to its regional jet and engine industries, Brazil to the regional jets, Japan and Singapore to parts and components manufacturing and its position as an MRO, warehouse and logistics provider.

The regional redistribution of employment

The most striking trend that affected the evolution of global aerospace employment, the drastic cut in US aerospace jobs, was already discussed in this chapter. The question that remains to be addressed is whether these jobs "migrated" to other countries, or were lost or migrated to other sectors. Roughly counting (that is, not distinguishing the space segment and defense segments), 470,000 jobs were lost globally between 1990 and 2011. North America and Europe lost even more than that, at 480,000 aerospace jobs (with much of it affecting the United States; aerospace employment in Europe has remained roughly stable since the mid-1990s) due to the cuts in military spending after the end of the Cold War and due to an overall consolidation of the industry. Only a fraction of these jobs were recovered elsewhere in the world, suggesting that fears in the industrialized countries may be exaggerated. As demonstrated by Figure 1.6, China, the second largest aerospace employer, followed a path of its own, and employment levels where shaped by internal dynamics rather than global trends. Growth in the early 1990s and the subsequent decline is most likely the outcome of a reshuffling of state-owned enterprises. Previously identified as numbered "machine building industries" with heterogeneous activities and at numerous locations across the country, the mostly military-oriented firms were regrouped in 1999 into two conglomerates, AVIC I and II. The process of consolidation that has yet to be finalized saw a gradual and limited opening to the market and the removal of only some of the duplication of activities, but complexities in ownership remain, according to the still limited information available on firm-level dynamics (Goldstein 2006; Eriksson 2011). The most recent years once again brought employment growth in China, but it is important to emphasize the persistent qualitative differences in the education and skills of the labor force, making international comparison somewhat problematic. Elsewhere in Asia, aerospace employment has remained relatively low compared to Europe and North America, so considering global developments, at least for now, the regional redistribution of employment has remained limited.

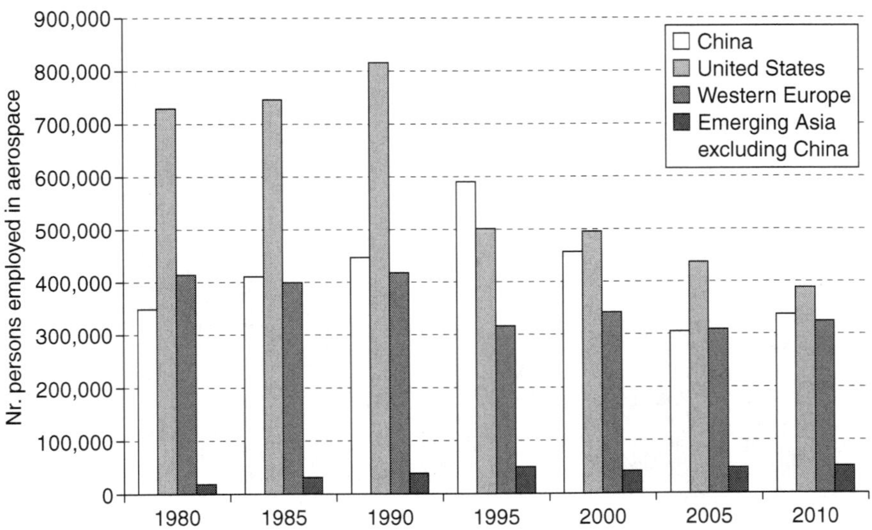

Figure 1.6 Trends in the global distribution of aerospace jobs, 1980–2010 (sources: OECD, EUKLEMS, Eurostat, UNIDO, national statistical offices).

Note
Includes air and space segments.

A special focus on emerging actors in the aircraft manufacturing industry

To better understand the most recent trends in internationalization, one should take a closer look at the developments in emerging economies that are also emerging as producers of aircraft or their parts. These, mostly Asian but also Latin American, countries are responsible for a rapidly growing share of global aircraft imports (more than one in four aircraft in value terms, as shown in Figure 1.7). Although, as we have seen above, their ~10 percent share in global output is relatively small, they show rapid growth through a new kind of export specialization. From many aspects, these countries show little commonality. Some, like Brazil and Mexico, run a positive trade balance in aircraft, while others, such as Singapore, China, India, South Korea, Thailand, Malaysia or Turkey are net importers (Figure 1.8). Some of these countries have longer traditions in producing aircraft or parts (owing to Embraer in Brazil, ST Aerospace and other transnational companies in Singapore, military and civilian state-owned producers in China or IPTN/IAe in Indonesia), while others are relative newcomers (such as Mexico or Malaysia). Production has so far not followed demand, but this imbalance provides ambitious governments with some leverage to gain access to technology and production capacity to force sellers to source at least some of the value of their aircraft from these countries. Yet changing the international division of labor in such a high-tech industry does not happen

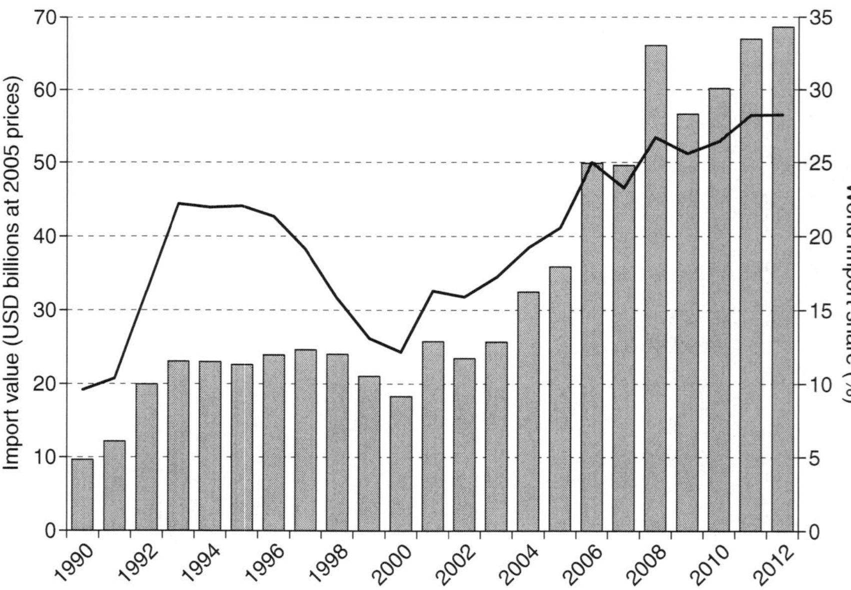

Figure 1.7 Aircraft imports of emerging economies (source: UN Comtrade).

Note
Aircraft industry defined by ISIC Rev.3 sectors: 792, 7131, 714 and 87411.

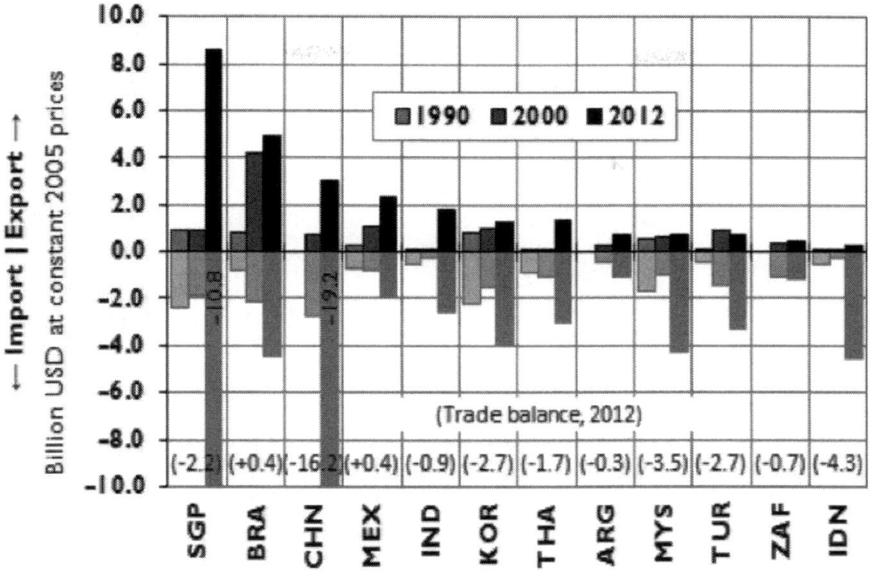

Figure 1.8 Balance of trade in aircraft for selected emerging economies (source: UN Comtrade).

Note
Aircraft exports defined by ISIC Rev.3 codes 792 (excl. 7925), 7131, 714 and 87411.

overnight, and depends on the successful implementation of policy and business strategies. These strategies show a common pattern, or a new wave of latecomer entry, which can be described as *entry to the aircraft industry through the supply chain.*

In an era when companies are more often producing goods and services through supply chains that span various countries, traditional trade statistics become less capable of measuring the contribution of each country to the total value of a good or service in the supply chain. Recent attempts by the OECD and the WTO tried to address this gap by compiling statistical data on the end use of exports (Zhu *et al.* 2013). Data on intermediate trade in aircraft offers interesting insights into ways countries become integrated in the global aircraft industry. Figure 1.9 shows two distinct patterns. One trading pattern is followed by a single country, Brazil, the only emerging market exporter specialized in assembling and selling entire aircraft. In fact, this corresponds to a strategy that we called the "first wave" of internationalization, which is entry from the top of the supply chain for an "indigenous aircraft" developer and producer – a process in which Embraer of Brazil turned out to be more successful than most others (Eriksson 1995; Vertesy 2011).

The other countries have become increasingly specialized as parts and component suppliers, among them China, South Korea or Mexico. They have done so following the model established by Japan, which, after a failed attempt to

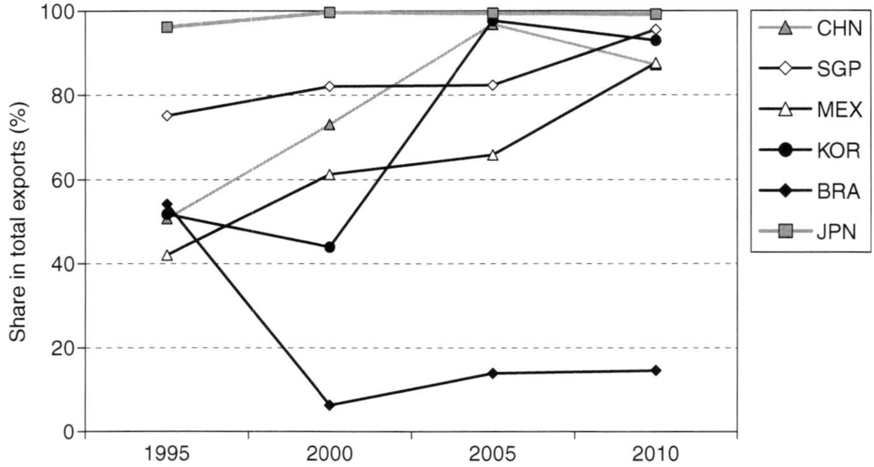

Figure 1.9 Share of intermediate goods in aerospace exports of selected countries (source: OECD Bilateral Trade by End Use database).

Note
Data for entire aerospace industry.

produce entire airliners (i.e. the YS-11 by Nihon consortium) shifted to parts and components manufacturing, and has become one of the leading suppliers of advanced composite materials.[14] Singapore followed a similar strategy in the establishment of its aerospace industry in the 1970s, when, leaving behind its single role of an entrepot trading post, it became a provider of MRO services and an important producer of parts and subsystems. Figure 1.9 offers further explanations for the difference between the size of production and exports of China: although it can sell aircraft in the domestic market, when it comes to exports China's current strength lies in supplying parts and components. If China's other strategy, that is, indigenous aircraft development, comes to fruition and Comac succeeds in exporting the ARJ-21 or C-919 jets, this picture will change. In any case, as for now, Figure 1.9 indicates that most of the aircraft-industry exports (more than 80 percent in 2010) of China, as well as the other selected countries, are used as intermediate goods by producers in their partner countries.

Yet, there are important differences between how countries of this latter group have integrated in global supply chains. Figure 1.10 offers more details on the structure of intermediate exports of two selected countries, China and Mexico. It distinguishes the five largest foreign users of their aircraft industry products, and looks at their evolution over time. In the case of China, we see a slower start, yet a more balanced geographic distribution: only after 2000 did the process of integration into global supply chains take off, but intermediate exports grew rapidly in the following decade, and its customers include US and European

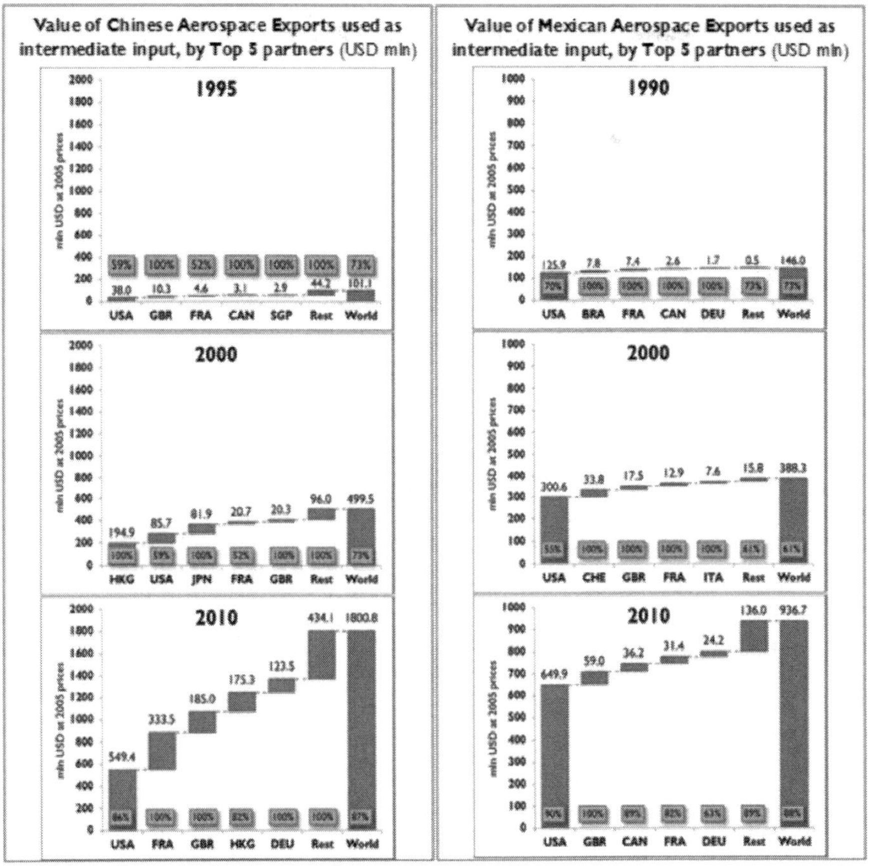

Figure 1.10 Evidence of latecomer entry through the supply chain (source: OECD Bilateral Trade by End Use database, WDI).

Note
Data include the entire aerospace industry. The percentage values in gray boxes show the share of intermediate products in selected export relations.

producers. Mexican aerospace exports to the US amounted to 300 million USD in 2000 – owing, to some extent, to the establishment of NAFTA. This further doubled by 2010, but the United States still remained the dominant trading partner.

The limits to internationalization

The relatively slower speed of internationalization of the aircraft industry compared to others can be attributed to a number of economic and political factors. First of all, new entrant companies cannot gain competitiveness overnight, but through the outcome of a longer learning process. This depends on joint efforts by the company as well as the host governments, by establishing a learning and innovation system, with the provision of specialized human resources, the availability of education, training and research institutes and the availability of linkages to other industries and leading producers. The provision of a specialized labor force is crucial (Niosi, 2005). Establishing stand-alone institutes is not enough, as long as there is a lack of interaction (flow of finance, skilled human resources, ideas, products, etc.) between the key actors of the innovation system (Vertesy, 2011). Second, if the high costs of continuously financing these efforts were not a big enough barrier to entry, latecomers have to reach markets limited by strong standards and political obstacles. The more complex the activities latecomers aim for (e.g., an entire aircraft), the greater the obstacles they face. At the same time, political obstacles are a double-edged sword; as latecomers can trade market access to foreign producers for access to technology and localizing higher value-added production activities. It also needs to be emphasized that developing and manufacturing a modern aircraft are extremely complex processes, and so is optimizing supply chains, thus any decisions that are made affect the life-cycle of an entire aircraft program.

Third, scale economies favor established trading patterns, and at least in short and medium term, it is much cheaper to buy aircraft and their components rather than make them. To a similar degree, the returns to R&D spent by incumbents is expected to be higher than to recent entrants, making it a race against a target that is moving away faster than the latecomers are gaining. The largest aerospace R&D spenders happen to be incumbents: the United States, France, Germany and the United Kingdom (see the left panel of Figure 1.11). US companies are by far the largest aerospace R&D spenders; they spend far more than those of the next ten countries combined. It has to be underlined that even if reported figures include military and space R&D, their outcomes are important sources of new technology used in commercial aircraft. But the R&D landscape has also seen important recent changes. China is emerging as a new major aerospace R&D spender as well as an employer of scientists and engineers. At some distance, India has also increased its aerospace research spending (this concerns mostly the space sector), and so have Singapore and Brazil. As the right panel of Figure 1.11 demonstrates, the growth of R&D expenditure by emerging aircraft producers has outperformed that of incumbents by some three percentage points per year since 2000. Direct or indirect public support plays a crucial role in these developments, and in fact a number of American and European companies have made strategic attempts to benefit from these programs. The emergence of world-class R&D capacity beyond the traditional locations, and the "competition" by governments to support them also increases the pool of available risk-sharing partners for incumbent system integrators, which will further increase international specialization along the supply chain.

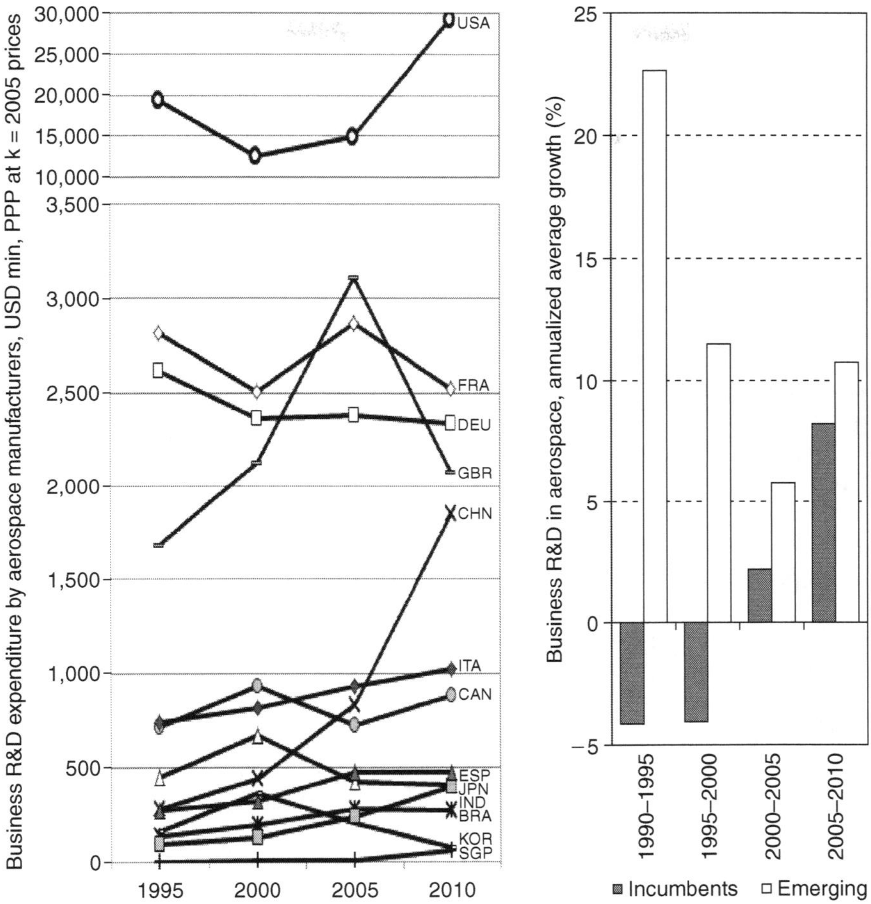

Figure 1.11 Evolution of business R&D expenditures by aerospace manufacturers in selected economies (sources: OECD, national statistical offices).

Notes
Emerging producers include Brazil, China, India, Mexico, Singapore and South Korea. Available data do not allow for distinction between civilian and military R&D.

Conclusion

The global commercial aircraft industry is undergoing a major transformation. The market for new aircraft and their maintenance has become truly global, driven to a large extent by the particularly strong demand by airlines in East Asia and in the Persian Gulf. Still, today, despite significant attempts made by governments around the world, the aircraft industry is not as internationalized as other high-tech sectors. The large majority of commercial aircraft families are designed and produced in America and Europe, as shown by production and export statistics. We can already observe turbulence in the aircraft manufacturing industry, a slow but profound change as the industry expands towards East Asia. Strong aerospace clusters have emerged from Singapore to Shanghai, Xian and Chengdu, Shenyang and Harbin in China, in South Korea, and are emerging in India and Malaysia, while Mexico is on the rise in Latin America. These new production centers are creating real competition for incumbent producers.

Over the past half-century, new entrants to the aircraft industry tried two distinct strategies. The first one aimed at achieving the capacity of indigenous aircraft design. This strategy, pursued from the 1960s to the early 1990s failed to produce commercially successful aircraft, despite the huge investments made by Japan, China and Indonesia. An exception was the market-niche-oriented Embraer of Brazil.

Another strategy was to build up the technological capability to produce parts and components, assemble aircraft under license or attract leading producers by applying a variety of economic and political means. This latter strategy was first introduced by Japan in the 1980s, and was followed by many after the end of the Cold War; it proved to be more successful for new entrants. Apart from following the technologically less demanding bottom-up approach, the other reason for success was the right timing. Entering at a time when incumbent producers of industrialized countries were forced to rationalize costs and when new information and communication technologies reduced distances, access to the market was easier. This way, by further deepening mutual dependence, new entrants could gain a foothold in an industry otherwise protected by high barriers of entry. The interplay of these developments, which we propose to call the "second wave of internationalization", triggered a substantial reorganization of the entire global aerospace industry, the end of which process we are yet to see. Nevertheless, statistics on the end-use of exports already show how countries have specialized along the supply chain as intermediate exporters.

As in the case of all abstractions, the world is more complex and countries tend to follow a mix of these strategies. For instance, while attracting leading companies of all tiers to produce locally, China also strives to design and manufacture "indigenous" aircraft (the ARJ-21 and the C-919), which would typically be the hallmark of a "first-wave" strategy. Considering, on the one hand, the serious delays in receiving international airworthiness certification for both of these programs, and the advances made by establishing final assembly lines and component manufacturing centers for leading global producers, we see that, at least for now, the advantages of the "second wave" strategy are more tangible. But needless to say, in a country the size of China and with declared regional security goals, the motivations for selecting strategies go beyond what concerns the commercial segment of the aircraft industry. But as technology complexity, capital intensity and the long lead time of product development continue to pose significant barriers of entry to this industry, all countries try to exploit political influence to support the industry, so strategies vary. Clearly, a fierce battle is fought for every percent of market share, and gaining and sustaining competitiveness depends on many more aspects, as also shown in other chapters of this book.

Production data show that the United States remains the distant leader in aircraft manufacturing. Fears of North America losing its position are therefore exaggerated. It is evident that the United States maintains its strong competitiveness while gradually reducing aerospace jobs, a process underway since the early 1990s. There is, however, little evidence on whether these jobs go to other parts of the world; we observe a general reduction of employment in the sector due to consolidation and possibly efficiency gains due to information and communication technologies. Countries of Western Europe have managed to maintain a relatively larger share of aerospace jobs while increasing exports, but in terms of total output they face stronger competition from Asia. A future change in competitiveness could also be expected in light of the significant increases in aerospace R&D spending in China, India and other Asian countries.

This chapter focused only on the commercial aircraft industry, but it needs to be emphasized that it is inherently connected to both the military and the space industry due to the technological proximity. In many of the statistics presented above, it was impossible to distinguish commercial aircraft manufacturing from these other two segments. It is true that the civilian segment is mostly shaped by business cycles, but military orders continue to play a crucial role in supporting new product development, and are an important driver of internationalization of the industry. However, if their role becomes excessive, they also have the potential to reverse the waves and shift back from globally distributed supply chains to greater domestic concentration. This is a future scenario that one cannot exclude. Another future scenario to consider is linked to the fate of the particularly strong current demand for new aircraft. In the wake of the recent financial crisis, demand for new aircraft did not decline to the same degree as would be expected considering the effect of previous macroeconomic cycles on the industry. On the contrary, new orders for more economic new aircraft have created what some industry analysts see as a bubble that could soon burst. How such an event would affect the speed of the internationalization process remains to be seen.

Acknowledgments

The author gratefully acknowledges the valuable inputs of Professor Adam Szirmai to an earlier version of this chapter, which formed part of the author's PhD thesis, and the comments and suggestions of Professor Sören Eriksson. All views expressed in this chapter, and any remaining errors or omissions, remain the responsibility of the author.

Notes

1 See Crooks, Ed "GE to sign slew of China deals in jobs boost" *Financial Times* 18 January 2011; Reed, John "Aerospace: Manufacturing takes off" *Financial Times* 16 April 2012.

2 The term "aircraft industry," unless otherwise specified, will henceforth refer to the commercial aircraft manufacturing industry.

3 Peterson, K., 2011. "Special Report: A wing and a prayer: outsourcing at Boeing" *Reuters*, 20 January, www.reuters.com/article/2011/01/20/us-boeing-dreamliner-idUSTRE70J2UX20110120.
4 Of course, the reasons why only Embraer of Brazil succeeded in becoming a successful exporter of commercial aircraft in the 1970s and 1980s are far more complex than structural (see Ramamurti 1987; Frischtak 1992; Cassiolato *et al.* 2002; Goldstein 2002; Marques 2004; Vertesy 2011).
5 China is a special case here. Although producers from the country have made more successful inroads into the industry through the supply chain than in previous attempts for indigenous innovation in earlier decades, the government in parallel is also pushing large-scale aircraft development programs – see the ARJ-21 and the C-919 projects. But the choice to include in these aircraft components designed by incumbent (foreign) suppliers shows a strategy of simultaneously gaining competence at all levels of the supply chain.
6 Based on data from the World Bank World Development Indicators.
7 The rough military aircraft export trend indicator values published by SIPRI show the highest export activity between 1972 and 1989, with a peak in 1980. This corresponds to the production pattern observable in the most successful commercial planes (the Tu-134 and Tu-154). The drop by the 1990s in both military and commercial production may have been as much as two-thirds of the previous rates. If we added these trends to the global aggregate figures, the 1970s and 1980s levels would be higher by at least 50 percent and the slump between 1990 and 1995 would look even more dramatic. The impact would be far less significant from the 1990s onward.
8 Official series begin only from 1995. Chinese production statistics were back-cast to 1981 using limited information on military and civilian aircraft deliveries and aggregate production indices. For details, see Vertesy (2011).
9 For a 2012 edition, see "Aerospace and defence top 100 special report" in *Flight International* 24–30 September 2013. Hindustan Aeronautics was the 33rd largest aerospace company with 3.1 bln USD revenue; AVIC – publishing its audited financial results for the first time in 2012 – was 37th with 2.7 billion USD in revenue, driven by helicopter sales; ST Aero was 53rd with 1.5 bln USD revenue and KAI was 55th with 1.4 bln USD. We also note that Fortune Global 500 ranks AVIC well ahead of many companies, although revenues stated are overestimated compared to the officially released annual reports.
10 This is based on the Balassa formula that measures the relative advantage of a set of goods within a country's total merchandise exports.
11 For the sake of consistency, "newly industrializing countries" refers to a group of 20 Asian (exc. Japan and Russia), Latin American and African countries that have at some point in the past five decades produced aircraft or aircraft parts.
12 Data source: 2011 Production Statistics of the International Organization of Motor Vehicle Manufacturers (http://oica.net/category/production-statistics/2011-statistics, retrieved: May 2013). Note that the share of emerging economies would probably be smaller based on turnover or value added, but these figures and a real industry-of-origin exchange rate are not available to allow for a proper global comparison.
13 Data presented below refer to aircraft imports obtained from UN Comtrade data, and were adjusted for inflation.
14 For instance, Kawasaki, Fuji and Mitsubishi Heavy industries produce structural parts for the Boeing 787 *Dreamliner*.

References

Aerostrategy, 2009. Aerospace Globalization 2.0: The Next Stage. [online]. Available from: www.fac.org.uk/wp-content/uploads/2013/01/200909-AeroStrategy-Globalization-Commentary.pdf.

Amsden, A.H., 2001. *The Rise of "the Rest": Challenges to the West from Late-Industrializing Economies*. Oxford and New York: Oxford University Press.

Cassiolato, J.E., Bernardes, R. and Lastres, H., 2002. *Transfer of Technology for Successful Integration into the Global Economy: A Case Study of Embraer in Brazil*. New York and Geneva: UNCTAD and UNDP.

Craypo, C. and Wilkinson, F., 2011. The low road to competitive failure: immigrant labour and emigrant jobs in the US. In: Michie, J. ed. *The Handbook of Globalisation*. 2nd edition. Cheltenham: Edward Elgar, 356–379.

Eriksson, S., 1995. Global shift in the aircraft industry: a study of airframe manufacturing with special reference to the Asian NIEs. PhD Thesis (Series B, No. 86). University of Gothenburg.

Eriksson, S. 2011. Globalisation and changes of aircraft manufacturing production/supply-chains: the case of China. *International Journal of Logistics Economics and Globalisation*, 3(1), 70–83.

Esposito, E. 2004. Strategic alliances and internationalisation in the aircraft manufacturing industry. *Technological Forecasting and Social Change*, 71(5), 443–468.

Frischtak, C.R., 1992. *Learning, Technical Progress and Competitiveness in the Commuter Aircraft Industry: An Analysis of Embraer*. Washington, DC: The World Bank.

Goldstein, A. 2002. EMBRAER: From national champion to global player. *Cepal Review*, 77, 97–115.

Goldstein, A. 2006. The political economy of industrial policy in China: The case of aircraft manufacturing. *Journal of Chinese Economic and Business Studies*, 4(3), 259–273.

Golich, V.L. 1992. From competition to collaboration: The challenge of commercial-class aircraft manufacturing. *International Organization*, 46(4), 899–934.

Hagedoorn, J. 2002. Inter-firm R&D partnerships: An overview of major trends and patterns since 1960. *Research Policy*, 31(4), 477–492.

Hobday, M. 1995. East Asian latecomer firms: Learning the technology of electronics. *World Development*, 23(7), 1171–1193.

Kim, L., 1997. *Imitation to Innovation: The Dynamics of Korea's teChnological Learning*. Boston, MA: Harvard Business School Press.

MacPherson, A. and Pritchard, D. 2003. The international decentralisation of US commercial aircraft production: implications for US employment and trade. *Futures*, 35(3), 221–238.

Maddison, A. 1998. Measuring the performance of a communist command economy: an assessment of the CIA estimates for the U.S.S.R. *Review of Income & Wealth*, 44(3), 307–323.

Maddison, A., 2007. *Chinese Economic Performance in the Long Run, 960–2030 AD*. 2nd, revised edition. Paris: OECD Publishing.

Marques, R.A., 2004. Evolution of the civil aircraft manufacturing innovation system: A case study in Brasil. In: Mani, S. and Romijn, H. eds. *Innovation, Learning and Technological Dynamism of Developing Countries*. Toky and New York: United Nations University Press, 77–106.

Mowery, D.C. and Rosenberg, N., 1989. *Technology and the pursuit of economic growth*. Cambridge and New York: Cambridge University Press.

Niosi, J. and Zhegu, M. 2005. Aerospace clusters: Local or global knowledge spillovers? *Industry & Innovation*, 12(1), 5–29.

Ramamurti, R., 1987. *State-owned enterprises in high technology industries: Studies in India and Brazil*. New York: Praeger.

Vertesy, D., 2011. Interrupted innovation: Emerging economies in the structure of the global aerospace industry. PhD Thesis. Maastricht University.

Wade, R. 2010. After the crisis: Industrial policy and the developmental state in low-income countries. *Global Policy*, 1(2), 150–161.

Wade, R.H. 2011. Emerging world order? From multipolarity to multilateralism in the G20, the World Bank, and the IMF. *Politics & Society*, 39(3), 347–378.

Zhu, S., Yamano, N. and Cimper, A. 2013. Compilation of bilateral trade database by industry and end-use category. *OECD Science, Technology and Industry Working Papers*, (2011/06).

Statistical sources

China Statistical Yearbook, various editions, National Bureau of Statistics, China.

Eurostat Structural Business Statistics, Annual detailed enterprise statistics for industry (NACE Rev. 2, B-E).

EU KLEMS Database, November 2009 Release, updated March 2011, see Marcel Timmer, Mary O'Mahony and Bart van Ark, The EU KLEMS Growth and Productivity Accounts: An Overview, University of Groningen and University of Birmingham; downloadable at www.euklems.net.

OECD, STAN database (according to ISIC Rev.3 and Rev.4). (www.oecd.org/sti/stan).

OECD STAN BTDIxE Bilateral Trade Database by Industry and End-use category (www.oecd.org/sti/btd).

UN Comtrade, DESA/UNSD, United Nations Comtrade database online (http://comtrade.un.org).

UNIDO INDSTAT Industrial Statistics Database, various editions.

United States Census Bureau (www.census.gov).

World Development Indicators (WDI), the World Bank.

2 Regional aircraft

Harm-Jan Steenhuis

Aircraft can be divided into several categories – for example, large aircraft such as the Airbus and Boeing jets, regional aircraft such as the Embraer jets, business aircraft such as the Gulfstream, general aviation aircraft such as Cessna and Piper, etc. The focus of this chapter will be regional aircraft. The time period since 1980 will be our focus – thus the last 35 years are covered. One main reason to do so is that there has been airline industry deregulation in this time period which has affected the type of airlines that operate regional aircraft and rise of the regional jets (see also Chapter 3). This chapter covers some general information about the regional aircraft industry, some insights into characteristics of producing aircraft and finally the regional aircraft manufacturers and their products and developments will be discussed.

General characteristics

The first important thing to do is to define what is meant by regional aircraft. This definition is somewhat dependent upon time. For example, in the 1930s, aside from some anomalies such as the Dornier Do X and the Tupolev ANT-20, the successful piston propeller powered Douglas DC-3 would probably have been classified as a 'large' aircraft even though in today's terms its capacity of around 30 passengers was limited. In today's terms, regional aircraft can be defined as having a capacity of up to about 100 passengers and are primarily used for the following types of routes (Heerkens *et al.*, 2010):

- 'Feeder' routes between smaller airfields and large 'hub' airports. For example, there are no direct connections between Edinburgh and Tokyo, so passengers would first travel to, say, London Heathrow with a regional aircraft, and then board a (usually large) long-distance aircraft to fly to Tokyo. In this way, routes that do not yield enough passengers for large aircraft can still be flown economically.
- 'Point-to-point' routes over distances from 300 to 2,000 km between destinations that warrant no large aircraft and that are so widely separated that at least some travellers prefer aircraft to trains or cars.

In this chapter the focus will be on aircraft that compete in the segments between 30 and 100 seats. This means that aircraft such as the smaller British Aerospace Jetstream, the Fairchild Merlin and Metro, the Dornier 228, as well as the larger Bombardier CSeries and the COMAC C919[1] will not be included in the analysis, even though the manufacturers of these aircraft will be included.

Regional aircraft can be further divided into categories based on their region of origin, i.e. 'Western' versus 'non-Western' or 'Eastern', and the method of propulsion. Western aircraft are manufactured by companies such as Bombardier, based in Canada, and British Aerospace, based in England. Several aircraft manufacturers are based in non-Western countries. Examples are Antonov, which is based in the Ukraine, and Tupolev, which is based in Russia.

Traditionally, the non-Western companies have used different manufacturing and quality-control philosophies and their aircraft have typically not been certified by Western aviation authorities such as the Federal Aviation Administration (United States) and the European Aviation Safety Agency (EASA), which limits their sales to these territories. Because of this, these aircraft will not be part of the discussion in this chapter, but Chapters 8–10 provide some discussion. Those companies that have explicitly aimed to sell aircraft in Western countries, such as Embraer, which is based in Brazil, will be included.

This leads to seven manufacturers who were active in the aforementioned time period and market segments. Three other manufacturers will be added to the discussion.[2] Comac, Sukhoi and Mitsubishi aircraft will be discussed because they are new entrants. Thus, the focus is on ten manufacturers. Their locations are shown in Figure 2.1. Figure 2.1 should be interpreted with some caution because aircraft manufactures sometimes have a different location for their headquarters compared to where manufacturing takes place. Also, manufacturing

Figure 2.1 Location of regional aircraft manufacturers.

facilities are sometimes spread over several locations; for example, parts might be produced in several locations while final assembly takes place in a different location. It is not usual to have more than one final assembly line, although Embraer, in order to enter the Chinese market, has assembled some aircraft in China.

Figure 2.2 provides a chronological display of the first deliveries of these regional aircraft. In many instances a particular type of aircraft gets improved over time with, for example, slightly different engines or small improvements in wing design. It can also get more elaborate modifications, such as derivative aircraft. For example, a stretched version allowing more passengers. This can lead to a 'family' of aircraft. This modification aspect causes some complications when determining aircraft performance characteristics or comparing aircraft because it depends on which version of an aircraft is taken under consideration.

Most of the new entrants into the market are based in non-Western countries. Note that Figure 2.2 includes the Sukhoi Superjet but does not include first deliveries of the Comac ARJ21 (expected in 2014) and the MRJ (expected in 2017).

Figure 2.3 shows the total number of aircraft deliveries of the manufacturers and their aircraft types from Table 2.1.[3] This illustrates how regional aircraft sales have increased overall since 1980, with a peak in 2001 when 418 regional aircraft were delivered. It is also characterized by phases of growth as well as decline.

Figure 2.4 illustrates that companies in the Western countries have been reducing production or halted production altogether for most of their aircraft types. In some instances the manufacturers still exist because they are either producing parts for other manufacturers (British Aerospace, Fokker and Saab) or continued production with other types of aircraft (Embraer).

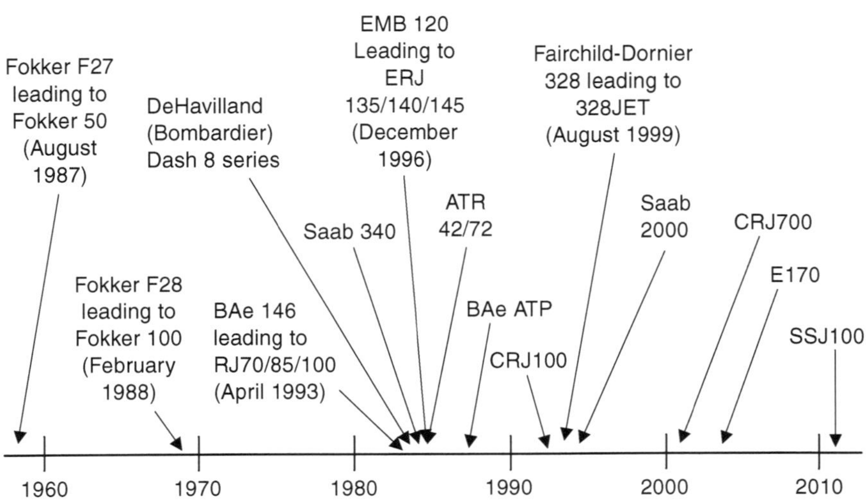

Figure 2.2 First deliveries of regional aircraft.

Table 2.1 Regional aircraft manufacturers

Company	*Aircraft*	*Website*
ATR (France)	ATR-42 and ATR-72 (prop)	www.atraircraft.com
Bombardier (Canada)	Dash 8 (prop), CRJ 100/200/440 (jet), CRJ 700/900 (jet)	www.bombardier.com
British Aerospace (England)	ATP (prop), Avro RJ85/100 (jet)	Not applicable
Embraer (Brazil)	EMB-120 (prop)	
	ERJ 135/140/145 (jet), E-170/175/190/195 (jet)	www.embraer.com
Fairchild Dornier/AvCraft (Germany/China)	328 (prop), 328JET (jet)	Not applicable
Fokker (Netherlands)	Fokker 50 (prop), Fokker 70/100 (jet)	Not applicable
Saab (Sweden)	Saab 340 (prop) and 2000 (prop)	Not applicable
Sukhoi (Russia)	Superjet (jet)	www.sukhoi.org/eng
COMAC (China)	ARJ21 (jet)	English.comac.cc
Mitsubishi (Japan)	MRJ (jet)	www.mrj-japan.com

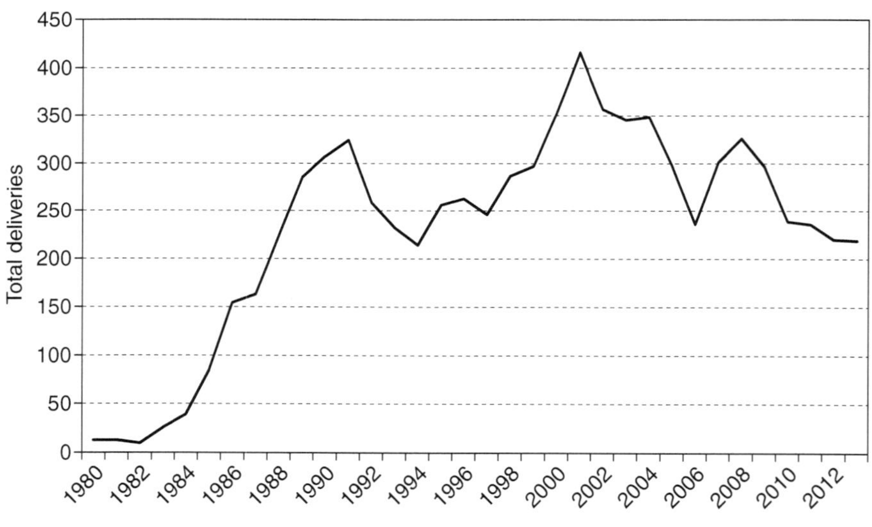

Figure 2.3 Total regional aircraft deliveries 1980–2013.

Another way of looking at this type of information is by separating aircraft deliveries from Western and Eastern manufacturers. This is done in Figure 2.5, which shows how the dominance of the West has been declining.

Another distinction that can be made for regional aircraft is the method of propulsion, the location of the engines and the number of engines. The location

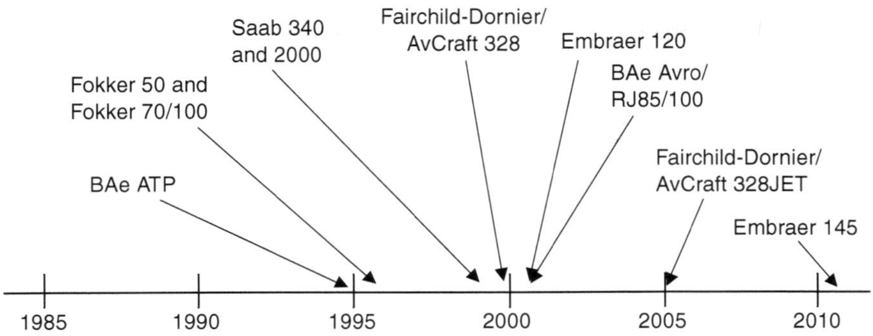

Figure 2.4 Serial production of aircraft ended.

of the engine can differ from on top of the wing, such as for the Saab 2000, below the wing, such as for the British Aerospace Regional Jet, or at the end of the fuselage, such as for the Embraer ERJ 145. The number of engines varies from two to four. See Chapter 4 for more discussion on engine aspects.

Two methods of propulsion are distinguished: aircraft with propellers versus those that use jet engines. Regional aircraft in the 1980s were primarily propeller aircraft, but since then more jet aircraft have been developed. Chapter 4 provides more information on the differences between these types of engines. Figure 2.6 shows a comparison of propeller and jet aircraft deliveries.

Especially during the 1990s, smaller jet aircraft were developed. The CRJ100 was the first small regional jet aircraft introduced to the market in 1992. This

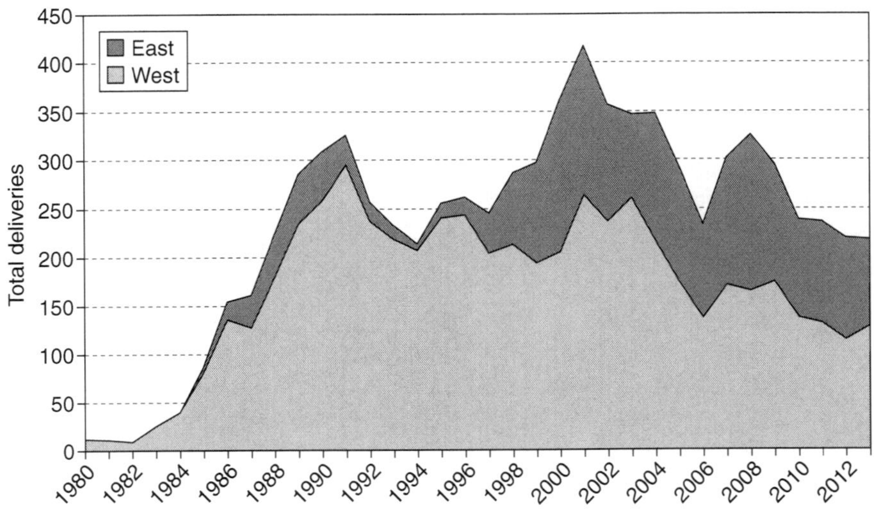

Figure 2.5 'Western' produced versus 'Eastern' produced regional aircraft deliveries.

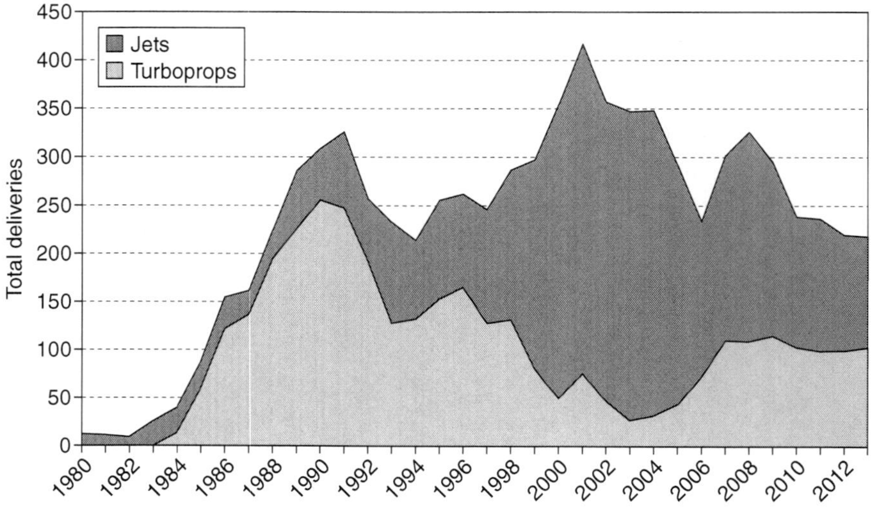

Figure 2.6 Regional jet versus turboprop deliveries.

was followed by the Embraer 135/140/145 family and the Fairchild Dornier 328JET (see also Figure 2.2). These introductions coincided with increasing demand in the 30–50-seat segment. The more recent entrants were in the 70+ seat segment of regional aircraft.

Figure 2.7 provides an overview of aircraft deliveries in the 30–50-seat segment. It shows that in the mid-1990s the number of deliveries of prop aircraft

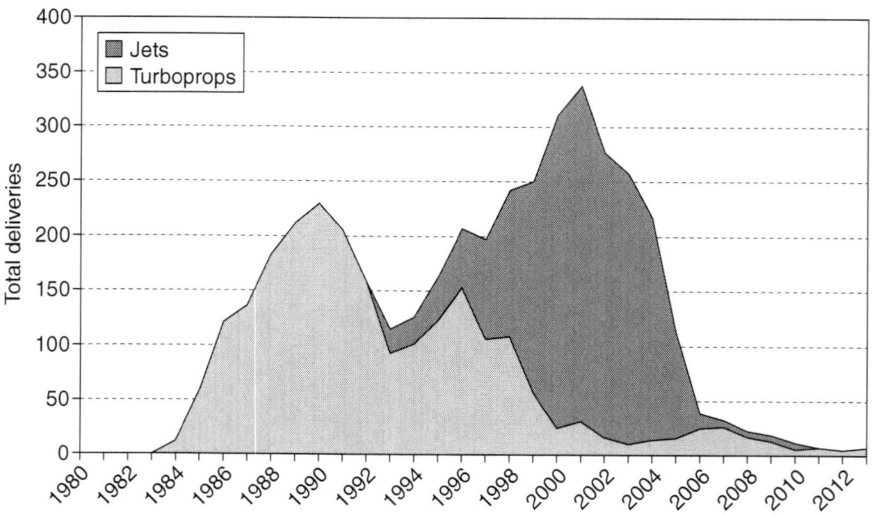

Figure 2.7 Jet versus prop regional aircraft deliveries in the 30–50-seat segment.

was higher than that for jet aircraft. This proportion reversed and, especially in the early 2000s, there was a high proportion of jet aircraft deliveries. When combining this with Figure 2.3, it becomes clear that most of the aircraft deliveries in this period were in the 30–50-seat segment (see also Figure 2.11 later in this chapter).

In recent years there has been a resurgence of turboprop aircraft (Richfield, 2011). This resurgence can be viewed in light of oil prices, since higher oil prices make the turboprop a more economical option than a jet aircraft for short-haul transport aircraft (Trimble, 2012f). By July 2012 several manufacturers were looking into developing new turboprop aircraft. For example, a 90-seat aircraft was under consideration by ATR, Bombardier (in talks with KAI from Korea for a joint production); also Saab, which is not producing commercial aircraft any longer, was rumoured to be considering a re-entry (Trimble, 2012a; Toh, 2013i), although SAAB later dismissed this (Kaminski-Morrow, 2012d). Potential new entrant National Aerospace Laboratories from India was considering a 70-seat turboprop (Waldron, 2013). In contrast with this, Embraer decided against turboprops as it considered the market too small to support the two main competitors, ATR and Bombardier (Trimble, 2012g).

Before getting into a more specific discussion of the aircraft manufacturers, their aircraft and the developments, there is one more additional characteristic that helps us identify regional aircraft: their size. Size of aircraft varies depending upon specific aircraft type, its generation, etc. Table 2.2 provides some comparisons to illustrate some dimensions of regional aircraft.

Lastly, a word of caution with regard to (regional) aircraft and what appears in publications. The regional aircraft industry is characterized by frequent announcements of manufacturers' 'plans'. These plans might, for example, show cabin cross-sections, possible aircraft dimensions or flight characteristics; it might mention plans for mergers or acquisitions, etc. In this industry, maybe more so than in other industries, a lot of this is going on but eventually much of it does not get materialized. Some of that will be illustrated in the discussion of the manufacturers.

Table 2.2 Comparison of regional aircraft

	Turboprop			*Jet*	
	Saab 340	*Fokker 50*	*ATR 72*	*CRJ-100*	*Fokker 100*
Wingspan (ft)	70	65	89	70	92
Height (ft)	23	21	25	21	28
Length (ft)	65	66	89	87	116
Passengers	35	30	74	52	107
Max. range (miles)	1,123	633	2,416	973	2,222

Understanding regional aircraft programme success

Before discussing the different regional aircraft manufacturers, their products and an analysis of their success in the market place, this section contains a general discussion of several characteristics that can help explain financial success (or failure) of an aircraft manufacturer. In general terms, financial success or failure for aircraft programmes can be attributed to three interdependent areas: design, production and sales.

Design-related issues

One characteristic in aviation that can contribute to the failure of an aircraft programme is the cost of aircraft design, and in particular the development of cashflows associated with this. Figure 2.8 provides an example of the general pattern.

The aircraft manufacturer is initially faced with negative cashflows as it is designing and launching the programme. The process of aircraft design and development is very expensive. For example, the development cost of the Embraer 170/190 was estimated at $850 million (Lewis, 2003). Furthermore, the initial aircraft that are produced are used for testing purposes required for certification (see also Chapter 7) and can typically not be sold to customers. The certification processes add to the very high cost involved for new aircraft

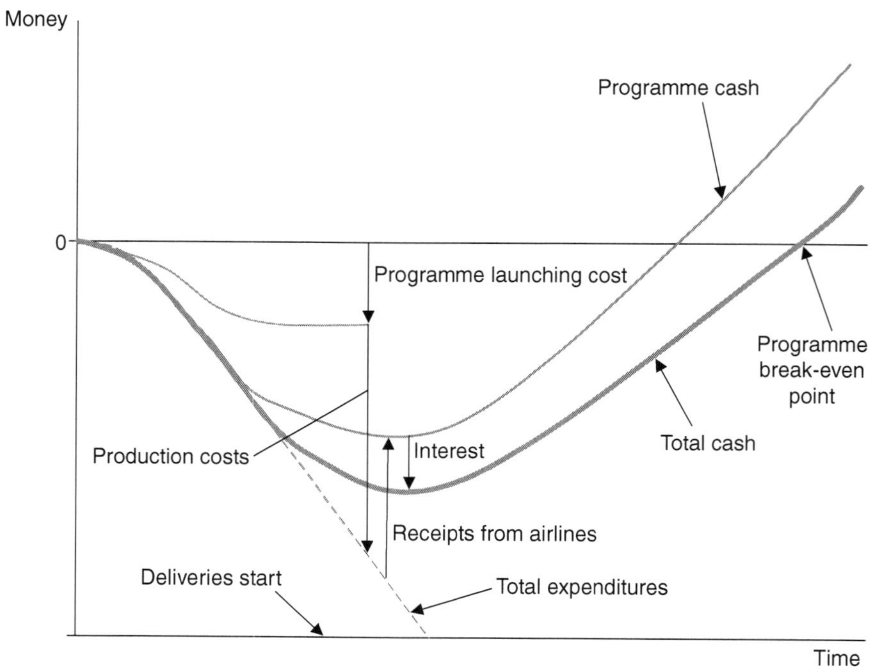

Figure 2.8 Typical cash flow curve for large transport aircraft programme (source: US Civil Aviation Manufacturing Industry Panel (1985)).

programmes. With many man-years of engineering work involved in the design and with high costs in the production of large, complex products leading to costs in the tens of millions of dollars for a single plane (depending on size), one can easily see how expensive it is in this industry to develop a new aircraft programme.

When a new aircraft programme is being considered, cashflow development has to be taken into consideration. This is not only because finances have to be secured for the programme but also because a break-even point has to be established (or at least an expected break-even point) and the break-even number of aircraft has to be considered in terms of market size, i.e. whether it is realistic. One advantage of a derivative aircraft instead of an all-new aircraft is that the cost of design will be much lower. This is therefore an appealing option for manufacturers, although an all-new design has the potential for greater improvements.

A delay compared to the initial plan in the design process because it takes more time, i.e. engineering man-hours, than originally envisioned to design the aircraft has two consequences. First, the cost of the programme goes up and therefore the expenditures are higher. The result of this is that the bold line (total cash) in Figure 2.8 makes a deeper dip and its minimum shifts to the right. Second, and related to this, it means there is a delay to when aircraft can be delivered, and thus a delay in receiving money from airlines. In addition, with loans now extended over a longer period of time, the interest cost goes up. The result of this is similar to the first issue (and thus exacerbates it), i.e. the bold line (total cash) in Figure 2.8 makes a deeper dip and shifts to the right. Combining these two effects means that the break-even point shifts to the right and thus more aircraft have to be produced before a programme becomes profitable. This situation can be made worse if changes in the aircraft are required after production has started. For example, in early 2013 Boeing was facing challenges with its 787 Dreamliner. This required additional engineering resources, thus adding to the overall cost of the aircraft programme. Third, a delay in design typically also means that production is delayed as well as entry to the market. This, due to competitors, can negatively affect the possibility of reaching the break-even point.

Production-related issues

A second characteristic that can contribute to the failure of an aircraft programme relates to the production of the aircraft and in particular the costs and margins that a manufacturer can achieve. For aircraft manufacturing the learning curve[4] is an important concept in this regard and early studies on the learning curve concept actually came out of the aircraft industry (Wright, 1936). The learning curve concept essentially means that when you perform a task multiple times, you become faster at doing it and thus the cost goes down. More precisely, the learning curve is defined as a constant reduction for every doubling in production. Figure 2.9 provides an illustration involving an 80 per cent learning

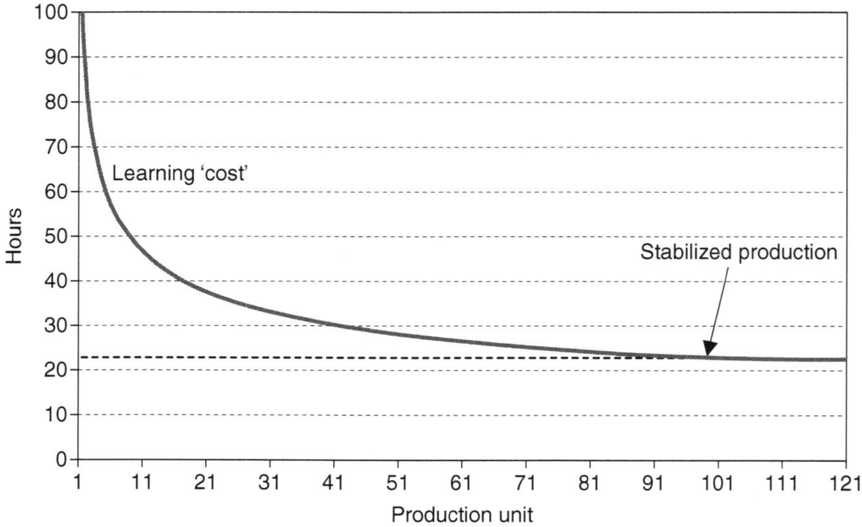

Figure 2.9 The learning curve.

curve. For simplicity sake, if the first unit of some type of product takes 100 hours to produce, then with an 80 per cent curve, the second unit (doubling) takes 20 per cent less to produce, i.e. 80 per cent of 100 hours is 80 hours. The fourth unit (doubling again) takes again 20 per cent less to produce, i.e. 80 per cent of 80 hours is 64 hours, etc. This means that the more you produce, the lower the cost of subsequent units and, consequently, the lower the average cost per unit.

The learning rate is influenced by, among other things, the scope of the task, the complexity of the task and the frequency of repetition. Doing a small task once per year will have limited learning effects compared with many frequent repetitions. Also, the learning 'ends' at some time. This is when production is stabilized – after this point there is no further significant reduction. For aircraft manufacturing, a stabilized production line typically occurs at 100 or 200 units. For an aircraft manufacturer the learning curve is an important concept because early in an aircraft programme it is practically impossible to charge customers a price for aircraft that is related to the actual production cost. In other words, with a development cost of an aircraft programme in the hundreds of millions of dollars, the initial cost of aircraft would be so high that sales would not exist. Therefore, the manufacturers apply the learning curve for planning and cost estimates. Experienced manufacturers can estimate their curves based on past performance and in the industry there are guidelines to help engineers make calculations – for example, average cost per weight. In the case of completely new aircraft programmes such as the Boeing 787, it becomes a much more tricky issue. The learning curve is another illustration of why it is financially beneficial to develop a derivative aircraft instead of an all-new aircraft, because there will be similarities in production, i.e. less learning is required to reach stable production.

Three potential problems can be identified. First, the aircraft manufacturer might find that the actual learning curve (the percentage) is less progressive than initially estimated (thus, a higher percentage which equates with less improvement). This means that the line in Figure 2.9 is flatter. With the same initial point for the first aircraft and the same (vertical axis) ending point in terms of cost or hours for a stabilized production line, this means that there are higher learning costs[5] than initially estimated. This also means that it will take longer to reach a stabilized production line. Thus, the average cost per aircraft ends up being higher than anticipated. Second, it may take longer to produce an aircraft on a stabilized production line than originally anticipated. This means that the dotted stabilized production line in Figure 2.9 moves up. Consequently, with a similar learning curve as initially expected, this means that the entire line in Figure 2.9 moves up, i.e. representing higher learning cost as well as higher overall cost for the aircraft. A consequence of this is that a particular aircraft unit is deliverable at a later date than initially estimated because it takes more time to produce any particular aircraft. This goes back to Figure 2.8 and results in delays in programme cash and a change in the break-even point. Another key aspect which is related to this is the ability of the manufacturer to ramp-up its production. If a manufacturer can ramp-up its production in a meaningful way, then more aircraft will be available sooner. Although the curve in Figure 2.9 may look the same, in terms of calendar time, it is achieved faster. This lowers the interest portion in Figure 2.8.

Sales-related issues

The third important characteristic of an aircraft programme is related to the sales of the aircraft. Sales depend upon typical aspects in any market place, such as performance and quality characteristics in terms of speed, payload, range, fuel consumption, etc. It also depends upon offerings of competitors, and since the customers, i.e. airlines, can be located anywhere in the world, the aircraft manufacturer need to have a global sales and service support network. Furthermore, aircraft have a lifetime of 30 years or more so customers are concerned with the long-term viability of a manufacturer. For any new potential entrant in the industry, the availability of a global support network and uncertainty over long-term viability will be obstacles to overcome. Lastly, the cost of the aircraft will impact potential sales. This is connected to the design and production issues because these not only influence overall cost, but also the timing of the programme, which influences the combination of the cost of the aircraft and the programme break-even point.

Manufacturers and their aircraft

In this section, the ten manufacturers will be discussed. The discussion will follow the sequence of their first deliveries as illustrated in Figure 2.2.

Fokker

The Fokker company was initiated by Anthony Fokker from the Netherlands. Fokker was one of the pioneers in aviation and built the Fokker Spin in the first decade of the 1900s. The company played an important role for military aircraft during the First World War, but the focus here will be on the commercial aircraft. The relevant history starts with the F27 Friendship, a turboprop aircraft. The first delivery of this aircraft was in November 1958. The F27 was a very popular aircraft that could replace the very successful but ageing DC-3. As a side note, the first DC-3 was delivered in the 1930s and in total over 16,000 commercial and military versions were produced. This is an extremely high number. For the present-day most successful aircraft (Boeing 737), almost 8,000 were sold between 1968 and the end of 2013. Many aircraft programmes do not reach sales of 1,000 units (see also Figures 2.10, 2.13 and 2.14). The F27 was produced in the Netherlands and also in the United States through a licensing agreement with Fairchild. The United States, due to its geographical size, the population size and increasing popularity of air travel was, and is, a very important market for aircraft manufacturers. Being able to sell the F27 in the United States was therefore an important factor in its success. Over 700 F27s were sold globally. Although this number is significantly lower than the numbers for the DC-3, it was a successful aircraft programme – i.e. profitable.

In the 1960s Fokker started to look at producing a commercial jet aircraft. The initial feasibility studies were looking at around 40 seats, but eventually it was concluded that capacity had to be around 60 seats to be economically feasible. Continued work led to the development of the F28 Fellowship. The first delivery of this aircraft was in February 1969. The aircraft sales were disappointing and although attempted by Fokker, a licensing agreement with Fairchild for the F28 was not reached. Several different versions of the F28 were developed, such as a stretched Mk 2000 which accommodated almost 80 passengers. In the end, fewer than 250 F28s were sold, but this aircraft programme passed the break-even point in 1981 and so after that was generating profits for the company.

In the early 1980s Fokker initiated studies for follow-up products for both the F27 and the F28. In November 1983 it decided to simultaneously develop the Fokker 50 to replace the F27 and the Fokker 100 to replace the F28.

Several improvements were made to the F27, such as new engines which reduced fuel consumption compared to the F27 by 30 per cent. Different propellers were used which reduced the noise level. More composite materials were used and slight modifications in the wing design as well as more automation in the cockpit were implemented. Several partners were used, such as SABCA from Belgium for the wing; parts of the fuselage were produced by Dassault from France; (West) Germany's Messerschmitt-Bölkow-Blohm (MBB) produced the flaps and some other parts; and Fuiji Heavy Industries (Japan) produced the vertical and horizontal stabilizers. The Fokker 50 programme faced significant delays and although the last F27 was delivered in June 1986, the first

Fokker 50 was not delivered until August 1987. A stretched version, the Fokker 60, was also developed but only a handful of them were delivered to the Dutch airforce.

Similarly, several improvements were incorporated into the Fokker 100 and in some instances demands from launch customers pushed Fokker beyond its initial ideas. For example, the first customer, Swissair, demanded the incorporation of the latest technologies with regard to automated landings (available in larger aircraft) so that the aircraft could be better utilized in different weather conditions. Compared to the F28 the Fokker 100 had new engines, a longer fuselage and an improved cockpit (navigation systems etc.) Several risk-sharing partners were also involved in the development of the Fokker 100, such as Shorts (Ireland) for the wing, MBB (Germany; later Deutsche Aerospace Airbus DAA) for fuselage sections and the tail, and Grumman for the engine nacelles (cover housing for the engines). The first Fokker 100 was delivered in February 1988. A smaller version, the Fokker 70, was also developed. A major success was achieved with the Fokker 100 when American Airlines ordered 75 aircraft in 1989. This entering of the US market was very promising.

In 1996 Fokker went bankrupt and production stopped in 1997 when 213 Fokker 50s and 283 Fokker 100s had been delivered. To understand the causes of this bankruptcy we have to go back to the decision made in 1983 to simultaneously develop two aircraft programmes.[6] Note that a full analysis goes beyond the scope of this chapter.

The plan for the Fokker 50 and the Fokker 100 was to have further developments of the F27 and F28 and to improve no more than 20 per cent of the parts. Based on this, initial costs for development were estimated (see Table 2.3). The Dutch government gave approval and the financing structure was 45 per cent for NIVR (Dutch Institute for Aircraft Development and Aerospace), 45 per cent through government secured loans and 10 per cent by Fokker.

By 1987 Fokker faced bankruptcy due to the earlier than expected withdrawal of the F27 and F28 aircraft and the later than expected introduction of the Fokker 50 and Fokker 100 into the market. The Dutch government supported Fokker by a cash injection of Hfl. 212 million. Furthermore, Fokker started to look for

Table 2.3 Financial characteristics of the Fokker 50 and the Fokker 100

Characteristic	*Fokker 50*	*Fokker 100*
Estimated development cost 1982 ($1 ≈ Hfl. 2.50 beginning of 1982)	Hfl. 380 million	Hfl. 530 million
Approved by Dutch government	Hfl. 383 million	Hfl. 579 million
Real cost by 1992 ($1 ≈ Hfl. 1.80 beginning of 1993)	Hfl. 634 million	Hfl. 1045 million
Estimated aircraft cost in 1983	Hfl. 17.6 million	Hfl. 38.5 million
Estimated aircraft cost by 1993	Hfl. 28.1 million	Hfl. 51.4 million

partners and in 1992 reached an agreement with Deutsche Aerospace (DASA), which became a majority shareholder. As history has shown, these approaches offered only a temporary relief.

Table 2.3 shows that the real development costs by 1992 were significantly higher than initially estimated in 1982. A main reason for this was that the 20 per cent rule could not be maintained. When the programme was developed, Fokker discovered challenges with its customers. This was due to a different type of customer, especially for the Fokker 100, i.e. much more demanding than what Fokker was used to with the F28. Additional changes and updates were required in order to be able to have an aircraft that could be sold in the marketplace. The amount of additional design work also led to the need to recruit more people who, due to lack of availability, were less experienced. This led to a further increase of the amount of time needed for the design. Overall, the design portion cost almost twice the amount of money initially budgeted. Furthermore, the cost portion for the company became Hfl. 755 million instead of the initially planned Hfl. 96 million!

In addition to higher design cost and timing delays, production also faced delays. The initial units suffered from delays in parts. Also, Fokker had estimated a learning curve based on its previous experiences, but the actual learning was initially less progressive partly due to the need to hire new personnel. This caused a combined estimated Hfl. 300 million extra in the production of the first 100 Fokker 50 aircraft and of the first 125 Fokker 100 aircraft.

In addition to the problems that arose with design and production, the market place also posed several challenges. First, there were costs involved with launch customers, i.e. offering a reduced price. For the Fokker 50 this amounted to costs of Hfl. 180 million and for the Fokker 100 to Hfl. 178 million. Another complicating factor was increased competition in the market place; for example, the ATR-42 posed a serious threat to the Fokker 50. Figure 2.10 illustrates the introduction of the Fokker 50 into the market as well as its main propeller-oriented competitors. This illustrates how the Fokker 50 (August 1987) was late into the market compared to the Saab 340 (June 1984), the Dash-8 (October 1984), the Embraer 120 (August 1985) and the ATR-42 (December 1985). As explained earlier, the delay in design also led to increased costs for the overall programme. Thus Fokker was not competitive in the market.[7] Some aircraft were sold below cost and in 1990 the first white-tails came out of the factory (aircraft without a customer). The estimates for break-even points in 1985 were 225 for the Fokker 50 and 175 for the Fokker 100, but by 1989 this had changed to 300 and 450, respectively.

To counter some of these effects the monthly production rates had to be increased. In the last years before Fokker went bankrupt, it had indeed dramatically improved efficiencies in production but by this time it was too late and the market was changing. For example, one of the changes was a demand for smaller jet aircraft. Attempts were made to get additional money from DASA and from the Dutch government, but for a variety of reasons this was not successful. DASA's mother company Daimler Benz was, for example, facing difficulties in

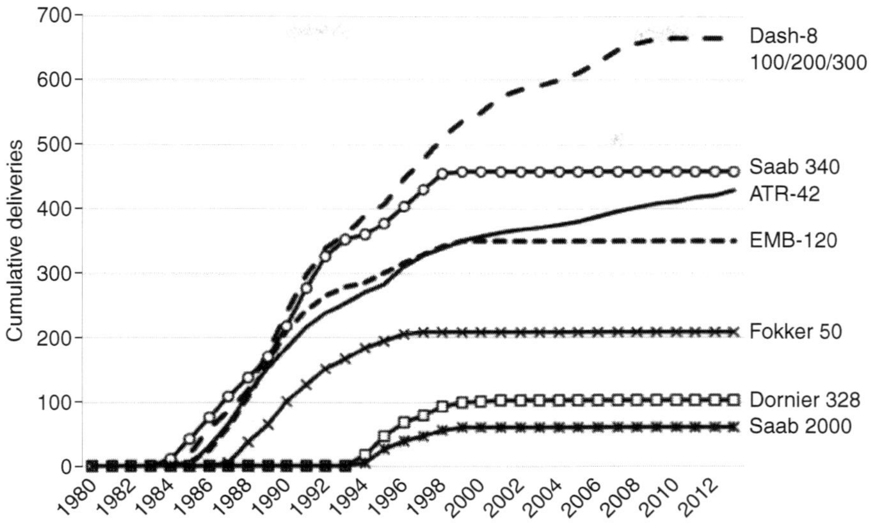

Figure 2.10 Cumulative deliveries of prop aircraft in 30–50-seat segment.

another core business – cars. Talks were also conducted with several other parties such as Bombardier (Canada), Samsung (Korea), AVIC (China) and Tupolev and Yakovlev (Russia), but nothing materialized.

Thus, Fokker provides an example of the inter-dependency of the three issues (design, production and sales) and how this can cause serious problems for an aircraft programme. After the bankruptcy Fokker was split into two parts. One part related to aircraft parts production, maintenance, etc. This was acquired by Stork and is currently a first-tier supplier to companies such as Airbus and Gulfstream. The other part related to the assembly of the existing Fokker aircraft. For the Fokker 100 this went through several parties, was initially named Rekkof (Fokker in reverse) and by 2012 attempts were still being made to restart production. The latest development in this regard is the F-120 Next Generation of modified and improved Fokker 100 aircraft (see www.ngaircraft.com). In particular, engine selection seemed to be a challenge (Kaminski-Morrow, 2012a).

British Aerospace

British Aerospace was formed in 1977 through the merger of four companies: Hawker Siddeley Aviation, Hawker Siddeley Dynamics, Scottish Aviation and British Aircraft Corporation. British Aircraft Corporation and Hawker Siddeley both had a history of mergers and acquisitions before being merged into British Aerospace.

Scottish Aviation was the producer of the Jetstream. This aircraft was originally designed by the Handley Page company but Scottish Aviation acquired the rights after the demise of Handley Page. There were two main versions of this prop aircraft: the Jetstream 31 and Jetstream 41. These aircraft had a capacity of fewer than 30 passengers. The first delivery of the Jetstream 31 was in 1982, while the last Jetstream 41 was delivered in 1999. In total more than 300 of these aircraft were produced and delivered (Roach and Eastwood, 2001).[8]

The British Aircraft Corporation was the producer of the BAC 1-11, which was a jet engine aircraft with a capacity of around 100 passengers. It was first delivered in 1965. After British Aerospace was formed, its product portfolio included two 100-seat jet (essentially competing) aircraft: the HS 146 and the BAC 1-11. British Aerospace decided to conclude the BAC 1-11 programme and a licensing agreement was reached in 1978 with the Bucharest Aircraft Factory (Intreprinderea de Avioane Bucuresti) in Romania (which was later renamed Romaero). This agreement included the purchase of three BAC 1-11 aircraft and allowed British Aerospace to phase out production. Production ended in the early 1980s after slightly over 230 aircraft had been delivered (Jet Information Services, 2003). The last BAC 1-11 was delivered in 1982 to Romania.

Hawker Siddeley was the producer of the HS 748. This was originally designed by the Avro company. It was a 36-seat propeller aircraft. The first version was delivered in 1962. In the 1960s Hindustan Aeronautics had a licensing agreement to produce the aircraft in India. It did so primarily for Indian Airlines and the Indian Airforce. The last HS 748 was delivered in 1967 to the Royal Air Force. In total, almost 300 of these aircraft were delivered (Roach and Eastwood, 2001). The ATP, a turboprop aircraft for almost 70 passengers which was first delivered by British Aerospace in 1988, was a derivative of the HS 748 and was later further improved under the name Jetstream 61. ATP deliveries ended in 1998 after a total of only 62 aircraft deliveries.

Hawker Siddeley was also the producer of the HS 146. The first delivery of this aircraft was in 1983. This was an aircraft with four small jet engines for around 100 passengers. British Aerospace further developed this into the Avro Regional Jet family RJ70, RJ85 and RJ100. The last delivery of this aircraft was in 2001. In total 385 of these aircraft were delivered (Jet Information Services, 2003).[9]

Figure 2.11 shows the deliveries in the 30–50-seat segment compared to the 70–100-seat segment. This shows that for most of the time period the majority of the deliveries have been in the 30–50-seat segment. In 1993 deliveries in both segments were about equal and deliveries in the 70–100-seat segment have outpaced the 30–50-seat segment since 2005. Based on this, it can be concluded that manufacturers such as British Aerospace, with aircraft in the 70–100-seat segment, before 2000 were essentially at a disadvantaged position in the industry. As a reminder, the Regional Jet family was first delivered in April 1993 (derived from the BAe 146, which was first delivered in 1983) and the ATP propeller aircraft was first delivered in 1988. Thus both were introduced at an inopportune time into the market.

Nevertheless, some aircraft were sold in the 70–100-seat market segment, so it is interesting to delve a little deeper to find out why BAe was not so successful

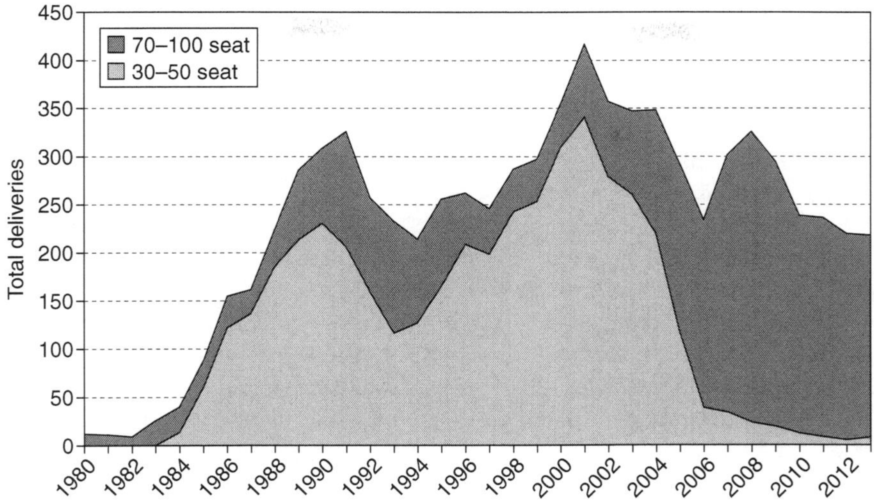

Figure 2.11 Deliveries of 30–50-seat regional aircraft compared to 70–100-seat aircraft.

with its products. Figure 2.12 provides an overview of deliveries for the 70–100-seat regional aircraft.

With regard to the failure of the ATP programme, Figure 2.12 illustrates how the market grew somewhat in the early 1990s then declined a little and grew again during the first decade of the twenty-first century. Most of this growth

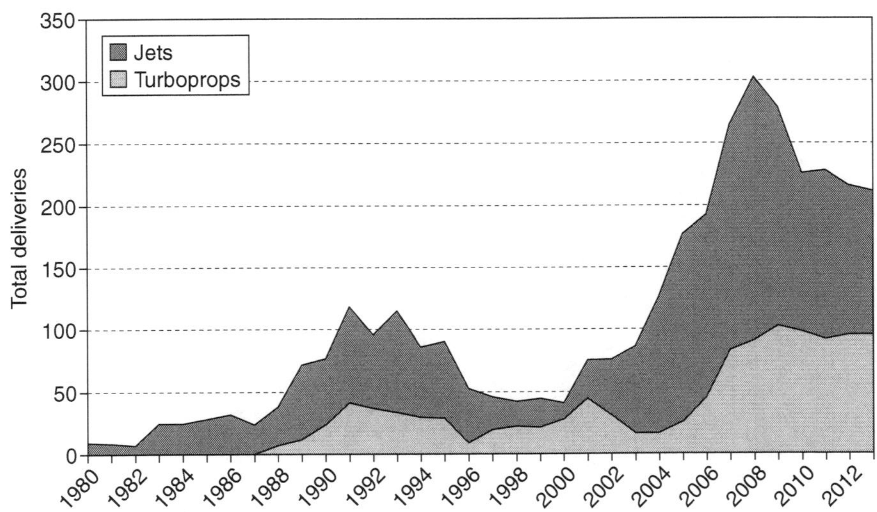

Figure 2.12 Deliveries of 70–100-seat regional aircraft.

occurred for jet aircraft, not propeller aircraft. This illustrates in particular the difficulties for the ATP programme, and can explain why so few of these aircraft were sold. Figure 2.13 provides a different type of information, i.e. cumulative deliveries.

Based on Figure 2.13, two groups of product introductions in the 70–100-seat market can be distinguished. The first group from roughly 1980 until 1990 covers Fokker, the BAe ATP and Regional Jets and the ATR-72. The second group, near the beginning of 2000, contains the Embraer 170/190 family, the CRJ 700/900 family and the Dash-8 400. The two least successful programmes in terms of deliveries are both propeller aircraft (Dash-8 400 and the ATP). The ATP, with its unfortunate timing, did worse than the Dash-8. As can be seen from Figure 2.13, both the CRJ 700/900 family and the ERJ 170/190 family had quick success, i.e. the line in the graph has a high slope compared to the other, earlier, programmes. This relates to the ability to ramp-up production and have high annual delivery rates. High annual delivery rates reduce the time period in which cost is recovered and reduces the overall interest cost, thereby lowering the total programme cost (see Figure 2.8). Thus, in terms of time, it can lead to a lower break-even point that will also be reached quicker.

Another part of the explanation for the weak performance of the British Aerospace aircraft has to do with the performance of the aircraft. Comparing, for example, the Fokker 100 with the ATP and the Regional Jets shows that the speed and range of the ATP, as well as the Regional Jets, is less than that of the Fokker 100. Thus, essentially British Aerospace had uncompetitive products and hence the lead in cumulative deliveries of the Fokker 100 until it ceased production in 1996.

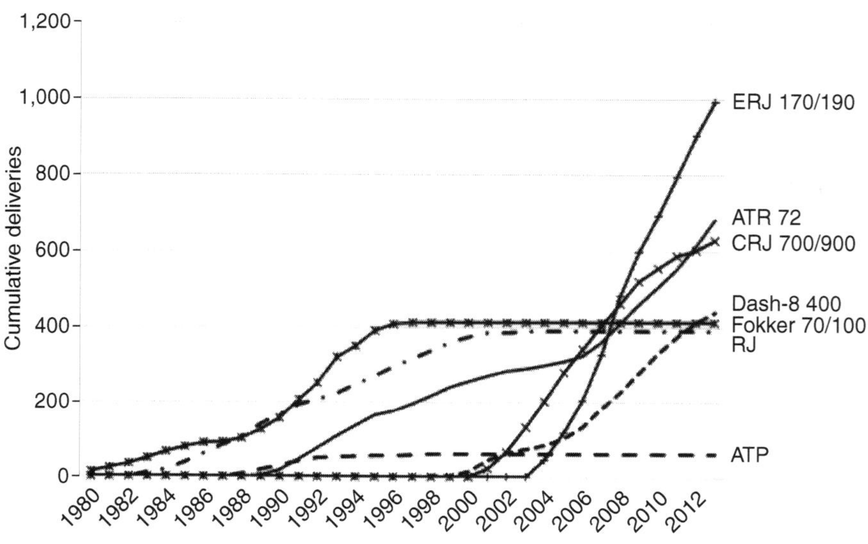

Figure 2.13 Cumulative deliveries of aircraft in the 70–100-seat segment.

The poor timing and the lack of competitiveness of the aircraft programmes had financial consequences for British Aerospace. Part of this can be explained through the learning concept (see Figures 2.8 and 2.9). When a product is not well received by the market, then consequently the production rates (and delivery rates) are low. This means that the costs stay relatively high because the learning effects are not (quickly) achieved. Because initial aircraft are typically sold at prices that do not reflect costs, this can lead to a loss-making situation. The evidence indicates that British Aerospace was probably in this position. For example, in 1993 the Jetstream and ATP businesses (the propeller aircraft) were running losses of about $93 million per year (Anonymous, 1993) and in the first half of 1994 losses for BAe's regional aircraft activities amounted to $124.8 million (Anonymous, 1994).

During 1997 and 1998 BAe made several attempts to boost its business. Among them were plans for a $1.2 billion programme for a new 54–84-seat jet aircraft as part of AIR (the AIRjet programme) (Sparaco, 1998a); plans for upgraded and re-engined versions of the Regional Jet family (new versions were indicated as the RJX) with a launch late in 1999, but these dates kept shifting (Morrocco, 1999); and there were plans for a joint undertaking with Malaysia's Kazanah Nasional Berhad which may have included technology transfer and investment in the Avro RJ product line (Sparaco and Morrocco, 1998). None of these plans materialized. Furthermore, during the early 1990s BAe and the Committee for Aviation and Space Industry Development (CASID) of Taiwan had also negotiated about production of the Avro RJ in Taiwan, but in this regard contract negotiations were also stopped. In 2001 BAe made the decision to exit the regional aircraft market (Kingsley-Jones, 2002). This coincided with a turboprop market that had been declining in the previous five years and where more jet aircraft had been delivered (see Figure 2.6), although as Figure 2.6 illustrates that would be changing in the next five years. This halting of production did not lead to the end of British Aerospace, as the company was still successfully involved in aircraft parts production – for example, as a partner in Airbus, as well as in defence-related products.

Saab

Saab (Svenska Aeroplan AB) was founded in 1937 at Trollhättan in Sweden. The original plan was to make military aircraft and this has also been the main business for most of the time since then. It was merged with the Aircraft Division of Svenska Järnvägsverkstäderna rolling stock factory at Linköping in 1939 and renamed Saab Aktieblolag in May 1965. It later merged with Scania-Vabis in 1969 to combine automotive interests.

With regard to civil aircraft, a collaboration between Saab and Fairchild Industries was announced in January of 1980. This collaboration entailed the joint development of the Saab-Fairchild 340 (SF 340), a 35-seat propeller aircraft. Fairchild was responsible for the manufacture of some of the parts such as the wings, tail unit and engine nacelles, while Saab was responsible for 75 per cent of the development cost, systems integration and certification (Hewson, 1994). The initial flight of the SF 340 was in 1983. The launch customer was Crossair from Switzerland, which received the first aircraft on 6 June 1984. An interesting side note is that almost a week later the airline carried out its first flight with a paying passenger: Pope John Paul II. A year later, Fairchild had to withdraw from the project (October 1985) due to its poor financial situation. Production was then gradually transferred to Saab's Linköping base. By 1987, as the linkage with Fairchild was completely removed, the product became the Saab 340 (Hewson, 1994). The last Saab 340 was delivered on 8 June 1999 (Jackson *et al.*, 2000); by that time almost 460 had been delivered.

During the late 1980s Saab perceived a market for an advanced, high-speed regional turboprop aircraft (Hewson, 1994). The idea was for an aircraft that could match jet performance over a range of sectors. Two disadvantages of jets are that they fly at a higher altitude, which adds to flight time, and that the fuel cost is higher. Thus, over relatively short distances jet aircraft have less of an advantage over turboprop aircraft. Saab launched the Saab 2000 programme in December 1988. The Saab 2000 was a 50-seat aircraft which was an extended and modified version of the Saab 340, i.e. a derivative and not an aircraft designed from scratch. Agreements were reached with partner manufacturers such as CASA (Spain) to build the wing and Valmet (Finland) to build the tail unit. The first Saab 2000 flew on 26 March 1992. Some delays occurred with certification of the aircraft, but on 30 September 1994 Crossair (which was again the launch customer) received the first Saab 2000 (Hewson, 1994). The last Saab 2000 was delivered on 29 April 1999. In total, a little over 60 were delivered.

Why did Saab withdraw from commercial aircraft manufacturing? Compared with the Fokker and British Aerospace aircraft, in terms of speed the Saab 340 was competitive and the Saab 2000 was in fact faster than the two jet aircraft (Fokker 100 and RJ100). However, in terms of range and payload, results were a little mixed. Figure 2.14 illustrates the cumulative deliveries of aircraft in the 30–50-seat market segment.

Figure 2.14 illustrates the similarity of the initial success of the Saab 340 and the Dash-8. The ATR-42 and the EMB 120 also show a similar pattern, but around 1990 their delivery rates are slower than the Saab 340 and the Dash-8. The two steep curves in Figure 2.14 are from the CRJ 100/200 and the ERJ 135/140/145. Both of these aircraft were introduced in the first half of the 1990s and both were targeting the 30–50-seat segment. This segment had previously not experienced jet aircraft (see earlier in this chapter). The competition with these two jet aircraft led to declining sales and caused Saab by 1998 to decide to stop producing the Saab 340 and the Saab 2000. The jet aircraft, at that time, offered better performance for about the same price. The president of the Continental Express airline stated this as follows: 'the big appeal of the ERJ-135 is that it appears to have jet-like revenues and turboprop operating costs' (Lopez and Norris, 1998). In short, it isn't so much that Saab had excessive cost or poor quality (although the Saab 2000, with its low total number of units sold, probably was not cost competitive nor reached its break-even point) but rather, better

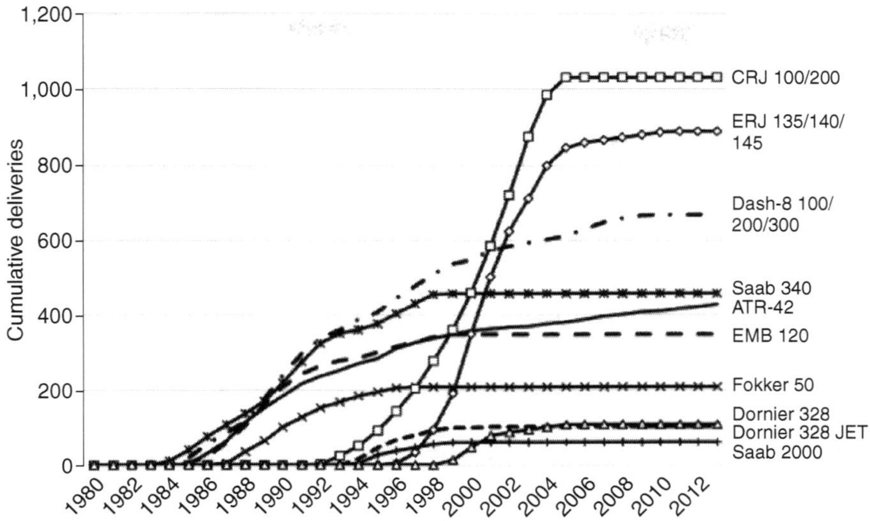

Figure 2.14 Cumulative deliveries of aircraft in the 30–50-seat segment.

competitors came onto the market which outcompeted Saab's products on performance. The 'mistake' Saab made, if it can be called such, is that it went for a turboprop aircraft and did not have the foresight to move towards jet aircraft. During the 1990s jet aircraft were rising in popularity (see Figure 2.6) and especially in the 30–50-seat market airlines increasingly preferred jet aircraft (see Figure 2.7). So Saab was, by that time, poorly positioned in the market. This preference for jet aircraft was not only an economic issue. For example, one airline's decision process when comparing the CRJ and the ERJ did not include the Saab 2000 'simply because it has propellers, and we are seeking to improve passenger appeal' (Kingsley-Jones *et al.*, 1998). A Bombardier executive stated on the comparison of jets and turboprops: 'Cost isn't so much of a factor right now. But when a downturn comes, I think you'll see the so-called turboprop avoidance factor reduced significantly' (Polek, 1998a). Figure 2.7 demonstrates that around 2006 turboprops had the highest market share in the 30–50-seat market again, which shows that some of this is a matter of timing (see also later in this chapter).[10] Note also that it was difficult to predict the preference for jet aircraft. For example, by 1998 industry publications frequently discussed the future of turboprop aircraft and were not sure that jet aircraft were going to win in the smaller 30–50-seat segment (see, for example, Lopez, 1998).

ATR

ATR stands for Avions de Transport Regional. ATR is a collaboration between Aerospatiale (France) and Aeritalia (Italy, later changed to Alenia). Aerospatiale was formed in 1970 by a French government-directed merger of Sud-Aviation (producer of the Caravelle), Nord-Aviation and SEREB (Jackson *et al.*, 2000). Alenia was part of the Finmeccanica company in Italy (Jackson *et al.*, 2000).

The first agreement for the collaboration between Aerospatiale and Aeritalia was in July of 1980. The ATR programme started in November 1981, while the economic joint venture (50:50) was formally established on 5 February 1982 with the purpose of developing turboprop regional aircraft (Jackson *et al.*, 2000).

The ATR-42 was launched in October 1981; the first flight of the aircraft took place on 30 April 1985; and deliveries began on 3 December 1984 (Jackson *et al.*, 2000). The ATR-72 was launched on 15 January 1986. The ATR-72 was a stretched and improved version of the ATR-42, i.e. it was not designed from scratch. The first flight took place in October 1988 and deliveries began in October 1989 (Jackson *et al.*, 2000). Production for both aircraft is presently (2014) ongoing.

During the latter half of the 1990s ATR had a collaboration with British Aerospace, i.e. AI(R) Aero International (Regional). This collaboration combined sales, marketing and customer service activities of ATR and the British Aerospace subsidiaries Avro and Jetstream (Condom, 1995). AI(R) examined the possibility of jointly developing a new jet airplane. After AI(R) was dissolved ATR investigated the possibility to develop the 70-seat regional jet (Airjet) by itself and also looked into possibilities of a collaboration with Fairchild Dornier around the 728JET, but none of these plans materialized (Jackson *et al.*, 2000).

ATR had several agreements with the Xian Aircraft Company in Xian, China (Eriksson, 1995). The Xian Aircraft Company was part of AVIC (Aviation Industries of China). The first agreement was reached in 1985 and involved ATR-42 outer wing boxes. In 1997 an agreement was reached for the production of the ATR-72 rear fuselage. During the 1997 Paris Air Show a memorandum of understanding was signed between ATR and AVIC for the establishment of a joint venture in China. This involved industrial cooperation in the form of licensed production. The idea was to have an increasing share of production at the Xian Aircraft Company, which would eventually lead to an ATR-72 assembly line in Xian (Sparaco, 1997a; Anonymous, 1998a). Around 1998 the market forecast for regional aircraft with passenger capacities up to 90 seats in China showed a market potential of about 500 new deliveries up to the year 2015. The anticipated demand for the ATR was about 200 aircraft for a 15-year period. A little over a year later, in December 1999, the market for large regional turboprop aircraft was forecasted to be substantially smaller. It was expected not to fall below 100 units in the following 15 years, of which ATR was expected to get the lion's share (Yu'An, 1999). The ATR-72 assembly line in China was never realized. In 2007 ATR announced new, improved versions of the ATR-42 and ATR-72 (i.e. the ATR-42-600 and ATR-72-600). First deliveries of the ATR-72-600 took place in 2011 and for the ATR-42-600 in 2012.

Why has ATR been able to survive where other manufacturers such as Saab have not been able to do so? Figure 2.13 showed the deliveries of aircraft in the 70–100-seat segment. This segment had mostly jet aircraft, except the British

Aerospace ATP and the ATR-72. The ATP and the ATR-72 were introduced around the same time. The ATR-72 had better characteristics than the ATP, that is, about the same number of passengers but a slightly higher speed and a better range. The Dash-8 400 was faster but had a shorter range than the ATR-72 but was introduced later in the market.

Figure 2.14 showed the deliveries of propeller aircraft in the 30–50-seat segment. The figure shows how the ATR-42 initially had similar success in terms of deliveries as the Dash-8, Saab 340 and EMB-120. By 1989 the cumulative deliveries of these companies were in the same ballpark, but with a lead for the Saab 340, i.e. 138 (Saab 340), 117 (Dash-8 100/200/300), 114 (ATR-42) and 107 (EMB-120). After 1989 the Dash-8 and the Saab 340 remain successful, while the EMB-120 and ATR-42 have slightly lower growth in cumulative terms. The Fokker 50 is clearly less successful. In terms of performance, the ATR-42 could carry more passengers for a greater distance, although at slightly lower speeds. The ATR-42 also had better performance characteristics than the EMB-120, that is 30 passengers, maximum range 633 miles and maximum operating speed 313 mph (Hewson, 1994; see also the discussion for Bombardier). Despite the apparently better success of the Saab 340, with the entry of jets in this market Saab, Embraer (for the 120), Fokker and Fairchild Dornier all exited the market. By early 2000 this left only Bombardier (Dash-8) and ATR to compete with turboprops. Figure 2.7 shows how the market for propeller aircraft declined significantly during the 1990s and deliveries reached a minimum of 50 units in 2000 (split about evenly between the Dash-8 and the ATR). By 2000 ATR had delivered 358 ATR-42s, 255 ATR-72s, while Bombardier had delivered 549 Dash-8 100/200/300 series and had just started deliveries (total of 15) of the Dash-4 400 series. Thus, the ATR and Dash-8 programmes probably reached their break-even point, had achieved low production cost due to the learning curve (Figure 2.9) and thus were likely to be able to sustain the production of these aircraft even with a low number of deliveries. Furthermore, the ATR-72 was a derivative of the ATR-42 and thus had production similarities, and Bombardier was not dependent upon the turboprops because it was also producing regional jets. The real intriguing question is whether Saab would have been able to continue to compete if it had not sustained its production. If Saab had stayed in the market, and assuming that demand would have stayed the same, this might have meant that either demand would have been split among the three manufacturers (Saab, Bombardier and ATR) or that it would have caused the exit of one of the other two parties (Bombardier or ATR). Table 2.4 shows the deliveries and orders for these main competitors in the few years before Saab decided to stop production.

Based on Table 2.4 one might conclude that the Saab 340 was still competing favourably compared to the ATR-42. However, another signal from the market is order cancellations. Saab faced 15 and 18 cancellations of orders for the 340 in 1995 and 1996, respectively, whereas ATR faced 0 and 1 cancellations for the ATR-42 in the same years. Thus, although Saab was still delivering more 340s than ATR was delivering ATR-42s, and although Saab was receiving more net

Table 2.4 Net orders and deliveries of turboprop aircraft around exit of Saab from the market

Manufacturer	*Type*	*1995*		*1996*		*1997*	
		Ordered	*Delivered*	*Ordered*	*Delivered*	*Ordered*	*Delivered*
ATR	42	24	13	13	27	20	17
	72	26	28	11	11	34	19
Bombardier	Dash-8 100	34	18	60	39	26	30
	Dash-8 400	N.A.	0	15	0	17	0
Saab	340	33	16	14	27	21	26
	2000	5	21	6	12	12	8

Sources: O'Toole and Moxon, 1996; O'Toole, 1997a; 1998; Roach and Eastwood, 2001.

orders for the 340 than ATR was receiving for the ATR-42, Saab might have perceived the market more negatively due to its experience with the cancellations. In addition, the Saab 2000 was not very successful, whereas the ATR had the better selling ATR-72. This might explain why Saab decided to exit the market whereas ATR remained in the market.[11]

Bombardier

Bombardier is a company that is a little different to the other companies in this chapter. While all the other companies have mainly a focus on aerospace-related activities, which in some instances includes military aircraft, Bombardier has a transport orientation. For example, besides commercial aircraft (it also produces business aircraft, amphibious aircraft (for example used to fight forest fires) and specialized aircraft with, for example, special navigation systems) it also produces trains.

Bombardier was named after Joseph-Armand Bombardier who, in 1937, obtained his first patent for the development of a tracked vehicle for travelling over snow. In 1959 the Ski-Doo snowmobile was launched and in 1968 the Sea-Doo jetski was launched. Other types of vehicles such as the ATV (all-terrain vehicle) also became part of Bombardier's product range. Bombardier's Recreational Product Division was sold in 2003 and became a separate entity.

Bombardier entered the railway industry in 1971, when it acquired Lohnerwerke (Austria). The aviation industry followed in 1986 when it purchased Canadair. This was expanded upon in 1989 with the acquisition of Shorts Brothers (Ireland), followed by Learjet (United States) in 1990 and then de Havilland (division from Boeing located in Canada) in 1992. Canadair and de Havilland, the relevant companies for the analysis, have a complex international ownership history. In the following only the main aspects are highlighted. More information can be found in Todd and Simpson (1986) and Jackson *et al.* (2000).

The de Havilland factory in Canada was originally a subsidiary of de Havilland, a British company. In 1961, with several other companies, de Havilland was merged into Hawker Siddely Aviation. The Canadian government nationalized it in 1974. Two of the main products were the DHC-7 (introduced in 1975) and the DHC-8 (Dash-8). The DHC-8 was a derivative of the larger DHC-7 and had its first flight in June 1983 and first delivery in October 1984. During the 1980s, the Canadian aviation industry had increasing difficulties and, for example, de Havilland lost $226 million in the last seven months of 1982. By 1986 de Havilland was sold to Boeing. Boeing decided to focus on the DHC-8 and stopped producing the DHC-7. On 22 January 1992 Boeing sold de Havilland to Bombardier.[12] At that time Boeing had lost nearly $1 billion building Dash-8 aircraft (Symonds, 1997). Several versions of the Dash-8 exist, i.e. the series 100, 200 and 300. The later series provide improved performance over the 100 series and, in addition, the series 300 is a stretched version that allows more passengers (50 versus 37). Bombardier launched the Dash-8 400 in 1995, for which it received a $57 million (Canadian) loan from the Canadian government (Polek, 1998a). This was a stretch of the series 300 that allowed 74 passengers. Later models had an added designation of a Q for quiet, e.g. 8Q 400, indicating the incorporation of the company's proprietary noise and vibration suppression system (Shifrin, 1997).

Canadair had several owners but by 1976 it was part of General Dynamics (United States), when it was nationalized by the Canadian government. One of its products at that time was the CL-215, an amphibious aircraft that could scoop water. During the 1980s, as mentioned previously, the Canadian aviation industry had difficulties and, for example, Canadair lost $1.4 billion on sales of $429 million in 1982. The Canadian government saw business aviation as the key to success for Canadair and invested in developing a business jet. This was the Canadair Challenger, which first flew in 1979. de Havilland and Canadair were subsidized for about $828.3 million per year through the 1981–1983 period. Bombardier acquired Canadair on 23 December 1986, and in 1987 design studies were initiated for a passenger jet based on the Challenger. This led to the CRJ-100. The CRJ-100 was launched based on the belief that a minimum of 400 aircraft could be sold (Godfrey, 1990). The break-even point for the CRJ-100 was probably relatively low for Bombardier because Bombardier had a history of acquiring companies that were in trouble and being rewarded by governments for doing so. For example, when Bombardier bought de Havilland and Canadair, it received two billion Canadian dollars from the Canadian government. When Bombardier purchased Shorts Brothers (Ireland) in 1989, it received guaranteed loans from the British government equivalent of 1.3 billion Canadian dollars (Anonymous, 1996a). In June 1990 Bombardier completed the purchase of the bankrupt company Learjet for $75 million (Jackson *et al.*, 2000). Based on this it is likely that much of the development costs of the Challenger were written-off, lowering the CRJ-100 cost. In addition, the projected operating cost of the CRJ-100 was lower than that of the comparable turboprops, i.e. Fokker 50, ATR-42, Dash-8 300 (Godfrey, 1990).

The CRJ-100 first flew in 1991 and first delivery took place on 29 October 1992. The CRJ-100 was the first jet aircraft that was introduced at the higher end of the 30–50-seat market segment. The CRJ-200 had improved performance characteristics such as lower fuel consumption, increased cruise altitude and increased cruise speed. Another version, the CRJ-440, had lower capacity, i.e. 44 passengers.

In 1995 Bombardier initiated design and market evaluation for a stretched derivative of the CRJ. This $475 million programme became the CRJ-700 (Symonds, 1997). Bombardier received an CAD$87 million loan for this from the Canadian government (Anonymous, 1999). This is a 70-passenger jet; its first delivery was in 2001. At the Farnborough Air Show on 8 September 1998 Bombardier announced the BRJ-X. This was a plan for an all new 90-seat class regional aircraft (Anonymous, 1998b). This plan was shelved by 2000 as Bombardier's conditions worsened and instead it opted for a stretch of the CRJ-700, i.e. the CRJ-900. First delivery of this 86-passenger aircraft, was in 2003. In 2002, Bombardier signed a tentative agreement with AVIC I to co-produce the CRJ700/900 jets in Shanghai (a counter move to the Embraer joint venture with AVIC II to produce the ERJ 145 in Harbin under licence) but this line never materialized (Lewis and Ionides, 2002).

By the beginning of the first decade of the twenty-first century Bombardier's Aerospace business' good fortunes seemed to have come to an end. Although it had previously purchased poorly performing companies, it now was in severe financial trouble itself. In October 2002 Bombardier started to temporarily close its business jet lines (Anonymous, 2002a). By early 2003 it faced the risk of an asset sale to secure funding (Dunn, 2003a) and the future of the Dash-8 production was in doubt as the backlog shrank to 26 aircraft, i.e. the equivalent of eight months of work. Union issues exacerbated its problems (Lewis and Dunn, 2003). After cutting 3,800 aerospace jobs in 2001, it cut another 3,000 jobs in 2003 (Walker, 2003). Luckily Bombardier could count on the Canadian government for help as it allocated $860 million in loans to buyers of Canadian aircraft in an effort to help Bombardier secure more foreign sales (Dunn, 2003b). By early 2004 pressure was mounting on Bombardier to create an all-new 90–110-seat aircraft in order to be able to compete with the EMB 170/190 and the Fairchild Dornier 728 (Dunn and Flores, 2004), but initially Bombardier did not believe in a viable market until at least 2008 or 2009 (Trimble, 2004). Nevertheless, it asked the Canadian government for more financial support and hinted at the possibility of producing a new 100-plus seat regional jet family at its Shorts facility in Ireland if incentives offered there were better (Dunn, 2004a). By mid-2004 Bombardier revealed details of a new proposed $1.53 billion 100-plus seat aircraft programme, the CSeries (Anonymous, 2004a). Subsequently it invited US states to bid for assembly of this aircraft, thereby putting pressure on Canada and Ireland (Dunn, 2004b).

Bombardier has been one of the consistent performers in the regional aircraft industry. What explains the success of Bombardier? There seem to be several explanations for Bombardier's success. First, it is not only dependent upon aircraft, so even if the aircraft industry has a downturn, it has other divisions which can 'carry' the aerospace division. Second, it acquired several of its aircraft-producing facilities for very low prices and was able to get additional funding. Furthermore, the CRJ-100 was based on an already existing design and therefore had a cost advantage. Third, it was first in the market and therefore had excellent timing with the CRJ-100 family (the initial smaller versions as well as the 70-seat and higher variants). All of this means that compared to, for example, Fokker, where the inter-dependency of design, production and sales exacerbated the situation, in the case of Bombardier it helped a good situation get even better.

Fairchild Dornier

The Fairchild Dornier history relates to both Fairchild from the United States and Dornier from Germany. The history of Fairchild is complex due to many mergers, acquisitions and diversifications in many different types of products, as well as aircraft-related divisions with different names and name changes. The original Fairchild Aviation Corporation was founded in 1924 by serial entrepreneur Sherman Fairchild. Aside from aviation he was involved in many other industries, such as semiconductors – the Fairchild Semiconductor company is attributed as a main contributor to the start-ups that eventually created the Silicon Valley region (Kenney and Patton, 2006). Over time, Fairchild Aircraft Inc. produced small aircraft such as the Metroliner and the Merlin (Jackson *et al.*, 2000). Fairchild also produced the Fokker F27 under a licensing agreement starting in the late 1950s and was involved in the joint development of the Saab 340 during the 1980s. In the period from 1992 until 1995 Fairchild held negotiations with LET (Czech Republic) for the creation of a joint-venture to produce and market a family of aircraft, including the L-410/-420, L-610 and Metro 23, but by 1995 negotiations broke down.

Dornier GmbH was formed in 1922 by Professor Claude Dornier under the original name of Dornier-Betallbauten. It operated as Dornier GmbH from December 1972. One of the products developed by Dornier was the 228. The Dornier 228 could accommodate 19 passengers (Hewson, 1994). The first Dornier 228-100 flew in Germany on 28 March 1981. Hindustan Aeronautics Limited (HAL) signed a contract for licensed manufacture of up to 150 Dornier 228s in November 1983. This included a phased technology transfer. Daimler-Benz (DASA) acquired a majority stake (65.5 per cent) in 1985 but reduced this to 57.55 per cent by 1 January 1989. Development of the Dornier 328 started in the mid 1980s but was suspended and then relaunched in 1988. The first flight was in 1991, with production aircraft following a couple of years later (Jackson *et al.*, 2000). DASA concluded that there were too many players in the market and that the 328 could not remain a stand-alone aircraft. It had planned to develop a 50-seat derivative in 1993 but dropped the idea. In 1995 it considered the 428, a 40–45-seat version of the 328 (Sparaco, 1995). The 428 never materialized. One complication with this plan was that this stretched version would compete with the Fokker 50 and Fokker was also partly owned by DASA in 1995.[13] In 1996 it was announced that production of all Dornier 228s would move to India (Jackson *et al.*, 2000).

In June 1996 Fairchild Aerospace (100 per cent owner of Fairchild Aircraft Inc.) and Daimler Chrysler Aerospace concluded an agreement to create a joint-venture company (Fairchild Dornier) in which Fairchild would acquire 80 per cent of Dornier Luftfahrt GmbH (Jackson *et al.*, 2000). On 5 February 1997, Fairchild Aerospace launched the 328JET, a jet-powered version of the 328. The first 328JET flew on 20 January 1998 and the first delivery was made in July 1999 (Jackson *et al.*, 2000).

In March 1997 Fairchild Dornier announced plans for a stretched 328JET, i.e. the 528JET (48–50 seats) (Sparaco, 1997b). Shortly afterwards it started looking for partners for the 528JET and in November 1997 announced plans for an all-new 70-seat aircraft; the 728JET, a potential 90-seat stretch, was also envisioned (Taverna, 1997). Subsequently a programme for a stretched version of the 328JET, i.e. the 428JET (42 seats), was officially launched at the Berlin Air Show in May 1998 (Jackson *et al.*, 2000) while the 528JET became part of the 728JET family (Jeziorski, 1998), which was also formally launched at the Berlin Air Show (Anonymous, 1998c). Fairchild Dornier looked for risk-sharing partners for the 728JET but had some difficulties (Anonymous, 1998d). Over the years Fairchild Dornier explored potential customers for the different jets as well as other collaboration opportunities. For example, in 1999 Fairchild Dornier and ATR discussed a potential collaboration for joint marketing and a potential 728JET industrial collaboration was discussed with AVIC I and AVIC II in 2000, whereas a 528JET production collaboration was discussed with AVIC in early 2001. In March 2002 Boeing was rumoured to be close to acquiring a significant stake in Fairchild Dornier. None of these materialized. A similar result was achieved for the different aircraft programmes. The 428JET, 528JET and 928JET were never produced, but on 21 March 2002 the first 728JET was presented to the public.

Shortly after having completed the first 728JET Fairchild Dornier filed for insolvency. To understand what caused this, the Dornier 328 programme under DASA management will be analysed.

By 1995 it became clear that the 328 was almost a decade late into the market compared to competitors such as the Saab 340 and the Embraer 120 (see also Figure 2.14). Thus, in terms of the section on regional aircraft success earlier in this chapter, it is clear that Fairchild Dornier was struggling with the sales of its 328. This is related to the production of the aircraft and the financial development, as illustrated in Figure 2.8. Due to limited sales, Fairchild Dornier would have trouble reaching its break-even point for the 328, which had an estimated development cost of one billion German marks (North, 1995b). Its estimated break-even point was above 150 units (Hewson, 1994), and as Figure 2.14 shows the total deliveries for the 328 did not reach that number of sales. With a low sales volume a programme does not reach its break-even point, while at the same time the design cost is not recovered from the sales. Thus, technically, if a manufacturer would want to recover the cost of the design, and the sales are disappointing, i.e. lower than forecasted, then the manufacturer would have to increase the sales price to recover the same amount of design cost. This, of course, would make the aircraft even less appealing, leading to even lower sales. Part of the lack of sales had to do with a 14 per cent drop in the value of the US dollar against the German mark (North, 1995b), which made the aircraft more expensive in international markets. In addition, the Fairchild Dornier 328 had relatively high production cost because of relatively high German labour costs. By the time of the sale to Fairchild Aerospace in June 1996, Dornier had annual losses of almost $325 million (Shifrin, 1996).

After Fairchild Aerospace became the majority stakeholder of Fairchild Dornier in 1996, it started to revamp the Dornier company by slashing production cost, and cutting the workforce from 2,300 to 1,800 employees. This may have been too late to help the 328 programme also because the 328 programme came too late to the market.

The 328JET was a somewhat similar story. The 328JET was first delivered in 1999; when looking at Figure 2.14 it can be seen that this aircraft was introduced into the regional jet market much closer to the CRJ 100/200 and the ERJ 135/140/145. In fact, the 328JET was the first jet aircraft in the smallest segment, i.e. in the 30-seat range (Polek, 1998b). The 328JET's break-even point was better than that of the 328 (fewer than 100 aircraft) (Sparaco, 1998b), and the direct operating costs per seat-mile were slightly lower than the 328 turboprop (Alcock, 1998). However, Figure 2.14 reveals that by the time of the introduction of the 328JET, hundreds of CRJs and ERJs had already been sold. Thus both of these products had a market advantage of being an established product and both companies were offering (over time) a range of products with similarities which provided airlines with benefits related to maintenance and pilot training. In addition, both the CRJ and ERJ probably had passed their break-even points, which gave them a cost advantage. Note that in the case of these CRJ and ERJ jet aircraft, the initial sales (and deliveries) of these regional jets were quite steep, so even a slight delay in entry into the market had a bigger impact than a decade earlier. Lastly, the sales of the 328JET may have suffered from 'image' problems with the 328. Although the 328 had a good reputation with pilots, its performance in terms of fuel efficiency, maintenance cost (both worse than what was advertised), cargo space and overall product support was not so good, leading to, for example, Horizon Air returning the aircraft (Polek, 1998b).

The 728JET is a different story. The estimated development costs for the 728JET were $500 million and a potential 90-seat stretch was also envisioned (Taverna, 1997). Unfortunately, similar to the situation at Fokker, Fairchild Dornier ran out of money. A $1.2 billion debt was expected to disappear through a bankruptcy, but potential investors would have to invest hundreds of millions of dollars to move the 728JET programme to first delivery (Flottau, 2002). Thus, any party interested in taking over the 728JET programme had to have sufficient funds to make it a success. To find such a party, as the evidence shows, was near impossible.

At the time of the bankruptcy, similar to the situation at Fokker, several parties seemed to be interested in Fairchild Dornier. This included Dimeling Schreiber and Park, a private US equity firm; a Russian consortium (including Irkutsk APO aircraft factory); a Swiss concern (RUAG); and Bombardier. Just as with Fokker, the Fairchild Dornier company was eventually split up into four parts.

1 RUAG acquired Airbus subcontract work and the maintenance and spare-parts divisions, and has the type certificate for the Dornier 228-212. After the acquisition, RUAG launched a re-vamped Do 228 Next Generation in 2007, which was certified in 2010 (Collins, 2012).
2 M7 Aerospace acquired the US-based operations.
3 The Chinese conglomerate D'Long International Strategic Investment bought the 728JET programme in June 2003 (Anonymous, 2004b). This was renamed Fairchild Dornier AeroIndustries and it tried to secure investments for the 728JET (Sobie, 2003a). In June 2004 Fairchild Dornier Aerostructures filed for insolvency (Anonymous, 2004b).
4 AvCraft Aviation and Dimeling Schreiber and Park bought the 328 and 328JET programme and rights to the 428JET. AvCraft delivered its first 328JET around September 2003 (Sobie, 2003a) and secured financing to restart 328JET production (Sobie, 2003a). In June 2004 328JET assembly resumed (Kingsley-Jones, 2004). In March 2005 AvCraft filed for insolvency[14] (Kaminski-Morrow, 2005). This essentially ended the production of the Fairchild Dornier aircraft.

Embraer

Embraer was created on 19 August 1969 and started operating on 2 January 1970. Embraer was originally a state-owned enterprise but was privatized in 1994 (Jackson *et al.*, 2000). The privatization was challenging and in the first years of operating as a private company Embraer was faced with difficulties. In particular, its operating expenses were too high, its production times too long, it had too many employees and it incurred losses. By 1996 losses had reduced to \$40 million from more than \$300 million in the two previous years (O'Toole, 1997b). As a result of the privatization, production times improved, for example lead times for the EMB-120 was reduced from 15 months to 8 months, and the workforce was reduced from a high of 12,800 in 1990 to 3,800 by 1997 (O'Toole, 1997b). Embraer produced military and civil products but the emphasis here is on civil aircraft.

When Embraer was created in 1969, it was already producing the EMB-110, a small propeller aircraft. The history of the EMB-110 goes back to 1965, when a new project was started to develop a Brazilian design small, twin-engine turboprop transport aircraft. The project was headed by Max Hoste, a French aeronautical designer who had moved to Brazil. He had already designed the MH-250, which became the Nord 262. Under Hoste's leadership the Brazilian project led to the EMB-110, which can be considered a derivative of the Nord 262 (Baranson, 1978). It flew for the first time in 1968 and was quite a successful aircraft in terms of sales.

The EMB-120 was launched in 1985. This was a 30-seat turboprop aircraft which was derived from the EMB-110. Deliveries of the EMB-120 stopped in 1999 after 350 were delivered. Thus, it can be concluded that this was a successful aircraft programme.

After the EMB-120, Embraer worked on another small, 19-seat aircraft; the CBA-123. This was a collaboration with Argentina's state-owned Fábrica Militar de Aviones, a component of the Argentine Air Force. This aircraft made its first flight in 1990, but the programme was a failure and was abandoned due to being relatively expensive, combined with there being a lack of demand in the market.

In 1989 Embraer moved into what at the time was considered a niche market, i.e. jet-powered regional aircraft. It developed the ERJ-145, a 50-seat jet aircraft, which was a $300 million investment (McKenna, 1995). Embraer expected to sell the ERJ-145 to airlines upgrading from the EMB-120 (McKenna, 1995). The ERJ-145 can be considered a derivative of the EMB-120 because Embraer essentially stretched the fuselage and mounted it on a new wing (Warwick, 1999). Some technology was also used from the CBA-123 (North, 1995a). The programme initially had some difficulties. In 1989 Embraer had already received more than 100 firm orders, but as delays mounted many orders were cancelled. Furthermore, Bombardier launched the Canadair regional jet, which grabbed the initial market (Anonymous, 1996b). However, the price of the ERJ-145 was about $2.5 million lower than the Canadair regional jet, even though the latter travelled slightly farther and faster (Anonymous, 1996b). This price point made it almost equal to the price of the Saab 2000 (North, 1996). The ERJ-145's first flight was in August 1995 and deliveries began in 1996.

In 1997 Embraer announced a smaller derivative of the ERJ-145, i.e. the 37-passenger ERJ-135 (cost of development was estimated at $100 million (Anselmo, 1998)). The first flight of the ERJ-135 was in July 1998 and first delivery in July 1999. This was followed in 2000 by another derivative, the 44-passenger ERJ-140. The first delivery was in 2002. In December 2002, Embraer reached an ERJ-145 licensed production agreement with China Aviation Industry Corporation II (AVIC II). In this joint venture (Harbin Embraer Aircraft Industry) Embraer holds a 51 per cent stake and AVIC II the remaining 49 per cent (Ionides, 2002). Demand in China for the ERJ-145 was expected to pick up, and producing in China avoided excessive import tariffs (Ionides, 2002). Since 2010 Embraer and AVIC II negotiated about the future of the Harbin line. Embraer initially offered to produce the ERJ-190 in Harbin, but AVIC II rejected this offer as the ERJ-190 would compete with the Comac ARJ21. In July 2012 an agreement was reached to convert it into a business jet production facility, i.e. the Legacy 650 (Hashim, 2012).

In 1998 Embraer started to study the 70+ market segment for larger regional jets (Warwick, 1998). This led to the E-170/190 family. The first flight of the E-170 was in February 2002. First delivery was in March 2004. The E-175,

E-190 and E-195 are derivatives. At the Paris Airshow in June 2013, Embraer launched updates for this family of aircraft, known as E2. This involved new engines (Pratt & Whitney geared-fan engines, see also under Mitsubishi Heavy Industries), new wings and upgraded avionics. It received 365 orders for this second generation of its E-170/190 family (Anonymous, 2013a).

As of 2014 Embraer is still operating as one of the largest civil aircraft manufacturers in the world. Initially it operated as a state-owned enterprise for many years. This, with a determined government, can help with survival under tough conditions. However, by 1994 Embraer was privatized and, aside from the early years, it has operated successfully for the last 20 years. What explains the success of Embraer where some of the other, especially Eastern, manufacturers have failed?

A couple of things are noticeable about the approach Embraer has taken. First, when it was privatized it already had the successful EMB-120. Figure 2.10 shows how the EMB-120 was introduced around the same time as the Saab 340, the Dash-8 and the ATR-42, and that sales were similar to those aircraft in the early years. This is an important observation for a product that was produced in a developing country. The introduction of the ERJ-135/140/145 family was timely in the market. It was a little later than the CRJ 100/200, but as noted it had a cost advantage. This can explain the success of the ERJ-135/140/145. Note also that the EMB-120 design was related to an older aircraft and that the ERJ-135/140/145 were related to the EMB-120. Consequently, the cost of development was lower than if a whole new aircraft had been designed and developed. At the same time, it offered similarities for airlines. Figure 2.14 shows the rapid market development for the CRJ and ERJ aircraft and possibly the largest accomplishment of both manufacturers was the production ramp-up to keep up with demand. In short, Embraer had a design process that did not entail excessive costs (partly due to being a derivative product) and had relatively low production costs (probably some carry-over of learning from producing the EMB-120) which led to a cost-competitive product which was very timely with its market entry, while at the same time the market was developing very rapidly. In terms of Figure 2.8 this means that the low point on the curve was not as low as some of the other manufacturers faced. Furthermore, due to rapid sales, the curve to the right of the low point had a steeper angle, which leads to a quicker achievement of the break-even point and faster recovery of investments.

Commercial success allowed Embraer to develop a completely new line of aircraft, i.e. the ERJ-170/175/190/195 family. Figure 2.13 shows that in this market segment Embraer was also later than Bombardier, with its CRJ-700/900 series. In this regard Bombardier probably had a cost advantage as the CRJ-700/900 was a derivative versus the all-new ERJ-170/175/190/195. Competition in this market segment was limited between the two manufacturers. Figures 2.11 and 2.12 show that for regional aircraft the market was predominantly oriented on 30–50-seat aircraft in the late 1980s and early 1990s, which is when both Bombardier and Embraer focused on that segment. The market for the larger 70–100-seat aircraft started to develop more after 2002, which is when both manufacturers had introduced their larger aircraft. Possibly both were fortunate with their timing or, rather, had a very good sense of how the market was going to develop (in contrast with, for example, Saab's 2000 development) and/or the introduction of its products led to the development of the different market segments due to the products on offer.

Sukhoi

Traditionally, the Russian aircraft industry had several characteristics that made it different to that in Western countries. One difference was the centralized approach to aircraft production, which led to, for example, separating design from production (Todd and Simpson, 1986). Since 1999 plans were circulating in Russia to consolidate its aircraft manufacturing industry. The process of integration was started in 2005 and led, in February 2006, to AOK (or United Aircraft Corporation) as a government-owned corporation that covers design, manufacture and marketing of aerospace products. Sukhoi is the forefront of this organization, but it also involves other parties such as Yakovlev, Ilyushin and Irkutsk Aircraft Production Organization (Massy-Beresford, 2007).

Another difference between Russian aircraft and Western aircraft was that Russian aircraft typically did not have FAA or JAA/EASA certification, thus limiting the ability of Russian manufacturers to sell their products internationally. One noticeable change to this came with the Russian Regional Jet. The RRJ was the first Russian aircraft designed from scratch with the intention to meet Western certification standards (Goold, 2004).[15] Russian studies into the regional jet began in 2001 (Kingsley-Jones, 2007a). In 2002 the Russian government launched an initiative to replace the country's ageing fleet of short-haul airliners with a request for tenders from the local industry for the supply of 200 large regional jets (Duffy, 2002). The RRJ was chosen over the Tupolev TU-414 and the Myasishchev M-60-70 for this in March 2003 (Karnazov, 2003a).

The RRJ programme is led by Sukhoi and from an initial range of versions (RRJ-60, RRJ-75 and RRJ-95) Sukhoi eventually concentrated on two 98-seat SSJ-100 models (formerly RRJ-95, basic and long-range versions). Boeing was involved in an advisory role on marketing, certification and customer support (Goold, 2004). Several (risk-sharing) foreign suppliers were involved for parts of the aircraft, for example Goodrich, Honeywell, Hamilton Sundstrand (Karnozov, 2004). In 2006 Alenia Aeronautica (Italy) took a 25 per cent stake in Sukhoi Civil Aircraft and a corresponding financial stake in the Superjet programme (Turner, 2007).

Initial development cost was estimated at over $600 million and in the original schedule first flight was envisioned in May 2006, with first deliveries in the middle of 2007 (Endres, 2006; Karnozov, 2004). Sukhoi forecasted a market for 800 units (Karnozov, 2003b) but internationally this was questioned, i.e. if based on sales in Eastern Bloc countries it might be realistic but not if based on penetration of Western markets (Kirby, 2008). By early 2005 the Siberian airline Sibir was to be the launch customer (commitment for 50 aircraft) while Aeroflot also had a requirement for 30 aircraft (Endres, 2006). By June 2007 the latter had transformed into a firm order for 30 95-seat SSJ-95Bs and a memorandum of understanding for an additional 15 aircraft. At this time Aeroflot was also pushing Sukhoi to expand the Superjet 100 family with the introduction of a 130-seat stretch and a 70-seat shrink (Karnozov, 2007).

Funding of the programme was an issue, but in January 2005 the Russian parliament allocated funds for the government to issue guarantees worth $100 million. This was the first time in Russian commercial aerospace history that any manufacturer received development funds with state help on a refundable basis (Karnosov and Norris, 2005). In early 2012 Sukhoi announced a 12 per cent rise in its prices, but according to Sukhoi this was still a 15 per cent cost advantage over comparable rivals (Thisdell, 2012). In 2011 Sukhoi had a net loss of $17 million and in the first six months of 2012 Sukhoi had an operating loss of $45 million and a heavy interest expense pushed the net loss to $100 million (Kaminski-Morrow, 2012c). By 2013 Sukhoi's civil aircraft division's debts had surpassed $2 billion (O'Keeffe, 2013). Nevertheless, it maintained that it could fulfil all its commitments and was expecting to reach the programme's break-even point in 2015, when total revenue was expected to be in excess of $1.5 billion (O'Keeffe, 2013).

First flight of the SSJ took place in May 2008 and by July 2008 Sukhoi reportedly held 73 secure orders (Kirby, 2008). Expected first delivery had slipped to end of 2008 (Kirby, 2008). Due to the global economic downturn, in May 2009 Russia reduced output targets for 2009–2012. The SSJ was affected by this and output targets for those years went from 230 to 7, although at that time the programme had 98 firm orders (Anonymous, 2009a). Despite having Alenia as a foreign partner in the programme, it was a disappointment for the alliance that Alitalia, in December 2010, opted for the Embraer E-jets instead of the SSJ (Thisdell, 2012). By January 2011 the backlog for the SSJ was reported at 170, but by that time Sibir was no longer on the list, and the initial first Western customer (ItAli from Italy) was also dropped from the list, but it disclosed an unnamed customer for 20 aircraft which was suggested as being a Western company. Several other previously mentioned orders had also changed (Reals, 2011). Later in January 2011 Mexico's Interjet became the first international customer for the SSJ, with a firm order for 15 Superjets and an additional five options (Dron, 2011), so this may indeed have been the undisclosed customer on the earlier list. First delivery, to the Armenian carrier Armavia, was in April 2011 (Thisdell, 2012). At the Paris Airshow in June 2011, another Western airline, Italian Blue Panorama,[16] placed a 12-aircraft order (Karnozov, 2011) while in the same month the second SSJ was delivered (to Aeroflot). At that time Sukhoi planned to deliver another ten aircraft before 2012, but industry sources questioned whether it could deliver more than an additional four (one for Armavia, three for Aeroflot) (Karnozov, 2011). By the end of 2011 Sukhoi had delivered only five aircraft in total, i.e. one to Armavia and four to Aeroflot, and in early 2012 it received EASA certification (Thisdell, 2012).

On 9 May 2012 Sukhoi was faced with a big set-back when one of the SSJs that was on an Asian promotion tour crashed into a mountain in Indonesia.[17] In the same year, a disagreement between launch customer Armavia and Sukhoi arose. Armavia stopped flying its first SSJ and postponed acceptance of a second aircraft, citing operational performance of the twinjet as an issue, i.e. needing repairs. But Sukhoi suggested that the real problem had to do with financial arrangements (Kaminki-Morrow, 2012b). In 2012 a completion facility for Western customers was opened in Venice, initially working on Interjet aircraft (Peruzzi, 2012). Interjet received its first aircraft at the Paris Airshow in June 2013 (Anonymous, 2013b) while at the same time signals were received that Western suppliers (Finmeccanica) viewed the relationship with Sukhoi as significantly unsatisfactory (Anonymous, 2013b). In 2012 Sukhoi delivered eight aircraft (Thomas, 2013). In November 2014 Belgian airline VLM was to become the first European Union operator of the Superjet, which at that time had delivered 50 aircraft and had a total of 166 orders (Morrison, 2014).

Thus the first flight and the first delivery were significantly delayed compared to the original plan. The Superjet also has been suffering from incidents with the landing gear. For example, aircraft delivered to Aeroflot had issues (Kaminski-Morrow, 2013b) as well as a test aircraft (Kaminksi-Morrow, 2013c). This has affected airline perception of the aircraft.

Comac

China has a long history of producing aircraft and has targeted aviation as one of its key industries (see also Chapter 8). By May 2001 an idea had formed to develop a 50–70-seat regional aircraft: the New Regional Jet (NRJ). Further developments led by 2002 to two indigenous Chinese regional jet programmes. AVIC II focused on a 30–50-seat aircraft[18] while AVIC I set up a dedicated company, AVIC I Commercial Aircraft (ACAC), to manage development of a Chinese 79–99-seat regional jet aircraft: the ARJ21 (Doyle, 2002).

The ARJ21 was initially unveiled in September 2001, involving a $600 million commitment (Sobie, 2003b), with an expected first flight in 2006 and first delivery in 2008 (Goold, 2004). The ARJ-700, a 78–85-seat version was the first model that was manufactured (Francis, 2004).

AVIC I hoped that enormous domestic market potential would lead to sales of at least 500 aircraft (Goold, 2004). Ultimately, it was also seeking overseas orders (Goold, 2004). Several Western parties were involved, such as Honeywell, Hamilton Sundstrand, Goodrich and Liebherr (Goold, 2004). Boeing Commercial Aviation Services was initially included as an engineering consultant (Anonymous, 2002b) and Antonov from Russia was contracted for the wing (Anonymous, 2002c). Alenia Aeronautica was looking at a possible partnership that could result in European assembly of the ARJ21 (Sobie, 2003c).

At the Aviation Expo China in September 2003, three Chinese customers (Shangdong Airlines (launch customer), Shanghai Airlines and Shenzhen Financial Leasing) ordered 35 ARJ21 aircraft (Anonymous, 2003). By 2004 the order book had grown to 41 (Goold, 2004). In 2008 the Chinese government merged AVIC I and AVIC II and created a new company, Commercial Aircraft Corporation of China (Comac) (Francis, 2008). First flight was in November 2008 (Yeo, 2010) a delay of several years. By 2010 the orderbook for the ARJ21 was reported at more than 200 orders, but continuing delays in the certification (due to unresolved design issues and lack of experience of the Civil Aviation Administration of China (CAAC) with the certification process) caused the first delivery to be delayed to the end of 2011 (Yeo, 2010). The FAA was conducting a shadow certification simultaneously which was expected to lead to faster FAA certification. By February 2012 the ARJ21 was still undergoing (flight) tests but positive news for Comac was that Indonesian Merpati signed a tentative deal for up to 40 aircraft (Toh, 2012a). However, in May 2012 it appeared that Merpati might be cancelling its plans (Toh, 2012c). At the Farnborough show in July 2012, officials stated that it would be unlikely that regulatory approval would be achieved before 2013. Faults were identified with the wings, wiring and computer systems. In March 2013, as a result of flight tests, landing gear changes were made (Toh, 2013a); delivery to launch customer Chengdu was now expected in 2014 (Toh, 2013b) but a few months later, in June 2013, the certification was not expected until late 2014 (Toh, 2013c). The order book by mid-2013 for the ARJ21 was reported at 252 commitments, most of them from Chinese airlines and leasing companies (Toh, 2013c). By November 2014 the order book was reported at 258 and the ARJ21 had completed the necessary ground tests and 95 per cent of all flight test modules but still had not achieved certification (Toh, 2014b). Construction was also taking place near Shanghai's Pudong International airport for a second assembly line and combined capacity of the two assembly lines was estimated as 50 aircraft per year (Toh, 2014b).

Mitsubishi Heavy Industries

In 1945 the once formidable Japanese aircraft industry was dissolved under the American occupation, but since 1952 it was slowly revived (Todd and Simpson, 1986). In terms of civil aircraft, Japan developed the YS-11 in the 1960s, a 60-passenger turboprop aircraft for which final assembly was carried out by Mitsubishi Heavy Industries (MHI) (Todd and Simpson, 1986). The YS-11 was a loss-making programme.

In the 1980s and early 1990s a consortium of Japanese firms, Japan Aircraft Development Corporation (JADC), of which MHI was a part, was looking into developing a 90–110-seat regional jet: the YS-X with Boeing as a partner (Mecham, 1995). Uncertainty about the 100-seat market led to initial delays with the programme (Sekigawa and Mecham, 1996) and the economic crisis in Asia led to eventual abandonment of these plans in July 1998 (Lewis, 1998). An alternative plan was a collaboration between MHI and Bombardier. The idea was to use the wing MHI built for Bombardier's Global Express business jet as the basis for a 90–110-seat regional jet. This would reduce the development cost to $463 million (Sekigawa and Mecham, 1996). MHI had already joined Bombardier in 1995 as a risk-sharing partner in developing the de Havilland Dash-8 Series 400 (Hughes, 1995).

These plans did not materialize; instead, in June 2007, MHI unveiled an all-new regional jet (Govindasamy, 2007a). The programme launch was backed by a 25-aircraft order from All Nippon Airways (Kingsley-Jones, 2007b). Two MRJ versions were initially offered, the 86–96-seat MRJ90 (ordered by ANA) and the 70–80-seat MRJ70. MRJ aircraft were claimed to offer up to 30 per cent lower operating costs than existing aircraft at the time (Kingsley-Jones, 2007b). Expected development cost for the aircraft were $1.5 billion, with up to one-third of this provided by Japan's Ministry of Economy, Trade and Industry as refundable launch aid (Kingsley-Jones, 2007b). First flight for the MRJ was targeted for late 2011 (Govindasamy, 2008) and first delivery to ANA was expected in 2013 (Anonymous, 2009b). Mitsubishi projected sales of 1,000 units for its new regional jet family (Govindasamy, 2007b), although its initial target was reaching the projected break-even point of 300 units (Govindasamy, 2008). After initial discussions with potential customers in Europe and the United States, Mitsubishi Aircraft (an MHI subsidiary formed to develop the MRJ) extensively redesigned the MRJ and revealed plans for a 100-seat stretch version in September 2009 (Anonymous, 2009a), while the first flight was delayed until the second quarter of 2012 (Trimble, 2013) The 100-seat stretch was intended to be introduced around 2017–2018 (Trimble, 2012c). By May 2012 Mitsubishi had only orders from three customers and the first flight was delayed to around the last quarter of 2013. This was due to fabrication processes and to provide sufficient time for technical studies. The company needed more time to review the industrial processes involved in producing the aircraft and these processes needed to be approved by the Japan Civil Aviation Bureau (Waldron, 2012a). This delay was because Mitsubishi Aircraft needed more time to certify its production system with Japanese regulators (Trimble, 2012e). First delivery was scheduled for 2015 (Trimble, 2013). By mid-2012 the order book for the MRJ had improved. In addition to the order from ANA, Trans States Holdings had agreed to buy 50 MRJs with another 50 options, and ANI Group Holdings had signed an MOU for five MRJs (Trimble, 2012c). At the Farnborough Airshow in July 2012 Mitsubishi Aircraft reached a tentative agreement with US-based SkyWest Airlines for 100 aircraft, thereby surprising competitors Embraer and Bombardier, bringing its order book to 170 firm orders with another 60 options (Anonymous, 2012). SkyWest apparently like the Embraer cabin but not its fuel burn, while Bombardier offered a good fuel burn but not a nice cabin (Toh, 2012b). The availability of the MRJ from 2017 was another issue for SkyWest (Toh, 2013g). Within the next six months additional orders from SkyWest were expected (Trimble, 2012a). Despite these orders, industry analysts stressed the importance of aftermarket services (global customer support network) which has proven a greater issue than programme delivery in the past. In addition, aircraft financing was considered another issue as banks and investors would perhaps be nervous about the aircraft in early stages of delivery (Waldron, 2012b).

By April 2013 the order book had grown to 165 firm orders and 160 options (Toh, 2013e) although on 7 May 2013 Hong-Kong based Aero Nusantara Indonesia cancelled an MoU for five MRJs which it had signed in June 2011 (Toh, 2013f). On 22 August 2013 Mitsubishi Aircraft announced additional delays, its third. First flight was pushed back to the second quarter of 2015 and first delivery to launch customer ANA was pushed back two years to the second quarter of 2017. The reasons for these delays were cited as the development and certification processes having taken greater resources than expected, which in turn impacted component deliveries and aircraft fabrication (Toh, 2013g). Part of this had to do with adopting the US FAA's new certification and approval process, i.e. the organizational delegation authorization which came into effect in 2009 and which was partly used for the Boeing 787, but the MRJ is the first aircraft to fully apply it (Toh, 2013h). Analysts expected that this delay would impact the MRJs orderbook as the new timetable would introduce the aircraft only one year ahead of Embraer's E-Jet E2, which would be powered by the same engine (Toh, 2013g). On 18 October 2014 the first flight-test example of the MRJ was rolled out and by November 2014 its order book was at 375 aircraft, which represented 191 firm orders and 184 options (Toh, 2014a).

In order to reach its production target, Mitsubishi Aircraft started investigating options for a second manufacturing line in 2012. This was necessary because its production target was 125 annually or around ten per month. One option being considered was the United States (Toh, 2012b). In 2013 it seemed that the second assembly line would be located at Nagoya in Japan (Toh, 2013d).

Conclusions

In this chapter the regional aircraft industry was discussed. The chapter showed how the 30–100-seat segments have developed over the last 30 years, how jet aircraft in particular became popular during the 1990s and especially in the 30–50-seat segment. It was also explained how, in particular, design, production and sales affect the financial success of a programme.

Several of the Western manufacturers have ceased commercial aircraft production. In particular, Fokker, British Aerospace, Fairchild Dornier and Saab. In three of the cases (Fokker, British Aerospace and Fairchild Dornier) this seems to have been caused by products that were not cost competitive in the market, which goes back to high design and production costs. Saab seems to have suffered mostly from an untimely decision to focus on developing a new turboprop aircraft when jet aircraft were gaining in popularity, which was helped by low oil prices.

Companies that have survived so far are ATR, Embraer and Bombardier. ATR has been able to focus on turboprop aircraft and its survival was helped with the exit of several of the other manufacturers. Both Bombardier and Embraer were able to capitalize on changing market conditions (smaller jet aircraft). Both had good timing with their products into the market. Both also had relatively lower design costs due to lower overall costs (Bombardier buying bankrupt companies) and using derivatives (CRJ 100 family and the ERJ-145 family).

For the new entrants into the market – i.e. Comac, Mitsubishi and Sukhoi – it remains a question how successful they will be. All three have suffered from similar issues which sealed the fate of Indonesian Aerospace 15 years ago. That is, problems with getting aircraft certified. If nothing else, this has caused extensive delays with the aircraft programmes. Such delays in themselves cause the overall cost of aircraft programmes to go up, the break-even point to go up, and it affects the timing as well. As the example of Fokker has shown, cost of design is very expensive and delays exacerbate the situation, which may ultimately lead to an unsustainable situation. Currently, this seems to be what especially Comac and Sukhoi are facing.

Notes

1 As an aside, Bombardier and COMAC have engaged in discussions to jointly develop one aircraft – see Ranson (2011).

2 Another company that has been active is IPTN (renamed as Indonesian Aerospace), which had three relevant products. The CN235 was a joint project between CASA (Spain) and IPTN. The Spanish version had primarily military customers and the IPTN version was not successful in Western countries. The N250 and the N2130 were both aircraft programmes in development which did not have global sales. This is covered in Chapter 8.

3 Sources used for determining the deliveries include Jet Information Services (2012), Roach and Eastwood (2001) and industry publications such as *Flight International*.

4 There are some differences in the learning curve, experience curve and cost or cumulative cost curve, but this is beyond the scope of this book. The importance is the general concept.

5 Learning cost can be viewed as the area below the graph and above the stabilized production line.

6 Main sources used for this analysis are Deterink *et al.* (1997), Martijn (1996) and general industry sources such as *Flight International*.

7 Additional issues were the transfer prices charged by DASA for fuselage sections and the exchange rate for selling globally.

8 As explained earlier in this chapter, the Jetstream aircraft are not included in the analysis due to the size of these aircraft.

9 It should be mentioned that British Aerospace is and has been involved in several alliances. First, British Aerospace was involved in the creation of Airbus Industries. Airbus is a producer of large aircraft, i.e. not regional aircraft. The Airbus consortium is worth mentioning because some of the decisions taken by British Aerospace in the 1990s and beyond may have been influenced by being part of a, by that time, successful European consortium. Another collaboration that British Aerospace was involved in was AI(R). This was a collaboration with ATR partners Aerospaciale (France) and Alenia (Italy). An initial protocol accord was signed in January 1995. This collaboration combined sales, marketing and customer service activities of ATR and the British Aerospace subsidiaries Avro and Jetstream (Condom, 1995). The agreement was formally signed on 6 June 1995 and became functionally operational on 1 January 1996. It was dissolved in July 1998 (Jackson *et al.*, 2000).

10 It was pointed out earlier in the chapter that around 2010, with high oil prices, the popularity of turboprop aircraft was increasing again and several manufacturers were looking into developing a 90-seat turboprop aircraft.

11 Note also that the purchasing behaviour of airlines is influenced by operating cost – for example, cost per seat-mile as well as the purchase price of the aircraft. The assumption made here is that these were fairly similar for the ATR-42 and the Saab 340.

12 A new structure was formed where Bombardier owned 51 per cent and the government of Ontario 49 per cent. In 1997, Bombardier bought the 49 per cent from the government of Ontario for $49 million (Anonymous, 1997).

13 Interestingly, DASA was involved in managing both Dornier and Fokker in the mid-1990s but both Dornier and Fokker do not exist anymore and DASA is not involved in manufacturing complete aircraft any longer.

14 It is interesting to observe that Dornier, under DASA management, was financially in trouble and was bought in 1996 by Fairchild Aerospace. Despite slashing production costs and laying off workers, Fairchild Aerospace was unable to turn the tide and filed for bankruptcy six years later in 2002. Two rescuers bought parts of the company but Fairchild Dornier Aerostructures filed for insolvency a year after the acquisition, and AvCraft two years after its acquisition. A similar pattern was observed with the troubled Canadair and de Havilland companies, which were purchased by Bombardier in 1986 and 1992; but as the previous section shows, Bombardier faced financial difficulties by early 2000. Bombardier survived, but the financial conditions for the purchase of Canadair and de Havilland were better than those for the purchase of Dornier. Similarly, in early 1999 an announcement was made that Britten-Norman acquired a stake of 72.9 per cent in Romaero (for $80.5 million) but subsequently Britten-Norman faced financial difficulties and was acquired by the Oman-based investment group Zawawi in May 2000.

15 Only one other Russian aircraft previously received FAA certification: the Ilyushin Il-96M/T (Karnozov, 2004).

16 Blue Panorama had its air operator's certificate revoked in October 2012 after it entered the Italian equivalent of chapter 11 bankruptcy protection (Trimble, 2012b). Thus, it is unclear whether the aircraft will be delivered.

17 This had nothing to do with the capabilities of the aircraft itself. It was later determined that the passenger jet was incorrectly coded as a Sukhoi Su-30 military fighter in the Air Traffic Control system which let the air traffic controllers allow the aircraft to fly where it essentially shouldn't have been flying. This, in combination with the captain silencing terrain-avoidance warnings, believing them to be erroneous, contributed to the crash (see also Chapter 7 and Kaminski-Morrow, 2013a).

18 Eventually leading to the joint venture with Embraer in Harbin.

References

Alcock, C. (1998), 'Jet-driven Do 328 commuter preps for first flight this month', *Aviation International News*, 1 January, p. 3.

Anonymous (1993), 'First-half profit of BAe', *Aviation Week & Space Technology*, 20 September, p. 37.

Anonymous (1994), 'BAe profits triple', *Aviation Week & Space Technology*, 26 September, p. 15.

Anonymous (1996a), 'Bombardier away', *The Economist*, 24 February, pp. 75–76.

Anonymous (1996b), 'Turbofanning the embers', *The Economist*, 22 June, pp. 73–74.

Anonymous (1997), 'News breaks', *Aviation Week & Space Technology*, 3 February.

Anonymous (1998a), 'Doubts raised by Xian plans for ATR production', *Flight International*, 16–22 September, p. 26.

Anonymous (1998b), 'Bombardier unveils plan for 90-seat jet family', *Flight International*, 16–22 September, p. 6.

Anonymous (1998c), 'Fairchild Dornier launches 728JET', *Flight International*, 27 May–2 June, p. 14.

Anonymous (1998d), 'Fairchild Aerospace names 728JET risk share partners', *Flight International*, 16–22 September, p. 13.

Anonymous (1999), 'Bombardier wins and loses in trade battle with Embraer', *Flight International*, 24–30 March, p. 25.

Anonymous (2002a), 'Bombardier starts to shut down lines', *Flight International*, 15–21 October, p. 20.

Anonymous (2002b), 'GE wins battle to power ARJ21', *Flight International*, 12–18 November, p. 20.

Anonymous (2002c), 'Antonov to develop wing for China', *Flight International*, 19–25 November, p. 10.

Anonymous (2003), 'Three carriers place ARJ21 orders', *Flight International*, 23–29 September, p. 23.

Anonymous (2004a), 'Bombardier reveals plans for 100-seat-plus family', *Flight International*, 27 July–4 August, p. 21.

Anonymous (2004b), 'Fairchild Dornier', *Flight International*, 2–8 November, pp. 65–66.

Anonymous (2009a), 'Superjet suffers most as Russia slashes output plan', *Flight International*, 12–19 May, p. 16.

Anonymous (2009b), 'MRJ set for wide-ranging redesign', *Flight International*, 15–21 September, p. 12.

Anonymous (2012), 'Mitsubishi's SkyWest MRJ win stuns regional rivals', *Flight International*, 17–23 July, p. 10.

Anonymous (2013a), 'Embraer throws down the gauntlet', *Flight International*, 25 June–1 July, p. 14.

Anonymous (2013b), 'Strains show in Superjet relationship', *Flight International*, 25 June–1 July, p. 24.

Anselmo, J.C. (1998), 'Embraer rolls out RJ-135 regional jet', *Aviation Week & Space Technology*, 18 May, p. 39.

Baranson, J. (1978), *Technology and the Multinational, Corporate Strategies in a Changing World Economy*, Lexington Books, Lexington.

Collins, P. (2012), 'Spying a niche', *Flight International*, 4–10 September, pp. 38–41.

Condom, P. (1995), 'Regionals on the move', *Interavia*, February, p. 3.

Deterink, A.A.M., Knüppe, B.F.M., Leuftink, A.L. and Schimmelpennick, R.J. (1997), *Onderzoek van curatoren naar de oorzaken van het faillissement van N.V. Koninklijke Nederlandse Vliegtuigenfabriek Fokker*, Amsterdam, 15 July.

Doyle, A. (2002), 'Lure of the East', *Flight International*, 29 October–4 November, pp. 42–44.

Dron, A. (2011), 'Super flexible', *Flight International*, 14–20 June, p. 74.

Duffy, P. (2002), 'Russia seeks bids for regional jets', *Flight International*, 1–7 October, p. 8.

Dunn, B. (2003a), 'Bombardier faces asset sale to beat cash crisis', *Flight International*, 28 January–3 February, p. 19.

Dunn, B. (2003b), 'Canada offers Bombardier loans', *Flight International*, 29 July–4 August, p. 5.

Dunn, B. (2004a), 'Bombardier wants more help from government', *Flight International*, 24 February–1 March, p. 28.

Dunn, B. (2004b), 'Bombardier to invite US states to bid for the CSeries assembly', *Flight International*, 26 October–1 November, p. 16.

Dunn, B. and Flores, J. (2004), 'Bombardier urged to enter 100-seat market', *Flight International*, 6–12 January 2004.

Endres, G. (2006), 'Back to stay', *Flight International*, 31 October–6 November, pp. 37–66.

Eriksson, S. (1995), Global shift in the aircraft industry: A study of airframe manufacturing with special reference to the Asian NIEs, PhD dissertation, University of Gothenburg.

Flottau, J. (2002), 'Fairchild Dornier will not be split German administrator says', *Aviation Daily*, 10 April.

Francis, L. (2004), 'ARJ21 suppliers plan for local plants', *Flight International*, 28 September–4 October, p. 14.

Francis, L. (2008), 'All change for China', *Flight International*, 28 October–3 November, pp. 46–47.

Godfrey, D. (1990), 'A jet for the regionals…' *Air International*, September, pp. 134–142.

Goold, I. (2004), 'Jets surge', *Flight International*, 2–8 November, pp. 52–74.

Govindasamy, S. (2007a), 'MHI tests the water for its planned regional jet', *Flight International*, 19–25 June, p. 20.

Govindasamy, S. (2007b), 'Mitsubishi takes aim for 1,000 sales', *Flight International*, 4–10 December, p. 21.

Govindasamy, S. (2008), 'Japan flies solo again', *Flight International*, 23–29 September, pp. 30–38.

Hashim, F. (2012), 'Embraer seals China Legacy 650 deal', *Flight International*, 3–9 July, p. 36.

Heerkens, H., de Bruijn, E.J. and Steenhuis, H.J. (2010), 'Common factors in the withdrawal of European aircraft manufacturers from the regional aircraft market', *Technology Analysis & Strategic Management*, Vol. 22, No. 1, pp. 65–80.

Hewson, R. (ed.) (1994), *Commercial Aircraft and Airliners*, Airlife, England.

Hughes, D. (1995), 'Mitsubishi to share risk on Dash 8-400', *Aviation Week and Space Technology*, 30 October, p. 46.

Ionides, N. (2002), 'Botelho: breaking ground in China', *Flight International*, 10–16 December, p. 27.

Jackson, P., Munson, K. and Peacock, L. (eds) (2000), *Jane's All the World's Aircraft*, Jane's Information Group Limited, Surrey.

Jet Information Services (2003), *World Jet Inventory, Year-End 2002*, Jet Information Services, Woodinville, WA.

Jet Information Services (2012), *World Jet Inventory, Year-End 2011*, Jet Information Services, New York.

Jeziorski, A. (1998), 'Fairchild Dornier gives the go-ahead to 428JET project', *Flight International*, 20–26 May, p. 4.

Kaminski-Morrow, D. (2005), 'AvCraft looks for options in the face of insolvency', *Flight International*, 15–21 March, p. 6.

Kaminski-Morrow, D. (2012a), 'Geared fan may power Fokker stretch', *Flight International*, 24–30 July, p. 13.

Kaminski-Morrow, D. (2012b), 'Sukhoi row spurs Armavia to stop Superjet flights', *Flight International*, 14–27 August, p. 10.

Kaminski-Morrow, D. (2012c), 'Sukhoi dreams on despite red marks', *Flight International*, 4–10 December, p. 10.

Kaminski-Morrow, D. (2012d), 'Saab dismisses return to building civil turboprops', *Flight International*, 28 August–3 September, p. 13.

Kaminski-Morrow, D. (2013a), 'Silenced warnings doomed Superjet', *Flight International*, 8–14 January, pp. 10–11.

Kaminski-Morrow, D. (2013b), 'Aeroflot technical snags prompt Superjet defence', *Flight International*, 19–25 February, p. 14.

Kaminski-Morrow, D. (2013c), 'Sukhoi unruffled by latest mishap', *Flight International*, 30 July–5 August, p. 6.

Karnazov, V. (2003a), 'Sukhoi-led RRJ wins Rosaviakosmos tender', *Flight International*, 18–24 March, p. 13.

Karnozov, V. (2003b), 'Sukhoi-led RRJ team upbeat on forecast', *Flight International*, 9–15 December, p. 13.

Karnozov, V. (2004), 'Western values', *Flight International*, 20–26 April, pp. 46–49.

Karnozov, V. (2007), 'Aeroflot urges additions to SSJ family', *Flight International*, 19–25 June, p. 30.

Karnozov, V. (2011), 'Courting Western favour: and certification', *Flight International*, 2–8 August, p. 42.

Karnosov, V. and Norris, G. (2005), 'Russian reality', *Flight International*, 15–21 February, pp. 38–41.

Kenney, M. and Patton, D. (2006), 'The coevolution of technologies and institutions: Silicon Valley as the iconic high technology cluster', in: Braunerhjelm, P. and Feldman, M. (eds), *Cluster Genesis, Technology-based Industrial Development*, Oxford University Press, Oxford.

Kingsley-Jones, M. (2002), 'Regional orders plummet as jet output growth slackens', *Flight International*, 26 February–4 March, p. 31.

Kingsley-Jones, M. (2004), 'Dornier 328JET assembly resumes after two years', *Flight International*, 15–21 June, p. 16.

Kingsley-Jones, M. (2007a), 'Russian revolution', *Flight International*, 6–12 February, pp. 36–39.

Kingsley-Jones, M. (2007b), 'Will MRJ change the game?' *Flight International*, 4–10 December, p. 20.

Kingsley-Jones, M., Moxon, J. and Norris, G. (1998), 'Brazilian workout', *Flight International*, 13–19 May, pp. 39–42.

Kirby, M. (2008), 'Bridging the divide', *Flight International*, 8–14 July, pp. 100–104.

Lewis, P. (1998), 'Back to basics', *Flight International*, 2–8 September, pp. 85–87.

Lewis, P. (2003), 'Changing circumstances', *Flight International*, 13–19 May, p. 60.

Lewis, P. and Dunn, B. (2003), 'De Havilland reopens as Bombardier studies costs', *Flight International*, 11–17 February, p. 9.

Lewis, P. and Ionides, N. (2002), 'Bombardier and Chinese to build the CRJ together', *Flight International*, 10–16 December, p. 4.

Lopez, R. (1998), 'Survival of the fastest? The market for regional aircraft is growing rapidly, but will jets be the ultimate winners?', *Flight International*, 13–19 May, p. 46.

Lopez, R. and Norris, G. (1998), 'Continental ERJ-135 order leads regional move to 30-seat jets', *Flight International*, 13–19 May, p. 5.

Martijn, C. (1996), *Vleugellam*, F&G Publishing, Bunnik.

Massy-Beresford, H. (2007), 'Growing a great OAK', *Flight International*, 14–20 August, pp. 30–32.

McKenna, J.T. (1995), 'EMB-145 to test Embraer's mettle', *Aviation Week & Space Technology*, 29 August, pp. 28–29.

Mecham, M. (1995), 'Asian manufacturers bid for "prime" time', *Aviation Week & Space Technology*, 13 March, p. 63.

Morrison, M. (2014), 'Breakthrough for Superjet', *Flight International*, 4–10 November, p. 19.

Morocco, J.D. (1999), 'RJX upgrade on track for autumn launch', *Aviation Week & Space Technology*, 10 May, p. 55.

North, D.M. (1995a), 'Embraer to shorten EMB-145 flight test program', *Aviation Week & Space Technology*, 12 June, pp. 147.

North, D.M. (1995b), 'Dornier 328 fights to break even', *Aviation Week & Space Technology*, 9 October, pp. 38–45.

North, D.M. (1996), 'EMB-145 success pivots on price, performance', *Aviation Week & Space Technology*, 15 July, pp. 48–51.

O'Keeffe, N. (2013), 'Debt-laden SCAC denies difficulties', *Flight International*, 23–29 July, p. 10.

O'Toole, K. (1997a), 'In search of a new jet age', *Flight International*, 5–11 March, pp. 25–26.

O'Toole, K. (1997b), 'Embraer reduces losses and expects return to profitability', *Flight International*, 23–29 April, p. 13.

O'Toole, K. (1998), 'Regional revolution', *Flight International*, 11–17 February, p. 27.

O'Toole, K. and Moxon, J. (1996), 'Regional dilemma', *Flight International*, 7–13 February, pp. 26–27.

Peruzzi, L. (2012), 'Interjet awaits first Sukhoi delivery', *Flight International*, 30 October–5 November, p. 10.

Polek, G. (1998a), 'Bombardier hopes to heat a cold market with the Dash 8Q-400', *Aviation International News*, January, p. 64.

Polek, G. (1998b), 'Embraer may broaden lead in 30-seat jet race', *Aviation International News*, September, pp. 128.

Ranson, L. (2011), 'Can Bombardier–Comac link-up work?', *Flight International*, 5–11 April, p. 12.

Reals, K. (2011), 'Superjet vows to win over the West', *Flight International*, 25–31 January, p. 10.

Richfield, P. (2011), 'Supersize this', *Flight International*, 3–9 May, pp. 24–25.

Roach, J.R. and Eastwood, A.B. (2001), *Turbo Prop Airliner Production List*, 4th edition, The Aviation Hobby Shop, Middlesex.

Sekigawa, E. and Mecham, M. (1996), 'Mitsubishi sees 100-seater in Global Express' wing', *Aviation Week & Space Technology*, 26 August, pp. 29–30.

Shifrin, C.A. (1996), 'Fairchild, Dornier merger plans outlined at RAA', *Aviation Week & Space Technology*, 27 May, pp. 27–28.

Shifrin, C.A. (1997), 'Bombardier bets on new regional turboprop', *Aviation Week & Space Technology*, 15 December, pp. 38–40.

Sobie, B. (2003a), 'D'Long seeks funds to restart 728', *Flight International*, 16–22 September, p. 32.

Sobie, B. (2003b), 'Local heroes', *Flight International*, 16–22 September, pp. 46–48.

Sobie, B. (2003c), 'Alenia aims for role in ARJ21 assembly', *Flight International*, 30 September–6 October, p. 12.

Sparaco, P. (1995), 'DASA assessing market for 40–45-seat Dornier 328', *Aviation Week & Space Technology*, 5 June, p. 42.

Sparaco, P. (1997a), 'AIR strengthens links with China', *Aviation Week & Space Technology*, 1 September, p. 40.

Sparaco, P. (1997b), 'Fairchild Dornier plans regional twinjet family', *Aviation Week & Space Technology*, 24 March, pp. 44–47.

Sparaco, P. (1998a), 'Europeans mull twinjet', *Aviation Week & Space Technology*, 30 November, p. 48.

Sparaco, P. (1998b), 'Fairchild Dornier seeks big role for small 328JET', *Aviation Week & Space Technology*, 2 March, pp. 56–57.

Sparaco, P. and Morrocco, J.D. (1998), 'AIR's failure may boost Avro', *Aviation Week & Space Technology*, 2 March, p. 45.

Symonds, W.C. (1997), 'Bombardier is doing barrel rolls', *Business Week*, 3 March, p. 40.

Taverna, M.A. (1997), 'Fairchild Dornier considering 70-seat regional jet', *Aviation Week & Space Technology*, 24 November, p. 48.

Thisdell, D. (2012), 'Breaking barriers', *Flight International*, 10–16 April, pp. 32–35.

Thomas, A. (2013), 'Geared up for a fight', *Flight International*, 30 April–6 May, pp. 42–44.

Todd, D. and Simpson, J. (1986), *The World Aircraft Industry*, Croom Helm, London.

Toh, M. (2012a), 'ARJ21 starts ice tests as Merpati signals interest', *Flight International*, 6–12 March, p. 12.

Toh, M. (2012b), 'Ambitious order goal will require MRJ plant growth', *Flight International*, 14–27 August, p. 8.

Toh, M. (2012c), 'Merpati expansion rethink threatens ARJ and Sukhoi', *Flight International*, 22–28 May, p. 14.

Toh, M. (2013a), 'Landing-gear changes add to ARJ21's headaches', *Flight International*, 12–18 March, p. 14.

Toh, M. (2013b), 'Comac's tardy ARJ21 inches closer to certification', *Flight International*, 7–13 May, p. 15.

Toh, M. (2013c), 'Delays continue to dog ARJ21 certification timescale', *Flight International*, 28 May–3 June, p. 10.

Toh, M. (2013d), 'Second line at Nagoya could support MRJ demand', *Flight International*, 5–11 February, p. 10.

Toh, M. (2013e), 'Mitsubishi defends MRJ in face of E-Jets overhaul', *Flight International*, 26 March–1 April, p. 12.

Toh, M. (2013f), 'MRJ to have seven-aircraft test fleet', *Flight International*, 21–27 May, p. 13.

Toh, M. (2013g), 'Mitsubishi bullish despite MRJ delay', *Flight International*, 3–9 September, p. 20.

Toh, M. (2013h), 'MRJ delay pinned on FAA paperwork', *Flight International*, 10–16 September, p. 15.

Toh, M. (2013i), 'Bombardier talks 90-seater with Korea', *Flight International*, 29 January–4 February, p. 13.

Toh, M. (2014a), 'Certification challenge ahead for MRJ', *Flight International*, 28 October–3 November, p. 16.

Toh, M. (2014b), 'ARJ21 on verge of certification after delays', *Flight International*, 4–10 November, p. 30.

Trimble, S. (2004), 'Bombardier cool on 100-seat jet', *Flight International*, 3–9 February, p. 11.

Trimble, S. (2012a), 'Big question', *Flight International*, 3–9 July, pp. 66–68.

Trimble, S. (2012b), 'Superjet retains confidence in Blue Panorama commitment', *Flight International*, 30 October–5 November, p. 10.

Trimble, S. (2012c), 'Mitsubishi reveals five-year plan for 100-seat MRJ', *Flight International*, 29 May–4 June, p. 13.

Trimble, S. (2012d), 'SkyWest expects further orders to follow MRJ90', *Flight International*, 24–30 July, p. 13.

Trimble, S (2012e), 'MRJ engine approval takes back seat', *Flight International*, 18–24 September, p. 19.

Trimble, S. (2012f), 'Return of the power turboprop', *Flight International*, 28 February–5 March, pp. 32–34.

Trimble, S. (2012g), 'Embraer shuns tight turboprop market', *Flight International*, 17–24 April, p. 12.

Trimble, S. (2013), 'Mitsubishi patient on MRJ engine slip', *Flight International*, 15–21 January, p. 8.

Turner, A. (2007), 'Sukhoi advances composite use for stretched SSJ', *Flight International*, 10–16 July, p. 8.

US Civil Aviation Manufacturing Industry Panel, Committee on Technology and International Economic and Trade Issues (1985), *The Competitive Status of the U.S. Civil Aviation Manufacturing Industry*, National Academy Press, Washington, DC.

Waldron, G. (2012a), 'MRJ reels as one-year hitch delays deliveries to 2015', *Flight International*, 1–7 May, p. 11.

Waldron, G. (2012b), 'Big break', *Flight International*, 9–15 October, pp. 30–31.

Waldron, G. (2013), 'Money worries delay Indian 70-seater', *Flight International*, 18 December 2012–7 January 2013, p. 15.

Walker, K. (2003), 'Profits alert as Bombardier jobs go', *Flight International*, 11–17 March, p. 4.

Warwick, G. (1998), 'Embraer studies market for larger regional jet', *Flight International*, 20–26 May, p. 5.

Warwick, G. (1999), 'Shorter story', *Flight International*, 5–11 May, pp. 42–46.

Wright, J.P. (1936), 'Factors affecting the cost of airplanes', *Journal of Aeronautical Science*, Vol. 3, No. 2, pp. 122–128.

Yeo, G.L. (2010), 'Flying high', *Flight International*, 9–15 November, p. 43.

Yu'An, Z. (1999), 'Italian plane maker eyes China', *China Daily*, 3 December.

3 Airline companies

Strategies and trends

Isabelle Dostaler and John Fiset

On December 18, 2012, Air Canada was very proud to announce the launch of its brand new leisure low-cost airline, daringly named "Rouge," the French word for red (Deveau, 2012). This was not Air Canada's first attempt at setting up a low-cost subsidiary. Zip, created in 2002 to compete with WestJet, ceased to operate in 2004. Tango, created in 2001, was designed to serve a no-frills service in Central and Eastern Canada, and is now one of the fare classes offered by the Canadian carrier. Air Canada has had its ups and downs in terms of financial performance since coming out of bankruptcy in 2004. Characterized by its adversarial labor relationship, the Canadian carrier is not applauded for the quality of service it offers to its clientele (although its safety track record commands respect). The chances are that a large proportion of the nearly 35 million passengers that have flown with Air Canada and its regional partners in 2012 (Air Canada, 2013) have smiled at the idea of a no-frills (referred to as a "casual feel" by the company) subsidiary when its introduction was announced. Frills? What frills? Indeed, the low-quality snacks and sandwiches sold on board could hardly be considered as "frills." Nevertheless, there is evidence that this new business venture has begun to pay off with Air Canada in terms of financial performance (CBC, 2014). Rouge is accelerating its expansion of service into a number of leisure destinations, with sights set on further European expansion and a potential foray into Asia (Marowits, 2014). The main difference between Air Canada and Rouge is their payroll. Rouge benefits from a larger breathing space than its parent company, courtesy of the new collective agreement that was signed during the bargaining session in which the Canadian government participated during the summer of 2012.

For the majority of the traveling public that cannot afford the pampering offered in first or business classes, air travel has become a rather unpleasant affair. We can all relate to the taste of unappealing snacks, the hassle of lost luggage and the endless lines at security check points. Yet, as indicated by the passenger traffic statistics presented in Figure 3.1, the demand for air travel continues to increase: the threshold of two billion passengers was passed in 2005 and traffic has steadily increased since. In 2010, 2,281,000,000 passengers were carried by airlines and in 2011 this figure increased to over 2.8 billion. Passenger traffic could reach 5.9 billion in 2030 (Air Transport Action Group, 2011).

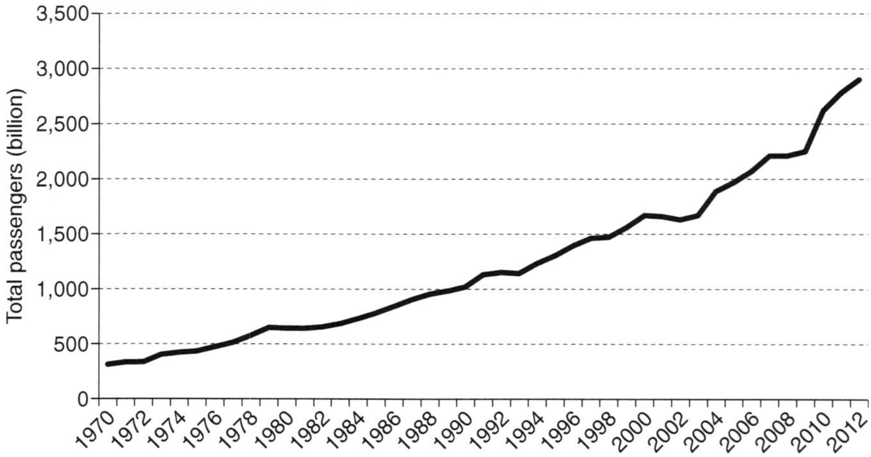

Figure 3.1 Passenger traffic (source: http://data.worldbank.org/indicator/IS.AIR.PSGR?order=wbapi_data_value_2012+wbapi_data_value+wbapi_data_value-last&sort=desc).

However, high passenger traffic does not always translate into larger profits. The first decade of the twenty-first century, punctuated by the terrorist attack on the twin towers, the Severe Acute Respiratory Syndrome (SARS) threat, increasing fuel costs and the 2008 crisis in the banking system was indeed challenging for all airlines. Interestingly, while airlines often struggle financially, air travel-related business such as aircraft-makers, travel agents, global distributions systems providers, airports, caterers and maintenance firms continue to do quite well. As *The Economist* (2012) states: "Airlines are wonderful generators of profit – for everyone except themselves."

Knowing the exact number of air carriers operating throughout the world, including small regional ones, is a difficult task. According to Flightstats, the total number of airlines registered with either the International Civil Aviation Organization (ICAO) or the International Air Transport Association is 1,457.[1] Most major airlines are members of the International Air Transport Association (IATA). The association was created with 57 founding members in 1945. Today, 240 airlines from 115 countries, and accounting for 84 percent of all air traffic, are members of IATA.[2] The world distribution of IATA members is presented in Figure 3.2; Figure 3.3 indicates how the members of the three major alliances (Star Alliance, Skyteam and oneworld) are spread across various regions of the globe. It is interesting to note that IATA has been losing members since 2003 in most regions of the world, with the exception of the Middle East. This makes sense considering that so many airlines have merged or folded due to the economic collapse between 2003 and 2013.

In this chapter we will present a brief review of the changes in the operating environment of air carriers, starting with the Big Bang that marked the deregulation

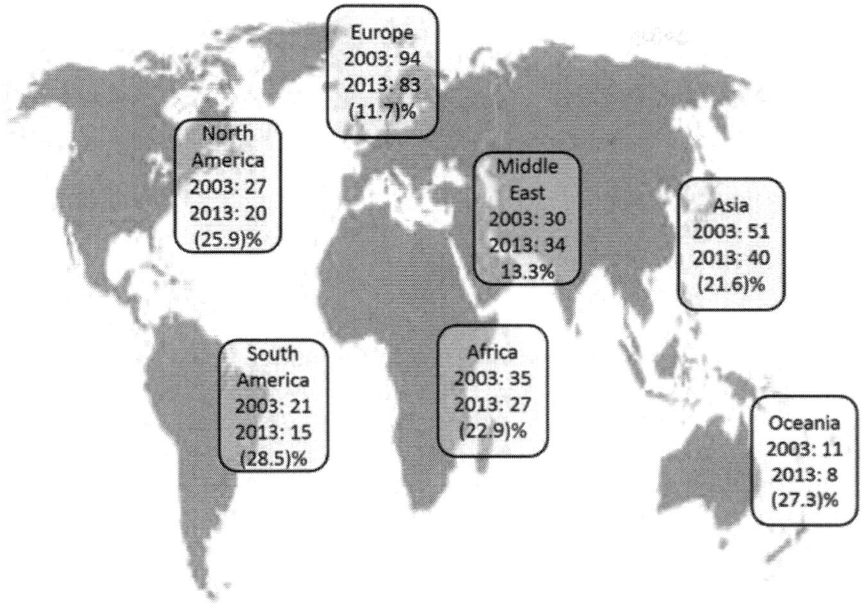

Figure 3.2 World distribution of IATA members: 2003–2013 (based on IATA Annual Report membership).

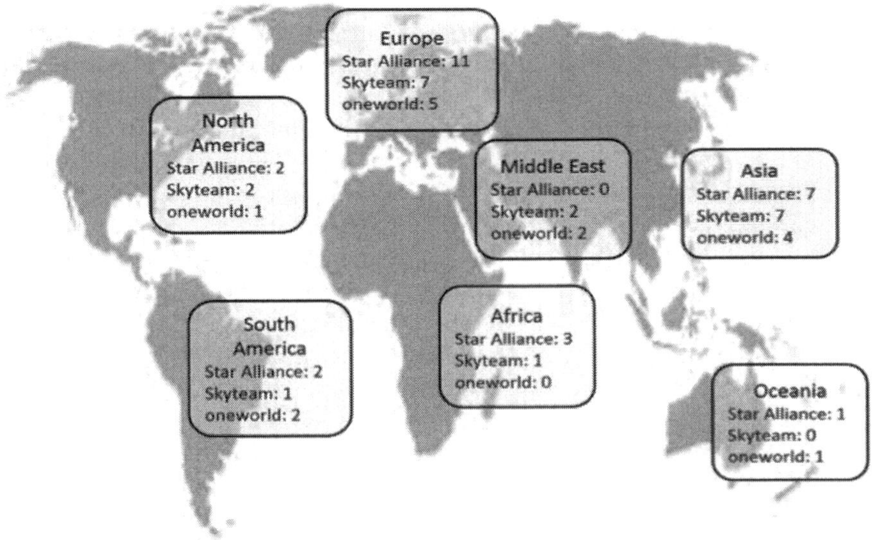

Figure 3.3 World distribution of IATA members: alliance partners by region.

of the US aviation market in 1978 during Carter's presidency. We will discuss the rise of the low-cost carriers and the retaliation tactics used by traditional carriers as well as the so-called "hybridization" or "dual" strategies that some airlines now claim to be using. We will then present the cases of three airlines operating in various regions of the world. This cross-section of carriers will vary in terms of age, size, geographic scope, business strategies, and performance. The presentation of these cases will be followed by a discussion of the key factors that have determined the survival and success of carriers over the years.

Deregulation, competition and business models

A true paradigm shift took place in air transportation when the Airline Deregulation Act was enacted in 1978 in the United States under the Carter presidency, changing the competitive aviation landscape in an irreversible manner. It is therefore not surprising that the air transport community refers to 1978 as the year of the "Big Bang" (Sheth *et al.*, 2007). Since then, numerous airlines have entered the market and numerous others have disappeared. As we will see in this chapter, survivors have either successfully seized the opportunities to create new business models or managed to thwart the threats posed by deregulation.

To regulate or not to regulate

Economists can be roughly divided into two camps with regards to the benefits for society of the deregulation of air transportation. The first camp claims that too many firms are attracted to the sector and tend to concentrate on profitable routes impairing the emergence of an integrated air transportation network, a problem that regulation can solve. Air transportation can also be seen as a natural monopoly and should be regulated to lower fares. To the contrary, advocates of liberalism consider air transportation as a competitive sector and believe that the arrival of new entrants is likely to lower the price of the services offered. Before the Big Bang, although US airlines were widely held publicly listed firms, operational decisions such as flight schedules, frequency and pricing were determined by public authorities. Walker *et al.* (2002) argued that airline employees benefited considerably from this regulatory framework but other stakeholders such as consumers and stockholders suffered from it, as price options were limited and profitability tended to be low. The Airline Deregulation Act promised to improve this situation. Interestingly, Sabourin and Fagnan (2000) posit that air carriers' typical strategic response to deregulation and the resulting competition was to try to obtain a dominant position and to thwart as much as possible the effect of deregulation. This claim is supported by Prince and Simon (2009), who have found the existence of a mutual forbearance phenomenon in the US airline industry. These authors have studied the services offered by ten main US carriers[3] on the 1,000 business domestic routes liaisons between January 1995 and August 2001 and found a link between the number of multi-market contacts and the amount of delays. Their research results suggest that mutual forbearance, like a monopoly situation, enable air carriers to allocate fewer resources to ground services, baggage handling and aircraft maintenance. The savings allow carriers who compete together on several markets to increase their profitability.

Before the Big Bang, the vast majority of airlines outside the United States were wholly state-owned national flag carriers. Deregulations had a major impact on Western countries and Canada and Europe followed suit with the privatization of several flag carriers such as British Airways in 1987 and Lufthansa seven years later, although foreign ownership continued to be regulated. In Canada, where long distance and low population density pose notable transportation challenges, the air transport deregulation process happened through more or less judicious half-measures triggering numerous recriminations from various stakeholders, ranging from large airport CEOs accusing the government of treating aviation as a "cash cow" to remote communities complaining about the low flexibility and high price of regional air transport services. A former crown corporation privatized in 1989, Air Canada continues in many ways to bear the stamp of a flag carrier. In Europe, the air transport deregulation process happened gradually and culminated in 1997 (Fan, 2010) with full freedom with regards to pricing, capacity, routing, service levels, and cabotage. This means that any member of the European Union can fly any route within Europe without a home country origin or destination. The EU is the first region in the world where airline ownership caps were eventually completely removed (Hsu and Chang, 2005), which created attractive business opportunities for airlines and gave several options to travelers.

Regulatory frameworks and levels of state intervention vary elsewhere in the world, in emergent and transitional economies, with many countries still owning partly or completely their flag carriers. Interestingly, Japan is considered to be "one of the last bastions of the legacy industry" (Thomas, 2010). The Japanese airline industry and Japan as a whole was considerably shaken in 2010 when Japan Airlines went bankrupt and was later revived under a smaller company operating under a rather different business model. Despite their limited size, regions like the Arab Emirates and Singapore have caught their fair share of the global increase in passenger traffic in the last decade thanks to finely orchestrated policies with regards to tourism, airport and airline development (Lohmann *et al.*, 2009). Needless to say, the autocratic nature of the political system in these countries translates to substantial state intervention in the air transportation system.

The aftermath of the Big Bang

In the United States, the Big Bang meant that new players were free to enter the industry and offer lower fares than incumbent firms. The examples of People Express and Southwest Airlines are particularly telling. The former operated from New Jersey from 1981 to 1987 and enjoyed some success until it was absorbed by Continental Airlines. People Express pursued a cost leadership strategy in the purest sense of the word (Porter, 1980): travelers enjoyed the lowest fares possible and did not have any expectations with regard to the quality of service and were willing to pay extra small fees for snacks and checked luggage. The no-frills carrier started its operation in the domestic market and eventually flew to Canada and Europe. The downfall of People Express could be attributed to its aggressive acquisition strategy, although Sheth *et al.* (2007) argue that it did not survive because of the predatory pricing practices of legacy carriers. These authors argue that American legacy carriers, such as American Airlines, United Airlines and Delta, also responded to the threat of deregulation by putting in place the hub-and-spoke model, allowing them to create entry barriers and benefit from economies of scale. In-house feeder subsidiaries brought passengers from secondary airports to main airports where legacy carriers had established their base, and large aircraft used for long-haul international flights could be filled with regional passengers. The advent of this business model created opportunities for Bombardier Aerospace to develop and sell more than 900 CRJ-100 and -200 regional jets since 1991 (see also Chapter 2).

As mentioned above, prior to deregulation, airlines' routes and prices were determined by the US Civic Aeronautics Board (CAB). Other coordinating mechanisms had to be put in place when the industry was deregulated (Lee *et al.*, 2000). This is when computer reservation systems (CRS), the ancestor of global distribution systems (GDS) were developed by airlines themselves as they wanted to avoid travel agents taking control of the coordination role played so far by the regulator.

Combined with international alliances and supported by global distribution systems, the hub-and-spoke model represented the promise of a "seamless" air travel experience from any regional location in a given continent to any regional location in another continent. Wanting to gain an increasing share of their passengers' traveling budget, traditional carriers started to move away from their core business and invested in hotels and car rental services. For example, in 1987 the UAL Corporation, the parent company of United Airlines, announced a plan to create Allegis, a travel conglomerate comprising the airline itself, both Hilton and Weston hotel chains and the Hertz car rental agency. This plan never took off due to serious complaints by internal stakeholders (Salpukas, 1987). Although business theorists such as Chandler (1990) would have argued that diversifying in fields in which they did not know much was an ill-advised strategic move, legacy carriers were motivated by the desire to protect themselves against the threat of deregulation by creating higher entry barriers. They also made sure to hold on to grandfather clauses allowing them to keep coveted airport slots. The connection between domestic and international passenger networks into seamless and globally ubiquitous multinational systems slowly became the legitimate "industry recipe" (Spender, 1989) that airlines identify with. Articulating a convincing rationale for growth that reflected the conventional wisdom was necessary for publicly traded airlines to positively affect stock prices movement and attract capital (Carney and Dostaler, 2006).

While several discount carriers established after deregulation were not able to survive in front of the incumbents' retaliation described above, the success of companies such as Southwest and Air Tran, two companies that merged in 2011 (Ranson, 2011), is very impressive. Southwest Airlines has become a mythical organization, skillfully managed by a charismatic leader, Herb Kelleher, who led the startup company through multiple court battles with American Airlines and Continental before it could offer air travel service beyond Texas (Grantham, 2007). Kelleher was perceived by employees as a genuine hero who successfully protected their jobs. The dedication of Southwest employees is vividly illustrated in testimonials and videos in which they can be seen singing, dancing and showing loyalty to their beloved CEO, Herb Kelleher. The success of Southwest was not only explained by its colorful leader, but also as a cohesive assemblage of practices including the concentration on point-to-point flights between less congested secondary airports, a uniform fleet favoring quick turnaround time and a flexible non-unionized workforce exemplified by pilots eager to help the crew with cabin cleaning. As a result, Southwest and the numerous low-cost carriers that emulated it, starting with Ryanair, benefited from marked cost advantages compared with traditional incumbent carriers. Low-cost carriers tended to be privately held small entrepreneurial firms free from the financial market constraints. As such, they had strong incentives for parsimony as well as the freedom to pursue novel opportunities. These entrepreneurial firms eventually imposed themselves with a business model that was rather revolutionary at the time (Carney and Dostaler, 2006).

Stuck in the middle revisited

The typology of business strategies developed by Porter (1980) can be useful to better understand the business models described above. Porter has argued that companies can choose between two types of competitive advantage: low cost and differentiation. These competitive advantages are combined with either a broad competitive scope (companies target large mass markets) or a limited one (companies focus on a small niche) to create four well-known business strategies: cost leadership, differentiation, focused low cost and focused differentiation. Cost leadership is the typical business strategy pursued by companies in the consumer electronics or compact cars industries. Each one of the cost leader's value chain activities has to be conducted in the most efficient way in order to generate a profit margin, despite the low price of the product or service offered. In contrast, differentiation is the business strategy of companies that offer a product or service that customers perceive as different and for which they are willing to pay a higher price. Selecting the bases of differentiation, in other words the features of the product offered or the way in which it is offered, and developing the organizational capabilities needed to achieve the bases of differentiation, is a key challenge for companies. Interestingly, in order to offer acceptable value to customers, cost leaders must not ignore the bases of differentiation for which customers are willing to pay a premium. However, cost leaders must not try to offer features that differentiated products or services possess, for fear of being "stuck in the middle". According to Porter (1980), this is what happened to Laker Airways in the 1970s. The British airline offered a successful no-frills/low-fare service but eventually started to add more destinations and fancier in-flight services. To maintain its profitability, Laker Airways had to raise its fares up to the point where travellers felt that they had more value for money when flying with traditional carriers. According to Porter, a firm that tries to pursue each generic strategy but fails to achieve any of them is "stuck in the middle." Porter (1990) argued that being stuck in the middle was "a recipe for strategic mediocrity and below-average performance, because pursuing all the strategies simultaneously means that a firm is not able to achieve any of them because of their inherent contradictions" (Porter, 1990: 40). This could explain why many of the in-house low-cost subsidiaries created in the 1990s by legacy carriers, such as KLM's Buzz or US Airways' Metrojet, struggled so much that many were either sold off or dissolved.

The "stuck in the middle" prescription has generated much debate through the years. Gilbert and Strebel (1988) did not consider cost leadership and differentiation as mutually exclusive, and argued that companies in mature industries can rejuvenate themselves by shifting to product differentiation and innovation while preserving strengths in cost reduction and process efficiency. Similar arguments could be found with Pettigrew and Whipp (1991), who observed that in many industrial sectors, bases of competition in one era became the essential prerequisites for new organizational capabilities in the next. They stated that "the popular notion of a single competitive edge appears at best wrong-headed and at worst downright alarming" and stressed the danger of "pinning all hopes and resources on one main ability" (Pettigrew and Whipp, 1991: 289). This strong argument echoed the "value for money" paradigm introduced by Pitelis and Taylor (1996), who are considered as fervent advocates of the need for companies to try to achieve both cost leadership and differentiation (Kanitakis, 2002).

Contributing to the debate on whether cost leadership and differentiation can be combined, Cronshaw *et al.* (1994) proposed a different interpretation of the "stuck in the middle" prescription. They suggested that firms that do not establish lower costs or better or differentiated products, overall, rarely succeed. In other words, "stuck in the middle" was less a prescription than a way to analyze strategic outcomes. In his comparison of the competitive advantage of nations, Porter (1990) himself claimed that whether a firm will be able to sustain its advantage depends on the source of the advantage, the number of distinct sources and constant improvement and upgrading. The author made a distinction between lower-order advantages, such as low labor costs or cheap raw materials, and higher-order advantages such as proprietary process technology or product differentiation based on unique products or services, arguing that pure cost advantages are often less sustainable than differentiation. In a sense, the author appeared to treat cost leadership like the poor cousin in the competitive strategy family. The underlying message seemed to be that differentiation is the best strategy. In keeping with Cronshaw *et al.* (1994), it could be argued that being able to successfully combine differentiation and cost leadership would be even better. Therefore, it is not surprising that most strategy textbooks now offer a fifth choice, namely the "integrated cost leadership/differentiation strategy" (Coulter, 2002; Hitt *et al.*, 2003) or the "best-cost provider strategy" (Thompson and Strickland, 2004), a strategy "in which an organization develops a competitive advantage by simultaneously achieving low-costs and high levels of differentiation" (Coulter, 2002: 228). Interestingly, while Southwest is widely recognized for having invented the low-cost carrier business model, Hitt *et al.* (2003: 6) argued in the opening of their textbook that Southwest succeeded despite poor economic conditions "because of its integrated cost leadership/differentiation strategy." The authors observed that Southwest offered low fares, like many other carriers, but also had fewer customer complaints than major carriers and was able to attract employees that treated customers well and had excellent on-time performance.

Other carriers have been recognized as successfully pursuing an integrated cost leadership/differentiation strategy. In their case study of Singapore Airlines, Heraclous and Wirtz argue that the Asian carrier pursue a "dual strategy"; "differentiation through service excellence and innovation, together with simultaneous cost leadership in its peer group" (2009: 274). To achieve this, Singapore Airlines manages to be "just a little bit better in everything" than their competitors (2009: 276). Some industry observers now use the expression "hybridization" (Airline Leader, 2011–2012) to refer to the process by which some low-cost carriers, such as Gol, WestJet and JetBlue, have started to add differentiating features to their business models. In keeping with Cronshaw *et al.* (1994), the success of these carriers seem to support the hypothesis that Laker Airways, Buzz or Metrojet did not fail because of a poor strategic choice, but because of poor strategy implementation.

Seamless travel as a basis of differentiation

Whereas the cost leadership business strategy is self-explanatory (companies pursuing it want to offer the lowest price possible compared to their competitors), the notion of differentiation needs to be specified. A differentiated product or service is something for which customers are willing to pay a premium. Companies pursuing a differentiation strategy need to have a clear understanding of the rules of the game in their business sector (namely the key success factors), as this will allow them to define the very product or service features for which customers will be willing to pay a premium. Therefore, the strategic fit between the key success factors in the competitive environment, the bases of differentiation that the company uses and the core competence (hopefully difficult to imitate) that the company has developed is recognized as a key determinant of business performance in the strategic management literature.

As mentioned before, the deregulation of air travel resulted in the creation of the hub-and-spoke system designed by legacy carriers as entry barriers. Beyond seeking protection against new entrants, it could be argued that legacy carriers calculated that passengers would be willing to pay more to have access to seamless multinational networks. The promise of a seamless travel experience was therefore used as a basis of differentiation and favored the development of global air carrier alliances. Airlines have been making route-sharing deals for decades. For example, in the 1980s SAS, Swissair, Austrian Airlines and Finnair tried without much success to establish the now defunct European Quality Alliance. In 1988, SAS bought an 18.4 percent stake in the Texas Air Corporation, which was the holding company for Continental and Eastern Airlines, and created an alliance that resulted in a financial disaster for SAS.

It was not until the 1990s that groups of airlines began to test international aviation regulations in an effort to create large-scale alliances which would result in efficiencies for all members as well as an extended list of destinations without the additional financial burden. The results of these partnerships were three major alliances that continue to exist to this day: Star Alliance, created in 1997; oneworld created in 1999; and Sky Team, created in 2000. A fourth, Global Excellence, was created in 1989 between Singapore Airlines, Swissair and Delta, and dissolved in 1998 (Li, 2000). As indicated in Table 3.1, their sizes vary from

Table 3.1 Major alliances members and year of entrance

Star Alliance	*SkyTeam*	*oneworld*
Lufthansa (Founder)	Air France (Founder)	American Airlines (Founder)
Scandinavian Airlines (Founder)	Delta Air Lines (Founder)	British Airways (Founder)
United Airlines (Founder)	Aeromexico (Founder)	Cathay Pacific (Founder)
Thai Airways International (Founder)	Korean Air (Founder)	Quantas (Founder)
Air Canada (Founder)	Czech Airlines (2001)	Finnair (1999)
All Nippon Airways (1999)	KLM (2004)	Iberia Airlines (1999)
Air New Zealand (1999)	Aeroflot (2006)	LAN Airlines (2000)
Singapore Airlines (2000)	Air Europa (2007)	Royal Jordanian (2007)
LOT Polish Airlines (2003)	China Southern Airlines (2007)	Japan Airlines (2007)
Asiana Airlines (2003)	Kenya Airways (2007)	S7 Airlines (2010)
Adria Airways (2004)	Alitalia (2009)	Air Berlin (2012)
Croatia Airlines (2004)	TAROM (2010)	LAN Columbia (2013)
TAP Portugal (2005)	China Airlines (2011)	Malaysia Airlines (2013)
South African Airways (2006)	China Eastern Airlines (2011)	SriLankan Airlines (2013)
Swiss International Airlines (2006)	Vietnam Airlines (2011)	Qatar Airways (2013)
Air China (2007)	Aerolineas Argentinas (2012)	TAM (2014)
EgyptAir (2008)	Middle East Airlines (2012)	US Airways (2014)
Turkish Airlines (2008)	Saudia (2012)	
Brussels Airlines (2009)	Xiamen Airlines (2012)	
Aegean (2010)	Garuda Indonesia (2014)	
Ethiopian Airlines (2011)		
Copa Airlines (2012)		
TACA/Avianca (2012)		
Shenzhen Airlines (2012)		
EVA Air (2013)		
Olympic Air (2013)		

17 to 26 carriers. They went through difficult times punctuated by economic downturns, terrorist attacks and pandemic fears, and appeared particularly outdated when the low-cost model gained popularity in the 2000s. The global alliances have nevertheless survived and have a strong hold on transatlantic routes, so much so that they are referred to as "transatlantic cartels" in which airlines agree on cost and artificially boost prices (*The Economist*, 2011b). While it could be argued that the existence of alliances prevents the inefficiencies resulting from fragmented air travel systems (*The Economist*, 2011c), the extent to which passengers benefit from this industrial structure, which is protected by the regulatory framework, is not clear.

It should be added that alliances are not static and have changed over time, beyond adding new members. Several airlines have left alliances due to a variety of reasons, such as bankruptcy, strategic changes, mergers or dissatisfaction with other members. For example, VARIG Brazil joined the Star Alliance in October 1997 and left when the company went into bankruptcy protection and restructuring and was eventually divided into two companies in 2006. Similarly, Ansett Australia became a Star Alliance member in 1999 but went into bankruptcy a few years later. Other examples include Mexicana, which joined Star Alliance in 2000, left in 2004, then joined oneworld in 2009, but ceased operation in 2010; and Shanghai Airlines which joined Star Alliance in 2007 and left in October 2010 after merging with China Eastern.

The business strategies pursued by alliance members is based on the underlying assumption that passengers are willing to pay a premium to have access to the international network that they can offer. However, the value that customers place on these networks is unclear. Furthermore, poor strategy implementation by legacy carriers often results in delays, missed connections and lost luggage, causing high levels of customer dissatisfaction. Networks are also not as seamless as they claim to be, given that some members resist the tightening of partnerships. For example, many do not agree to joint check-in, although this would save time for passengers, for possible fear of weakening their brand. The fear of eroding the brand might also exist for Asian airlines whose North American partners do not offer the same levels of business class services.

It therefore seems difficult for legacy carriers and alliance members to achieve strategic fit. Either they do not seem to have a clear understanding of the key success factors in the competitive environment that they should be using as a basis of differentiation or, in cases where they do understand customers' needs, they seem unable to develop the organizational capabilities that will allow them to meet these needs. The consequence is that many customers use online portals to build their own flight itineraries (*The Economist*, 2011a). Not only does this option sometimes result in savings, but the possibility of keeping control on luggage and allocating enough time between flights to buffer the risk of delays can be very appealing. Some travelers seem to be redefining the concept of seamless travel.

Changing business models

As exemplified by Air Canada's Rouge, some legacy carriers are currently trying their luck again with in-house low-cost subsidiaries. In the meantime, low-cost carriers, such as Brazilian carrier Gol, which has several codeshare arrangements with members of various alliances, feel the need to offer more connectivity (Airline Leader, 2011–2012). Different airline business models therefore seem to be meeting in the middle of the low-cost–differentiation continuum. This raised the following question: is it easier to successfully implement a low-cost–differentiation business strategy starting from a low-cost position or from a differentiation position? In other words, can Rouge succeed where Zip failed and can Gol avoid the sad fate of Laker Airways? Will evolving carriers avoid getting stuck in the middle?

The situation may or may not be different now than in the beginning of the 2000s when, on one side, legacy carriers started to reduce their service levels in the hope of reducing costs, while, on the other side, carriers with a low-fare mandate, such as JetBlue, flew with aircrafts fitted with leather seats and satellite TV. A JetBlue manager described the early 2000 competitive landscape as follows: "It's one of those situations where for a lower price you get a better product, which is really hard to compete with" (Bonné, 2003). Evidently, passengers who were flying legacy carriers and expected the frills that had been removed were bound to be less happy than passengers paying lower fares and being pleasantly surprised by extra perks. Bonné (2003) referred to this as the "expectation game." His analysis suggested that legacy carriers were better at playing that game in 1939 when they introduced "Conditional Passage": "Sell cheaper airline tickets to passengers who wouldn't pay for a full-fare or a full-service ticket. There was, of course, one big caveat: It had to be made clear to these passengers that they were getting a second-class ride" (Bonné, 2003). This is a rather different proposition than the "de-bundling" or "ancillary revenue" strategy that some legacy carriers[4] started to implement in the mid-2000s (Garrow *et al.*, 2012) when passengers were offered a basic fare to which they could add various options such as checked baggage, reserved seats and assistance in the case of flight cancellation. Asking passengers to pay for service features to which they felt entitled is a questionable way to manage their expectations.

Southwest's growth path is another illustration of a move towards the middle of the low-cost–differentiation continuum.[5] The carrier went from organic growth (and occasional acquisition of small players) to absorbing AirTran in 2011 and hence becoming the largest low-fare carrier in the United States (Southwest Airlines, 2013). Some commentators noted that low-cost and legacy carriers are more and more similar to each other (Knowledge at Wharton, 2010). In fact, it could be argued that the main advantage that low-cost carriers had compared to legacy carriers was that of youth, an advantage bound to erode. Indeed, the acquisition of AirTran brought a number of challenges typical to those faced by legacy carriers. The harmonization of seniority lists and potential labor unrest, which could be a threat to Southwest's culture – one of its key strengths – as well as the information systems integration, are examples of these challenges. While for AirTran, the acquisition resulted in the elimination of its first-class service, it forced Southwest to move away from the key features of its successful low-cost model, such as the concentration on one type of aircraft and the use of small secondary airports which both contributed to reduce turnaround time.

Another differentiating feature of low-cost and legacy carriers is the distribution system that they use. As mentioned before, global distribution systems (GDS) were coordination mechanisms developed in the wake of deregulation, given that until then routes and prices were determined by civil aviation authorities. Developed by legacy carriers themselves, the early GDS were another illustration of how these carriers tried to mitigate the effect of deregulation and competition. American Airlines developed Sabre, United Airlines owned Apollo, while European carriers developed Amadeus and Galileo. Travel agents used these information systems to check flight availability and pricing information, to make bookings and issue tickets. These systems, however, did not guarantee impartial comparisons between available flights because of a "halo effect," namely "the travel agents' tendency to book flights on owner airline(s) of CRS's they operated" (Lee *et al.*, 2000: 4). Each system was subject to a bias, as the flights offered by the CRS owner would be displayed on the top of the screen while the number of flights listed on a screen was limited. Legacy carriers were trying to mitigate the effect of deregulation by creating entry barriers. At the same time, travel agents benefited from CRS to the detriment of the airlines. Larger travel agencies were able to connect to multiple CRS systems and played the systems against each other by generating "passive bookings" that did not generate sales but from which airlines had to pay nevertheless. It is understandable that, at some point, airlines were hoping to get rid of travel agents. Given that regulatory authorities had started to look into airlines' anti-competitive way of handling reservations, the obvious strategic decision for legacy carriers was to divest the CRS business and sell the reservations systems:

> At the dawn of the internet age, airlines assumed that the middlemen who came between them and their passengers were headed for extinction. Travelers would eventually buy tickets either from the airlines' own websites or from price-comparison engines which hooked up directly to the airlines' computers over the web. So why pay commissions to agents?
>
> (*The Economist*, 2012)

Unfortunately for legacy carriers, things did not unfold as they had planned and, while carriers often struggled financially, the GDS has proved to be a very profitable business. Furthermore, travel agents have not disappeared. Airlines currently pay average fees of approximately $12 per round trip booked through a GDS and a portion of these fees go to travel agents (either physical or online) for flights booked by them (*The Economist*, 2012).

With a business model based on point-to-point service, low-cost carriers were lucky enough to operate without travel agents and GDS, therefore saving on distribution cost. However, as they move along the low-cost–differentiation continuum toward a so-called "hybrid" position, low-cost carriers want to offer more connectivity. They will no longer be able to rely on a stand-alone website; more connectivity means paying the middlemen as legacy carriers always had to do. The acquisition of AirTran by Southwest illustrates this well. This acquisition connected Southwest to a network, including its first international connections, but also brought the challenge of integrating two information systems (Knowledge at Wharton, 2010).

Even if the global picture depicted above seems to be one in which low-cost and legacy carriers are starting to look more and more like each other, individual companies do exhibit unique characteristics. In the next section, we will present the cases of three airlines operating in various regions of the world.

Airline profiles

The three carriers portrayed in this section, namely United Airlines, AirAsia and Gol were selected because they each vary significantly in terms of age, size and geographic scope, in addition to operating according to different strategy. United Airlines is a legacy carrier that uses international scale to its advantage. AirAsia is a firmly rooted airline that focuses on providing low-cost fares and high-quality service to passengers across southern Asia, while Gol is currently transitioning into an international carrier, while concurrently shifting from a low-cost carrier to a hybrid strategy. To highlight this point, Table 3.2 provides data on revenue, profitability, number of passengers carried and fleet size of each of the three organizations.

United Airlines

United Airlines and United Express, with the 2011 merger with Continental Airlines, operates an average of 5,472 flights per day to 381 airports across six

Table 3.2 Key 2012 airline statistics (all currency in million USD)

	United Airlines[1]	*Gol*[2]	*AirAsia*[3]
Revenue	\$3,715	\$3,484	\$1,500
Profitability	\$(723)	\$(653)	\$553
Passengers (millions)	93.6	39	19.7
Fleet	702 aircraft	131 aircraft	125 aircraft

Notes

1 http://ir.unitedcontinentalholdings.com/phoenix.zhtml?c=83680&p=irol-newsArticle&ID=1777521&highlight=

2 www.mzweb.com.br/gol2009/web/conteudo_en.asp?idioma=1&tipo=28005&conta=44&id=170228

3 www.airasia.com/iwov-esources/my/common/pdf/AirAsia/IR/annual-report-2012.pdf

continents (United Continental Holdings, 2013). In 2012 United Airlines flew more total scheduled passenger-kilometers than any other airline in the world, tallying up over 288 million, both domestically and internationally (IATA, 2013). United Airlines, now traded as United Continental Holdings on the New York Stock Exchange, had become the largest airline in the world. However, this did not last for long as, in February 2013, the anticipated merger between American Airlines and US Airways became a reality, changing yet again the competitive landscape of the US airline industry to one that is a three-way battle for global airline supremacy (Schlangenstein, 2013).

Based in Chicago, United Airlines was one of the "Big Six" airlines (which, after a series of mergers, has been reduced to three) in the United States that dominated commercial travel for much of the twentieth century and were known as "legacy carriers," a label that refers to the fact that they existed prior to deregulation (Holloway, 2008). This group of large airlines has long been viewed as being lax on their air service offerings. For example, although they had among the five-highest fees, American Airlines and United Airlines also had the worst customer service rating according to the American Customer Satisfaction Index (ACSI). In comparison, Southwest, which had among the lowest fees, scored as one of the best on the ACSI (Sauter, 2013). Many United Airlines' passengers have horror stories to share and can relate to the author of "United breaks guitars," a video put on YouTube in 2010 and viewed almost 13,000,000 times (Sonofmaxwell, 2009) and followed by a book on the power of social media (Carroll, 2012).

The origins of United Airlines provides us with an excellent case of the benefits and pitfalls of vertical integration. The air carrier was originally named United Aircraft and Transport Corporation, a partnership between Boeing Airplane Company and Pratt & Whitney (Garvey *et al.*, 2001; United Continental Holdings, 2013). The corporation originated with the opening of United Air Lines on July 1, 1931. At the time, the company advertised itself as being the largest air carrier in the world. Soon after, on March 30, 1933, the organization took the lead in introducing what many consider the world's first modern civil airliner, the Boeing 247. This vertical integration of air carriers and aircraft makers was greatly facilitated by the McNary-Watres Act of 1930, which served to regulate the air mail industry. Prior to the 1930 Act, mail delivery services were provided by over a dozen carriers vying for these same contracts. As reported by Vietor, profit limitations "prevented the development of any significant passenger service" (1990: 64), as mail was the prime profit driver for these early airlines. Regulation therefore appeared to be needed to create favorable conditions for business development. The McNary-Watres Act of 1930 led to the development of three large vertically integrated air transportation companies that brought together aircraft manufacturers and that formed what many called a government-sponsored cartel (Vietor, 1990: 65), as only the largest firms were awarded contracts.[6] Although this industry structure stimulated the development of passenger service, it was dismantled under the 1934 Air Mail Act as allegations of collusion created a national outcry. The act stipulated that all existing aviation holding companies had to break-up or risk never receiving a mail contract again.[7] United Aircraft and Transport Corporation was then divided into its three legally distinct parts: Boeing, United Aircraft and United Air Lines.

Although not initially an early adopter of jet engine aircraft, United was the very first operator of the Boeing 720 in 1960 and, four years later, of the Boeing 727. In the 1990s, the carrier was going to be closely involved in the development of the 777, a program during which Boeing implemented innovative product development practices including close interaction with customers from the early stage of the development process (Brown *et al.*, 2002). As a result, United was the first carrier to fly the Boeing 777 internationally in 1995.

A major player in the development of United Air Lines and in the creation of an industry for air passenger transportation was "Pat" A. Patterson, the president of the airline for over 30 years from the 1930s to the 1960s. In addition to being a major voice for developing new technologies, he was also credited with the invention of the role of flight attendant in the United States. By the end of his tenure, United was the US airline enjoying the highest number of passenger-miles, a privileged position that it maintained right up to the point of deregulation. The Deregulation Act of 1978 forced the organization to cut its flight offerings in an effort to become more profitable. As described earlier, legacy carriers responded to the threat of deregulation by creating entry barriers. Like the other major airlines, United Airlines focused its activities around several major hubs such as Los Angeles, Chicago and Tokyo. At the same time, like many other legacy carriers, United embraced a diversification strategy, expanding into other areas such as computerized reservation systems, hotel chains and rental car companies. United also entered new markets in the Pacific, Australia and Europe using a fleet of Boeing 747-400 jumbo jets (Garvey *et al.*, 2001).

The carrier has also been making major inroads in the international market. In 1997, for example, it partnered with Air Canada, Germany's Lufthansa, the Scandinavian Airlines System (SAS) and Thai International to create the Star Alliance and provide a common network of world-spanning routes. United posted several years of profits in the late 1990s but, due to the economic recession in Asia, the airline's growth in profits has slowed. At the turn of the century, United continued to be one of the most important players in domestic commercial aviation. However, the first decade of the twenty-first century, marked by the SARS epidemic, the liquid bomb episode, the 2008 banking crisis, as well as the rise of the low-cost carriers in addition to the September 11 terrorist attack, was extremely challenging for legacy carriers. The challenge was particularly critical for United Airlines as two of the four aircraft used on September 11 were part of its fleet. When it became impossible to obtain the necessary capital to continue to operate, United had to go through a major cost-cutting exercise. For United Airlines and several other legacy carriers, the only way to achieve this was to seek bankruptcy protection.

With its 85,592 employees and its fleet of 703 aircraft, composed of various Airbus and Boeing models including the Dreamliner, United Airlines is still alive and relatively well (United Continental Holdings, 2013), with load factors and revenue passenger miles slightly on the rise as a result of decreased capacity. However, the restructuring process it went through, as well as the recent merger with Continental Airlines, has taken its toll on labor relationships. Labor relationships are far from a strength of legacy carriers and largely explain the poor service their passengers often receive. United Airlines did improve its employer image in January 2013 when it rewarded employees who helped the world's largest carrier achieve its best on-time performance in ten years with a $100 on-time bonus (Lazare, 2013). However, it should be noted that the effectiveness of such an extrinsic motivation tool is limited according to the organizational behavior literature (Deci *et al.*, 1999) and can probably not measure up to the strong high service quality culture that low-cost carriers such as Southwest and JetBlue have successfully implemented.

The four American major carriers are now American, United Continental, Delta and Southwest – three of these are legacy carriers. It could be argued that following the mergers that brought down the number of US legacy carriers from six to three, and in the context of an international "cartel" (e.g. the three international alliances), the business environment in which American major carriers operate is not particularly threatening. This could explain why 2012 airline fees had been on the rise compared to 2011, according to TravelNerd (2013). United Airlines is also adding to its ancillary revenue by offering new services, such as the BagsVIP program, which allows travelers to skip baggage claim and have their luggage delivered directly to their final destination. United is also the first US legacy carrier to offer Wi-Fi on its international flights (TravelNerd, 2013) and has been recognized for its treatment of elite flyers through its Global Services Program (Nicas, 2013). Interestingly, the airline decides which flights to give priority to during air traffic or flight delays, using an algorithm that assigns a score to each flight based on passenger count and their connections, as well as the number of elite-level frequent fliers on the flight (Elliot, 2012).

Although many commentators argue that US airlines would support more freedom in the industry, it could be argued that the environment in which they operate is a rather friendly one. There is still a fair level of regulation in the United States, mainly in the form of the foreign ownership cap: "The foundation or airline regulation is the premise that unfettered access to a nation's markets and infrastructure should be limited to airlines of that nation" (Cosmas *et al.*, 2011: 18). The rationale for this is the maintenance of the strong safety record of US carriers and the protection of the US competitive position, labor and national security (Cosmas *et al.*, 2011: 21). The threat of reducing the access of isolated communities to transportation networks could also be added to this list. The extent to which US airlines are satisfied with the level and nature of regulations is unclear. While there is an argument that US airlines may see in a positive light the way foreign carriers have their capacity, frequency and fares restricted by the US regulator, the limited access to foreign capital hinders the potential for growth of American carriers. It could also be argued that the friendly US regulator artificially allows weak carriers to survive and to continue to offer poor service and higher fares.

AirAsia

Having won the title of the "world's best low-cost airline" for five consecutive years (Voyagers World, 2013), AirAsia attracts considerable attention, while Kuala Lumpur where the carrier is based is recognized as the "birthplace of Asia's LCC movement" (Thomas, 2011). With its remarkably uniform fleet of more than 100 Airbus 320 of an average age of 4.2 years, AirAsia does seem to fit well in the low-cost carrier category. AirAsia was originally created in December 1993 by DRB-Hicom, a Malaysian government-owned conglomerate. It started to operate in 1996 and offered full service air transportation to domestic destinations within Malaysia. This strategy did not work well, however, and by December 2001 the full service carrier had accumulated US$11 million worth of debts. This is when former Time Warner executive Tony Fernandes came into play: his company Tune Group – which also owns hotels, a Formula One racing team and a football league – acquired AirAsia for the token sum of one ringgit (about US$0.26 at the time).

Just as William Patterson had a significant impact on United Airlines between 1933 and 1963, it could be argued that Tony Fernandes, ranked #53 in 2011 in *FastCompany* Top 100 most creative people in Business (*FastCompany*, 2011), played a major role in AirAsia's turnaround after he acquired it. Fernandes is believed to have been influenced by Michael O'Leary who himself modeled Ryanair on Southwest[8] (Lohmann *et al.* 2009). Instrumental in the implementation of the low-cost carrier model in Asia, Fernandes has contributed to enabling Pacific Asian populations to fly just like years before American low-cost carriers had stimulated the demand for regional air transport and actually competed with ground transportation. From their inception, one of AirAsia's major strategies was to focus on enticing first-time flyers (*Aviation Strategy*, May 2003), as it was estimated that prior to the entrance of their firm only six percent of Malaysians had ever traveled in a plane (*Real Leaders*, 2009). AsiaAir continues to focus and build on this strategy with the creation of subsidiaries in other Asian countries, including Thailand and Indonesia (AirAsia, 2013). This gives a measure of the growth in the demand for regional air travel that can be expected in the Asia Pacific region.

As mentioned earlier, North American legacy carriers have acquired a reputation as providers of low-quality air travel services. In stark contrast, Asian carriers are renowned for the high quality of service that they offer and also have a very positive opinion of themselves as indicated by the director general of the Association of Asia Pacific Airlines (AAPA) in his opening speech of the 56th Assembly of Presidents in Kuala Lumpur in November 2012 (AAPA, 2013): "Asia is at the heart of innovative thinking in our industry, the place where new business models are being refined, new partnerships created, and new service standards implemented." Operating outside the three global air alliances, AirAsia's business practices illustrate well the "innovative thinking" described by AAPA's DG. For example, AirAsia has started to use social media to sell seats on domestic and international flights, effectively bypassing traditional global distribution systems. The air carrier is able to combine low fares with differentiating features, such as offering a route between Makassar, Indonesia and Jeddah, Saudi Arabia via Kuala Lumpur, Malaysia to accommodate religious travelers. AirAsia operates 142 routes to 78 destinations and employs more than 8,000 people. As mentioned before, passengers on board traditional carriers are moving away from a differentiation strategy and resent having to pay for services that they perceived themselves to be entitled to. AirAsia's customers also have to pay to check baggage and buy snacks during flights. However, AirAsia manages to make its offering of food and drink appealing by referring to it as the "Snack Attack" program. The carrier is also accredited by the KL Syariah Index which means that it does not serve pork or alcohol on board. It would therefore be argued that although AirAsia is referred to as a low-cost carrier, it is successfully using an integrated cost leadership–differentiation strategy, as other Asian carriers do.

AirAsia enjoys solid financial and operational performance. In 2012 the airline carried 19.68 million passengers, generated sales of $1.5 billion and a $562 million net profit (AirAsia, 2013). It is also renowned for achieving an average aircraft utilization rate of 13 hours and operating the world's lowest unit cost of US$0.023 per available seat kilometer (ASK). As a result, AirAsia has a remarkably low passenger break-even load factor of 52 percent (O'Connell and Williams, 2005). AirAsia has six subsidiaries,[9] including AirAsiaX, identified as AirAsia's long-haul low-fare affiliate that started to operate in 2007. It is interesting to see that while several legacy carriers started to operate low-cost subsidiaries in an attempt to compete with low-cost carriers, AirAsia took the opposite path. This path was not always smooth, however, and AirAsiaX had to consolidate their route network in early 2012 after having incurred losses (*The Star*, 2013). However, AirAsiaX seems to be as innovative as its parent AirAsia and attracted media attention with the recent introduction of a kids-free quiet zone (Dorman, 2013).

Asia's aviation regulatory environment is still considered to have an "often unbalanced and restrictive entry system." The way the Malaysian government divided the domestic routes between Malaysia Airlines and new entrant AirAsia in 2006 to make sure the two airlines would not compete with each other after the flag carrier had lost half a billion dollars illustrates this (Hoffer Gittell *et al.*, 2009). Things are changing, however, and in 2015 Southeast Asia's Open Sky Agreement will become a reality. The ten ASEAN members (Brunei, Cambodia, Indonesia, Laos, Malaysia, Myanmar, the Philippines, Singapore, Thailand and Vietnam) will enjoy unrestricted flights to each other's countries. Tony Fernandes is renowned for having played a major role in this effort towards liberalization when he convinced the prime minister of Malaysia to sign the Open Skies Agreement with neighboring countries such as Indonesia, Singapore and Thailand. It is interesting to know that while ASEAN countries are moving away from protectionism, the Association of Asia Pacific Airlines is complaining that "when it comes to making rules that govern this industry, the US and the EU still exert a very strong, some would say dominant, influence" (AAPA, 2013: 3).

Gol Airlines

Based in Sao Paulo, Gol Airlines is the second-largest Brazilian airline. It was founded in 2000 as a subsidiary of the Constantino family's conglomerate that owned the largest urban and long-distance coach services in Brazil. It is interesting to note that this related diversification strategy allowed the conglomerate to establish an intermodal network by connecting air and surface transportation. Gol was the first low-cost carrier in Latin America and its market entry mode was similar to the one established by Southwest Airlines: it carefully selected the routes where it was going to operate and offered a no-frills transportation service. By controlling its costs, Gol was able to offer lower prices and therefore represented a major threat to Brazil's Varig, Vasp, Tam and Transbrasil. Today, Vasp and Transbrasil no longer exist; Tam has been acquired by the Chilean carrier Lan; and in a move that was unusual for low-cost carriers, Gol acquired Varig in 2007.

Gol was very successful during its early days and its CEO, Constantino de Oliveira Junior, was named "Most Valuable Executive" by a Brazilian newspaper in 2001 and 2002 (*Businessweek*, 2013). Gol Airlines diversified shortly after its foundation. It started to offer a larger portfolio of routes and focused on longer-haul markets, actually moving away from Southwest's business model to replicate JetBlue's approach.[10] Indeed, Gol Airlines realized that it was not possible to attract as many lower-income consumers as it had originally planned. As a result, the airline added several medium- to long-haul routes between 2001 and 2002 and increased its fleet to 22 aircraft. It also started to move away from its point-to-point business model by offering more connecting flights (Oliveira, 2005). In order to finance its rapid growth, Gol launched initial public offerings on the Sao Paulo and New York Stock Exchange in June 2004.[11] While it is common to see legacy carriers put together low-cost subsidiaries, Gol did a completely different move in 2007 when it acquired struggling Varig, one of Brazil's four legacy carriers. The plan was for the two companies to be managed separately, each focusing on their respective business models (Wheatley, 2007). Gol itself (i.e. without Varig) now has a fleet of 30 Boeing 737-700 and 85 Boeing 737-800 and offers 62 destinations in 13 countries. According to its website, the airline employs 18,706 people (Gol, 2011). Although it has engaged in various partnerships with different airlines, Gol operates outside of the three global alliances. This could change in the near future, as there are rumors that it could join SkyTeam (Wall, 2013). In early 2013, Gol had entered into an agreement with Delta Airlines, one of the founding members of SkyTeam, to support each other's frequent flyer loyalty programs (Zacks, 2013a).

Some industry observers now identify Gol as a "hybrid" carrier, noting that the company has managed to digest Varig and uses GDS distribution, which is a major roadblock when trying to move from LLC to a hybrid position. Comparing small samples of low-cost and hybrid carriers, Airline Leader (2010–2011) identified Gol as the hybrid airline having achieved the highest operating margin. However, altogether the low-cost carriers enjoyed a better financial performance than the hybrid carriers that Airline Leader looked at. As a matter of fact, Gol's financial performance has been rather poor since 2011. Would it be fair to say that Gol Airlines has successfully achieved the shift from the low-cost position to the integrated low-cost/differentiation strategy discussed earlier? The answer to this question is unclear since, in many ways, Gol shares some of the characteristics of North American legacy carriers. On his blog, consultant Simon Robinson (Robinson, 2013) blamed Gol for having only retained the cost control elements of the Southwest model, leaving to one side the caring attitude toward the workforce which is believed to have a positive impact on customer service. This is why, according to blogger Robinson, Gol has been losing ground to Brazilian airline Azul, founded in 2008 by JetBlue's David Neeleman.

The poor labor relationships at Gol are illustrated by the court battle that followed the acquisition of its competitor Webjet. Gol obtained regulatory approvals to conclude the acquisition of Webjet in October 2012, only to shut it down shortly after. This resulted in the layoff of approximately 1,000 employees who went ahead and sued Gol for moral collective damage. The court ordered the airlines to re-integrate these employees (Bevan, 2012). The airline has embarked on a major restructuring exercise after losing US$368 million in 2011 and US$20.3 million in the first quarter of 2012 (Marketwatch, 2012). Later that year, Gol argued that closing down its subsidiary would allow it to focus on international expansion. Gol's strategy was designed to seize the opportunity of rising international traffic driven by the holiday season across America (Zacks, 2013b).

Gol has experienced mixed financial performance since its foundation. After some successful early years, the airline's rapid expansion and the acquisition of Varig took its toll on its financial health. The negative results in 2008 were followed by a period of profitability until 2011. It should be added that Gol operates in a complex and challenging regulatory environment as illustrated by the decision of the Brazilian government to "re-regulate" the aviation industry in 2003. Before the industry was deregulated in 1992, the market was divided between four national airlines and five regional carriers, prices were fixed and entry into the industry was not allowed. During the first wave of deregulation that started in 1992, the regional monopolies were dismantled; however, major city pairs continued to be regulated. A second wave of deregulation began in 1997 when the two last regulatory instruments, the fare bounds and the rights to operate on major cities pairs, were removed. By 2001, entry, frequencies and fares were almost completely liberalized (Bettini and Oliveira, 2008). A year later, however, most airlines were in financial crisis and the authorities decided to re-regulate the industry in 2003, "aiming at controlling an alleged excess capacity and over-competition in the market" (Bettini and Oliveira, 2008: 291). The daring attitude of Gol, which decided to continue its expansion strategy by introducing red-eye flights despite the government's policy to limit airlines' growth (Oliveira, 2005) should be noted.

Public intervention in the Brazilian aviation system decreased in recent years, as illustrated by the increase in the foreign ownership cap from 20 percent to 49 percent in 2010. In early 2013 there were rumors that Brazil's aviation regulator was going to force airlines to limit prices. This was denied by the authorities, who otherwise announced that they planned to revise the rules for distribution of takeoffs and landing slots available in Brazilian airports (Leite, 2013).

Conclusion

American Airlines' CEO Bob Crandall is believed to have said that the best way to make a small fortune in aviation was to start out with a big one. The three cases presented above demonstrate that aviation is indeed a challenging field. AirAsia has experienced solid operational and financial performance since it was acquired and turned around by Tony Fernandes; however, AirAsiaX, the long-haul subsidiary launched in 2007, has been struggling. Meanwhile, although it offers poor service but charges high prices, legacy carrier United Airlines is still alive after having merged with Continental Airlines. Soon after its early success, the Brazilian low-cost carrier Gol had embarked on a rapid expansion path, leading to the acquisition of legacy carrier Varig in 2007. The airline performance had been mixed and the last two years were particularly difficult.

Despite the huge challenges that they faced, some airlines were able to develop solid business models. As illustrated by the various examples in this chapter, the integrated cost leadership–differentiation strategy is the most effective business strategy. Strategy writers have argued that it is the ability to offer both low fare and a pleasant travel experience that largely explained Southwest's success (Hitt *et al.*, 2003). Other successful players such as Singapore Airlines, JetBlue and AirAsia were also able to combine lower fares with differentiating features. While the successful implementation of the integrated cost leadership–differentiation strategy, based on a clear understanding of what customers value and expect, may lead to a superior performance, a failed attempt to implement this strategy can lead carriers to be "stuck in the middle" (Porter, 1980). Traditional carriers that tried to house low-cost subsidiaries were good examples of this, but so was the acquisition of Varig by Gol or even AirAsia's long-haul subsidiary AirAsiaX. The legendary Southwest has acquired AirTran and is now one of the four largest American carriers; the chances are that it will eventually very much resemble its three large counterparts. Could Southwest end up being stuck in the middle of low cost and differentiation and failing to achieve any of them? Time will tell.

While airline companies' success and survival is determined by the quality and innovativeness of their business models, the evidence presented in this chapter suggests that success and survival also largely depends on the ability of airlines to mitigate competition. The predatory pricing practices that legacy carriers used against the first generation of low-cost carriers was an example of this. The creation of the hub-and-spoke system, as well as the development of computerized reservation systems, also proved to be efficient approaches used by incumbent firms to deter new entrants in the aftermath of deregulation. The mergers of US legacy carriers from six down to three could also be seen as a way to mitigate competition, together with holding on to grandfather clauses allowing old carriers to keep control over airport slots. International alliances, perceived by some as transatlantic cartels surviving with the help of a friendly regulator, further reduce the intensity of competition. In addition, the friendly regulator helps incumbent firms by imposing limits to foreign ownership of airline companies and by offering bankruptcy protection to low-performance carriers that need temporary breathing space.

Survival, and occasional success, in the airline industry seem to be determined by mutual forbearance in the hope of reducing the intensity of competition between rivals, and/or by the development of innovative business models combining low fares and differentiation. Any airline can combine the two approaches (mitigating competition and innovating). The extent to which an air carrier will rely on one approach versus the other may vary at different points in its history. Aviation is such a challenging industry that the temptation to try to reduce the intensity of competition once the innovative features of a business model have started to erode is understandable, although not excusable. However, the evidence presented in this chapter indicates that strong leadership is an important element in the equation and may determine the extent to which the airline will rely (consciously or not) on mitigating competition or on innovating. For example, Tony Fernandes appeared confident enough in the superiority of AirAsia's business model to advocate for more liberalization in South East Asia. Similarly, Herb Kelleher was not afraid to fight American Airlines and Continental in court to gain permission to venture outside Texas.

It should also be added that in the shadow of the fairly large scheduled air carriers discussed in this chapter, there are numerous general aviation services providers that are gaining momentum. At a time when security screening measures often contribute to making air travel a rather unpleasant affair, small carriers can offer a very fluid travel experience with the help of fixed-based operators who provide ground handling services away from main terminals. Travelers are sometimes surprised to see that the regional aviation services offered by these small firms are not all that more costly than the scheduled flights offered by regional subsidiaries of traditional carriers, particularly in regions where population density is low. Similarly, in the long-haul market, the fractional ownership of business jets or the services offered by business jets charter operators, such as VistaJet, provide a viable alternative to first- and business-class travel. Legacy, low-cost and even hybrid airlines should closely monitor how this new form of competition will evolve. As discussed in Chapter 11, they should also be attentive to the growing environmental concerns of the traveling public. Travelers are becoming more and more aware of the carbon footprint of air transport and could one day choose to travel less or travel more slowly using ground transportation as much as possible.

Notes

1 www.flightstats.com/go/Airline/airlinesOfTheWorld.do.
2 www.iata.org/about/members/Pages/index.aspx.

3 American, Alaska Airlines, Continental, Delta, America West, Northwest, TWA, United, US Air, and Southwest.

4 It should be noted, however, that de-bundling strategies are also used by low-cost carriers, the extreme case being Ryanair's 2011 plan to ask passengers to pay a fee to use lavatories. While this plan was abandoned, the carrier is now proposing to replace two of the three toilets by extra seats (Calder, 2011).

5 Southwest has always combined low fares and excellent service, as noted by Hitt *et al.* (2003) in their strategy textbook; it could therefore be argued that it was always very close to the middle of the low-cost–differentiation continuum.

6 As reported by Vietor (1990: 65): "three transcontinental routes were designated and awarded: a southern route to American Airways, a central route to TransContinental and Western Air (TWA; and 1950, Trans World Airlines), and a northern route to United Airways."

7 Vietor interestingly argues that since airlines were no longer allowed to be vertically integrated, the 1930 Act resulted in the creation of the "horizontal oligopoly that would last until 1978" (1990: 66).

8 It should be noted that there is a clear distinction between labor relations at Southwest, renowned for treating is employees particularly well, and Ryanair's "attempt to control their employees" (Hoffer Gittell *et al.*, 2009: 295). AirAsia seems to be following that latter's approach and manages to operate in a non-unionized environment.

9 The whole AirAsia group flies to 85 destinations across 21 countries (Voyagers World, 2013).

10 As indicated in the earlier discussion, the notion of "hybridization," some low-cost carriers, such as Gol, WestJet and JetBlue, have started to add differentiating features to their business models. It can therefore be argued that they are moving away from the "pure" Southwest low-cost model.

11 Although publicly traded, Gol remains under the control of CEO Constantino De Oliveita Jr's family.

References

AAPA, 2013. 2012 Speeches and presentations, *Association of Asia Pacific Airlines* [online]. Available at: www.aapairlines.org/2012_Speeches_and_Presentations.aspx [accessed March 7, 2013].

Air Canada, 2013. *Air Canada Overview, March 2013* [online] Available at: www.aircanada.com/en/about/acfamily/ [accessed March 12, 2013].

Air Transport Action Group, 2011, *Aviation benefits beyond boarders* [pdf] Montreal: International Air Transport Association. Available at: www.aviationbenefitsbeyondborders.org/sites/default/files/pdfs/ABBB_Medium%20Res.pdf [accessed March 6, 2013].

AirAsia, 2013. *Press Release Quarter 2 2012* [online]. Available at: www.airasia.com/iwov-resources/my/common/pdf/AirAsia/IR/AA_4Q12_Press_Release.pdf [accessed March 7, 2013].

Airline Leader, 2011–2012. Low-cost airlines, hybridisation and the rocky path to profits, January 11, Available at: www.airlineleader.com/index_issue_11.htm [accessed November 27, 2012].

Aviation Strategy, 2003. Asia's emerging low-cost carriers, *Aviation Strategy*, May, 2–5.

Bettini, H.F.A.J. and Oliveira, A.V.M., 2008. Airline capacity setting after re-regulation: The Brazilian case in the early 2000s, *Journal of Air Transport Management*, 14: 289–292.

Bevan, S., 2012. Brazilian airline Gol expands daily service to MIA. *South Florida Business Journal*, [online] December 18. Available at: www.bizjournals.com/southflorida/news/2012/12/18/brazilian-airline-flies-first-route-to.html [accessed June 18, 2013].

Bonné, J., 2003. Making sense of the airline business; Fewer frills and a focus on economic fundamentals, *MSNBC*. Available at: www.msnbc.msn.com/id/3073566/ns/business-us_business/t/making-sense-airline-business/ [accessed November 28, 2012].

Brown, K.A., Ramanathan, K.V. and Schmitt, T.G., 2002. The Boeing commercial airplane group: Design process evolution. In: N. Harrison and D. Samson (eds.), *Technology Management*, New York: McGraw Hill.

Businessweek, 2013. Gol Linhas Aereas Intel-adr. Available at: http://investing.businessweek.com/research/stocks/people/person.asp?personId=10244623&ticker=GOQ:GR [accessed June 17, 2013].

Calder, S., 2011. Ryanair unveils its latest plan to save money: Remove toilets from plane. *The Independent* [online]. October 12. Available at: www.independent.co.uk/travel/news-and-advice/ryanair-unveils-its-latest-plan-to-save-money-remove-toilets-from-the-plane-2369232.html [accessed June 17, 2013].

Carney, M. and Dostaler, I., 2006. Airline ownership and control: A corporate governance perspective, *Journal of Air Transport Management*, 12: 63–75.

Carroll, D., 2012. *United Breaks Guitars: The Power of One Voice in the age of Social Media*, Carlsbad, CA: Hay House.

CBC, 2014. Air Canada stock dives 20% on record 2013 results. *CBC News* [online] February 12. Available at: www.cbc.ca/news/business/air-canada-stock-dives-20-on-record-2013-results-1.2533756 [accessed April 1, 2014].

Chandler, A., 1990. The enduring logic of industrial success, *Harvard Business Review*, 68: 131–139.

Cosmas, A., Belobaba, P. and Swelbar, W., 2011. Framing the discussion on regulatory liberalisation: A stakeholder analysis of open skies, ownership and control. *International Journal of Aviation Management*, 1(1): 17–39.

Coulter, M.K., 2002. *Strategic Management in Action*, 2nd edn, Upper Saddle River, NJ: Prentice Hall.

Cronshaw, M., Davis, E. and Kay, J., 1994. On being stuck in the middle or good food costs less at Sainsbury's. *British Journal of Management*, 5:19–32.

Deci, E.L., Koestner. R. and Ryan, R.M., 1999. A meta-analytic review of experiments examining the effects of extrinsic rewards on intrinsic motivation. *Psychological Bulletin*, 125(6): 627–668.

Deveau, S., 2012. Air Canada targets new leisure destinations with low-cost carrier Rouge. *The National Post* [online]. Available at: http://business.financialpost.com/2012/12/18/air-canada-targets-new-leisure-destinations-with-low-cost-carrier-rouge/ [accessed March 6, 2013].

Dorman, C., 2013. Kid-free zones on planes: It's about time. *The Age Traveller*, [online] February 11. Available at: www.theage.com.au/travel/blogs/travellers-check/kidfree-zones-on-planes-its-about-time-20130211-2e7nb.html#ixzz2KdP7bhkA [accessed March 6, 2013].

The Economist, 2011a. The airmiles-high clubs, *The Economist* [online] November 12. Available at: www.economist.com/node/21538152 [accessed November 25, 2012].

The Economist, 2011b. Open the skies, *The Economist* [online] November 12. Available at: www.economist.com/blogs/gulliver/2011/12/airline-alliances [accessed November 25, 2012].

The Economist, 2011c. Airline alliances, *The Economist* [online] December 12. Available at: www.economist.com/node/21538149 [accessed November 25, 2012].

The Economist, 2012. The ineluctable middlemen, *The Economist* [online] August 25. Available at: www.economist.com/node/21560866 [accessed December 17, 2012].

Elliot, C., 2012. 5 Fascinating facts about the new United Airlines. [online] August 4. Available at: http://elliott.org/blog/5-fascinating-facts-about-the-new-united-airlines/ [accessed June 15, 2013].

Fan, T.P.C., 2010. De novo venture strategy: arch incumbency at inaugural entry, *Strategic Management Journal*, 31: 19–38.

FastCompany, 2011. The 100 most creative people in business: Tony Fernandes. [online] Available at: www.fastcompany.com/most-creative-people/2011/tony-fernandes-tune-group [accessed May 13, 2012].

Garrow, L.A., Hotle, S. and Mumbower, S., 2012. Assessment of product debundling trends in the US airline industry: Customer service and public policy implications. *Transportation Research Part A: Policy and Practice*, 46: 255–268.

Garvey, W., Fisher, D., and Johnson, R., 2001. *The Age of Flight: A History of America's Pioneering Airline*. Greensboro: Pace Communications.

Gilbert, X. and Strebel, P., 1988. Developing competitive advantage, in J.B. Quinn, H. Mintzberg and R.M. James (eds.), *The Strategy Process: Concepts, Contexts, and Cases*, Englewood Cliffs, NJ: Prentice-Hall.

Gol Airlines, 2011. Data and statistics. [online] Available at: www.voegol.com.br/en-us/a-gol/quem-somos/dados-e-estatisticas/paginas/default.aspx [accessed June 16, 2013].

Grantham, J., 2007. A free bird sings the song of the caged: Southwest airlines' fight to repeal the Wright Amendment. *Journal of Air Law &Commerce*, 72: 429–462.

Heraclous, L. and Wirtz, J., 2009. Strategy and organization at Singapore Airlines: Achieving sustainable advantage through dual strategy, *Journal of Air Transport Management*, 15: 274–279.

Hitt, M.A., Ireland, R.D. and Hoskisson, R.E., 2003. *Strategic management: Competitiveness and globalization*, 5th edn., Cincinnati , OH: Thomson South-Western.

Hoffer Gittell, J., von Nordenflycht, A., Kochan. T.A., McKersie R. and Bamber, G.J., 2009. Labor relations and human resources management in the airline industry, in: Belobaba, P., Odoni, A. and Barnhart, C. (eds) *The Global Airline Industry*, Chichester: Wiley.

Holloway, S. (2008). *Straight and Level: Practical Airline Economics*, 3rd edn., Aldershot: Ashgate Publishing Limited.

Hsu, C.J. and Chang, Y.C., 2005. The influences of airline ownership rules on aviation policies and carriers' strategies, *Proceedings of the Eastern Asia Society for Transportation Studies*, 5: 557–569.

IATA, 2013. Scheduled passenger-kilometers flown [online]. Available at: www.iata.org/publications/pages/wats-passenger-km.aspx [accessed August 26, 2013].

Kanitakis, E., 2002. Stuck in the middle: Fact or myth? The case of Easyjet. Unpublished MA Dissertation, Nottingham University Business School.

Knowledge at Wharton, 2010. By acquiring AirTran, will Southwest continue to spread the LUV. [online] October 13. Available at: http://knowledge.wharton.upenn.edu/article. cfm?articleid=2614 [accessed May 13, 2012].

Lazare, L., 2013. United Airlines notches best on-time performance in a decade. *Chicago Business Journal* [online] February 5. Available at: www.bizjournals.com/chicago/news/2013/02/05/united-airlines-notches-best-on-time.html [accessed March 7, 2013].

Lee, A., Lee, L. and Farhoomand, A.F., 2000. *Computer Reservation Systems: An Industry of its Own*, Centre for Asian Business Cases, School of Business, University of Hong Kong.

Leite, J., 2013. Rumors of a Brazilian airfare cap send Gol stock price tumbling. *Bloomberg* [online] February 1. Available at: http://skift.com/2013/02/01/rumors-of-brazilian-airfare-cap-send-gol-stock-price-tumbling/ [accessed June 17, 2013].

Li, M.Z., 2000. Distinct features of lasting and non-lasting airline alliances. *Journal of Air Transport Management*, 6, 2: 65–73.

Lohmann, G., Albers, S., Koch, B. and Pavlovich, K., 2009. From hub to destination: an explorative study of Singapore and Dubai's aviation-based tourism policies, *Journal of Air Transport Management*, 15, 5: 205–211.

Marketwatch, 2012. Union says Brazil's Gol Linhas laid off 84 pilots. *Marketwatch* [online] June 26. Available at: www.marketwatch.com/story/union-says-brazils-gol-linhas-laid-off-84-pilots-2012-06-26 [accessed June 17, 2013].

Marowits, R. 2014. Air Canada moves to lower costs by expanding Rouge service to Vancouver, Calgary, *The Gazette* [online] March 25. Available at: www.montreal-gazette.com/business/Canada+moves+lower+costs+expanding+Rouge+service+Vancouver/9658735/story.html [accessed April 1, 2014].

Nicas, J., 2013. Inside United's secret club for top fliers [online] August 22. Available at: http://online.wsj.com/article/SB10001424127887323423804579025120455867410.html [accessed August 26, 2013].

O'Connell, J.F. and Williams, G., 2005. Passengers' perceptions of low-cost airlines and full service carriers: A case study involving Ryanair, Aer Lingus, Air Asia and Malaysia Airlines, *Journal of Air Transport Management*, [online]. Available at: http://dspace.lib.cranfield.ac.uk/handle/1826/1453 [accessed May 12 2012].

Oliveira, A.V.M. 2005. An empirical model of lost cost carrier entry: The entry patterns of Gol Airlines. In: *9th World Conference of the Air Transport Research Society (ATRS)*, Rio de Janerio, Brazil July 3.

Pettigrew, A. and Whipp, R., 1991. *Managing Change for Competitive Success*, Oxford: Blackwell.

Pitelis, C. and Taylor, S., 1996. From generic strategies to value for money in hypercompetitive environments. *Journal of General Management*, 21: 45–61.

Porter, M.E., 1980. *Competitive Strategy: Techniques for Analyzing Industries and Competitors*, New York: The Free Press.

Porter, M.E., 1990. *The Competitive Advantage of Nations*, New York: The Free Press.

Prince, J.T. and Simon, D.H., 2009. Multimarket contact and service quality: Evidence from on-time performance in the U.S. airline industry. *Academy of Management Journal*, 52: 336–354.

Ranson, L., 2011. Southwest closes AirTran acquisition. *Flight Global* [online] May 2. Available at: www.flightglobal.com/news/articles/southwest-closes-airtran-acquisition-356148/ [accessed May 8, 2013].

Real Leaders, 2009. A new and responsible business model is showing that flying can be guilt-free [online]. Available at: www.real-leaders.com/articles/a-cut-above/ [accessed May 15, 2012].

Robinson, S., 2013. A tale of two airlines: Brazil's Gol and Azul. [online] March 21. Available at: http://transitionconsciousness.wordpress.com/2013/03/21/a-tale-to-two-airlines-brazils-gol-and-azul/ [accessed June 17, 2013].

Sabourin, V. and Fagnan, M.D., 2000. Les pratiques stratégiques et le développement d'avantages structurels dans un contexte de déréglementation, IXe Conférence de l'Association Internationale de Management Stratégique, Montpellier, May.

Salpukas, A., 1987. Allegis Corp. replaces chairman and plans to sell Hertz and Hotels. *Net York Times* [online]. Available at: www.nytimes.com/1987/06/10/business/allegis-corp-replaces-chairman-and-plans-to-sell-hertz-and-hotels.html [accessed March 6, 2013].

Sauter, M., 2013. Airlines charging the highest fees. *24/7 Wall St.* [online]. Available at: http://247wallst.com/2013/02/05/airlines-charging-the-highest-fees/ [accessed March 6, 2013].

Schlangenstein, M., 2013. US Airways leads AMR merger to create largest airline. *Bloomberg News* [online] February 14. Available at: www.bloomberg.com/news/2013-02-14/us-airways-leads-amr-merger-to-create-largest-airline.html [accessed March 6, 2013].

Sheth, J.N., Allvine, F.C., Uslay, C. and Dixit, A., 2007. *Deregulation and competition: Lessons from the airline industry*, New Delhi: Response Books, Sage.

Sonofmaxwell, 2009. United breaks guitars. [video online]. Available at: www.youtube.com/watch?v=5YGc4zOqozo [accessed June 23, 2009].

Southwest Airlines, 2013. *Southwest Corporate Fact Sheet*. Dallas: Southwest Airlines. Available at: www.swamedia.com/channels/Corporate-Fact-Sheet/pages/corporate-fact-sheet [accessed March 7, 2013].

Spender, J.C. 1989 *Industry Recipes: An Enquiry into the Nature and Sources of Managerial Judgement*, Oxford: Blackwell.

The Star, 2013. AirAsia X records 41% growth in passengers in fourth quarter. *The Star (Malaysia)* [online]. Available at: http://biz.thestar.com.my/news/story.asp?file=/2013/2/7/business/12681943&sec=business [accessed March 6, 2013].

Thomas, G., 2010. Asia's rising low-cost tide, *Air Transport World*, October.

Thomas, G., 2011. Squeeze play, *Air Transport World*, June.

Thompson, A.A. and Strickland, A.J., 2004. *Strategic Management: Concepts and Cases*, 13th edn, New York: McGraw Hill.

TravelNerd, 2013. TravelNerd study finds over 50 U.S. airline fee changes since last year [online]. Available at: www.nerdwallet.com/blog/travel/2013/travelnerd-study-finds-50-airline-fee-changes/ [accessed June 15, 2013].

United Continental Holdings, 2013. *United Fact Sheet*. [pdf] Chicago: United Continental Holdings. Available at: www.unitedcontinentalholdings.com/documents/FactSheet.pdf [accessed March 6, 2013].

Vietor, R.H.K., 1990. Contrived competition: Airline regulation and deregulation, 1925–1988. *The Business History Review*, 64: 61–108.

Voyagers World, 2013. AirAsia & AirAsia X clinch awards at World Airline Awards 2013 [online] June 20. Available at: http://voyagersworld.in/article/airasia-airasia-x-clinch-awards-world-airline-awards-2013 [accessed June 17 2013].

Walker, G., Madsen, T.L. and Carini, G. 2002. How does institutional change affect heterogeneity among firms? *Strategic Management Journal*, 23: 89–1004.

Wall, R., 2013. Skyteam alliance may add Gol and Virgin Atlantic following Delta investment. *Bloomberg* [online] February 1. Available at: http://skift.com/2013/06/03/skyteam-alliance-may-add-gol-and-virgin-atlantic-following-delta-investment/ [accessed June 18, 2013].

Wheatley, J. 2007. Brazil's Gol buys rival Varig for $320m. *Financial Times* [online] March28. Availableat: www.ft.com/cms/s/0/0176074c-dd7a-11db-8d42-000b5df10621.html#axzz2Xq8poyph [accessed June 17, 2013].

Zacks, 2013a. Gol's new partnership with Delta [online] February 11. Available at: www.zacks.com/stock/news/92447/gols-new-partnership-with-delta [accessed June 16, 2013].

Zacks, 2013b. Increased December traffic for Gol [online] January 22. Available at: www.zacks.com/stock/news/90951/increased-december-traffic-for-gol [accessed June 16, 2013].

4 Engines

Daniel Todd and Sören Eriksson

Introduction

The most striking aspect of the famous flight of the Wright brothers at Kitty Hawk in 1903 was not that it was the first successful attempt of mankind to become airborne, but that it was the first in which powered flight was accomplished. Man venturing aloft into the ether had been going on long before Orville and Wilbur Wright introduced their 'Flyer'. Countless pioneers of ballooning and gliding had preceded them. One has only to think of such luminaries as Etienne Montgolfier, responsible for the first balloon ascent in 1783, and Sir George Cayley, who achieved the first recorded manned glider flight in 1853 and became the 'father of aerodynamics' into the bargain. The conspicuous feature setting apart the Wright Flyer from other pioneering efforts was its means of propulsion: in the event, a very modestly powered inline engine assembled by Charlie Taylor, the Wrights' mechanical engineer. To be sure, the Wrights' persistence in developing aerodynamic adjustments to their airframe promised great advances in aircraft efficiency, but without an effective power source these innovations would have come to nought. Over the course of aviation history, all the aircraft designs that are fondly remembered as being a cut above their contemporaries are held in high esteem precisely because of the effectiveness of their means of propulsion. Quite simply, an aircraft's capability was strongly determined by its propulsion system: with efficient power, its success was virtually guaranteed; without it, the aircraft was doomed to failure. Examples vindicating this cardinal rule are not hard to find.

Two examples associated with the famous Rolls-Royce Merlin engine drive home that fact. The first concerns the story of the North American P-51 Mustang, one of the best fighter aircraft to emerge from the Second World War. Its origins and initial service record were certainly not auspicious. With service entry in 1941 around the Allison V-1710 engine of 858 kW (1,150 hp), the early Mustangs proved disappointing. Engine limitations restricted the flight envelope, confining them to low-level operations. The superb aerodynamic properties of the airframe were thus largely negated. They came into their own, however, when the power source was replaced by the Merlin. This 1,186 kW (1,590 hp) engine transformed the Mustang's prospects, granting it that combination of manoeuvrability and long range that was sought by every fighter designer (Gunston, 1990). A contemporary of the Mustang was the Avro Lancaster. This aircraft, the backbone of the British bombing offensive against Germany, also experienced a less-than-promising start. The Lancaster was originally conceived as an aircraft known as the Manchester, equipped with twin engines. It entered combat operations in 1941 with disastrous results. The root problem was the Rolls-Royce Vulture engines, notoriously underpowered and prone to reliability problems. Redesigning the aircraft with four, instead of two, engines promised to eradicate the power performance, while switching to the Merlin ensured reliability. The redesign, restyled the Lancaster, exceeded all expectations in service (Jackson, 1990).

The instances cited were drawn, of course, from the annals of military aviation when wartime circumstances set a premium on the prompt remedying of defects in aircraft performance. Yet commercial aviation is equally prone to technological shortfalls in aircraft propulsion, leaving aeronautical designers no alternative but to abandon one engine type in favour of another so as to restore the fortunes of an aircraft type. This is aptly demonstrated in the story of the Sud-Est Caravelle, a twin-engine French airliner of the 1950s and 1960s. A pioneer in the field of turbojet-powered airliners, the Caravelle initially relied on the Rolls-Royce Avon, an axial-flow engine rated at 50.7kN (11,400lb) of thrust. While the early versions attracted modest orders among world airlines, lasting success was not thought to be possible without entry into the American market and that, in turn, was felt to be incumbent on the aircraft adopting American engines of superior performance. The engine eventually selected, the Pratt & Whitney (P&W) JT8D incorporated new turbofan technology and gave the Caravelle a useful spurt in performance. Ironically, orders from American airlines failed to materialize, falling victim to intense pressure from American airframe manufacturers who wished to retain the domestic market for their own products. Nevertheless, the revamped Caravelle was successfully employed by European airlines (Chillion *et al.*, 1980, pp. 36–67).

It is as well to remember that engine technology is essentially 'dual use' in nature; that is to say, it is applicable both to aircraft designed from the outset at the request of the military and to those designed with the object of fulfilling commercial criteria. This is not to say that certain engines are better fitted for one role rather than the other, but either by design or good fortune, most engines are sufficiently versatile to find applications across the spectrum of aviation (or, failing that, have technology embodied in them that can be adapted to uses well beyond their targeted uses). The Merlin can once again be cited in corroboration. This engine was designed with the express purpose of equipping such warplanes as the Supermarine Spitfire and the Hawker Hurricane which, like all fighter aircraft, set great store by the Merlin's high performance rating and reliability. However, later developments of the engine – particularly the 1,320kW (1,770hp) Merlin 621 – were held in such regard that they found applications on several post-war four-engine transport aircraft. The aircraft in question, the Avro Lancastrian, Avro York, Avro Tudor and Canadair North Star, saw significant usage in airline service (Lumsden, 2003). Of course, 'dual use' technology has persisted to the present day and is just as relevant to turbine engines. The GE TF34 turbofan is a case in point. Designed for the American military to power the Fairchild Republic A-10A and Lockheed S-3A Viking anti-submarine aircraft, the engine emerged in 1972 as a 41.3 kN (9,275 lb) thrust turbofan (Gunston, 1986, p. 67). In short order, however, it was found suitable for commercial uses, especially by business-aircraft manufacturers who were actively extending their area of operations into regional jets. Introduced as the CF34 on the Canadair Challenger executive jet in 1980, the engine was subsequently employed in a whole range of regional jets emanating from Bombardier and Embraer. In this guise, its current manifestation is an 81.3 kN (20,000 lb) thrust enlargement of the original TF34, which GE is producing for the latest generation of single-aisle airliners (such as the Comac ARJ21, the Bombardier CRJ1000 and the Embraer 190).

These examples, which throw light upon the adaptability of engines, affirm the tendency of military-inspired technology to migrate to commercial uses. However, the reverse situation is also possible, although in general engines designed for commercial purposes do not lend themselves to applications in combat aircraft. Fuel efficiency, an overriding consideration in civil-engine design, and one that is frequently emphasized at the expense of performance, is regarded far less highly in military engines, where performance is valued above all else. Nevertheless, the military has a need for transport aircraft and often 'militarizes' engines appropriate for them. Two American instances, nearly half a century apart, bear witness to this occurrence. The first, dating from the piston-engine era, concerns one of the most celebrated of all aircraft, the Douglas DC-3 airliner. An incremental development of earlier Douglas aircraft, the DC-3 appeared in 1935 equipped with a pair of Wright R-1820 Cyclones. However, the engine type was switched to the P&W R-1830 Twin Wasp of 895 kW (1,200 hp). Providing greater reliability and better performance at higher altitudes, the DC-3 now offered an unrivalled combination of airframe and aero-engines, one that so impressed the military that immense orders flowed into the Douglas factories (Holden, 1996). Such was its acclaim by the military that the aircraft (as the C-47, C-53 or Dakota) became the premier transport in the Allied air forces. Post-war, numerous airlines around the world chose the DC-3 as their 'work-horse', ensuring that it pioneered most of the world's commercial air services. Much of that acclaim could be imputed to the Twin Wasp powering the aircraft; so much so that the engine conceived to fulfil all markets, both civil and commercial, became a major element in wartime production, being built in large numbers to power the four-engine Consolidated B-24 Liberator bomber, the twin-engine Consolidated PBY Catalina maritime patrol aircraft and the single-engine Grumman F4F Wildcat naval fighter.

The second instance shows that the practice holds good to this day. It turns on the development of the Boeing C-17, the US Air Force's latest heavy transport aircraft that is used to sustain the NATO effort in Afghanistan. This aircraft has the merits of long range, heavy lift and short take-off and landing capability; all of these ultimately dependent on its four P&W F117-PW-100 turbofans each giving 180kN (40,400lb) of thrust. These engines are simply military versions of the tried and trusted PW2000 series, the engines specifically designed to meet the requirements of the Boeing 757 airliner, along with the competing engine, Rolls-Royce RB211. The RB211, the first three-spool engine, was originally developed for the Lockheed L-1011 TriStar passenger aircraft, but was later applied to several other airliners. The PW2000 also powered one version (Il-96M) of the Ilyushin Il-96, Russia's first wide-body airliner that entered service in 1992.

A third instance, that of the British Rolls-Royce Tyne, illustrates that the practice is neither confined to American engine designers nor is it restricted to piston or turbofan technology. The Tyne was designed specifically to power the four-engine Vickers Vanguard, an airliner that first flew in 1959. The engine was a big twin-spool turboprop that was also applied to the Canadair CL-44 commercial transport. Its merits, however, were quickly appreciated in the defence field, and in the 1960s the engine went on to equip the Breguet Atlantic maritime patrol aircraft and the Transall C-160 transport, both used extensively by European militaries.

In the light of these observations, it is impossible to hold to a sharp division between military and civilian aero-engines. The two broad markets clearly overlap and that fact must be borne in mind when contemplating the history of aviation propulsion. While the substance of this chapter is directed towards commercial engines, those vested with military interest will not be deliberately ignored. This pragmatic approach is apparent in what follows, the evolution of aircraft engines.

An overview of aero-engine evolution

Fundamentals

The fundamental challenge facing the Wrights in their pioneering attempts was to contrive a way of countermanding the effect of aircraft weight, which had the unfortunate propensity to neutralize the machine's forward motion and plunge it to the ground. They famously managed to contain the weight problem by manipulating the aircraft's lift – the force needed to support its weight in flight – through adjusting the shape and cross-section of its wings. Previous airborne ventures had either avoided the gravity problem altogether by settling for lighter-than-air ballooning or had resorted to sailplanes. Sailplanes or gliders nullify most of the force of gravity associated with weight by obtaining forward motion (thrust) through transforming the energy accumulated in gaining altitude (from uplifts in air currents) into kinetic energy. The energy, however, is not limitless, bleeding away as the glider loses height with distance. The powered aircraft, in contrast, at once offers level flight over much greater distances with a potentially much greater payload, provided it can satisfactorily resolve the power-to-weight ratio. This arose from the inescapable fact that a powered aircraft, in order to take-off, must reconcile the four forces bearing on it; specifically, it must have sufficient engine power to ensure that the thrust comfortably exceeds the drag (air resistance), while at the same time maintaining a greater lift than weight. The power-to-weight issue haunted the Wrights ever afterwards and continues to preoccupy aeronautical designers to this day.

A chronic cause of concern in the early decades of aviation was the seeming 'law' that every improvement in power rating required a proportionate increase in engine size and weight; and therein lay the rub, since heavier engines necessitated either bigger airframes or airframes devoted largely to carrying the engine with little left over for anything else. To be sure, bigger airframes permitted bigger payloads, but at the price of reduced efficiency for commercial operators. They also were deficient in such flight characteristics as agility and manoeuvrability, so essential to military aviation. Smaller airframes, while grudgingly accepted by the military as being better than the alternative, were judged less than ideal in promoting performance at the expense of range and endurance. Overcoming these dilemmas was of utmost importance to aero-engine designers; to such an extent, indeed, that progress in engine technology was seen to consist, for the most part, in boosting the power-to-weight ratio. Improvements in this all-important ratio have usually come about in an incremental fashion. Occasionally, however, transformative breakthroughs in technology have occurred, the most outstanding of which was the inception of the aircraft gas turbine, which heralded the jet age. In view of the signal importance of that innovation, it is convenient for the purposes of this chapter to divide the following discussion into two portions, with the first referring to the era when piston (reciprocating) engines held sway and the second concentrating on the impact of jet engines.

Reciprocating engines

The original Wright engine was built around four cylinders arranged in line after the fashion of typical automotive gasoline engines of the day. Capable of generating 8.9 kW (12 hp) of thrust from its 79 kg (174 lb) weight, the engine's power-to-weight ratio stood at a very unexceptional 0.11:1 kW/kg. By 1910 the Wrights had steadily raised the performances of their engines, achieving ratios of the order of 0.17–0.18:1. They had also diversified the inline engine into the V-type. This they accomplished by rearranging the cylinders from a straight alignment into two rows tilted towards each other. The inline engine in the meantime was falling out of favour with engine builders, who were becoming increasingly frustrated at the growth in weight. This frustration caused them to dismiss the inline engine's chief advantage; namely, that of conferring a narrow frontal area on the aircraft containing it, thus ensuring a low drag. Impatient for new technology, they looked instead to the rotary engine. Its advent promised, at one fell swoop, to boost power rating while cutting engine weight substantially. It was straightforward to make and cheaper to boot, which also set it apart from the inline. An innovation of the French Gnome firm, the rotary had made its appearance in 1908. It differed from the inline engine in having the cylinders positioned in a circle around the crankcase, with the crankshaft bolted to the airframe. The upshot was that the entire cylinder block rotated around the stationary crankshaft when the engine was in operation, furnishing the additional benefit of more than enough airflow to prevent over-heating. Unfortunately, the rotary movement of the engine was to render the aircraft carrying it difficult to fly (owing to the torque effect), but that was of little account in the First World War, when production considerations took priority over pilot survivability.

Despite its structural failing – a defect it did not share with the broadly similar radial engine – developments of the rotary surged ahead, fuelled by the immense impetus given to aviation by the war. The largesse of belligerent governments not only paid for production of engines on a scale unimaginable in peacetime, but provided lavish funds for experimentation of every kind. In fact, thousands of rotary engines poured from the factories, and incremental improvements in them were implemented at a moment's notice (Setright, 1971). The designs of French firms Clerget and Gnome et Rhône were especially prominent, and widely disseminated among a multitude of engine makers. Typical was the Gnome Monosoupape 9N of 1916, which was used to great effect by, among others, the legendary Sopwith Camel fighter. Achieving 112 kW (150 hp) of power on an engine weighing 137.4 kg (303 lb), it attained a power-to-weight (p/w) ratio of approximately 0.81:1 kW/kg. In the event, the war years sounded the death knell of the rotary engine, for the intensity of attention devoted to it merely brought forward the date of its expiry. In short, by war's end the engine had reached the limits of its potential. Practically, it was found that it could not be improved beyond the 180 kW (240 hp) mark, since rotary motion in excess of that performance sharply curtailed the amount of fuel and air needed to be injected into the cylinders. Fortunately, parallel developments had removed the obstacles that had hitherto hindered the wholesale adoption of the alternative radial engine.

The radial had emerged well before the war, powering, for example, the aircraft that Louis Blériot had flown across the English Channel in 1909. It differed basically from the rotary in having a conventional rotating crankshaft fixed to the engine block. Marked improvements in the means of cooling cylinders and in the metals (aluminium alloys) applied to engine construction – both the upshot of wartime experimentation – had borne fruit by the early 1920s. Leading exponents of the new engines were the Armstrong Siddeley Jaguar and the Bristol Jupiter. Both the military and the newly emergent civil airlines eagerly embraced them. One of the pioneering commercial operators was Imperial Airways, the ancestor of British Airways. It was at the forefront of introducing both the Jaguar and the Jupiter, pressing them into service on its prestigious London–Paris route. The Jaguar was featured on the Armstrong Whitworth Argosy, a three-engine biplane in operation from 1926 until 1935. At its best, this radial was capable of generating 365 kW (490 hp) from its 413 kg (910 lb) mass, implying a p/w ratio of 0.88:1 kW/kg. The Jupiter replaced it, equipping Imperial's Handley Page HP42 four-engine biplane airliners. Giving forth 414 kW (550 hp) and weighing 451 kg (995 lb), the Jupiter represented a modest improvement in the p/w ratio to

0.91:1. While outstanding for their era, the Jaguar and Jupiter were destined to be outclassed by P&W's Wasp and Twin Wasp families of engines. Already remarked on with respect to the DC-3, this engine series had first been conceived in 1926.

In fact, the original Wasp (R-1340) was the first product of the P&W concern. It was a single-row radial containing nine cylinders arranged in a circular fashion around the crankcase. Its attractive feature, shared with all radials, was a fairly compact, and hence relatively light, crankcase. This enabled it to attain a p/w ratio of 1.05:1 (kW/kg), which was exceptional in comparison with its competitors. Early models were rated at 447 kW (600 hp), but this rating was doubled when the engine was transformed into the Twin Wasp (R-1830) of DC-3 fame. Reconfigured as a two-row, 14-cylinder engine, the Twin Wasp registered a p/w ratio of 1.58:1. Among the best engines of its day, the Twin Wasp (and its R-2000 improvement) was built in vast numbers. Nevertheless, its potential was far from exhausted, and in its Double Wasp (R-2800) manifestation the engine was customized to meet the higher performances demanded in wartime. A two-row, 18-cylinder engine, the Double Wasp achieved a power output of 1,567 kW (2,100 hp), but at the expense of the p/w ratio, which was lowered to 1.46:1. Besides its military applications, the engine was pressed into service on the post-war Douglas DC-6, a four-engine aircraft widely used by the airlines. The engine's evolution culminated in the R-4360 that stretched the power output to 3,210 kW (4,300 hp). By this juncture, however, the piston aero-engine was facing a bleak future, struggling with the challenge posed by turbine technology, on the one hand, while rapidly running up against the technical limitations of reciprocating technology, on the other. The appearance of the former and its subsequent rapid assumption of pre-eminence in aircraft propulsion is a topic warranting consideration in detail. As a footnote, it is worth remarking that piston technology survives today in reduced form, powering the multitudes of light aircraft and the smaller helicopters that characterize general aviation.

Gas-turbine engines

The application of the gas turbine to aviation truly heralded a revolution in air transport. As with many of the innovations incidental to aviation, it owed its inspiration to military rivalry and, in particular, to the persistence of two pioneers – Frank Whittle and Hans Pabst von Ohain. The two, independent of each other, were directly responsible for the inception of the aircraft jet engine, the turbojet (Hünecke, 1997). Built around three basic components (the so-called engine core) – the compressor (where air enters and is pressurized), the combustion chamber (where the air is mixed with a burning fuel and converted into gas) and a single or multiple-stage turbine (in which the airflow is taken and subsequently ejected) – the turbojet was theoretically elegant but notoriously difficult to effectively integrate. Whittle first patented the turbojet in 1930 and von Ohain, toiling in his wake, registered his patent six years later. Both, however, succeeded in trying out their prototype engines in 1937. The German, though, outdid the Englishman in having his creation flown in 1939, two years ahead of Whittle's W1. Accordingly, the first aircraft powered by turbine technology were, respectively, the Heinkel He 178 and the Gloster E28/39; both test vehicles for operational combat aircraft. Emblematic of the aircraft in question were the Messerschmidt Me 262 and the Gloster Meteor, the two proving beyond any shadow of doubt the superiority of the new propulsive technology. At the end of the Second World War the jet engines representing the state of the art were the Rolls-Royce Derwent and the Junkers Jumo 004, which together embodied all the turbojet's chief particulars. The former relied on centrifugal compression, wherein compressed air is discharged radially outward at 90 degrees to the spool axis. At the time, it was the preferred technology, but in the event was found inadequate for high thrust levels and from the 1950s was confined mostly to turboprop and turboshaft applications. Nevertheless, the Derwent was relatively simple (and inexpensive) to manufacture. In its Mark IV guise, it was able to achieve a thrust of 10.7 kN (2,400 lb) and a thrust-to-weight (t/w) ratio of 2.1:1 (20.1 N/kg). The Derwent was noteworthy in powering the Avro Canada C-102, an early jetliner. First flown in 1949, the four-engine airliner was intended for Trans Canada Airlines (now Air Canada), but fell victim to its manufacturer's military priorities and its prospective customer's doubts as to the capability of its power-plants (Campagna, 2003; Molson and Taylor, 1982, pp. 81–85). The Jumo, which was the first jet engine to be mass produced, adopted the alternative axial compression in which the air is discharged parallel to the spool axis. Inherently highly efficient and capable of handling large mass flow rates, this engine held great promise for attaining the high-thrust levels consistent with high performance. It was, however, handicapped by its complexity (and expense). In its 'D' version the Jumo 004 was able to generate 10.3 kN (2,315 lb) of thrust and recorded a t/w ratio of 1.38:1. The technology incorporated in the Derwent and the Jumo was eagerly adopted by other jet aspirants. For example, the progressive development of the Derwent (the Nene) was built in both the United States (as the P&W J42) and the Soviet Union (as the Klimov RD-45). For its part, the Jumo was built in Czechoslovakia and the Soviet Union (as the Klimov RD-10).

With the onset of the 1950s the diffusion of the turbojet into all branches of aviation began in earnest, and where the military led, the commercial operators were keen to follow. The first jetliner to fly in commercial service was the De Havilland Comet, which took to the air in 1949. While experiencing a chequered career marked by crashes that blighted its prospects, the re-engineered Comet (the Mark 4) finally emerged in 1958 equipped with four axial-flow Rolls-Royce Avon turbojets. These, primarily used in combat aircraft, were also selected for France's first jetliner, the aforementioned Caravelle. The most powerful Avon, the 301R, was rated at 56.4 kN (12,690 lb) without reheat and achieved a t/w ratio of 5.66:1. Its near contemporary, the P&W JT3C axial-flow turbojet, had comparable antecedents. Initiated at the military's request (as the J57) to power the Boeing B-52, the engine first ran in 1952. Typically, it attained a maximum thrust of 52 kN (11,700 lb) without reheat and a t/w ratio of 3.32:1. Fortuitously, the engine was also chosen for the Boeing KC-135, the four-engine aerial tanker complementing the B-52. One may say fortuitously because the KC-135 shared many design features – including the engines – with a commercial initiative, which emerged in 1958 as the Boeing 707. Thereafter the 707 took commercial aviation by storm, igniting a race by all the world's chief airlines to initiate long-haul services by pressing it (and the similar Douglas DC-8) into service.

Two other variations on the gas turbine owed their beginnings to the 1940s: the turboprop and the turboshaft. The turboprop, the earlier of the two, extracts excess hot gas from the turbine and uses it to drive a propeller. It operates on a principle diametrically opposite that of the turbojet; rather than accelerating the air mass flow to a high exhaust velocity, it is designed to convert the air mass flow to a low velocity (using reduction gears). The outcome is much-enhanced fuel efficiency (provided air speed is kept below about 725 km/h), rendering the engine attractive to users on account of its cost-efficiency. However, it pays a price for this efficiency in comparison with turbojet-powered aircraft in terms of reduced air speed and boosted cabin noise, both detrimental to passenger satisfaction.

The Hungarian physicist and mechanical engineer György Jendrassik developed the world's first bench run and functioning turboprop engine (Cs-1). A senior engineer at Ganz Wagon Works, Budapest, he began the design of an experimental gas turbine engine 100 hp unit in 1932 and ran it in 1937 (Gunston, 1986, p. 81). His next move was to start the development of the larger turboprop engine, Jendrassik Cs-1, an axial-flow design with a 15-stage compressor, annular combustion chamber, cast inlet housing and many other modern features. The 400 hp engine ran in August 1940, and although the Cs-1 was an underperformer, there were plans to fit an improved version in the domestic proposed Varga RM1 fighter/bomber aircraft. Hungary joined the Tripartite Pact in November 1940, and with the pact in place, both the Cs-1 engine and the Varga aircraft were shelved and with that the world's first designed turboprop aircraft never went into production. In November 1940 Hermann Göring proposed to the Hungarian Ministry of Defence to build a new large aircraft plant in Hungary, beyond the range of the British bombers. A contract was signed in June 1941 and with that started the production, at different sites, of the Messerschmitt Bf109 fighter and the Me 210 fighter/bomber, both for the German Luftwaffe and the Hungarian Air Force, both using the Daimler-Benz DB605 V12 piston engines manufactured in Hungary (Vajda and Dancey, 1998, p. 252)

The first practical turboprop, the RB.50 Trent, was devised by Rolls-Royce as an offshoot of the Derwent turbojet (Gunston, 1986, p. 142). Further development led, in 1946, to the Dart, which after a protracted development became the engine of choice for the outstanding Vickers Viscount (Gunston, 1989, pp. 121–124). A four-engine airliner, the Viscount was a miracle of modernity when it entered service in 1952, offering the last word in passenger comfort and aircraft reliability. It flew for many airlines around the world, convincingly demonstrating the superiority of turboprop power over the older piston technology. Much of the aircraft's reputation could be credited to the Dart, an engine so highly respected that it remained in production for more than half a century.

Apart from the Viscount, it powered a brace of highly successful twin-engine airliners, the Fokker F-27 and the Hawker Siddeley 748 (to say nothing of their less-successful counterparts, the Handley Page Dart Herald and the Japanese NAMC YS-11). A typical example, the Dart RDa7, was able to generate 1,354 kW (1,815 hp) and exhibited a p/w ratio of 2.48:1.

Following the trail blazed by the Viscount was the Lockheed L-188 Electra, a four-engine airliner that emerged in 1958. Despite a promising start, the Electra suffered a series of mishaps and, besides, paled in comparison with the contemporaneous turbojet-powered Boeing 707. Its career, accordingly, was cut short; not so, however, the aircraft's Allison (now Rolls-Royce) 501-D single-shaft turboprops, which went from strength to strength, and was also used in the Convair 580 aircraft. Designed as the T56, the engine powered two very successful military aircraft: the Lockheed C-130 Hercules transport (along with its civil variant) and the Lockheed P-3 Orion maritime patrol aircraft, a derivative of the L-188. The Allison's characteristic rating was 3,915 kW (4,350 hp), with a p/w ratio of 4.45:1 (kW/kg). Occupying the other end of the turboprop size spectrum is the P&W Canada PT6A. Development work started in the late 1950s and the engine ran in early 1960 as a modest 373 kW (500 hp) free turbine (minus a clutch); with a 2.45:1 p/w ratio, the engine proved equally suitable as a turboprop or a turboshaft (as the PT6B, C and T). The PT6 has remained in continuous production ever since, powering a host of aircraft from light general-aviation types to trainers, commuters and a number of helicopters. Developed into three dozen or so variants, its latest mark can generate in excess of 1,432 kW (2,000 hp) (Garvey, 2012, p. 14).

The larger P&W Canada PW100/150 engine family is a series of larger turboprop engines (1,500–3,700 kw) used in a number of regional turboprop aircraft: ATR-42/72, BAe ATP, Bombardier Dash-8, Dornier 328, Embraer EMB Brasilia, Fokker 50 and the Chinese Xian MA60. It is also used in the EADS C-295 military transport and the Bombardier 415 Superscooper (former Canadair CL-415) and was used in the Ilyushin-114 regional turboprop aircraft.

A more recent engine is the Rolls-Royce AE 2100, a turboprop engine developed for high-speed regional aircraft. SAAB 2000 was the first commercial aircraft to use this engine (then developed and built by Allison), driving six-bladed Dowty-propellers. It was also used in the Indonesian N-250 aircraft, an aircraft that never developed beyond the prototype phase (see Chapter 8). It is also used in the Lockheed Martin C-130J Hercules military transport, the Alenia C-27J Spartan medium-sized military transport and the ShinMaywa US-2 amphibious search and rescue aircraft. The AE2100 engine was an innovative design and was the first to use dual FADECs (full authority digital engine control) to control both engine and propeller.

The turboshaft, for its part, was designed expressly for application to rotary-winged aircraft; that is to say, helicopters. Subscribing to the same principle as the turboprop, the turboshaft differs in having two separate turbines, with the first driving the compressor and the second linking to a transmission system that drives the helicopter's rotors. The genesis of the turboshaft was a small 74.6 kW engine designed in 1948 by Joseph Szydlowski on behalf of the French Turboméca concern. A further development, the Artouste, emerged in 1950 to power the Sud Aviation (later incorporated into Aérospatiale, the French precursor of EADS) Alouette II, the first practical turbine helicopter. Subsequent maturing resulted in the Artouste III, which was employed in the Alouette III, a helicopter that was widely used by civilian operators. At its most powerful, the Artouste recorded a power rating of 640.3 kW (and a p/w ratio of 3.6:1). The Artouste, in turn, gave rise to the Turmo, which was taken up by the Puma, a twin-engine medium transport helicopter, in 1968. In its Super Puma form, that helicopter continues in production today, much favoured by energy companies intent on servicing offshore production platforms. Equally adept in that role is the Sikorsky S-61, a helicopter dating from 1961 and powered by two GE CT58 turboshafts of 1,044 kW rating (and a p/w ratio of 4.6:1). Coeval with the appearance of the S-61 was the Soviet Mil Mi-8 (Mi-17 in its export version), which went on to become the commonest twin-engine medium transport helicopter in the world. It relied on the Klimov (ex-Isotov) TV2-117, a 1,268 kW (1,700 hp) turboshaft with a p/w ratio of 3.84:1. Another venerable type originating in 1961 and still very much in production is the Boeing CH-47 Chinook. This military machine has a commercial variant, the Model 234, and is capable of heavy-lift duties. It is powered by a pair of Honeywell (ex-Lycoming) T55s, each of which is capable of generating 3,631 kW (4,867 hp) and achieving a p/w ratio of 9.63:1. The T55s is basically a scaled-up version of the smaller Lycoming T53, an engine used in civil and military helicopters, such as Bell 204/205 and Bell AH-1 Cobra. It was also applied to the Taiwanese turboprop-powered military trainer (T-CH-1 Chung Hsing) built by AIDC, Taichung, Taiwan, an aircraft derived from the piston-engined North American T-28 Trojan.

Turbofan technology

As the 1950s unfolded and commercial aviation increasingly turned to the turbine form of propulsion, a looming problem began to assume major proportions. It made itself evident as airlines became habituated to running their aircraft at high subsonic speeds, for they had simultaneously exceeded the speed limits and efficiency of the turboprop while failing to reach the speeds necessary to induce power efficiencies in the turbojet. The issue persisted until the technology behind the turbofan was mastered. Overcoming the challenge posed by low efficiencies at high subsonic speeds was of critical importance to cost-conscious airlines. Yet the military was equally keen to back the turbofan, since it offered the prospect of high-endurance, fuel-efficient combat aircraft. The turbofan embodies aspects of the turbojet and the turboprop, but without incorporating any of their inefficiencies in the crucial speed range of 720–1,100 km/h. Like a turboprop, it draws excess hot gases from the turbine, but differs in using them to drive a fan. The air that is drawn into the engine and then circumvents the core turbine gives the turbofan its by-pass ratio (BPR). Generally, the greater the proportion of this airflow relative to the amount directed to the core turbine, the greater the resultant fuel efficiency. In the name of efficiency, then, designers seek to create engines of high BPR. In any case, lower BPR engines generate excessive noise levels, a factor detracting from their use in commercial aviation (which must adhere to strict airport noise levels).

The high BPR engine can overcome this defect much more effectively and at the same time grow in size to accommodate larger-sized aircraft. Unsurprisingly, then, the inception of the high BPR turbofan was instrumental in rendering possible the wide-body airliner of unprecedented size, while keeping its operating costs manageable. Unfortunately, the first by-pass engine, the Rolls-Royce Conway of 1956, was intended for in-wing mounting on aircraft and thus had a low BPR (initially 0.25:1, later 0.60:1) that was consistent with the restricted fan widths imposed by the mounting. This, together with the ease with which JT3C turbojets could be converted to the turbofan equivalents (JT3D of 1.4:1 BPR) on 707s and DC-8s, hamstrung the innovative Conway (although it was successfully employed in a rear-fuselage mounting on the four-engine Vickers VC-10 airliner). The aviation industry had to await another decade before turbofans in the high by-pass class (BPR over 5:1) became available.

Instigated at the behest of the US Air Force, which was searching in vain for an appropriate power-plant (one combining high thrust and economical cruise characteristics) for its massive Lockheed C-5 transport, two aero-engine makers submitted designs that resulted in the selection of GE's TF39. The TF39 made by-pass ratios of eight-to-one possible, resulting in fuel consumption that was 25 per cent lower than other engines available. The design effort was forthcoming with more dramatic results, however, which eventually came to fruition as the commercial GE CF6 and the P&W JT9D.

Joined by the Rolls-Royce RB211, the three engines burst onto the scene just as the four-engine wide-body Boeing 747 was transforming the airline business (in 1969). Consequently, they were readily available for installation in the 747's wide-body descendants, the three-engine Douglas DC-10 and Lockheed L-1011. As it happened, they proved crucial in the establishment of Airbus, justifying the concern's first aircraft, the A300B jetliner. Upon maturation, the CF6-80C2 from GE had a maximum rating of 263 kN (59,000 lb) whereas P&W's JT9D-7R could attain 249 kN (56,000 lb) and Rolls' RB211-524D was capable of 240 kN (54,000 lb) of thrust (Taylor, 1984). In the succeeding decade these big turbofan engines were supplemented with engines tailored for smaller narrow-body airliners. As with their big brethren, the lower-thrust turbofans offered improved efficiencies in specific fuel consumption. For good measure, they sharply lowered the noise level of aircraft operations. Standing out among them were the CFM56 (BPR of 5.96:1; rating of 118 kN (26,500 lb) of thrust) and the V2500 (BPR of 5.44:1; rating of 110 kN (24,800 lb) of thrust). Together, they breathed new life into the venerable Boeing 737 twin-jet while firmly consolidating the establishment of Airbus by powering its highly successful twin-engine A320 airliner. All in all, the turbofans, big and small, have set the standards of aero-engine practice that hold good to this day.

It is now necessary to take a completely different course. Hitherto attention has been directed to the properties of the engines themselves, highlighting the hallmarks of the technologies that distinguished them. Little has been said about the platforms – the aircraft – for which the engines were intended, and in particular, the considerations that must be taken into account when positioning them on or within the airframe. In fact, an airframe's configuration can impact – and impact negatively at that – an engine's design and performance; a point that has already been affirmed, specifically with respect to the Rolls-Royce Conway. By the same token, an engine's placement on an airframe can make all the difference to the effectiveness of the aircraft end-product. Just how this occurs is the subject of the next section.

Engine placement

The most arresting aspect of the engine-placement issue is the limited number of choices available to the aerodynamicist. Ultimately, they are governed by the prime function accorded to the aircraft itself. Thus the classic fighter warplane, devised under the harsh operational conditions of the First World War, was given the function of besting other combat aircraft by dint of its superior speed, manoeuvrability and agility, the last facilitated by small size. The two overriding factors of aircraft control and weight distribution – of critical importance then as now – had to be reconciled to this function and the practicalities stemming from it. Aircraft control, it was discovered, was best accomplished by having the engine positioned on the centre-line of the fuselage, for drag was thereby mitigated. Any deviations from an engine location close to the fuselage detracted from the pilot's ability to fly the aircraft; specifically, requiring him to exert more rudder movement to countermand the unbalanced thrust that inevitably resulted. Practically, the upshot was the single-engine fighter scout (like the Sopwith Camel) that adhered to a configuration in which the engine was mounted at the front on the aircraft's centre-line and buried within the fuselage. Of course, an engine positioned at the aircraft's front end threw in bold relief the problem of weight distribution, which called for attention to the aerofoil's centre of gravity. The solution to this problem required, in turn, arriving at the appropriate arrangement of counter-weights to balance the mass of the engine and ensure flight stability.

These concerns of centre-line placement and weight distribution remain cogent factors in combat aircraft design. They also strongly influence general aviation; an arena where small, light aircraft design remains prevalent. In commercial aviation, however, the age of the single-engine, modestly sized aircraft has largely passed away, although single-engine turboprops continue to fulfil a useful niche role. One need only think of the Cessna Caravan and Pilatus PC-12 to appreciate their importance as small commuter airliners and light air-freight transports. For the most part, though, commercial aviation today is the preserve of the large, multi-engine airliners and air freighters, and that fact presents issues of engine placement that dwarf those that tried the designers of single-engine aircraft.

The early jetliners, the four-engine Comet and the twin-engine Soviet Tupolev Tu-104, achieved an approximation of the centre-line ideal by burying the engines in wing roots abutting on the fuselage, so curtailing the amount of drag. Unfortunately, this imposed severe constraints on the dimensions of engine intakes, constraints which, as mentioned, became serious liabilities when turbofans were introduced. Besides limiting the aircraft's potential, the in-wing placement, owing to engine proximity to the cabin, burdened the aircraft with noise levels antagonistic to passenger comfort. Furthermore, the airlines voiced their dissatisfaction with the configuration on account of the difficulty of access to the buried engines for maintenance purposes, a fact that exacerbated aircraft running costs. For these reasons, the in-wing layout of engines fell out of favour in the 1960s. Consequently, aircraft designers were left with three main choices for engine placement: first, they could mount them in nacelles and place the nacelles under the wings; second, they could elect to mount them aft on the fuselage; third, they could combine the two, an option particularly relevant for three-engine airliners. Each choice had its advocates and detractors, depending on the onus given to the primary function of the envisaged aircraft and the degree of compromise judged appropriate in meeting its design specifications. Their strengths and weaknesses will be outlined below.

The first choice, that of placing the engines in nacelles under the wings, was proven in the post-war generation of jet bombers emanating from Boeing (the B-47 and B-52) and carried over into commercial aviation by that manufacturer with its seminal 707. Experience demonstrated that aircraft so equipped enjoyed good results in propulsive efficiency and longitudinal stability without suffering from excessive wing bending. The distribution of weight is probably optimized with this configuration. Added to this, the engine positioning offered excellent access for maintenance and, in the event of an aircraft crash, provided the passengers and crew with a high probability of survival. Diminishing the configuration's attractions, however, was the low ground clearance afforded by the engines, a reality that rendered them susceptible to damage from debris acquired during aircraft take-off and landing. The ground-clearance problem increased when high BPR engines – with their big intakes – became commonplace. Despite this reservation, the under-wing placement of twin-engine and four-engine airliners remains popular, as is borne out by the currently produced aircraft of Airbus (A320, A330 and impending A350 of the former category and A380 of the latter) and Boeing (737, 767, 777 and 787 twins and the 747 with four engines).

The second choice was granted credibility by the Caravelle jetliner in the late 1950s. The French aircraft underscored the usefulness of aft placement, with an engine appended to each side of the rear fuselage just ahead of the tail-plane. In one fell swoop, this placement eliminated the problems associated with low ground clearance that had plagued under-wing mounting. At the same time, dispensing with the under-wing configuration resulted in the aircraft experiencing far less drag, since it avoided altogether the interference that followed from the pylons attaching the nacelles to the wings. Furthermore, the nuisance of cabin noise was sharply diminished with the engines moved to the rear of the aircraft. By any measure, the mitigation of passenger discomfort was an important consideration in boosting the appeal of air travel, but there is no denying that it was bought at a high price. Specifically, aft-mounted engines create balance problems for the aircraft, for its centre of gravity when empty lies far behind its loaded centre of gravity. This imbalance is compounded by the aircraft requiring a disproportionately large T-shaped tail-plane, a structure judged essential for preventing damage from the exhaust gases issuing from the nearby engines. These reservations have strongly influenced modern aircraft designers, who are much less likely than their predecessors to champion the configuration. Indeed, since the glory days of the Douglas DC-9, and its successor the MD-80/90/B717 series of aircraft, and the Russian counterpart the Tupolev Tu-134, the layout seems to have been reserved for smaller commercial aircraft.

It is true that a second heyday for the aft-engine layout occurred in the 1990s with the widespread diffusion of the first generation of regional jets from Bombardier and Embraer. It needs stressing, however, that these were intentionally designed to smaller dimensions than airliners earmarked for the main routes. Practically, then, the most common application of the configuration today is in business jets, most notably the Bombardier Challenger series, some Dassault Falcons, Gulfstream and Hawker twins.

The third configuration also appears to have lost ground, the result of the unfavourable economies of three-engine wide-body airliners in comparison with newer twin-engine wide-bodies powered by larger high-BPR turbofans. The configuration was originally advocated as a good compromise that captured the attributes of both previously mentioned configurations. Its popularity coincided with the entry into service of the Douglas DC-10 (and its later spin-off, the McDonnell Douglas MD-11) and the Lockheed L-1011. These aircraft retained the conventional under-wing installation for two of the engines, but mounted the third engine aft, either within the fin (the Douglas preference) or at its base with the engine incorporated within the rearmost part of the fuselage (the Lockheed preference). The first positioning of the central engine had the advantage of offering an inlet free of aerodynamic distortion, whereas the second positioning succeeded in dispensing with part of the tail-plane and thus reduced drag. Neither positioning, however, was entirely problem free, for the Douglas design imposed extra structural weight on the fin while the Lockheed design risked structural failure of the rear fuselage. Significantly, the problem of placement of the central engine had first emerged in the 1960s with the Boeing 727, a narrow-body airliner much in demand at the time. The 727 was powered by three engines, all aft, with two slung in nacelles on either side of the rear fuselage. The centre-line engine received its air flow from an intake at the base of the fin, feeding it through an S-shaped duct to the turbine buried in the fuselage (in a similar fashion to the Lockheed L-1011). With the demise of the 727 and the eventual retirement of similarly equipped jetliners (such as the Tupolev Tu-154 and Yakovlev Yak-42), the aft-mounted centre-line engine is best exemplified today in the Dassault Falcon 7X and 900 business jets.

Yet another, a fourth configuration, emerged in the German VFW-Fokker 614, a twin-engined short-range/regional aircraft, with its engines mounted above the wings. The Rolls-Royce/SNECMA M45H turbofan was specifically developed for this aircraft. This aircraft was the first passenger jet developed in Germany, but it was an unsuccessful aircraft, with only 19 built (three prototypes and 16 production aircraft; some of the latter found no customers). The first flight took place in 1971 and the programme was cancelled in 1977. The position of the engines was favourable in particular for take-offs and landings on poorly reinforced runways. Additionally, the high engine position means better protection from dust and dirt, which can be whirled up by the soil. Another motive for this design was to avoid the structural weight penalties of rear-mounted engines. Initially the aircraft was prone to engine problems and it was too expensive for the small airlines for which it was planned. This configuration has never turned up again and can be looked upon as an odd but innovative design.

Clearly, the question of where to place the engines is one of fundamental importance to the aircraft designer. It is equally critical to the aero-engine designer, who must ensure that the engines perform in the manner stipulated for the aircraft. In other words, the two design traditions must work in step together. Failure to do so could result, on the one hand, in an aircraft equipped with unsuitable power-plants regardless of their placement, and on the other hand, in the development of an engine without due reference to aircraft designs appropriate to hosting it. The latter contingency is one that engine enterprises wish to avoid at all costs, since it would compound the daunting financial and environmental challenges that they already face. The nature of those challenges is now considered, beginning with the steep financial commitments that are unavoidable in engine development.

Development, cooperation and supply chains

Since the beginnings of a recognizable aero-engine industry, the enterprises comprising it were compelled to come to terms with a stark reality; namely, that the burdensome costs of tooling and engine development could not be justified economically by the low-volume production typical of their aircraft recipients. In other words, non-recurring costs almost always exceeded revenues from engine sales. Only in exceptional times, such as during hostilities or the build-up to hostilities, were production runs for the military of sufficient volume to comfortably cover development (and production) costs. In essence, the enterprises became wards of the state, depending on it for subsidizing their technical advancement and underpinning their productive activity. That situation, inherited from the early days, still persists, for the costs associated with engine development have climbed remorselessly even as the market has tilted more in favour of commercial aviation. The underlying harsh logic remains: exacting development costs need to be recouped despite low production volumes. By common consent, development costs of an engine are pegged at about US$2 billion, sufficient to impose forbiddingly high barriers to entry and compelling firms to think twice about indulging in aero-engines. The incumbents, in spite of being spared the competition of new entries, must still tackle the worrisome risk that is entailed in new engine development. The upshot of this state of affairs is twofold: a small number of enterprises dominate the global aero-engine industry in the first place and these enterprises, while competing vigorously with each other, are paradoxically forced to collaborate in order to mitigate risk (Todd and Humble, 1987, pp. 46–48).

A few firms – the so-called first tier – straddle the aero-engine spectrum, engaging in the design and manufacture of gas turbines of the turbofan, turboprop and turboshaft variety. As one might expect in view of America's military dominance and prominence in commercial aviation, two of the biggest are American: GE and P&W. Europe is represented in the big league by Rolls-Royce and the Safran Group's SNECMA (Société nationale d'études et de construction de moteurs d'aviation) and Turboméca, since 2001 a subsidiary of SNECMA. A distinctive feature of first-tier firms, one that sets them apart from all other engine enterprises, is their ability to master the complexities of design and integration of big turbofans.

Russian aero-engine enterprises are currently coordinated through the United Engine Corporation (UEC), which is a vertically integrated company producing engines for military and civil aviation and many other applications (United Engine Corporation, 2014). It includes all the major Russian aero-engine producers, Klimov, NPO-Saturn, Aviadvigatel/Perm, although they still work, manufacture and sell the engines using the established names. The Ivchenko-Progress enterprise, located in Ukraine, once a part of the Soviet aero-engine industry, is a part of the Ministry of Industrial Policy of Ukraine (Ivchenko-Progress, 2014). Collectively they offer impressive capabilities, but compared with the leading Western companies they are very small actors on international markets and basically only deliver engines to aircraft developed in Russia and Ukraine.

A select clutch of firms constitutes the second tier of aero-engine enterprises. They offer one or all of the following: first, specialist expertise in the design and development of engine components; second, well-equipped facilities that the first-tier enterprises can use to supplement their own plant and labour resources (by means of licensing contracts); and third, expertise in the design and production of a limited range of engines. Regarding the first offering, they are increasingly valued by first-tier firms, who resort to them in order to expedite their own engine programmes and reduce risk by sharing it across several participating enterprises. The most well-known of these firms are Honeywell and Williams International of the United States, MTU Aero Engines of Germany, and the Japanese trio of Ishikawajima-Harima (IHI), Kawasaki (KHI) and Mitsubishi (MHI) Heavy Industries. Of these, Honeywell has the most impressive portfolio of in-house designs, the result of its absorption of Lycoming and Garrett: the former known for turboshaft engines (especially the T55 and LTS101) and the latter renowned for expertise in small turbofans (TFE731 family) and small turboprops (TPE331 series).

A third tier of firms consists of raw material supplier to Tier 2 and Tier 1 companies, such as Alcoa and Hexcel, and many others. In some cases it is difficult to draw a line between Tier 2 and Tier 3 suppliers as the aero-engine industry has gone through a number of structural changes in recent years, including acquisitions, mergers, and firms in Tier 3 moving into Tier 2 operations by not only delivering raw and semi-finished material. It can be exemplified with Alcoa's announcing its portfolio transformation by signing a definitive agreement to acquire Firth Rixson, a well-known manufacturer of jet engine components (Alcoa, 2014).

Among other things, Firth Rixson is the world's largest producer of seamless rings for the aerospace sector. The acquisition further strengthens Alcoa's aerospace business. It positions the company to capture additional aerospace growth with a broader range of high-growth, value-added jet engine components. The acquisition is strategically aligned with the company's objective to continue to build its value-added businesses (Alcoa, 2014)

Altogether, the structure of the commercial aero-engine industry can be exemplified by a basic and simplified supply-chain structure (Figure 4.1).

The Tier 2 suppliers include a variety of competences and firms, from producers of limited numbers of components to firms with a broad expertise in design and development, including engine system integration competences. One very obvious development within this industry is an increased specialization among many firms, which can be exemplified by Volvo Aero, the former wholly owned subsidiary of AB Volvo, Sweden, acquired by the British GKN in 2012, becoming GKN Aerospace Engine Systems.

It was founded in 1930 as NOHAB Flygmotorfabrik AB to produce aircraft engines for the Swedish Board of Aviation. In 1937 it became a part of the newly formed SAAB, but was sold to Volvo in 1941, and the name was changed to Svenska Flygmotor and later to Volvo Aero (VAC). For about 50 years the

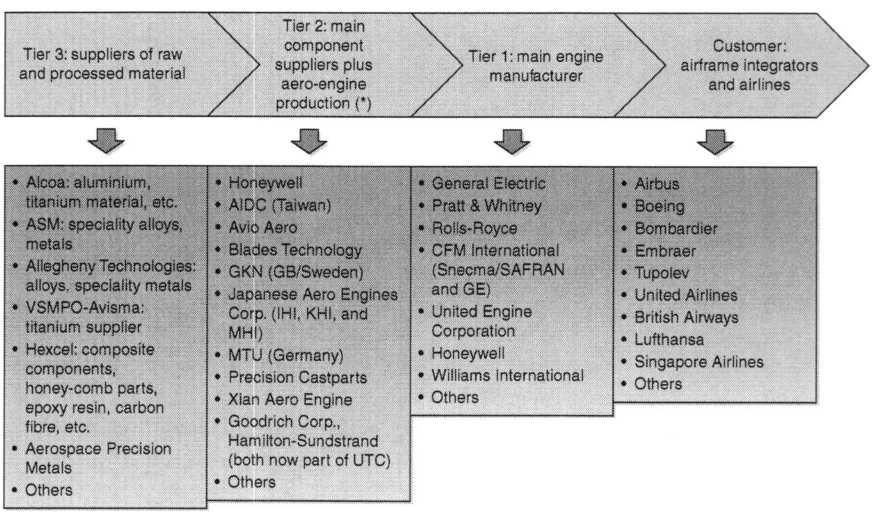

Figure 4.1 A basic supply chain in the commercial aero-engine industry.

'core business' was the development, production, technical support and maintenance of engines for the Swedish Air Force (Eriksson, 2000). Declining military volumes led the company to an increased interest in commercial engines and, based on its experiences and core competences, it led to a new strategy focusing on structures, rotating parts and combustion chambers. In the late 1990s VAC was engaged in a collaborative programme with all major aero-engine manufacturers, Allied Signal (TFE731, TPE331, TPF351), BMW–Rolls-Royce (BR-715) General Electric (CF6–80), Pratt & Whitney (JTD8, V2500, PW2000, PW 4084/90/98) and Rolls-Royce (Tay) (Eriksson, 2000, p. 659). Currently components from GKN Engines (pre-VAC) are installed in nearly all large commercial aircraft engines sold.

In spite of efforts to ensure comprehensive coverage, each firm exhibits gaps in the engine-size spectrum, indicating that it falls short of full capability. As a counter-measure to this evident weakness, the firms resort to cooperation with other enterprises – which are often rivals in all other respects – in order to make good the deficiency. Three reasons are usually advanced in justification of this collaboration. The first is to spread the capital costs of designing and developing a new engine and is based on the conviction that sharing the costs between two (or more) firms is better than shouldering the burden alone (risk-revenue sharing). The prospective partners, dismayed by the projected costs, calculate that collaboration is the only way in which a new engine is possible. They are willing to overlook competitive rivalries, provided that each is simultaneously contemplating adding engines of the envisaged size and function to its portfolio. The second reason has a similar motivation to the first, namely to save non-recurring development costs. However, it assumes an asymmetry between the collaborating partners, with one firm acknowledging the other as the overall systems designer and conceding that it fulfils the niche, albeit specialist, subsidiary role. On the face of it, the third reason is not so much to do with mitigating capital costs as it is with acquiring market access. However, implicit in the acquisition of market share is the underlying imperative of amortizing high development costs from revenues that are garnered from increased production runs in markets that otherwise would be out of bounds. To that end, a partner is sought who offers the other collaborator privileged access to the desired market in question. In return, the collaborative instigator promises to promote the sought-for partner's presence in markets previously closed to it. Both partners, therefore, conceivably benefit from market enlargement and, what is more, the weaker partner may gain immeasurably from advanced technology transferred from the stronger. In reality, two or more of these reasons may coalesce to reinforce collaboration among engine firms. Establishing which is paramount may be difficult, especially when the opaqueness of official pronouncements (inevitable in the case of international collaboration) is taken into account. This becomes apparent in the examples subjected to enquiry.

The dominant engine manufacturers participate in various joint ventures, which are formed to capitalize on emerging market demand for engines, while at the same time allowing partners to share development and production costs along with risk (Table 4.1).

Table 4.1 Major joint ventures in the large commercial aero-engine industry

Joint ventures	*Partners and ownership percentages*
CFM	GE (General Electric) – 50 per cent SNECMA (Safran) – 50 per cent
Engine Alliance	General Electric – 50 per cent Pratt & Whitney – 50 per cent
International Aero Engines (IAE)	Pratt & Whitney – 25.00 per cent Pratt & Whitney Aero Engines International GmbH – 24.50 per cent MTU Aero Engines – 25.25 per cent The Japanese Aero Engine Corporation – 25.25 per cent: Kawasaki Heavy Industries Ishikawajima-Harima Heavy Industries Mitsubishi Heavy Industries
PowerJet	Snecma (Safran) – 50 per cent NPO Saturn – 50 per cent

A pre-eminent example of the first reason for this was when, in 1974, the formation of CFM International began. Quite independently, GE and SNECMA decided that a market existed for an engine in the 98–120 kN (22,000–27,000 lb) thrust class. Each had carried out preliminary design work but had arrived at the conclusion that engine completion would be greatly aided by combining their efforts in a joint company. The outcome was the CFM56, the product of a carefully crafted division of labour that saw GE assume responsibility for the engine core and SNECMA for the rest. Becoming operational in 1979, CFM56 engines first found military applications (as the F108), but quickly gained commercial prominence powering Boeing 737s and Airbus A320s. A much modified development, the LEAP-1A/B/C, which is destined for the 737 MAX, A320NEO and Chinese Comac C919, promises future benefits for the joint company (Flottau, 2012, p. 46). Spurred by the CFM example, P&W and Rolls-Royce chose to sink their differences and form a joint enterprise with the express purpose of producing an engine that could compete with the CFM56. The result was International Aero Engines, registered in Zürich and formed in 1983. Besides the two originators (initially holding 30 per cent each), a number of other firms were invited to join; namely, the three Japanese companies (IHI, KHI and MHI, collectively holding a 23 per cent stake), MTU (11 per cent holding) and Italy's FiatAvio (the residual).

FiatAvio withdrew as a shareholder of the programme early on, and in 2003 the Fiat Group, grappling with the crisis in the automobile sector, sold Fiat Avio S.p.A. to a consortium formed by the American private equity fund the Carlyle Group (70 per cent) and Finmeccanica S.p.A. (30 per cent) (Fiatgroup, 2014). Renamed Avio S.p.A., it remained as a supplier that continued through the next ownership change that took place in 2006, when the English private equity fund Cinven announced that it had acquired Avio S.p.A. from Carlyle. The latest change in ownership and structure was when Avio S.p.A. was sold to Nuovo Pignone Holding S.p.A. (General Electric Group) on 1 August 2013, which makes up an integral part of the GE Aviation activities (Avio Aero, 2014). This is one more example of the fast and complex ownership, strategic and supplier changes taking place in this industry. IAE's current ownership structure is included in Table 4.1.

The partners assumed responsibilities that played to their strengths. Thus, Rolls-Royce was charged with the compressor, P&W dealt with the combustor and high-pressure turbine, the Japanese trio focused on the low-pressure spool, MTU handled the low-pressure turbine and Avio assumed responsibility for the accessory gearbox. These combined efforts were forthcoming with the V2500 engine, which became operational in 1988 and found immediate application on the A320. Interestingly, P&W switched allegiance from Rolls to partner with its erstwhile rival, GE, in the design and production of a big turbofan. In this instance, both American firms were intent on countering Rolls-Royce's lead in powering the Airbus A380 (with the Trent 900). Their collaboration, styled Engine Alliance, also involved MTU (which procured a 22.5 per cent stake in the GP-7000 engine programme, while SNECMA has 10 per cent stake). These partners pooled their expertise – GE contributing the engine core and P&W (aided by MTU) the fan and low-pressure system – to create the GP7200, a 363 kN (81,500 lb) thrust engine with a BPR of 8.7:1 and a t/w ratio of 4.73:1.

Emblematic of the second reason underscoring collaboration was the historically significant case of the Olympus 593, the engine conceived to power the Anglo-French Concorde supersonic transport of the late 1960s. The engine collaborators, Bristol Siddeley (now part of Rolls-Royce) and SNECMA, saw fit to develop a military version of the former's Olympus turbojet into the definitive Concorde engine. In so doing, they produced a power-plant capable of 142 kN (32,000 lb) dry thrust and t/w ratio of 5.4:1. In faithful recognition of each partner's competence, Bristol was assigned the lion's share of the engine with SNECMA concentrating chiefly on the afterburning section. The Olympus saga is illustrative of an alliance of unequal partners, but another venture involving SNECMA puts the matter in a different light: one that is both contemporary and demonstrative of the third reason for alliances. The venture, PowerJet, is erected to build the engine for the Russian Sukhoi Super 100 regional jet and unites the French firm with NPO Saturn. In this case SNECMA commands the stronger position, using the technical prowess it gained from the CFM56. Accordingly, it is responsible for the engine core, while its Russian partner is charged with the low-pressure section. The outcome is the SaM146, which first ran in 2008. The engine is capable of 76.8 kN (17,270 lb) of thrust, has a BPR of 4.43:1 and a t/w ratio of 5.3:1. However, the reason for collaboration owed less to technical considerations and more to market accessibility. In short, the prospect of gaining orders from Western users was sufficient to convince NPO Saturn of the advantages stemming from teaming with a Western engine company and granting concessions in order to secure it.

Dominant West versus the 'rest'

The aero-engine market is very complex and is made harder to understand by the fact that the firms compete ferociously in one part of the market while working together elsewhere. CFM International and its US shareholder General Electric are the lead producers in their respective markets, delivering about 70 per cent of commercial engines in 2012 (*Flight Global*, 2013). Looking at total deliveries of all aircraft in use, the CFM/GE figure is close to 60 per cent market share (Figure 4.2). Engine manufacturers' market shares differ a lot between various aircraft manufacturers and market segments. For instance, CFM supplies all the engines for Boeing's 737 (B737 Classic 300/400/500 and B737 Next Generation 600/700/800/900), including the future 737 Max, using a CFM Leap engine, currently under development. The CFM56 is an engine option for the B737's main rival Airbus A320 family, together with the IAE V2500 engine (not offered for A318). Based on deliveries, CFM had a market share of 53 per cent and IAE's share was 47 per cent in 2012 (*Flight Global*, 2013).

A few other aircraft types show that of the 97 Airbus A330 aircraft delivered in 2012, 70 per cent used Rolls-Royce engines, while of the 46 Boeing 787 aircraft delivered the same year, 59 per cent were fitted with the General Electric GEnx and 41 per cent with the Rolls-Royce Trent (*Flight Global*, 2013). The GEnx is also offered in the latest Boeing 747 (B747-8). The B747's successor as the world's largest passenger aircraft, the Airbus 380, has two engine options: the Rolls-Royce Trent 900 series or the Engine Alliance GP7000s. Of the 30

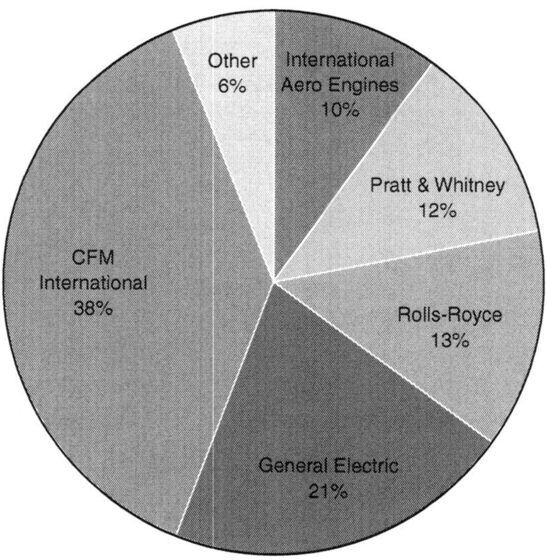

Figure 4.2 World market share of commercial aircraft engines 2013. Figures include narrowbody, widebody, regional (incl. Russian) jets in passenger, freighter, combi and quick change roles. Data is based on 20,606 aircraft and 44,607 engines (source: *Flight Global*, 2013, p. 15).

aircraft delivered during 2012, 16 aircraft (53 per cent) were delivered with Rolls-Royce engines and 14 (47 per cent) from the latter.

So far it is very obvious that the global commercial aero-engine industry is to a very large extent dominated by a small number of Western firms.[1] It becomes even clearer when looking at engines supplied to all current commercial aircraft in production (including new versions: Airbus A320 Neo, B737 Max and Embraer E-Jet Second Generation, not yet delivered) and the Chinese ARJ-21, expected to reach customers in 2015, and the Comac C919, which is under development (Tables 4.2, 4.3 and 4.4).

Looking at the wide-body aircraft, the only exception to a complete dominance of Western-built engines is the Ilyushin Il-96, of which only about 30 were made. This aircraft also has a Western-engine option, the PW2000 series for the Il-96M (PW2000) and IT-96T (PW2337). The same 'rule' applies to the narrow-body jet aircraft, i.e. the only exception is a Russian-made aircraft, the Tupolev 204/214,[2] which is delivered with Aviadvigatel (previously Soloviev) PS90A engines.[3] Compared with the IL-96, the TU-204/214 has been produced in close to 80 copies, but compared with Western-built aircraft these are very small numbers. China has moved into development and production of two narrow-body aircraft, the ARJ-21 and the C919, both using Western engines.

Regional jets are dominated by General Electric and Rolls-Royce as suppliers of engines for the two major aircraft manufacturers, Bombardier and Embraer.

Another newcomer into this segment is Pratt & Whitney, which has secured the supplier role in the Mitsubishi Regional Jet. There are two other engines used in regional jet aircraft; the SaM146 (SNECMA/NPO Saturn) in the Russian Sukhoi Super Jet and the Ukraine Ivchenko-Progress D-436 in the likewise Ukraine Antonov An-148/158. The Power-Jet joint venture (SaM146) between SNECMA (France) and NPO Saturn is very dependent on Western technology as SNECMA is in charge of the core, control system (FADEC), power transmission (accessory gearbox, transfer gearbox), engine integration and flight testing, while NPO Saturn is responsible for the components in the low-pressure section, engine installation on the aircraft and ground testing (SNECMA, 2014).

The Ivchenko-Progress D-436 is a turbofan engine originally develop for a few Yakovlev and Antonov (then Russian) aircraft in the 1980s. The first run took place in the middle of the 1980s; it was also planned for the Tu-334 airliner (programme cancelled in 2009 with only two aircraft built). Currently it is used in the Antonov An-148/158,[4] an aircraft only built in 33 copies until July 2014. The Chinese decided to use Western engines (GE and CFM) in their two current aircraft programmes as they currently have no commercial engine of their own that can be supplied to these aircraft.

The supply of engines for regional turbo-prop aircraft in production is mainly a business handled by the Canadian branch of Pratt & Whitney (US), itself a business unit of United Technologies Corporation (UTC). The only exception is the Russian Klimov engine supplied to the Antonov An-140 aircraft.

The commercial aero-engine industry has not seen any major changes in the global development and manufacture of engines. Contrary to the airframe/

Table 4.2 Engines currently used in wide-body and narrow-body aircraft in production or planned delivery

	CFM	*GE*	*Engine Alliance*	*IAE*	*P&W*	*Rolls-Royce*	*Aviadvigatel*
Wide-body aircraft							
A330		CF6			PW4000	Trent 700	
A350						Trent XWB	
A380			GP7000s			Trent 900	
B747–8		GEnX-2B67					
B767		CF6			PW4000s		
B777		GE90			PW4000s	RR895	
B787		GEnX-IB				Trent 1000	
Ilyushin Il-96					PW2000s		PS90-A
Narrow-body commercial aircraft							
A318	CFM56–5				PW6000		
A319/A320/A321	CFM56–5			V2500			
A320 Neo	LEAP-1A				PW1100G		
ARJ21		CF34					
B737NG	CFM56–7						
B737 Max	LEAP-1B						
Bombardier CSeries					PW1500G		
Comac C919	LEAP-1C						
Embraer E-Jet Family (E-170/175/190/195)		CF34–8E/10-E					
Embraer E-Jet Second Generation					PW1000G		
Tupolev 204/214						RR RB-211–535E4	PS90A

Table 4.3 Engines used in regional jets in production or planned delivery

	GE	*P&W*	*Rolls-Royce*	*Power-Jet (SNECMA/ NPO Saturn)*	*Ivchenko-Progress*
Antonov An-148/158					D-436
Bombardier CRJ-700/900/ 1000	CF34/8C				
Embraer ERJ-145 family (ERJ-135/ ERJ-140/ERJ-145)			AE3007		
Sukhoi Superjet 100				SaM146	
Mitsubishi Regional Jet		PW1217G			

Table 4.4 Engines used in turboprop aircraft currently in production

	P&W Canada	*GE*	*Klimov*
ATR-42/72	PW120-series		
Bombardier Dash-8	PW120-series PW150A (series-400 aircraft)		
CASA-IPTN CN235		CT7–9C	
Antonov An-140	PW127		TV3-117 VMA-SBM1
Xian MA-60	PW127		

aircraft sector, where Embraer from Brazil has developed into a large global player, and several other emerging countries have made large investments, the aero-engine sector has seen very few changes, except the ones accounted for below.

The role of the former Soviet Union, now represented by Russia and Ukraine, has diminished as their commercial aircraft programmes have contracted, with fewer aircraft built during the last decades. Furthermore, the loss of the inherent markets, i.e. communist countries in various parts of the world, has had a negative influence on business and sales.

During the communist period (Comecon bloc, until 1991) Russia's aircraft industry delivered nearly all commercial aircraft (including engines) to the national airlines in Bulgaria, Czechoslovakia, East Germany, Hungary, Poland and Romania.[5] Other countries with close political (communism) connections such as Cuba and Vietnam also relied on Soviet-made aircraft and engines, as did some countries in Africa and Asia with close ties to the Soviet Union. Since the fall of the Iron Curtain starting in 1989, and the subsequent political changes, nearly all the previous 'Eastern Bloc' flag-carriers have abandoned Russia/ Ukraine aircraft in favour of Western aircraft (Boeing, Bombardier, Airbus,

Embraer, etc.). The same applies to a large number of private airlines established in recent years. Vietnam's national airline, undergoing a major renewal and expansion in recent years, relies on Airbus, Boeing and ATR aircraft, and even Cubana, the national airline of Cuba, has started to switch to Western-built aircraft, although still using Antonov, Ilyushin and Tupolev aeroplanes.

Besides the core companies and nations accounted for, only China has the ambition to develop an advanced commercial aero-engine industry.

China already has a rather big engine industry, but it is for the most part based on older foreign designs, mainly from the Soviet era. Some are based on licensed manufacturing, while others are reversed engineered. This applies to all kind of engines (piston, turbo-prop, turbo-shaft, turbo-jet and turbofan). Most engines are for military aircraft, but some are applied to commercial aircraft. The large current interest and efforts of China to develop a competitive engine industry applies both to military and commercial engines; although the military is strategically more important, the commercial market is potentially much bigger, with China as the world's fastest growing civil aviation market. China has a clear ambition to end, or at least diminish, its dependence on Russian and Western power-plants.

China has no turbofan engine available for fitting on modern commercial aircraft. All turbofans manufactured are applied to various military aircraft types. While most of the military turbofans are based on Soviet designs, one is a licensed manufacture of the Rolls-Royce Spey.[6]

China is investing huge resources, human as well as financial, to develop the aerospace industry, not least aircraft manufacturing. China has huge ambitions in the aero-engine sector, but China, as well any other new entrants, has to cope with the enormous entry barriers. There are only a few companies in the world with the technical expertise and economic resources to develop a new state-of-the-art turbofan engine, i.e. to master the whole process from design to final production requires a complete system-integration knowledge and ability. The huge development costs in this industry have forced engine producers to cooperate in a network of partnerships, mainly directed towards risk/revenue sharing (Eriksson, 2000). There are thousands of parts and small components that need to function under extreme temperatures and pressures. To reach that level you need to master state-of-the-art technologies in design, machining, casting, composite materials, exotic alloys, electronic performance monitoring and quality control, and then apply it to various aircraft designs and the final flight-testing. Even when you have reached that level you still have to cope with a carefully coordinated and exhaustive documentation to satisfy aviation certification authorities. Then you have to master the commercial side (sales, trust, after-sales, logistics knowledge, etc.) of the aero-engine business, which often is an underrated factor in the aircraft/aero-engine sector. Thus, catching up and overtaking established technological leaders poses formidable problems for imitators and aspirants for leadership, since they must aim at a moving target (Eriksson, 2010). All these high-level barriers force new entrants, such as China, to cooperate with the leading corporations, mainly located in the United States and Europe. In some ways it is more demanding to develop an advanced engine than to make an airframe.

China's aero-engine industry still lacks many parts of the aero-engine jigsaw to be able to develop a competitive commercial aero-engine; but some parts are very obvious, such as state-of-the-art compressors, turbine blades, as well as process quality and standardization.

Yet another obstacle is the fact that the established manufacturers have laboured on R&D for about 60 years to build reliable and safe engines, and since the 1950s the leading companies in Europe and the United States have collected vast stores of performance and operational data from existing engines that give them a head start in designing new versions with improved fuel efficiency and reliability, which airlines demand (Lague and Zhu, 2012).

In a written inlay/opinion by Cao Chunxiao (2014), member of the Chinese Academy of Sciences and professor at the Beijing Institute of Aeronautical Materials, he discusses the role of the new Comac C919 in advancing China's competence and ability in aircraft and aero-engine manufacture. He says that an advanced foreign engine will be used at first (see Table 4.2), but the ambition is to develop their own engine in later stages. Often the engine is looked upon as the heart of an aircraft and he compares the Chinese 'engine problems' to heart troubles. He also acknowledges the tremendous difficulties in developing a suitable engine, which is more difficult than the airframe, and that the materials are also more challenging.

Foreign aero-engine manufacturers are less likely than aircraft manufacturers (airframe integrators such as Airbus, Boeing, Embraer) to share their industrial secrets with China, limiting the transfer of know-how and opportunities for intellectual property theft. Another reason for the restrictions of technology transfer is the risk of dual-use technology, i.e. that advanced technology find its way into Chinese military aircraft programmes.

The Chinese government is treating engine development as a high priority and has decided to invest huge amount of economic resources into this field, but China is still very dependent on foreign assistance. AVIC Commercial Aircraft Engine Co (ACAE),[7] established in 2009, was mainly created for the purpose of developing an engine, the-1000, for the C919 and future Chinese large passenger aircraft. Foreign cooperation was front and centre in ACAE's business plan when it was set up and the company even had a 30 per cent equity structure reserved for foreign strategic investors, but it quickly discovered that the leading Western engine makers – General Electric, Pratt & Whitney, Rolls-Royce and SNECMA – would not assist. Instead, the Chinese turned to the German MTU[8] asking for assistance, but after pressure from the main Western companies they reduced this to a mere gas cycle study (Perrett, 2014).

The future of China's commercial aero-engine programme seems unsure and a bit shaky and it will probably take a few more decades until Chinese engines will be used in main commercial airliners.

Environmental challenges

Arguably, the greatest challenge facing the aero-engine industry, one that can certainly prejudice its fortunes, is that of ameliorating adverse environmental consequences. Pollution mitigation, be it of noise or of damaging emissions (carbon dioxide, nitrogen oxides and others) deriving from aircraft propulsion, is of paramount importance. Regarding noise, technological advances have done much to reduce levels. By all accounts, engines with BPRs of 10:1 have the property of reducing noise levels by half (Hünecke, 1997, p. 210). The adoption of the high BPR turbofan sharply curtailed levels in accordance with targets mandated by the FAA and ICAO. Formalized in 1972 by the US Noise Control Act, the first two targets, stipulating the withdrawal of loud airliners (Stages 1–2), were accomplished by 2002. Less-noisy (Stage 3) aircraft, meanwhile, were subject to 'hushkitting' or new-engine installation. Thereafter, new aircraft (Stage 4) would be obliged to operate at noise levels 10 dB below previous standards. While only in force in developed countries, these controls compel airlines from elsewhere to conform or face the consequences of being barred from accessing airports in the developed world.

Aircraft engine emissions pose a trickier problem. Governments and airlines are divided as to appropriate measures, with some of the former (European Union members) insistent that the latter must conform to emission trading and the financial costs and penalties attaching to it. All are united, however, in clamouring for 'cleaner', more efficient engines. Consequently, the engine firms are focusing on delivering engines with reduced fuel burn while simultaneously supporting government initiatives aimed at producing alternatives to conventional kerosene-based jet fuels (United States, 2012). Typical of the efforts directed at the first objective is P&W's PW1000G (BPR 12.1:1) geared turbofan that promises a 15 per cent efficiency improvement over existing engines. This engine, including variants, has currently been selected to power several new commercial jets: Bombardier CSeries (PW1500G), Mitsubishi Regional Jet (PW1217G), Embraer E-Jet E2 family (PW1700G and PW-1900G). The engine will also be available as an option on the new Airbus A320 Neo. In a geared turbofan a reduction gearbox between the fan and the LP shaft allows the latter to run at a higher rotational speed, thus enabling fewer stages to be used in both the LP turbine and the LP compressor, implying increased efficiency. However, energy will be lost as heat in the gear mechanism. Also, the weight saved on turbine and compressor stages is offset to some extent by the mass of the gearbox.

Pursuing that line, but attempting to eliminate its shortcomings, is work on open-rotor engines. By common consent, diminishing returns has set in with high-BPR engines, the upshot of weight and drag increases accompanying the growth in nacelle size needed to house the large-diameter fans of such engines. Open rotors eradicate nacelles altogether, since they have propellers that operate freely. One collaborative project, sponsored through the European Commission's Sustainable and Green Engine programme, has fired the enthusiasm of engineers at companies such as Rolls-Royce and SNECMA. They believe that an open-rotor engine can be devised in the next few years that will unequivocally demonstrate the technology's viability. This effort, together with improvements in composite materials, is expected to substantially lighten turbine blades and, correspondingly, significantly boost engine efficiency (Norris, 2012).

General Electric demonstrated the GE36 Unducted Fan in flight in the late 1980s, but the concept was shelved when the fuel crisis ended. The design is intended to offer the speed and performance of a turbofan, with the fuel economy of a turboprop. It is basically a hybrid between a turbofan and a turboprop, also known as a propfan. The GE propfan was later revived with funding from NASA, but the latter withdraw from the project, leaving SNECMA and General Electric in the CFM International (engines for narrow-body aircraft) and Europe's Clean Sky programme to take the lead in advancing the maturity of open-rotor as a possible successor to CFM's Leap Engines (Warwick, 2014). Key to economic viability will be the weight penalty incurred to protect the aircraft from damage caused by a rotor-burst or blade release. A turbofan can contain a released blade, but an open-rotor will require shielding of the airframe and systems. In the end, the operators, regulators and public will decide whether this kind of engine will be a success or failure.

The search for alternative fuels has sparked much debate and spawned many research ventures. While appearing to have merit on first appearances, many of the proposed alternatives leave much to be desired. Chief among them is cost, for all alternatives present huge bills associated with erecting production plants. These costs are multiplied when attention switches to their supply and distribution (Warwick, 2012). Biomass alternatives, for instance, raise issues of opportunity costs, specifically the sacrifices to society implicit in setting aside food-growing land for producing transportation fuels (to say nothing of apportioning shares between biodiesel for road transport and feedstock for aviation bio-fuels). Furthermore, these alternatives leave unanswered the question of how to transport them to airports in the event that installed pipeline networks prove unsuitable. Despite such strong reservations, encouraging developments have occurred with two technologies: Fischer-Tropsch (FT) on the one hand and the processing of hydroprocessed esters and fatty acids (HEFAs) on the other. FT is an older technology pressed into service to convert natural gas or biomass into liquid fuels. The newer and more complex HEFA technology is capable of transforming oilseeds (carmelina and jatropha) and algae into liquid fuels. Both FT and HEFA fuels have been approved for aircraft use (in 2009 and 2011), provided they are blended in equal proportions with conventional jet fuel. The ultimate goal is to have aircraft fuelled wholly from such alternatives, and at costs that do not throw airline finances into disarray. For their part, the engine makers are acutely aware of the fact that, beholden as they are to commercial aviation, their future well-being rests on hopes that the goal is achievable. In the meantime, they are focused on developing efficient engines fully compatible with the bio-fuels in question.

Notes

1 This also applies to the very large majority of Tier 2 and 3 firms, although a few suppliers, mainly from China (Xian Aero Engine) and Taiwan (AIDC) have established themselves as Tier 2 suppliers. A unique occurrence was when Rolls-Royce, UK, decided to invest in an aero-engine assembly facility in Singapore, building the large commercial Trent aero engines, The first was delivered to Airbus in November 2012.
2 The Tu-214 is technically a variant of Tu-204-200, built in Kazan by Kazan Aircraft Production, while all versions of the Tu-204 are built in Ulyanovsk by Aviastar-SP.
3 Two variants of this aircraft, the Tu-204-120/220 versions were supplied with Rolls-Royce RB-211-535 engines, mainly to appeal to a broader international market.
4 An-158 is a stretched version of the aircraft, accommodating up to 99 passengers.
5 An exception was the use of the British BAC 1-11 One-Eleven aircraft, including a number of licensed manufactured BAC 1-11s, labelled Rombac 1-11, used by the government airline Tarom.
6 Chinese designation WS-9 Qin Ling, used in the Xian JH-7 fighter-bomber. Rolls-Royce Spey was originally intended for commercial aircraft applications when the design was initiated in the late 1950s, but was mainly adapted and used in military aircraft (F-4K Phantom and Blackburn Buccaneer). It was used in the BAC 1-11 airliner. Rolls-Royce and Allison (United States) cooperated on an US-built licensed version, labelled Allison TF-42, used in the Vought Corsair A-7 military aircraft.
7 ACAE, headquartered in Shanghai, is a joint venture between the Aviation Industry Corporation of China (AVIC) and Shanghai Electric (Group) Corporation and Shanghai Guosheng (Group) Company. This organization is a deviation from the mainstream organization of China's aerospace industry, which is completely organized within AVIC. Due to the disappointing results of ACAE, there are discussions taking place in China (2014) to put it back into the main organization, implying full control by AVIC.
8 The main focus was on the assistance on the low-pressure turbine. MTU and ACAE even signed an MoU, which was later cancelled.

References

Alcoa (2014) Home page. Online, www.alcoa.com/global/en/news/news_detail.asp?pageID= 20140626000215en& newsYear=2014 (accessed 5 July 2014).

Avio Aero (2014) Avio Aero: A GE aviation business. Online, www.aviogroup.com/?lang=en (accessed 6 July 2014).

Campagna, P. (2003) *Requiem for a Giant: A.V. Roe Canada and the Avro Arrow*, Toronto: Dundurn.

Cao, C. (2014) C919 will help china make giant leap, *Aviation Week & Space Technology*, 13 January.

Chillon, J., Dubois, J-P. and Wegg, J. (1980) *French Postwar Transport Aircraft*, Tonbridge: Air-Britain (Historians) Ltd.

Eriksson, S. (2000) Technology spill-over from the aircraft industry: The case of Volvo Aero. *Technovation*, 20(12), 653–664.

Eriksson, S. (2010) China's aircraft industry: Collaboration and technology transfer – the case of Airbus, *International Journal of Technology Transfer and Commercialisation*, Vol. 9, No. 4, pp. 306–325.

Fiatgroup (2014) Fiatgroup, Cessioni FiatAvio and Avio S.p.A. Online, www.fiatgroup.com/it-it/mediacentre/press/Documents/2003/Cessione FiatAvio ad Avio.pdf (accessed 6 July 2014).

Flight Global (2013) Commercial engines, flight global analytics, special report.

Flottau, J. (2012) Transitioning leap, *Aviation Week & Space Technology*, 22 October, p. 46.

Garvey, W. (2012) 'Golden turbine', *Aviation Week & Space Technology*, 30 July, p. 14.

Gunston, B. (1986) *World Encyclopaedia of Aero Engines*, Wellingborough: Patrick Stephens.

Gunston, B. (1989) *Rolls-Royce Aero Engines*, Wellingborough: Patrick Stephens.

Gunston, B. (1990) *North American P-51 Mustang*, New York: Gallery Books.

Holden, H.M. (1996) *The Legacy of the DC-3*, Warrendale, PA: Society of Automotive Engineers.

Hünecke, K. (1997) *Jet Engines: Fundamentals of Theory, Design and Operation*, Osceola, WI: Motorbooks International.

Ivchenko-Progress (2014) Home page. Online, http://ivchenkoprogress.com/?page_id=22&lang=en (accessed 28 June 2014).

Jackson, A.J. (1990) *Avro Aircraft since 1908*, London: Putnam.

Lague, D. and Zhu, C. (2012) Unable to copy it, China tries building own engine, *Reuters*. Online, www.reuters.com/article/2012/10/29/us-china-engine-idUSBRE89S17B20121029 (accessed 18 August 2014).

Lumsden, A. (2003) *British Piston Engines and their Aircraft*, Marlborough: Airlife Publishing.

Molson, K.M. and Taylor, H.A. (1982) *Canadian Aircraft since 1909*, London: Putnam.

Norris, G. (2012) Family fortunes … composite club, *Aviation Week & Space Technology*, 15 October, pp. 52–53.

Perrett, B. (2014) China considers setting up an independent engine maker, *Aviation Week & Space Technology*, 12 May, pp. 32–33.

Setright, I.J.K. (1971) *Power to Fly: The Development of the Piston Engine in Aviation*, London: Allen and Unwin.

SNECMA (2014) Home page. Online, www.snecma.com/-sam146-.html?lang=en. (accessed 16 August 2014).

Taylor, J.W.R. (1984) *Jane's All the World's Aircraft 1984–85*, London: Jane's Publishing.

Todd, D. and Humble, R.D. (1987) *World Aerospace: A Statistical Handbook*, London: Croom Helm.

United Engine Corporation (2014) Home page. Online, www.uk-odk.ru/eng (accessed 2 July 2014).

United States (2012) *Aviation Greenhouse Gas Emissions Reduction Plan*. Online, www.faa.gov/about/office_org/headquarters_office/apl/environ_policy_guidance/policy/media/Aviation_Greenhouse_Gas_Emissions_Reduction_Plan.pdf (accessed 1 November 2012).

Vajda, F.A. and Dancey, P. (1998) *German Aircraft Industry and Production, 1933–1945*, Bath: Bath Press Ltd.

Warwick, G. (2012) Fueling debate, *Aviation Week & Space Technology*, 8 October p. 54.

Warwick, G. (2014) Open answers, *Aviation Week & Space Technology*, 31 March, pp. 22–23.

5 Airports

Daniel Todd, James Maquire and Harm-Jan Steenhuis

In common with other modes of transportation, commercial aviation turns on networks of routes and terminals. The former constitutes the connections between origins and destinations of air travel, whereas the latter embodies the embarkation/disembarkation points from and to which the connections emanate. It is the terminals that are usually thought of when considering the transportation role of commercial aviation, for they render possible the transhipment or inter-modal exchange that is the essence of transport systems. In this familiar respect, they bear comparison with railway stations, bus stations, seaports and all the other terminals at work in the transport system. Unlike routes in the rail and road modes, however, those in aviation do not conform to fixed links; rather, not being earth-bound, they readily assume new configurations in response to weather and other environmental conditions. Represented on a non-planar graph the routes occur as temporary edges. The terminals, by contrast, are practically permanent features on the graph, serving as nodes that anchor the impermanent edges. Better known as 'airports', the terminals form the centrepiece of this chapter. That said, however, it is important to bear in mind that the terminals cannot function alone, but operate in conjunction with two necessary activities: the landing ground or the airfield; and the radar and navigational aids permitting the airport access to the non-planar routes or airways. While all three elements collectively constitute airport infrastructure, only the terminals and the airfields are of direct concern in this chapter. This stems from the fact that air traffic management, which features significantly in dictating the routes of airways, is largely a government preserve. As the arbiters of the airways, governments determine the navigational equipment and the personnel necessary to uphold them. Mindful of this qualification, the subject of airport infrastructure provision is the first major topic of this chapter. It is followed by topics on airport classification, airport finances, airport performance and airports as instruments of economic development.

Airports as infrastructure

Infrastructure costs associated with aviation are high (Canadian Institute of Traffic and Transportation, 2008).This is a characteristic that it shares with sea and rail transport, but is widely at variance with the road mode. Moreover, most airport infrastructure costs are attributable to airfields and their attached terminals, with the latter assuming greater than proportionate relevance as the significance of the airport increases. Figure 5.1 provides a schematic illustration of the shape of some of these structures. It illustrates how airports can have several runways which can have many different layouts. The Chicago and Dallas-Fort Worth airports are among those with the most runways.

Two fundamental issues have to be addressed before delving into the various components of infrastructure. They are, quite simply, instrumental in determining whether a new airport is a worthwhile venture. These issues refer to the viability of the airport as a whole, for the entire facility is contingent on the wise selection of a suitable site in the first place and of the adoption of a plan that allows it to grow in tandem with market forces. The site issue blends geographical and economic factors, balancing such obvious desirable features as a vibrant local economy with possession of an environment (expressed in weather conditions) amenable to flying. It also requires an appreciation of the airport's location relative to other airports, for the insertion of a new airport too close to the others brings with it problems of crowded airspace (Horonjeff and McKelvey, 1994: 193). Not only will this complicate air traffic control, imposing restraints

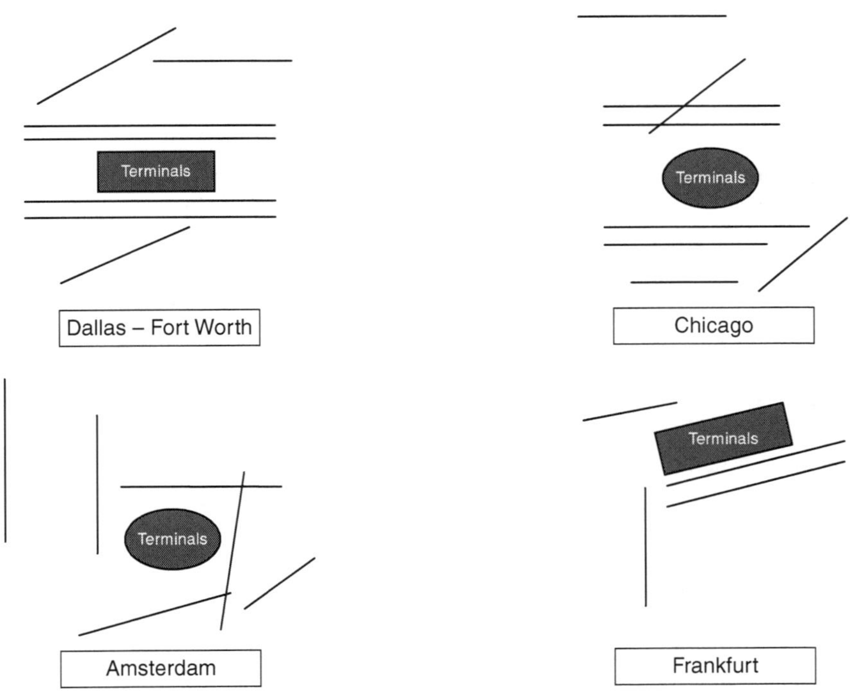

Figure 5.1 Schematic examples of airport runway layouts (source: based on www.faa.gov/airports/runway_safety/diagrams/ and airport websites).

(and attendant costs) on air carriers, but it can seriously impair the capacity of a new airport from the outset, hampering the number and direction of flights that will be permitted to operate from it (with grave consequences for its revenues). Should these concerns be allayed, the onus switches to the availability of land, and reasonably priced land at that. Associated with it is the question of the ease with which utilities – power, water supply and waste disposal – can be procured. More telling yet is the accessibility of the airport to the land modes of transportation, since straightforward and speedy communication are highly valued by customers, be they passengers or freighting firms. In short, congestion in the area surrounding the airport must be mitigated as a matter of priority.

Market forces, of course, are implicit in these geographical considerations, but they are subordinated to the economic case for or against pressing ahead with the airport project. The primary objective is establishing beyond doubt that the locality has the economic base to justify the cost entailed in inaugurating an airport. Evidently, the investors attach much weight to the market potential derived from the economic base, for the credibility of their investment rides on the long-term viability of the airport. Put plainly, the locality must support a robust mix of economic activities, together with the population and jobs attendant on them. Practically, techniques are available to convert the economic base into measures of current and projected traffic patterns; the 'life-blood' of the airport's sustainability (Foster, 1974: 3–20). Ideally, a significant threshold of traffic would have to be achieved before airport initiation would occur. In reality, though, airport advocates bent upon bringing their plans to fruition are sometimes blinded by their own optimism and are willing to accept marginal traffic volumes. For example, no fewer than 162 American airports were said to survive on three or fewer daily scheduled airline departures (Fiorino, 2004: 47).

Once the market potential for the proposed airport has been found acceptable, the 'lumpy' investment required for constructing and operationalizing the facility must be forthcoming. It is at this juncture that the scale of the venture comes to the fore, since airport size determines the amount of land required. Including a buffer zone around the airport, judged necessary to reduce the noise nuisance, an airport envisaged as a small hub would typically occupy at a minimum 4,900 ha, whereas one planned as a large hub would need at least 13,000 ha of land to be set aside (Blankenship, 1974: 18). Acquiring that amount of land in a dense urban region can be something of a tall order, presenting the airport planner with almost insurmountable difficulties and vastly inflating project costs. The experience of London Heathrow drives home the fact: its fifth terminal was opened in 2008 no less than 19 years after inception at a cost of about $8 billion, and its proposed third runway, ten years in planning, would require a staggering $13 billion to complete (Sparaco, 2009: 46). Another example is the sixth runway (Polderbaan) at the Schiphol (Amsterdam) airport. From the initial idea until opening of the runway took over 30 years and due to space and environmental constraints the runway is far removed from the terminal, i.e. taxi-times are roughly 20 minutes. Other illustrations are several Japanese airports such as Kitakyushu, Kobe and the Nagasaki airport, which were constructed on (artificial) islands.

Airports in large urban areas such as London's Heathrow have already experienced considerable difficulties expanding their airside facilities. The addition of the Airbus A380 'Superjumbo' has further complicated and often driven the need for large capital investments for expansion. Key airports around the world have similarly had to come to terms with expensive modifications consequent upon the introduction into service of the Airbus A380. The A380 was designed by Airbus for the purpose of transporting large numbers of passengers from various hubs, separated by great distance. Many of these hubs already have problems with slot availability and other congestion-related issues. Airports that seek to accommodate the A380 were required to make significant investments such as for expanded runways, realigned taxiways and terminal modifications. Furthermore, due to the size of the airframe, airports had to modify the taxi, take-off and landing movements of other aircraft to accommodate the A380. This affects the airports' ability to timely navigate aircraft. This could result in additional costs for other airport users at large hub airports, which is primarily where the A380 will be utilized. There is also the already mentioned issue of land availability and cost to expand runways at large and congested international hubs.

As a result, airports' current capabilities may be strained, leading to a higher marginal cost for the operation of the A380 (Forsyth, 2005). Essentially, by modifying terminal and runway infrastructure, it is likely that the opportunity cost of serving the A380 could complicate the current weight-based pricing structure. In the event that weight-based rates increase as a result of the investment costs, it is also possible that airport users without A380s in their fleet will have to pay fees, essentially subsidizing those flying the A380. There are many who argue that A380 users would need to pay an add-on fee to avoid this cross-subsidization effect. In turn, this could impact airlines' purchasing and usage decisions if the fees reduce the economic benefit of utilizing the A380. Many argue that the fees associated with the use of the A380 should reflect the costs they impose on the airport so that airlines will choose an aircraft mix that minimizes costs overall.

These above-described difficulties have implications for an airport's financing and directly influence the authority governing its development and operation. Traditionally a preserve of government, airport ownership in recent years has been amended to allow greater private-sector involvement. Indeed, the airport authority may be turned over entirely to the private sector (inspired by the privatization of the British Airports Authority in 1987), but governments loathe to give up ownership may resort to corporatization instead (Doganis, 1992). Privatization, of course, lifts the burden of airport financing from the shoulders of governments, whereas corporatization is applied in hopes of instilling private-sector cost efficiencies into public enterprises. Examples of airports fully privatized include London's Heathrow and Gatwick, and Sydney Kingsford Smith. Numbering among those corporatized are Manchester, Oslo and Singapore Changi. In some instances, of which India's New Delhi and Mumbai airports stand out, the construction and management of the facility is let as a concession to private interests for a limited period before reverting to government control

(Productivity Commission, Australia, 2011: 327–333). American airports have largely ignored these initiatives, persisting with public ownership. They mainly rely on the bond market for their capital projects, but have recourse to the government's Airport Improvement Program (responsible for about 29 per cent of the annual $12 billion requirement) to significantly boost this funding (Unnikrishnan and Wilson, 2009).

The same joint issue of steep costs and lengthy lead times holds true for ground transportation linking the airport to its host community. Ground access to the airport has predominantly rested on the road mode. Ironically, however, boosting highway capacity has usually exacerbated the congestion problem instead of relieving it. Almost invariably, saturation of the road network has occurred as soon as the additional capacity is brought on stream: the upshot of tardiness in its provision (often the result of popular opposition) and the stimulus that the extra capacity provides to traffic unconnected with the airport (Blankenship, 1974: 24). Keen to overcome the bane of remorseless road-traffic growth, airports have increasingly turned to the rail mode as a means of redress. This includes the 'train' type as well as the underground/subways (for instance, London and Singapore, where the latter connected the MRT-system to Changi Airport in 2002). Besides promising to reduce road congestion appreciably, train transport offers improved economies in people movement (provided that the volume is high enough). Furthermore, in requiring less space than highways it enjoys the bonus of reduced land-acquisition costs, to say nothing of being more environmentally benign than vehicular traffic (and thus appeasing the environmental lobby).

Some countries attach sufficient importance to railways to have integrated airports into their national rail networks. The most celebrated instances are found in Europe, where Paris Charles de Gaulle, Frankfurt and Amsterdam Schiphol (Europe's second, third and fourth in terms of passenger traffic) offer high-speed rail connections to a host of major cities. Terminal 2 at Paris has a station offering high-speed train service to cities as distant as Brussels, Marseilles and Toulouse. For its part, Frankfurt's airport rail station directly accesses the Cologne–Frankfurt high-speed line. Amsterdam Schiphol, meanwhile, offers high-speed rail services to Berlin and Paris from a station immediately beneath the airport's terminal complex. Demonstrably successful in reducing the time associated with ground travel to the airports, these connections have had the further effect of diverting some passenger demand from the airlines to the railways. That outcome is a mixed blessing, allowing airports to concentrate on long-distance flights at the expense of environmentally damaging short hauls, but threatening their overall passenger volumes. The latter can become detrimental to airport fortunes when transport policy is not coordinated. China exemplifies the danger. Despite enormous growth in aviation and airports, China has espoused high-speed railways in a monumental way, with a multiplicity of intercity lines springing up across the country. Already Chinese airlines are feeling the effects: for example, the premium domestic route, Beijing–Shanghai, is expected to lose 45 per cent of its traffic to the new 380 km/h train service.

Moreover, half the air-passenger traffic has switched to high-speed rail on the Guangzhou–Wuhan route. All told, although this is a deliberate choice by the government due to the increase in air traffic, it is estimated that the airlines risk losing nearly half of their traffic base to the rail alternative on routes of 600 km or less (Perrett, 2011: 76).

Other jurisdictions have been content to settle for dedicated high-speed commuter lines linking airports with city centres, as is most spectacularly illustrated by Hong Kong. Currently the world's busiest cargo-handling terminal and one of Asia's dominant passenger terminals, Hong Kong International was created in 1998 on two small islands. From the beginning, it was linked to downtown Hong Kong, 34 km away, by a high-speed rail service capable of whisking passengers to the airport in just 24 minutes. Hong Kong serves as a template for American airports. Since 2001, when Newark Liberty opened its train station, air–rail connections have undergone a spirited revival. Eleven airports across the country had implemented rail services by 2011, including Philadelphia International, Fort Lauderdale, Miami International, Dallas-Fort Worth and Chicago O'Hare (Johnston, 2011: 18). Notably, these were airports experiencing large passenger volumes, the indispensable requirement for ensuring the viability of the rail option. In short, these examples happen to conform to a certain class of 'large hub' airports, invested with particular characteristics. This raises the question of what determines how airports are classified, the subject of the next section.

Airport classifications

The interested reader searches in vain for a classification of airports that is universally accepted. Instead, there are several ways of distinguishing between airport types, depending on the combination of circumstances that gave rise to their existence. This combination embraces many causes, ranging from the historical, the functional, the geographical and, not infrequently, the machinations of politicians. These causes are interactive, complicating any grouping procedure. The resultant classification is of necessity a simplification of the true role of any airport, trading sophistication for clarity. For example, it has long been noted that a typical airport handles both passengers and cargo, posing a puzzling predicament for the taxonomist desirous of assigning it unequivocally to the passenger-serving function or the cargo function (Button, 1982). Nevertheless, classification is resorted to in order to impose some means of categorizing the infrastructure so as to allow generalization. It follows that nobody should be blind to the fact that any airport, conceivably, could be legitimately assigned to multiple categories spanning several classifications. As always with such exercises, classifications are merely descriptive devices for aiding the understanding of the analyst.

Historical classification

To begin with, it is expedient to contemplate classification grounded in historical fact. This kind of classification is at once the vaguest and the most compelling means of separating airports into distinct groups. Consistent with most historical analysis, it lacks the rigour and accuracy of scientific classifications but, unlike them, it is always predicated on events that have occurred in the past and have heralded the formation of facilities that now are held to be airports. Furthermore, it does not stop with the causes accounting for the foundation of airports, for implicit in classification of this nature is an evolutionary aspect, one allowing for changes over time. These events, whether inaugurating airports in the first place or unfolding in response to changing circumstances latterly, ultimately touch on geographical factors. Geography influences decisions concerning the selection of suitable sites in any given locality, to say nothing of the larger issue of facility location in relation to the country's economic and trade links (Sealy, 1957: 183–204). The part played by geography in airport formation and evolution is a constant, though understated, theme, so the reader must always be mindful of the geography underscoring historical classification.

Perhaps the most coherent historical classification assumes that airports fall into just two basic categories (albeit with some allowance for variation on the two); namely, they either abide by the characteristics of 'national gateways' or else owe their origins and subsequent development to their ability to function as 'way-stations'. 'National gateways' are major airports serving as international hub facilities for global cities. Each exists to ensure that the city-region to which it is geographically attached is fully interconnected with comparable facilities elsewhere. In short, 'national gateways' are indispensable to national well-being, fulfilling a vital trade function. In fact, their importance frequently extends beyond the borders of their host nations to incorporate extensive catchment areas in contiguous national economies of smaller stature. Contemporary examples are well-known. The likes of Washington Dulles, New York Kennedy, London Heathrow, Amsterdam Schiphol, Paris Charles de Gaulle, Beijing Capital and Tokyo Narita stand out as the main access points for the cities in question, cities which act as magnets to the traveller and commercial interests alike.

In the above instances – and indeed in virtually all cases that can be cited – the current airport locales are merely the latest round in the evolution of airport sites deemed capable of fulfilling the function of the 'national gateway'. In other words, various sites in the vicinity of a global city have been tried and judged satisfactory, only to be later found wanting. As a rule, the pattern conforms to one in which larger sites increasingly further removed from the city centre replace smaller more centrally located sites that have outlived their usefulness. The lack of room for expansion is the driving force behind this pattern. Finding the necessary space usually – but not invariably – leads to sites that are embedded in the rural hinterland where land is far easier to amass. Prior to Heathrow's inception at the end of the Second World War, for instance, London's premier airport was Croydon, a facility dating from the dawn of commercial aviation. Oddly, Croydon was further away from central London than its replacement site at Heathrow (19.3 km as opposed to 16.5 km). However, constrained by urban developments in its immediate vicinity, Croydon had run up against real limits, unable to expand its landing ground to accommodate the latest generation of aircraft. At best, its longest runway could be extended (at a considerable cost) from 1,200 m to 1,846 m. Heathrow suffered no such constraints in 1945, planning to operate from a 2,770 m main runway and two 1,846 m subsidiary runways from the outset. Over the succeeding decade airlines were forced to migrate to the newer facility, leaving Croydon devoid of traffic. Declared obsolete, it was turned over to housing and commercial activities. More than half a century later, Heathrow finds itself suffering from the same affliction as its predecessor: space constraints denying future expansion. This brake on its growth has enormous implications for the national economy, triggering a frantic – and highly politicized – search for solutions.

Other global cities saddled with equally obsolete or obsolescent facilities have followed suit. Paris is a spectacular case in point. There, the body charged with overseeing airports (Aéroports de Paris) switched most of the international traffic from Orly Airport (opened in 1932) to Charles de Gaulle Airport at Roissy in 1974. A more than adequate facility in its heyday, Orly was judged to be too cramped for expansion, despite occupying an area of 15.3 km^2 with enough space to host a main runway 3,650 m in length. The Roissy site, in marked contrast, sprawled over 32.4 km^2 and gloried in more long runways (the longest running for 4,215 m). This vast area was procured at the expense of distance from central Paris: some 25 km as against the 13 km of Orly. Interestingly, Orly itself had earlier usurped Le Bourget as the city's main airport. True to the pattern, Le Bourget was just 11 km from central Paris and, over time, found itself beset all around by space limits. As an aside, in terms of commercial air transportation, Le Bourget was closed in 1977 for international traffic and in 1980 for regional and national traffic. It is currently used for business aviation and as a host for the world's largest airshow, the Paris Airshow, which is hosted once every two years. Needless to say, during the airshow Le Bourget faces a lot of traffic.

Berlin exemplifies this relocation pattern too, albeit with a peculiar twist. The post-war history of the erstwhile German capital, whereby it was partitioned among the three Western powers and the Soviet Union, imposed an overriding political complexion on the structure of air transportation – as with everything else. The upshot of this division was the maintenance of airports in each zone. Consequently, the newly restored German capital was left, as a legacy of the Cold War, with no fewer than three international airports, each deficient in one aspect or another. The best of the three – Schönefeld – was partly incorporated in a single new replacement, Brandenburg Airport, but the other two – Tempelhof and Tegel – were earmarked for disposal. Freed from Cold War political constraints, the planners of Berlin Brandenburg found a more spacious site 18 km south of the city. When it opens, the new airport will offer international airlines the benefits of a 4,000 m runway, significantly longer than the 3,000 m structure available at Schönefeld (which, upon lengthening to 3,600 m will enjoy a new lease of life as part of the Brandenburg site). When this opening of the Berlin Brandenburg airport will take place is unclear. Initially it was planned for 2011 but it has faced numerous delays and it is now expected not to open until 2016 (von Bullion, 2013).

A variation on the 'national gateway' class of airports is what might be termed the 'secondary gateway'; that is to say, an airport acting as an auxiliary to the main facility. As intimated, 'national gateways' are apt to succumb to massive increases in traffic, the timely alleviation of which tends to defy the best efforts of airport planners. The outcome is congestion, with terminal facilities bursting at the seams and aircraft movements at a maximum. Such full-capacity usage runs the risk of prejudicing safety and efficiency. Passenger disaffection often proves to be the last straw, forcing airport authorities to seek redress in solutions that appear manageable and less costly than those entailed in a comprehensive expansion of the main airport. Therefore, recourse is had to neighbouring airports that promise moderate costs and which can be pressed into service at a moment's notice (or what passes for quick implementation in the air transport business). These facilities assume the role of relief or overflow airports, seeing their traffic patterns as integral aspects of the larger 'national gateways'. Often, they are as well-known to the travelling public as their grander counterparts. The aforementioned Orly, for instance, is widely accepted as a gateway to Paris, in large part because it continues to handle a portion of the international traffic diverted from Charles de Gaulle Airport. Other examples abound around global cities. Consider the three global financial centres: New York, London and Tokyo. New York has Newark to help out Kennedy. London, the leading international destination in the world, relies on Gatwick, Stansted and City Airports to supplement capacity-stretched Heathrow. Tokyo, for its part, allocates domestic traffic and a modicum of international flights to Haneda while confining Narita to long-haul services.

Some airports are envisaged from the outset as 'secondary gateways' and are built as stripped-down versions of their larger brethren. The majority that fall into this sub-class, however, were conceived with other purposes in mind – typically, as military bases or general-aviation airfields – and are elevated to 'secondary gateway' status almost as an afterthought. As a result, they have new life infused into them. London City Airport exemplifies the purpose-built version to a nicety. It is salutary in other respects too. Besides conforming to the strict stripped-down model, it illustrates how the opportunity can be seized to redevelop 'brownfield' sites for aviation purposes. This versatility is especially relevant to large global cities where land shortage is an acute problem, available space is at a premium and in consequence is extremely costly. Located 11 km east of central London, it was built on land made redundant by the closure of the city's docks. It began operations in 1987 with aircraft movements inhibited by the single short runway (even now just 1,500 m long), to say nothing of the required steep climbs and descents. By 2009, though, it was offering jet service to as far afield as New York Kennedy, as well as maintaining a multiplicity of connections to European cities. Note that British Airways uses an A318 for the flight from London City Airport to New York Kennedy and this requires a refuelling stop at Shannon in Ireland. Shannon can be considered another type of airport – a way-station, as will be discussed below. All things considered, it demonstrates the usefulness of 'secondary gateways' even in the face of severe operating restrictions and minimum infrastructure.

It has to be conceded, however, that most 'secondary gateways' began life in a different guise. Air bases surplus to military requirements often form a convenient foundation for resurrection as civilian airports. After all, they come complete with basic infrastructure, readily adaptable for commercial-aviation purposes. In some instances, the infrastructure in question includes the all-important runway that is of adequate length and strength to entertain jet airliner traffic from the outset. In exceptional cases the redundant military base may be fitted up in accordance with the most recent airfield architecture and navigational approach equipment, rendering it suitable for conversion to civilian usage at short notice. Above all, their very existence allows the airport authority to dispense with the difficult and costly process of land acquisition. By the same token, it inherits a situation in which the neighbouring population, already inured to the nuisance aspects of aircraft movements, can be expected to acquiesce to continued aviation activities. The assumption is that the NIMBY (not-in-my-backyard) phenomenon is far more likely to arise in localities new to aviation – although, in truth, that expectation is not always borne out in reality.

Located 48 km northeast of London, Stansted Airport bears all the hallmarks of a 'secondary gateway' with military origins. Built at the height of the Second World War for use by the American air forces, it was quickly run down after hostilities ended and soon turned over to a batch of start-up air-freight operators and charter carriers. At this time it was also designated the chief diversion airfield for London, coming into its own when more active Heathrow and Gatwick were fogbound. In the 1950s it was the recipient of renewed attention from the military, becoming a US Air Force reserve base. Practical benefits followed, not least of which was a major new runway, some 3,049 m long. This intervention failed to disrupt its continued usage for charter flights and airline-pilot training. The new runway was not overlooked by government planners, however. They contemplated developing the airfield into a 'national gateway' in the 1970s, envisioning Stansted as Britain's fourth major airport after Heathrow, Gatwick and Manchester. In the event, their grand plans went awry, defeated by spirited (and unanticipated) opposition from the local community. Instead, the airport was subjected to more modest development in the 1980s, insidiously going from strength to strength. By the 1990s Stansted had been fully tested and found equal to the role of 'secondary gateway', hosting increasing numbers of airlines operating scheduled services. Currently, it handles flights to numerous European airports, the majority of which are performed by low-cost carriers of the likes of Ryanair and Easyjet. These activities are supplemented by significant air-cargo services that regularly link the airport to destinations far beyond Europe, including several in the United States (Atlanta, Chicago, Houston, Memphis, Newark and Philadelphia).

The fact that a majority of the flights handled at Stansted are performed by low-cost carriers points out another development which may have played a role in the growth of the secondary gateways. Part of their rise is related to deregulation. For example, throughout the 1970s to the 1990s the airline services industry within the United States went through a period of deregulation which drastically modified or even eliminated many of the price controls that governed airline economic decision making. The deregulation which began with the Airline Deregulation Act of 1978 eliminated the governmental restrictions and requirements of airfares, city-to-city markets and mergers and acquisitions. Prior to the Act, airlines were required to file for a certificate of public convenience and necessity from the Civil Aeronautics Board (CAB) before they could establish new or service points. Additionally, the airfares charged to the travelling public were subject to CAB oversight and approval. Upon passage of the Act, the CAB's regulatory authority was drastically reduced, granting airlines wider flexibility to set fares and determine routes (Creager, 1983). This led to the rise of low-cost airlines. A similar development took place in Europe since 1997, leading to the rise of low-cost airlines such as Ryanair and Easyjet, which followed different strategies in terms of airports. Instead of flying to the national gateways, these airlines negotiated with and serviced the secondary airports such as Stansted and Faro, which allowed these airports to grow (Almeida, 2011).

General-aviation airfields generally have much less to recommend them as candidates for conversion into 'secondary gateways'. This is on account of their Spartan facilities in comparison with better-appointed surplus air bases, some of which come complete with long runways, sophisticated navigational aids and extensive maintenance shops. By virtue of their history of catering to small, usually propeller-driven, aircraft, the operators of general-aviation airfields have tended to shun needless investment in long runways, the key pieces of infrastructure required for jet airliner flights. Nevertheless, circumstances sometimes result in the overlooking of such handicaps and efforts are made to transform general-aviation airfields into 'secondary gateways'. Several with such antecedents have sprung up in the last few years. Toronto Island Airport furnishes a perfect example. Rebranded as Billy Bishop Toronto City Airport to reflect its newly granted status, this airport has carved out a niche for itself as the centre for regional flights, complementing the comprehensive domestic and international network of flights offered from Toronto Pearson Airport, Canada's principal gateway. Ironically, when planned in the 1930s, Toronto Island was intended as the main airport of the city. Upon opening in 1939, however, it had been usurped by a much more spacious site at Malton, the future home of Pearson International. Resigned to undertaking flight training during the war, the airfield settled into a long period post-war of limited usage, being dedicated to air freight and charter flights as well as training. Confined within the strict dimensions of its island site, the airfield was greatly overshadowed by developments at Pearson. Yet it was not entirely neglected, for paved runways were laid between 1959 and 1963, the longest of which reached a modest 1,219 m. Their existence, together with the attraction stemming from the airfield's convenient location in relation to the city's downtown, were sufficient to induce pioneer operators of STOL turboprop aircraft to begin scheduled services in 1980. Against the odds, these operations have stood the test of time. Accounting for the lion's share of the airport's contemporary traffic, STOL services have expanded to embrace a number of Canadian cities, not to mention such US destinations as Boston, Chicago Midway, Newark and Washington Dulles.

We come at length to the airports composing the 'way-stations' class. Rather than acting as major hubs in the manner of 'national gateways' or being set up as 'secondary gateways' to arrest the decline of their more important brethren, 'way-stations' were established to promote long-distance connections between the great hubs. Only latterly did 'way-stations' frequently undergo the transition into sizeable hubs in their own right. Some, though, never accomplished the transition, but remain to this day as refuelling points. Anchorage in Alaska, Bangor in Maine, Gander in Newfoundland, Shannon in Ireland and Prestwick in Scotland are by and large still 'way-stations' in the classic mould. They all existed because of the combination of 'fog and propellers'; that is to say, their ability to offer clear weather in regions notorious for cloudy maritime climates that were liable to obscure flying operations of the then prevalent piston-powered aircraft. Bangor, to this day, bills itself as a diversion airport for trans-oceanic traffic. Its single 3,487 m runway is capable of handling airliners entering US airspace that are reluctant to proceed to their planned destination owing to bad weather. While waiting for weather clearance at Bangor, the diverted aircraft can seize the opportunity of taking on competitively priced fuel and their passengers can use the time gainfully to satisfy customs and immigration requirements.

At their height, the members of this class faithfully reflected the limits of aviation technology of the day, being located at the furthest range of the largest practical commercial aircraft then flying. Commonly, the long-range aircraft of choice was the flying boat, an aircraft that simultaneously offered the advantages of size while operating from water, thus dispensing with the need for runways. Along with infrastructure in general, runway provision was scanty on global routes that disproportionately crossed underdeveloped territories. A solution was found in marine airports that could be established at relatively low cost. Provided they employed the facilities needed for refuelling aircraft and accommodating passengers in transit, the solution proved more than adequate. A perusal of the renowned flying-boat services of the 1930s sheds light on the 'staging posts' vital for their effectiveness.

Prominent among them were Honolulu in Hawaii, Fiji in the South Pacific, Foynes in Ireland and Botwood in Newfoundland; all notably either at the land extremity preparatory to a trans-oceanic crossing or occurring as 'stepping stones' along the route of that oceanic crossing. The first of these is now a busy leisure destination. A conventional airport today, it initially saw service in 1935 as the first stopover on Pan Am's 'China Clipper' flying-boat run from San Francisco to Manila and, subsequently, to Hong Kong. Assigned to the latest Martin and Boeing aircraft, the run was unequalled in length and endurance, requiring refuelling stops at Midway Island, Wake Island and Guam, as well as Honolulu. Fiji, which currently brands itself as the air hub of the South Pacific, had similar origins, started life as a stopover on the TEAL (now Air New Zealand) flying-boat service that began in Auckland and proceeded via Fiji, Samoa, the Cook Islands and Tonga to its terminus in Tahiti. For their part, the fortunes of Foynes and Botwood were far less auspicious, since their replacement land-based airports (Shannon and Gander) were devoid of local markets capable of justifying alternatives to the refuelling role.

Other airports once reliant on the 'way-station' role have capitalized on their locations to an enormous extent. Singapore stands head and shoulders above the others in this respect. Echoing its vital location as a coaling-station on world sea lanes, it was pressed into service on the long-haul route of Imperial Airways (an ancestor of British Airways) to Australia. This rose to prominence in 1938 with the inauguration of Short Empire flying boats, among the best equipped airliners of the era and unsurpassed in the lavish facilities made available to their passengers. Beginning at Southampton in England, the route proceeded in stages compatible with the aircraft's range of 1,216 km to arrive in Singapore. There, passengers transferred to an Empire flying boat belonging to Qantas, the Australian carrier that undertook the last leg of the flight to Sydney. This transfer operation was accomplished at Seletar, which was also used by the military for flying-boat purposes. With the phasing out of flying boats after the war, Singapore's international airport was switched, successively, to Paya Lebar and Changi, the latter now constituting one of the world's leading aviation terminals, transferring travellers between flights to Australasia, South East Asia and Europe.

While admittedly dwarfed by Singapore's experience, Bahrain can lay claim to a comparable evolutionary path. It, too, owed its genesis to Imperial Airways. Established in 1932 as a 'staging post' on the link from London to India, it became the first international airport in the Persian Gulf. As with Singapore, it was soon to cater to the Empire flying boats that dominated the airline's long-haul routes. The discontinuance of flying boats in favour of land-based aircraft after the war was greatly assisted by the military construction of landing grounds, now made available to civilian airlines. In Bahrain's case this resulted in aviation activities moving from Mina Salman to the island of Muharraq. From there, growth of air services gradually increased, accelerating after the kingdom's independence in 1971. The airport began to assume hub proportions, overseeing flights to destinations as far away as Hong Kong. Symbolic of this vibrancy was the fact that Bahrain was chosen to host Concorde flights from London in 1976.

Functional classification

The foregoing account has provided a fair description of historical classification in all its chief particulars. At best, it is a rough and ready device for partitioning airports according to their designed purpose. In addition, it faithfully makes appropriate allowance for succeeding, specific events encroaching on their operations. At worst, this historical predilection threatens to destroy the generalization that is fundamental to classification. Given this deficiency, the formulation of a classification that intentionally eschews historical circumstance to focus on current airport activities was eagerly anticipated. The best known classification of this type is associated with the FAA and is widely used for American airports.

Not only is this classification fully comprehensive, but it is easily compiled, resting on data of critical importance to the effectiveness of all airports – those referring to annual traffic figures.

Spurred by its responsibility for implementing the Airport Improvement Program (AIP), the FAA was compelled to devise a straightforward means of distinguishing among the nearly 3,400 diverse airports that fell under its jurisdiction. The agency saw fit to set up a subsidiary planning organization (under the auspices of the National Plan of Integrated Airport Systems, or NPIAS) which was charged with the task of formulating an airport classification that aided coherence in the distribution of government grants (Horonjeff and Mc Kelvey, 1994: 35). The NPIAS planners responded by adopting a hierarchical approach, first sorting the numerous candidates for infrastructure assistance into four categories: commercial-service airports; primary cargo-service airports; reliever airports; and selected general-aviation airports. As their name implies, commercial-service airports are preoccupied with scheduled passenger traffic; specifically, they are held to be such when, each calendar year, they record a minimum of 2,500 passengers boarding and disembarking through their facilities. Their counterparts dealing with air freight, the primary cargo-service airports, must register an annual throughput of 45.4 million kilograms. In practice, the NPIAS recognizes that some airports combine the requirements of the two classes, boasting the passenger and cargo figures to qualify as both. For the most part the final two classes function as necessary adjuncts to the first two. Reliever airports are judged to exist largely to relieve congestion at commercial-service airports. In some respects, then, they can be likened to the 'secondary gateways' highlighted in the previously discussed historical classification. Finally, a minority of general-aviation airports are regarded by the NPIAS as fulfilling a commercial-service role, albeit of minor proportions. In this light, those credited with housing at least ten aircraft and handling fewer than 2,500 scheduled passengers per year are deemed worthy of consideration for AIP grants.

By any measure other than sheer numbers (where they are eclipsed by general-aviation airports), the commercial-service airports stand out as the most important: so much so that NPIAS has elevated them above the other classes to proceed to the second step in the functional hierarchy, which discriminates among commercial-service airports according to their relative significance, dividing them into two groups. The more significant are termed 'primary airports', which exhibit throughputs in excess of 10,000 scheduled passengers per year. Offsetting them are 'non-primary airports', which accommodate between 2,500 and 10,000 scheduled passengers in the same period (leaving the selected general-aviation airports to account for the residual passenger flows). This procedure is preparatory to the third step, which gives rise to the most compelling part of the classification: the accent on hub size. The criterion governing airport designation is simply its percentage share of the national total number of passengers carried by scheduled airlines in a year. The outcome is a declining order of classes: namely, hubs defined as large, medium and small, followed by two kinds of non-hubs, the second of which is assigned to the 'non-primary airports' group.

In this respect, the 'large hub' towers over all, conveying 1 per cent or more of the passenger total. Currently, no fewer than 33 American airports qualify as 'large hubs', with Hartsfield Atlanta, Chicago O'Hare, Los Angeles International, Dallas-Fort Worth, Denver International and New York's Kennedy occupying the top places. By virtue of the substantial regions that they serve, these five airports bear comparison with the 'national gateways' highlighted in the historical classification. Less reminiscent of 'national gateways', however, are the remaining 28 'large hubs'. The state of Florida, out of all proportion to its economic and political weight, alone holds title to four. The airports in question – Miami International, Orlando International, Fort Lauderdale and Tampa International – are testimony of the overwhelming importance of the tourism industry. Even more at odds with 'national gateways' are Metro Oakland International, the pair of Ronald Regan Washington and Washington-Baltimore International, to say nothing of Newark Liberty and La Guardia. Since the first is clearly overshadowed by San Francisco International, the second pair is found within the zone dominated by Washington Dulles, and the final pair is bound up with the operations of New York Kennedy, these 'large hubs' correspond more to the 'secondary gateways' of the historical classification. Yet the fact remains that the very quantity of 'large hubs' is a striking commentary on the pervasiveness of commercial aviation in the United States.

The 'large hubs' are matched by an almost equal number of 'medium hubs', some 35 all-told. While subordinate to its larger counterpart, the 'medium hub' is still an airport to be reckoned with. Each is responsible for handling between 0.25 per cent and 1 per cent of the national tally of passengers. Prominent among them are Memphis, San Jose, Portland, Raleigh-Durham, Kansas City and Cleveland Hopkins; all count as legitimate 'international' airports. In marked contrast, the 'small hub' is decidedly more modest in its traffic ambitions. Each is credited with between 0.05 per cent and 0.25 per cent of the grand total of passengers travelling annually. Leading exponents of the class include the airports located in Albany, Birmingham (Alabama), Colorado Springs, El Paso, Long Beach, Oklahoma City, Richmond and Spokane. Altogether, membership of the class amounts to 66 airports. Even smaller are the 'non-hubs'. Those branded as 'primary airports' aim to handle at least 10,000 scheduled passengers per year. They serve as the outlying 'spokes' of hub airports, aiming to attract regional and commuter services. Typical of them are Toledo Express Airport, Helena Regional Airport and Wilmington International Airport. Languishing below them in the hierarchy are the 'non-hubs' without any meaningful scheduled traffic. Their irregular role within the national airport system is sufficient to see them condemned to the 'non-primary airports' class.

Other countries follow suit, albeit after instituting appropriate amendments. Canada and Britain are cases in point. Canada, as befits a nation of vast size but small population, makes do with a functional classification stripped of the embellishments of its much more populous neighbour. The country's National Airports System divides airports among five classes: international, national, regional, local commercial and local. Traffic flow, established by the NPIAS and upheld by the National Airport System, is judged to be key in determining an airport's significance. However, traffic flow alone is not sufficient; rather, it is supplemented in the Canadian instance by consideration of the geographical origins of arriving passengers and the location of the destinations of departing passengers. American origins and destinations warrant their own 'trans-border' category distinct from other international traffic. The 13 international airports, accordingly, are seen as vital in maintaining overseas links. They embrace the obvious gateways of Toronto, Montréal and Vancouver, together with the national capital, Ottawa, and the chief provincial capitals such as Edmonton and Winnipeg. Also included in their number is Gander, an airport that has outlasted its 'way-station' origins to fulfil a useful reliever function akin to Bangor in Maine. The nine national airports, meanwhile, are dedicated to country-wide communication on the one hand and cross-border traffic to and from the United States, on the other. Saskatoon and Regina, two medium-sized cities in the province of Saskatchewan, are characteristic of this class. Regional airports are mini-hubs, for the most part dedicated to collecting local traffic and feeding it into the nexus of national and international hubs. Red Deer and Fort McMurray in Alberta are very active regional airports. The two remaining classes correspond closely with the NPIAS lower-order classes. Thus local-commercial airports (such as La Ronge, Prince Albert and Uranium City in Saskatchewan) concentrate on local services, frequently of the charter kind, leaving local airports to confine themselves to private flying.

Britain, while geographically only a small fraction of America's size, employs a diverse collection of airports that are comparable in scope to those across the North Atlantic. Not surprisingly, then, similar classification patterns hold true for Britain and the North American countries. First and foremost are the 'Category A' airports, also known as the 'international gateways'. As is to be expected, these airports are major points of access for flights to Britain arriving from foreign countries and, equally, marshal domestic passengers for destinations beyond Britain. Notably, a number of airports in combination constitute the London gateway. Besides the three familiar facilities at Heathrow, Gatwick and Stansted, this single Category A cluster also encompasses Luton. The overriding importance of the category is endorsed by its very scarcity; for, outside the London group, only Manchester is deemed of sufficient stature to justify designation as an 'international gateway'. Appearing next in the hierarchy are 'Category B' facilities, the 'regional airports'. Unlike their Canadian namesakes, they assume a prominence in the national economy, with each serving a leading city-region. The airports at Glasgow, Birmingham, Cardiff, East Midlands, Newcastle and Leeds/Bradford bear witness to this importance. This dominant position in their regions grants them considerable tourist traffic, mostly consisting of British passengers vacationing overseas. Occupying a lower order, in turn, are the 'Category C' or 'local airports'. Their relevance also derives from tourist traffic, although the volume of passenger flows and the choices of destination are more limited. Chief among them are Bristol, Exeter, Liverpool, Southampton and Teesside. Finally, residing at the bottom of the hierarchy are the 'Category

D' airports, those confining their activities to general aviation. With the understanding of national classifications of airports and the relationship with size, the largest airports can be analysed. But before doing that, a brief intermezzo will discuss the financial side of airports.

Airport finances

The Act and its deregulation of the US airline services industry did not occur with respect to airports. Airports remained largely under the regulatory authority of the Federal Aviation Administration (FAA). To this day the FAA still governs the regulatory environment of airport services and aviation safety (Creager, 1983). This has had implications for airport fee structures and their associated revenues. The fee structure is a result of significant FAA influence due to the dependence upon federal subsidies for airport infrastructure and operation. In order to obtain those subsidies, which are critical for the economic health of airports, grant agreements must be made which require airport revenues to be spent on capital or operating cost (Creager, 1983).

The airport fee structure is based upon marginal cost pricing, which often results in long-run break-even revenues or even deficits if airport capacity is not maximized. Airport finances are primarily based on runway fees and terminal fees. Traditionally, airport landing fees have been established based upon aircraft weight. For example, Spokane's landing fees are \$1.73 per 1,000 lb, Seattle's landing fees are \$3.00 per 1,000 lb.[1] In the United States maximum certified landing weights are used to establish landing fee rates (Morrison, 1982). As landing fees have been primarily based upon aircraft weight, they are set the same for all carriers despite differences in usage level among those carriers and regardless of airport congestion level (Morrison, 1982).

There has been a great deal of discussion to transition from weight-based fees to pricing based upon user charges. These charges would seek to address airport congestion which has been, and will continue to be, a serious concern as global travelling volumes continue to climb. The fee structure for runway fees is set based upon marginal-cost pricing due largely to regulatory influences, as well as the monopolistic forces of the airlines. Airport competition has also been increasing steadily within the United States and globally, which has diminished the overall market power for airports. Airports must compete with one another to serve as hubs or even service points for cities with multiple airports (Airports Council International, 2009). The overall result of the landing fees is a fee structure that is based upon marginal cost, often resulting in budgetary deficits with respect to runway fees.

To overcome the budgetary shortfalls from the runway fee structure, airports often rely on terminal fees (in addition to public subsidies). Terminal fees often include revenue generated from such operations as parking facilities, restaurants and shops (Creager, 1983). Airports have worked to increase their competitive strength by adding unique amenities to enhance the travelling experience of the travelling public. It has become more common to enjoy wide offerings of extensive food courts and restaurants, specialty stores, technological conveniences and other services one would expect to find in an upscale mall or shopping centre. For example, Schiphol Amsterdam Airport features a museum containing Dutch art and historical pieces. Austin-Bergstrom International Airport holds over 12 live concerts each week to entertain travellers. Taiwan Taoyuan International Airport has an e-book library available to help passengers pass time as they wait for their flights (Becker, 2012). These unique types of terminal amenities not only draw direct revenue for the airport, but also serve to differentiate themselves from possible competing airports. Terminal fees do not typically have regulatory pricing restrictions, unlike landing fees; therefore, airports often use competitive bidding to collect a portion of the monopolistic profits enjoyed by airport vendors (Creager, 1983). The use of terminal fees has been a useful way for airports to obtain sufficient revenues and mitigate any shortcomings from the landing fee pricing structure.

Airports have become increasingly savvy when it comes to revenue generation and cost savings. For instance, San Francisco International Airport has installed 2,800 solar panels on one of its terminals to contribute to a portion of the airport's power demands. Long Beach Airport in California has also adopted a solar approach to mitigating its electricity costs. The airport has installed 'solar trees' that follow the sun throughout the day. Alternatively, Boston's Logan International Airport installed wind turbines modelled after aircraft propellers in 2008 to help meet their energy demands. These cost-saving measures will likely become more commonplace as airports struggle with revenue generation amid the required changes to airport infrastructure and pricing (Briggs, 2012).

Airport 'performance'

The performance of airports can be evaluated in terms of several different variables. One method of measuring airport performance is to measure and track the aircraft movements, i.e. take-off and landings. Another method of evaluating airport improvements is through measuring the quality of the airport. For example, Skytrax conducts an annual survey of passenger satisfaction – see www.worldairportawards.com. Table 5.1 provides an overview of the ten best airports for the last five years.

Yet another method of evaluating airports is to look at passenger and/or cargo traffic. That means looking at how many passengers or how much cargo gets transported through airports. The Airports Council International (ACI) keeps track of this. Figure 5.2 shows the top-ten airports in terms of passenger traffic in 2000 and 2013 (the last year available), while Table 5.2 shows the top-30 airports.

Figure 5.2 illustrates that the top-ten busiest airports in terms of passenger traffic has remained largely stable over the last 14 years. Seven of the ten airports have consistently been ranked in the top ten. These airports are: Atlanta, London (Heathrow), Tokyo (Haneda), Chicago, Los Angeles, Paris (Charles de Gaulle) and Dallas-Fort Worth. Atlanta has consistently ranked first in all of these years.

Table 5.1 Best airports in the world

	2009	*2010*	*2011*	*2012*	*2013*	*2014*
1	Seoul	Singapore	Hong Kong	Seoul	Singapore	Singapore
2	Hong Kong	Seoul	Singapore	Singapore	Seoul	Seoul
3	Singapore	Hong Kong	Seoul	Hong Kong	Amsterdam	Munich
4	Zurich	Munich	Munich	Amsterdam	Hong Kong	Hong Kong
5	Munich	Kuala Lumpur	Beijing	Beijing	Beijing	Amsterdam
6	Osaka	Zurich	Amsterdam	Munich	Munich	Tokyo
7	Kuala Lumpur	Amsterdam	Zurich	Zurich	Zurich	Beijing
8	Amsterdam	Beijing	Auckland	Kuala Lumpur	Vancouver	Zurich
9	Nagoya	Auckland	Kuala Lumpur	Vancouver	Tokyo	Vancouver
10	Auckland	Bangkok	Copenhagen	Nagoya	London	London

Source: based on www.worldairportawards.com.

Figure 5.2 The world's ten busiest airports by passenger traffic (source: based on ACI).

Notes

● Top-ten airport in 2000 and 2013.
▲ Top-ten airport in 2000 but not in 2013.
■ Top-ten airport in 2013 but not in 2000.

Three airports appeared in the top ten in 2000 but have since disappeared. These three airports have been among the top-ten busiest airports for many of the years but have experienced a relative decline compared to the other top-ten airports. They are Frankfurt (ranked 7th in 2000 and 12th in 2013), Amsterdam (ranked 10th in 2000 and 14th in 2013) and San Francisco (ranked 9th in 2000 and 22nd in 2013).

There were also three airports that were not among the top ten in 2000 but they appear in the top ten in 2013. These three airports were not included in the top 30 for several years and all have experienced high growth. The Beijing airport appeared first in the top 30 in 2002 and is currently ranked 2nd. It is remarkable that in terms of passenger traffic, the Beijing airport has grown by more than 200 per cent since 2002; this compares with less than 25 per cent growth for Atlanta in the same time period. The Dubai airport first appeared in the top 30 in 2007 and is currently ranked 7th. In terms of number of passengers, Dubai grew by almost 95 per cent between 2007 and 2013, compared to less than 6 per cent for Atlanta in the same time period. The Jakarta airport first appeared in the top 30 in 2009 and is currently ranked 10th. The Jakarta airport grew by a little over 60 per cent between 2009 and 2013 compared to a little over 7 per cent for Atlanta in the same period. This illustrates the high growth of travel in the developing economies. Many of these countries are still faced with relatively low income levels; with continuous improvements travel is likely to increase even more. Table 5.3 illustrates this as well, and demonstrates the

Table 5.2 Top-30 world's busiest airports by passenger traffic

	2000			*2013*		
	Airport/city	*Country*	*Passengers*	*Airport/city*	*Country*	*Passengers*
1	ATL, Atlanta	USA	80,162,407	ATL, Atlanta	USA	94,430,785
2	ORD, Chicago	USA	72,144,244	PEK, Beijing	China	83,712,355
3	LAX, Los Angeles	USA	66,424,767	LHR, London	UK	72,368,030
4	LHR, London	UK	64,606,826	HND, Tokyo	Japan	68,906,636
5	DFW, Dallas	USA	60,687,122	ORD, Chicago	USA	66,883,271
6	HND, Tokyo	Japan	56,402,206	LAX, Los Angeles	USA	66,702,252
7	FRA, Frankfurt	Germany	49,360,630	DXB, Dubai	UAE	66,431,533
8	CDG, Paris	France	48,246,137	CDG, Paris	France	62,052,917
9	SFO, San Francisco	USA	41,040,995	DFW, Dallas	USA	60,436,266
10	AMS, Amsterdam	Netherlands	39,606,925	CGK, Jakarta	Indonesia	59,701,543
11	DEN, Denver	USA	38,751,687	HKG, Hong Kong	China	59,609,414
12	LAS, Las Vegas	USA	36,865,866	FRA, Frankfurt	Germany	58,036,948
13	MSP, Minneapolis/Saint Paul	USA	36,751,632	SIN, Singapore	Singapore	53,726,087
14	GMP, Seoul	South Korea	36,727,124	AMS, Amsterdam	Netherlands	52,569,250
15	PHX, Phoenix	USA	36,040,469	DEN, Denver	USA	52,556,359
16	DTW, Detroit	USA	35,535,080	CAN, Guangzhou	China	52,450,262
17	IAH, Houston	USA	35,251,372	BKK, Bangkok	Thailand	51,363,451
18	EWR, Newark	USA	34,188,468	IST, Istanbul	Turkey	51,172,626
19	MIA, Miami	USA	33,621,273	JFK, New York	USA	50,413,204
20	MAD, Madrid	Spain	32,893,190	KUL, Kuala Lumpur	Malaysia	47,498,157
21	JFK, New York	USA	32,856,220	PVG, Shanghai	China	47,189,849
22	HKG, Hong Kong	China	32,752,359	SFO, San Francisco	USA	44,944,201
23	LGW, London	UK	32,065,685	CLT, Charlotte	USA	43,456,310
24	MCO, Orlando	USA	30,823,509	LAS, Las Vegas	USA	41,856,787
25	STL, Saint Louis	USA	30,561,387	ICN, Seoul	South Korea	41,679,758
26	BKK, Bangkok	Thailand	29,616,432	MIA, Miami	USA	40,563,071
27	YYZ, Toronto	Canada	28,930,036	PHX, Phoenix	USA	40,318,451
28	SIN, Singapore	Singapore	28,618,200	IAH, Houston	USA	39,865,325
29	SEA, Seattle	USA	28,408,553	MAD, Madrid	Spain	39,729,027
30	BOS, Boston	USA	27,412,926	MUC, Munich	Germany	38,672,644

Source: based on ACI.

Table 5.3 Airports by region

Region	*Number of airports in 2010*	*Number of airports in 2013*
North America	19 (63.33%)	12 (40.00%)
Asia	5 (16.67%)	10 (33.33%)
Europe	6 (20.00%)	7 (23.33%)
Central America	0	0
South America	0	0
'Arab nations'	0	1 (3.33%)
Australia-Oceania	0	0

Source: based on ACI.

decline in the top 30 of North American airports and the rise of the Asian airports.

Other notable airports with high growth are Guangzhou in China (first entered the top 30 in 2010 and ranked 16th in 2013, with growth of almost 30 per cent in those years), Istanbul in Turkey (first entered top 30 in 2011 and ranked 18th in 2013, with growth of over 35 per cent during those years), Kuala Lumpur in Malaysia (first entered the top 30 in 2011 and ranked 20th in 2013, with growth of over 25 per cent during those years). Seoul (ranked 25th in 2013)[2] and Sao Paulo (ranked 33rd in 2013) also show high growth. In contrast to this, airports that have shown a relatively high decline are Newark in the United States (ranked 18th in 2000 and 39th in 2013, with 2 per cent growth during that time period), Minneapolis/St. Paul in the United States (ranked 13th in 2000 and 42nd in 2013, with more than 7 per cent decline in the number of passengers during that time period) and Detroit in the United States (ranked 16th in 2000 and 45th in 2013, with an almost 9 per cent decline in passenger traffic during that time period).

With the perusal of some national classifications of airports and aircraft 'performance' and size, it is opportune to examine how airports have been conceived by governments as infrastructure essential to furthering the national economy.

Airports as instruments of economic growth

Of late there has arisen a kind of airport markedly different from anything considered under the standard classifications. In short, the airport is seen as the centre of a newly planned city and, what is more, is held to be the source of that community's economic well-being. An example is the Ciudad Real Airport, located roughly 200 km south of Madrid. This airport was completed and began operation in 2008. Completion of the Ciudad Real Airport was expected to create 6,000 jobs and a boom for the local economy (Harter, 2012). Ciudad Real was created with the intention of acting as a 'secondary gateway' to both supplement Madrid's Barajas International Airport and to attract travellers to Ciudad Real. The facilities were quite impressive, with a 4.2 km runway and other capabilities to support the Airbus 380 (Harter, 2012). Unfortunately, the airport failed to live up to its lofty expectations. Ciudad Real lacks appeal relative to other Spanish destinations, as the city is more of a working town than a tourist destination. With the lack of demand for leisure travel and the economic crisis which peaked in 2008, the year the airport was opened, the airport failed to meet the demand necessary for sustainment. As of December 2013, the airport is vacant and under auction (Busch, 2013). The airport was privately owned, but had the political backing necessary to secure loans from Spain's local savings banks, of which local politicians sat on the boards. Many of those same banks have now had to merge or be taken over as a result of the Ciudad Real failure (Harter, 2012). The actual cost of the project is a point of contention, with estimates ranging from €356 million to over €1.5 billion (Busch, 2013).

In this economic development context, the prime role of an airport is seen in a very different light from that of being merely the infrastructure servicing aviation; rather, it is regarded as the engine of growth for an entire economy and is planned as such from the outset. The resultant composite of airport and city is styled an 'aerotropolis'. Intricately bound up with the unique advantage of air transport – its ability to 'shrink' time-distance – the composite entity is especially valued by businesses that depend on time-sensitive freight of high value (Rodrique, 1999). These businesses have prospered in the era of globalization, and their instrument, the 'aerotropolis', is seen as both a cause and a consequence of the trade that they have engendered. The superior growth of such a composite entity, by definition exceeding the growth prospects of other planned entities, is largely an article of faith, based on the fortuitous combination of circumstance working to the advantage of a select number of airports that have concentrated on handling air cargo. The expectation is that planned development of airports of this kind will ensure that growth stimuli will flow in the manner associated with these celebrated cases. While this supposition smacks of 'wishful thinking', it is typical of planning initiatives that border on offering panacea-like solutions.

Airport growth poles

A cautionary tale is provided by Mirabel, the first planned growth pole to rest on new-airport foundations and to reach completion of sorts. Its story shares similarities with the Ciudad Real airport and illustrates very well the sequence of raised expectations followed by dashed hopes. Based on wildly optimistic traffic-growth projections, Mirabel was initiated in 1970 with the objective of providing a new airport for Montréal while, at the same time, generating economic stimulus into a corner of Québec province that was in dire need of development. A project jointly championed by the Canadian federal government (under the aegis of its Department of Regional Economic Expansion) and the Québec provincial planners, the Mirabel site was located 55 km from central Montréal. It would assume the trappings of an international gateway from the outset, totally replacing the existing Dorval airport, which was deemed unsuitable for expansion owing to its suburban position, a mere 20 km from downtown Montréal. Dorval was relegated to ministering to domestic passengers only. At the time of its opening in 1975, Mirabel boasted the largest area of any airport in the world, some 39,660 ha, the majority of which was zoned for industrial sectors (a record held until the rise of Riyadh's King Khalid International in 1982). To safeguard its success, all international flights bound to and from Montréal were redirected to Mirabel, much to the chagrin of Dorval and its loyal customer base. This resistance of passengers to the inconvenience of travelling to the new airport by inadequate ground links was compounded by the disaffection of airlines forced to transfer their international passengers to Mirabel flights while retaining domestic services in Dorval. Such popular dissatisfaction with the planners' efforts was matched by the patent failure of Mirabel to foster a dynamic industrial complex around it (Higgins, 1992: 201–206). Only Bombardier Aerospace and Bell Helicopter Textron were willing to serve as anchor tenants, using airport premises to assemble regional jets and commercial helicopters, respectively. Bowing to the inevitable, the planners acknowledged that their grand design had failed and began to retrench. Fully 32,780 ha of airport land, unused for airport expansion and industrial development alike, were released to the previous landowners. By the same token, international flights were no longer compelled to operate from Mirabel (in 1997) and the airlines responded with alacrity, returning all their scheduled services to Dorval. Mirabel today is just a pale shadow of its glory days, surviving on charter flights, air-cargo movements and general-aviation activities. Its growth-pole ambitions, equally thwarted, continue in reduced form as an aerospace complex.

The precedents for the aerotropolis stem from the aforementioned growth-pole concept. This is a theoretical notion and practical instrument that was introduced by Perroux in the 1950s and gained currency in planning circles in the 1960s and 1970s (Christofakis and Papadaskalopoulos, 2011). Envisaged as a collection of activities that benefited both from a common location (the outcome of external economies) and from backward and forward linkages to one another, the planners saw these 'complexes' as instruments for restructuring regional economies. In particular, their supposed versatility was applauded, for they were judged capable of not only fomenting growth in the communities hosting them, but in the wider region as well. They contrived, in a word, to provide an instrument that proved mutually beneficial, uniting urban and rural interests with the promise of planned development (Todd, 1974). Inspiring the proponents of planned growth poles, who credited the emergence and phased maturity of a cluster to deliberate inducements provided by government, was the vivid example of spontaneous growth poles; that is to say, those that market forces had spawned naturally in locations abounding in fecund conditions.

The first growth pole expressly tied to aviation was thrown up in the deliberations for a future London airport in the late 1960s. The planners for that grand project, ultimately stillborn owing to what they saw as an unholy alliance between nascent environmentalists and NIMBY campaigners, could point to the existing airport at Heathrow and argue that the benefits it showered on the surrounding region were bound to be replicated at the new site (Great Britain, 1971;

Howard, 1974: 542–569). Guided by the principles of cost–benefit analysis, the planners nominated a site at Cublington on the grounds that it scored best of the four sites under consideration. Much to their dismay, however, the planners were soon forced to defend their methodology. Among a myriad of defects exposed by the critics was its obsession with economic criteria at the expense of environmental concerns, not to mention its inability to satisfactorily rank social issues (Pearce, 1998; Self, 1970; Thompson, 1972). The critics then turned their attention to the weaknesses inherent in growth-pole theory. On the one hand, they readily conceded that airports were substantial 'growth magnets' in their own right, responsible for stimulating sizeable labour markets. After all, Heathrow had a workforce in 1969 amounting to 46,000, which made it one of the greatest concentrations of workers in the country. Jobs associated with directly linked aviation activities were plentiful and well remunerated by the standards of the local labour market. These activities were then, and continue to be, varied in kind but broadly conforming to three occupation groups (Wells, 1984). The first kind are the services indispensable to airline operations, especially their management, the catering, the fuelling of aircraft and the maintenance of them in the hangars. Beyond the airline/passenger interface is a second legion of support services needed to conduct air-freight operations. Chief among these are freight forwarders, agents, storage firms and the government personnel (customs and security) inevitably in attendance. Finally, overseeing them all is the airport authority, complete with its own specialist labour. These managers, technicians and workers are preoccupied with ensuring that the airport is operating safely and efficiently. All told, the multiplier effect imputed to airports credits them – as a crude generalization – with generating 1,000 airport jobs and 200 off-airport jobs for every million passengers that passes through their terminals. Under the most optimistic scenario, those 1,000 airport jobs are likely to give rise to an additional 600 indirect and induced jobs in the community at large (Hilling, 1996: 126–127).

On the other hand, the critics were much more sceptical of an airport's ability to generate jobs in activities only indirectly connected with aviation – the litmus test that would affirm or deny growth-pole stimuli. These indirect activities were businesses one and two steps removed from those directly concerned with aviation. The evidence for their existence in the vicinity of airports was less than convincing, to say nothing of their formation as a result of access to an airport. Again, the critics turned to Heathrow to vindicate their doubts and misgivings. In this instance, Heathrow's long-standing record of encouraging business creation was subjected to close inspection. By one reckoning (Hoare, 1974), this was unimpressive; indeed, the author went so far as to claim that indirect activities – particularly in the manufacturing sector – were downright disconcerted by proximity to the airport. The firms in question regarded themselves as the victims of externalities, especially those deleterious effects arising from inflexibilities in the job market. Put succinctly, they felt disadvantaged in having to compete with the airport for quality employees in a tight labour market and, to add insult to injury, being compelled to pay high wages in order to procure them.

Compounding the disadvantage of airport proximity was the prevalence of that other neighbourhood effect, noise pollution. This was perceived by firms, both those engaged in manufacturing and those undertaking services, as being generally detrimental to their productivity, deterring all but the most dependent on aviation from locating close to the airport boundary. Curiously – and ironically in the light of subsequent airport experience – the adverse effect of congestion in ground transportation was not identified by the firms as a major hindrance to locations adjoining Heathrow. On balance, it appeared that a location in the shadow of the airport was desirable only for a limited range of firms. Specifically, they fell into three categories: those making frequent use of air transport; those belonging to foreign firms appreciative of the glamour of a location close to a well-known international airport; and those having contracts with enterprises directly involved in airport operations.

These matters rested for the next 40 years, leaving unresolved the issue of a new 'greenfield' London airport. In the meantime, the problems besetting Heathrow were allowed to accumulate, assuming grave proportions. Forced to consider growth within the bounds of the existing site, the airport authority plans on incremental expansion centred round a third runway. Reminiscent of old times, the battle lines were immediately drawn up between NIMBY lobbyists and environmentalist opponents on the one side and supporters of airport growth in the national interest on the other. Significantly, the growth-pole rationale has been totally eclipsed in the contemporary stand-off. However, that situation is far from the case elsewhere, for, rather than disappear, the planned growth pole has been reborn in different guise – that of the aerotropolis, itself an outgrowth of the popularity of 'cluster' thinking.

Clusters and the aerotropolis

Truth to say, the new version, commonly styled the 'cluster' notion, bears only a superficial resemblance to the old growth-pole theory. To be sure, it too rests on spatial external economies (also known as agglomeration economies) to account for the emergence of like activities in the same locations. Yet, these co-located activities exist less as the products of forward and backward links from a key actor and more as the beneficiaries of a business climate compatible with their interests. Above all, the components of the cluster remain in vigorous competition with each other (rather after the fashion of Japanese keiretsu). It is this keen competitiveness that lies at the heart of their survival and prosperity. A natural rider of this state of affairs is that only the more successful clusters will undergo transformation into specialized zones fully capable of competing in global markets (Porter, 1990; 2000). The emphasis on international trade, strongly reminiscent of the classical notion of comparative advantage, elevated the 'cluster' notion to concerns far beyond the somewhat parochial regional-development remedial action that had prompted growth-pole theory. 'Cluster' notions, in contrast, could be used, no less, as an indicator of any country's standing in the global-competitiveness stakes. It has to be said, though, that the detection of 'clusters' is no more than the identification of empirical regularities, and a fairly crude one at that.

It is against this backdrop of renewed enthusiasm for identifying – and then promoting – aggregations of activities prospering from a common location that the case for the aerotropolis arose. Like 'cluster' thinking in general, it poses no threat to conventional ideas of international competitiveness in a globalized economy. Indeed, its lack of a rigorous theoretical structure only tells in its favour. Aerotropolises emerge when certain locations, which lend themselves to air-cargo operations, become the kernels of clusters of businesses that join forces with the airports nurturing them (Kasarda and Lindsay, 2011). While the local circumstances impacting such airports vary enormously, they all share one or two features. Thanks to either the strategic location of the airport or to the predilection of its owners to devote it at all costs to air freight – or preferably to both – each airport contrives to grow by leaps and bounds in this specialized role. All obstacles encountered in the airport's progress are effectively overcome, implying that single-minded airport management and appropriate political backing is promptly forthcoming. The instances where this situation first became apparent were found in the United States. Not for nothing, then, is the aerotropolis known as an American concept that can only really be replicated beyond American shores in those countries enjoying free trade and extolling the virtues of dynamic capitalism. In a similar manner to the old growth-pole concept, examples of 'spontaneous aerotropolises' are held up to stimulate interest in 'planned aerotropolises' in other jurisdictions.

The two usually cited as leading exponents of the spontaneous kind are Memphis and Louisville. Their rise to fame is inextricably linked with the growth of air-cargo and particularly overnight parcel services. More specifically, it is tied in with the emergence of air-freight operators specialized in carrying it. The decision makers charged with running the two airports were prescient in seeing the opening that air freight presented and willing to cooperate unstintingly with the expansionist ambitions of the carriers. In Louisville's instance, the airport managers succeeded in enticing UPS, which concluded in 1980 that the site would be ideal as its hub operation. In this respect it was vying with Memphis, an airport that had blazed the trail in 1973 by attracting Federal Express (now FedEx). Not to be outdone, Memphis was awarded 'superhub' status by its key tenant in 1985. Each airport, clearly aping one another, depended on the business strategies of the freight firm acting as its dominant client.

As well as exhibiting similar competitive traits, the two rival airports had other things in common. Geographically, they were both found at inland locations; thus avoiding the congestion and weather-related problems that tended to characterize airports located in coastal areas. Furthermore, being more centrally positioned in the continental land mass, they occupied locations convenient for dispatching flights timed to arrive at their destinations early in the working day (a situation that worked most advantageously for Memphis). These destinations were not only scattered throughout the United States, but accessed leading cities elsewhere. FedEx began services from Memphis to Europe (Cologne, London and Paris), the Middle East (Dubai), Northeast Asia (Seoul and Tokyo) and South America (Campinas in Brazil). In emulation, UPS used its Louisville 'Worldport' as the origin of flights to Africa (Casablanca) and to foreign destinations in the Americas (Mexico City and the Canadian pair of Montréal-Mirabel and Toronto).

Both had been created by the military in the Second World War and retained a residual military presence (Air National Guard) ever afterwards. Similarly, they both pursued commercial aviation in the years that followed, encouraging passenger services. They eventually qualified as 'medium hubs' in the NPIAS classification. While respectable (currently amounting to over three million departing passengers at each airport), the growth in passenger traffic fell short of airport capacity and therein was a source of frustration to airport managers. Granted that efforts to boost passenger volumes encountered obstacles, the managers turned their attention to the air-freight alternative. In short, they were willing to offer generous inducements to appropriate firms. Emblematic of that willingness was Louisville's construction of two new parallel runways (the longest reaching 3,620 m) in order to appease UPS. The firm was threatening to quit the airport because of its wartime runway pattern, singularly unsuitable for intensive jetliner operations. With the modern runway layout, the airport retained the goodwill of UPS and, along with it, safeguarded the 21,000 jobs that the firm brought to the city. Looked at in this light, the decision of the airport authority, which incurred considerable costs to implement, has been judged to be money well spent (Kasarda and Lindsay, 2011: 86–87). With that quantity of direct employment, the other spin-offs of an aerotropolis are virtually guaranteed. Thus the airport literally transforms its urban host, spawning clusters of logistics parks, distribution centres, office campuses and industrial zones that all indirectly depend on the core air-freighting business. That is not all, for the bulk of the city's services – ranging from retail establishments to entertainment outlets – owe their well-being to the continuing success of the airport and its chief user.

However, this ultimate reliance on air freight in general and a single prime user in particular is both a boon and a potential threat, risking the community's future. Remove the chief user and the consequences for the community are dire, as the example of Wilmington attests (Kasarda and Lindsay, 2011: 87). The cornerstone of that Ohio airport was Airborne Express, another leading air-cargo carrier. In 1979 Airborne Express bought the former air base with the intention of completely transforming it into an air-cargo hub. Having obtained the site for a fraction of its value, the firm then invested a sizeable sum into making it into a well-appointed and efficient operation. However, in 2003 Airborne Express was acquired by DHL, a rival express parcels enterprise, and soon after matters began to go awry. Compelled to retrench, DHL elected to abandon its Wilmington hub in 2008. At one fell swoop, 8,000 jobs at the airport were declared redundant, devastating the neighbouring community.

Despite such pitfalls – and the increasing opposition of the environmental movement to carriage of cargo by air – some jurisdictions remain undismayed and heartily embrace the idea of founding new cities on the coat-tails of new airports. India, for example, has officially adopted the aerotropolis concept, nominating Durgapur as its pioneering venture. The allure of a prospective 90,000 jobs, together with the backing of Singapore Airport, proved highly persuasive. However, it is especially in the booming economies of East Asia where the 'planned aerotropolis' has been taken up with gusto. South Korea and Taiwan, both keen to have their designated airports serving as offshore gateways into China, have implemented plans that aim to invest them with all the trappings associated with the concept. The chosen recipients are Incheon International and Taiwan Taoyuan International airports. Not known for settling for half measures, the Korean authorities first built a large airport (completed in 2001) on a reclaimed island and then proceeded to set up a huge development zone (the Incheon Free Economic Zone) on the adjoining coastal mud-flats. An integral part of that development was a brand-new city, New Songdo, envisaged as environmentally friendly in the extreme and linked directly to the airport by an 11 km highway bridge. The first phase of New Songdo, costing more than $10 billion, was opened in 2009. Incheon airport, in the meantime, became a hub for Korean Air Lines (which claimed to be the world's largest carrier of air cargo) on the strength of its abundant space readily available for unlimited expansion. All the benefits of airport-related and indirect activities were expected to flow in the next decade as a matter of course, fuelled by more than $40 billion of investment.

In Taiwan's case the incentive for appointing Taoyuan airport as an aerotropolis was different; rather than buttress the natural growth stimuli that arose from a new airport's establishment, the situation for Taoyuan (an airport dating from 1979) was of slowing growth: indeed, growth had eluded it in recent years. It had given ground to Beijing Capital, Tokyo Haneda and Hong Kong International in the critical gateway stakes, and had even lost out to the much smaller (but much more conveniently located) Taipei Songshan airport. Nor was its air-freight side performing as hoped, since its air-cargo appendage was failing dismally to spark economic development. Determined to revitalize airport-related growth, the local county government in conjunction with the airport authority embarked on a 'planned aerotropolis', breath-taking in scope. In total, the planned area consists of 4,115 ha, including the airport itself, with zones dedicated to direct and indirect activities, high-technology clusters and new urban settlements (Francis, 2012: 44). The $13 billion project, of which a start was made in 2008, is predicted to generate 80,000 jobs, split evenly between airport-related employment and other activities.

China, while expressing neither acquiescence nor dissent with these offshore gateways, has made it abundantly clear that it fully intends to develop its enormous aviation potential in its own right. Passenger traffic alone is expected to grow at an average annual rate of 12.2 per cent until 2020. The infrastructure necessary to support this potential is of vast proportions, embodied in more than 200 new or enlarged airports. There is scope within this massive initiative to contemplate laying down airport infrastructure that is consistent with urban-economic development, and the opportunity to develop 'airport cities' has been seized upon in some circles, generally influential at the provincial level. However, these airports-cum-airport cities are not, strictly speaking, aerotropolises. They differ fundamentally in eschewing market forces as determinants, turning instead to 'scientific development', which is how the planners set their growth targets to coincide with the official design for distributing well-being (Perrett, 2012: 31). The principal examples of these 'airport cities' are to be found at regional hubs (Chengdu, Chongqing and Xian) and not at the main gateways of Beijing Capital, Shanghai Pudong and Guangzhou Baiyuan. Evidently, Chinese central government planners set a high value on the role of 'airport cities' in promoting the economic development of some interior provinces, but it is striking that their belief in the effectiveness of such growth stimuli does not extend to the front-ranking provinces. To be sure, the impending airport at Beijing Daxing, destined to be the world's biggest, is reputedly to include an affiliated 'airport city', but it remains to be seen how this is regarded in official plans.

Notes

1 www.spokaneairports.net/Business/2013_Budget.pdf.

2 Seoul, as well as several other airports, may not be representative in this regard. This is because in these instances an existing airport has been replaced by a newer airport but obviously pre-existing passenger traffic already existed for the older airport. For Seoul this involved the replacement of the Gimpo (or also Kimpo) international airport with the Incheon international airport. Another example is Bangkok, where the Suvarnabhumi airport took on much of the traffic previously going to the Don Mueang international airport.

References

Airports Council International (2009) *Policies and Recommended Practices Handbook 2009*, Geneva: Airports Council International.

Almeida, C.R. de (2011) 'Low cost airlines, airport and tourism: The case of Faro Airport', *ERSA Conference Papers*, European Regional Science Association.

Becker, J. (2012) '14 airport amenities that will make you long for a layover', CNN, 19 June Retrieved from: www.cnn.com/2012/06/18/travel/outstanding-airport-amenities, 16 September 2014.

Blankenship, E.G. (1974) *The Airport: Architecture, Urban Integration, Ecological Problems*, London: Pall Mall Press.

Briggs, J. (2012) 'How airports make money' presented at *Federal Aviation Administration Northwest Mountain Region Airports Conference*, 16–18 April, Seattle.

Busch, S. (2013) 'Spanish "ghost airport" goes on the block', CNN. Retrieved from www.cnn.com/2013/12/10/travel/spanish-ghost-airport, 16 September 2014.

Button, K.J. (1982) *Transport Economics*, London: Heinemann Educational.

Canadian Institute of Traffic and Transportation. (2008) *Transportation Distribution and Logistics: A Canadian Perspective, vol 1: Transportation Systems*, Toronto: CITT.

Christofakis, M. and Papadaskalopoulos, A. (2011) 'The growth poles strategy in regional planning: the recent experience of Greece', *Theoretical and Empirical Researches in Urban Management*, Vol. 6, No. 2, pp. 5–20.

Creager, S.E. (1983), 'Airline deregulation and airport regulation', *The Yale Law Journal*, Vol. 93, No. 2, pp. 319–339.

Doganis, R. (1992) *The Airport Business*, London: Routledge.

Fiorino, F. (2004) 'The new reality', *Aviation Week & Space Technology*, Vol. 160 (26 April), pp. 46–47.

Forsyth, P. (2005) 'Airport infrastructure for the Airbus A380: cost recovery and pricing', *Journal of Transport Economics and Policy*, Vol. 39, No. 3, pp. 341–362.

Foster, J.A. (1974) 'The elements of planning necessary for the development of a major civil airport', in Howard, G.P. (ed.) *Airport Economic Planning*, Cambridge, MA: MIT Press.

Francis, L. (2012) 'Heart of Asia: Taiwan renews its push to be an Asia-Pacific hub', *Aviation Week & Space Technology*, Vol. 174 (9 April), pp. 43–44.

Great Britain. (1971) *Commission on the Third London Airport (Roskill Commission), Report, vol 1 and 2*, HMSO: London.

Harter, P. (2012) 'The white elephants that dragged Spain into the red', *BBC News Magazine*, 26 July. Retrieved from: www.bbc.com/news/magazine-18855961, 16 September 2014.

Higgins, B. (1992) *All the Difference: A Development Economist's Quest*, Montréal: McGill-Queen's University Press.

Hilling, D. (1996) *Transport and Developing Countries*, London: Routledge.

Hoare, A.G. (1974) 'International airports as growth centres: a case study of Heathrow Airport', *Transactions Institute of British Geographers* Vol. 63, pp. 75–96.

Horonjeff, R. and McKelvey, F.X. (1994) *Planning and Design of Airports*, 4th edn, New York: McGraw-Hill.

Howard, G.P. (ed.) (1974) *Airport Economic Planning*, Cambridge, MA: MIT Press.

Johnston, B. (2011) 'Where trains and planes meet', *Trains*, Vol. 71 (June), pp. 18–19.

Kasarda, J.D. and Lindsay, G. (2011) *Aerotropolis: The Way We'll Live Next*, Toronto: Viking Canada.

Morrison, S.A. (1982) 'The structure of landing fees at uncongested airports', *Journal of Transport Economics and Policy*, Vol. 16, No. 2, pp. 151–159.

Pearce, D.W. (1998) 'Cost–benefit analysis and environmental policy', *Oxford Review of Economic Policy*, Vol. 14, pp. 84–100.

Perrett, B. (2011) 'Gathering storm: Chinese airlines are facing the greatest assault from high-speed rail in history', *Aviation Week & Space Technology*, Vol. 173 (7–14 March), pp. 76–77.

Perrett, B. (2012) 'Now hear this: Beijing pushes for accelerated reforms for civil aviation, notably in airspace management', *Aviation Week & Space Technology*, Vol. 174 (23 July), pp. 30–31.

Porter, M.E. (1990) *The Competitive Advantage of Nations*, New York: Free Press.

Porter, M.E. (2000) 'Location, competition and economic development: local clusters in a global economy', *Economic Development Quarterly*, Vol. 14, pp. 15–34.

Productivity Commission, Australia (2011) 'Economic regulation of airport services', draft inquiry report of the Productivity Commission, Canberra, August 2011.

Rodrique, J.-P. (1999) 'Globalization and the synchronization of transport terminals', *Journal of Transport Geography*, Vol. 7, pp. 255–261.

Sealy, K.R. (1957) *The Geography of Air Transport*, London: Hutchinson.

Self, P. (1970) '"Nonsense on stilts": cost–benefit analysis and the Roskill Commission', *The Political Quarterly* 41, 249–260.

Sparaco, P. (2009) 'Runways are forever', *Aviation Week & Space Technology*, Vol. 170 (2 February), p. 46.

Thompson, F.P. (1972) 'Statistics and the environment: the Third London Airport study', *Journal of the Royal Statistical Society D* 21, 19–30.

Todd, D. (1974) 'The development pole concept in regional analysis', *Environment and Planning A* Vol. 6, pp. 291–306.

Unnikrishnan, M. and Wilson, B. (2009) 'On hold: credit forces airports to place some projects on back burner', *Aviation Week & Space Technology*, Vol. 169 (15 December), pp. 25–26.

von Bullion, C. (2013) 'Verloren in der Entrauchungsmatrix', *Süddeutsche Zeitung*, 23 October.

Wells, A.J. (1984) *Air Transportation*, Belmont, CA: Wadsworth.

6 Aircraft maintenance, repair and overhaul

Andrew Potter, Hamad Al-kaabi and Mohamed Naim

Introduction

In achieving reliable and safe operations, maintenance, repair and overhaul (MRO) activities are critical for airlines. The main objective of MRO is to provide safe and serviceable aircraft while maintaining minimum costs, maximum quality and the best lead-time (Knotts, 1999). While maintenance failures only account for a very small number of serious accidents, failures can potentially put an aircraft at risk. It is this risk that is behind the European Union having a 'blacklist' of airlines that cannot operate in European airspace due to maintenance concerns. According to IATA (2013), maintenance costs represent around 12 per cent of total annual operating costs for airlines, making it the third greatest cost centre behind fuel and the cost of operations. Taking a longer-term perspective, Spafford *et al.* (2012) calculate that maintenance represents 27 per cent of lifecycle costs over ten years of ownership, and 38 per cent of lifecycle costs over 20 years. This increased proportion reflects the increased maintenance requirements of aircraft as they get older.

In terms of quality and lead time, this can be measured in terms of the extent to which technical delays impact upon an airline's schedule. At a macro level, the Association of European Airlines (2012) highlights that, for European airlines, technical delays disrupted around 2.6 per cent of all departures. They are the most time consuming cause of delay, averaging 42.1 minutes. Focusing purely upon delayed flights, Table 6.1 presents data from an airline on the root causes of delays to their flights over a 12-month period. What can clearly be seen is that technical delays are the cause of over 20 per cent of disruptions to flight schedules, which is comparable to operational factors. However, when considering the percentage of delay minutes, it can be seen that this increases to almost 40 per cent and is significantly more than the other causes identified.

Economic forces accompanied by fluctuating passenger demand have forced many carriers to evaluate their business models to ensure that MRO operations continue to meet the three goals outlined above. In doing so, the trend towards outsourcing has been increasing. Globally, Marcontell (2013) estimates that the percentage of outsourcing has risen from about 25 per cent to around 70 per cent of maintenance activities between the mid-1990s and 2012. For US-based airlines the percentage of expenditure with outsourced providers has increased from 20 per

Table 6.1 Impact of delay types, frequency of events and time

Type of delay	*Per cent of delay events*	*Per cent of delay minutes*
Technical	22.3	39.2
Operations	20.5	17.3
Air traffic control	16.7	11.7
Airport and authorities	11.3	6.3
Passengers and baggage	10.9	6.0
Weather	8.0	12.1
Ramp handling	7.5	4.2
Damage to aircraft	1.2	1.7
Equipment failure	1.1	0.9
Cargo and mail	0.1	0.1
Miscellaneous	0.2	0.5
Unallocated	0.1	0.1

Source: based on data from Al-kaabi, 2006.

cent in 1990 to 44 per cent in 2011 (Tang and Elias, 2012). In particular, many airlines have outsourced non-core, labour-intensive activities (such as base maintenance) and focused on providing fewer value-added MRO activities themselves. This has led to the growth of major independent MRO providers, as indicated in Table 6.2, which shows the largest MRO providers globally. This is measured on the basis of airframe man-hours, which represents actual activity carried out on aircraft. Ownership refers to whether the company is part of an airline group or is not affiliated to a particular operator. Finally, the base country for the company is identified. However, these businesses have global networks of facilities and operations, as shown in Figure 6.1 for the case of Lufthansa Technik.

Historically, if an airline decided to outsource its MRO activities, this would be to a specialist independent provider such as those shown in Table 6.2. More recently, airframe and engine manufacturers have moved into this area as a way of improving their customer service. As an example, Boeing has developed its GoldCare solution, whereby airlines can outsource the maintenance and engineering activities to the airframe manufacturer. Initially offered on the Boeing 787 (Flint, 2006), this integrated role enables the airline to focus purely on operating the aircraft and leaves the manufacturer, who should understand the technical side of the aircraft better, to focus on making the asset available for use. Interestingly, the actual maintenance activities are delivered by a global network of MRO providers, including British Airways Engineering, Monarch Aircraft Engineering, FL Technics, Thales and Nayak Aircraft Services.

Given the degree to which the MRO activity is outsourced, this chapter first considers the different types of maintenance activity undertaken by airlines, before identifying the main business models adopted for MRO operations. It is important for an airline to identify which of these is the most appropriate for its operations, and therefore some key decision variables and performance metrics are identified. Finally, a number of key trends affecting the MRO industry into the future are described.

Table 6.2 Largest airframe MRO providers

Rank	*Company*	*Airframe man-hours*	*Ownership*	*Home country*
1	Singapore Technologies Aerospace	11.5 million	Independent	Singapore
2	Haeco Group	7.4 million	Independent	Hong Kong
3	AAR Corp.	4.6 million	Independent	United States
4	SIA Engineering Co.	4.2 million	Airline	Singapore
5	Lufthansa Technik	4.1 million	Airline	Germany
6	AFI KLM E&M	3.9 million	Airline	France/Netherlands
7	Timco Aviation Services	3.2 million	Independent	United States
8	Ameco Beijing	2.8 million	Airline	China
9	Mubadala Aerospace	2.5 million	Independent	United Arab Emirates
10	Iberia Maintenance	2.3 million	Airline	Spain

Source: adapted from Tegtmeier, 2013.

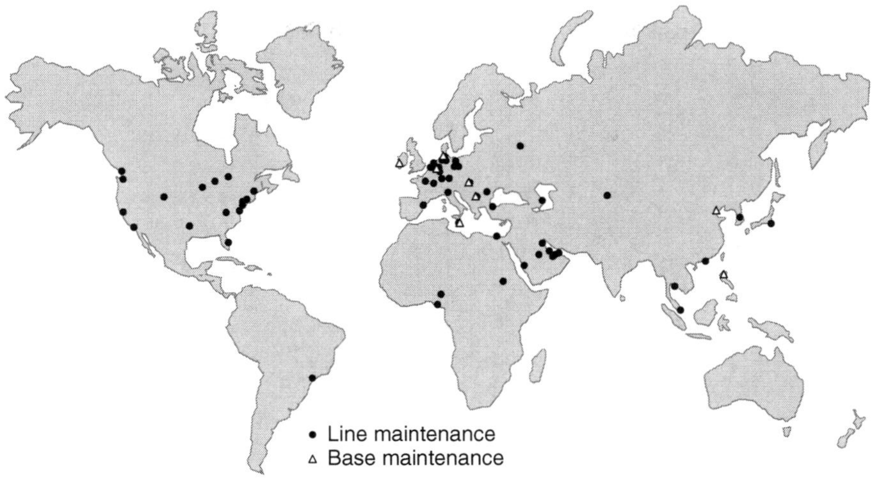

Figure 6.1 Line and base maintenance locations for Lufthansa Technik (source: authors – data from Lufthansa Technik, 2013).

Types of maintenance activity

Maintenance has evolved from being seen as a necessary and costly activity to a perception that it now offers the opportunity for organisations to make profits (Waeyenbergh and Pintelon, 2002; Alsyouf, 2007). Different maintenance concepts have been developed and are used in different industrial sectors, but generally maintenance may be categorised as either reactive, or unplanned, and proactive, or planned (Alabdulkarim *et al.*, 2014, Kothamasu *et al.*, 2006). Proactive maintenance may be further divided into preventative and predictive approaches. The former approach entails the establishment of a fixed schedule, based on either predetermined time intervals or related to the age of a particular component or system, with the aim of avoiding potential malfunctions. In a predictive approach the time schedule is not fixed, but based either on the condition of or reliability estimates for a component or system. This is also known as reliability centred maintenance (RCM).

RCM originated in the aircraft industry (Alabdulkarim *et al.*, 2014; Kothamasu *et al.*, 2006). In the process of gaining certification for the new Boeing 747 in the 1960s, it was foreseen that applying the maintenance strategy in existence at that time would never make the aircraft profitable (Smith, 1993). Reviewing the failure history database for commercial aircraft, United Airlines proved the misconception of 'Bath tub shape failure rate' to aircraft as it found that only 11 per cent of all non-structural components failures could be attributed to the ageing factor, while 89 per cent failed for reasons other than fatigue (Smith and Hinchcliffe, 2006). The four main features of RCM as described by Smith (1993) are: preserve function, identify failure modes that can defeat the function; prioritise function needs (via failure modes); and select only applicable effective preventive maintenance tasks. RCM applications have contributed to improving system availability and reliability, and reducing the amount of preventive and unplanned maintenance (Backlund and Akersten, 2003). Criticism of RCM includes its complexity and therefore price, although the cost involved in implementing RCM is justifiable in airlines (Waeyenbergh and Pintelon, 2002).

An alternative approach to RCM that has found favour in many industry sectors is total productive maintenance (TPM). The TPM concept was introduced in the United States in the early 1950s and exported to Japan where it further developed in the late 1960s (Tsang and Chan, 2000). TPM is defined as 'productive maintenance involving total participation' (Nakajima, 1988); in this, the TPM objectives are:

- to achieve maximum equipment effectiveness;
- to establish a thorough system of preventive maintenance (PM) for the equipment's entire life;
- implementation by various departments (engineering, operations and maintenance);
- involvement of every single employee, from top management to workers on the floor;
- promotion of preventative maintenance through motivation and management of autonomous small-group activities.

In measuring equipment effectiveness, TPM uses overall equipment effectiveness (OEE), which is the product of equipment availability, equipment efficiency and equipment quality. OEE measures system waste, which Nakajima (1988) traced to six losses: equipment failure; set-up and adjustment; speed losses; idling and minor stoppage, reduced speed; reduced yield at early stage of production; and quality defect and rework. Nakajima (1989) contend that for any TPM programme to be successful it should be based on the following six pillars:

1 increased equipment efficiency through implementing improvement activities;
2 reducing or eliminating the 'six big losses';
3 a system of autonomous maintenance to be performed by equipment operators;
4 planned maintenance system;
5 training courses in order to enhance equipment operators' skill levels;
6 a preventative maintenance system.

One of the criticisms of TPM is that it focuses primarily on equipment efficiency and ignores cost and profit (Waeyenbergh and Pintelon, 2002). Nevertheless, implementation of TPM has impacted organisations beyond improving equipment efficiency and effectiveness, since it has contributed to reducing manufacturing cycle time, inventory reduction and customers' complaints, which can be measured in monetary terms (Ahmed *et al.*, 2005).

Within aircraft MRO, there are four distinct activities that can be identified: base maintenance and modifications, engine maintenance, line maintenance, and spares and rotables. The former two types are proactive approaches, while the latter two may be classified as a combination of proactive and reactive. Table 6.3 provides an overview of how these costs have changed over time. While there has been an increase overall, it is noticeable that in the early 2000s costs fell and remained fairly stable. This period represented the start of the move towards outsourcing and an initial reduction in MRO costs. Table 6.3 also includes the total aircraft fleet at the end of each year. From this, it can be seen that this has consistently increased over the period, the result of this being that average expenditure per aircraft has fallen by over 10 per cent.

Line maintenance represents the routine aircraft inspections. This type of maintenance covers visual checks of major aircraft systems, rectifying discrepancies and monitoring aircraft systems performance. On a day-to-day basis, line maintenance involves a daily visual inspection as well as checking the maintenance log book for any issues or responding to failures while in service. This activity is also seeing a move towards preventative maintenance, whereby potential failures are being detected through on-board diagnostics, with the aircraft being replaced in service before the component actually fails.

Further, two types of maintenance inspections are carried out as part of line maintenance:

1 A-checks, which includes a general inspection of the aircraft, checking and servicing of oil, changing filters and lubrication. Depending upon factors such as aircraft type and usage, these checks occur every 3–6 weeks and take 1–2 days to carry out.
2 B-checks, where additional work is carried out to check the functioning of operating systems. The aircraft needs to be placed in a hanger and requires around 200 man hours of work over 1–3 days. The frequency of these checks is every 2–4 months.

Nowadays, more balanced maintenance programmes have been introduced whereby the activities from B-checks are spread across several A-checks. By doing this, the schedule of line maintenance checks are distributed evenly over time and take a similar duration each time. This helps airlines plan their operations more effectively.

By contrast, base maintenance includes more intensive maintenance checks, involving the dismantling of major aircraft components along with comprehensive inspections of the airframe. Again, there are two main maintenance inspections that take place as part of base maintenance – C-checks and D-checks. C-checks take place every 15–30 months, depending upon the type of aircraft and the airline's operations, and will generally last about 1–2 weeks and use around 6,000 man hours. The whole aircraft is inspected and serviced, with minor structural works and modifications required by the manufacturer undertaken. C-checks can be categorised as 'light' or 'heavy', depending upon the scale of work undertaken. A 'heavy' check is needed approximately every fourth C-check, although again balanced maintenance programmes are being introduced to spread the workload more evenly. Table 6.4 gives typical costs for these checks.

Table 6.3 Estimated global MRO expenditure (US$ billions) and global fleet size

Year	*MRO expenditure (US$ billions)*					*Global aircraft fleet*
	Line maintenance	*Base maintenance and modifications*	*Spares and rotables*	*Engine maintenance*	*Total*	
2001	9.2	14.1	7.4	11.5	42.2	15,271
2002	8.5	12.0	6.9	10.4	37.8	15,612
2003	8.2	10.7	6.7	10.5	36.1	16,168
2004	8.5	11.6	6.9	10.1	37.0	16,800
2005	8.9	11.5	7.2	10.7	38.3	17,330
2006	8.0	10.0	7.4	13.5	38.8	18,230
2007	7.3	8.6	7.9	17.1	41.0	19,000
2008	8.1	9.6	8.7	18.8	45.1	18,800
2009	8.3	9.9	9.0	18.5	45.7	18,890
2010	7.8	8.7	7.8	18.0	42.3	19,410
2011	8.0	8.7	8.6	21.6	46.9	19,890
2012	8.9	8.7	9.5	22.4	49.5	20,310

Source: cost data from IATA, 2013, fleet information from Boeing's Commercial Market Outlook, various years.

Table 6.4 Estimated costs of C-checks

Aircraft type	*Cost of 'light' C check*	*Cost of 'heavy' C check*
Regional jet	$60,000–90,000	$100,000–180,000
Narrow-body aircraft	$120,000–180,000	$220,000–350,000
Wide-body aircraft	$375,000–550,000	$550,000–700,000

Source: adapted from Ackert, 2010.

By contrast, a D-check occurs about every five years, and sees the aircraft entirely taken apart. Engines and landing gear are removed, while the paint will often be removed to check on the state of the fuselage. The structure is checked for material fatigue and cracks. As part of this process, the aircraft are subjected to other changes such as modifications or cabin refits. Due to the amount of work undertaken, an aircraft will often be out of service for up to six weeks. This high level of downtime means that a D-check may be planned over a year in advance to ensure that there is no disruption to the airline's schedule.

Engine maintenance covers engine shut-downs due to defects during operation and life-limited part replacements through to full repair of the engine. Engine maintenance tends to be the most expensive type of MRO activity, and will often be outsourced to organisations that are better equipped to deal with the complexities of this technology. This outsourced provider may be the original equipment manufacturer, as they look to increase the customer service offered to airlines.

Finally, spares and rotables are needed to support any aircraft maintenance. Essential spares and rotables are distributed throughout an airline's network, while others are held more centrally. Spares may be owned by an airline or pooled between operators. Recent trends towards cost reduction have seen greater outsourcing of spare part holdings, with 77 per cent of airline MRO cost in this area being outsourced. An example of an airline undertaking this is Finnair (Gubisch, 2012).

Airline MRO business models

Decisions as to whether to keep the different MRO activities in-house or outsource them to a third party have led to a number of different airline MRO business models. They range from a fully integrated MRO within the airline that has the capability to undertake all of the different MRO activities, often over a range of sites and increasingly on a global scale, through to a wholly outsourced model where MRO activities are managed but not physically undertaken by the airline. Figure 6.2 provides an overview of these different models, and each is now described in turn.

Fully integrated MRO

Line and base maintenance is provided internally within the airline. The MRO activities may be vertically integrated, allowing maintenance to be a core activity

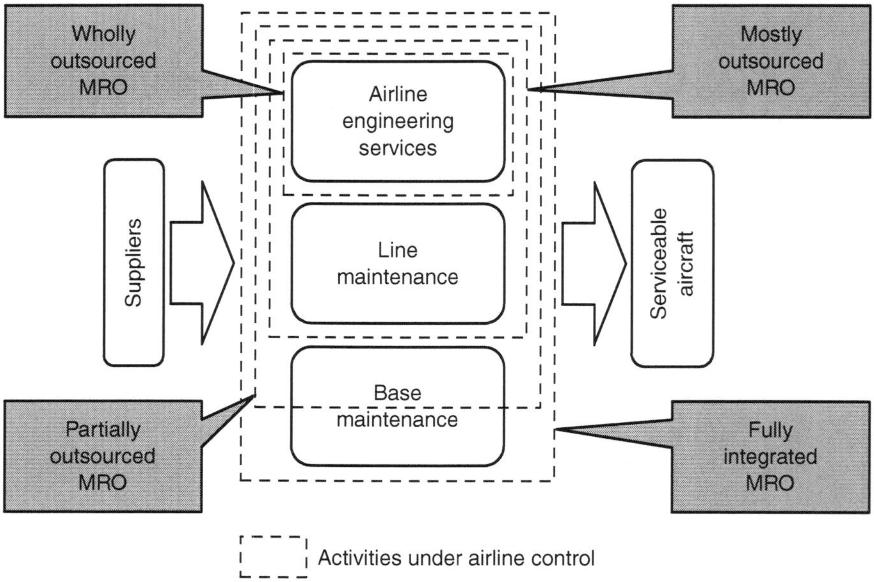

Figure 6.2 Airlines MRO models (adapted from Al-kaabi *et al.*, 2007a).

for the airline. While many airlines have viewed MRO as an expense, others, such as Lufthansa Technik, have successfully turned their MRO to a profit-generating unit. In these instances, the MRO operation is considered as an independent subsidiary, with separate financial accounts. In many cases the profits gained by the MRO are healthier than the airline itself (Heracleous *et al.*, 2004). A key attribute of the fully integrated MRO model is the scope of activities undertaken and the extensive experience of the airline in undertaking MRO.

While the overall level of outsourcing in the airline industry has been increasing, the larger airline groups have maintained the fully integrated MRO model. This can be seen by the ownership of the organisation in Table 6.2. The parent airlines share common characteristics such as a large fleet size, operating a range of aircraft types and a global network. The MRO operation has capacity built into the system that enables services to be provided to other airlines. In order to expand, some airlines have established joint ventures with partners in other regions of the world to increase the global presence of their services, and potentially access other markets that they would not otherwise be able to. For example, Ameco (ranked 8 in Table 6.2) is a joint venture between Air China and Lufthansa, providing substantial maintenance facilities in Beijing as well as a wider presence for line maintenance activities.

Partially outsourced MRO

With this business model, the airline retains control of all line maintenance and base maintenance activities related to the airframe. Base maintenance of specialist systems, such as engines, is outsourced. Similarly to the fully integrated approach, this business model, which is also a separate cost centre, also provides the scale to offer services to other carriers. Given the advancements associated with aircraft technology, such an MRO model has associated high costs, especially where an airline has a wide range of different aircraft types to maintain.

Nevertheless, a number of airlines have exploited the inherent economies of scale associated with a partially integrated model to lower upstream costs and supplying to downstream competitors for specific MRO activities (Chen, 2005). A benefit of being vertically integrated is that the function can be flexibly deployed to service the parent company's own fleet or to other airlines operating the same type of aircraft. This model also exploits its volume flexibility capability and can cater for fluctuation seasonal demand changes (Rosenberg, 2004). Medium- to large-sized airlines have adopted the partially outsourced model. An example is Delta Airlines from the United States, which has outsourced 24 per cent of its MRO operations (Rosenberg, 2004), mainly engine maintenance, and at the same time providing third-party MRO support for other carriers.

Mostly outsourced MRO

In this business model configuration only critical MRO activities are retained; all remaining activities are outsourced. Typically, this encompasses line maintenance activities as they provide some assurance to the airline of ensuring punctuality of passenger services (Seidenman and Spanovich, 2005). As airlines grow in size the need to have some MRO capabilities becomes crucial. This MRO configuration will include activities where supplier accessibility and/or delivery performance is not assured.

Wholly outsourced MRO model

All MRO activities are outsourced in this business model. The airline focuses on its core competence, namely providing an air transport service to passengers. Both line and base maintenance are outsourced. Many low-cost airlines and new entrants adopt this business model as the cost of having their own MRO capability is a higher percentage of their total operational costs.

The degree of outsourcing of the MRO function also varies depending on the activity being undertaken, as shown in Table 6.5. Table 6.6 summarises the

Table 6.5 Level of outsourcing of MRO activities

Maintenance activity	*Percentage of outsourcing by cost (2008)*
Line maintenance	16
Base maintenance	53
Engine maintenance	75
Spares and rotables	77

Source: adapted from Phillips, 2008.

Table 6.6 SWOT analysis of MRO business models

MRO model	*Strength*	*Weaknesses*	*Opportunity*	*Threats*
Fully integrated	• Profit centre • Better control of MRO activities • Large knowledge base	• Inflexible structure • Tolerance to market demands • Not focused	• Utilising capabilities and expertise to expand • Focusing on new markets • Alliance or joint venture to optimise capabilities	• Fluctuating MRO demands • OEM market penetration • New technology
Partially outsourced	• Tailored in respect to available capabilities • Profit centre • Excellent level of expertise	• Slightly rigid system • Intolerant to market demands • Difficulties in managing MRO activities	• Securing long-term contract • Focusing on specific MRO activities • Providing creative support package to other airlines • Integrating suppliers	• Under-optimised capacity • Technology advancement • Change in aircraft types demand
Mostly outsourced	• Model is dynamic with MRO market supply and demand • MRO activities tailored to support airline's own operations • Provide more control over essential activities	• Airline dependent on suppliers • Short-term perspectives	• Turning in-house capabilities to core competency • Supplier base reduction • Long-term relationship with key suppliers	• Dependence on suppliers' performance • Selection of MRO activities to outsource is vital • Relationship with suppliers
Wholly outsourced	• Efficient • Cost focused • Takes advantage of supplier's pool • Suits new entrants and low-cost airlines	• Dependence on suppliers' availability • Performance measures mostly based on cost • Dependent on suppliers' performance	• Retaining essential MRO activities • Long-term contracts with key suppliers	• Model is very dependent on suppliers' performance • Could be costly if suppliers' availability is low • Risk of supplier opportunism

Source: authors.

strengths, weaknesses, opportunities and threats (SWOT) of the four types of MRO business models.

A decision-making framework for outsourcing MRO

Given the above discussions, it is important for airlines to choose the most appropriate outsourcing model. Based on Franceschini *et al.* (2003), Al-kaabi *et al.* (2007a) provide a generic framework to give some guidance, as depicted in Figure 6.3.

The first stage, in common with most of the outsourcing literature, is to identify the core activities of the business. It is not necessary for an airline to be able to provide all of the different MRO services outlined earlier, but it is important to identify which are the core activities that should remain under the airline's control, particularly where they affect performance. Any activities that are viewed as non-core and where risk can be controlled should be outsourced. For example, airlines may outsource base maintenance activities, especially where the size of the fleet means that the resources may not be used constantly.

The second stage is to evaluate the level of demand for the activity as, if this is insufficient, outsourcing may represent a viable alternative. Within the context of MRO, demand can be influenced by a number of factors. Fleet size will have a direct influence on the demand for MRO, with larger fleets potentially supporting an airline's own operation (Sobie, 2007). Fleet mix is also considered an important factor, with Al-kaabi *et al.* (2007b) highlighting that a higher fleet mix was consistent with a lower level of outsourcing. If an airline is able to maintain a range of different aircraft types, then a greater opportunity exists to sell spare MRO capacity to other airlines.

Two other factors that may be important are aircraft age and fleet utilisation (Gramopadhye and Drury, 2000). The structure of an aircraft is affected by its age, with in-depth inspections becoming more important as the aircraft gets

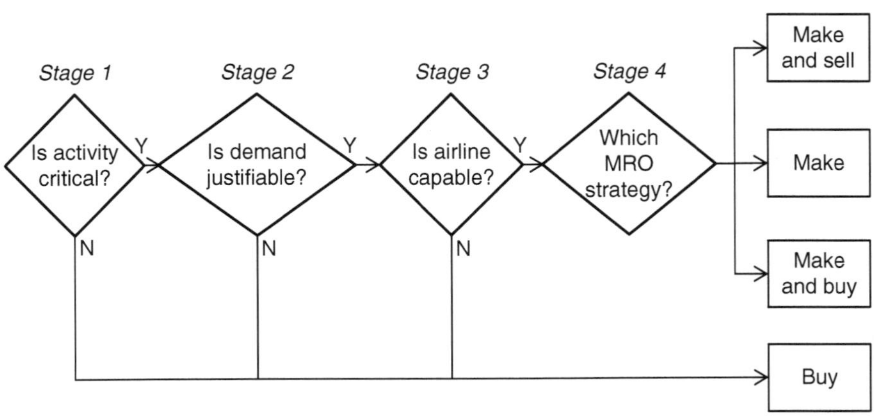

Figure 6.3 An outsourcing decision framework for MRO (source: adapted from Al-kaabi *et al.*, 2007a).

older. On the other hand, aircraft utilisation affects the frequency of maintenance checks, which are based on flight hours and cycles. As aircraft utilisation increases, the interval time between scheduled maintenance visits reduces. However, in their survey of European airlines, Al-kaabi *et al.* (2007b) found no statistical relationship between outsourcing level and these variables. Finally, the level of leasing could affect demand for MRO. Aircraft leasing is becoming more popular, as airlines look to increase their flexibility while reducing their exposure to risk (Gibson and Morrell, 2004; Oum *et al.*, 2000). These contracts may contain maintenance provisions, while also indicating that an airline is willing to consider outsourcing.

At the third stage, the airline needs to assess whether it has the capability to undertake maintenance in-house. Capability can be aligned with the strategic direction of the company. Traditional, scheduled airlines with established MRO support networks will often retain the activity in-house, selling spare capacity to other airlines. However, other business models may be more supportive of outsourcing. For example, Arnoult (2010) identifies low-cost carriers as preferring to outsource their MRO activities. At an operational level, there may be certain systems within an aircraft that an airline does not have the capability to maintain. As has already been highlighted, engine maintenance is one such activity that is often outsourced.

Depending upon the responses to the above questions leads to a decision as to the level of outsourcing within MRO operations. These are:

- Make and sell: airlines have turned their MRO activity into a profit centre. Excess capacity is provided so as to provide for the airline's own needs while allowing the remaining capacity to be 'sold' to other airlines. An example would be Lufthansa Tecknik, where Lufthansa provides 45 per cent of its work with the remainder from outside customers (Arnoult, 2010).
- Make: MRO capacity is designed to satisfy the airline's own MRO needs for a particular activity.
- Make and buy: although there is a capacity to perform part of a particular MRO activity internally, there is a need for other parts to be supported through external suppliers/contractors.
- Buy: a fully outsourced scenario where the MRO demand for a particular activity is met externally.

These decisions, combined with consideration as to the different types of MRO activity, influence an airline's decision on the configuration of its MRO operations. However, there are many external factors that can also influence this decision, and some of the future trends are now considered.

Trends and developments in MRO

Finally, it is important to consider some of the trends in MRO that are affecting the sector currently.

Globalisation in MRO operations

Table 6.3 showed that global expenditure on MRO activities has increased between 2002 and 2011. However, there are regional differences that exist, as can be seen in Figure 6.4.

One of the most rapidly growing markets is Asia, where the regional growth rate in MRO expenditure as a whole between 2013 and 2022 is predicted at 5.5 per cent (Berger, 2013). However, in certain parts of the region, such as India and the Middle East, this growth rate is over 8 per cent. By contrast, the global average is 4.1 per cent. There are several factors behind this predicted growth.

This particular region is predicted to see a substantial growth in air transport services, with annual growth in revenue passenger kilometres in the period 2012 to 2032 varying between 5.5 per cent (Airbus, 2013) and 6.9 per cent (Boeing, 2013). This expansion is faster than the predicted global growth rate. This will have an impact on the demand for aircraft, although with increasing reliability and airlines up-scaling to larger aircraft, maintenance requirements will not grow at the same rate.

Another factor in the growth within Asia is that the region currently offers the potential for cost savings, particularly in the context of base maintenance. This is because the lower labour costs make the region more attractive to airlines. Normalised survey data from Oliver Wyman (2013), presented in Table 6.7, highlights the cost differences between North America and other regions in the world for MRO activities. Labour costs in China and South East Asia can be as much as 30 per cent lower and so, when also including the cost of a ferry flight to the region from North America, it is still possibly to save 18–20 per cent. However, Marcontell (2013) suggests that this cost difference is closing and that, by the early 2020s, wage rates will be comparable to North America.

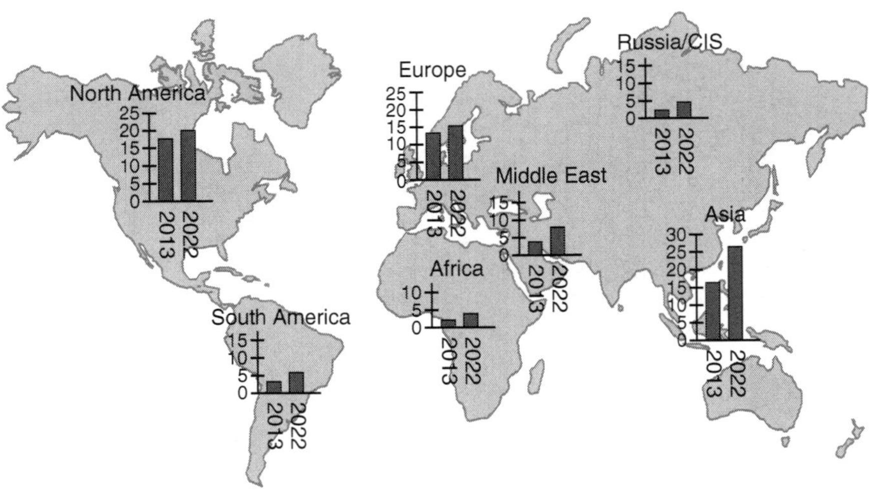

Figure 6.4 Global MRO expenditure by region for 2013 and predictions for 2022, US$ billions (source: based on data from Berger, 2013).

Table 6.7 Cost difference for airframe work when compared to the United States

Location	*Base man-hour rates*	*Additional costs including on-site management and aircraft ferrying costs*
North America	1.00	1.08
Latin America	0.78	0.90
Western Europe	1.26	1.48
Southern Europe	1.17	1.33
Eastern Europe	1.02	1.16
Middle East	0.90	1.04
Singapore and Hong Kong	0.96	1.11
Mainland China and South East Asia	0.72	0.88

Source: data from Oliver Wyman (2013).

As an example of an airline benefiting from this wage rate differential, Lufthansa Technik has a facility in the Philippines to undertake base maintenance. As well as servicing their own aircraft, the facility has contracts with airlines such as Virgin Atlantic and LAN Chile to ensure that capacity is used effectively. Another example is United Airlines, which carries out base maintenance on its aircraft in Hong Kong. Their behaviour is reflective of North American airlines in general, with up to 25 per cent of base maintenance being outsourced to the Asia-Pacific region (Tang and Elias, 2012).

Increased outsourcing

Throughout this chapter, the growth of outsourcing has been highlighted as a major driver of change in MRO activities. This is likely to continue as airlines focus upon the activities that are critical to their own operations. In addition, the industry is seeing the growth of airframe and engine manufacturers moving into the provision of maintenance services. As can be found with consumer goods, these companies offer discounts on the initial acquisition cost of the equipment, on the basis that they will make more substantial profits from the MRO activities associated with the item over its lifespan. Spafford and Rose (2013) highlight that currently 28 per cent of airframe maintenance decisions and 54 per cent of engine maintenance decisions are taken before the purchase decision is made. Their survey suggests that in the future these figures may rise to 45 per cent and 59 per cent, respectively.

Focus on cost reduction

While airline yields have always been quite small (Doganis, 2010), the global economic downturn from 2008 has required airlines to focus even more intently upon their cost base. While some aspects of operations offer good opportunities for cost reduction, the concern with MRO activities is that lower expenditure could compromise safety or reliability. Nonetheless, opportunities for cost reduction do exist. Many airlines have been simplifying their fleet structure. A consequence of this is that fewer spare parts are needed, reducing the stock holding costs. Where this is not possible, then outsourcing of spares and rotables enables economies to be achieved through effectively pooling requirements with other operators of the same aircraft types. There is some evidence of this occurring between airlines belonging to the same global alliance. For example, airlines in Star Alliance can trade surplus spare parts through a web-based exchange (Buyck, 2013).

Within MRO operations, there has been significant interest in the adoption of lean thinking, whereby the operation should focus on eliminating waste activities and delivering what the customer wants; an example can be found in Srinivasan *et al.* (2007). However, Ayeni *et al.* (2011) note that the lean thinking in aircraft MRO operations is more oriented only towards reducing waste, and therefore cost. Where lean thinking is effectively implemented, then financial benefits have been reported by MRO operators. For example, Delta TechOps has used lean thinking to reduce the time each engine has been under maintenance by 20 per cent (McAuliffe, 2007). This has halved the number of items being repaired, offering a cost saving in terms of the value of the parts. Further, more engines can be repaired each month, increasing revenues and improving profitability.

Fuel burn reduction

With fuel representing a significant element of airlines' operating costs, MRO activities can help in reducing this burden. One particular way in which this can be achieved is through modifying the airframe to include new technologies that offer a reduction in fuel burn. For example, many airlines have taken to fitting winglets to their aircraft to reduce the drag around the end of the wing and therefore reduce fuel consumption.

Engine maintenance can also help to reduce fuel burn. Beck (2012) shows that by refurbishing engines during base maintenance slightly more frequently, the amount of extra fuel used due to the deterioration of the engine can be reduced by 7 per cent. However, when balanced against the cost of servicing the engine more frequently, the total cost is actually more. There may be more opportunities with line maintenance activities, where it is suggested that washing the engine core every six months would reduce fuel burn by 0.5 per cent (Beck, 2012).

Newer generation aircraft

With each new generation of aircraft, additional maintenance cost savings are achieved. Ali (2011) shows that for wide-body aircraft, maintenance costs reduced by about 25 per cent between designs from the 1980s and 1990s, while aircraft such as the Boeing 787 should offer a similar level of reduction over the 1990s designs. One of the reasons for this is that maintenance considerations are designed into the aircraft, from the inclusion of diagnostic systems to detect failures earlier through to the positioning of critical components for ease of access.

There are also other implications for MRO operators. For example, newer designs increasingly make use of composite materials. Therefore, MRO operations need to develop new expertise in the maintenance and repair of such materials. With increased use of information technology within the aircraft, there is also the need to train maintenance workers in the effective use of this technology to complement the physical repairs that may need to take place. Finally, as newer generation aircraft often provide significant operational cost benefits, particularly in terms of fuel, so the industry is seeing the average retirement age for aircraft reduce. The consequence of this for MRO providers is that there is less demand for base maintenance checks as aircraft are requiring fewer of these before reaching retirement age.

Increased number of leased aircraft

The size of the leased aircraft fleet is continuing to grow, with many airlines now choosing this route to fund their new aircraft deliveries rather than buying them outright. Research by Al-kaabi *et al.* (2007b) showed a positive relationship between the level of outsourcing and percentage of leased aircraft. Leasing also creates additional demand for MRO services. For example, once an aircraft is returned to a lessor, it may need modifications, such as a new interior or repainting, before being used again. Further, there may be requirements for base maintenance outside of the scheduled programme in order to make the aircraft more attractive to lessors in the future.

Increased asset utilisation

While airlines have always looked to keep their aircraft airborne as much as possible, this strategy is becoming increasingly important in keeping overall costs under control. The low-cost airlines, in particular, have proved effective in achieving this, often getting two more flight sectors out of their aircraft each day when compared to traditional airlines. There are various consequences of this for MRO operations. The first is the need to try to reduce the failure rates of components so that there are fewer instances of technical delays. When failures do occur, MRO responses need to be swifter to ensure the aircraft can take off as close to scheduled as possible, given that there is less downtime planned within the system. Finally, given that the maintenance requirements are based on either the number of flying hours or take-off and landing cycles, increased utilisation has the potential to reduce the time between maintenance checks.

Conclusion

This chapter has demonstrated the continuing importance of MRO to airline operations. While outsourcing of this function has grown significantly, it is clear that certain critical activities such as line maintenance remain within the control of the airline. After this, key factors include whether the airline can generate enough demand for the service, and whether it is strategically important. Consequently, some activities will remain in-house but, particularly for engines where maintenance costs are higher, outsourcing will also occur.

For the larger airlines, which have substantial integrated MRO facilities, the extent of their service provision now stretches globally. While this supports the activities of the owning airline group, such a network also enables the operations to take advantage of the lower operational costs in some countries. Looking to the future, the impact of MRO on cost will be important, especially where it can improve aspects such as fuel consumption. It is clear that outsourcing will continue to be important, but that original equipment manufacturers will have a bigger role to play in this market.

References

Ackert, S.P. (2010) 'Basics of aircraft maintenance programs for financiers: evaluation & insights of commercial aircraft maintenance programs'. Online. www.aircraftmonitor.com/uploads/1/5/9/9/15993320/basics_of_aircraft_maintenance_programs_for_financiers___v1.pdf (accessed 8 November 2013).

Ahmed, S., Hassan, M.H. and Taha, Z. (2005) 'TPM can go beyond maintenance: excerpt from a case implementation', *Journal of Quality in Maintenance Engineering*, 11(1): 19–43.

Airbus (2013) Global market forecast 2013–2032. Online. www.airbus.com/company/market/forecast (accessed 27 March 2014).

Alabdulkarim, A.A., Ball, P.D. and Tiwari, A. (2014) 'Influence of resources on maintenance operations with different asset monitoring levels: a simulation approach', *Business Process Management Journal*, 20(2): 195–212.

Ali, K.M. (2011) 'Trends in aviation and impact on MROs', presentation to the 7th Maintenance Cost Conference. Online. www.iata.org/whatwedo/workgroups/Documents/MCC-2011-SIN/Day_02/1400-1430_Boeing_Trends_in_Aviation_and_MRO_Opportunities.pdf (accessed 26 July 2013).

Al-kaabi, H. (2006) 'Airlines maintenance, repair and overhaul (MRO) configurations', PhD thesis, Cardiff University.

Al-kaabi, H., Potter, A. and Naim, M. (2007a) 'An outsourcing decision model for airlines' MRO activities', *Journal of Quality in Maintenance Engineering*, 13(3): 217–227.

Al-kaabi, H., Potter, A. and Naim, M.M. (2007b) 'Insights into the maintenance, repair and overhaul configurations of European airlines', *Journal of Air Transportation*, 12(2): 27–42.

Alsyouf, I. (2007) 'The role of maintenance in improving companies' productivity and profitability', *International Journal of Production Economics*, 105(1): 70–78.

Arnoult, S. (2010) 'The MRO quandary', *Airline Business*, November 2010: 48–50.

Association of European Airlines (2012) Punctuality statistics 08/2012. Online. www.aea.be/AEAWEBSITE/STATFILES/RB11-12-08.pdf (accessed 22 March 2013).

Ayeni, P., Baines, T., Lightfoot, H. and Ball, P. (2011) 'State-of-the-art of "Lean" in the aviation maintenance, repair, and overhaul industry', *Proceedings of the Institute of Mechanical Engineers Part B: Engineering Manufacture*, 225(11): 2108–2123.

Backlund, F. and Akersten, P.A. (2003) 'RCM introduction: process and requirements management aspects', *Journal of Quality in Maintenance Engineering*, 9(3): 250–264.

Beck, A. (2012) 'Engine maintenance and fuel burn', presentation to the 8th IATA Maintenance Cost Conference. Online. www.iata.org/whatwedo/workgroups/Documents/MCC-2012-ATL/Day2/1150-1230-snecma-eng-mtce-vs-fuel-consumption.pdf (accessed 22 July 2013).

Berger, J. (2013) 'Global MRO market: Forecast and trends', presentation to Aircraft Maintenance Russia and CIS 2013, Moscow, 20–21 February.

Boeing (2013) Commercial market outlook. Online. www.boeing.com/boeing/commercial/cmo/ (accessed 27 March 2014).

Buyck, C. (2013) 'Untapped potential', *Aviation Week & Space Technology*, 11 November: MRO10.

Chen, Y. (2005) 'Vertical disintegration', *Journal of Economics & Management Strategy*, 14(1): 209–229.

Doganis, R. (2010) *Flying Off Course: Airline Economics and Marketing*, 4th edition, London: Routledge.

Flint, P. (2006) 'Boeing GoldCare aims to take MRO, supply chain burden off 787 customers', *Air Transport World*, 14 May. Online. http://atwonline.com/operations/boeing-goldcare-aims-take-mro-supply-chain-burden-787-customers (accessed 22 July 2013).

Franceschini, F., Galetto, M., Pignatelli, A. and Varetto, M. (2003) 'Outsourcing: guidelines for a structured approach', *Benchmarking: An International Journal*, 10(3): 246–260.

Gibson, W. and Morrell, P. (2004) 'Theory and practice in aircraft financial evaluation', *Journal of Air Transport Management*, 10: 427–433.

Gramopadhye, A.K. and Drury, C.G. (2000) 'Human factors in aviation maintenance: how we got to where we are', *International Journal of Industrial Ergonomics*, 26(2): 125–131.

Gubisch, M. (2012) 'In a state of flux', *Airline Business*, 28(11): 28–34.

Heracleous, L., Wirtz, J. and Johanston, R. (2004) 'Cost-effective service excellence: lessons from Singapore Airlines', *Business Strategy Review*, 15(1): 33–38.

IATA (2013) Airline maintenance cost executive commentary. Online. www.iata.org/whatwedo/workgroups/Documents/MCTF/AMC-ExecComment-FY11.pdf (accessed 26 July 2013).

Knotts, R.M.H. (1999) 'Civil aircraft maintenance and support fault diagnosis from a business perspective', *Journal of Quality in Maintenance Engineering*, 5(4): 335–348.

Kothamasu, R., Huang, S.H. and VerDuin, W.H. (2006) 'System health monitoring and prognostics: a review of current paradigms and practices', *International Journal of Advanced Manufacturing Technology*, 28(9–10): 1012–1024.

Lufthansa Technik (2013) 'Lufthansa Technik interactive'. Online. www.lufthansa-technik.com/worldmap (accessed 30 October 2013).

Marcontell, D. (2013) 'MRO's offshore edge shrinking', *Aviation Week & Space Technology*, 175(22): 56.

McAuliffe, G. (2007) 'Aftermarket: the ascendency of lean in MRO', *Aviation Today*, 1 June 2007. Online. www.aviationtoday.com/am/categories/commercial/Aftermarket-The-Ascendency-of-Lean-in-MRO_12094.html (accessed 26 July 2013).

Nakajima, S. (1988) *Introduction to a Total Productive Maintenance*, Cambridge, MA: Productivity Press, Inc.

Nakajima, S. (1989) *TPM Development Programme*, Cambridge, MA: Productivity Press.

Oliver Wyman (2013) Is it time to consider bringing some overseas aviation work back home? Online. www.oliverwyman.com/mro-survey-2013.htm (accessed 28 June 2013).

Oum, T.H., Zhang, A. and Zhang, Y. (2000) 'Optimal demand for operating lease of aircraft', *Transportation Research Part B: Methodological*, 34: 17–29.

Phillips, E. (2008) 'Throttling back', *Aviation Week and Space Technology*, 14 April: 74–75.

Rosenberg, B. (2004) 'Everybody's doing it', *Aviation Week Space and Technology*, 19 April: 68.

Seidenman, P. and Spanovich, D.J. (2005) 'Leveraging line maintenance', *Overhaul & Maintenance*. 12 December: 22.

Smith, A.M. (1993) *Reliability-Centred Maintenance*, New York: McGraw-Hill.

Smith, A.M. and Hinchcliffe, G.R. (2006) 'Beware of the fallacy of the bathtub curve', *Plant Engineering*, 60(2): 35–38.

Sobie, B. (2007) 'Outer limits', *Airline Business*, October: 46–53.

Spafford, C. and Rose, D. (2013) MRO survey 2013: thrive rather than survive. Online. www.oliverwyman.com/mro-survey-2013.htm (accessed 26 July 2013).

Spafford, C., Hoyland, T. and Lehman, R. (2012) MRO industry landscape 2012: market dynamics and new points of leverage. Online. www.oliverwyman.com/media/373424_NYC-AGE98201-001_P1_-_Press_Proof.pdf (accessed 26 July 2013).

Srinivasan, M.M., Best, W.D. and Chandrasekaran, S. (2007) 'Warner Robins Air Logistics Center streamlines aircraft repair and overhaul', *Interfaces*, 37(1): 7–21.

Tang, R. and Elias, B. (2012) 'Offshoring of airline maintenance: implications for domestic jobs and aviation safety', Congressional Research Service. Online. www.hsdl.org/?view&did=729477 (accessed 27 March 2014).

Teigtmeier, L.A. (2013) '*Aviation Week* ranks biggest airframe MROs', *Aviation Week*, 26 June. Online. www.aviationweek.com/Article.aspx?id=/article-xml/awx_06_26_2013_p0-591584.xml (accessed 26 July 2013).

Tsang, A.H.C. and Chan, P.K. (2000) 'TPM implementation in China: a case study', *International Journal of Quality and Reliability Management*, 17(2): 144–157.

Waeyenbergh, G. and Pintelon, L. (2002) 'A framework for maintenance concept development', *International Journal of Production Economics*, 77(3): 299–313.

7 Safety in commercial aviation

Hans Heerkens

Introduction

Why devote a chapter to safety in commercial aviation? On first sight, safety is not a problematic issue in present-day aviation, very much unlike the profitability of airlines, airport capacity and the like. Measured in the number of fatalities, injuries or hull losses, commercial aviation – hereafter simply called 'aviation' – has never been safer than in the last decade. Even if aviation would by some miracle become perfectly safe, this would save only 500–1,000 lives per year worldwide (Learmont, 2012a). In the small country of Belgium there were 770 fatalities due to traffic accidents in 2011.

Yet it is imperative to continue the struggle for increased safety, as will become clear in this chapter. Threats to safety continue to evolve. New actors enter the industry and have to work hard to attain the safety level of their peers. Satisfaction with the current safety level may all too easily breed complacency, endangering what has been achieved at such tremendous cost. So, aviation safety remains as relevant as it has ever been.

This chapter starts with some statistics on, and a short historical overview of, aviation safety resulting in a simple framework for safety analysis. After that, we address some of the main issues and challenges relevant for aviation safety at present and in the near future. We end with some concluding remarks.

Safety and aviation

Definitions and some statistics

Let's start with a definition of 'safety' and some statistics. A definition often used is: the number of hull losses (aircraft destroyed) in accidents (whereby no fatalities need occur) per 100 million kilometres, flight hours or departures. This is the definition we will mostly use, although occasionally we will also refer to the number of accidents or fatalities per year or per 100 million flights, because some sources use this measure. Of course, people on the ground can also be affected; several aircraft crashes in built-up areas have caused great loss of life. Steps can be taken to protect people on the ground, for example, by avoiding climb-out routes over built-up areas and by providing adequate rescue personnel and equipment in case of an accident. However, space constraints prevent us from going into this subject.

There is no universally used definition of 'accident', but in this chapter we will use the following broad definition: an accident is an occurrence whereby either an aircraft is damaged to such an extent that it has to be taken out of service for an extended time, or even permanently, or one or more passengers or crew are seriously wounded. A fatal accident is an accident in which at least one passenger or crew member is killed.

How safe is civil aviation? Table 7.1 shows the worldwide highest and lowest number of accidents and accompanying fatalities for each decade since 1950. Table 7.2 shows the worldwide numbers of accidents and fatalities plus the hull loss rate (number of aircraft lost per million departures) in the period 2003–2012, the latter being the last year for which data were available at the time of writing. Table 7.2 points to a problem when interpreting safety figures; not all sources use the same definitions and units. In Table 7.2, the numbers of accidents and fatalities (source: Aviation Safety Network, 2013) are given for all aircraft, while the hull loss rate (source: IATA, 2013) is only for Western-built aircraft. Since Western-built aircraft tend to have a better safety record because of their more modern electronic equipment, the hull loss rate in Table 7.2 is slightly optimistic compared to the numbers of accidents and casualties. Also, the definition of 'hull loss' leaves room for interpretation. It is possible that an aeroplane is written off because repair is deemed not to be economically viable, even though the plane can be repaired without having to rebuild it

Table 7.1 Best and worst years in terms of hull losses per decade, 1950–2012

Best and worst year for each decade	*Number of accidents*	*Number of fatalities*
2011–2012; best	2012: 23	475
Worst	2011: 36	524
2001–2010; best	2004: 33	454
Worst	2002: 43	1,112
1991–2000; best	1999: 46	696
Worst	1996: 56	1,831
1981–1990; best	1984: 39	676
Worst	1985: 42	2,010
1971–1980; best	1975: 55	1,186
Worst	1972: 71	2,375
1961–1970; best	1964: 45	1,017
Worst	1962: 70	1,681
1951–1960; best	1955: 53	562
Worst	1960: 64	1,395

Source: http://aviation-safety.net/statistics/period/stats.php?cat=A1, 8 May 2013

Table 7.2 Accidents, fatalities and hull loss rate per year, 2003–2012

Year	*Accidents*	*Fatalities*	*Hull loss rate (only Western-built jets)*
2012	23	475	0.20
2011	36	524	0.37
2010	31	847	0.61
2009	31	760	0.71
2008	34	589	0.81
2007	31	773	0.75
2006	33	905	0.65
2005	39	1,073	0.77
2004	33	454	0.80
2003	33	703	0.87

Sources: http://aviation-safety.net/statistics/period/stats.php?cat=A1, 8 May 2013; www.iata.org/pressroom/facts_figures/fact_sheets/Pages/safety.aspx, 8 May 2013.

completely. In this case the associated accident will not appear in safety statistics if there are no injuries involved.

Although Table 7.1 only shows the absolute level of safety, and not safety per departure or flight hour, it shows that the number of accidents and fatalities has generally declined in absolute figures, despite an average yearly growth of 5 per cent in seat-kilometres produced, meaning a tripling of air traffic about every 20 years. Incidentally, ticket prices have seen a similar development. A return Amsterdam–London ticket cost 250 then-guilders in 1920. Presently, the same ticket can be bought for about €150, whereas €1 was worth 2.2 guilders at the time of its introduction. This shows the immense progress made in civil aviation in less than a century.

Table 7.2 shows a gradual improvement in hull loss rate over the last decade, but it also shows that this figure can vary considerably. This is because the absolute number of hull losses is so low (generally between 30 and 40 per year) that a few more or fewer accidents can make the difference between a good and a bad year.

Table 7.3 points to a lingering problem in civil aviation safety; the disparity in safety figures between best and worst performing regions. Europe, the United States and North Asia score best on safety, Russia and Latin America in particular have shown significant improvement in hull-loss rate in recent years. Africa trails in rate of improvement. Problems often found in relatively unsafe regions include: poor safety cultures at airlines, lack of independent oversight capabilities (separation of rule-making and oversight, aviation regulators unburdened by political interference), deficient infrastructure (navigation aids, air traffic control) and shortages of trained crews and maintainers due to fast traffic growth. These problems are often compounded by challenging operating environments, like airports surrounded by mountains or being subjected to rapidly changing weather. Several safety enhancement programmes established by international organizations like IATA (addressed later) are aimed at elevating

Table 7.3 Hull loss rate per region, Western-built jets, 2006–2012

Region	*2006*	*2007*	*2008*	*2009*	*2010*	*2011*	*2012*
Africa	4.31	4.09	2.12	9.94	7.41	3.27	3.71
Asia-Pacific	0.67	2.76	0.58	0.86	0.80	0.25	0.48
Russia and CIS	8.60	0.00	6.43	0.00	0.00	1.06	0.00
Europe	0.32	0.29	0.42	0.45	0.45	0.00	0.15
Latin America	1.80	1.61	2.55	0.00	1.87	1.28	0.42
MENA	0.00	1.08	1.89	3.32	0.72	2.02	0.00
North America	0.49	0.09	0.58	0.41	0.10	0.11	0.00
North Asia	0.00	0.88	0.00	0.00	0.34	0.00	0.00
Industry	0.65	0.75	0.81	0.71	0.61	0.37	0.20

Source: www.iata.org/pressroom/facts_figures/fact_sheets/Pages/safety.aspx, 8 May 2013.

the safety of airlines, countries and regions worldwide to the level of the best performers.

Although mainline and regional airlines are generally not distinguished in safety statistics, and we will not make that distinction either, smaller airlines, especially those operating turboprop aircraft, face special safety challenges. Regional flights are generally short, making the relatively unsafe take-off and landing phases more significant. Turboprop aircraft are not always capable of flying 'above the weather', making turbulence and icing a matter of extra concern. The airports used are often less elaborately equipped with instrument landing systems and the like, and pilots regularly leave regional airlines after having gained enough experience, in the form of flight hours, to be able to secure a job with a national or international airline. So, while the challenges facing regional airlines and their mainline peers do not differ in principle, the impact of these challenges may vary. We will not go deeper into this subject, but make mention of the differences between mainline and regional airlines when appropriate.

A question that may interest the reader is whether there are 'safe' and 'unsafe' aircraft. In the view of the author, so few accidents happen relative to the number of hours flown and passengers carried, and the causes of those accidents can so seldom be traced back to design flaws that cannot be corrected once known, that there is no justification for speaking of 'unsafe' aircraft. Two examples of design flaws that led to fatalities are a cargo door of the McDonnell Douglas DC-10 that was somewhat prone to being insecurely locked, and actually opened in flight on at least two occasions; and a flaw in the rudder control system of the Boeing 737 that could lead to uncommanded rudder deflections. Both flaws were corrected to the extent that no further fatalities have occurred to this day, so we cannot say that these two aircraft types are unsafe, if they ever were. There have been other examples of design flaws, sometimes discovered before fatal accidents occurred. Aircraft built in the former Soviet Union have a somewhat tarnished reputation, but as far as the author can judge on the basis of accident statistics, the problem is not with the aircraft themselves, but with the way they are used. Because these aircraft often are no longer in production and are cheap to acquire on the second-hand market, they are presently generally used by second-tier operators in countries with limited safety resources and oversight. The aircraft are not always operated and maintained properly (some accidents have happened due to overloading the aircraft) and they are often not fitted with the most modern avionics. In conclusion, we can say that every airliner that is flying today on passenger revenue services can be considered a safe aircraft by design, if not always by way of operation.

Safety until the arrival of the jet engine

In the first decade of powered flight, safety was subordinate to being able to fly at all. The first aircraft were generally so unstable and difficult to control that they were impossible to get into the air in all but the calmest weather, and then with only the pilot on board. Accidents, even fatalities, were accepted as long as flights were no more than spectacular entertainment. This changed during the First World War, during which 150,000–200,000 aircraft were built (Ellis and Cox, 2001). Aircraft with bad safety reputations sometimes caused a lowering of morale in the units that flew them. Losses in accidents broadly matched those in combat (see, for example, Hooton, 2010), and hindered operations. For example, the weak construction of the lower wing of the German Albatros D.III and D.Va fighters made pilots apprehensive to dive after opponents, potentially saving many British and French pilots' lives and inhibiting the offensive and defensive effectiveness of the German fighter arm (Guttman, 2009). Safety became a factor in operational effectiveness. It was believed that training was key to both safety and pilots' fighting ability, and especially the British training system became an example for the rest of the world (Hooton, 2010). Much remained to be improved; pilots sometimes entered combat with a mere seven hours of flying time in their logbooks.

After the Great War, there were many young pilots wanting to keep flying regardless of the risks. It was the time of 'aircraft made of wood flown by men made of steel'. But again operational concerns made their mark. In the United States, airlines were earning money by transporting post, subsidized by the government. The loss of airmail was more prosaic but at least as personally important to the general public as the loss of pilots. In Europe, air travel became a prerogative for the well-to-do and for prosperous businessmen. These elite groups wanted safe and reliable travel, although the norms for safety were basic by today's standards, not merely for air travel. Although accidents were common (all four pilots who founded the Dutch Airline Pilots' Association died while performing their profession), aircraft accidents received wide media coverage and hurt the reputation of the industry. In both the United States and Europe, operational concerns made striving for safety imperative. This is still the case today. As a former head of the safety department of the Royal Netherlands Air Force told the author: 'Every accident has almost happened three hundred times before.' Long before accidents happen, their omens haunt airlines in the shape of delayed and cancelled flights due to, for example, system defects, lack of spares and maintenance anomalies.

The most important contributor to aviation safety since those heady days, since known as the Golden Age of aviation, must be the jet engine. The accident rate has decreased significantly since its introduction, from more than 50 in the 1950s (Boeing, 2010), when commercial jets were a rarity, to 1.07 in 1999 (Baberg, 2001), when regional jets had replaced propeller aircraft on all but the shortest flights. Other innovations, such as the all-metal aircraft, radio navigation aids like Decca and improved aircrew selection methods, made important but less significant contributions. In the first ten years of commercial jet operations in the United States and Canada, the number of accidents with fatalities per million departures decreased from more than 40 to fewer than two (Boeing, 2011), and this was after the introduction of Decca and other navigation methods but before the age of Cockpit Resource Management and automation. The significance of engine technology is illustrated by the fact that one of the last-generation, long-distance piston-engined aircraft, the four-engined Lockheed Constellation, had the nickname 'the world's best three-engined airliner'. The increased productivity of jet airliners, at least 50 per cent bigger and faster than their predecessors (see Table 7.4 for two typical examples), made mass travel possible, making safety even more important as the number of potential casualties per accident rose.

With the coming of the jets, safety evolved from being a sought-after attribute to something that should be taken for granted. In the late 1950s an airline withdrew an advertisement in which a plane was shown above the ocean between Europe and the United States, seemingly connecting the two continents. The management assumed that the expanse of water shown in the advertisement might put travellers off. KLM Royal Dutch Airlines long used the publicity phrase 'safety first' but changed it to 'the reliable airline'. Safety should not be an issue for prospective travellers

Since the coming of the jets, several real or perceived safety issues have emerged, some of which were solved, some of which still pose challenges to this day. We will deal with the latter in a later section, but a few words on the former are in order here to set the stage. They are: the transition from the three-person

Table 7.4 Typical last-generation propliners and first-generation jets compared

Aircraft type	*Cruising speed (km/h)*	*Number of passengers (high density)*	*Range (km, with maximum payload)*
Last-generation long-range propliner: Douglas DC-7C	555	105	5,810
First-generation long-range jetliners: Boeing 707-120B	897	179	6,820

Source: www.airliners.net/aircraft-data/, 8 December 2012.

cockpit to the two-person flightdeck; ageing aircraft; extended-range twinjet operations (ETOPS); and controlled flight into terrain (CFIT).We address these issues in the temporal order in which they came into significance.

The two-person flightdeck

Until the introduction of the Airbus A310 in 1982, the flight crew of a jet airliner consisted of two pilots and a flight engineer. Airbus, the European aircraft manufacturer, saw the increasing maturity of automation and display technology as an opportunity to reduce the number of flight crew. Since up to 12 crews may be needed to utilize one long-distance airliner efficiently, reduction of the flight crew by one-third can yield significant savings. But there can be consequences for safety. The most important are: a reduced level and diversity of expertise, less intellectual capacity for taking decisions, and less available manpower to share the workload. Also, if one of the crew is incapacitated, in a three-person cockpit there are still two people who can fly the plane, whereas in a two-person flightdeck there is only one; a reduction of 50 per cent.

But how much do these arguments matter in practice? Specifically: is there any empirical proof that aircraft with two flight crew members are less safe than aircraft with three, or that task saturation or the quality of decision making are more problematic in the latter than in the former? The answer is that this proof is lacking. According to Baberg (2001), 'the lack of manpower was more than compensated' (by technology; author's comment). Presently, two-person flightdecks are the norm, and the safety level of commercial aviation is higher than ever, despite the fact that the skies are more crowded than ever. It can, however, not be said that two-person flightdecks have been good for safety, for so many other variables have changed that the influence of the number of flight crew is impossible to determine. Examples of such changes are: more emphasis on crew resource management (so that available human resources can be utilized more effectively), more reliable and user-friendly navigation systems like digital terrain databases and GPS (satellite) navigation, better health monitoring systems, and so forth. Also, the number of pilots who have flown in two-person flightdecks during a major part of their career increases year after year. From informal interviews conducted with pilots, the number of flight crew simply is not an issue any more; transition problems are a thing of the past. Task saturation remains a contributing cause of accidents, but it is empirically impossible and logically hazardous to presume that tasks can be divided in such a way that a three-person flightdeck would lead to a meaningful reduction of saturation compared to a modern two-person cockpit in those situations where it matters. Besides, it is generally agreed that humans are better in action than in monitoring, and especially monitoring tasks have been transferred from humans to computers in the two-person flightdeck. It is sometimes assumed that automation may reduce workload when it is already low, and increase it when it is already high, but there seems to be no conclusive evidence for this (Funk *et al.*, 1998).

The three- versus two-person flightdeck case shows us several things. First: that safety problems can be transitional. That is to say; the transition to a new technology, working practice or organization causes problems that disappear when the transition is completed. The technological and other changes themselves are not the problem, but the fact that people have to adapt to them. Second, it can be observed that safety problems can be largely potential problems. There is no doubt that the decreased intellectual and decision-making capacity in a two-person cockpit can reduce safety in certain situations. But it has not been proven that these potential hazards manifest themselves in such a way as to make two-person flightdecks intrinsically less safe than three-person ones. This is partly due to the many other changes that accompanied the transition, but also because the number of accidents in commercial aviation is so low, and the combination of contributing factors in most cases so unique, that statistical proof of the safety effect of complex developments like the transition from three- to two-person flightdecks is almost impossible to obtain. It is harder still to identify the cases in which either a three- or two-person cockpit layout may have contributed to preventing accidents. Accidents that do not happen cannot be reported. Incidents that are successfully contained can. But even if there were more incidents in two-person flightdecks, apparently so many of them are contained that the total number of accidents does not seem to be higher than that of three-person flightdecks.

The coming of the two-person flightdeck shows that, in modern jets, technology can successfully replace human crewmembers.

Ageing aircraft

In 1988 a Boeing 737 of the Hawaiian airline Aloha suffered a major structural failure; the front end of the fuselage roof detached from the aircraft. Miraculously, the plane landed safely. Apart from one stewardess who was caught in the slipstream, all occupants of the aircraft survived. The cause of the incident was metal fatigue that was neither detected in time during maintenance nor mitigated by failsafe construction, and was exacerbated by the humid environment in which the aircraft operated. This made aircraft manufacturers and airworthiness authorities realize that jet airliners, which generally accumulate many more flight hours during their lifetime than their piston-engined predecessors, may require monitoring and maintenance beyond that envisaged during their design. Since then, tailored monitoring and maintenance programmes have been designed for each aircraft type and sub-version, and as far as Western commercial aircraft are concerned, there are no further known cases of fatal accidents with civil aircraft attributable to ageing of the airframe (as opposed to aircraft with obsolescent avionics), and without defective maintenance playing a role as a root cause. So, despite – or, in this case, because of – the increasing maturity of the aviation industry, technological measures have overcome this challenge.

In a way, the ageing aircraft case is a transitional problem, in the sense that it surfaced when aircraft began accumulating large numbers of flight hours for the first time in aviation history, and was adequately solved. But since the measures taken are permanent (stricter inspection regimes for older aircraft), it can also be seen as a framing problem. People framed the problem of accidents with ageing aircraft as a problem specific to ageing aircraft, whereas it can be seen as a problem concerning unexpected safety hazards, the solutions of which are similar to unexpected safety hazards with other (younger) aircraft. After all, the measures taken are essentially not different from measures taken to maintain the airworthiness of not-so-old aircraft: scheduled inspections and airworthiness directives when specific problems arise with particular aircraft types. As we shall see, with the Airbus A380, younger aircraft can have the same problems as older ones. However, the fact remains that defective maintenance (addressed later) will often not immediately lead to accidents, due to the elaborate 'built-in' safety of modern airliners. In this sense, older aircraft should continue to receive extra attention, not because age itself is a hazard, but because maintenance errors may manifest themselves only over time, as was the case with the Aloha 737.

Extended-range twinjet operations

In the age of piston-engined aircraft, it was an internationally observed rule that twin-engined airliners should not fly beyond a 60-minute radius of the nearest available airport, assuming single-engine cruising speed at optimal single-engine altitude. The reason was, of course, the limited reliability of the engines of the day. But as jet engines grew more powerful and reliable, more and more airliners had only two engines. While the first generation of Western long-distance jetliners all had four engines (De Havilland Comet, Boeing 707, DC-8, Vickers VC-10 and Convair 880/990), since then only three Western long-distance aircraft had four engines (Boeing 747, Airbus A340 and A380), and two had three engines (DC-10/MD-11 and Lockheed TriStar). All others had two engines, i.e. Airbus A330, Boeing 757 and 767. Apart from the Airbus A380, which needs four engines because of its size, there is no need any more for more than two engines. Two engines are more efficient than four, so airlines started pushing for the '60 minute rule' to be relaxed. The American Federal Aviation Administration (FAA) took the initiative and allowed designated airlines to deviate up to 120 minutes from the nearest available airport, provided that aircraft, equipment, crew and procedures – i.e. maintenance – fulfil specific requirements. Examples of these requirements are that the generators that drive avionics and such can be driven by either engine or by one of the engines and the auxiliary power unit (APU). The latter should be operable even after having been cold-soaked after hours at high altitude. This regulatory regime, adapted by aviation authorities worldwide, is known as Extended-range Twinjet Operations (ETOPS). The consequences for safety can be easily summarized: no accident with a twin-engined jet airliner has ever been caused by failure of both engines due to different causes. There have been accidents in which all engines failed, but that was because of a common cause, such as fuel starvation, and then the number of engines does not matter. Over time, ETOPS rules have evolved. In 1988 the

FAA granted the first 180-minute ETOPS clearances. Since then, 240-minute clearances have been regularly granted and the new Boeing 787 Dreamliner is designed for 330-minute ETOPS flights plus 15 minutes diversion time. As with the case of the three- versus two-person flightdeck, when ETOPS operations were started there was much debate in trade journals like *Flight International* about whether the ETOPS regime compromised safety. Fortunately, no ETOPS-related accidents happened in those crucial years and long flights with twinjets away from airports seem to be completely accepted. A strong indicator is the lack of orders for the four-engined A340, which was completely eclipsed by the Boeing 777 and A330 twinjets and was taken out of production as a consequence (Parker Brown, 2012). From this, it can be deduced that the safety of twinjets is no longer a concern any more than is the safety of airliners in general.

Although ETOPS safety concerns also seem to be a transitional problem, this is not entirely true. The driver behind the ETOPS regime is that the safety of a twinjet should be at least equivalent to that of a four-engined aircraft. But it is conceivable, although by no means certain, that these 'quad-jets' could be safer than twinjets if built to the same technical standards. The development of twin-jets has progressed, while that of the quad-jets has essentially stopped except for the Airbus A380 (the new Boeing 747-8 is a modernized version of a design conceived in the 1960s). Another way of looking at the comparison between twins and quads is that the savings that twins generate are now largely passed on to the customers in the form of lower ticket prices, but they could also be invested in further safety measures. All this comes down to the question 'How safe is safe enough?' Or, more to the point: what is the monetary value of safety?

Controlled flight into terrain

No matter how reliable airliners have become, occasionally they crash into mountains or even in flat terrain. This can happen even when there is nothing wrong with the aeroplane – for instance, because of navigation errors. This type of accident is called 'controlled flight into terrain' (CFIT). In the 1990s this type of accident began to attract significant attention. The main reason was that the relative frequency of these accidents went up. This was partly because the number of accidents where technical issues played a major part decreased, partly because more and more flying took place in potentially hazardous regions and partly because it fit in a more general trend of paying more attention to non-aircraft-related causes of accidents.

Contrary to the situation with the two-person flightdeck and ETOPS, CFIT was not a potential safety problem but a real one. For several years it was the most prevalent cause of fatal accidents. But it was largely cured by a combination of technology and cockpit resource management. First, satellite-based navigation was introduced. At present only the American Global Positioning System (GPS) gives worldwide coverage, and that is why in this chapter 'satellite-based navigation' equals GPS. In the future, the European Gallileo satellite constellation will perform the same function. This form of navigation is not only accurate to a few hundred feet, but its accuracy is consistent, except at high latitudes and under conditions where the reception of satellite signals is hindered by mountains, etc. Navigation equipment utilizing ground-based radio transmitters, like VOR/DME, becomes less accurate as the distance from the transmitter increases. These characteristics enabled GPS to be combined with digital terrain navigation, where a digital representation of the world's surface, including human-made objects, is stored in a computer. By using GPS, or by comparing radar altimeter data with elevation data of the digital database, the position of an aircraft can be accurately determined. Computer technology has made it possible to reliably automate the necessary calculations and to integrate data from various sensors (GPS receiver, radar altimeter, inertial navigation systems). This made seamless transition between navigation systems possible (above water digital terrain navigation is impossible for want of elevation data) and data from the various sensors can be automatically compared for integrity monitoring. The combination of satellite navigation and digital terrain databases resulted in the Enhanced Ground Proximity Warning System (EGPWS) that is carried by every modern airliner. With this system, pilots do not merely see how high they are above the ground, but they can see how close to terrain their intended course will bring them. This makes it easier to anticipate terrain clearance problems.

The introduction of the new navigation systems was not entirely trouble-free. Incidents and accidents occurred because maps from different producers were not always compatible with each other, and at least one accident was due to a digital map having a wrong airport identification code, which was subsequently inserted in the flight management system. But these problems have been, to all practical intents and purposes, overcome, and CFIT accidents occur less and less often (Boeing, 2011). Although these accidents still occur, other types of accidents have overtaken them in terms of frequency, and the cause of CFIT nowadays is not the lack of resources of the involved crews to establish their position, but loss of control (addressed later) or issues like not following established approach and landing procedures. Even in 2006, when CFIT accounted for one-quarter of all fatalities, none of the aircraft involved in CFIT accidents were fitted with modern EGPWS (Heerkens, 2007).

This is also due to the second type of improvement made, besides better navigation equipment. This comprises the improvements made in presenting information to the pilots. Figure 7.1 shows a digital map, with a dot indicating the position of the aircraft. On the map, terrain that reaches above the aircraft's altitude is coloured red. Terrain at the same and lower altitude is displayed in yellow and green, respectively. It is easy to see that, even if a pilot does not know his or her position, high terrain can easily be anticipated and avoided. 'Anticipated' is a keyword here. Prior to the era of digital terrain navigation, aircraft were often equipped with a Ground Proximity Warning System (GWPS, the forerunner of EGPWS) that alerted the pilots if a pre-set minimum height above terrain was reached. But if the terrain slopes steeply, there may be insufficient

Figure 7.1 Example of a moving map (reproduced with the permission of Garmin; copyright 2013 Garmin Ltd or its subsidiaries; all rights reserved).

time to react, and is may well be unclear in which direction a pilot has to turn so as to avoid high terrain. It is clear that navigation and display technology are closely intertwined; only digital terrain navigation can provide the data needed to display images like those in Figure 7.1.

Intuitive as the display images in Figure 7.1 may seem, designing a display format is far from straightforward. For example: are three colours enough for the pilot to be able to avoid terrain? The transitions between green, yellow and red can be quite abrupt. But adding more detail can lead to information overload at moments when workload is already high. After all, pilots should normally not need 'height above terrain' information; their flight plan should keep them far from dangerous terrain. When they are dependent on the display for avoiding terrain, something obviously has gone wrong, so the displayed information should be kept as simple as possible. This points to a subject that will be elaborated on later: the relationship between crew and aircraft. For now, we can conclude that CFIT is perhaps the clearest case in which technology played a central role in solving a serious safety problem.

Conclusions so far

In 2012 a telling milestone was reached. The number of fatal accidents – accidents with fatalities – dropped to fewer than one per ten million flights. The significance is that this '10^{-7} rule' originally applied merely to aircraft components. Now entire aircraft, made up of thousands of components, are as safe as one component was until now meant to be (Learmont, 2012b). We can indeed say that aviation has not only become much safer since the advent of the jet engine in the 1950s, but also since the coming of present-generation jets with two-person flightdecks and computerized navigation, display and flight control equipment in the 1970s (Baberg, 2001). Even so, new challenges to safety have continued to emerge. This is, of course, partly due to old problems being overcome. CFIT was always a cause for concern, but other safety problems attracted more attention and, in the beginning of the 1990s technologies became available that made it possible to effectively combat CFIT, rendering it logical to make the necessary efforts to do so. But new challenges constantly emerge, some not intrinsically related to safety but linked to it through the laws of economics. The two-person flightdeck and ETOPS were not technical or safety imperatives; they were driven by the desire to lower operating costs and hence ticket prices, and so to induce more people to fly. Sometimes, technologies that would logically increase safety created new safety hazards, as will be shown when we address computerized flight control systems later in this section. Furthermore, safety varies greatly across world regions. In Western Europe, the number of hull losses per million departures was zero in 2011. In North America it was 0.10. But in Latin America and the Caribbean it was 1.43. And in Southern Africa it was 3.93 (Learmont, 2012a). The picture that emerges from these figures has been consistent for a long time. Specific problems in these regions are: lack of safety oversight and of independence of safety oversight organizations, lack of expertise and funds for, for example, training, unfavourable geographical and climatic conditions and, perhaps, other priorities for the limited funding available. Steps have been taken to improve safety in these regions, for example, by holding safety audits by the IATA, and helping airlines to address problems found during these audits. But results have been slow in coming. The conclusion must be that the quest for safety is a never-ending battle.

Another conclusion is that technology can indeed make flying safer. Despite the reservation expressed about the two-person flightdeck and ETOPS, flying has continued to become safer. Of course, stricter flight and maintenance procedures also contributed, but they can be seen as adjuncts to technology. Besides, it is information technology that makes today's maintenance procedures possible. Also, accident investigation research and studies on, for example, man–machine interaction, are heavily dependent on data-gathering, storage and processing technologies.

Finally, we can deduce from the four safety issues described in the previous sections the elements for a simple framework aimed at classifying flight safety problems and linking them to possible causes. The first element is the accident, characterized in the type and the phase of flight in which it occurs. The type of accident can be, for example: CFIT, disintegration in the air (as a result of a fire or structural failure) or loss of control (for example, when the plane enters a stall and is not recovered). The failure of both engines of a twinjet, the ETOPS nightmare, can also be seen as a case of loss of control. There are three phases of flight in which an accident can take place: take-off, cruise and landing. Historically, 70–80 per cent of accidents take place during take-off and landing (Boeing, 2010). There is some logic in this. In these phases the workload of the crew is high; there is little time for correcting errors; there may be interference not only from other aircraft but also from ground vehicles; obstacles and terrain are in close proximity; during take-off engines are operating at full power and thus relatively likely to develop trouble; and during landing equipment defects have accumulated, the aircraft is operating close to stalling speed, fuel is low and the crew may be tired. The reservations regarding the two-person flightdeck are especially relevant during take-off and landing.

The second element is the type of cause of the accident. We can distinguish between direct, indirect and contributing causes. A direct cause is a cause that has the shortest possible causal link to the accident. Icing, leading to loss of control, is a good example. An indirect cause is related to the accident through several intermediate phenomena. A defect in the de-icing equipment of an aircraft may lead to icing and hence loss of control. Contributing causes do not by themselves lead to accidents, but shape the causal links between direct and indirect causes and the accident. If the pilot of a two-person flightdeck is so immersed in navigating in bad weather that he or she does not notice that the de-icing equipment is not functioning despite it having been activated, the high workload is a contributing cause. In the cases of the two-person cockpit and ETOPS, contributing causes played a significant role in the minds of opponents. The example of high workload makes this clear for the two-person flightdeck. In the case of ETOPS, there was concern that, when one engine would fail, systems redundancy would be lowered to an unacceptable level. The ETOPS regime therefore demands that there is redundancy in power supply to essential systems, so that the failing of one engine (the contributing cause in this example) cannot lead to, for example, loss of power for navigation systems, resulting in the aircraft running out of fuel (the direct cause of the accident) and crashing.

An important distinction within types of causes is the one between technical and human causes of accidents. The latter are collectively called 'human factors'. An older term was 'pilot error', but in modern aviation safety research and practice the word 'error' has too much of a normative connotation. Besides, pilots are not the only humans relevant for aviation safety. The cabin crew, maintainers, suppliers of spare parts, airworthiness and safety oversight authorities and designers of aircraft and their components all play their part. Essentially, of course, humans are always at the beginning of the causal chain of factors leading to an accident. Even if an aircraft part fails, it is the maintainer that installed it, the airworthiness authority that approved it, the oversight organization that monitored compliance, the designer who decided that the part should be used in the aircraft. Devices like the flight data recorder and the cockpit voice recorder, but also automated part tracking systems, often make it possible to pinpoint precisely where events leading to an accident began to deviate from normal practice, and what the human involvement was at that point. Regrettably, exceptions remain, as the case of Air France flight AF447 (described later) shows.

Causes can be further classified as originating in the aircraft or in the environment: air traffic control (ATC), weather, airfield (particularly runway) conditions and terrain features. As noted before, the prominence of these factors varies over time. In the 1990s weather and terrain features were especially important because CFIT was a prominent class of accident. At the moment the most prominent classes of accidents are loss of control (LOC), runway incursions (aircraft entering the runway inadvertently) and runway excursions (aircraft sliding off the runway), and hence airport conditions play an important role.

Whatever the temporal importance or prevalence of the various causes, one class of causes was never driven from first place. Human factors are either a direct, indirect or contributing cause in 70 per cent or more of all fatal accidents, even if the total number of accidents has remained fairly constant in absolute terms over the past two decades and has decreased per million passenger miles. It is clear that the human factor is a prime target for safety improvement. This will be addressed in the next section.

The final element of our framework concerns the consequences of an incident or accident. We confine ourselves in this chapter to accidents leading to injuries or fatalities to occupants of the aircraft involved, and do not go into the consequences for people on the ground.

This leads to the model of factors influencing aviation safety shown in Figure 7.2.

However appropriate the model is for displaying causal chains of accidents, its disadvantage is that it does not display the organizational context in which aircraft operate and accidents occur. Organization makes, and organizations make, aircraft fly. The sheer complexity of aircraft and their operations require trained personnel, procedures, division of responsibilities and the like. Causes of accidents do not occur in isolation. They originate, and hopefully are dealt with before doing harm, in interactions between actors performing their duties within organizations. The model in Figure 7.3 (Wagenaar *et al.*, 1990) shows how unsafe acts (behaviour potentially leading to accidents) originates within the organization of human interaction.

An example may clarify the model. With the introduction of the Airbus A320, Airbus decided to largely automate the 'stall protection' system that prevents pilots from flying so slow that the wing suddenly loses lift, which may render the aircraft uncontrollable and may require more altitude to recover than is available during the approach for landing. This is a policy decision in terms of the model in Figure 7.3. Airbus did this by limiting the angle of attack, or alpha (the angle of the wing relative to the airstream), that the pilot can command. When the pilot pulls the joystick aft, the nose of the plane will go up until the alpha reaches a certain value. Then the plane will stabilize. This policy decision induced a general failure type: pilots may not completely understand, or concern

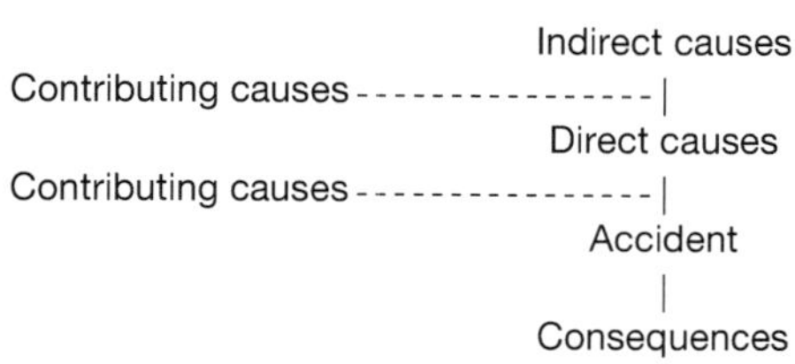

Figure 7.2 Factors influencing aviation safety.

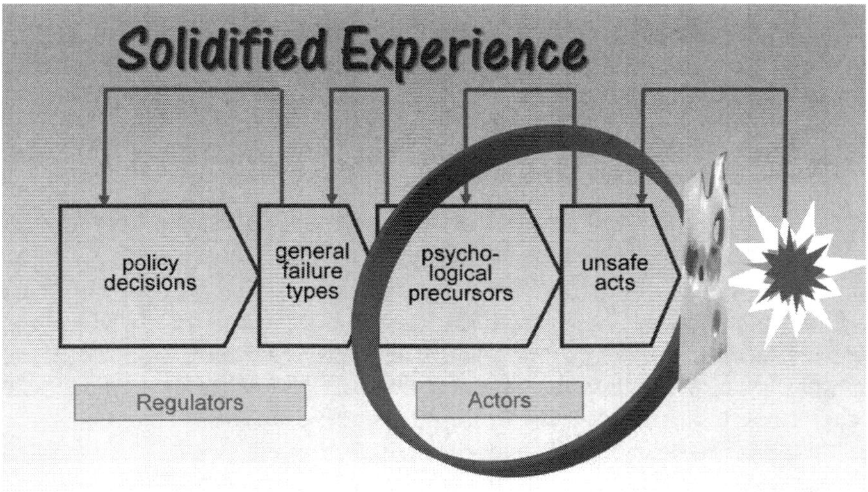

Figure 7.3 Organizational model of safety factors (drawing by B. Baksteen).

themselves with, the workings of the stall protection system and not realize its limitations, leading to the general failure type of not properly preparing pilots for the new technology. The psychological precursor may be that pilots, for example during the approach for landing, do not adequately monitor all flight parameters of the aircraft in the assumption that the incident every pilot dreads – a low-altitude stall – can no longer occur. This is what happened in a few cases. Pilots retarded the throttles shortly before landing – the unsafe act – believing they could reach the runway with reduced power, but failed to monitor their vertical speed. Even if an A320 will not stall under these circumstances, without enough engine power vertical speed will build up quickly. At least one A320 hit the ground in front of the runway before the pilots could correct their mistake (Funk *et al.*, 1998).

We now have two models with which to analyse aviation safety issues; a causal model and an organizational model. With these models, we will in the next section look at a number of present-day issues in aviation safety.

Present-day issues and dilemmas in aviation safety

The issues addressed in this section were chosen because they represent some of the current foci in the field of aviation safety, because they illustrate the eternal struggle to make an already extremely safe industry still safer, and because there are some recent accidents that can be used as examples. The issues we address are: the man–machine relationship in aircraft, training, design, production and maintenance, safety oversight and the role of technology. We do not discuss runway incursions (aircraft inadvertently entering a runway occupied by another aircraft) and runway excursions (aircraft departing from the runway because of, for example, aquaplaning). These incidents occur quite frequently, but we feel that what can be learned from this subject is already sufficiently covered in the other issues we address.

The man–machine relationship in aircraft

On 1 June 2009, Air France flight AF447 was flying at 35,000 feet over the South Atlantic when it encountered turbulence, low visibility and icing. The pitot tubes of the airspeed measurement system iced up, depriving the pilots and the autopilot of reliable airspeed data. The autopilot disconnected and the aircraft descended. The pilot flying pulled the sidestick back (lifted the nose), presumably to get back to the cruise altitude. Because of the high altitude, the maximum cruising speed of the Airbus A330 was close to the stalling speed, and in the process of climbing the plane stalled. The nose-high attitude associated with the stall was maintained by the crew despite the aircraft descending rapidly, until it eventually hit the water. None of the passengers or crew survived. The direct cause of this accident was thus loss of control, but its occurrence cannot be explained without looking at indirect and contributing causes, which we will address shortly.

This accident is of interest for several reasons. First, it happened outside direct radio contact with air traffic controllers, over water so deep that it took a long time to find the flight data recorders. So, for quite some time, there was no reliable data on the basis of which to discover the cause of the accident. Second, it was one of those rare accidents that did not happen during take-off and landing and did not involve either CFIT or a collision with another aircraft. Third, to the extent that the causes of the accident were established, a complex mixture of mechanical and human factors was involved, a few of which will now be discussed.

Cockpit instruments as information sources

The direct cause of the accident, i.e. the final factor that, had it been mitigated or had it not appeared, would have prevented the accident, was the sustained stall that led to a catastrophic loss of altitude. As far as could be determined, the aircraft was not damaged in any way that would have prevented the pilots from recovering from the stall. The French accident investigation body BEA stated in its final accident report that the pilots had perhaps mistaken the buffeting that must have accompanied the stall for an indication of overspeed (BEA, 2012). This impression may have been reinforced by the fact that the aural stall warning system of the aircraft was automatically de-activated in case the airspeed dropped below 60 knots so as to prevent unreliable warnings; a contributing cause. So, the pilots may have thought that they had exited the stall while in reality the speed had dropped instead of increased, which would have been necessary to exit the stall. The stall warning sounded several times, which might have added to the pilots' confusion. Also, an altitude alert warning sounded at the same time, another contributing cause. The sounding of these two alarms logically points to a high-altitude stall, but at the same time the flight director (an instrument that gives information about airspeed and attitude) advised a nose-up attitude. According to standard operating procedures this instrument should have been disengaged because speed measurements had become unreliable due to pitot tube icing (an indirect cause), but the crew presumably continued to rely on the instrument. The BEA observed that there are indications that in high-workload conditions pilots rely more on visual than on audio cues. Furthermore, the flight director appeared to reconnect after an initial disconnection, presumably leading the crew to believe that its indications were valid (BEA, 2012).

There is much more to this accident than was related above, but a few points stand out. First, that in a modern airliner the pilots are completely dependent on their cockpit instruments for situational awareness (knowing their position in space and their velocity), especially at night and in low visibility. The small flightdeck windows offer insufficient field-of-view for either assessing the spatial position of the aircraft under all conditions or detecting other traffic with any reliability, even if the speed of that traffic would not be in itself problematic. This places heavy demands on the reliability and clarity of the instruments. The manufacturer of the A330 announced after the publication of the final accident report that it would review whether letting the stall warning sound even at speeds below 60 knots would enhance safety, although it doubts whether it would have prevented the AF447 accident (Learmont, 2012c). After all, the aircraft had wandered so far outside its normal flight envelope that a continuous alarm probably would have made little difference. A better understanding by the crew of the cues that were available probably would have been far more important. This goes further than the crew merely being able to interpret the instruments. It concerns both the quality of the man–machine interface and the crew's understanding of the workings of the aeroplane.

Man–machine interface problems related to safety come in many shapes and forms. Sometimes they are cruelly futile – with the benefit of hindsight that is. For example: in January 2002 an Airbus A320 descended to the airport of Strasbourg (France). One of the crewmembers wanted to set a 3.3 degrees descent angle to the runway for the autopilot and did this by rotating a knob on the instrument panel. But he was one click off; instead of a descent angle of 3.3 degrees he selected a 3,300 feet per minute descent rate. The aircraft flew into a mountain (BEA, n.d.)

This accident, while not impossible in an aircraft with electromechanical instruments, is indicative of the challenges in modern aircraft where knobs, switches and displays can have many functions, the logic of which may not always be self-evident. This may cause errors like in the example above. In a modern cockpit there can be as many as eight or more displays, hence it is often called the 'glass cockpit'. Whereas with electromechanical instruments, like the

Figure 7.4 Example of a non-ergonomic altimeter (drawing by B. Baksteen).

altimeter shown in Figure 7.4, the display format is fixed, on a display like the one shown in Figure 7.1 various data can be displayed in several formats. For example, altitude can be represented in the form of a clock, with hands showing the hundreds, thousands and tens of thousands of feet, like a traditional electro-mechanical instrument, or digitally, as figures. Both have their advantages and drawbacks. A 'clock' format is prone to misinterpretation; the altimeter in Figure 7.4 may seem to indicate 21,800 feet, but it shows 20,800 feet. But a digital representation does not show the direction and speed of change in altitude as clearly as moving hands do. In a modern display, all primary flight data – speed, course, altitude, attitude, turn and slip angles and rate of climb or descent – can be shown in one single instrument, thus limiting the number of instruments a pilot has to scan. And there is redundancy; when one display fails, its information can be presented on another. Furthermore; only the information needed for the phase of flight at hand needs to be displayed, which decreases the pilot's workload. Also, data from multiple sources can be integrated and presented in a user-friendly manner on a display. For example, the aircraft position as measured by satellite navigation can be displayed on a digitally generated map showing high terrain, the position of landmarks and airports and so on. The map can be zoomed in and out as desired. When properly used, this yields high reliability (satellite navigation data can be automatically correlated with data from radio beacons, inertial navigation systems, the radar altimeter and the digital map).

Furthermore, additional systems can be integrated. A potentially important example is the Synthetic Vision System (SVS). SVS uses digital terrain maps and GPS data to construct an image of the environment as seen from the perspective of the pilot. The resulting image is presented on a head-down or head-up display (HUD). In the latter case, the pilot can look out of the cockpit window and see the terrain as on a clear day, even at night or in bad weather, albeit with less detail. SVS is being introduced on business aircraft presently, where it can prove its worth in the coming years. It is not yet used on airliners, but research has shown the benefits for pilots' terrain awareness (Bailey *et al.*, 2002).

For all these advantages of modern displays, there are also drawbacks. If there is a power failure, the crew may instantly lose all essential information, as has happened several times in the past decades. This drawback is mitigated by installing a few basic standby instruments like airspeed indicator and altimeter. Also, if an accident occurs, it may not always be clear which information was displayed to the pilots at crucial moments. A significant but decreasing problem is that pilots who were flying 'steam gauge' aircraft in the past may sometimes have difficulty in adapting to digital displays. But there are fewer and fewer of these pilots around. A phenomenon observed by an experienced aircraft commander in an interview with the author is that sometimes younger pilots, used to digital displays on their home computers tend to take the information from those displays for granted. For example, they see their position as a dot on a map and do not care to validate if by examining the raw data that the display information is derived from (radio beacons, satellite information, the old-fashioned compass and so on). It is not known how widespread this phenomenon is.

Mode confusion

The man–machine interface is about more than making clear that data is communicated unambiguously to the crew. It also concerns ensuring that the crew understands what the aircraft is doing. Modern aircraft have two features that make this potentially problematic. The first is that the logic of an aircraft's equipment often is no longer physically visible but is hidden in computers and databases. The second is that the logic of equipment is no longer fixed. For example, a modern passenger plane can have several flight control logics. The most sophisticated one decouples the movements of the pilot's joystick from the movements of the control surfaces. So, when the pilot pulls the joystick back, he or she does not pull the elevator up, but merely tells the flight control computer that he or she wants the aircraft's nose to come up. The computer works out the necessary movements of the control surfaces and also takes care that the pilot does not overstress or stall the aircraft. If there is an incident, like unreliable altitude or airspeed data because of malfunctioning equipment, the flight control computer has several other modes, for example a mode with or without stall protection, or even 'direct mode' where the computer does not calculate the required control surface movements anymore, but merely generates a fixed control surface movement for a given joystick displacement, like a classic hydraulic system would do. It is, of course, vital that the crew is aware of the mode that the flight computer uses. In the case of flight AF447, the pitot tube icing degraded the reliability of the airspeed data so that the flight control computer had switched to an alternate mode in which the normal stall protection was no longer active.

In modern aircraft there are so many instruments with so many operating modes that 'mode confusion' is an identified safety hazard (Baberg, 2001). For example; the Boeing 747-400 has nine pitch modes, ten roll modes, five autothrottle modes and six autoland modes, plus combinations of these (Baberg, 2001). Apart from the fact that pilots may seldom use some of these modes or combinations, the danger exists that pilots are not aware of the mode the autopilot or autothrottle is in at a certain point in time. If, for example, the autopilot is in altitude-hold mode but the autothrottle is not engaged and insufficient power is given, airspeed may decay without the pilots being aware of it. This is because, if there is insufficient power to maintain both altitude and speed, the autopilot will try to maintain altitude by raising the nose so as to increase lift, thereby increasing drag which will decrease speed. This is, of course, a dangerous situation if it happens at low altitude.

If crews have insufficient insight in the way their aircraft work, several solutions present themselves, although the problem may never be adequately solved. One solution is more or better training, which is the subject of the next section. Another is reducing the role of the crew. This can be done by automation of certain tasks or by 'envelope protection'. The latter, mentioned earlier, means that the aircraft systems react in such a way to pilot inputs as to prevent actions that are potentially unsafe. Both automation and envelope protection are controversial since they reduce the freedom of action of pilots. Suppose an aircraft has to climb steeply in order to avoid hitting high ground. In an aircraft with the most common form of envelope protection – stall protection – the maximum angle of attack, and thus lift, that the pilot can generate is limited. No matter how hard the pilot pulls the yoke or stick back, the nose of the aircraft will not go up any further when the critical angle of attack is reached. With no envelope protection, the pilot might be able to increase the angle of attack with that one-tenth of a degree that was built in as a safety margin in the envelope protection system, thereby saving the plane. Or he might stall and crash. What is best? The clinical answer would be: do not rely on automation as long as more passengers are saved by pilots acting beyond the limits that an envelope protection system would give than are killed by pilots performing actions that an envelope protection system would have prevented. But the data to support either choice do not exist. And, obviously, pilots have more faith in their own skills than in automated aircraft systems. Passengers seem to share that sentiment.

Making flying more intuitive

The last way to make crews more proficient in operating their aircraft that we discuss here is reducing the complexity crews have to deal with. This is partly achieved with specific forms of automation; computers can in many cases detect and diagnose defects in complex aircraft systems faster and more reliably than humans can. But the operation of aircraft can in theory be made much more intuitive. An example that has been around for decades in military aviation and is now finding its way into the commercial world is the Head-Up Guidance System (HGS) on which certain flight information is presented. The HGS, like its military cousin the Head-Up Display (HUD), is a piece of glass in the field of view of the pilot on which data are presented, so that he or she can see information like airspeed, course and altitude while looking outside the cockpit at the same time. What makes the HGS intuitive is the symbology, most important of which is the velocity vector or Flight Path Marker (FPM). This symbol, usually a circle with a dash through it, displays the direction in which the aircraft is flying (see Figure 7.5). Without an HGS featuring an FPM, the pilot has to mentally calculate where the aircraft will, for example, touch the runway based on the artificial horizon, which shows where the nose is pointing, the indication of engine power, the angle-of-attack indexer, the airspeed indicator, which shows the speed in the direction the aircraft is moving, and the vertical speed indicator (VSI). Any combination of data from these instruments, plus wind force and direction, gives a unique indication of the direction in which the aircraft is moving. It goes without saying that the HGS greatly reduces workload, especially when it is highest, during landing. An added advantage of the HGS is that SVS images (addressed earlier) can be presented on it. Ideally, this gives the pilot a view of the environment (albeit not in colour) as he or she would see on a clear day, regardless of rain, mist or darkness, without reliance on off-board systems like radio beacons.

Another way of making flying more intuitive that is being developed presently is the 'Highway in the Sky' symbology, to be presented either on an HGS or on head-down displays. The symbology consists of a series of squares or

Figure 7.5 A head-up guidance system. The Flight Path Marker shows the touchdown point.

circles that the pilot has to 'fly through', not unlike a computer game. Theoretically, this eliminates the need for flying from waypoint to waypoint using data like changes in course and altitude, although in practice these data remain necessary for communicating with air traffic controllers. The Highway in the Sky symbology is not past the experimental stage yet. Despite its apparent simplicity, the right way to present the symbology is not straightforward (Newman, 2003). Are circles better than squares? Should only the edges of the squares be presented so as not to obscure other information? How does one make sure that the pilot is not mistaken about which squares are in the front and which are further away? And all this in various lighting conditions and various sizes of displays. But, when fully developed, the symbology has the potential to make piloting airliners simpler and perhaps safer. Think of, for example, approaches in mountainous areas. There may be another advantage that has so far received little attention: the potential to serve as a check on the performance of both pilots and aircraft systems. In modern aircraft, the communication between crew and aircraft systems is often via keyboards. This is the case with, for example, the insertion of courses, speeds and such into the flight management system (the modern and intelligent cousin of the autopilot). Not only do typing errors sometimes occur, but if information has to be inserted under time pressure it may add greatly to workload, and mistakes may be made. If such a mistake takes the aircraft on a course that will make it, for example, collide with high ground, this would in many cases be readily visible if a Highway in the Sky is presented on a display.

The interface between crew and air traffic control operators

Errors in inserting data into aircraft systems take us to the last item to be discussed in this section: the communication between crew, aircraft and air traffic control (ATC). This communication is often challenging because of dense traffic, time pressure, atmospheric conditions that hinder radio communications and the complexity of instructions to be exchanged. A solution that is being implemented at present is to send ATC instructions digitally to the aircraft. The instructions appear on a display and the crew can accept or reject them or ask permission for modifications. When the crew accepts the instructions, a press on a button sends the instructions to the flight management system to be executed. Obviously, some safety hazards associated with spoken instructions are avoided, like mishearing instructions or making errors in inserting the instructions in the FMS. But whether digital instructions are safer than the spoken word is not yet clear; not enough experience has been gained yet. Nothing should be taken for granted. For example, if there are no spoken instructions anymore to be read back verbally, ATC errors may go unnoticed. It is too early to determine whether the number of accidents where digital ATC instructions play a role is higher or lower than the number of accidents where spoken instructions are involved.

There is an aspect of the communication between ATC and aircraft crews that tragically surfaced above southern Germany in 2002. A Tupolev Tu-154M and a

Boeing 757 were approaching each other at 36,000 feet at approximately right angles. When the duty controller realized the danger of collision he instructed the Tu-154 to descend. A few moments later, the on-board Traffic Alert and Collision Avoidance System (TCAS) of the Tu-154 gave a collision alert and instructed the pilots to climb, whereas the TCAS of the Boeing 757 instructed its crew to descend. The crew of the Tu-154, following Eastern European procedures then in use, obeyed the air traffic controller and continued to descend, ignoring the TCAS instructions. The Boeing 757 crew, following the Western reasoning that if TCAS gives an alarm, ATC integrity has apparently broken down and hence cannot be relied on, followed the instructions of its TCAS. The two descending planes collided, killing all occupants (Bundesstelle für Flugunfaluntersuchung, 2004). Apart from other contributing causes, it is clear that procedural differences (follow ATC versus TCAS instructions) played a key role here. Since then, this ambiguity has been resolved; TCAS instructions take precedence worldwide. One could say that the introduction of TCAS, meant as a safety measure, introduced a new hazard since responsibility for safe aircraft separation was no longer shared between crews and ATC, but between those two and the TCAS equipment in all planes involved. Whereas ATC and crews can communicate verbally, exchange views and discuss options, the TCAS equipment has a very limited number of instruction options, and no meaningful method of two-way communication. There are no known accidents attributable to conflicting TCAS instructions, but the possibility of such accidents cannot of course be excluded (Brooker, 2005). This accident can be explained with the model of Wagenaar *et al.* (1990), displayed in Figure 7.3. The policy decision was to set rules concerning which instructions should be followed in case of a conflict between ATC and TCAS. These rules were ambiguous. The general failure type resulting from this ambiguity was that different actors operate according to different rules. The psychological precursor was to selectively follow these rules (in the case of the Tu-154 crew), despite the clear and unambiguous TCAS warning that this was dangerous, and not asking ATC for a course deviation that would have enabled them to follow the ATC instruction and still avoid a collision course. The psychological precursor in the case of the Boeing 757 crew was opposite but similar; to keep following the TCAS instructions despite the collision alert continuing. The unsafe act was the descent by both crews. The policy decision was the issue to be eliminated to prevent recurrence – setting a worldwide standard for prioritizing ATC and TCAS instructions.

We conclude, from this limited treatment of the subject, that the relationship between crew and aircraft is a complex one, with technology both holding the promise of increasing safety by, for example, making some aspects of flying more intuitive, and creating hazards by its limits and the failure of the crew to completely understand it. An obvious remedy for the latter hazard is training; the subject of the next section.

Aircrew training

Given space constraints, we do not discuss the entire range of crew training subjects relevant for aviation safety. We confine ourselves to those aspects that are related to some of the most important safety issues that currently are the focus of safety experts, aviation authorities, airlines and pilots' associations. These are: basic flying skills in highly automated aircraft, the man–machine interface and cockpit resource management. Issues like selection of aircrew are not covered because they, important as they are, are no longer posing significant safety hazards. For example, the present aircrew selection methods seem very reliable in keeping people unsuited to the job of flying aircraft out of the cockpit. Problems of pilots incapable of doing their job because of faulty training on type or because of physical disabilities are more a matter of oversight than of training. It is clear that, in terms of the model in Figure 7.3, the design and organizing of training concerns policy decisions, primarily aimed to eliminate or mitigate certain general failure types.

Basic flying skills in highly automated aircraft

In today's highly automated passenger aircraft, there is little need for the pilot to touch the controls. Some maintain that flying, and especially landing, can be done better, or at least more consistently well, by autopilot or FMS. Some airlines even discourage their pilots from landing manually since they believe that the passenger experience is, on average, better with automated landings. But this raises the question of whether pilots have enough routine in basic flying skills to apply them adequately when needed. In the case of Air France Flight 447 that we addressed previously, it was discussed at length by professional pilots in trade journals like *Flight International* and *Aviation Week & Space Technology* whether the apparent inability to either recognize the Airbus A330 was in a stall or reacting appropriately to it was due to a lack of basic flying skills. We will not give a definitive answer here for, to our knowledge, a universal answer is not known at present and may not even exist. Still, a few observations can be made.

First, it is possible that a lack of basic flying skills indeed is an issue. Even if the lack of practice in flying in automated aircraft may not be the problem, these aircraft are flown in such a narrow part of the flight envelope that, apart from landings, few other challenging situations requiring basic flying skills are to be encountered. So, pilots may not be prepared for flying an airliner 'by hand' if the need arises. It has been suggested that airline pilots should periodically be exposed to what is generally called 'unusual attitude situations' in light or aerobatic aircraft. 'Unusual attitudes' can be stalls, spins, steep dives and the like. Ebbatson *et al.* (2010) observed indications of a relationship between handling performance and recent flying experience, especially with one of the two engines of a twinjet inoperative; the type of condition when taking manual control might be in order.

Second, airline training sometimes is at fault. For example, some airlines train their pilots to focus on minimum loss of altitude when reacting to a stall (Crider,

2010). Whether this is recommendable or even feasible at low altitudes, where most stalls occur (during landings), is open to discussion, but it can make getting out of a stall more difficult. The essence of getting out of a stall is to reduce the angle of attack (the angle at which the airstream hits the wing). This means pushing the nose down. The other method, increasing engine power to gain speed and only then decreasing the angle of attack, gives a much slower recovery because modern jet engines react slowly to throttle movements and because the drag associated with a stall impedes acceleration. At cruising altitude there is always enough air under the aircraft to lower the nose in case of a stall. Hence, this would have been the appropriate action for the crew of Flight AF447 (BEA, 2012). Still, the crew seemed to concentrate on maintaining altitude.

Third, training for unusual attitudes is problematic with passenger aircraft. To do it with real aircraft can be outright dangerous, and even during test flights aircraft are not deliberately brought into a situation like AF447; an angle of attack so great that speed decays below the range within which it can be reliably measured. This point is not trivial, since no two types of aircraft behave the same. For example, the McDonnell Douglas MD-11 is more prone to hard landings than other passenger aircraft if speed and flare height kept very close to the prescribed values. Aircraft with swept-back wings are more prone to Dutch roll and often have less benign stalling characteristics than the light aircraft that could be used for training how to deal with unusual attitudes. Simulators offer an alternative, but only to a limited extent. General aviation pilots may benefit from unusual attitude simulator training (Rogers and Boquet, 2012), but in simulator training pilots tend to overestimate G-loads, and hence undercorrect while giving control inputs (Ledegang *et al.*, 2011). Motion cues are notoriously difficult to simulate. Furthermore, the behaviour of simulators is modelled after that of the aircraft they are to simulate, but only limited data are available for modelling unusual attitudes (Gingras and Ralston, 2012). So, even if pilots train basic flying skills on a light or aerobatic aircraft, there is no guarantee that they will do the right thing in a crisis situation in a passenger aircraft.

Fourth, the real problem may not be a lack of basic flying skills at all. In the AF447 accident report (BEA, 2012) the possibility was raised that pilots suddenly confronted with a crisis situation could suffer 'startle' or an emotional shock that makes them incapable of taking appropriate action. This hypothesis has to our knowledge not yet been empirically tested, but it may offer great potential. After all, many basic flying skills, like pushing the stick forward in case of an impending stall, are not physically difficult. There are also indications that pilots sometimes focus more on the (automated) aircraft systems than on maintaining the correct flightpath (Learmont, 2012d). Recognizing the need for applying certain flying skills, realizing that standard procedures do not cover a certain crisis situation and actually taking control of the aircraft may be the real issues. This warrants further research, and a solution is not straightforward. When should procedures be followed and when should pilots rely on their own skills and initiative? It is unlikely that there is a universal answer. And when an accident has happened, it is often easier for a pilot to justify having followed procedures than it is to explain idiosyncratic behaviour in a situation that may not even be reproducible. This relates to the issue of 'just culture' that will be touched upon in a separate section. In the case of AF447 some feel that the crew bears a greater responsibility for the accident than can be deduced from the accident report. After all, the aircraft was in full working order except for a brief lack of speed data, which should be manageable by any competent and well-trained pilot. The author, however, while understanding this point of view, thinks that the confusion that can develop in a cockpit subject to turbulence and unfamiliar aircraft attitudes and movements, on a dark night with little or no external references for orientation, should not be underestimated. Yes, if the actions of even one of the crewmembers had been just a little bit more adequate the accident might have been prevented, but here we enter the realm of chance and speculation. The author is of the opinion that, given the fact that we will never know exactly what happened in the cockpit of the doomed aircraft, and on the principle that any person should be considered not guilty unless proven otherwise, the accident report should be taken as a reference for judging the crew.

So, it is unclear whether more emphasis on basic flying skills will make flying safer. Fred Smith, founder of shipper FedEx, recently stated that humans on the flightdeck make the airways more dangerous, not less, and supports the idea of unmanned cargo aircraft (Pierobon, 2012a), a statement with which we intuitively fully agree but which cannot be tested empirically at present. If it is true, the availability of basic flying skills is not the problem, since a computer can do the job of flying just as well. But as long as pilots are in the cockpit they have to have the flying and decision-making skills necessary for safe flight. And in order to be able to properly apply those skills, they need to be fully familiar with their aircraft. This brings us to the next subject: training and the relationship between pilots and aircraft.

Training and the man–machine interface

Modern airliners are not only complex machines, but, as we have already seen, the logic of its many systems is far from transparent to its crew. How much insight in the workings of an aircraft does a crew need for safe flight? What is the balance between knowing what to do and knowing why to do it? Between rule-based and knowledge-based behaviour? Opinions differ, not only on what is required, but also on what is achievable. A training approach that seems to be gaining wide acceptance after initial apprehension is the Multicrew Pilot License Training System (MPL), developed by Boeing subsidiary Alteon. The system is strongly competence-based. Student pilots do not fly solo in order to practise specific skills and procedures; they fly in pairs together with an instructor, taking turns in flying, observing and evaluating their fellow students. This should yield a more thorough understanding of the interaction between aircraft and crew. Hopefully, students take the routine of observation and evaluation with them to the flightdecks of the airliners they fly after graduating. As the system was introduced only in the past few years, it is too early to assess how pilots trained in this way will perform in command positions.

Training crews to perform adequately is one approach to increasing safety; evaluating and improving performance based on empirical safety hazard data is another. This is the idea behind the Line Operations Safety Audit (LOSA). Randomly selected crews are observed during real-world flights in a structured way, by using formal observation protocols. Helmreich *et al.* (2001) observed that in 64 per cent of the flights on which LOSA data were collected in their research, errors were made by the crew. Fifty per cent of these errors involved non-compliance ('breaking the rules'), but only 6 per cent of those led to an undesired aircraft state (incorrect speed, heading, etc.). Conversely, proficiency errors (bad execution of tasks because of insufficient knowledge or skills) made up only 5 per cent of the errors, but more than 60 per cent of these were consequential. So, both types of errors are equally threatening to flight safety, but the mechanisms through which they work are vastly different. This makes devising countermeasures difficult.

Training and crew resource management

In the 1970s and 1980s a number of accidents occurred that drew attention to serious crew resource management (CRM) problems in passenger aircraft. The worst accident in commercial aviation history, a ground collision between a jumbo jet of KLM (Netherlands) and one of PanAm (United States) at Tenerife airport in Spain, was caused by the captain of the KLM aircraft starting his take-off roll without ATC clearance. The engineer was unsure whether the PanAm aircraft had cleared the runway but was overruled by the captain (Bruggink, 2000). This and other accidents pointed to issues like flawed communication between crewmembers, inadequate division of tasks in emergencies, overly authoritive captains and unassertive crewmembers. The result was increased attention to CRM, partly as part of regular training, partly by means of special programmes like LOSA. The techniques in these programmes differ, but their common denominator is that they aim to:

- make crewmembers conscious of the fact that not only technical but also CRM skills are essential for a safe flight;
- provide CRM skills in areas like communication and leadership;
- train crewmembers to evaluate their own and their colleagues' behaviour.

Besides these general programmes, specific CRM issues have been addressed over the years. A recent example is 'the sterile cockpit environment'. This means that during take-off and landing, or below certain altitudes, all communication between crewmembers not concerning the execution of the flight is forbidden, and the communication that is allowed must be in standardized phrases whenever possible. This also pertains to communication with ATC. This not only is aimed at reducing the chances of communication errors, but should increase focus and discipline as well.

No matter how much training is provided, CRM, or lack thereof, is likely to remain a safety hazard. Time will tell whether the Multicrew Pilot License Training System, described earlier, which trains pilots to fly as a team from the start, will improve the CRM performance of new generations of pilots. And even with the best of training, there will be occasional mistakes and slips of discipline. AF447 provides a telling example. Shortly before the incident that led to the disaster (the decoupling of the autopilot), the captain had left the cockpit to take a rest. When the replacement pilot arrived, it was not explicitly stated who was in command; the pilot flying or the replacement pilot. It is customary – but not a given – for the pilot who replaces the captain to be in command. When the captain left for his rest period, he pushed his seat fully backward so as to be able to rise. The replacement pilot sat down but left the seat in the aft position, rendering him unable to reach the controls from a normal seating position. All this may have contributed to the confusion that reigned on the flightdeck once the aircraft entered the stall (BEA, 2012).

Design, maintenance and safety

The crew of an aircraft is the ultimate goalkeeper as far as safety is concerned. But many accidents have their roots in the drawing-board or the hangar. Some aircraft are known to have had in-designed faults that have led to accidents. The McDonnell Douglas DC-10 trijet widebody had a cargo door that could be secured improperly without the groundcrew noticing. Although design faults rarely lead to accidents, they are systemic in the sense that they affect all aircraft of a certain type. Usually, two design principles ensure that design faults are discovered before they lead to accidents. The first principle is failsafe design, meaning that no failure of a single component or subsystem can lead to loss of vital functions of an aircraft. This is mostly achieved by redundancy in airframe structures, avionics and, of course, crew (two pilots instead of one). The second principle is 'safe life', meaning that aircraft components are designed not to fail within a number of flights, flight hours or within a certain time. For example, shortly after the Airbus A380 entered service, fatigue cracks were discovered in some wing structure parts. This required corrective action but did not lead to any accidents because the cracks grew so slowly that they could be discovered before the parts in which they occurred failed (safe life) and because the wing consists of so many redundant parts that it would not have failed under cracks in just a few parts (failsafe).

Corrective actions for design errors can take many more forms than just re-designing or replacing defective parts. A good example is the McDonnell Douglas (now Boeing) MD-11, a developed version of the DC-10. The aircraft has the reputation of being prone to hard landings and bounces if not flared at exactly the right altitude and airspeed. The combination of a hard landing and bouncing is especially vicious because when a pilot does not make a go-around in time each bounce can be harder than the last one. A really hard landing can even lead to wing fracture. Given the fact that re-designing the out-of-production aircraft so that it becomes less prone to hard landings is impracticable, measures were taken to reduce the chances of a hard landing and mitigating its consequences (Kaminski-Morrow, 2013a). Measures, either proposed or implemented, include: improving the longitudinal stability system protecting pitch attitude; additional training for crews; fitting head-up displays so that the crew is better aware of horizontal and vertical speed and the flight path of the aircraft; installing cockpit indicators to advise the crew on whether the landing gear has fully touched the runway; and increasing flare altitude (Kaminski-Morrow, 2013a).

Maintenance is meant to guarantee safety, thus it is not surprising that defective maintenance has led to accidents (see the Aloha Boeing 737 example described earlier). Although sometimes maintenance procedures are faulty (for example, if critical parts fail sooner than assumed when setting inspection intervals), the main cause of maintenance-related accidents is the human factor. Two recurring themes present themselves here: organizational culture and work pressure. Both are important responsibilities of the management of airlines and maintenance organizations. Fogarty and Shaw (2010) found that the perception of management attitudes had a direct effect on workers' attitude, group norms and work pressure. In other words, if management has the attitude of 'safety works until we are busy' (an old saying cited by Fogarty and Shaw (2010)), one cannot expect workers to see safety as their number-one priority. This notion has lost none of its relevance now that airlines are under more pressure than ever to maximize utilization of their aircraft (to reduce capital cost per seat-mile) and minimize delays (which may easily lead to loss of departure slot times on busy airports). Of course, errors are possible in the most safety-oriented cultures. Modern technology can play a beneficial role in this respect. For example, portable online computer devices presently in development are capable of generating checklists that allow maintainers not only to check which actions to take when making a repair, but also to check whether the actions were completed successfully (Liang *et al.*, 2010). Grissom and Done (2008) investigated a prototype of an Automatic Communication Exchange (ACE) system that collects maintenance data while interacting with personnel working on the aircraft. Prognostic health monitoring systems can predict impending failures in flight and automatically send maintenance data to home base by datalink. Not only does this increase safety, but replacement parts can be ordered quickly and may be waiting to be installed when the aircraft lands.

But technology cannot solve all problems. When maintenance is found to be a factor in accidents, frequently errors turn out not to be one-off events but manifestations of systemic problems. The accident with a British Airways BAC 1-11 on 10 June 1990 is a good example. At altitude, one of the cockpit windows blew out, partially sucking out the captain. He was restrained by cabin staff while the co-pilot made a quick descent and landing. There were no fatalities. It turned out that during replacement of the window shortly before the flight, a number of the bolts used to secure the window in place were either too short or of a thinner diameter than prescribed. The fault went unnoticed, no inspection of the work by a supervisor was carried out afterwards and the repair was not tested before the aircraft was used on a passenger-carrying flight. The accident report noted that the person who made the repair was fully responsible for its quality (no back-up), the shift maintenance manager employed poor trade practices and did not adhere adequately to company standards, which reduced his ability to 'achieve quality in the windscreen fitting process', and the airline and other relevant actors had not monitored the working practices of shift maintenance managers (Air Accidents Investigation Branch, 1992). This is a clear example of systemic shortcomings in a maintenance organization eventually leading to an accident. Since then, safety management, including human factors, has received much attention. It is, for example, incorporated in airline audits performed by international organizations like ICAO and IATA (see the next section), but it remains an area in need of attention to this day (see, for example, Baldwin, 2013).

The above addresses just a few challenges, and solutions, that confront maintainers. In a sense they are the same as the challenges aircrew face: handling information, working in line with procedures, developing and maintaining a safety-oriented culture and coping with work pressures. No matter how much modern technology comes to the aid of pilots and maintainers, they are the ones who let aircraft fly, and, seldom, let them crash.

The safety issues discussed so far have left out one important group of actors: rule-making and oversight authorities. These will be addressed in the next section.

Safety oversight

We will not go deeply into this subject, and only touch on some subjects that are either typical for aviation (as opposed to oversight in general) or of particular relevance at present. We address: the general organization of oversight, exclusion and blacklisting, accident investigation and just culture.

The general organization of oversight

National states have their own oversight authorities, like the FAA in the United States. The independence of these organizations should be sufficiently guaranteed, and rule-making and oversight should be separated. Many countries have separate transport safety organizations that can investigate accidents independent of aviation authorities. An example is the US National Transport Safety Board (NTSB). Accident investigation will be addressed later. In Europe, the European Aviation Safety Agency (EASA) has taken over some tasks from national aviation authorities. The main rules set by aviation authorities relevant for aviation safety are the following:

- Airworthiness requirements: conditions that an aircraft has to fulfil in order to be allowed to fly.
- Operating requirements for individuals or organizations who operate aircraft and infrastructure, like airports.

- Inspection and maintenance procedures, including safety management procedures. Following these procedures is one condition for an operator to keep his operating certificate.
- Airworthiness directives (ADs): when a defect in an aircraft is discovered, either during maintenance or after an accident, and this defect is deemed not to be an isolated case, aviation authorities can order modifications, extra inspections and the like. Modifications can pertain to all aircraft of a certain type, or can be restricted to certain subtypes (perhaps fitted with certain types of engines or equipment) or individual examples that have, for example, accumulated a certain number of flight hours or flight cycles. In extreme cases, all aircraft of a certain type or subtype may be grounded immediately. In urgent cases, inspection before or after each flight may be required, but sometimes aircraft operators may have more than a year to carry out certain inspections or to make modifications. A feature of modern aircraft that is both a help and a hindrance is that aircraft design is so well understood that aircraft generally behave very predictably. Even if an unexpected defect occurs, it often may occur only after a certain number of flight hours or flight cycles. This means that aircraft approaching the same number of flight hours or cycles should be inspected immediately, but other aircraft are likely to be safe in the short term, so no immediate action is necessary for them. Also, when the cause of a defect is determined, the number of aircraft affected can be narrowed down quickly. This is, of course, important for airlines. Extra inspections not only mean extra costs, but also lost income from cancelled flights, fewer passengers on connecting flights, and unsatisfied passengers who may avoid the airline in the future.

Worldwide commercial aviation standards are set by ICAO (International Civil Aviation Organization). Many of these rules cover other subjects than safety (e.g. rules for landing right treaties), but quite a few pertain to safety, e.g. runway lay-out and lighting, separation between aircraft taking off and landing, etc. Between the United States and Europe there is a high degree of harmonization of, for example, aircraft airworthiness standards. Since the aviation markets in these regions have dominated the world since the dawn of aviation, and because many of the most important aircraft manufacturers (e.g. Boeing and Airbus) are located there, European and US airworthiness standards are de facto worldwide standards. The IATA, a worldwide association of airlines, conducts the IATA Operational Safety Audit (IOSA), the passing of which is a condition for membership (Learmont, 2011). It also established the STEADES worldwide anonymous incident reporting system, where aircrew, air traffic controllers, maintainers and others can report events relevant for preventing or explaining accidents. Low-cost airlines are generally not members of IATA.

The rule-making and rule-enforcing powers of aviation authorities generally are confined to the countries in which they operate, but they have some powerful instruments to influence the behaviour of airlines and even peers worldwide. This is the subject of the next section.

Exclusion and blacklisting

Both Europe and the United States have taken measures to avoid foreign airlines that are considered unsafe entering their airspace. One is exclusion: forbidding aircraft of certain airlines to enter European or US airspace. Reasons can be: serious defects found during inspections of aircraft, or accidents revealing systemic safety problems. It is also possible to deny all airlines of certain countries access to one's own airspace because the safety oversight system (i.e. the functioning or independence of the aviation authorities concerned) is deemed to be inadequate. Exclusion is no trivial matter. It can potentially have political repercussions, and it is thus a political decision. There have been accusations that countries with little significance to European states are more likely to have their airlines excluded than their more powerful peers, but those accusations have never been substantiated or conclusively proven. Nonetheless, some African countries, for example, feel discriminated against (Pierobon, 2012b). Also not proven is the desired long-term positive effect on safety: airlines and oversight authorities paying more attention to safety to prevent being excluded. But the effect may well be there, and may be more important than the direct effect of preventing 'unsafe' flights.

Blacklisting is another measure to coerce foreign airlines or oversight authorities into taking safety seriously. The essence of blacklisting is to 'name and shame' unsafe airlines by designating them in public as unsafe. Not only government authorities can do this, but also consumers' associations and the like. The aims of blacklisting are to force airlines to ensure safety, and to enable travellers to make informed choices concerning safety when planning their trips. Since blacklisting often goes together with exclusion, its effects cannot easily be determined. But they are debatable. The possibility of blacklisting may cause airlines to be less open about incidents that did not lead to accidents but could have had potential effects on safety. For prospective travellers the safety information has little practical meaning, since even relatively unsafe airlines still experience extremely few accidents. And in areas where travelling by air is relatively unsafe, it may still be safer than other transport modes like travelling by car. This is especially relevant since blacklisting affects an entire airline, not just an airline's flights into Europe and the United States.

Exclusion and blacklisting are aimed at preventing accidents based on past experiences. An important instrument to give meaning to past experiences is accident investigation – a currently much debated aspect of which is the subject of the next section.

Incident and accident investigation

No matter how safe aviation is, accidents do happen. When they happen they should be reported to the oversight authorities. This is, incidentally, also the case with 'incidents' in which an unsafe or irregular situation develops (for example, a near-collision) without damage, injuries or loss of life. The first priorities of an aviation authority, and other involved parties like police and ambulance services, are: taking care of survivors; preventing further accidents by, for example, removing dangerous cargo; and securing any material that can shed light on the causes of the accident. At the same time it may be necessary to ensure the safe continuation of other flights, for example by diverting traffic from the airport where the accident happened. Communication with next-of-kin and the media is also an important responsibility of, especially, aviation authorities and the airlines involved. Here, a dilemma presents itself. Naturally, the next-of-kin want to know the condition of passengers, crew and people on the ground involved in the accident, but sometimes reliable information is simply not available, for example when human remains are so severely burnt that identification is not immediately possible. Also, the media, and increasingly legal representatives of casualties and next-of-kin, want to know the cause of the accident, to seek justice or financial compensation. But establishing the cause of an accident can take months. In the case of flight AF447 it took two years to retrieve the flight data recorders from the ocean floor. The dilemma is to provide as much information as possible and accept the risk that it has to be rescinded later, with a possible loss of credibility or even legal consequences, or to provide only information that is either verified or inconsequential, risking the suspicion that information is being withheld so as to, for example, protect interested parties like airlines or aircraft manufacturers.

After the immediate consequences of an accident have been taken care of, the accident investigation proper can start. The chief aim of the investigation is to prevent a recurrence by identifying the causes of the accident so that corrective measures can be taken. The secondary aim is to identify individuals or organizations who bear responsibility for the accident. The accident investigation process can be broadly divided into the following phases:

1 Establishing the circumstances under which the accident took place; time, position, weather, altitude, maintenance history and known condition of the aircraft, qualifications of the crew and the like.
2 Establishing the chain of events that led to the accident; performance of aircraft systems, crew and air traffic controller actions and such. The result is a second-to-second overview of events pertaining to the accident.
3 Identifying the causes of any of these events that were relevant for the accident. Key areas are: the way the crew was trained (which may determine their ability to deal with problems that presented themselves), the way the aircraft was maintained and prepared for its flight (were proper spare parts used and installed correctly? Was the crew provided with all information needed for a safe flight?).
4 Identifying systemic factors influencing the causes of the accident. For example, if a repair was carried out improperly, was this a one-off incident of was it the consequence of a sloppy maintenance culture?
5 Determining the direct, indirect and contributing causes of the accident.
6 Recommending measures to be taken so as to prevent repetition of this accident or accidents in which similar causes are involved.

Often, an interim report is released as soon as plausible causes of the accident have been identified. This is done to cater for the need for information of next-of-kin and other interested parties, to provide a maximum of transparency to the general public, to expedite the implementation of safety-enhancing measures, and to invite relevant parties, like the airline involved, to comment on the preliminary findings. After that, the definitive report is published.

Just culture

As stated in the previous section, aircraft accident investigations have as a primary aim the prevention of recurrence of an accident. This is done by establishing the cause or – nearly always – causes of an accident. So, finding the cause of an accident is merely a means to the end of improving safety in the future. However, for victims of accidents or their relatives, finding the cause of an accident may imply finding the party responsible for their misfortune. And for judicial authorities it may mean finding evidence for a trial against persons or organizations suspected of criminal negligence or even involuntary manslaughter. Unfortunately, the goals of these parties can be, and often are, at odds with each other. It is essential for establishing the cause of an accident that all parties involved freely provide precise and reliable information. But they may not do so if they know, or fear, that the information they provide may find its way into a criminal trial and be used as evidence against them. So, as a rule, accident investigations should be conducted separately from judicial action taken against those involved in the accident. In practice, this leads to several problems. First, judicial authorities generally lack the means to assemble information about accidents, and the expertise to interpret it. So, they are to a large extent dependent on the work of the accident investigators. Second, information collected by accident investigators has to be disseminated if it is to be of any use in preventing future accidents. Given that the parties involved in an accident are often easily identifiable, it may be practically impossible to shield individuals who provided information for the accident investigation from the actions of judicial authorities based on that information. Third, judicial authorities and politicians are under real or imagined pressure from the media and victims or relatives communicating through the media, to 'see to it that justice is done', or at least to identify a party to which damage claims can be addressed. And lastly, the line between making a mistake with deadly consequences and negligence of duty can be razor-thin. Take the crash of a Concorde supersonic airliner at take-off from Charles de Gaulle Airport (Paris, France) in July 2000. The root cause turned out to be a metal strip that had separated from a previously departed McDonnell Douglas MD-11 airliner. The strip, lying on the runway, punctured one of the Concorde's wheel tires, fragments of which penetrated a wing fuel tank, causing a fatal fire. The technician responsible for making sure the metal strip was securely fastened to the MD-11, and some other personnel, were charged with involuntary manslaughter. They were convicted, but this was overturned on appeal, although the airline involved was sentenced to pay compensation. There is no reason to suppose that the technician had deliberately neglected his duty; it was a case of inadvertently making a mistake, or sloppiness at worst. The consequences were unique and almost impossible to foresee. But they were severe, mistakes had been made and the dangers of debris lying on the runway are well-known.

Whether judicial action against those involved in an accident seems justified or not, it can be problematic if it leads to people not wanting to cooperate with accident investigators. The same goes for confidential incident reporting systems, like IATA's STEADES (mentioned earlier). These systems, of which there are several worldwide, are essential in gaining knowledge to prevent accidents (as related previously, many incidents happen that could, but do not, end in accidents). There have been occasions where judicial authorities wanted access to data from confidential incident reporting systems. Aviation organizations are pleading for a 'just culture' in aviation organizations, where employees are trusted to do their best unless there is strong evidence of the contrary. After all, as the saying goes, a pilot (or other crewmember) is always the first on the scene of the crash. When a 'just culture' prevails, employees can report incidents, including the ones in which they are involved themselves, without undue fear of repercussions.

But the tension between confidentiality and transparency remains, and a universally accepted solution is not in sight. It is not even clear how big the problem actually is. Cases like the Concorde accident seem to be an exception, but they may still cause widespread reluctance to report incidents, as has been implied in trade journals. It is also not known whether there are accidents that could have been avoided if similar incidents that went unnoticed had been reported.

In the preceding sections we addressed several current issues in aviation safety. There is one issue that impacts several of these subjects: the role of technology. Aspects of this were already mentioned when basic flying skills and the relationship between crew and aircraft were discussed, but what does technology in general have to offer in terms of safety, and what are its limitations?

Man versus machine: the role of technology

Has technology made flying safe, or safer? If we combine the two trends mentioned earlier; the decreased number of hull losses per million flights in the last decades and the persistent share of 70 per cent of human factors as direct, indirect or contributing causes of the accidents that do occur, the answer must in our view be affirmative. But it must not be forgotten that it is man who chooses to employ technology to increase safety. It is conceivable that other choices could have been made, for example to use technology more to decrease cost or to increase productivity, than has actually been done. But such choices were not made by aircraft manufacturers or by aviation authorities, and for good reasons. Even with emphasis on safety as it is, productivity and efficiency gains have been enormous. And efficiency and safety often go together. Keeping aircraft and other equipment in proper condition is as essential for optimal utilization of these expensive systems as it is for safety.

If the development of technology has benefited safety, how did this happen? And does technology also provide challenges for safety? In the remainder of this section, the main benefits and challenges that technology provides for safety will be briefly outlined.

Does technology increase aviation safety?

Technology has made aircraft and their systems more reliable. The first mass-produced jet engine, the German Junkers Jumo 004 of 1944, needed to be completely overhauled after ten flight hours. The Wright Duplex Cyclone piston engine of the Lockheed Constellation needed an overhaul every 3,500 flight hours (Wikipedia 2012). A modern, high-time RB211-535 spent 42,743 hours on the wing of an aircraft without a visit to the maintenance shop (Rolls-Royce, 2012). But technology has had other benefits. Modern displays, flight envelope protection and digital terrain databases, to name but a few technologies, have shown great safety-enhancing potential. Even if some maintain that systems like envelope protection has its dangers because it limits pilots' freedom of action or may lead to loss of basic flying skills, technology at least gives aircraft manufacturers the choice to install such systems or not. But the safety benefits of technology go further. High-fidelity flight simulators enable crews to practice – to a certain extent – emergencies that are too dangerous to train in real flight, and make it possible to 'replay' accidents to find their causes. Digital recorders store flight data that can reveal the causes of accidents.

Technology does not make aircraft perfect. The latest creations of both Boeing and Airbus have had engine failures due to design and production problems. But this has not yet led to fatalities or even injuries, and the problems, rare but not completely unknown with new aircraft, seem to have been overcome. The A380 is a case in point. In August 2010, the outer starboard engine of an A380 suffered an in-flight failure. Some turbine blades, due to their high rotational speed, slashed through the engine nacelle and penetrated the wing. Fortunately the fuel carried in the wing was not ignited and the aircraft made a successful emergency landing. No-one was hurt. This kind of engine failure is one of the most dangerous hazards for airliners because of the damage it can do to the aircraft (fire, structural failure to the wing, penetration of engine debris in the pressurized passenger cabin, rupture of hydraulic or electric lines). From what is known from open sources, the biggest problems for Airbus were not safety-related, but had to do with the compensation airlines demanded for the unforeseen downtime of their aircraft. The situation was similar when it was discovered during repair of the damaged aircraft that certain small parts in the wings of A380's were insufficiently strong. Again, the biggest problems for Airbus were not safety-related but concerned the cost of modifying aircraft that had already been built. For airlines, the downtime associated with inspections and repairs was an issue.

All in all, we conclude that technology has indeed made aviation safer. But as the example of the A380 shows, with each new aircraft, or any other system for that matter, there will be new safety challenges.

A particular aspect of technology worth mentioning is its role in managing information. Modern airline operations would probably be impossible, or very likely less safe, without modern information systems, not only for managing spare parts and information as such, but also for managing documentation. Operation and maintenance manuals need to be distributed, updated and tracked (so that non-updated manuals are identified). For a long time, when a manual was to be updated, this was done by inserting a new page in a binder, sometimes replacing, sometimes complementing a previous one. This was and is a cumbersome process, prone to errors. More and more, manuals for both aircrew and maintainers are digitized and carried on, for example, Apple iPad tablet computers or dedicated Electronic Flight Bags (EFBs). This is relatively cheap and reliable and has the added advantage that information can be found much easier than with paper manuals. But this relatively new technology has its pitfalls.

In April 2012 a Boeing 737-300 hit the runway with its tail during take-off because the speed at which the pilot rotated the aircraft was too low. The reason turned out to be that a too-low take-off weight had been used to calculate the take-off speed with the help of an EFB. The take-off weight in question had been used for the previous flight and had remained in the memory of the EFB because the crew had not turned off the equipment completely after landing but had merely put it in stand-by mode (Kaminski-Morrow, 2013b). The crew were apparently not aware of the subtle workings of the EFB; something that would not have been an issue with paper documentation.

Conclusions

In this chapter we have briefly discussed safety developments since the beginning of powered flight, a little over a century ago. This resulted in a classification of safety factors. Then, we addressed the most important present-day safety issues. On this basis we conclude that:

1 Commercial aviation safety is higher than it has ever been in terms of hull losses per million flights. Even in regions with a relatively bad safety record (South America, Africa, some regions of Asia), the safety level is better than it was in the Western world in the beginning of the 1950s, when air travel was already soundly established as a viable mode of travel.
2 Many developments in aviation are, or were, controversial with regard to the consequences for safety (the two-person cockpit, envelope protection, digital displays, automation). Yet, the aggregated positive effects on safety of these combined developments seem to outweigh the negative consequences. None of the aforementioned developments can be proven to have structural detrimental effects on safety, partly because some of these effects seem to have been transitional.
3 Safety is an ongoing concern. New technologies, new players and new demands on air travel will continue to generate safety challenges.

4 An issue that was not mentioned before because it probably is at least a few decades away from manifesting itself is that of pilotless flight. The statement of Fred Smith, founder of shipper FedEx, that aircraft are probably safer without than with pilots was mentioned earlier. If true, it raises important questions. Should there always be at least one pilot on board? Should that pilot be capable of controlling the aircraft directly or should he or she merely give ‘strategic’ commands, like the destination to fly to, and let an intelligent flight management system decide how to execute those commands? If this is the way to go, could such a task not be delegated to a specialized member of the cabin crew? And, the most important question of all: will passengers accept aircraft without pilots? At present, the answer is a resounding ‘no’, but what if pilotless aircraft make flying cheaper, or indeed manifestly safer?

But pilotless passenger aircraft are far into the future. For the near term, our view on safety can perhaps best be guided by the observation of Captain Benno Baksteen, former president of the Dutch Airline Pilots’ Association: ‘Flying is not safe.... You have to make it safe.’

References

Air Accidents Investigation Branch (1992). *Report on the Accident to BAC One-Eleven G-BJRT over Didcot, Oxfordshire on 10 June 1990*. London, HMSO.

Aviation Safety Network (2013). Statistics. Retrieved from http://aviation-safety.net/statistics/period/stats.php?cat=A1, 8 May 2013.

Baberg T.W. (2001). Man–machine interface in modern transport systems from an aviation safety perspective. *Aerospace Science & Technology*, Vol. 5, pp. 495–504.

Bailey, R.E., Parish, R.V., Arthur III, J.J. and Norman, R.M. (2002). Flight test evaluation of tactical Synthetic Vision display concepts in à terrain-challenges operating environment. In: Verly, J.G. (ed.) *Enhanced and Synthetic Vision 2002. Proceedings of SPIE*, Vol. 4713, pp. 178–189.

Baldwin, H. (2013). EASA’s new human factors roadmap. *Aviation Week & Space Technology*, Vol. 175, p. MRO20 (digital edition).

BEA (2012). *Final Report on the Accident on the 1st June, 2009 to the Airbus A330-203, Registered F-GZCP, Operated by Air France, flight AF447 Rio de Janeiro–Paris*. Le Bourget, BEA.

BEA (undated). *Rapport de la commission d’enquete sur l’accident servenu de 20 Javier 1992 pres du Mont Sainte-Odile (Bas Rhin) à L’Airbus A320 immatricule F-GGED exploite par la compagnie Air Inter*. Accident report. Retrieved from www.bea.aero/docspa/1992/f-ed920120/htm/f-ed920120.html, 15 November 2013.

Boeing (2010). *Statistical Summary of Commercial Jet Airplane Accidents; Worldwide Operations 1959–2010*. Seattle, Boeing.

Boeing (2011). The industry’s role in aviation safety. Retrieved from http://web.archive.org/web/20110629092157/www.boeing.com/commercial/safety/manufacturers_role.html#controlledFlight, 5 October 2013.

Brooker (2005). STCA, TCAS, Airproxes and collision risk. *Journal of Navigation*, Vol. 58, pp. 389–404.

Bruggink (2000). Remembering Tenerife. *Air Line Pilot*, August.

Bundesstelle für Flugunfaluntersuchung (2004). *Investigation Report AX001-1-2002.* Braunschweig, BSU.

Crider, D.A. (2010). Upset recovery training; learning from accidents and incidents. *Aeronautical Journal*, Vol. 114, No. 1160, pp. 629–636.

Ebbatson, M., Harris, D., Huddlestone, J. and Sears, R. (2010). The relationship between manual handling performance and recent flying experience in air transport pilots. *Ergonomics*, Vol. 53, No. 2, pp. 268–277.

Ellis, J. and Cox, M. (2001). *The World War I Databook.* London, Aurum Press.

Fogarty, G.J. and A. Shaw (2010). Safety climate and the theory of planned behavior: towards the prediction of unsafe behaviour. *Accident Analysis and Prevention*, Vol. 42, pp. 1455–1459.

Funk, K., Suroteguh, C., Wilson, J. and Lyall, B (1998). Flight deck automation and task management. systems, man, and cybernetics. *1998 IEEE International Conference*, vol. 1, pp. 863–868.

Gingras, D.R. and Ralston, J.N. (2012). Aerodynamic modeling for training on the edge of the flight envelope. *Aeronautical Journal*, Vol. 116, No. 1175, pp. 67–86.

Grissom, T. and Done, R. (2008) Hands free data collection for aircraft maintainers. *IEEE Autotest Conference*, Salt Lake City, UT, 8–11 September.

Guttman, J. (2009). *SE5a vs Albatros D.V.* New York, Osprey.

Heerkens, J.M.G. (2007). Onbemand bestaat niet. Met stewardess aan stuurknuppel wordt vliegen veiliger. *Piloot en vliegtuig*, Vol. 14, No. 3, p. 44.

Helmreich, R.L., Klinect, J.R. and Wilhelm, J.A. (2001). Systems safety and threat and error management: the line operations safety audit (LOSA). In *Proceedings of the Eleventh International Symposium on Aviation Psychology*. Columbus OH, Ohio State University, pp. 1–6.

Hooton, E.R. (2010). *War over the Trenches*. Hersham, Midland Publishing.

IATA (2013). IATA safety statistics. Retrieved from www.iata.org/pressroom/facts_figures/fact_sheets/Pages/safety.aspx, 8 May 2013.

Kaminski-Morrow, D. (2013a). Japan seeks stability gains on MD-11. *Flight International*, Vol. 183, No. 5389, p. 18.

Kaminski-Morrow, D. (2013b). False data cause 737 to strike tail. *Flight International*, Vol. 183, No. 5387, p. 11.

Learmont, D. (2011). Airlines achieve safest year ever for air travel. *Flight International*, Vol. 179, No. 5280, p. 9.

Learmont, D. (2012a). Lessons still to learn. *Flight International*, Vol. 181, No. 5324, pp. 26–33.

Learmont, D. (2012b). Modern jets reach safety milestone. *Flight International*, Vol. 182, No. 5359, p. 8.

Learmont, D. (2012c). AF447 prompt alarm review. *Flight International*, Vol. 182, No. 5351, p. 12.

Learmont, D. (2012d). Training is failing. *Flight International*, Vol. 179, No. 5277, pp. 30–33.

Ledegang, W.D, Groen, E.L. and Wentink, L. (2011). Pilot performance in centrifuge-based simulation of unusual attitude recovery. *Journal of Aircraft*, Vol. 49, No. 4, pp. 1161–1167.

Liang, G.F., Lin, J.T., Hwang, S.L., Wang, E.M. and Patterson, P. (2010). Preventing human errors in aviation maintenance using an on-line maintenance assistance platform. *International Journal of Industrial Ergonomics*, Vol. 40, pp. 356–367.

Newman, R.L. (2003). Advanced display certification issues. *Digital Avionics Systems Conference*, 12–16 October.

Parker Brown, D. (2012) Farewell to the Airbus A340. Retrieved from www.airlinereporter.com/2012/01/a-farewell-to-the-airbus-a340/, 8 December 2012.

Pierobon, M. (2012a). Unmanned issues. *Aviation Week & Space Technology*, Vol. 174, No. 40, p. 34.

Pierobon, M. (2012b). Inspecting inspections. *Aviation Week & Space Technology*, Vol. 174, No. 45, p. MRO27.

Rogers, R.O. and Boquet, A. (2012). The benefits and limitations of ground-based upset-recovery training for general aviation pilots. *Aeronautical Journal*, Vol. 116, No. 1184, pp. 1015–1039.

Rolls-Royce (2012). RB211-535. Retrieved from www.rolls-royce.com/civil/products/largeaircraft/rb211_535/, 20 December 2012.

Wagenaar, W.A., Hudson, P.T.W. and Reason, J.T. (1990). Cognitive failures and accidents. *Applied Cognitive Psychology*, Vol. 4, No. 4, pp. 273–294.

Wikipedia (2012). Wright R-3350 Duplex Cyclone. Retrieved from http://en.wikipedia.org/wiki/Wright_R-3350_Duplex-Cyclone, 23 December 2012.

8 Newly industrialising economies and the aircraft industry

Economic and industrial policy views in Asia

Sören Eriksson

Introduction

Major shifts have taken place in global manufacturing and trade during the last decades. Internationalisation throughout the 1950s and the 1960s was mainly an activity within the old industrial core (OIC) – the industrialised countries in Western Europe and North America (United States, Canada) and a few other countries such as Australia and Japan.

International economic integration until the 1960s was essentially a shallow integration, manifested largely through arm's-length trade in goods and services between independent firms and through international movement of portfolio capital and relatively simple direct investment. In today's world we see more deep integration, organised primarily within and between geographically extensive and complex global production networks, and through a variety of mechanisms, increasingly becoming the norm (Dicken, 2011).

Such qualitative changes are simply not captured in aggregate trade and investment data used by the sceptics. There has been a huge increase in both intra-industry and intra-firm trade, both of which are clear indicators of more functionally fragmented and geographically dispersed production processes (Dicken, 2011). These developments have also been seen in the global aircraft manufacturing industry (Eriksson, 1995). Globalisation processes, implying both extensive geographical spread and a higher degree of functional integration, embrace many parts of the world, especially newly industrialising economies (NIEs).

There are no universal agreed-upon criteria of what makes a country a developing or newly industrialised economy, but NIEs are nations undergoing rapid economic growth and industrialisation (usually export-oriented). They can also be defined as countries with more advanced economies than other developing nations, but which have not yet developed country status. Other criteria include the size of a nation's GDP per capita compared to other nations or those economies that have in a macroeconomic sense outpaced their developing counterparts. Other designations used for this heterogeneous group of countries are advanced developing countries and emerging economies.

In the 1970s and 1980s, this group included the first generation of Asian NIEs – Hong Kong, South Korea, Singapore and Taiwan. Examples from the 1990s and early twenty-first century are China, India, Malaysia, the Philippines, Thailand and Turkey. Economists and political scientists sometimes disagree over the classification of these countries. Various organisations, such as the World Bank, IMF, United Nations and WTO have their own definitions.

The number of countries that have tried to foster an aircraft industry in 'the shadow' of the leading aerospace nations has steadily increased (Todd and Simpson, 1986; Eriksson, 1995; Vértesy, 2011), thus implying an increased globalisation in this industry. The aerospace/aircraft industries have in recent years frequently been used as a target and tool in many developing and emerging economies as a means for economic and industrial development. There are a few main reasons for this development (Eriksson, 1995, pp. 122–123),

- Political isolation and/or national independence: from the political point of view there is no doubt that the various embargoes that have been imposed on various nations have been a push-factor for initiating development of an aircraft industry, especially the military one. National independence may also aim at economic and industrial independence, implying a nationalistic view of development.
- Economic development: this is a main argument for many countries when they start investing in this industry. They have the desire to foster economic and industrial development and to create 'spin-off' and 'spill-over' effects to other industries and sectors of society. These effects include creation of jobs, development of new firms and technologies.
- Economies that want to maintain the growth of their industrial sector have to consider two options: either to reduce or increase their participation in international trade. This first option means to deepen the *import substitution* process and the second way means to *encourage production for export*. In the context of the aircraft industry, import substitution implies saving money by producing domestic aircraft and in the case of export promotion the domestic industry can act as an earner of foreign currency and create new markets for the industry.
- Prestige: the development of an aircraft industry is based on several factors, some rational, other less so. To the latter we can attribute the factor of prestige. Without doubt there is such a factor (Eriksson, 2003), although it is very difficult to prove.

Aircraft, whether military or commercial, are assembled in many countries, but few of them have the capability to design, develop and produce an entire aeroplane. Much of the expenditure to develop a new aeroplane is spent on integrating numerous technologies and systems with origins from various fields and industries, i.e. systems integration. Technology used in modern aircraft is extremely demanding due to the high levels of functional performance, reliability, safety and efficiency required at the system level (Eriksson, 2010).

Thus, emerging aerospace firms and nations have a great dependency on established companies in the leading aerospace nations because of the needs for transfer of technology, but the success of technology transfer is determined both by the installation of a technology at the destination site and by the utilisation of the technology after it has been transferred (Steenhuis and de Bruijn, 2001). Steenhuis and de Bruijn (2002) discuss the concept of international technology transfer in the aircraft industry based on learning curves as international transfer of technology still encounters great difficulties. One conclusion was that inappropriate and unrealistic learning curves sometimes were applied to the destination companies. Building up an aircraft industry is much more than thinking about technology itself – it is very much a highly complex process that can be understood in terms of 'explicit' and 'tacit' knowledge. Explicit knowledge can be transmitted in formal, systematic language, while tacit knowledge is based on experiences, rooted in action or a specific context in individuals and organisations.

Technology transfer is consequently more than the movement of machines, equipment and tools to new locations. It is a socio-technical process implying the transfer of machinery, equipment and tools, as well as socio-cultural knowledge and skill (Levin, 1993). Long-term competitiveness in advanced technology industries, such as aerospace, is also based on innovative capability. Thus, catching up and overtaking established technological leaders poses formidable problems for imitators and aspirants for leadership, since they must aim at a moving target. It is no use simply importing today's technology from the leading countries, for by the time it has been introduced and assimilated, the leaders have moved on (Freeman, 1988). Applied to the aircraft industry, Steenhuis *et al.* (2007) discuss such issues concerning catch-up and technology transfer strategies in four industrially developing countries, including the leader companies' improvement of technologies or moves to newer technologies.

It is well-known that there are linkages between civil and military aircraft development and production. Many producers develop and manufacture both kinds of aircraft, and many systems and technologies that are used are applied to both civil and military aircraft. Historically, there are a number of examples from the United States and Europe where aircraft manufacturers have started as military aircraft producers, but later moved into civil aircraft manufacturing. Thus, in this chapter the military activities will be dealt with when they are a part of the historic development into commercial activities.

This chapter will focus on economies in Asia with manufacturing activities in the commercial aircraft sector. It will include a wide range of countries (heterogeneous group), using a broad definition of NIEs. Some of the countries are by some definitions no longer counted as 'emerging' economies (although they have been for a long period) due to their successful economic and industrial development. They are nonetheless interesting industrial examples and can be looked upon as emerging, or newly industrialising, aerospace economies. By definition, the 'old industrial core' Japan is excluded from this chapter.

The main focus of this chapter is to investigate:

- the background and origin of commercial aircraft industrial activities;
- economic and industrial policy arguments used;
- commercial aircraft developments;
- development of commercial subcontracting as indicators of more functionally fragmented and geographically dispersed production processes.[1]

West Asia

Israel

Israel, previously defined as a newly industrialising country, is nowadays usually ranked as a 'highly developed' economy and became an OECD country in 2010. Israel has a very competent aircraft industry, producing aerospace systems both for civilian and military use.

Israel Aircraft Industries (IAI), the nation's prime aerospace company, was established in 1953 as Bedek Aviation Company in order to maintain Israel Defense Forces (IDF) aircraft. In 1959 the state-owned company started licensed manufacturing of the French Fouga Magister, a two-seat turbo-jet trainer, locally named Tzukit. In response to the French embargo imposed on the region after the Six-Day War in 1967 Israel started developing its own derivatives (Nesher and Kfir) of French Mirage fighters. In 1980 the government of Israel took the decision to use the experience IAI had accumulated to develop and manufacture a modern fighter aircraft, the Lavi, but the project was cancelled in 1987. The closure of the Lavi project led to a serious crisis at IAI that led to job cuts and a reorganisation of the company, implying increased focus on commercial activities.

In the middle of the 1960s the company had started a diversification of the business, moving into civil production. IAI's first own-design was the Arava, a utility STOL transport aircraft intended both for civil military and aircraft markets. Design work started in 1966 and production ceased in the late 1980s when 103 aeroplanes had been manufactured (Globalsecurity, 2014).

In 1961 the Aero Commander Bethany Division of Rockwell Standard Corporation (United States) announced the development of a new executive transport aircraft, the Jet Commander 1121. The merger that joined North American Aviation and Rockwell Standard in 1967 brought a sales conflict of similar aircraft: North American Sabreliner and Rockwell's Jet Commander. It was decided to continue production of the longer-established Sabreliner, and all tooling and production rights were sold to Israel Aircraft Industries (Mondey, 1981). It became the basis for the IAI Westwind (1121/1122/1123/1124) business jets manufactured until the late 1980s.

The Astra series of business jets (1125/SP/SPX) were developed from the Westwind. In the late 1980s the original 1125 Astra was replaced by the Astra SP, which included a new airframe and wing design. The Astra SPX was introduced in 1994, with new engines and winglets (Jetadvisors, 2014).

With the start in the early 1990s, Galaxy Aerospace, a subsidiary of IAI, developed a new business jet with an intercontinental range, Astra Galaxy. Delivery of this aircraft started in 1999, but a few years later the IAI product line of business jets were sold to the US Gulfstream Company. At the end of the 1990s, General Dynamics, the large US aerospace and defence industry, purchased Gulfstream, a main US manufacturer of business jets. The company focused on enhancing product performance and lowering costs. In 2001 it acquired Galaxy Aerospace and with it Astra SPX and the new Galaxy, which were later rebranded the G100 and G200, respectively (Gulfstream, 2014).

In 2006 the 22-year production run of the Astra SPX/G100 ended, and the improved G150 entered service to take its place, while the larger Galaxy/G200 was produced from 1999 to 2011. In 2005, Gulfstream and IAI began designing a follow-on aircraft to the Gulfstream 200. The new model, then known as the G250, was launched in 2008 (Croft, 2008). In July 2011 the G250 was renamed the G280.

The G150 and G280 are still manufactured by IAI in Tel Aviv, Israel, although it is since 2001 an integral part of the Gulfstream family of business jets.

Gulfstream owns the type certificate for both the G150 and G280, while IAI owns the production certificate. The initial phase manufacturing (green aircraft) is done at IAI's facility in Tel Aviv and then the aircraft are flown to the final phase manufacturing (interior and paint) at Gulfstream's completion centre in Dallas, United States. A total of 442 Jet Commanders (1121) and Westwind series (1122, 1123, 1124) of aircraft were produced under IAI's designation. Below are the number of Astra and Galaxy aircraft that have been produced (as of December 2013):[2]

- 145 Astra/Astra SPX/G100
- 104 G150
- 250 Galaxy/G200
- 23 G280.

As a part of extending commercial activities, IAI began developing the Airtruck, a cargo turboprop aircraft capable of carrying five standard-sized containers over a range of about 1,850 km (1,000 nm). It was designed to meet a requirement from US express parcels carrier FedEx for a new-generation freighter to replace Boeing 727s and Fokker F27s on hub feeder services. FedEx had pledged a requirement for around 100 aircraft, but IAI sought more sales to enable it to launch the aircraft. The Israeli company also looked for risk-sharing subcontractors to manufacture major sections of the aircraft. Negotiations for sales and partners were conducted in Europe and the Far East (*Flight International*, 11–17 August 1999, p. 5). After several attempts to launch the aircraft it was later cancelled.

Another attempt to expand the commercial aviation business came when US aircraft manufacturer Fairchild, then the owner of aircraft manufacturer Dornier, signed an agreement whereby IAI would assemble in Israel the new proposed

Dornier 428 regional jet aircraft. The IAI–Fairchild agreement was for the design, manufacture and assembly of the fuselage. It comes on top of an agreement signed in June 1999, under which IAI was entrusted with engineering planning, flight-testing and licensing (Globes, 1999). In early 2000 it was revealed that IAI was increasing its participation in the programme, expanding into design and manufacturing of additional components such as electrical components and air-conditioning systems (*Flight International*, 22–28 February, 2000, p. 17). The first supply was planned for 2003, but the project was cancelled in August 2000 due to changing market conditions (official explanation) but certainly too few orders was a contribution to the cancellation.

For the future, the emphasis for IAI will be on exploring opportunities for producing longer-range executive jets (Fulgham, 2012).

IAI's Commercial Aircraft Group is involved as a subcontractor to several international commercial aircraft projects:

- Boeing 777: empennage (sole supplier, leading-edge assemblies, tip and skin panels).
- Boeing 787: section 46/47 (pax floor grid assembly and cargo floor assembly, door surrounds), section 48 (pivot bulkhead), horizontal stabilizer (tip assembly, LE assembly and strakelet, trailing edge).

IAI is also a subcontractor to major international engine programmes, producing engine nacelles, fan cowls and barrels. IAI's Bedek Aviation Group is one of the largest specialists of the conversion of Boeing passenger aircraft (B737, B767, B747) to cargo aircraft.

Turkey

Turkey is located both in Asia and in Europe, although about 97 per cent of the land area is located in Asia, and the Asian part is home to about 88 per cent of the nation's population. Although mainly an Asian country in area and population views, Turkey has strong economic and political connections to Europe and the Western world. Turkey became a NATO member in 1952 and long saw itself as the eastern bulwark of the NATO alliance; it is a major regional power in the Middle East.

Turkey's aircraft industry is centred on the Turkish Aircraft Industries Corporation (TUSAS), established on 28 June 1973 under the auspices of the Ministry of Industry and Technology in order to reduce the foreign dependency on the defence industry in Turkey (TAI, 2014). Very limited development took place during the first decade, but since the foundation of the Republic Turkey had sought to have its own national aerospace industry. There were several false starts over the years, but the Turkey Air Force needs for a modern fighter led in 1984 to the US Peace Onyx Program and the subsequent formation of TUSAS Aerospace Industries (TAI) and the new TAI plant at Murted, outside Ankara (Wanstall, 1990a).

The Peace Onyx Program was the US agreement on sales and licensed production of the General Dynamics F-16 fighters to Turkey. Initially TAI was 51 per cent Turkish-owned and 49 per cent US-owned (General Dynamics 42 per cent and General Electric 7 per cent, the latter the maker of the F110 engines for the F-16). Construction of the facility in Murted began in mid-1984, and the first locally manufactured F-16 left the facility in early 1988. The F110 engines were produced by TUSAS Engine Industries (TEI) in a large custom-built plant at Eskesehir, 240 km west of Ankara (Wanstall, 1990b).

Since then, the Turkish government through TAI has made large investments in a number of military aircraft projects, mainly various modernisation and upgrading programmes of various military aircraft, but also licensed manufacturing of foreign military helicopters. The military aircraft activities have been closely connected to offset deals, implying that foreign aircraft sales to Turkey have created a number of subcontracting works for TAI.

During the 1980s discussions were taking place about the Turkish government's need to replace the ageing fleet of C-47s (military version of the Douglas DC-3) and to provide additional tactical airlift to supplement its Lockheed C-130 Hercules and Transalls (French/German military transport aircraft). This led to an agreement to buy, and assembly under licence, the Spanish-Indonesian CN-235 light civil/military transport aircraft. Fifty aircraft were produced between 1991–1998, all of them delivered to the Turkish Air Force (*Hurriyet Daily News*, 8 May 1998).

In the 1990s, it became evident that TAI wanted to use the knowledge and technical resources at its facilities to move into commercial production.

During the middle of the 1990s, Turkey, as so many other countries, had plans to develop a small twin-engine commuter aircraft to meet a market demand that was due to the government's initiative to open 40 regional airports (*Flight International*, 18–24 October, 1995, p. 13). This project was never realised.

In an interview (Moxon, 2000) with TAI's managing director, Brig. General Kaya Ergenc, he says that TAI wants to move away from dependence on military production and within ten years increase international commercial programmes sales to 40–50 per cent of the turnover. The civil aircraft production performed during the 1990s had mainly been offset against the purchase of aircraft by state-owned Turkish Airlines. Such contracts included 600 737 wingtips and 400 flight panels for Boeing (Moxon, 2000).

TAI was restructured in 2005, meaning the current shareholders are the Turkish Armed Forces Foundation (54.49 per cent), the Undersecretariat for Defence Industries (45.45 per cent) and the Turkish Aeronautical Association (0.06 per cent).

Current civil aircraft production in 2014 is as follows (TAI, 2014):

- Airbus: risk-sharing partnership contract for design and manufacture of Aileron for Airbus' new developing A350XWB. Another contract was signed in 1998 between TAI and EADS-CASA, covering the manufacture of 200 ship sets of section 18 fuselage panels for A319/320/321 aircraft. The first programme was completed with the delivery of the last set on 18 August 2004. Since then the deliveries have continued.

- Boeing: a contract was signed with Boeing in 2003; a total of 200 sets of B777 dorsal fins were manufactured at TAI's facilities. A new contract was signed in 2006 in regard to meeting December 2007–December 2012 requirements of Boeing. With the additional order, the number of total sets to be manufactured reached 350. Another commercial programme is the production of the Boeing 787 'elevator', 'cargo barrier' and 'body seal' components.
- Bombardier: manufacturing of the Bombardier C series fixed trailing edge (FTE). Assembly programme activities have been started with GTA (general terms agreement) signed on 17 December 2011 and STA (special terms agreement) signed on 21 January 2011 between Bombardier and TAI.
- Spirit Aero Systems Program: a production programme that started in 2002 for various sub-assemblies for 737, 747,767 and 777 Boeing Aircraft.[3]
- AgustaWestland 139 helicopter programme: manufacturing of various configured fuselages of this helicopter. A total of 42 fuselages were delivered to AgustaWestland in the year 2012, whereas 50 fuselages with two different configurations were delivered in 2013. TAI also manufactures the canopy, radome and tail boom skin.

Iran

Iran's Aircraft Manufacturing Industrial Company (HESA), located at Shahin Shahr, Isfahan, was established in 1976 to produce the Bell 214ST helicopter.

The 214ST was developed as a military project from the Bell 214B BigLifter, specifically for production in Iran. Bell's development costs for the new derivative were funded by the Iranian government (Apostolo, 1984, p. 54).

The factory was initially planned for production of 350 STs plus other versions of the Bell 214 (*Air International*, 1982, pp. 165–166). Development of three prototypes started in 1978 (Donald, 1997), but the work ended due to the Iranian Revolution and subsequent sanctions against Iran.

The first civil aircraft activities taking place at this facility were when, in 1995, an inter-governmental agreement was signed between Iran and Ukraine on licensed assembly of the Antonov An-140 by HESA. The first An-140 (dubbed IrAn-140) of the Iranian assembly was rolled out in 2001. Only seven of the IrAn-140 had been assembled between 2001 and 2008 (Aviacor, 2014). Until 2013 HESA had only produced 14 aircraft, though initially it was planned to manufacture 12 airplanes yearly (Muravsky 2013).

The aircraft was billed as being a symbol of Iran's achievement in the aviation industry, but from the very beginning the IrAn-140 programme was riddled with engine failures, safety concerns and complaints from Iranian aviation experts about the licensed production contract, and the weak performance of the aircraft. When the sole airworthy HESA IrAn-140 turboprop crashed on take-off from Tehran in August 2014, Iran's hopes of becoming an aerospace-manufacturing nation appeared to crash with it (*Flightglobal*, 25 November 2014).

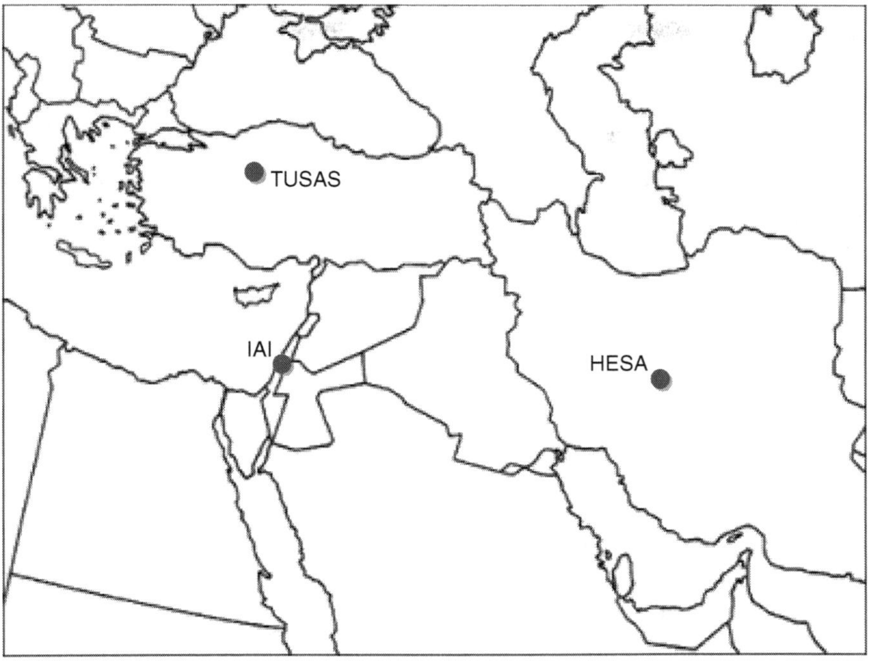

Figure 8.1 Location of aircraft industries in West Asia.

No fewer than four accidents involving the type led to a regulatory ban on all flight operations by the aircraft. One of many issues was the aircraft's Klimov TV3-117VMA engines – they were not suited to Iranian meteorological conditions and the weak performance of the aircraft's engines restricted IrAn-140s to carrying a maximum of 37 passengers. Antonov had been offered the Pratt & Whitney Canada PW127A engine as a replacement for the TV3-117VMA-SBM1s, but sanctions meant that HESA could not implement the engine change (*Flightglobal*, 25 November 2014)

After the accident, the Iranian Civil Aviation Organisation banned all flight operations of the IrAn-140 until investigation teams from HESA and Antonov could determine the cause of the crash.

Another failed project was the planned licensed assembly of the Antonov An-148 regional jets, which was not realised. A letter of intent was signed for the production of 50 An-148s, with the bulk of the 70-seaters to be assembled locally from kits, although an initial few were to be supplied directly from the main plants in Kiev and Voronezh (*Flight International*, 13 November 2008). The contract, expected to be finalised in 2009, called for an increasing level of local production as the programme progressed (*Flight International*, 13 November 2008). Nothing has happened since the agreement was signed.

South Asia

India

Introduction

India has a large aerospace industry with a strong emphasis on military aircraft and defence products. The industry is to a great extent associated with Hindustan Aeronautics Limited (HAL), a government company managed by the Indian Ministry of Defence. It is one of the largest aerospace companies of any developing or newly industrialising country, with more than 30,000 employees.

HAL is involved in many parts of the aerospace industry, such as manufacture and assembly of aircraft, avionics, engines and helicopters, but also MRO and operating of airports.

The company can trace its roots to the creation of Hindustan Aircraft Ltd (HAL) in Bangalore in 1940. The company was a private start-up, but India's government bought one-third stake shortly after establishment. During the Second World War the Bangalore factory was handed over to the United States Army Air Forces (Air Technical Service Command) and used as a depot-level maintenance facility, including overhaul and repair. The USAAF left and handed over to the Indian government in October 1945. In 1964 Hindustan Aircraft Ltd merged with the Indian company Aeronautics India to form Hindustan Aeronautics Ltd, retaining the HAL identity (Eriksson, 1995).

A large number of foreign aircraft models have been licence-manufactured in India. It started with the assembly of the American military trainer Harlow PC-5 during the Second World War and continued with the British Percival Prentice trainer aircraft after the war. The first aircraft designed by HAL was the H-2 two-seat primary trainer that entered production in the early 1950s. In the late 1950s a domestic two-seat monoplane, the Pushpak, was developed, although based on a foreign design.

In 1956 India signed an agreement to licence-manufacture its first jet aircraft, the British Folland (Hawker Siddely) Gnat fighter/trainer aircraft, which later went through some modifications and was given the name Ajeet (Eriksson, 1995). Since then a number of foreign military aircraft have been manufactured under licence in India, most notably Soviet/Russian fighter aircraft Mig-21s, Mig-27s and more recently the Sukhoi Su-30MKI. The Anglo-French SEPECAT Jaguar ground attack aircraft and the British BAE Hawk jet trainer aircraft have also been assembled by HAL.

HAL has its head office, and a large number of facilities in Bangalore (Aircraft Division, Overhaul Division, Aerospace Division, Airport Services Centre, Engine Division, Foundry and Forge Division, Industrial & Marine Gas Turbine Division, Facilities Management Division, Helicopter Division, Helicopter MRO Division, Composites Manufacturing Division).

Other facilities are located throughout India: Nasik, Koraput, Hyderabad, Kanpur, Korwa, Lucknow and Barrackpore (Calcutta/Kolkata). Nasik (Aircraft

Division, Aircraft Overhaul Division) and Koraput (Engine Division, Sukhoi Engine Division) comprise the Mig Complex, a name used for the licensed production of Soviet/Russian military aircraft and engines and associated MRO activities.

The Hyderabad and Korwa divisions manufacture aviation electronics (avionics), mainly for military aircraft. The Lucknow Accessories Division manufactures various kinds of parts and system (hydraulics systems, environmental control systems, various instruments, wheels and brakes, etc.), while the Barrackpore Division is mainly an MRO facility for the French licence-built Cheetah and Chetak Helicopters.

Civil aircraft activities

In 1960 HAL's Transport Aircraft Division, in Kanpur, was established to manufacture the British Hawker Siddeley HS-748 passenger transport aircraft. This medium-haul turboprop aircraft was originally designed in the late 1950s by the British firm Avro (then a part of the Hawker Siddeley Group) as a potential replacement for the enduring but ageing Douglas DC-3s. The project had a slow start, with few orders, but encouragement came in July 1959 when the Indian government announced its intention to assemble the HS748 under licence at Kanpur (Munson, 1983, p. 283). A total of 89 aircraft were produced in Kanpur between 1960 and 1983.

A small agricultural aircraft, the HA-31 Basant, was developed by HAL, but only 19 were manufactured between 1975 and 1978. The HAL HPT-32 Deepak was a propeller-driven primary trainer, with 142 manufactured between 1983 and 1998 (HAL, Kanpur, 2014).

A licence agreement was signed in 1983 between Dornier, Germany and HAL for the production of the Dornier Do 228, twin-engine, multi-role light transport aircraft.[4] Production started in 1985 and the aircraft is still in production, with a total of 125 manufactured so far (HAL, Kanpur, 2014). While the German main production line ended in 1998, production continued in India.

Nowadays, the Aviation Division of the Swiss Technology Group RUAG owns the production rights for this aircraft, as it acquired the rights and licences when the parent company went into liquidation in 2002. A few years later a development programme for a new generation, the Do 228NG started. RUAG is turning out the new generation Do 228s from its facility in Oberpfaffenhofen, Germany. It is built in collaboration with HAL, which provides the basic airframe, while RUAG integrates the final product. The Do 228NG features a new glass cockpit, modified interior and five-bladed props, along with a number of other design tweaks (Airvectors, 2014).

In July 2014, an agreement was signed between RUAG and Tata Advanced Systems, India, that the latter will provide RUAG Aviation with fully assembled fuselage and wing structures out of their Hyderabad Facilities in India. Tata Advanced Systems will undertake the complete scope of part manufacturing and assembly required (*Business Air*, 2014). This is based on a joint-venture agreement with the formation of a joint-venture company, Tata HAL Technologies Ltd.

HAL manufactures components and parts for some foreign aircraft manufacturers. In recent years there has been a slight increase in civil aircraft subcontracting work and in 2014 the following parts were manufactured:

- Airbus A320 forward passenger doors (Airbus France)
- Boeing 767 bulk cargo doors (Boeing USA)
- Boeing 777 uplock box assembly (Boeing USA)
- Boeing 777 flaperon (Boeing USA)
- Boeing 737-300 cargo conversion door and kits (IAI, Israel)
- G-150 rear fuselage (IAI, Israel)
- Legacy 450/500 passenger door (Embraer).

Until 2004 HAL manufactured the Boeing 757 over-wing exit doors and previously it also manufactured the Dornier Do 228 undercarriages and the Fokker 50 horizontal stabiliser and the ATP tailplane (Eriksson, 1995).

Efforts to develop domestic aircraft designs

In the mid-1980s discussions were underway in India between government authorities, the National Aerospace Laboratories (NAL) and HAL to increase India's participation in civil aircraft manufacturing and implement a long-term strategy to develop a viable civil aircraft industry. The result of these discussions became a proposal to make a feasibility study of a small multi-role light transport aircraft (LTA). This twin turboprop aircraft (later re-named SARAS), powered by two Pratt & Whitney Canada PT6A-66 engines, was planned with a seating capacity of up to 14 passengers. It was aimed at various roles such as executive transport, light package carrier, remote sensing, coast guard, border patrol, air ambulance and other community services.[5]

After the feasibility study had been published a decision was taken to go ahead with the project. The search for a foreign partner that could provide both technological and financial support was initiated. It ended up with an agreement with the Russian design bureau Myasishchev, but ended in 1993 due to lack of investment (*Flight International*, 22–28 May 2001, p. 25). Instead, the project was funded by India's Technology Development Board, the Ministry of Civil Aviation and Hindustan Aeronautics (*Flight International*, 22–28 May 2001, p. 25).

Interviews (by the author) with officials from NAL and HAL in Singapore 1996 stated that they foresaw a market of at least 400 aircraft in India and 'hundreds' of aircraft for the international market.

The project was marred by delays and the first flight took place in May 2004, which implies a development period of about 15 years, which is extremely long for such an aircraft. The project came to an even bigger crisis when the second prototype crashed during a test flight in March 2009, near Bidadi, 40 km from

Bangalore, killing its three pilots. An inquiry report by the Directorate General of Civil Aviation (DGCA) identified 61 flaws that contributed to the crash of the SARAS aircraft. Barely a month before the fatal crash, the aircraft was used for flying in the Aero India 2009 air show for four days without the DGCA's permission (*Deccan Herald*, 2010).

Thus, the first attempt to develop and market a domestic civil passenger aircraft became a big failure. According to the *Times of India* (10 January 2014) the Indian Air Force will buy 15 SARAS aircraft of a modified and re-engined version. Yet in January 2014 the aircraft was not certified, neither by local or international authorities, after nearly 30 years of development!

In spite of all the failures throughout the SARAS project, India's government, NAL and HAL started to discuss new projects. In 2007, NAL and HAL announced the development of a 70-seat turboprop, the regional transport aircraft RTA-70. It was planned for roll-out in 2013, but nothing happened. It was not even decided if it would be a turboprop or a jet aircraft, which is of basic importance when initiating a development project.

Instead, the project has turned into a 90-seater regional jet, labelled the Indian Regional Jet (IRJ). India's dream project of building mid-size civilian aircraft is expected to get the nod at a high-level meeting convened by Prime Minister Manmohan Singh to discuss measures to boost the manufacturing sector (*India Today*, 8 July 2013). The project was also looked upon as a tool to catch up with China, Japan and Russia in building regional aircraft and reducing dependence on Bombardier and Embraer, which dominate the market for such planes (Livemint and *The Wall Street Journal*, 2014).

Referring to Satish Chandra, head of the aircraft programme at NAL, this project is also justified from a national industrial development view, i.e. build the expertise so that this aircraft project can create spin-offs to other sectors (Livemint and *The Wall Street Journal*, 2014). The project plan is for a roll-out in 2017, but it is not yet decided (early 2014) on the engine configuration, jet or turboprop, which was also a main issue on the RTA-70. Although it is labelled the Indian Regional Jet, NAL officially speaks about the use of a turboprop. The project seems to be very uncertain, and if the project goes ahead 'India' will find itself in a very competitive and crowded market.

Besides HAL, Taneja Aerospace & Aviation Ltd (TAAL) was established in 1994 as the first private-sector company in the country to manufacture general aviation aircraft (TAAL, 2014).

The initial business of the company was to manufacture the Italian Partenavia P68C, six-seat, twin-engine aircraft in India. Taneja licence-produced the Partenavia-designed P68 at its Hosur, India, plant from 1995 to 1998. The first five aircraft were built from Italian kits, with Taneja rolling out its first indigenously produced example in 1998 (*Flight International*, 28 October–3 November 2003, p. 57). When Partenavia became bankrupt in 1998, another Italian company, Vulcanair, established in 1996, purchased all the assets, type design, trademarks and rights of the Partenavia brand.[6] Vulcanair cancelled the agreement with Taneja (*Flight International*, October–3 November 2003, p. 57).

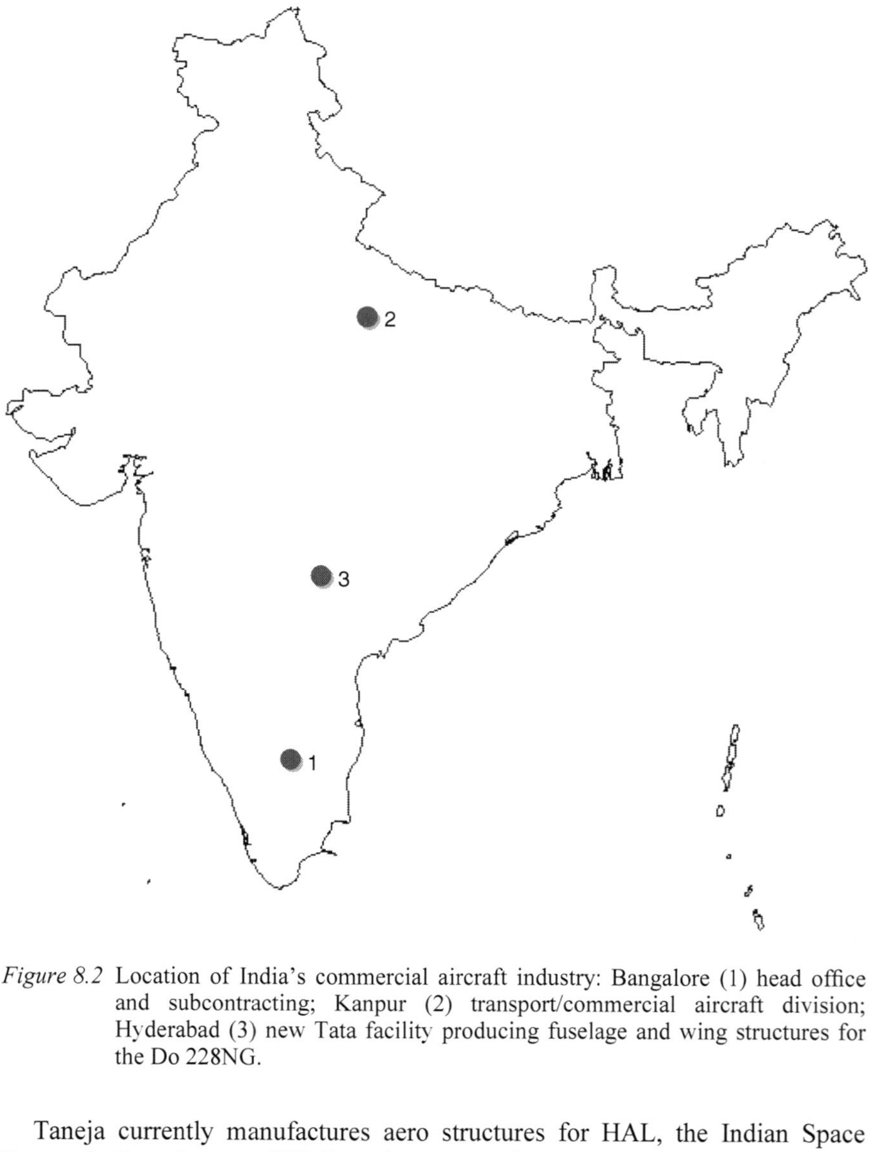

Figure 8.2 Location of India's commercial aircraft industry: Bangalore (1) head office and subcontracting; Kanpur (2) transport/commercial aircraft division; Hyderabad (3) new Tata facility producing fuselage and wing structures for the Do 228NG.

Taneja currently manufactures aero structures for HAL, the Indian Space Research Organization (ISRO) and NAL, and make modifications on Indian Navy and Air Force helicopters and aircraft. It also built major structures of the ill-fated SARAS aircraft.

Southeast Asia

Indonesia

Background

Following independence, Indonesia's economic policy was shaped by a strong sense of nationalism flavoured with anti-colonial sentiment. Indonesia's second president, Suharto, introduced the 'New Order', based on a series of five-year plans designed to support the strong development of industrial projects. Such a project was the establishment of commercial aircraft manufacturer IPTN, the largest and most ambitious investment by the Indonesian government to promote technology development in the country (Eriksson, 1995).

During Suharto's rule, the Indonesian government was characterised by two distinct and competing groups of economic advisers: the technocrats and a diverse group of economic nationalists. While the technocrats were strongly committed to markets and competition, the nationalists had reservations about free market ideology and pressed for active government intervention in market behaviour as well as regulation. The most forceful exponent of the nationalist view was the architect of Indonesia's high-technology strategy Dr B.J. Habibie, the former State Minister for Research and Technology, who also was the founder of IPTN (Eriksson, 2003).

According to Habibie, Indonesia could never catch up economically with industrialised nations without a strong government-led push to support a self-sustaining high-tech manufacturing base. Habibie saw Indonesia's future competitive advantage in value-added high technology and in the upgrading of human resources. He believed that Indonesia must focus on the 'competitive advantages' that only technology can provide rather than rely on its traditional and 'comparative advantages' of abundant land and labour (Smith, 1998).

Habibie's model of development rejected orthodox economic approaches, with their emphasis on cost–benefit analysis and comparative advantage. Instead, he relied on guiding principles such as a strong education base and the development of national R&D capacities as a tool to minimise reliance on imported technologies. An important part in this 'national strategy' was creating 'vehicle industries' as a way to develop 'hands-on' scientific competence (Eriksson, 2003).[7]

It is obvious that the main goal is technology itself, not the business that has been the priority. This can be exemplified by an interview (Elson, 1983, p. 15) in *Aviation Week & Space Technology*: 'Future programs will be selected largely for their ability to meet domestic needs and further the nation's industrialization and technology transfer objectives.' In another interview (Bailey, 1992, p. 51), Habibie said:

> The approach to making an aircraft industry in Indonesia is not new. There was a minister for aircraft industry under Soekarno, but none of them ever

> succeeded. The reason is very simple: no real preparation and background. It's not a matter of decision, it's not a matter of capital, it's a matter of know-how.

With this approach it is easy to forget that managerial capability and managing the whole project is an indispensable ingredient in technological development:

> The neglect of managerial know-how results in part from a bias at work in the way policy makers in most countries (not only Indonesia) think about 'innovation', 'technology transfer', and 'technological development'. Most are preoccupied with the tangible indicators of technological advance – the number of scientists and engineers, licensing agreements, new industries established – rather than coupling them with considerations about what it takes to be commercially viable, even in the long run. As a consequence, the 'softer' and less glamorous managerial skills associated with coordination, marketing, after-sales service, personal management, pricing, scheduling and inventory control are neglected.
>
> (McKendrick, 1992, p. 65)

Habibie's focus on high technology earned him plenty of criticism at home and abroad. The major arguments against his ideas concerned their limited effects on the economy as a whole, whether this kind of industry is an appropriate one for a country of Indonesia's economic and technological stage of development (Eriksson,

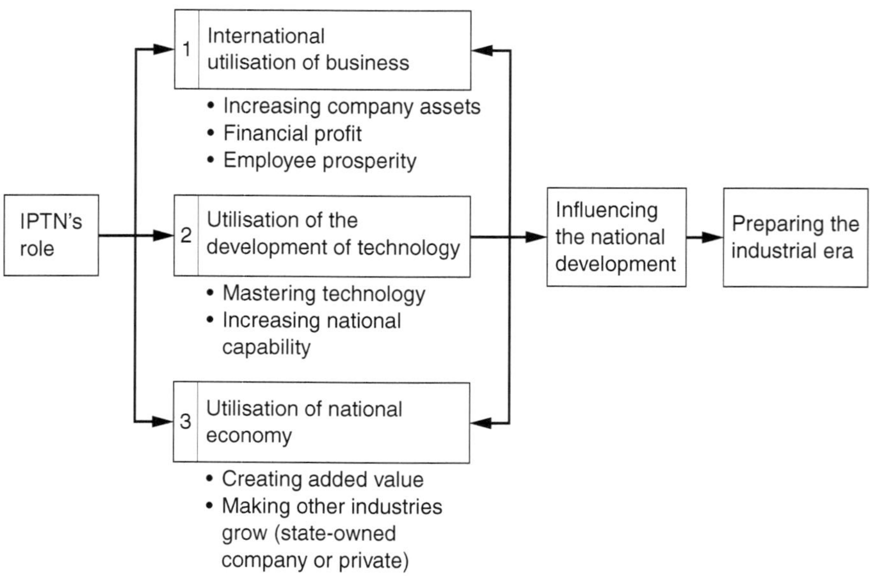

Figure 8.3 The role of IPTN in the national development (Habibie's perspectives) (source: Eriksson, 1995).

2003). The technocrats questioned the economic validity of high-technology production in a labour-surplus economy. There were also fears about the establishment of economic and technological enclaves with very limited links to the rest of society.

Establishment of IPTN

The city of Bandung, about 180 km southeast of Jakarta, became the location of Indonesia's emerging aircraft industry. In 1974, Habibie, with a background in the German aircraft industry, and a small team returned to Indonesia and established the Advanced Technology and Aviation Technology Divisions in the state-owned oil company Pertamina, which provided them with a working environment to get started. The Pertamina divisions and state-owned Lembaga Industri Penerbangan Nurtanio merged and the result became PT Pesawat Terbang Nurtanio (Nurtanio Aircraft Industry Ltd). In April 1976, President Suharto issued a decree giving Habibie the managerial responsibility for the company, which was established in August 1976. In 1978 he was also appointed Minister of State for Research and Technology (Eriksson, 1995).

It changed its name in 1985 to Industri Pesawat Terbang Nusantara, or IPTN. In August 2000, its name was once again changed to PT Industri Dirgantara for domestic use and Indonesian Aerospace (IAe) as its international identity. The name IPTN is used in this chapter. On various occasions Dr Habibie and President Suharto have given additional motives for justifying the large investments in the aircraft industry. In an interview with *Interavia* (Davidson, 1981, p. 1236), Habibie said about the future of aviation in Indonesia:

> Look at the spread of Indonesia, nearly 14 000 islands extending over a distance equal to that between Paris and New York, and equal in area to the whole of Europe, and a population of 163 million which is dependent on air transport. We are condemned to aviation – there is no other way. As we have to use aircraft for essential communications, why not build them on our own rather than buy them.

From an advertisement in *Fortune*, 3 September 1984:

> During the roll-out ceremonies for the CN-235, President Suharto gave five reasons why the aircraft industry is 'absolutely important' for his country: to further integrate and unify the archipelagic nation; for security and defence; to generate job opportunities; to develop new technologies; and, he concluded, 'to increase the confidence of other countries and the world in our ability to apply modern technology'.

Indonesia's technology projects were long decided and influenced by Habibie because of his position as State Minister for Research and Technology. His influence started to diminish after the IMF's intervention in 1998 and after he lost the presidential elections in 1999 and was succeeded by Abdurrahman Wahid. Some features of Habibie's approach stand out:

> One is the extremely personalized manner in which projects have been under-taken. With the exception of the N-2130 project, still in its infancy, all the initiatives have been directly under his control: no major decision can be taken without his approval; no credible financial performance statements have ever been released; none of the usual checks and balances (such as scrutiny by the Department of Finance) is present; and not even the most powerful 'technocrat' in the cabinet has been able to challenge Habibie's direct access to the President.
>
> (Hill, 1998, p. 44)

Additional policy tools to assist IPTN's development included an import ban on competing aircraft, exemption from government policies directing state enterprises to buy domestic inputs and considerable discretionary authority granted to Habibie (McKendrick, 1992, p. 42).

Officially, IPTN's long-range goals were as follows (Eriksson, 1995):

1 To become self-reliant in the design and manufacture of aircraft and aerospace products.
2 To be competitive on the international market.
3 To support national defence and security.
4 To foster the development of other domestic technologies and industries.
5 To establish R&D in advanced technology and new products.

IPTN's aircraft manufacturing business

In its efforts to establish an indigenous aircraft industry with a far-reaching ability, with the intention to design, develop and manufacture whole aircraft, IPTN followed a four-phase scheme for the transfer of aircraft manufacture technology (Figure 8.4).

Implementation of the first phase started with the licensed manufacture of the Spanish CASA 212 Aviocar, a STOL light transport aircraft, and the German MBB Bo 105 helicopter in 1976. Later, Nurtanio/IPTN obtained a licence to build a number of Aérospatiale SA 330 Puma helicopters for the Indonesian market. The production of this functioned as a learning programme for the bigger, more modern and complicated SA 332 Super Puma.

The next agreement, signed in 1982, was for the production of an American helicopter, the Bell 412. In September 1995, the production of this helicopter was halted after a joint audit of IPTN's Bandung plant by the US Federal Aviation Administration (FAA) and Indonesia's DGAC because IPTN had failed to conform to FAA regulations. The parties revealed that some Bell 412 design data were missing or outdated (*Flight International*, 6–12 December 1995, p. 30). The inspection also uncovered the misuse of manufacturing manuals and

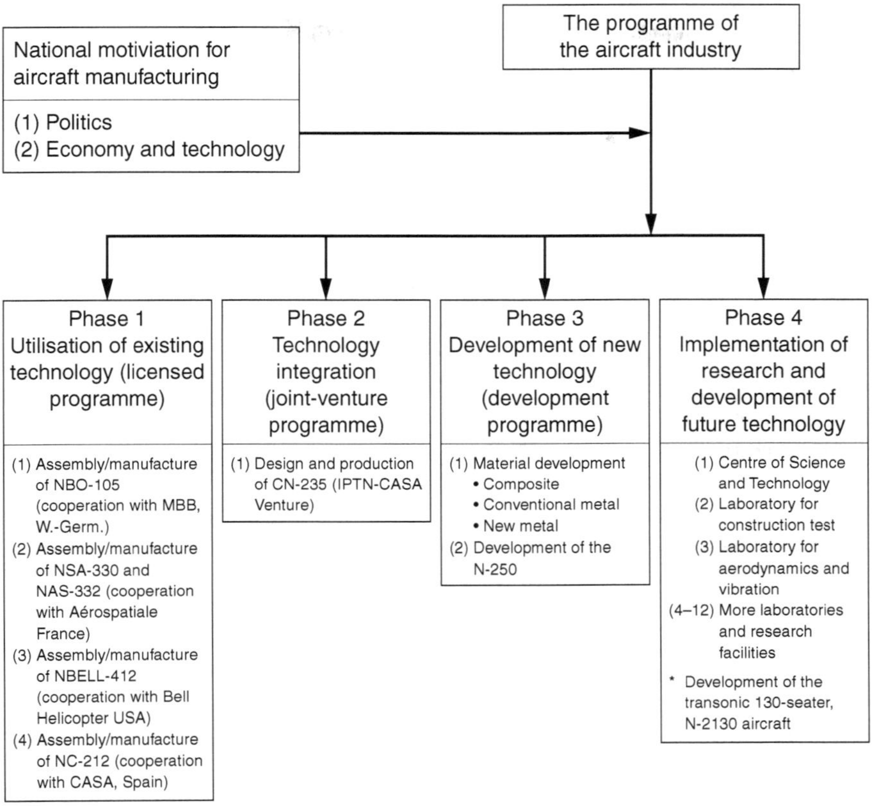

Figure 8.4 Implementation of technology at IPTN (source: Eriksson, 1995).

poor communication between IPTN and Bell Forth Worth (*Flight International*, 6–12 December 1995, p. 30). In the middle of the 1980s, IPTN received permission to build the MBB/Kawasaki BK-117 helicopter, but this programme was not successful and was terminated after only a few had been built.

Phase 2 (joint-venture programme) started in 1979, with the agreement to develop the CN-235 commuter/transport aircraft in collaboration with CASA of Spain. This phase was the integration of existing technology through the realisation of co-design and manufacturing programmes with the Spanish company CASA. The CN-235 was aimed at the regional airliner market, although the CN-235 very much looked like a compromise between commercial and military needs. The reason for this was that the design had a rear ventral door and sponson-mounted main undercarriage and shoulder-mounted wings. The aircraft was also planned to carry four LD-3 containers or a pair of 88-inch cargo pallets. A single management company, Air Technology Industries, was set up in Madrid in 1979, with Habibie as president. Design studies started in 1980 and prototype construction the year after. Simultaneous roll-outs were made in September 1983, and the first IPTN delivery was in 1986. Assembly lines were set up in Bandung and Spain (Eriksson, 1995). This programme was critical to IPTN as it was looked upon as a basis for the design of a larger and much more advanced aircraft.

The work-sharing agreement between the two companies was as follows: IPTN was responsible for the production of the main components of the tail unit (horizontal stabiliser, vertical stabiliser and rudder) and outer wing, outboard flap, aileron and door; CASA had responsibility for the production of the centre wing and power-plant, inner flap, main and nose landing gear and nose fuselage. The production and assembly of the fuselage, the centre and rear fuselage was the responsibility of each of the companies (Eriksson, 1995).

Until 1995 a major stumbling block for sales of the IPTN-built version of the CN-235 was its lack of an internationally recognised certificate of airworthiness. The company was finally granted Joint Aviation Rules Part 25 by the European Joint Aviation Authorities in 1995, but not before CASA had virtually cleaned up on the export front with its own FAA-certified CN-235 (Eriksson, 1995).

Up to 2001, about 35 CN-235s were produced in Indonesia. During the next ten years, up to early 2012, 22 more were manufactured, making a total of 57 aircraft. This is a very small number of aircraft produced from an international perspective and far from the break-even point. Around 250 CN-235s have been manufactured, most at CASA's (now EADS) Spanish assembly line in Seville. Fifty aircraft were manufactured under licence by Turkish Aerospace Industries (TAI) under an agreement signed between CASA and TAI. These aircraft were produced and delivered to the Turkish Air Force between 1991 and 1998 (*Hurriyet Daily News*, 8 May 1998).

One way to increase Indonesian orders for the CN-235 was to force a number of these aircraft onto Indonesian airlines, which resulted in the government's dismissal of Merpati Airline's president, as he refused to do so. A sales hurdle for the company has been its lack of export credit and thus it has instead resorted to barter trade, such as the counter-purchase agreement of rice with Thailand and Proton cars from Malaysia (Eriksson, 2003).

Phase 3 was the application of the acquired technology for the indigenous design and manufacture of entirely new products. It came into being with the announcement, in June 1989, to launch the fly-by-wire 50–54-seater N-250 regional turboprop. This was IPTN's first indigenously developed aircraft. In June 1993 Habibie abandoned the 50-seater design in favour of a stretched version, the 64–68-seater N-270, re-designated N-250-100. Apart from a fly-by-wire flight control system, full-authority digital engine control, composite propellers, engine-indication and crew-alerting system, the aircraft was equipped with other state-of-the-art technology such as a Doppler turbulence weather radar and a collision-avoidance system. The roll-out took place in November 1994 in Bandung, with flight testing starting in 1995 (Eriksson, 1995).

On several occasions during the 1990s, Habibie and IPTN released fictitious information claiming large letters of intent and orders of the N-250 aircraft, trying to give an impression of a successful project. Even before the aircraft had made its first flight, official talk started of establishing overseas production in the United States, choosing between Portland, Mobile or Phoenix (Eriksson, 2003). According Habibie, overseas production of the N-250 was a part of IPTN's long-term strategic vision, stretching over 15 to 20 years, and would be in addition to domestic production for the 'captive market' of up to 400 N-250 sales that were forecasted within Indonesia (*Flight International*, 2–8 March 1994, p. 16).

The second prototype of the N-250 (first certification prototype) was set to fly in May 1996, but as a result of component documents falling below FAA requirements, the maiden flight of this aircraft had to be delayed (*Flight International*, 9–15 October 1996, p. 10). The FAA refused to accept the aircraft until IPTN brought its vendor record system in line with international standards (*Flight International*, 9–15 October 1996, p. 10).

In early 1997, IPTN enlisted a team of European aerospace consultants to try to help secure Joint Airworthiness Authorities (JAA) type certification of this aircraft. Jakarta-based consultancy Bramadi Pratama recruited a group of former British Aerospace employees, ex-JAA officials and test pilots to assist IPTN and the Indonesian DGAC with certification (*Flight International*, 19–25 March 1997, p. 17). In 1998, during the Asian financial crisis, flight testing was frozen because of financial restrictions as the development programme ran into trouble when the IMF blocked further government support for IPTN.

As this project more or less came to a standstill, IPTN contacted a number of foreign companies in Asia and Europe to find industrial partners for the N-250 programme. In 1999 there were discussions between the Indonesian government and China about this project (*Flight International*, 29 August–4 September 2000, p. 16). IPTN was looking for an investor to supply US$90 million to complete the certification of the aircraft. For a few more years, two N-250 prototypes were used in flight testing, but the whole project was then closed down.

Phase 4 was in development for several years and thus overlapped the others. It can be described as the implementation and R&D of future technology. This phase included a plan for launching a transonic turbofan 130-seater, the N-2130.

The decision to start with the N-2130 was not taken as a result of successful sales in domestic or international aircraft markets. In fact, when the decision was taken in 1996, only a few CN-235s had been exported and IPTN had no orders for the CN-250, even though the company used all its efforts to give that impression. During the LIMA 1995 aerospace exhibition at Langkawi, Habibie announced that he had received government approval to develop the new jet when the N-250 made its first flight (*Aviation Week & Space Technology*, 11 December 1995, p. 37).

IPTN had intended building three different sizes of N-2130, seating 80, 100 and 130 passengers, and the aircraft was scheduled to enter the market in 2006. According to Habibie, there were no worries about demand as Indonesia had a big domestic market. A special company, PT Dua Satu Tiga Puluh, was founded to function as IPTN's fund-raising agency for the N-2130. The project continued for some years, including wind-tunnel testing and some work on a prototype, but in late 1999 it was officially dismissed and the project closed down (Eriksson, 2013a).

In spite of the unsuccessful history, IPTN/Indonesian Aerospace in 2010 started to work on a new commuter aircraft, the 19-seat turboprop N219, similar in size and appearance to the de Havilland Canada DHC-6 Twin Otter (now Viking Twin Otter). Development is expected to cost roughly US$80 million and will be funded by the Indonesian government; it is expected to be ready for the first flight in 2019, and will draw on the experience from the N250 aircraft (Osborne, 2014). If the aircraft enters the market it has to compete not only with the Twin Otter, but also with the Dornier Do 228NG (see section on India), the Chinese Harbin Y-12, the Czech Let L410 and Polish PZL M28 Skytruck, although the latter is mainly used by non-commercial operators.

Other activities

Besides the main objective to become a major international aircraft producer, IPTN also had a goal to develop as an international supplier of aircraft components and parts. Throughout the years, the company has carried out subcontracting work for international aircraft companies such as Boeing (B737 leading edge flap, B767 flaps), Fokker (speed brakes, lift dumpers, wing to fuselage fairings, pedestal frames), General Dynamics/Lockheed (F16: forward engine access door, wing flapperon, fuel pylon, weapon pylon, main landing gear door, graphite epoxy skin vertical fin) and Mitsubishi (B767 keel beams) (Eriksson, 1995, pp. 167–168). After 1995, the company also started to produce components for the Airbus consortium. A main business has been the continued production of airframe sections for the Spanish-built CN-235. According to the company (information received during a visit in 2001), it had delivered 159 shipsets of CN-235 components to CASA, worth US$77 million. Under an agreement signed in 2005, and ended in 2011, IAe manufactured the slat skin (leading edge) for the Bombardier Global Express aircraft.

In 2014, IPTN carried out international subcontracting as follows:

- Airbus A380: manufacture and sub-assembly of the inboard outer fixed leading edge (IOFLE) wing assembly. This project was signed in 2002 for 300 shipsets, based on a delivery rate of 36 each year.
- Airbus A350: manufacture and assembly of root end fillet fairing (REFF) assembly for A350 Airbus. This project was signed in 2010 for 805 shipsets.
- Airbus A320/A321: manufacture and assembly of D-nose skin, pylon and leading edge assembly.
- A330: manufacturing of various components, which also applied to the previous A340.
- Boeing 747-8: manufacture of the leading edge skin and wing tip extension for B747-8 aircraft, signed in 2008 and ending in 2017. The agreement is for 18 shipsets per year.

- Eurocopter Super Puma Mk II: the manufacture of fuselage and tail boom for 125 shipsets. Until now delivery recently implemented to tail boom of four sets. Target of delivery is 15 sets per year for tail boom, and ten sets per year for fuselage. The contract was awarded in 2008.

In the 1980s IPTN signed an agreement with the US engine manufacturer General Electric for assistance to establish a maintenance centre for repairing and overhauling aero-engines. The company also had ambitions to become a producer of aero-engine parts, but these hopes never came to fruition. The company is also engaged in various MRO services, both for its own produced aircraft and for different kinds of aircraft for various domestic and international operators. One way to create additional revenues is to carry out various kinds of engineering services to non-aeronautical companies (Eriksson, 2013a).

Despite its know-how and impressive technology resources, the company is struggling to right itself as state funding has been forced away and it still faces the challenge of defining its own raison d'être. The economic and political crises of the late 1990s worsened the situation for IPTN/IAe. Since then, the company has struggled to stay afloat mainly by keeping its lines from licensed production and international subcontracting work going.

Malaysia

Malaysia, the Southeast Asian country with well-endowed natural resources in areas such as agriculture, forestry and minerals, is one of the successful second generation 'Tiger economies' that experienced an economic boom and underwent rapid economic development during the late twentieth century. As an NIC, the manufacturing sector has had a growing influence and importance in the country's economy, not least the electronics sector and partly the automotive industry. Malaysia's economic and industrial development is closely connected to the former Premier Minister Mahathir Bin Mohamad's Wawasan 2020, or Vision 2020, that calls for the nation to become a self-sufficient industrialised nation by the year 2020. The government identified aerospace as one of ten broad areas of development in the Second Industrial Master Plan, 1996–2005.

The first 'loose' statements concerning the creation of a national aerospace industry in Malaysia were expressed in the middle of the 1980s (Eriksson, 1995). Until then the aircraft/aviation experience in Malaysia was mainly composed of MRO competence within Malaysian Airlines, the national airline, and the Royal Malaysian Air Force, the latter activities taking place within Airod, an acronym for Aircraft Inspection, Repair & Overhaul Depot, established in 1975.

The first step towards a more developed aircraft industry was taken when, in December 1983, AeroIndustries of Malaysia Sdn Bhd was incorporated as an investment holding company with the aim of becoming a body for future aerospace industries development. Already in January 1984 it changed its name to Aerospace Industries Malaysia Sdn Bhd (AIM).[8]

The first 'practical' effort to develop the industry was in 1985, when Airod (located at Subang Airport, Kuala Lumpur) became privatised and formed a joint venture with Lockheed Aircraft Service International, a wholly owned subsidiary of the Lockheed Corporation, United States. Lockheed held 49 per cent and the remaining 51 per cent was owned equally between the Malaysian government, Malaysian Airlines System and the United Motor Works (Eriksson, 1995).[9] Lockheed was able to develop technical competence, business and management skills, but later withdrew from Airod. Initially, the ambition was to develop Airod into a manufacturer of aircraft components, besides its main business as an MRO provider, but this was never realised.

Although Malaysia expressed interest in the aerospace sector, it was far from the large-scale ambitions seen in Indonesia. Already in 1987, before any kind of aerospace manufacturing competence (including certification of firms) had been established in Malaysia, a news item in *Flight International* (31 January 1987) said that Malaysia's new aerospace industry would make components for British Aerospace's civil aircraft under an agreement signed at Hatfield, UK. The idea was for Malaysia to become a long-term source of components for BAe civil aircraft, and ultimately for 'the whole range' of British Aerospace products. This preliminary agreement never came to fruition, probably because Malaysian Airlines did not buy BAe's ATP regional airliner; instead it decided to buy nine Fokker 50s (Interavia, 1990). A few years later an MoU was signed between the governments of Malaysia and Great Britain concerning a very large defence-related order, but the Malaysian aerospace sector did not receive any benefits from this (Eriksson, 1995).

The next step was taken in April 1993, when the government announced that it had agreed to acquire Eagle Aircraft Australia, producer of the single-engined two-seat aircraft XTS, almost entirely built of composites. Malaysia's involvement in the Australian company began in 1991, when the Perth-based company was scouting for a partner to inject equity. A joint-venture company, Eagle Aircraft International, emerged after Petronas, Malaysia's state-owned petroleum company, and the Malaysian Finance Ministry bought a 50 per cent stake in Eagle's Aircraft operating subsidiary, Composite Technology. The stake was acquired with A$3.5 million in cash and A$2 million in a loan (Vatikiotis, 1993). Then it was agreed that the Malaysian government was to pay A$4 million for the remaining 50 per cent share of its venture in the Eagle XTS project (Phelan, 1993). This laid the foundation for Composites Technology Research Malaysia Sdn Bhd, a company involved as a subcontractor in the aerospace industry and other non-aerospace sectors.

Yet another acquisition was when, in 1993, the Swiss Dätwyler MD-3 trainer aircraft was acquired and all rights to the design and production was taken over by SME Aviation in Malaysia. The two-seater, mid-wing monoplane was developed in Switzerland during the 1960s and 1970s. Renamed the Aero Tiga, it is manufactured by SME Aerospace (former SME Aviation, formed in 1992).

Another project initiated in the same year was the agreement with Dornier Composites, Germany, to establish production of the troubled Dornier Seastar aircraft in Malaysia (Eriksson, 1995). Development of the Seastar started in Germany in the early 1980s, but the project ran into financial difficulties. This flying boat, like the Eagle aircraft, was largely built of composites and that was a decisive factor as the government had targeted composites manufacturing as one important stage in its industrial development. A new company was set up, Dornier Seastar Malaysia, which consisted of Malaysian investors (including AIM) sharing 65 per cent, while Dornier retained 35 per cent.

Grand ambitions were laid out in Malaysia for the Seastar amphibious aircraft, such as using this project for recruiting fresh graduates from local universities to train as engineers and technicians at a new aircraft manufacturing plant at Bayan Lepas, Penang. In an interview (David, 1994), Dornier Seastars sales and marketing director, Rajinder Singh, said that the Penang factory would be operating in 1995 and would be able to build 20 planes each year. He claimed that they had received 57 letters of interest, which is no guarantee for real orders. He also claimed receiving 39 verbal orders! According to Rajinder Singh, the interest from customers would mean the company faced a busy manufacturing schedule.

Airod's managing director, Dato' Ariff Awang, said that this project would be a major step in propelling Malaysia into the aerospace age (*Flight International*, 15–21 December, 1993). Already in 1994 it became evident that the project was far from 'secured'. In early 1995 the programme was on the verge of collapse, because Malaysian shareholders refused to invest further funds in the project (Lewis, 1995). They probably understood that the programme was not technically or financially viable.

In 1995 the construction of the factory in Penang had not started. The prime minister had strongly backed the Seastar project as a part of his Vision 2020 project, but the project was then closed down which caused some embarrassment for him and the government. After Malaysia's withdrawal the project itself did not end. The Germans went on 'hunting' for new investors. Throughout the years numerous revelations have been 'disclosed', such as the following (Sarsfield, 2012):

> Dornier Seawings plans to select the final assembly base for its SeaStar CD-2 twin-engined amphibious turboprop in the third quarter of this year and will deliver the first of the 12-passenger aircraft 33 months later, the company says. 'We have got a shortlist of three candidates with whom we are in an advanced stage of discussion,' says Dornier Seawing's chairman Conrado Dornier. The choice is between bases in Quebec, Canada – the most advanced of the three options – China; and India. We are talking with three prospective partners in those countries who will also help to fund the programme.

When the Dutch aircraft manufacturer Fokker went into bankruptcy in 1996, there were numerous efforts to sell the operations to investors and manufacturers. Fokker Chairman Ben van Schaik said that the company had spoken to some 30 parties potentially interested in taking over all or part of its operations (*Flight International*, 14–20 February 1996, p. 12). Aérospatiale, Bombardier and British Aerospace were among the companies, as well as Hindustan Aeronautics (*Flight International*, 14–20 February 1996, p. 12). According to Fokker, the Russian aviation companies Tupolev and Yakovlev had offered about US$240 million to buy parts of its failed operations. A spokesman for Fokker said that there was a need to discuss the conditions with them; a good business plan was important (*Moscow Times*, 30 March 1996).

Not much was revealed for the next year about Fokker's future destiny when, not surprisingly, it was revealed that 'Fokker hopes focus on Malaysian rescue' (*Flight International*, 26 February–4 March 1997, p. 10). It was looked upon as a last-ditch rescue-plan, based on discussions between the Malaysian government and Malaysian and Dutch investment groups. The negotiations ended without any results and the Malaysian 'take-over' was not realised.[10]

Instead, a new proposal turned up in late 1997, namely discussions between British Aerospace and Malaysia's government, including the state-owned investment house Kazanah Nasional Berhad, about Malaysian interest, taking up to a 50 per cent stake in the UK company's Avro International Aerospace Division. The framework agreement included transfer of parts production to Malaysia and various agreements and measures to develop the nation's aerospace industry (*Flight International*, 10–16 December 1997). This effort to move into more advanced aircraft production was aborted after extensive negotiations. Since then, Malaysia has stayed away from uncertain aircraft projects, but has been able to develop a supplier industry.

Supplier industry/subcontractors

The government-owned Composites Technology Research Malaysia (CTRM), created for the manufacturing of the Eagle aircraft, has moved into various activities, of which aircraft component and parts manufacturing is a main activity. The main customers are Airbus/EADS, Goodrich, GKN Aerospace and Spirit Systems and the production consists of the following components and parts (commercial aircraft), all manufactured in composites (CTRM, 2014):

- Airbus A320: wing panels (covering about 20 per cent of the wing surface), wing spoilers and various fairings.
- Airbus A380: inboard outer fixed leading edge (IOFLE), fixed leading edge lower panels (FLELP) and inner inboard fixed leading edge (IIFLE).
- Airbus 350 XWB: aft cascade ring assemblies
- Boeing 737NG: saddle fairings
- Boeing 777: chine manufacturing (fuselage sideways extensions)
- Boeing 787: a few smaller components are manufactured for this aircraft; inlet aft bulkhead, inlet inner barrel parts and composites aft cascade ring assemblies.

Added to this is the manufacture of a few parts to the IAE V2500 engine nacelle.[11]

Another government-owned company, SME Aviation (SME Aerospace), a wholly owned subsidiary of the National Aerospace & Defence Industries (NADI) Bhd, formed in connection with the acquisition of the Swiss Dätwyler MD-3 trainer aircraft, is a metal-based aerospace parts manufacturer. According to its official webpage (2014) it has contracts to manufacture and assemble parts and components for various aircraft models, including Airbus A320, A340 and A380, and Boeing B777 and B747, but when looking at specific products (another page) it manufactures parts for the following commercial aircraft:

- Airbus A320: inboard/outboard falsework, leading edge subspars, edge details, fabricated parts for composites, spoiler hinge bracket assembly.
- Airbus A330/340: Airbus A340 aft pylon fairing, A330/A340 winglet fabricated parts.
- Boeing 777: a few smaller parts (outboard details, stiffener).
- Avro RJ/RJX: aircraft parts.[12]

Asian Composites Manufacturing Sdn Bhd (ACM) was founded in 1998 and is based in Alor Setar, Kedah, Malaysia. It changed its name to Aerospace Composites Malaysia Sdn Bhd in November 2013. Originally established by Boeing and a few domestic investors, it is a joint venture between Boeing Worldwide Operations Limited and Hexcel Corporation (*Businessweek*, 2014), a US materials company with an extensive involvement in the aerospace industry. Aerospace Composites Malaysia Sdn Bhd manufactures flat and contoured primary and secondary structure composite bond assemblies and sub-assemblies for aerospace industries. Its products include aileron skins, spoilers and spars, and flat panels, leading edges, trailing edges and miscellaneous components (ACM, 2014).[13]

A press release (Hexcel, 2013) stated that Boeing and Hexcel celebrated a 40 per cent factory expansion of their joint-venture Aerospace Composites Malaysia Sdn. Bhd (ACM) to support increased production by Boeing Commercial Airplanes. ACM produces flight surfaces for all of Boeing's commercial programmes, including the next-generation 737, 747-8, 767, 777 and 787 Dreamliner.

The large US company, Spirit AeroSystems, announced in 2007 the establishment of a facility at Subang Airport, near Kuala Lumpur. The new company, Spirit AeroSystems Malaysia Sdn Bhd, became operational in 2009. The facility is set up to provide a variety of manufacturing, engineering and support functions. Initial products include a number of composite sub-assemblies, principally on Airbus single-aisle aircraft. The operation is also providing design support for the A350 XWB leading edge lower panels (Spirit Aerosystems, 2014).

Singapore

Introduction

Singapore, one of the very successful examples of Asia's NIEs, has gone through an impressive economic development since its independence. From being dependent on a few economic pillars, mainly entrepot trade and the British military base, at the time of independence, it has now established itself as a nation with several competitive industrial and service clusters.

The foundations for today's successful economy were already laid with Singapore's model of development (SMD), which refers to nine major policies introduced by the PAP government during the 1960s to ensure political stability and economic growth. Among the policies were promotion of economic development, minimisation of corruption, heavy investment in education and learning from others, the latter meaning that you accept and encourage strong ties with the Western world, as you need them in your economic development programme. It included creating an investment climate for industrialisation, an export drive and incentives to attract foreign investments and TNCs. Singapore has been very successful in implementing a number of policies for economic and industrial programmes by modifying them to suit Singapore's local context (Eriksson, 2011a).

In the late 1970s, when Singapore's average annual growth rate of 9.4 per cent was one of the highest in the world, the second international oil crisis resulted in developed countries introducing protectionist measures. The government responded by launching the so-called 'second industrial revolution'. Compared with other Asian NIEs (Hong Kong, South Korea and Taiwan), the Singapore economy seemed to be slow in intensifying the use of capital and skill (Tan, 1995). By the late 1970s, the government changed its strategic focus to skill- and technology-intensive, high-value-added industries, moving away from labour-intensive manufacturing.

The prospects of being squeezed between these apparently more productive economies and lower-cost locations opening up in the region (Indonesia, Malaysia and Thailand) also contributed to implementing the new industrial strategy. The government defined new priority sectors, all linked to high technology and more advanced services. At the same time, the National Wages Council moved towards a substantial increase in pay, designed to delocalise industries that were the weakest in added value (Regnier, 1992, p. 56). Increases in research and development (R&D) and technical skills were given special focus. The government dramatically increased expenditure on education and special emphasis was placed on engineering studies.

The 1986 report of the Economic Committee of Singapore (1986) marked a watershed in the Singaporean leaders' vision of the future, from a strong industrial base to a much more diversified, mostly tertiary economy, concentrating on advanced services (Margolin, 1993, p. 93). Still, several parts of the manufacturing sector were identified as playing an important future role, but there was a need for general upgrading. The previous policy to attract foreign TNCs was further strengthened with an emphasis on more advanced manufacturing, attracting foreign HQs to undertake product development and advanced technical and management services.

In 1991 the Strategic Economic Plan – Towards a Developed Nation – was presented. It was partly a restatement of established goals, but also spoke about

Singapore as a global city, by making it a 'total business hub' for the Asia-Pacific, offering a business location on par with other leading global cities. The National Science and Technology Board (NSTB) was established in 1991, and development of technological abilities has since then been orchestrated through national science and technology plans (NSTPs), also accompanied by increasing investments in R&D and technological infrastructure (Blomqvist, 2005). Today, Singapore offers favourable corporate taxation, a very stable political environment and transparent regulations.

For instance, in 1999, 'Industry 21' was launched by the government to develop Singapore as a vibrant global hub of knowledge industries in manufacturing and traded services. Strategies for services were grouped under International Business Hub 2000, which aimed at developing the city-state as a global city and a hub for business and finance, logistics and distribution, and communication and information (Chia and Lim, 2003).

Along with its strategic geographical position, Singapore has for a long time developed into an important global transportation hub. The port of Singapore has been a strategic asset since the nineteenth century and is one of the world's largest and busiest ports. Singapore's Changi Airport has, since it opened in 1981, constantly been rated as one of the world's best airports and has received more awards than any other airport.[14] In 2013 it was the world's 13th largest airport by passenger and 12th largest cargo airport by freight tonnage. The aviation industry at large is a key component in Singapore's economy and is still a part of the nation's overall economic and industrial strategy, and also as a part of the travel and tourism industry.

An important element in Singapore's economic and transportation policy has been the growth of its national airline, Singapore Airlines (SIA); in 1990 the SIA Group contributed nearly 5 per cent to Singapore's GDP (Guillouët, 1990, p. 92). Singapore's geography provided the economic incentives to exploit its limited air space. Without the need to restrict aircraft movements over large areas, Singapore adopted an open skies policy that allowed international airlines to compete for passengers in Singapore. As a result, many international airlines use Changi Airport as a transit stop between Europe and the Asia-Pacific (Ling and Shaw, 2004). This advantage partly helped Singapore Airlines to secure reciprocal landing right to overseas destinations (Perry *et al.*, 1997). This has contributed to international connectivity and economic development initiated a long time ago by the port activities.

In 2012 the World Bank's Logistics Performance Index (LPI) ranked Singapore as first out of 155 countries. The LPI measures the on-the-ground efficiency of trade supply chains, or logistics performance. Supply chains are the backbone of international trade and commerce. Their logistics encompasses freight transportation, warehousing, border clearance, payment systems and many other functions. Singapore has always positioned itself as a business hub for companies wanting to do business in ASEAN or in the wider Asia-Pacific region.

In 2009 the aviation sector contributed S$14.2 billion to the Singaporean GDP, made up as follows (Oxford Economics, 2011):

- S$8.7 billion directly contributed though the output of the aviation sector;
- S$3.1 billion indirectly contributed through the aviation sector's supply chain;
- S$2.4 billion contributed through the spending by employees of the aviation sector and its supply chain

In addition there were S$9.3 billion in 'catalytic' benefits through tourism, which raised the overall contribution to S$23.5 billion or 8.9 per cent of GDP. The aviation sector supports 119,000 jobs in Singapore, plus an additional 78,000 people employed through the catalytic (tourism) effects of aviation (Oxford Economics, 2011).

The aircraft industry

In 1975 the government founded a domestic aerospace company, Singapore Aircraft Industries (SAI), to be involved in various activities such as manufacturing, MRO, warehousing and supplies (Eriksson, 1995). Initially SAI started the learning curve by developing MRO capabilities, mainly to support the national airforce's aircraft. Another ambition was to progress to aircraft assembly and parts manufacture. Although the bulk of SAI's work was connected with military aviation, the company had the goal of expanding civil activities.

A reorganisation of SAI took place in 1981, ending up in five subsidiaries and two associate companies. The most well-known aircraft programme during the 1980s was the re-building and re-engine programme of the McDonnell Douglas A-4 Skyhawk, aimed at Singapore's Air Force. The first production of complete aircraft was the assembly of the 24 Italian SIAI-Marchetti jet trainers, followed by the licensed assembly of the French AS-332 and A350 helicopters (Eriksson, 1995). These aircraft programmes were handled by SAI's subsidiary Singapore Aerospace Maintenance Company (SAMCO), while SAI's Singapore Aerospace Manufacturing (SAM) produced airframe and sub-assembly work.

In an interview (Rek, 1987, p. 1269), a senior officer responsible for aerospace at EDB said that Singapore wants to move closer towards manufacturing in the aircraft industry. Maintenance and overhaul operations were the mainstay business of Singapore Aerospace and made up 73 per cent of the Group's turnover in 1990 (Singapore Aerospace, Annual report, 1990, p. 22). From the late 1980s until the early 1990s SAI manufacturing activities increased and the following commercial aircraft parts were produced (Eriksson, 1995):

- Airbus A320: rear passenger door.
- BAe125: landing gear.
- Fokker 100/F70: passenger doors.
- Boeing 777: nose landing gear doors.
- Sub-assemblies, including MD-11 engine mount.
- Airbus A340: engine mount and thrust reversers.
- A few engine components were also manufactured (PW4000).

The increased focus on manufacturing and design, implying increased technological capabilities and higher value-added production, led SAI in the late 1980s to join the development of Aérospatiale (France) P120L helicopter (now EC120 Colibri), together with China's CATIC and Harbin Aviation Industries Group. SAI took a 16 per cent share, with the responsibility for design and manufacturing of access doors, the tail boom and the composite structure of the tail rotor (Eriksson, 1995).[15]

In late 1994, China and South Korea initiated a proposal to develop the Asian Air Express 100 (AE-100) twin-engine 100-seat regional jet, represented on the project by Aviation Industries of China (AVIC) and the Korea Commercial Aircraft Development Consortium. Early on many disagreements between the two partners, such as work shares, programme leadership and location of final assembly site, led to a Chinese ultimatum demanding South Korea concede programme leadership and final assembly site of the aircraft (Lewis, 1996a).

Shortly thereafter the Korean consortium withdrew from the project. Instead, Singapore Technologies Aerospace (STA) moved into the programme and this was seen as a unique opportunity to take another step in Singapore's ambition to move into commercial aircraft manufacturing. As there was a need for a leading Western company to offer technology transfer, marketing and after-sales support, China wanted Airbus to join the consortium (Lewis, 1996b).

Airbus joined the project and a period of intense discussions followed and the AE-100 was developed into the AE31X aircraft project. The partners discussed speeding up the development process in response to Boeing's re-launch of the former MD-95 twin-jets as the Boeing 717 (Lewis, 1998). Further negotiations didn't resolve all the complicated issues and later that year Singapore withdrew from the project, apparently exasperated with the failure to reach agreement (Moxon and Lewis, 1998). The final blow came in September 1998 when Airbus announced termination of the project, saying it was not economically viable.[16]

Since this failure Singapore Technologies Aerospace has not moved into any other large-scale international aircraft cooperation manufacturing programme. Since then, the focus has changed towards becoming an integrated service provider that offers a wide spectrum of maintenance and engineering services through its five capability areas: aircraft maintenance and modification; component total support; engine total support; aviation and training services; aerospace engineering and manufacturing (ST Engineering, 2014).[17]

ST Aerospace, with more than 8,000 employees, has developed into the world's largest airframe MRO provider (see Chapter 6), operating a global network within the Americas, Asia-Pacific and Europe.

The general government policy to attract foreign TNCs (more advanced manufacturing, etc.) was also implemented in the aviation/aerospace sector. Throughout the years a large number of foreign companies within the whole aviation/aerospace sector have been established in Singapore, but few of these pursue manufacturing in Singapore.[18]

Aerospace manufacturing took a further step, both in terms of technology sophistication and value-added, when Rolls-Royce unveiled its plans for building a new Trent engine assembly plant in Singapore. According to the 2007 announcement, the plant will produce the Trent engines for the Boeing 787 and the Airbus A350. The plant, covering 154,000 square metres, includes a Trent aero engine assembly and test unit; a wide chord fan blade manufacturing facility; an advanced technology centre; and a regional training centre. When fully operational the facility will create approximately 500 new jobs, bringing the total number of employees in Singapore to over 2,000 (Rolls-Royce, 2014).

In January 2013, Rolls-Royce US rival Pratt & Whitney (a subsidiary of United Technologies) decided to establish a Singapore facility for the manufacture of fan blades and high-pressure turbine disks for its advanced geared turbofan engine, which has been selected to power several new-generation aircraft platforms (Aerospace Factsheet, 2014). In total, Pratt & Whitney has nine businesses in Singapore, with over 2,400 staff (EDB, 2014a).

Another subsidiary of United Technologies, UTC Aerospace Systems,[19] was established in Singapore, through its former name Hamilton Sundstrand Pacific Aerospace Pte Ltd, in 1971. It has two manufacturing plants in Singapore. The Bedok plant, established in 1976, manufactures aerospace components, gears and gear shafts, overhaul and repair support on integrated drive generators, constant speed drives, lube and scavenge pumps and electronic engine controls. The Changi plant, established in 2005, manufactures compressor wheels, turbine wheels, QAD rings and gearbox housings or auxiliary power units; fluid pumps housing for main fuel and lube pumps and housing for integrated drive generators (UTC Aerospace Systems, 2014).

Other companies are involved in manufacturing various assemblies, invalves to seat actuators, electrical power systems, machines parts and galley equipment, etc.

MRO and aviation cluster

Although the MRO sector is not specifically dealt with in this chapter, there is a need to comment on the astonishing development of Singapore's MRO sector. Singapore's aerospace sector revolves around MRO activities, and thus it has become the region's MRO hub as a result of the government's industrial polices within the aviation industry during the 1990s (Ng *et al.*, 2012).

MRO accounts for one-quarter of the Asia-Pacific market share (Singapore Aviation Industry Directory, 2014). More than 100 international companies carry out a comprehensive range of MRO activities in Singapore, including airframe maintenance, engine overhaul, component repair, structural and avionics systems repair, as well as aircraft modification and conversion. This comprehensive 'nose-to-tail' suite of capabilities has established Singapore as a preferred one-stop solution provider for MRO needs (EDB, 2014b). Nine out of ten aerospace companies that have established bases in Singapore are involved in MRO services (EDB, 2014b). Two of the world's four largest airframe MRO providers come from Singapore: Singapore Technologies (no. 1) and Singapore Engineering Company (no. 4), which is a part of the Singapore Airlines Group.

Singapore's small size (700 km^2) and population of nearly 5.5 million (2014) makes it one of the world's most densely populated countries. The highly concentrated economic and industrial activities within such a limited area and the access to an adequate pool of labour, the existence of a large number of specialised suppliers and supporting functions, as well the existence of internal and external spill-overs, nearly makes Singapore a single large cluster on its own. The aerospace activities are located in various places, but with a high concentration in the eastern part of Singapore, close to Changi International Airport and Seletar Airport, the nation's first international airport.

Singapore's government often speaks about the aviation cluster in general, but in recent years the Seletar Aerospace Park, which is located around the Seletar Airport, has been the focus of a targeted integrated cluster of activities, including: aerospace MRO and manufacturing; business and general aviation activities; education, research and training. Launched in 2007, it has attracted a number of companies, mainly in the MRO sectors, but also some manufacturing companies, not least the new Rolls-Royce factory. In 2013, EDB announced the 1,080 ha expansion of Changi Airport, which will cater for new industrial zones for MRO and air cargo activities to grow when completed in the mid-2020s.

Singapore has implemented a large number of measures to sustain and further develop the nation's aviation-related activities. The Agency for Science, Technology and Research (A*STAR) runs the A*STAR Aerospace Programme to further strengthen Singapore's vision to be a leading aviation hub, both in MRO and new products manufacturing (Association of Aerospace Industries, 2014). The Civil Aviation Authority of Singapore provides support to the industry through various incentive programmes under the Aviation Development Fund (ADF). The Singapore Workforce Development Agency (WDA) enhances the competitiveness of the workforce by advancing various kinds of skills. Universities in Singapore have developed specific educational programmes aiming at various parts of the aviation/aerospace industries. In 2011 the US Embry-Riddle Aeronautical University expanded its activities to Singapore, with the aim of an increased focus on Southeast Asia. It offers Bachelors and Masters programmes in business administration and aeronautical science, all with an aviation focus.

The Philippines

Although the Philippines can be considered a very small country as an aircraft industry producer, it is nevertheless interesting as the Philippines already in the early 1970s had strong ambitions to build up a domestic aircraft industry and was thus an early starter in this region with regards to its intentions to focus on the industry (Eriksson, 1995).

The Philippine Aerospace Development Corporation (PADC) was established by Ferdinand Marcos in 1973 to promote development in the industry. The driving motives for its establishment were self-reliance, national security and technology transfer (Eriksson, 1995). The first project, which started in 1974, was assembly, on licence, of the German (MBB) Bo 105 helicopter (44 built

1974–1981). The same year the assembly of the UK Britten-Norman Islander, a small passenger/transport aircraft, started, with 67 assembled between 1975 and 1989 (Eriksson, 1995)

In the middle of the 1970s PADC revealed the PADC fixed-wing aircraft project, which was a joint-venture between PADC and the Philippines government's National Science and Development Board. They aimed at developing a four-seat utility aircraft but the project only entered the prototype phase (Eriksson, 1995). In 1988 the Philippine Air Force made public that it had placed an order for 18 SIAI-Marchetti S.211 jet trainers, which were to be assembled by PADC. A second batch was ordered in 1992. Assembly, and some component manufacture of another SIAI Marchetti aircraft, the SF 260 trainer, started in 1993. In June 1994 the first and only Philippine-assembled SF 600 Canguro was made by PADC (Eriksson, 1995) This Italian-designed, small passenger aircraft (maximum nine passengers) never became a success and only a few were produced. Since then, only 8 Lancair small aircraft, used by the national police, have been assembled by PADC.

Figure 8.5 Location of commercial aircraft industries in Southeast Asia: IPTN/IAe, Bandung Indonesia (1), Malaysia (2, various), Singapore (3, various), PADC, the Philippines (4)

For many years PADC's main business has been to provide MRO for small aircraft, such as the Britten-Norman Islander and various Cessna and Piper aircraft models. The commercial MRO sector in the Philippines is dominated by Lufthansa Technik Philippines and to a lesser extent by the Singapore Airlines (SIA) Engineering (Philippines) Company, which is owned by SIA Engineering Company (65 per cent) and Cebu Air (35 per cent).

East Asia

China

Introduction

The People's Republic of China (PRC) has the largest aircraft industry of any emerging/newly industrialising country, which is dominated by military aircraft production. In fact, it is the world's second largest industry in terms of employment. Most of the production has been designated for the domestic market. Historically, but even today, there are many uncertainties regarding China's industry. Previously it was identified as a machine-building industry with heterogeneous activities, which made it difficult to make accurate analyses of the specific production (see Chapter 1).

It is also known that throughout certain periods, and in some cases for considerable time, the aircraft industry has manufactured a large number of non-aerospace products, such as in the case of Chengdu: 'In the early 1980s, the Chinese aviation industry started to reorganize and diversify into other products. In Chengdu, this led to the manufacture of light vehicles, windows, motorcycles and dry-cleaning machines' (Eriksson, 2013b)

Due to its complexity and size, this part of the chapter will initially focus on the general historical development of China's aircraft industry and then narrow it down to the increased civil aircraft industry's main development in recent years, with a focus on China's emergence into global supply chains and the efforts to move into the airliner market.[20]

Before the 1949 Communist Revolution there was almost no aircraft industry in China, except for the assembly of a few foreign aeroplanes from ready-made parts. After 1949, the Communist government decided to develop an aircraft industry, mainly for defence. As the West had imposed an economic embargo in the wake of the revolution, China imported foreign technology from the Soviet Union. Starting in 1953, agreements were signed to manufacture, on licence, a variety of mainly military types such as the MI-4 helicopter, An-2 utility biplane and Yak-18 trainer (Eriksson, 1995).

At the end of the 1950s, relations between China and the Soviet Union began to deteriorate as ideological differences emerged. At the time of the abrupt Soviet withdrawal from China in 1960, China had just begun to manufacture on licence the next generation of Soviet military aircraft, such as the MiG-19 fighter and Tu-16 bomber. The imports of components and raw material ceased, and a period of reorientation towards technical and industrial independence began. At the beginning of the 1960s China set out to design its own aircraft, necessarily based on available Soviet designs. This task, along with the development of transport aircraft, became difficult with the onset of the anti-technology Cultural Revolution in 1966. Only well-established aircraft programmes were able to continue through the ten years of turmoil. The main strategy was to reverse-engineer foreign-developed aircraft and give them Chinese designations (Eriksson, 1995).

The aircraft industry and open-door policy

With the end of the Cultural Revolution and the emergence of the new leadership under Deng Xiaoping, China changed direction and adopted an open-door policy in 1979. It also brought changes in the aviation industry, such as an increased emphasis on civil air transport, supporting the expected growth of China's economy. The seventh Five-Year Plan, which covered the period 1986–1990, singled out improvements to transport, particularly air transport, as a national priority. This fact naturally stimulated the nation's aircraft industry. The establishment of a satisfactory air transport system was, and still is, vital for the development of China's economy, and apart from China's own industry, it gave great opportunities for foreign producers of aircraft and equipment. China represented a great potential market with its large territory and enormous population (Eriksson, 1995).

One of the great problems for the Chinese industry during the 1980s was the lack of the most sophisticated technology. Another important problem was the lack of management skills and methods. Up to the late 1980s, China had manufactured thousands of aircraft, mainly military but also civil, most of them based on old Soviet designs. A special case was when, in 1970, the local government of Shanghai and the Ministry of the Aerospace Industry decided to launch the Y-10 commercial aircraft programme. This closely resembled the old US Boeing 707 and similarly was equipped with two Pratt & Whitney JT3D turbofans. Only a few prototypes were built and it is considered by most experts to be a reverse-engineered project, although the Chinese deny it.

In April 1985 an agreement was signed between the Shanghai Aviation Industrial Group of China and McDonnell Douglas (United States) to start co-production of the MD-82 airliner. It was an offset agreement for the sale of McDonnell Aircraft to China and the assembly of 25 MD-82s, which started in 1986. An extension was granted for ten more MD-82s with a final delivery in 1994. It was to be followed by the production of the new MD-90, but the programme failed after only three aircraft were produced. The MD-80 assembly project was the first modern airliner ever built in China and thus it became an important learning experience for the emerging Chinese aerospace industry (Eriksson, 1995, 2010).

The gradually improving political relations with Western countries, not least the United States, opened possibilities for China to access advanced Western technology. One important obstacle disappeared when CoCom (Coordinating Committee for Multilateral Export Controls) restrictions on the sale of military technology to China were eased in 1985.

China's aerospace industries were restructured in June 1993. The former organisation headed by the Ministry of the Aerospace Industry was divided into two new profit-making bodies, Aviation Industry Corporation of China 1 (AVIC I) and Aviation Industry Corporation of China 2 (AVIC II), both under government control. AVIC I was established to develop and manufacture military and commercial aviation products. It focused on medium-sized and large aircraft (i.e. the bulk of China's military aircraft production), while AVIC II gave priority to smaller aircraft and helicopters. In October 2008, AVIC I and AVIC II merged because the previous separation resulted in a split of resources and led to redundant projects. After the merger, the new AVIC consisted of ten business units: aero engines, avionics, defence, general aviation aircraft, helicopters, transport aircraft, aviation R&D, flight test, trade and logistics and asset management. A major focus of AVIC is to develop indigenous military technologies as well as commercial aircraft to compete in domestic and international markets (Eriksson, 2013b).

Early internationalization: entering global supply chains

With the open-door policy in 1979 it became very obvious that the outdated Chinese aircraft industry was in great need of access to modern technology and production methods. A suitable way to start the modernising process was to initiate a development to become a supplier, i.e. subcontractor, to foreign aircraft manufacturers. In 1979 China signed its first agreement with a foreign aircraft manufacturer for the manufacture of landing gear doors for the MDC MD-80 (production started in 1980). This agreement, as many others that followed during the 1980s and 1990s, were based on the strategic tool of offset for aircraft sales of aircraft to Chinese airlines (Eriksson, 1995, 2010). In other words, China demanded technology transfer in exchange for market access. Later, this was complemented by the need to lower production costs by outsourcing the production of components and parts to China. In the early stages, the main jobs were 'simple' parts such as fairings and small doors; later, Chinese subcontractors increasingly became more involved in advanced components, systems, materials and technologies (Eriksson, 1995, 2010, 2011b). Such examples were when McDonnell Douglas, 'offshored' production of the complete MD-82 nose sections to Chengdu Aircraft Corporation and Boeing's production of the complex B737 vertical fin in Xi'an. In the early and mid-1990s China had more extensive supplier functions regarding airframe parts than any other emerging economy (Eriksson, 1995). Since then, China's importance as an international subcontractor has increased and involves production for a number of foreign companies, although Airbus and Boeing have especially strong connections to the Chinese aircraft industry.

Chengdu Aircraft Corporation supplies the Airbus A320's rear passenger door and parts of its nose section; Shenyang Aircraft Corporation manufactures the A320's emergency exit doors and fixed leading edges, wing interspar ribs, cargo doors and skin plates, as well as A330 cargo doors; the Xi'an Aircraft Company manufactures electronic bay doors for the A320 and A330, as well as the wing box and fixed trailing edges on wings for the A320 Family; Hong Yuan Aviation Forging & Casting (HYFC) supplies titanium forged parts; Shanghai Aircraft Manufacturing Factory produces the A320 family aircraft cargo door frames; Chengdu Aircraft Industries Group (CAC) manufactures the Boeing 737 forward entry doors and over-wing exit doors as well as the B747-8 ailerons/spoilers. CAC also produced the empennage of the Boeing 757 (ceased production in 2004). A few years ago, a new agreement was signed with Boeing for the production of the composite rudder of the new Boeing 787 'Dreamliner'.

In 2008 Boeing announced the decision to substantially increase 737 component production rates at Shanghai Aviation Industrial Corporation, Xi'an Aircraft Company and Shenyang Aircraft Corporation. Xi'an will now produce the whole empennage (tail section), including the horizontal stabiliser. There will also be an increased participation in the 777, 747 and 737 airplane programmes. In 2011 Boeing's China Office revealed that an expansion of its venture in north China's port city of Tianjin would be operational in 2013. The US$21 million project would double the size of Boeing Tianjin Composites Co. Ltd, a joint venture between Boeing and the China Aviation Industry Corporation, which produces components and parts for the Boeing 737, 747, 767, 777 and the 787 Dreamliner aircraft, bringing the venture's total employment to more than 1,000 (Eriksson, 2013b).

Another main aircraft industry player, Bombardier of Canada, signed a major cooperation agreement with Shenyang Aircraft Corporation (SAC) as a supplier of main components for the Q400 aircraft. The packages supplied by SAC represent approximately 12 per cent, by weight, of the Q400 aircraft (Bombardier, 2014). SAC is also manufacturing the fuselage of the new Bombardier CSeries of aircraft.

China's increased importance as a supplier of components and parts, implying movement up the technology ladder, getting access to various kinds of new materials, technologies and aerospace design skills, brings about a general increased competence of China's aerospace industry. This development has taken place alongside the increased ambitions to develop the nation's own commercial aircraft industry, but that step is much more complicated, demanding not only modern manufacturing skills, but also other kinds of knowledge, such as management, marketing skills, appropriate logistics knowledge, compliance to international rules and regulations of airworthiness and safety, and trust from the customers (airlines and passengers). One very demanding task remained – to develop and integrate all the complicated technology systems, and to work in an integrated way, i.e. system integration.

Commercial aircraft projects in the twenty-first century

In the 1990s, after the MD-80 programme experiences and a general modernisation and competence increase in China's aircraft industry, ambitions to move into the development and manufacturing of commercial jet aircraft have increased, albeit with foreign firms heavily involved in design and technology transfer. As China and other Asian countries became increasingly important as markets, but also potential financiers of joint projects, Western companies saw a possibility for cooperation with Asian partners. The first attempt for such a joint venture was made by Boeing in the early 1990s, with the NSA regional jet. This aircraft, resembling the B737, was planned to be a joint venture between the United States, China, South Korea and a few other Asian countries, but it never left the drawing board.

Instead, in 1994, China and South Korea initiated a proposal to develop the Asian Air Express 100 (AE-100) twin-engine 100-seat regional jet, represented on the project by Aviation Industries of China (AVIC) and the Korea Commercial Aircraft Development Consortium (discussed in the Singapore section). Many disagreements between the two partners early in the process led to the Korean consortium's withdrawal from the project. As there was a need for a leading Western company, China wanted Airbus to join the consortium (Lewis, 1996b). Airbus joined, and after a period of intense discussions the AE-100 developed into the AE31X aircraft project. The final blow came in 1998 when Airbus withdrew from the project. Yet, another attempt of China to move into the commercial aircraft industry had failed.

In 2000 the Commission of Science, Technology and Industry for National Defense acknowledged that China's aircraft industry lacked the capability to develop and manufacture modern medium-sized and large aircraft. Owing to the large demand for new aircraft in the Chinese market, now and in the foreseeable future, decision makers considered that the nation's aviation sector would be incomplete without developing its own civil aircraft. There are now several ongoing projects, domestic as well as joint ventures with foreign partners (Eriksson, 2010).

In May 2000 the Brazilian aircraft manufacturing company Embraer opened an office in Beijing, making it a base for increased cooperation and sales in China. At the 2002 Asian Aerospace in Singapore, Embraer made it clear that it aimed at establishing a final assembly line for its regional jets (Goldstein, 2006). The joint-venture company, Embraer Harbin Aircraft Industry, located in Harbin, is a part of the regional economic policy programme (Li, 2004).

The Brazilian president involved himself in the deal, which included discussions with the Chinese president, Jiang Zemin, without being able to solve some outstanding issues (*Aviation Daily*, 2001). In April 2002 the Chinese government increased import tax on foreign-produced aircraft from 5 per cent to 23 per cent, thus giving favourable conditions for domestically produced aircraft. This tax increase could be seen as pressure from the Chinese government to produce these Brazilian aircraft in China. The Harbin Aircraft Industry, producing the ERJ-145 regional jet, is a joint venture between Embraer (Brazil) and the Aviation Industry Corporation of China, in which Embraer holds 51 per cent and the Chinese partner 49 per cent. In June 2004 the first China-made Embraer delivery was made to China Southern Airlines.

In early 2011, Embraer's China managing director Guan Dongyuan said the joint venture had delivered 39 ERJ-145s and had two left on order, the last of which would be delivered in the second quarter that year (Francis, 2011). As Embraer had no follow-on orders from Chinese customers for ERJ-145s, it wanted to keep its Harbin Embraer manufacturing joint venture going by making the larger E-190s instead, but it required approval from China's central government. The E-190 competes in the Chinese market against the domestic ARJ-21 regional jet. There has been some political lobbying behind the scenes in which some parties have been pushing the government to stop Embraer from manufacturing in China, in order to protect the ARJ-21 (Francis, 2011).

The ERJ-145 assembly project ended in 2011, when 41 aircraft had been built. No agreement was reached concerning the assembly of the E-190. Instead, an agreement was reached after almost two years of negotiations to assemble the Legacy 650 business jet, which is a variant of the ERJ-135/ERJ-145 models, for the Chinese market. The company will convert its assembly line in Harbin, where it assembled the ERJ-145 regional jet from 2002 to 2011, into a Legacy 650 facility during 2013 (Hashim, 2012). The first Legacy 650 assembled in China made its first flight in 2013.

The first modern domestically developed jet aircraft, the ARJ-21 regional jet, was unveiled at the 2001 Beijing Airshow, representing China's most comprehensive effort to build a modern indigenous aircraft, although with a number of foreign partners and suppliers and technical assistance from large US and European companies. Although the Chinese advertising of the aircraft refers to the ARJ-21 as an independent design with independent intellectual property rights, all its main technologies are Western-based, such as its avionics, engines and the fly-by-wire system. Indeed, more than 20 American and European contractors supply a large number of critical materials and technical systems and parts. Included among the foreign supplying companies are CFM International (France/United States), Eaton (United States), General Electric (United States), Honeywell (United States), Goodrich (United States), Hamilton Sundstrand (United States), Moog (United States), Parker Aerospace (United States), Rockwell Collins (United States), Liebherr Aerospace (Germany/France) and SAFRAN (France) (information received at a seminar at Asian Aerospace 2007 Congress, Hong Kong, 5 September 2007).

In fact, the ARJ-21 has the same cabin cross-section, nose profile and tail as the US MD-80/90 aircraft (earlier licensed and manufactured in Shanghai) that ceased production in 1999 (Eriksson, 2013b). This implies that the ARJ-21 nose section uses the same tooling as for the manufacture of the MD-80/90 nose section between 1991 and 1999 (Eriksson, 2013b). Another technology input is that Ukraine's Antonov, which supplied the ARJ-21 with a new super-critical wing as well as integral analysis of the construction strength. It also performed additional wind tunnel testing (*Antonov News*, 2007).

Initially planned for delivery in 2007, it has been prone to a number of delays due to a variety of flaws and problems, such as wings wiring, computer systems, re-design of the landing gear, etc. During a stress test in mid-2010, the wings of the ARJ-21 broke, or 'cracked' (Reuters, 2012). Comac's chairman, Jin Zhuanglong, blamed delays in the ARJ-21 programme on China's inexperience in designing, building and certifying commercial jetliners (Bodeen, 2013). Now it seems that the aircraft is due to enter service in April or May 2015, eight years later than scheduled in the programme and 13 years after development began (Perrett, 2014a).

In 2006 the European aircraft consortium Airbus decided to build an aircraft assembly plant in Tianjin. The production site is a joint venture between Airbus and a Chinese consortium of the Tianjin Free Trade Zone, AVIC I and AVIC II (now AVIC). It is the first Airbus final assembly plant outside Europe, and it was a strategic decision to strengthen Airbus' position in China relative to its main competitor, Boeing (Eriksson, 2010). This project has so far been the most successful commercial aircraft industrial project in China. The facility was inaugurated in 2008 and the first aircraft was delivered to Sichuan Airlines in June 2009.

An Airbus press release (Airbus, 2014) dated 3 December 2014 stated that the 200th A320 family aircraft had been assembled by the Airbus Tianjin Final Assembly Line (FALC). In March 2014 Airbus, TJFTZ and AVIC agreed to extend the successful joint venture for another ten years, from 2016 to 2025. The extension, called 'Phase II', will include the final assembly of the A320 Neo family from 2017 onwards for delivery to the Asian region (Airbus, 2014).

The supply of aircraft parts and components used in Tianjin's production comes from Airbus Europe, but since 2010 the wings are supplied locally by the Xi'an Aircraft Company, which has built a facility very close to the Airbus assembly line. The structures are assembled in Xi'an and then equipped in Tianjin. Airbus has also established a logistics centre in Tianjin to support all the parts coming in and out of China (information received during a visit to FALC in October 2012).

The most recent domestic project aiming at becoming a global player in the commercial aircraft industry and China's long-term goal to break Airbus and Boeing's duopoly in the medium-sized jet aircraft market is the Comac C919 narrow-body jet airliner. It is a planned family of aircraft, resembling the Airbus A320 series, accommodating 158–174 passengers. When the programme was launched in 2008 the first flight was scheduled for 2014, with delivery to customers in 2016; however, the roll-out of the first assembled aircraft had not occurred by late 2014.

According to Comac, customers have ordered more than 400 C919s, but the contracts have little binding effect according to people who have seen some of them (Perrett, 2014b). All orders, except one, are Chinese, giving the impression that the orders are from national policy (Perrett, 2014b). One problem with the aircraft is the lack of clear path to endorsement of its airworthiness by the FAA or the EASA as originally intended, but the C919 is being developed to international standard according to Comac (Perrett, 2014b). If the aircraft does not receive the necessary international certification it will limit the aircraft to the Chinese market. The C919 project relies on a number of foreign suppliers, although the Chinese have the main responsibility for the system integration.

Production and challenges

China's commercial aircraft development is facing opportunities as well as big challenges. The industry has advanced over the past few decades. This can be attributed to rapidly growing governmental support for China's aerospace sector, but aerospace capabilities have largely benefited from the increasing participation of its aircraft industry in the international supply chains, and joint projects with the world's leading aerospace firms.

As regards commercial jet aircraft *produced* so far (except the Y-10; see Table 8.1), they have been foreign constructions assembled in China, although some with local parts production. The 'first' Chinese design, the ARJ-21, is partly based on a foreign construction, albeit redesigned in China, but using a large number of foreign suppliers for all critical parts systems. The Chinese have the responsibility for the system integration and it has been a very demanding task. There is a substantial risk that the ARJ-21 will be obsolete to most airlines by the time it is delivered.

The C919, the 'second' Chinese jet airliner is an even more demanding project. Only the future can tell the fate of this aircraft project, but the development so far also raises some questions.

The propeller aircraft produced in China, except the smaller Harbin Y-11 and Y-12, are all based on an old Soviet design, the An-2 (see Table 8.2).

A recurrent issue in China's aerospace industry has been low productivity and an overstaffed production system (Brömmelhörster and Frankenstein, 1997). Many

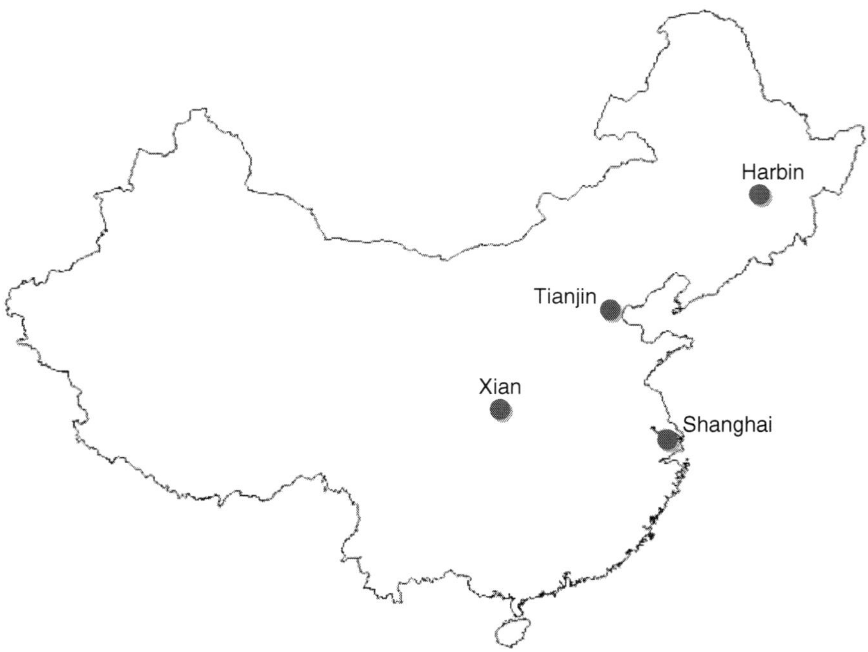

Figure 8.6 Locations of commercial aircraft production in China.

Table 8.1 Commercial jet aircraft produced in China

Aircraft	*Origin of aircraft*	*Production period*	*Engines*	*Production location*	*Maximum number of passengers*	*Number built*
Y-10	China (reversed engineered Boeing 707?)	1970s–1983 (project cancelled)	Four turbofans	Shanghai	178	3; never went into airline service
MDC MD-82	United States	1986–1994	Two rear-mounted turbofans	Shanghai	172	35
MDC MD-90	United States	1995?	Two rear-mounted turbofans	Shanghai	172	3; originally 40 planned
Embraer ERJ-145	Brazil	2004–2011	Two rear-mounted turbofans	Harbin	50	41
Embraer Legacy 650 Business jet	Brazil	2013 – in production	Two rear-mounted turbofans	Harbin	14	A few; 35 on order
Airbus A320 family	Europe: Airbus	2008: start of production 2009: first delivery	Two turbofans	Tianjin	180 (A320)	200 by early December 2014
Comac ARJ21	China 'influenced' by MDC MD-82/90	2007: roll-out; in production	Two rear-mounted engines	Shanghai	105	6–7 in flight-testing; additional aircraft have been produced, but not in service by 2014
Comac C919	China	Under development	Two turbofans	Shanghai	174	First flight planned for 2015?

Table 8.2 Commercial propeller aircraft produced in China (excluding the old Y-5/An-2 radial engine aircraft)

Aircraft	*Origin of aircraft*	*Production period*	*Engines*	*Production location*	*Maximum number of passengers*	*Number built*
Xian Y-7	Soviet Union: licensed manufacture of Antonov An-24. The Y-7H is an unlicensed version based on the An-26	1967/1968–?	Two turboprops	Xian	44	100+
Shaanxi Y-8	Reverse-engineered Antonov A-12	1981–early twenty-first century?	Four turboprops	Hanzhong	100–120; transport aircraft, mostly for military use very limited use as a commercial aircraft	100+
Xian MA60	Soviet Union: stretched version of Y-7	2000 – in production	Two turboprops	Xian	60	80–100?
Xian MA600	Improved MA60 (new avionics, cabin and engines)	2008 – in production	Two turboprops	Xian	60	Few
Xian MA700	Developed from MA600	Planned 2018	Two turboprops	Xian	70–80	None
Harbin Y-11	China	1977–1983?	Two piston-engines	Harbin	8	About 50
Harbin Y-12	China; larger and developed from the Y-11	1983 – in production: made in ten variants	Two turboprops	Harbin	19	100+?

Western industry specialists have reported an excessive number of people working in Chinese-managed aircraft factories, and with few incentives to increase efficiency. One problem in the factories is that managers are still struggling with the Soviet model in which the more employees you have, the more important you are (Perrett, 2013). There is a big difference when, for instance, comparing the Airbus facility in Tianjin that is built according to Western manufacturing and management systems (author's own observations). In reality such differences, if not dealt with, will have consequences for efficiency and international competitiveness.

South Korea

Introduction

South Korea, Hong Kong, Singapore and Taiwan constituted the very successful first generation of Asia's NIEs. South Korea adapted an export-oriented economic strategy and had one of the world's fastest-growing economies from the 1960s until the 1990s. In the early phases of industrialisation, the economic-industrial policy had an emphasis on primary import-substituting industrialisation, such as food, beverages, textiles, clothing, footwear, cement and various kinds of light manufacturing. The next industrial policy shift was towards secondary import-substituting industrialisation and secondary export-oriented industrialisation, with an emphasis on automobiles, shipbuilding, steel and metal products, petrochemicals, ICT and the consumer electronics industries (Eriksson, 2005). The 1990s saw an increased focus on high-technology industries, such as biotechnology, new materials and the aircraft industry.

Korea's involvement in the aircraft industry started with developing military maintenance capabilities in the 1950s and 1960s. In the early 1970s the government decided to support the development of an indigenous South Korean defence industry, which was supported by the 1973 Law on Defense Industry, which became a first push-factor to develop a manufacturing capability in the aircraft industry. During the 1980s government involvement in the aircraft industry increased. In 1984 the National Assembly promoted a law, Bill 552, Promotion Law for Korean Aerospace Technology, and the transfer of technology and the use of off-set was a key issue in the industrial strategy. In the early 1990s the aircraft industry was given priority in a new economic development plan, with ambitions to develop into a global player in the aircraft industry (Eriksson, 1995).

The ambitions could be summarised by the following statement: 'South Korea is attempting to propel itself to the top of the Asian aerospace industry league with a series of ambitious plans to turn its growing subcontract capabilities into a complete aircraft programme' (*Flight International*, 2–8 March 1994).

Commercial projects in the 1990s

In 1994 a few disclosures were made by Korean firms about their plans to develop a commuter aircraft, and in one of these statements the planned aircraft was dubbed Phoenix (Eriksson, 1995, p. 177). The aircraft's external design had an extreme similarity (author's view after seeing a small-scale model) to the French–Italian ATR-42. Samsung was to take the lead in the development, with Korean Air and Daewoo being named prime contractors. Only a mock-up was made and the project was later cancelled.

At about the same time, a much more ambitious project was revealed under the title Asia Air Express 100 (AE-100), previously discussed in the Singapore and China parts of this chapter. In Korea, a special organisation, the Korean Commercial Aircraft Development Consortium (KCDC) led by Samsung was created with the aim to take the lead in the development of the joint aircraft with China. From the very beginning a lot of disagreements arose between the two partners, such as programme leadership, work-shares and location of final assembly. The Chinese partner, Aviation Industries of China (AVIC) was arguing for taking the lead as China had more experience in aircraft production than South Korea and the domestic market was much larger. The Koreans were said to be shell-shocked by the uncompromising 'take it or leave it' position being adopted by the Chinese; they had lost face to the Chinese and were highly embarrassed (*Asian Aviation*, February 1996, p. 12). After a few years of discussions, Korea left the project, which later developed into the AE31X project (with new partners), which was also cancelled.

Before the Koreans left the AE-100 project, Daimler-Benz, then the owner of the troubled Dutch Fokker company, tried to secure a stake for Fokker in the AE-100 project (*Asian Aviation*, March 1995, p. 8), but it was not realised. After Fokker was declared bankrupt in March 1996, numerous attempts were made to sell the aircraft production abroad, which has been discussed earlier in this chapter (Malaysia section). Before the efforts to promote it to Malaysia, the Fokker rescue plan was for Samsung to take over the production:

> Fokker expects to be back in business before the end of the month, following Dutch Government's approval for the company's rescue by South Korea's Samsung. A detailed memorandum of understanding (MoU) has been agreed and is awaiting official approval by the South Korean Government.
>
> (O'Toole, 1996a)

The following week it was revealed that the proposed rescue was put on hold until the government and other domestic aircraft manufacturers had decided whether or not they should back the programme (Lewis, 1996c). A 15-man commission, consisting of university, state-funded institute and industry representatives was to judge the feasibility of the Fokker purchase. One senior aerospace executive complained that Samsung had so far failed to provide sufficient information, except a 15-page proposal that was rather more brief than the usual presentation material (Lewis, 1996c).

Fokker's administrators called a halt to the Samsung rescue plan as the Korean company had failed to meet a final deadline to restart Fokker by the end of October; there was a subsequent announcement by Shorts (Northern Ireland) that it would dismantle the wing-assembly line for the Fokker regional jets (O'Toole, 1996b). There was still a possibility for a new rescue plan if the wings could be built elsewhere, but the Koreans also withdrew from the project, making the entry into commercial aircraft production much more difficult than anticipated.

In 1997 South Korea, as were many other Asian economies, was hard hit by the Asian financial crisis, mainly due to foreign currency speculators. In reality there were several underlying problems in the Korean economy, such as structural distortions, both internal (such as over-borrowing by the chaebols, the large Korean business conglomerates) and external in origin, and weaknesses inherited from past industrial policy (Kim, 2000). Through the implementation of a range of structural reforms and good governance, Korea was able to overcome the crisis in a short time (Kim, 2000). The reforms were launched in 1998 in four areas: the public sector, the financial sector, chaebols and the labour market. Prior to the crisis, reform programmes had been discussed but never implemented because of inertia and resistance from stake-holders (Eriksson, 2005). One of the reforms, aimed at the chaebols, also had a direct influence on the aircraft industry when the government forced a merger of three aircraft companies (Daewoo Aerospace Division, Hyundai Aerospace and Samsung Aerospace), into a new entity, Korea Aerospace Industries (KAI), founded in 1999. Before discussing KAI, a short review follows of the aircraft activities of the three chaebols and the 'fourth' aircraft industry player, Korean Air, before 1999.

Korean Air

Korean Air (Hanjin Group) was the first company to set up an aerospace division (KAL ASD), established in 1976. The first activity was the assembly of the Hughes 500D/MD helicopter, followed by the assembly of the American Northrop F-5E/F fighters. The assembly of the US Sikorsky UH-60 military helicopters, for the armed forces, started in 1990. As part of the national aircraft industrial policy, a project was led by the Ministry of Science and Technology, aimed at developing a small four-seat aircraft. It ended up with the Chang-Gong 91 single-engined low-wing monoplane. Only three prototypes were manufactured by Korean Air, and it never went into production. During the late 1980s and the early 1990s, Korean Air developed its subcontracting business which also included commercial component and parts, such as fairings and wingtips for the Boeing 747, MDC MD-11 wing/fuselage fillets and composite spoiler, MD-80/82 nose-cap, bulkhead, doors, skin panels and fuel tank (Eriksson, 1995).

Boeing's long-lasting relationship with Korean Air has increased and varied over time, and now includes manufacturing for the B737 (empennages, flap support fairings), B747-8 (fairings, wingtip extension, radome), 777 (structural components) and B787 (cargo door, wing-tips, pivot bulkhead, aft body and a few structural fuselage parts). On the new Boeing 737 MAX it will also build the winglets (a second supplier is GKN, UK). Boeing and KAL ASD also have a considerable cooperation in military programmes (various sources).

The cooperation with Airbus is a newer event, and consists of the new A320 'sharklets', the wing-tip devices used for fuel saving. As the sole supplier, the company delivers (since 2012) to the final assembly lines in Toulouse, Hamburg and Tianjin. KAL ASD also currently supplies Airbus with fuselage skin panels and floor assemblies for the A330, as well as all-composite cargo doors for the new A350 XWB (various sources).

Korean Air has rather extensive commercial MRO activities in South Korea.

Samsung Aerospace

Samsung entered the aircraft industry in 1977 by overhauling engines for the Korean Air Force. Although Samsung initially had a focus on engines, the Korean government chose Samsung as the prime contractor for the Korean Fighter Programme (KFP), which in fact was the US F-16 aircraft. The assembly of the F-16 formed the basis for Samsung's aerospace activities throughout the 1990s, although some commercial subcontracting was performed, mainly a few parts for the MD-11, trailing edges for the Boeing 757 and 767 and a few small components for the B747 (Eriksson, 1995).

Daewoo

The next chaebol to enter the aerospace industry was Daewoo Heavy Industry, which established an aerospace division in 1983. Daewoo began its work in 1984 with off-set subcontracting from General Dynamics F-16 (now Lockheed Martin) sales to the Korean Air Force. In 1988, Daewoo entered a cooperation agreement with Dornier concerning a new turboprop commuter, the Do 328. It ended up with Daewoo producing the forward, centre and rear fuselage section for this aircraft (Eriksson, 1995). Discussions with the Russian Mil helicopter company about the manufacture of Mil Mi-8 and Mil Mi-17 in South Korea never came to fruition.

In the late 1980s Daewoo started the development of the KTX-1 turboprop military basic trainer. It continued during the 1990s, and when finally going into production it was the first indigenous Korean aircraft reaching that phase.

Daewoo was the second largest chaebol in South Korea when it, due to the financial crisis in 1997, ran into deep problems in 1998, leading to it being dismantled in 1999. The aircraft production was transferred to the new Korea Aerospace Industries.

Hyundai

The Hyundai Group was an aircraft industry latecomer, established in 1994 under the name of Hyundai Space & Aircraft Company. The aerospace activities were limited due to the short period of operations until the merger into KAI in 1999. The most important parts manufactured were the wings for the Boeing 717 (named MD-95 until Boeing merged with McDonnell Douglas in 1997). A few other components were manufactured, mainly for military aircraft.

Korea Aerospace Industries (KAI)

KAI is the only Korean company involved in aircraft manufacturing, albeit military aircraft (fixed wing) and helicopters, with a large dependency on foreign companies such as Lockheed Martin and Eurocopter. KAI is also engaged in a few other activities, such as MRO. The KTX-1 indigenous turboprop military basic trainer, once developed by Daewoo, is manufactured as KT-1.

In spite of the failure to move into commercial aircraft in the 1990s, KAI made new efforts just a few years after it was established. In 2001, KAI signed an MoU with the French aerospace design consultancy GECI International to study the development of a multi-purpose aircraft known as the Skylander (*Flight International*, 26 June–2 July 2001). It was planned that KAI should invest US$30 million in the project; meanwhile the company was discussing a project with Sukhoi Design Bureau to design a 25–50-seat passenger aircraft (*Flight International*, 23–29 October 2001, p. 22). The Skylander project never went further than a mock-up and the project was cancelled when GECI went into receivership in 2012. The discussion with Sukhoi did not produce anything.

In an interview (Sobie, 2005) KAI's president and chief executive, Chung Hae Joo, said that KAI has the goal to become one of the world's ten largest aerospace companies, fuelled by an anticipated boom in export and commercial sales. In line with that statement, yet another effort was made in 2007 when KAI initiated planning to design and manufacture an indigenous business for regional aircraft (Govindasamy, 2007). The plan was to raise an initial public offering in 2010, to be geared towards research and development efforts.

According to Chung Hae Joo, KAI started the feasibility study in 2007, looking at either a light aircraft that can carry up to ten passengers, or a 50- to 80-seat turboprop (Govindasamy, 2007)! A main motive behind the planning is revealed: 'The study is jointly conducted with the South Korean government, which is keen for the domestic aerospace industry to grow and match that of neighbouring Japan.'

In 2013 it was revealed that Bombardier (Canada) was in talks with three potential South Korean partners to jointly develop a 90-seat turboprop aircraft. Discussions began in early 2012, but the negotiations have not been smooth, resulting in a delay in the decision on whether they should launch the programme (Toh, 2013). Nonetheless, Korea Aerospace Industries Ltd wants to become a bigger player in the global supply chain for Airbus and Boeing commercial aircraft, and reduce its dependence on the South Korean defence market, its chief executive told Reuters (Reuters, 2013).

KAI has developed its activities as an airframe subcontractor for Airbus and Boeing. In 2014 the commercial production for Boeing aircraft was as follows (year of contract and time span in brackets) (Korean Air, 2014a):

- B737 (2004–2024): horizontal stabiliser and vertical fin.
- B747-8 (2008): fuselage frame and stringer.
- B767 (2009): fuselage upper panel, section 48 and fixed trailing edge.

Figure 8.7 Location of South Korea's aircraft industry: Seoul (1) Korean Air head office and Bucheon/Gimpo maintenance facilities; Incheon (2) Korean Air maintenance complex; Daejeon (3) Korean Air R&D Center; Busan/Gimhae (4) Korean Air Aerospace Divison (Tech Center), aircraft production and MRO (heavy maintenance); Sacheon (5) Korea Aerospace Industries (KAI) head office and production facilities.

- B777 (1999–2016): nacelle fitting; (2013–2024) fixed leading edge.
- B787 (2005–2021): section 11, centre wing box and fixed trailing edge.
- B787 (2012–2024): pivot bulk head.

KAI manufactures parts for the following Airbus aircraft (Korean Air, 2014b):

- A318/319/320/321 (1997–2014): fuselage section 15 upper shell.
- A318/319/320/321 (2012–life of the programme): wing bottom panel assembly.
- A318/319/320 (2001–life of the programme): wing top panel assembly.
- A320 (2006–life of the programme): fuselage section 16A shell.
- A330 (1997): wing machined stringer.
- A330 (1998–life of the programme): wing machined ribs.
- A330 (2001–life of the programme): bottom stringer.
- A350 XWB (2008–life of the programme): wing machined ribs.
- A350 XWB (2009–life of the programme): NLG door, NLG bay.
- A380 (2002–life of the programme): wing bottom panel.

Taiwan

Introduction and military background

Taiwan is widely known as a very successful economy based on an export-oriented development strategy. During the early 1970s it became apparent that internal and external challenges threatened the continuation of export-led growth. Based on Taiwan's economic needs and capabilities, the new policy plan 'Industrial Consolidation and New Export Growth' (1973–1980) focused on heavy investment in infrastructure, industrial upgrading and secondary import substitution (World Bank, 1993).

During the 1980s the Taiwan economy revealed structural weakness, particularly in the financial system's inability to match the increasing demands of industrialisation and external trade. It also began to reap the benefits of trade-promotion policies, and an increasing surplus was recorded in foreign trade. In the late 1980s Taiwan's exports faced additional losses of competitiveness due to the appreciation of the Taiwanese dollar and rising wages. As a first-generation East Asian NIE, Taiwanese manufacturers were squeezed between lower-wage NIEs in labour-intensive manufacturing, on the one hand, and high-technology products from industrial economies, on the other (Eriksson, 2005).

Once again there was a need to restructure the economy, moving into the fifth stage, 'High Technology and Modernization' (1981–1990), by developing such capital- and technology-intensive industries as electronics, information and machinery. The Six-Year National Plan (1991–1996) focused even more on high-technology industries, especially civil aerospace, biotechnology and electro-optics. Taiwan wanted to develop the civil aerospace industry into one of the most important industrial sectors in the new stage of economic growth

(Eriksson, 1995; Chiang, 1997). It was anticipated that the sector would grow in terms of employment, export, innovation and technology development, and that new companies and clusters were to be established as a result of growth in this sector.

The aircraft industry in Taiwan can be traced back to 1946, when the Bureau of Aircraft Industry was established in Nanking on the mainland. After the Kuomintang government's move to Taiwan, the Bureau followed. The first aircraft to be built in Taiwan was a slightly modified version of the American Pazmany PL-1. The Aeronautical Research Laboratory, then a branch of the Bureau of Aircraft Industry, assembled it in 1968. In 1969 the Aero Industry Development Center (AIDC) was established as a successor to the Bureau of Aircraft Industry. AIDC became a subsidiary of the Chung-Shan Institute of Science and Technology (CIST), the government's main, defence-related, research and development facility (Eriksson, 1995).

During the Nixon years, the United States' foreign policy underwent a change with regard to China. The integration of the PRC into the international system meant that many nations terminated their diplomatic relations with the Republic of China in Taiwan. During the 1970s Taiwan's isolation in the international community also meant that it had no access to foreign military equipment. This constituted an important impetus to try even harder to develop a domestic military aircraft industry (Eriksson, 1995).

In 1974 AIDC started licensed production of US Northrop F-5 fighter aircraft, under the name Chung Cheng. This project was initially an assembly of purely imported components, but these were gradually replaced by some local content production. The following year AIDC started, with the assistance of Northrop, to develop a new two-seater advanced training aircraft for the Air Force, the AT-3. The biggest project up to now was the development of the Indigenous Defence Fighter (IDF), designed with the assistance of General Dynamics. All of the 130 aircraft were manufactured between the late 1980s and January 2000, when production ceased.

Taiwan's civil aircraft: the early years

When the government decided to embark on the development of the civil aerospace industry it required access to advanced foreign technology and a huge amount of capital. In the projections, the output value of the whole Taiwanese aircraft industry was expected to escalate tenfold from 1991 to 2000. The aim was to obtain offset deals from foreign aircraft manufacturing companies, such as Boeing, McDonnell Douglas and Airbus, but also to become a producer of commercial jet aircraft. Several academics and experts with a background in the US aerospace industry returned to Taiwan in the early 1990s to take part in the bid to establish a domestic commercial aerospace industry (Eriksson, 1995).

The government, through the Ministry of Economic Affairs, introduced the 'Aeronautics and Space Industries Development Program' to function as a guide to the industry. The development of the industry was planned by an ad-hoc semi-governmental unit, the Committee for Aviation and Space Industry Development (CASID), which consisted of members from government units, universities, research organisations, etc. CASID became the most important actor/organisation in the process of building an international competitive aerospace industry.

Since only a small number of Taiwanese manufacturers were able to act as suppliers of aircraft components in the early 1990s, one important measure was to create a unit which could take the main responsibility for the integration of different subcontractors or suppliers. To fulfil these purposes, a semi-governmental company, the Taiwan Aerospace Corporation (TAC), was officially established in 1990 and started working in July 1991. The government provided 29 per cent of the initial capital, and private investors, including banks and manufacturing firms, covered the rest. Thus, TAC got the role, together with AIDC, of a main focal company in the future development of Taiwan's commercial aircraft industry (Eriksson, 1995).

Already in November 1991 an MoU was signed between McDonnell Douglas (MDC) and the newly established TAC. The aim was to set up a new commercial aircraft consortium and the key to the relationships between MDC and TAC was the launching of the proposed MD-12 wide-body airliner. MDC estimated MD-12 development costs at up to US$5 billion. Initially, MDC was offering co-development on major airframe sections in return for cash investments from the Asian partners in the project. There was a hope for a win–win situation – MDC was in desperate need of cash and Taiwan hoped to leapfrog into the aerospace industry. In the summer of 1992 the whole deal collapsed (Eriksson, 1995).

A new MoU turned up in mid-September 1992 when British Aerospace (BAe) announced a joint venture with TAC. The deal should have seen TAC become a risk-sharing partner when the BAe 146 regional jet was re-launched as the RJ family (see the Malaysia part of this chapter). In late 1993 it seemed that the talks had collapsed and in 1995 it was obvious that this second attempt to enter the fully fledged aircraft industry would not bear fruit. In late 1994 a deal was concluded between a consortium of private Taiwanese investors and the US firm Swearingen, regarding the development of the SJ30 business jet. This also ended up as a failure.

In 1995 AIDC was considering developing a six- to nine-seater turboprop aircraft for commercial and military use. AIDC's Aeronautical Research Laboratory (ARL) was conducting preliminary studies of the aircraft with funding from Taiwan's Ministry of Economic Affairs and Ministry of National Defence (*Flight International*, 23 August 1995). The aircraft never left the drawing board.

In 1997 AIDC signed an agreement with the Czech aircraft company Aero Vodochody to jointly manufacture and market the Aero Ae 270 Ibis aircraft, a single-engine turboprop utility aircraft carrying up to eight passengers. Early in this project troubles emerged because of disagreements about production, financing and strategies (discussions with various personnel at CASID, AIDC and Aero Vodochody). This project was later cancelled.

An evaluation (Eriksson, 2006) of the first ten years of efforts to establish a viable civil aircraft industry concluded that it was much more difficult than expected. One reason for that was the complete lack of experience from the civil aircraft industry, which differs considerably from the military equivalent. Commercial aircraft development and manufacturing are extremely complex, customised and engineered product systems, unfamiliar to most Taiwanese companies. It differs considerably from modularisation and disintegration, used by Taiwanese companies as a way to lower the entry barriers for their very successful semiconductor industry. In comparison with the aircraft industry, the semiconductor business has short product lifecycles and rapid company turnover. Another major obstacle was the obvious difference in business culture between foreign and domestic actors. In the 1990s the entry barriers to enter this industry had grown.

The early twenty-first century[21]

The failure to move into commercial aircraft projects with American and European companies did not dampen Taiwan's ambitions to achieve a higher status in the aerospace business. During the 1990s the focus was to a large degree to move into commercial aircraft manufacturing, but it had shown to be a very costly and difficult strategy. CASID (the government and private companies) still aims at moving into the industry, albeit at a slower pace and with a different strategy. In the future the target is a balanced share of manufacturing (50 per cent) and maintenance/overhauling (50 per cent).

After ten years, AIDC was still the only major company involved in the aircraft manufacturing business. Originally known as the Aero Industry Development Center, it changed its name to Aerospace Industrial Development Corporation, while still retaining the abbreviation AIDC. It was transformed from a military organisation into a state-owned company with a market-oriented commercial approach, under the authority of the Ministry of Economic Affairs (MOEA) from 1996. Due to declining military programmes, it transformed from mainly defence-related activities into a mix of military and commercial business.[22] Today, AIDC has achieved its privatisation objective; it was transformed into a private company in August 2014. In 2013 the commercial aircraft business had reached 32.6 per cent of the total revenues of US$763 million.[23]

AIDC's current commercial aviation production can be summarised as follows:

- Participation in various rotor wing programmes, i.e. manufacturing of fuselage parts of helicopters (Bell 412, Bell 429, Eurocopter EC120, Sikorsky S-76, Sikorsky S-92).
- Manufacturing of fuselage parts for business and regional jet programmes (Bombardier Challenger 300 rear fuselage and winglets, Bombardier CSeries elevator, rudder, H/S and V/S leading edges, Learjet 40/45 rear fuselage, Mitsubishi Regional Jet, Dassault Falcon 900/2000 rudder) (Figures 8.8 and 8.9).

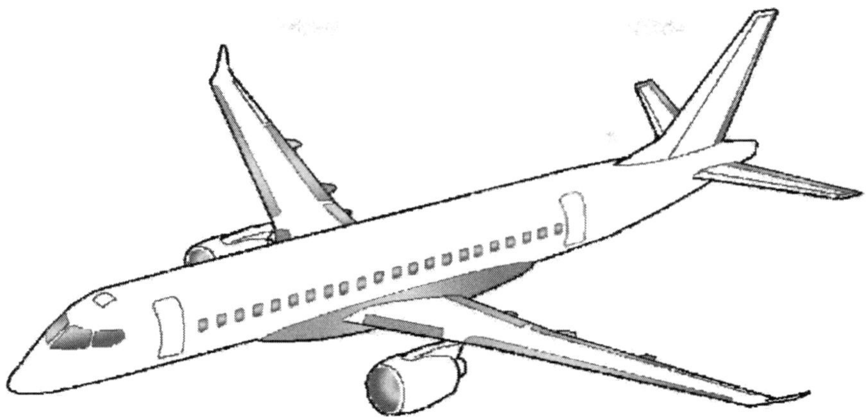

Figure 8.8 AIDC manufacturing of the Mitsubishi Regional Jet (belly fairing/support structure, flap track fairing, slats, flap, elevator, rudder, aileron, spoiler) (used with permission from AIDC).

Figure 8.9 AIDC manufacturing of the Bombardier Challenger 300 (rear fuselage, empennage) (used with permission from AIDC).

- Participation in Boeing programmes (B737 forward doors; Boeing 747 main entrance doors, crew door, equipment doors; Boeing 757 cargo door surroundings; Boeing 787 horizontal stabiliser auxbox and leading edge, composite parts for doors).[24]
- Participation in Airbus programmes (A320 vertical trailing-edge panels and belly fairings; A321 manufacturing of the section 16A barrel of the fuselage; A380 HTP tip assembly).

- Manufacturing of the Embraer 190/195 shroud panel, which was subcontracted by Kawasaki Heavy Industries (KHI).
- Main landing gear door (MLGD) for Bombardier's Global 7000 and Global 8000 business jets.
- Manufacturing of engine parts (such as GECF 34, GE/SNECMACFM 56, V2500 casing HPT & IPT casing for Rolls-Royce Trent XWB-97K engine etc.).
- Some commercial MRO activities are also performed.

Other manufacturing and MRO

With Taiwan's ambitions to create a competitive commercial aircraft industry, significant economic resources were used for building up an 'infrastructure' of possible suppliers, as only a small number of companies were able to act as suppliers of aircraft components in the early 1990s. In 1990, just before the large-scale effort to move into the commercial aircraft industry started, there were six Taiwanese companies involved (on a small scale) as subcontractors (military parts) in the aircraft industry, all of them working for AIDC (Eriksson, 2006). None of these companies had aerospace production as their main business. A few MRO companies were also within the aerospace sector, the largest being the China Airlines maintenance centre at Taiwan Taoyuan International Airport.

In 2001 the number of companies involved in aerospace manufacturing had increased to 19 (commercial and military production, excluding AIDC), including the six identified in 1990 (Eriksson, 2006). Some of them were newly established firms with the aircraft industry as the main focus, while others had a background in car, bicycle, machinery, or metal industries. A few had received subcontracting work directly from AIDC as a part of their supply chain, or indirect subcontracting works from foreign aerospace producers. Indirect implies that an order from a foreign company went through AIDC and then was forwarded to these 'new' suppliers.

During the visit to Taiwan in 2010, a follow-up was made concerning the companies identified by Eriksson (2006). Of the few companies involved as manufacturing subcontractors in 1990, three were still in the business in 2010. Of the 19 (excluding AIDC) manufacturing companies identified in 2001, only six remained in the aerospace industry. Most of the companies have closed down, while some are active but not in the aerospace business.

AIDC is still the only major aerospace manufacturing company in Taiwan. Of the about 5,000 employed in the manufacturing part of Taiwan's aerospace industry (2010), 4,745 worked for AIDC. From 2001 onwards a few other companies have entered this sector; they are all subcontractors to AIDC.

The MRO sector has showed a positive development compared with aerospace manufacturing. The MRO-companies identified in 1990 were still active in 2001. The largest actor in 1990, as well as in 2001, was the China Airlines MRO department. Since the late 1990s it has had steady growth, including expansion of its international customer base.

A highly specialised MRO provider in aero engines is the Asian Compressor Technology Services (ACTS) that was established in 1996. It is a joint venture between the US aero engine manufacturer Pratt & Whitney, which has a 51 per cent stake in the company, and Singapore Airlines and China Airlines, each holding 24.5 per cent. It specialises in the overhaul and repair of high pressure compressor (HPC) and low pressure compressor (LPC) components for the PW4000, PW2000/F117 and CF6 families of engines.

A successful establishment in the MRO sector is the development of EVA Airways MRO division. EVA Airways, a part of the Taiwanese Evergreen Group, started operations in 1991 and has since developed into an international carrier, now a main competitor to China Airlines. For several years EVA had around 100 technicians performing 'simple' maintenance checks on EVA's own aircraft. A big change took place in 1998 when General Electric (United States) went in with investments and formed a joint venture with EVA Airways MRO division. Since then it has had steady growth: 1,500 employed in 2005, 1,950 employed in 2008,[25] which had increased to 2,200 in 2013. EVA's MRO division was responsible for the extensive modifications of Boeing 747-400 aircraft used for transporting B787 parts between various manufacturers and to the final assembly plant in Seattle. The aircraft, named Boeing Dreamlifter, is the same concept as the Airbus A300-600ST Beluga.

Figure 8.10 shows the production value of Taiwan's aerospace sector. Of the production value in 2009, the manufacturing part accounted for 44 per cent, while the MRO part accounted for 56 per cent. Of the total MRO value, 84 per cent came from civil MRO activities. From an employment perspective around 5,000 people were employed in the manufacturing sector, while around 8,700 were employed in the MRO sector.[26]

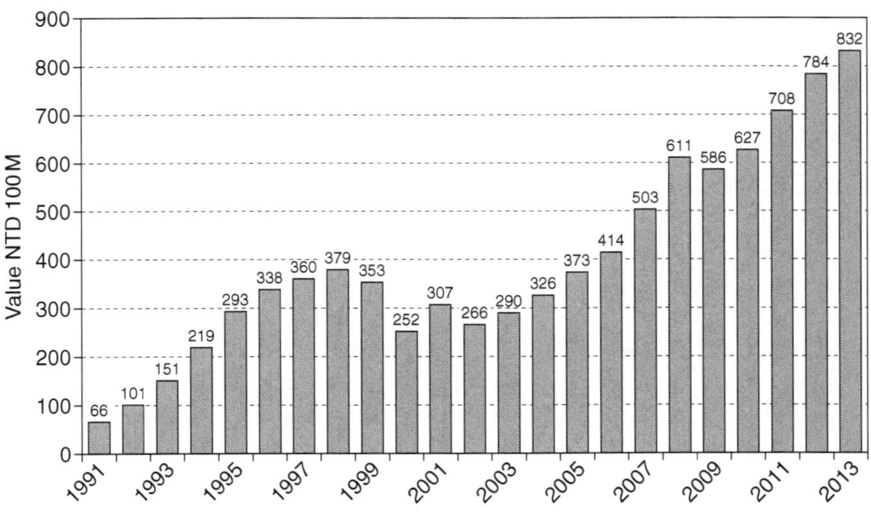

Figure 8.10 Total production value of Taiwan's aerospace sector, 1991–2013 (source: data provided by CASID).

Figure 8.11 Main location of Taiwan's aircraft industry: Taoyuan (main MRO area), Taichung (AIDC manufacturing and MRO), Kaohsiung (AIDC Kang-Shan Complex, aero engine assembly, parts production and testing).

Conclusions

In this chapter the development of commercial aircraft industry activities among Asia's NIEs is discussed. The background and origin of these industrial activities varies among the investigated countries. Some countries can trace its roots to military aviation activities, whereas a few started their aircraft industries due to political isolation. In other cases MRO activities constituted the initial starting point, while some cases can be considered green-field projects.

In reality, development and establishment of commercial operations has in all cases, but to various degrees, been a part of national economic and industrial policies. Various economic, industrial and technology policy arguments have been used in the efforts to invest in this industry, including spill-over effects, innovation and self-sustaining industrial development.

The results of all these efforts and investments in various countries show varying degree of success and failure. Especially striking are all the failures to move into the development and production of commercial turboprop and jet passenger aircraft. A few points stand out: the repeated efforts by troubled Western companies to sell aircraft projects to emerging countries; and the unawareness and ignorance among governments/politicians and companies about the difficulties involved in developing a viable aircraft industry.

In some cases it is possible to see a degree of prestige and national pride in the efforts to move into aircraft manufacturing. Market analysis and pure business dimensions often seem to be lacking and are subordinated to other factors.

It is very obvious that the development of a successful civil aircraft industry is more difficult than expected. This very complex industry is not only a matter of transferring technology – there are a large number of other dimensions, practices and skills needed for success. There is a need to develop and master management and marketing skills, working methods, logistics knowledge, compliance with international rules and regulations of airworthiness and safety. Finally, you need to master the development and integration of all advanced and complicated soft and hard skills and technologies, to allow functioning system integration.

China is now the main emerging actor in Asia, with great ambitions to develop into a global player in aircraft development and production. Commercial jet and turboprop aircraft manufactured in China have so far mainly been based on foreign constructions and technologies. China is now in the process of establishing its own domestic jet aircraft projects, albeit with considerable dependence of foreign suppliers and technologies. The current domestic projects still need to prove their legitimacy.

An interesting case is Singapore, which implemented a strategy to develop into a global leader in commercial MRO. Taiwan's large-scale commercial aircraft industrial plans have also ended up with the MRO activities outperforming the anticipated aircraft manufacturing activities.

A main observation from an industrial globalisation point of view is the extensive development of international subcontracting among the investigated economies.

In some cases the main jobs done are 'simple' sheet-metal fabrications, production of labour-intensive items or even basic five-axis machining works, which are associated with low-cost production typical for some of the investigated economies. In other cases there is a clear progress towards more advanced and complicated jobs, parts and systems. This implies more of a functional integration of development, design and manufacturing. Yet, the final assembly is still mostly taking place in the Western advanced economies.

Notes

1 In the case when the manufacturing part of industry has taken another route, i.e. into MRO, it will be dealt with. The same applies to some cases of aero engine activities.

2 Information from Steve Cass, vice president of Communications Gulfstream Aerospace 500, Savannah, Georgia, United States.

3 Spirit AeroSystems, headquartered in Wichita, United States, is one of the world's largest aircraft subcontractors (first tier), especially fuselage sections for Boeing and Airbus.

4 The Do 228 can be deployed in various configurations: passenger and cargo, air taxi, corporate purposes, maritime surveillance, border patrol and medical evacuation missions, etc.

5 Based on the original product-specification/advertisement leaflet, received at the Asian Aerospace Trade Fair, Changi, Singapore, February 1996.

6 In 1991 Partenavia became a part of the former Italian aerospace engineering group Aeritalia, but in 1993 it sold Partenavia to Aercosmos, yet another Italian aviation concern, following the collapse of an earlier attempt to transfer the enterprise to Piaggio (*Flight International*, 21–27 April 1993).

7 For an overview of the Indonesian politics during the Suharto era, especially the interaction between the state, industrial sectors and various interest groups, see *The Technological State in Indonesia* (Amir, 2013), which also deals with additional views of IPTN, previously not accounted for.

8 In 2004 AIM was converted to a public limited company as National Aerospace & Defence Industries Sdn Bhd (NADI).

9 Nowadays, AIROD is a fully Malaysian-owned company under the NADI group of companies.

10 During a national aerospace seminar at University Utara, 13 April 1997, among other things the Fokker deal was discussed and, based on the arguments from some of the participants, i.e. Malaysian Industry – Government Group for High Technology (MIGHT), it became clear (to the author) that a lot of prestige was involved if one could get hold of 'any' aircraft manufacturer to fulfil the Vision 2020.

11 I sent an e-mail asking for additional information about the parts and components manufacturing and a few other questions, such as whether the Eagle 150B was still manufactured. I received an e-mail response saying that a representative would respond shortly to my questions. They never did, even after two telephone calls and further promises.

12 The last Avro RJ/RJX aircraft was delivered in late 2003. The information about production of parts for this aircraft is outdated. Due to various ambiguities, contradictions and inaccuracies about the company, three e-mails were sent in June, July and August 2014, asking for clarification of a number of issues. None of the e-mails were responded to. During August and September 2014 four telephone calls were made to the company without any reply. Based on that I sent an email to the National Aerospace & Defence Industries Sdn Bhd (NADI), the government organisation that owns SME Aerospace and asked for clarification, but no response was received. A telephone call was made to NADI but the officer didn't understand or speak English. Thus, the information about this company is unreliable. As late as December 2014, the official webpage had not been updated since July 2012.

13 Various information regarding the production at ACM has been noted in a few journals. To sort out these issues, two e-mails were sent to ACM for additional information. No replies were received. After a telephone call to ACM they promised to reply, but never did.

14 In 2013 Changi served more than 100 international airlines, flying to about 70 countries and territories worldwide, and handled more than 53.7 million passengers (Changi Airport, 2014).

15 During the definition and early development phase Aérospatiale was the lead company with 54 per cent project share. In 1992 the German DASA and Aérospatiale merged their helicopter divisions and formed Eurocopter, which later became a part of EADS and was renamed Airbus Helicopters in January 2014.

16 Interestingly, a few years before the cancellation of the AE31X programme, Airbus had initiated a study of a smaller variant of the Airbus 319. A few years after the

AE31X cancellation, Airbus introduced the A318, having many shared features with the cancelled project. It is usually claimed that the A318 emerged from the failed AE31X.

17 ST Aerospace is nowadays a part of ST Engineering, formed in 1997, with a global network of over 100 subsidiaries and associated companies across 24 countries in the United States, Europe, Asia and Australasia.

18 By checking (in several cases also by direct contact via e-mail or telephone) a large number of companies listed in the Singapore Aviation Industry Directory 2014 it is clear that few companies are engaged in manufacturing in Singapore. Many of the foreign manufacturing companies are mostly performing MRO-related or trade activities in Singapore.

19 In 2012 Hamilton Sundstrand merged with Goodrich Corporation, creating UTC Aerospace Systems.

20 China's ambition to develop an advanced commercial aero engine industry is discussed in Chapter 4.

21 The following sections dealing with Taiwan are based on a two-week follow-up tour visiting companies and industrial organisations in Taiwan, from late September to early October 2010. After 2010, contacts have been made with companies and organisations for additional information.

22 Interviews at AIDC were held with the deputy director of business development, Jennifer Chuang, senior manager (commercial business development section), Carter Cheng, and assistant manager (commercial business development section), Vic Chen.

23 Information from Sylvia Chen, business manager AIDC/commercial business department, 30 December 2014.

24 Previously AIDC manufactured the rear fuselage of the Boeing 717; production ended in 2006.

25 Information from a meeting, 4 October 2010, with Dr Chong Kin-Hung, deputy senior vice president, and Own Wu-Cheng, junior vice president, Evergreen Aviation Technologies.

26 Information from visits to CASID in September 2010.

References

ACM (2014) Home page, www.acmsb.com.my, accessed 16 June 2014.

Aerospace Factsheet (2014) Singapore: Asia's home for aerospace, Singapore Economic Development Board.

Airbus (2014) Airbus celebrates 200th aircraft assembled in Tianjin, www.airbus.com/presscentre/pressreleases/press-release-detail/detail/airbus-celebrates-200th-aircraft-assembled-in-tianjin, accessed 4 December 2014.

Airvectors (2014) Dornier civil aircraft, www.airvectors.net/avdojet.html, accessed 4 October 2014.

Amir, S. (2013) *The Technological State in Indonesia: The Co-constitution of High Technology and Authoritarian Politics*, London and New York: Routledge.

Antonov News (2007) News page. www.antonov.com/news/index. Xml?news5antk-main/news_20071224.xml, accessed 29 October 2011.

Apostolo, G. (1984) *The Illustrated Encyclopedia of Helicopters*, New York: Bonanza Books.

Association of Aerospace Industries (2014) *Singapore Aviation Industry Directory 2014*. Association of Aerospace Industries.

Aviacor (2014) Introducing AN-140 regional aircraft, www.aviacor.ru/files/AN_140_Presentation_in_English.pdf, accessed 15 January 2014.

Aviation Daily (2001) 'Embraer sells 40 jets to China in $1 billion order', 18 April.

Bailey, J. (1992), 'Habibie's grand design', *Flight International*, 19–25 February, pp. 51–55.

Blomqvist, H.C. (2005) *Swimming with Sharks: Global and Regional Dimensions of the Singapore Economy*, Singapore: Marshall Cavendish Academic.

Bodeen, C. (2013) Delivery of the first China jetliner delayed again, http://bigstory.ap.org/article/delivery-first-china-jetliner-delayed-again, accessed 4 December 2014.

Bombardier (2014) Local partners and suppliers, http://cn.bombardier.com/local_partners.htm, accessed 28 November 2014.

Brömmelhörster, J. and Frankenstein, J. (1997) *Mixed Motives, Uncertain Outcomes: Defense Conversion in China*, Boulder, CO: Lynne Rienner Publishers.

Business Air (2014) RUAG Aviation contracts Tata Advanced Systems to manufacture Dornier 228 fuselage and wings, www.businessair.com/aircraft-press-releases/ruag-aviation-contracts-tata-advanced-systems-manufacture-dornier-228-fuselage-and-wings, accessed 15 November 2014.

Businessweek (2014) Company overview of Aerospace Composites Malaysia Sdn Bhd, http://investing.businessweek.com/research/stocks/private/snapshot.asp?privcapId=22127066, accessed 16 June 2014.

Changi Aiport (2014) Home page, www.changiairport.com, accessed 12 October 2014.

Chia, S.Y. and Lim, J.J. (2003) Singapore: a regional hub in ICT, in Seiichi Masuyama and Donna Vandenbrink (eds), *Towards a Knowledge-based Economy: East Asia's Changing Industrial Geography*, Tokyo: Numura Research Institute; Singapore: Institute of Southeast Asian Studies, pp. 259–298.

Chiang, J.-T. (1997) Defence conversion into a global system of proprietary technologies, *Technology Forecasting and Social Change*, 56, pp. 77–85.

Croft, J. (2008) NBAA 2008: Gulfstream know-how buoys G250 performance claims, www.flightglobal.com/news/articles/nbaa-2008-gulfstream-know-how-buoys-g250-performance-claims-316880, accessed 2 January 2014.

CTRM (2014) Home page, www.ctrm.com.my/main.php, accessed 12 August 2014.

David, A. (1994) Dornier scouts for Malaysian graduates. *New Strait Times*, 15 May.

Davidson, B. (1981) PT Nurtanio: the rising star of the Orient, *Interavia*, 12, pp. 1236–1239.

Deccan Herald (2010) Human error, faulty design behind Saras crash: report, 27 April.

Dicken, P. (2011) *Global Shift: Mapping the Changing Contours of the World Economy* (6th edition) London: Sage.

Directorate General of Civil Aviation (DGCA) Final Investigation Report, http://dgca.nic.in/accident/reports/VT-XRM.pdf, accessed 25 January 2014.

Donald, D. (1997) Bell Model 214ST, in *The Complete Encyclopedia of World Aircraft*, New York: Barnes & Noble.

Economic Committee, Singapore (1986) *The Singapore Economy: New Directions*, Singapore: Ministry of Trade and Industry.

EDB (2014a) Pratt & Whitney opens new engineering and repair centre at Seletar Aerospace Park, www.edb.gov.sg/content/edb/en/news-and-events/news/2014-news/pratt-and-whitney-opens-new-engineering-centre-at-seletar-aerospace-park.html, accessed 20 September 2014.

EDB (2014b) Aerospace Engineering Singapore, www.edb.gov.sg/content/edb/en/industries/industries/aerospace-engineering.html, accessed 14 October 2014.

Elson, B.M. (1983) Nurtanio leads industrial modernization, *Aviation Week & Space Technology*, 26 December.

Eriksson, S. (1995) Global Shift in the Aircraft industry: a study of airframe manufacturing with special reference to the Asian NIEs, Thesis, Gothenburg University.

Eriksson, S. (2003) Indonesia's aircraft industry: technology and management impediments, *International Journal of Technology Transfer and Commercialisation*, 2 (2), pp. 207–226.

Eriksson (2005) *Innovation policies in South Korea and Taiwan*, Stockholm: Vinnova Analysis.

Eriksson, S. (2006) Cluster creation and innovation within an emerging Taiwanese high-tech sector, *International Journal of Technology Transfer and Commercialisation*, 5 (3), pp. 208–236.

Eriksson, S. (2010) China's aircraft industry: collaboration and technology transfer – the case of Airbus, *International Journal of Technology Transfer and Commercialisation*, 9 (4), pp. 306–325.

Eriksson, S. (2011a) Can Singapore develop into a global media city? In C. Karlsson and R. Picard (eds), *Media Clusters: Spatial Agglomeration and Content Capabilities*, Cheltenham: Edward Elgar Publishing Ltd, pp. 328–353.

Eriksson, S. (2011b) Globalisation and changes of aircraft manufacturing production/supply-chains – the case of China, *International Journal of Logistics Economics and Globalisation*, 2, pp. 70–83.

Eriksson, S. (2013a) The aircraft industry as a tool for economic and industrial development: the case of Indonesia, in S. Eriksson, *Clusters and Economic Growth in Asia*. Cheltenham: Edward Elgar Publishing Ltd, pp. 141–164.

Eriksson, S. (2013b) Foreign knowledge transfer in the development of aircraft industry clusters: the case of Chengdu, China, in S. Eriksson, *Clusters and Economic Growth in Asia*. Cheltenham: Edward Elgar Publishing Ltd, pp. 165–181.

Flightglobal (2014) How Iran's aerospace dream began and ended with the licence-built Ir-An 140, www.flightglobal.com/news/articles/analysis-how-iran39s-aerospace-dream-began-and-ended-with-the-licence-built-406044/, accessed 28 November 2014.

Francis, L. (2011) Harbin Embraer nears end of ERJ-145 assembly: plans for E-190s uncertain, http://aviationweek.com/awin/harbin-embraer-nears-end-erj-145-assembly-plans-e-190s-uncertain, accessed 2 December 2014.

Freeman, C. (1988) Technology gaps, international trade and the problems of smaller and less developed economies, in C. Freeman and B.Å. Lundvall (eds) *Small Countries Facing the Technological Revolution*, London: Pinter Publishers.

Fulgham, D. (2012) Reviving the technology engine: IAI boosts spending on R&D and advanced technologies to win foreign customers, *Aviation Week & Space Technology*, 23 July, pp. 48–50.

Globalsecurity (2014) IAI-201 Arava. www.globalsecurity.org/military/world/israel/arava.htm, accessed 20 February 2014.

Globes (1999) Israel's business arena, 3 October, www.globes.co.il/serveen/globes/docview.asp?did=378552, accessed 2 January 2014.

Goldstein, A. (2006) The political economy of industrial policy in China: the case of aircraft manufacturing, *Journal of Chinese Economics and Business Studies*, 4 (3), pp. 259–273.

Govindasamy, S. (2007) KAI seeks funding for Korean airliner, *Flight International*, 3–9 April, p. 4.

Güillouët, A. (1990) *Booming Economies of South East Asia*, Singapore: Longman.

Gulfstream (2014) Gulfsteam history, www.gulfstream.com/history, accessed 2 January 2014.

HAL, Kanpur (2014) TAD-Kanpur Division, www.hal-india.com/TAD-Kanpur%20Division/M__120, accessed 5 November 2014.

Hashim, F. (2012) Embraer and China reach agreement on Legacy 650 line in Harbin, www.flightglobal.com/news/articles/embraer-and-china-reach-agreement-on-legacy-650-line-in-373358/, accessed 22 November 2014.

Hexcel (2013) Boeing, Hexcel expand Aerospace Composites Malaysia facility by 40 percent, www.hexcel.com/news/market-news/news-20131107, accessed 15 July 2014.

Hill, H. (1998) Introduction, in Hal Hill and Thee Kian Wie (eds) *Indonesia's Technological Challenge*, Singapore and Canberra: Institute of Southeast Asian Studies and Australian National University, pp. 1–52.

Jetadvisors (2014) Israel Aircraft Industries Astra SPX, http://jetadvisors.com/astra-spx/, accessed 22 February 2014.

Kim, K.S. (2000) The 1997 financial crisis and governance: the case of South Korea, Working Paper #272-March 2000, Kellog Institute.

Korean Air (2014a) Boeing business, www.koreaaero.com/english/product/boeing.asp, accessed 12 December 2014.

Korean Air (2014b) Airbus business, www.koreaaero.com/english/product/airbus.asp, accessed 12 December 2014.

Levin, M. (1993) 'Technology transfer as a learning and development process: an analysis of Norwegian programmes on technology transfer', *Technovation*, 13 (8), pp. 497–518.

Lewis, P. (1995) Seastar project could be sunk, *Flight International*, 19–25 July, p. 20.

Lewis, P. (1996a) China tackles S Korea on AE-100 leadership, *Flight International*, 24–30 January, p. 4.

Lewis, P. (1996b) China wants Airbus to join AE-100 programme, *Flight International*, 1–7 May, p. 5.

Lewis, P. (1996c) Fokker rescue plan on hold, *Flight International*, 20–26 November, p. 6.

Lewis, P. (1998) Airbus urges AE31X speed-up to compete with Boeing 717, *Flight International*, 4–14 February, p. 6.

Li, C. (2004) China's northeast: from largest rust belt to fourth economic engine? *China Leadership Monitor*, 9.

Ling, O.G. and Shaw, B.J. (2004) *Beyond the Port City: Development and Identity in 21st Century Singapore*, Singapore: Pearson/Prentice Hall.

Livemint and *The Wall Street Journal* (2014). India considers partnerships to end delays in aircraft project, www.livemint.com/Industry/Fjdkqfucn0MBPkH7tx5StI/India-considers-partnerships-to-end-delays-in-aircraft-proje.html, accessed 5 February 2014.

Margolin, J.-L. (1993) Foreign models in Singapore's development and the idea of a Singaporean model, in Garry Rodan (ed.) *Singapore Changes Guard: Social, Political and Economic Directions in the 1990s*, Melbourne: Longman Cheshire.

McKendrick, D. (1992) Obstacles to 'catch-up': the case of the Indonesian aircraft industry, *Bulletin of Indonesian Economic Studies*, 28 (1), pp. 39–66.

Mondey, D. (1981) *The World's Commercial and Private Aircraft*, London: The Hamlyn Publishing Group.

Moscow Times (1996) Russian companies bid for bankrupt Fokker, 30 March.

Moxon, J. (2000) TAI adopts multi-product strategy to boost orders, *Flight International*, 13–19 June.

Moxon, J. and Lewis, P. (1998) Airbus Industries and AVIC abandon AE31X, www.flightglobal.com/news/articles/airbus-industrie-and-avic-abandon-ae31x-39195, accessed 19 September 2014.

Munson, K. (1983) *Airliners from 1919 to the Present Day*, New York: Exeter Box.

Muravsky, A. (2013) Antonov receives an offer it can (not) refuse, www.day.kiev.ua/en/article/economy/antonov-receives-offer-it-cannot-refuse, accessed 16 January 2014.

Ng, H., Ndengabaganizi, D. and Shiou, J. (2012) *Singapore aerospace industry*, US Department of Commerce.

Osborne, T. (2014) Second try: Indonesia launches development program for a commuter aircraft, *Aviation Week & Space Technology*, 24 February, p. 30.

O'Toole, K. (1996a) Samsung steps closer to Fokker, *Flight International*, 13–19 November, p. 6.

O'Toole (1996b) Hopes fade for Fokker rescue, *Flight International*, 4–10 December, p. 5.

Oxford Economics (2011) Economic benefits from Air Transport in Singapore, Singapore Country report. www.iata.org/policy/Documents/Benefits-of-Aviation-Singapore-2011.pdf

Perrett, B. (2013) Many hands, *Aviation Week & Space Technology*, 9 September.

Perrett, B. (2014a) ARJ21 delayed again, due to enter service April–May 2015, *Aviation Week & Space Technology*, 30 January.

Perrett, B. (2014b) Into assembly, *Aviation Week & Space Technology*, 3–10 November.

Perry, M., Kong, L. and Yeoh, B. (1997) *Singapore: A Developmental City State*, Chichester: John Wiley & Sons Ltd.

Phelan, P. (1993) Malaysia takes control of Eagle, *Flight International*, 5–11 May, p. 23.

Regnier, P. (1992) *Singapore: City-State in South-East Asia*, Kuala Lumpur: Majeed.

Rek, B. (1987) Singapore aims for increased aerospace activity, *Interavia*, 12, pp. 1269–1273.

Reuters (2012) Wing cracks, other flaws delay China jet manufacture, http://in.reuters.com/article/2012/06/08/uk-airlines-china-comac-idINLNE85700Z20120608, accessed 28 November 2014.

Reuters (2013) S Korea's KAI eyes bigger role in aviation, http://news.asiaone.com/news/asia/s-koreas-kai-eyes-bigger-role-aviation, accessed 12 December 2014.

Rolls-Royce (2014) A strategic hub for Rolls-Royce, www.rolls-royce.com/country/singapore.jsp, accessed 17 September 2014.

Sarsfield, K. (2012) Dornier Seawings earmarks 2015 for first Seastar amphibian delivery, *Flight International*, 12–18 June.

Singapore Aerospace (1990) *Annual Report*. Singapore: Singapore Aerospace/Singapore Technologies

Smith, S.L. (1998) Batam Island and Indonesia's high-technology strategy, in Hal Hill and Thee Kian Wie (eds) *Indonesia's Technological Challenge*, Singapore and Canberra: Institute of Southeast Asian Studies and Australian National University, pp. 342–363.

Sobie, B. (2005) KAI keeps up fight to make top 10, *Flight International*, 5–11 April, p. 25.

Spirit Aerosystems (2014) Spirit's global locations, www.spiritaero.com/About_Us/Locations/Malaysia.htm, accessed 20 October 2014.

ST Engineering (2014) Products and solutions, www.stengg.com/our-business/aerospace/products-solutions, accessed 16 September 2014.

Steenhuis, H.J. and de Bruijn, E.J. (2001) Developing countries and the aircraft industry: match or mismatch, *Technology in Society*, 23, pp. 551–562.

Steenhuis, H.J. and de Bruijn, E.J. (2002) Technology transfer and learning, *Technology Analysis & Strategic Management*, 14 (1), pp. 57–66.

Steenhuis, H.J., de Bruijn, E.J. and Heerkens, J.M.G. (2007) Technology transfer and catch-up: lessons from the commercial aircraft industries, *International Journal of Technology Transfer and Commercialisation*, 6, (2–4), pp. 250–277.

TAAL (2014) Taneja Aerospace and Aviation, www.taal.co.in/, accessed 2 June 2014.

TAI (2014) Company profile, www.tai.com.tr/en/about-us/company-profile, accessed 20 April 2014.

Tan, C.H. (1995) *Venturing Overseas: Singapore's External Wing*, Singapore: McGraw-Hill.

Todd, D. and Simpson, J. (1986) *The World Aircraft Industry*, London & Sydney: Croom Helm.

Toh, M. (2013) Bombardier, South Korea in joint development talks for 90-seat turboprop, www.flightglobal.com/news/articles/bombardier-south-korea-in-joint-development-talks-for-90-seat-381329/, accessed 12 December 2014.

UTC Aerospace Systems (2014) Home page, www.hamiltonsundstrand.com.sg/index.html, accessed 16 November 2014.

Vatikiotis, M. (1993) Fledgling industry: Malaysia's Mahathir pushed aerospace venture, *Far Eastern Economic Review*, 13 May, p. 62.

Vértesy, D. (2011) Interupted innovation: emerging economies in the structure of the global aerospace industry (doctoral dissertation), University of Maastricht.

Wanstall, B. (1990a) Top-grade F-16 from Turkey, *Interavia*, 3, pp. 257–261.

Wanstall, B. (1990b) Turkish aerospace industry ready for take-off, *Interavia*, 1, pp. 55–58.

World Bank (1993) *The East Asian Miracle: Economic Growth and Public Policy*, New York: Oxford University Press.

World Bank (2012) The World Bank's Logistics Performance Index (LPI), http://lpi.worldbank.org/, accessed 12 November 2014.

9 The commercial aircraft industry in Russia and Ukraine

Strategic transformation and prospects

Alma Lozano and Sören Eriksson

Introduction

Aircraft manufacturing is characterised by technological complexity, high value-added, dual-use application, constant innovation and strategic relevance. Possessing an aircraft industry is therefore regarded as a matter of national interest that serves to fulfil both economic and security objectives. Nevertheless, the heavy R&D investments, high level of engineering expertise, sophisticated techno-industrial assets and advanced management skills required to develop aircraft production capabilities have resulted in few countries possessing the capacity to manufacture complete aircraft platforms. Those that do have traditionally relied on government intervention to keep the industry afloat in times of contracted demand, and constant political support to gain competitive advantages and increase international market shares. Indeed, aircraft enterprises operate in an atypical oligopolistic market influenced by political variables. As such, their performance is determined by both corporate strategy and government policy. Since the aircraft industry is typically associated with technological superiority, international prestige, and military and industrial prowess, it comes as no surprise that the USSR possessed a very robust aircraft manufacturing system that at its heyday produced 40 per cent of the world's military aircraft and 25 per cent of all aircraft platforms (De Kort and Kluiters, 2003, p. 381). This output had strong military production as its backbone and was therefore the result of high defence expenditures, representing 25 per cent of Soviet GDP (Gansler, 2011, p. 322).

During the Cold War, the USSR government controlled every aspect of aircraft production under a centrally planned system focused on developing advanced technologies to meet Soviet operational requirements. Driven by military and technological rivalry with Western countries, the Soviet aircraft production system was characterised by a strict division of labour in compartmentalised departments and over-specialisation, resulting in multiple inefficiencies and lack of synergies among the different organisations involved in the production process. The Ministry of Aviation was responsible for coordinating the operations of the entire industry and had six R&D institutes devoted to major aircraft production specialities: aerodynamics, engines, materials, equipment, production technology, and flight performance. Design bureaus were in charge of developing competing aircraft designs from which one would be selected on the basis of technical performance. And, finally, manufacturing plants undertook production to meet centrally assigned targets, but had no role to play in the research, design and development phases. In the absence of market-driven incentives, supply chains were structured on the basis of political interests, further preventing economic efficiency. Yet, economic rationality was clearly not part of the Soviet equation. Profitability was as inexistent as was competition, while demand was guaranteed by high domestic defence budgets and captive international markets in allied countries. In this context, military acquisitions were the basic support of the Soviet aircraft industry, fuelling constant technological development and production, and resulting in the USSR registering unmatched levels of military output that in 1989 reached 650 fighters and attack aircraft (Harned, 1995, pp. 43–53)

All that came to an end when the Cold War abruptly ceased. Suddenly, the world was no longer divided into two antagonistic spheres of influence, global military expenditures dropped and captive markets were essentially gone. International competition based on cost, quality and performance became the new rule of the game. The USSR was disintegrated into 15 republics and although Russia inherited 85 per cent of the former Soviet aircraft production assets (De Kort and Kluiters, 2003, p. 384), political disintegration meant that the once centrally coordinated industry was now fragmented and scattered across independent countries. Notably, the Antonov design bureau, a key component of the USSR aircraft production system specialised in airlifting capabilities, now belonged to Ukraine and in fact 30 per cent of the USSR aerospace and defence design, development and production facilities were located within Ukrainian territory (Kuznetsov, 1997, p. 551). Thus, Russia and Ukraine, as the largest heirs of Soviet industrial might, have at their disposal the technological and industrial resources to emerge as aircraft production hubs in their own right. However, the two countries faced serious challenges they had to overcome in order to survive in post-Soviet times. In particular, deep industrial, organisational and management restructuring would be necessary to adapt to new market conditions and remain positioned as major aircraft manufacturers in a world ruled by commercial imperatives.

To be sure, the adverse effects that the end of the Cold War had on aircraft production were felt globally. The US industry had to go through a process of consolidation to tackle overcapacity, relying on a strategy of mergers and acquisitions that resulted in the industry being reduced from more than 50 aerospace companies to four large national champions, namely Boeing, Lockheed Martin, Northrop Grumman and Raytheon (Murman *et al.*, 2002). A similar phenomenon occurred in continental Europe with the formation, in 2000, of the European Aeronautics Defence and Space Company (EADS), which in 2014 was reorganised as Airbus Group, combining the divisions for development and marketing of civil and military aircraft, as well as communications systems, missiles, rockets, helicopters, satellites and related systems.[1]

The UK was not immune and the national aircraft manufacturer, BAe, merged with Marconi Electronic Systems to become BAE Systems. Certainly, Russia and Ukraine were not the only countries that had to completely restructure their national aircraft industries to become viable commercial entities in post-Cold War market conditions.[2] However, what makes the cases of Russia and Ukraine particularly outstanding is the fact that they had to go through a process of total transformation. Indeed, while US and European companies were used to competing in commercial markets, former Soviet manufacturers simply were not. The world in which they were conceived to operate had literally collapsed and they had to re-learn how to function in a completely new environment. Russian and Ukrainian aircraft producers had no experience marketing their products internationally because exports had always been done by specialised Soviet export companies. Management teams that had always relied on central planning were for the first time required to react to market behaviour and meet the demands of customers driven by commercial interests. And, crucially, without a central authority, there was no coordination between the research, design, manufacturing and sourcing entities integrating the production system.

Under these conditions, how would the industry survive? How would industrial and organisational obstacles be overcome to effectively compete in international markets? Answering these questions is the objective of this chapter. The chapter analyses the strategies and processes whereby the Russian and Ukrainian aircraft industries transformed from protected military producers operating as part of a centrally planned economy to manufacturers of civil aircraft competing in a global market economy. The analysis focuses on examining the transition from a strategy based on over-reliance on a large domestic market and the use of political power to capture international market shares to one based on a mix of selective state intervention and strategic international collaboration with some of the world's leading aircraft-producing companies. The chapter is divided as follows. The second section looks at the modernisation strategies implemented at the end of the Cold War. The third section examines the policy reform based on industrial consolidation and international collaboration. The fourth section discusses the recent political developments and the influence on the aircraft industry and the future prospects of Russia's and Ukraine's commercial aircraft industry.

Surviving the post-USSR environment

Russia

In 1991 the Russian aircraft industry was in a disastrous state and in desperate need of restructuring and modernisation. Although this was the case for the entire Russian economy, the aircraft industry was likely the most affected of all (Daniels and Perez, 2007), not least because the drastic reduction in state funds resulted in aircraft production almost immediately dropping by 30–40 per cent in an environment where excessive bureaucracy, multiple inefficiencies and over-capacity were rampant (Elenkov, 1995). Upon disintegration, the Ministry of Aviation was in charge of approximately 400 aircraft firms that were 100 per cent state-owned (De Kort and Kluiters, 2003). The industry was dominated by a few elite design bureaus and producers that possessed advanced technological and industrial capabilities, but had a very low degree of integration among themselves, thereby preventing strategic collaboration. Furthermore, sourcing from traditional and trusted suppliers entailed high logistics costs, as many happened to be located in newly independent republics imposing international trade tariffs and requiring payment in a variety of currencies. In addition, Russian managers were not familiar with modern management practices and consequently were unable to do strategic planning. Essentially, there was a total absence of suitable mechanisms to competitively operate in an international market. Yet, becoming internationally competitive was a must and, importantly, with global defence demand on a downward trend, the focus had to be on commercial products.

However, the design bureaus and manufacturing plants were largely specialised in military production. Indeed, just before the Cold War ended, the aircraft industry was receiving approximately 20 per cent of the Soviet annual defence budget (Shaw, 1997, p. 733), inevitably resulting in most funds and development programmes being canalised to the military sector. In this context, the major challenge that industry faced was its limited expertise in the commercial sector, with civil output accounting for only 20 per cent of all Soviet aircraft production in 1990 (De Kort and Kluiters, 2003). The neglect of civil aircraft production would prove to be quite costly in post-Soviet times, as the economic crisis in the 1990s significantly reduced domestic demand and at the same time low import tariffs approved by Moscow resulted in Russian airlines placing most of their orders with Western suppliers.[3]

Thus, Russian firms found themselves in a totally unfavourable situation where they had to cope with competition in a domestic market that had always been exclusively theirs, but were unable to access Western markets due to the unreliability, inferior quality, shorter lifespan, higher maintenance costs and lack of international certifications of Russian products. This mix of circumstances caused the production of Russian civil aircraft to decline by 80 per cent in the early 1990s, with several firms registering an output of only one or two platforms[4] per year (Ecorys Research and Consulting, 2009, p. 236). It was under these conditions that a variety of strategies at the government and enterprise levels had to be implemented in order to ensure that Russian manufacturers could survive by establishing a position in a post-Cold War international market characterised by the prevalence of commercial products and the duopolistic dominance of Boeing and Airbus.

Moscow's first move was to privatise producers with the objective of increasing efficiency. The process of privatisation started in 1992 and by 1996 only 15 per cent of all aircraft manufacturers were owned by the state (De Kort and Kluiters, 2003). Privatisation, however, was not enough to enhance competitiveness, as in many instances former Soviet managers and workers were the new owners of the privatised entities, resulting in managerial and operational practices remaining basically unchanged. Aware that more had to be done, the Russian government committed to invest US$266 billion between 1993 and 2000 on new developments and the modernisation of production facilities (De Kort and Kluiters, 2003). In addition, to coordinate the strategies of the separate design and manufacturing enterprises and reduce overcapacity, both vertical and horizontal integration were required (Bek and Bek, 1998).

Thus, in 1997 Moscow initiated the process of industrial consolidation by grouping aircraft design bureaus and manufacturers into state holdings. This move was aimed at generating economies of scale through concentration, while enabling the canalisation of scarce state financial resources to large entities deemed capable of adapting to changing environments and successfully competing in international markets. This Russian strategy emulated that of the United States and Europe, and resulted in approximately 50 per cent of all Russian aircraft producers being integrated into joint stock companies, with the state owning key firms and banning the sale of its shares in 125 shortlisted companies deemed strategic (De Kort and Kluiters, 2003).

Although government support did help the Russian industry survive the collapse of the USSR, it did not make it internationally competitive. As such, in recognition that transformation was imperative for long-term survival and sustainable development, Russian aircraft enterprises implemented their own strategies to supplement government-mandated ones. These strategies included diversification into non-aircraft manufacturing, investment in R&D and development of new technologies, establishment of collaborative networks with the domestic supply base, and international strategic alliances. In general, the objective was to supply technologically advanced aircraft at internationally competitive prices.

With R&D and labour costs representing a fraction of those found in the United States and Europe, Russia had the advantage of lower fixed costs compared to Western manufacturers. Nevertheless, due to the lack of marketing expertise and familiarity with Western production and marketing practices, it was necessary for Russian industry to engage in international partnerships. This was known by industry leaders since the early 1990s, when international collaboration became a key instrument to access foreign markets, gain competitive advantages and fill technological, industrial and managerial capability gaps.

By 1995 Russian aircraft companies had established subsidiaries in Western countries, as well as FDI joint ventures and joint R&D, co-production, co-marketing and cross-licensing agreements with foreign companies (De Kort and Kluiters, 2003). All major design bureaus and manufacturers were actively involved in dozens of multinational operations (De Kort and Kluiters, 2003). Notably, the public Aviadvigatel design bureau partnered with the private company Perm Motors to undertake joint R&D with Pratt & Whitney and Germany's MTU. The two Russian enterprises also had co-production agreements with General Electric and France's SNECMA.

Adopting a similar approach, Sukhoi collaborated with the US company Gulfstream Aerospace in joint R&D projects, and the Yakovlev Design Bureau was engaged in cross-licensing with Textron Lycoming in the United States, co-marketing with Italy's Aermacchi and France's ATR, co-production with Collins Transport in the US, and joint R&D projects with Israel Aircraft Industries. Similarly, the Mikoyan undertook collaborative R&D with SNECMA and had a presence in Europe through co-production agreements with Hughes Rediffusion in the UK and MTU, as well as co-marketing collaboration with France's Thompson-CSF and Dassault Aviation.

At the Paris Airshow, in June 1993, Mikoyan announced they would co-produce the MiG-AT military jet with South Korea's Daewoo Heavy Industries (Warwick, 1993, p. 26), but this deal never came to fruition.

In 1991, Yakovlev and Aermacchi decided to jointly develop the two-seat jet-trainer/light-attack Yakovlev Yak-130 aircraft. It was the first time that a Russian and Western company cooperated in the design, manufacture and sale of military aircraft.[5]

For its part, Ilyushin established a subsidiary, Euro Ilyushin Aircraft Sales, in the UK as well as collaboration agreements with several US companies. Furthermore, the Russian Scientific Industrial Enterprise Energia and Khrunichev also established a subsidiary, NPO Energia, in the US as well as FDI joint ventures and co-production programmes with Lockheed and Rockwell Space, respectively.

International partnerships were complemented by offshore outsourcing practices that led to the incorporation of Western components and subsystems into Russian aircraft. For example, in the early 1990s Ilyushin integrated Pratt & Whitney engines into its Il-96M and Il-96T platforms. The two models were also equipped with Rockwell Collins traffic alert and collision avoidance systems, as was Tupolev's Tu-204. The latter was also equipped with Rolls-Royce engines[6] and a variety of other Western components. It was expected that offshore outsourcing would strengthen the competitiveness of Russian products in international markets and generate transfer of product and process technologies unknown to domestic manufacturers. Above all, by incorporating Western producers into their supply chains, Russian firms obtained constant access to international business networks; it made the process of international certification easier; and they learned to meet high quality standards (Shaw, 1997).

Collaboration with more advanced Western companies possessing abundant knowledge of international markets was indeed a major value-creating strategy that facilitated the transition from sheltered state-dependent Soviet producers to modern companies competing for shares of the international aircraft market. However, that came at a cost, as Western companies collaborated with their Russian counterparts because of their interest in obtaining access to Russian engineering skills, high-performance technologies and markets (Daniels and Perez, 2007). Thus, Western companies, including Boeing and Airbus, established a footprint in the Russian market by sourcing parts and components from Russian suppliers, opening subsidiaries in Moscow and obtaining contracts from local airlines. Having the competition at home, the Russian industry now had no choice but to prioritise the development of new designs and penetration of foreign markets, making use of both its own resources and international alliances.

Ukraine

The case of Russia is unique because while it possessed sophisticated aircraft technology and expertise similar to that of the world's most developed manufacturers, it lacked the extensive marketing expertise and in-depth knowledge of the best international practices that characterise Western companies. Therefore, the devised strategy consisted of maximising on existing capabilities to ensure that the accumulated industrial and technological advantages would not be lost, while simultaneously filling capability gaps by acquiring the required expertise to compete internationally through collaboration with foreign companies. This was feasible because Russian industry had attractive assets to offer foreign partners in return, notably high-tech products, low-cost manufacturing, and, importantly, a large market. Although also an heir of Soviet techno-industrial capabilities, the case of Ukraine was markedly different. This was the result not as much of initial infrastructural conditions as of government policy. Indeed, Ukraine had been fully integrated into the Soviet aircraft production system and had the potential to join Russia in pursuit of international competitiveness. Furthermore, due to their shared experience, the opportunities and challenges faced by the two national industries were very similar. Like Russia, Ukraine also had a strong scientific and industrial base, advanced manufacturing capabilities, a skilled workforce, was specialised in military production, and lacked modern management and international marketing skills.

However, an additional challenge that Ukrainian industry confronted was that production plants were not located in-country and therefore final assembly often had to be subcontracted to manufacturers located in Russia and other former Soviet countries. Development was further hindered by the fact that, unlike Moscow, upon disintegration, Kiev failed to accelerate the processes of economic reform, privatisation and industrial consolidation. To compound this, although in the early 1990s Kiev put in place a programme to propel the development of the civil aircraft industry, lack of sufficient financial resources meant that only 10 per cent of the necessary funds were available (Karnozov, 2004).

These conditions caused the Ukrainian aircraft industry to remain largely isolated from foreign partners, essentially limiting international collaboration to arrangements with other former Soviet producers, in turn leading to industrial decline throughout the 1990s and over-reliance on Russian suppliers (Dominese, 2005). Notwithstanding, aware of the imperative to establish a position in commercial markets for long-term sustainability, in the 1990s Antonov managed to release a commercial short-range turboprop airliner, the An-140, and started the development of a commercial regional jet, the An-148. Despite these feats, however, the Ukrainian aircraft industry remained focused on its core strengths: military production, exports to traditional markets, collaboration with Russia and provision of maintenance and upgrading services to Antonov aircraft in dozens of countries, particularly China, India, Libya and Russia (Karnozov, 2004).

One decade after the disintegration of the USSR it had become evident that government and enterprise efforts had not been enough to enable former Soviet industries to join the world leaders in the sector. Indeed, even though 70 per cent of all Russian aircraft manufacturing was done by private industry in 2000, the civil output was 90 per cent less than a decade earlier (De Kort and Kluiters, 2003). In addition, most domestic orders were not being placed with domestic manufacturers. This was not only because of the perception of superior quality and reliability associated with foreign platforms, but also because flying Boeing or Airbus made it easier for airlines to obtain certifications and rights to operate in Western airports. As a result, Russian civil aircraft producers Ilyushin, Tupolev and Yakovlev had to cope with decreased domestic demand. In this context, the danger was the potential decline and eventual loss of domestic aircraft production capabilities. To avoid such an outcome, it was necessary to develop new designs and implement more robust consolidation strategies to ensure that once industry had survived it would also be able to successfully compete in the twenty-first-century international market.

Further consolidation and international collaboration

Russia

Despite economic reform and industrial restructuring undertaken throughout the 1990s, in 1999 the Russian aircraft industry had barely changed and was still too large, unintegrated and inefficient: it comprised 335 enterprises and organisations, 9 design bureaus and 19 major manufacturing plants (Giles, 1999, p. 12). Moreover, low R&D investments and lack of orders had resulted in industry producing only 10 per cent of its Soviet output (Giles, 1999, p. 12). The state could only afford 14 per cent of the required R&D investments due to a drop in oil prices and there was 75–80 per cent overcapacity (Giles, 1999, p. 12). It was indeed a very dire scenario. Yet, the situation began to change in the early 2000s when local demand grew as national airlines needed to replace ageing platforms and there was a concomitant increase in the demand for international air travel.

However, it soon became evident that a new corporate structure suitable to operate in the hyper-competitive twenty-first-century international aircraft market would be required. The Russian industry was basically producing a few 'modern' commercial jets (Il-96, Tu-204/214, An-148), while the older Tu-154 and Yakovlev Yak-42 designs were phased out from the production line. The more recent commercial jets have not been successful in terms of number built, compared with the older Tu-154. The same applies to the rather recent Ilyushin Il-114 propeller aircraft, with only 20 built, when the production was terminated in 2012 (see Table 9.1).

New designs had to be developed, not least because in 2005 while Russia was producing only ten aircraft per year, Boeing and Airbus had orders for over 1,000 aircraft each (US Department of Commerce, n.d.).[7] There was therefore substantial catching-up to do and since the sector was recognised by Moscow as essential for the development of the Russian economy (Komarov, 2008, p. 41),

Table 9.1 Commercial aircraft produced in Russia from the 1990s onwards

Jet airliner	*Development started*	*Service entry*	*End of production*	*Engines*	*Maximum number of passengers*	*Number built*
Ilyushin Il-62 long-range, narrow-body airliner	Early 1960s	Aeroflot 1967	1995	Four rear-mounted turbofans	195	292
Ilyushin Il-86 medium-range wide-body airliner	Mid-1970s	Aeroflot 1980	1994/1995	Four turbofans	350	106
Ilyushin Il-96 long-range wide-body airliner	Mid-1980s	Aeroflot 1993	In production	Four turbofans	300	Around 30 until 2014
Sukhoi Superjet 100 regional airliner	2000	Armavia 2011	In production	Two turbofans	108	75 until November 2014
Tupolev Tu-154 medium-range narrow-body airliner	Mid-1960s	Aeroflot 1972	Unclear, airliner probably early 2000s, but a few have been built for the Ministry of Defence as late as 2013	Three rear-mounted turbofans	180	1,000+; probably 1,025 or 1,026
Tupolev Tu-204/214	Mid-1980s	Vnukovo Airlines 1996	In production	Two turbofans	215 (204SM)	76 in early 2014
Tupolev Tu-334 short- to medium-range airliner	Early 1990s	None	Project cancelled in 2009	Two rear-mounted turbofans	102	2
Yakovlev Yak-42	Early 1970s	Aeroflot 1980	2003	Three rear-mounted turbofans	120	185+
Propeller aircraft						
Ilyushin Il-114	1986	Uzbekistan Airways 1998	2012	Two turboprops	64	About 20

Note
The USSR ceased to exist in December 1991.

strong government intervention would shape industrial structure and development programmes.

As usual, the pursuit of sovereignty and indigenisation was very present, but now it was also confronted with the imperatives for international cooperation and industrial interconnectedness. Thus, upon consultation with a special commission, the Putin administration concluded that the best strategy to ensure the long-term sustainability and international competitiveness of the national aircraft industry was further industrial consolidation and rationalisation in the form of a conglomerate grouping all major design bureaus and manufacturers. Hence, in 2006 the government created the joint-stock company United Aircraft Corporation (UAC), encompassing the vast majority of Russian aircraft designers and producers, including Irkut, Mikoyan, Sukhoi, Ilyushin, Tupolev, Beriev and Yakovlev.

In total, UAC currently comprises 23 companies and those that do not belong to the conglomerate do not get to benefit from Moscow's financial support (Ecorys Research and Consulting, 2009). This decision to canalise all financial resources to a national champion is driven by the conviction that consolidation will enable the industry to overcome the problems caused by the lack of integration between design bureaus and manufacturers, reduce inefficiency, generate further economies of scale and expand the product line (Matthews and Lozano, 2012).

The consolidation of Russia's aircraft industry into UAC can be regarded as re-nationalisation, since private capital was reduced while the role of government officials was increased. The composition of the Board of Directors reflects this clearly, as eight out of the 14 appointed members are high-ranking government officials. In addition, although the state initially owned a 75 per cent stake, it has risen year after year, and as of 2013 the Russian Federation owns 84.33 per cent of UAC's chartered capital, valued at €4.7 billion (United Aircraft Corporation, 2013a). UAC was in effect conceived to be a government-controlled aerospace national champion and become the world's third largest aircraft manufacturer after Airbus Group and Boeing. This is to be achieved through a variety of corporate strategies, notably: strong collaboration with foreign companies, reduction of funding for non-priority programmes, canalisation of industrial and financial resources to the Sukhoi Superjet (SSJ) 100[8] and MS-21 programmes, and aggressive expansion into post-sale services (Ullrich, 2008). Initially, UAC planned to manufacture 2,600 commercial aircraft between 2008 and 2025, anticipating that 60 per cent would be for the export market (Komarov, 2009). But such an ambition soon proved to be, if not unachievable, certainly too big, not least because by 2013 the SSJ 100, had secured orders for only 179 aircraft, 30 of which were from Aeroflot (Sukhoi Civil Aircraft Company, 2013).

The SSJ, UAC's star commercial programme, encapsulates the Russian industrial aircraft strategy at large: national control of original designs and products supported by intensive international collaboration and strategic partnerships. The SSJ 100 was designed to replace Tu-134 and Yak-42 aircraft and be a competitor to Embraer's E-jets and Bombardier's CRJ series, with the Russian government financing 25 per cent of the development costs (Antonova, 2010). However, in an unprecedented move, national self-sufficiency was relinquished and an international strategic partnership was established between Sukhoi and Italy's Alenia Aermacchi to develop the SSJ family of regional planes through the Sukhoi Civil Aircraft Company, of which Sukhoi owns 75 per cent and Alenia Aermacchi 25 per cent. The programme is evidence of Moscow's strategy to enhance domestic capabilities by using international collaboration mechanisms, while simultaneously ensuring that the national champion owns the design and remains positioned as the system integrator (Komarov, 2008). It is estimated that 50–60 per cent of the SSJ components are foreign-sourced (ITAR-TASS World Service, 2010), but the most outstanding aspect of the programme is the fact that UAC has managed to reduce the negative stigma associated with Russian products by enlisting the world's leading companies in the sector as collaborators and suppliers.

Thus, not only was Boeing hired as a consultant, but all major subsystems are sourced from well-known European and American companies in the sector: Thales supplies the avionics, Germany's Liebherr the flight control systems, Honeywell the auxiliary power units, Hamilton Sundstrand the electrical systems, France's Intertechnique the fuel systems, Parker the hydraulic systems, SAFRAN the landing gear and Goodrich the wheel brakes and brake controls. Moreover, the SSJ's SaM-146 engines are designed and produced by the French–Russian PowerJet 50/50 joint venture between SNECMA and NPO Saturn, with the French and Russian governments contributing US$168 million and US$116 million to finance the programme, respectively (Ecorys Research and Consulting, 2009). Having successfully integrated an engine exclusively designed for the aircraft, Sukhoi markets the plane as 'the first airliner in which engine and airframe have been designed together to optimize performance' (Sukhoi Civil Aircraft Company, 2013).

Although sale volumes are still are much below targets, the programme is looked upon as an industrial success by the Russian partners. It has enabled Russian industry to make use of international collaboration to overcome deficiencies and produce an efficient platform whose operating costs claimed to be 6–8 per cent lower than those of its main competitor, Embraer's 190/195 (ATO.RU, 2010). The SSJ programme has made it possible to give Russia a chance to enter the international market with a new commercial aircraft. Key to this is the fact that the SSJ is not marketed internationally by Sukhoi, but by the SuperJet International joint venture between Alenia Aermacchi and Sukhoi, with the former owning 51 per cent of the shares and collaborating in the worldwide provision of after-sales services.

By combining domestic strengths with international partnerships, Russia has managed to emerge from its Soviet legacy, maximising on its own assets and capabilities while selectively enlisting the contribution of more advanced manufacturers to strategically fill pre-identified capability gaps. So far, the results are satisfactory. UAC has reported that between 2007 and 2013 revenue increased by 100 per cent, registering an annual growth of 20 per cent (SKRIN Newswire,

2013). In addition, the company claims orders for 740 aircraft, albeit only 33 per cent are civil (SKRIN Newswire, 2013). Indeed, 80 per cent of UAC's output corresponds to the military sector, but the corporation's objective is to reverse the trend until civil products account for 75 per cent of the total (ITAR-TASS World Service, 2013).

A fundamental success factor will be the extent to which Russia's most ambitious civil aircraft programme, the MS-21 family of commercial airliners, fulfils its objective of establishing a permanent presence in international markets alongside Boeing and Airbus. The MS-21 has been designed by Irkut, Tupolev and Yakovlev to compete with the Boeing 737, Airbus A320 and, eventually, China's C-919. Under the Russian industrial strategy, it is also expected that the programme will help modernise domestic design and manufacturing capabilities through the infusion of Western technology. Expectations are indeed high and this is justified by the fact that the programme targets the single-aisle class passenger aircraft market, which Boeing estimates will be worth US$2 trillion by 2040, with most demand coming from Asian countries experiencing very high levels of economic growth (Sanati, 2012).

Scheduled to hit the market in 2017, the MS-21 prospects seem promising, not least because it is US$20 million cheaper than similar Western designs,

Figure 9.1 Manufacturing locations (main assembly plants) of current commercial aircraft produced in Russia. (1) Voronezh aircraft plant – production of the Ilyushin Il-96 and the Antonov An-148 (Ukraine); (2) CJSC Aviastar-SP, Ulyanovsk – production of the Tupolev Tu-204; (3) Kazan Aircraft Production Association (KAPO) – production of the TU-214; (4) OJSC Aviakor, Samara – production of the An-140 (Ukraine); (5) Komsomolsk-on-Amur Aircraft Production Association (KnAAPO) – production of Sukhoi Superjet 100 (SSJ100).

offers 20 per cent lower operating costs and is 10–15 per cent more efficient (RIA Novosti, 2008). Furthermore, to enhance the competitiveness of the programme, potential national and international purchasers have been involved in the design process in order to guarantee that customers' requirements are fully met (United Aircraft Corporation, 2013b). As in the SSJ case, offshore outsourcing has been crucial and therefore the aircraft is powered by Pratt & Whitney's PW1000G engines, while the avionics and integrated control systems are supplied by Rockwell Collins and United Technologies, respectively. Yet, notwithstanding the extensive use of international collaboration, industry continues to heavily rely on government subsidisation. Indeed, both the SSJ and MS-21 programmes have received substantial government funds: RUB16 billion (US$355 million) were allocated to the SSJ development and more than RUB100 billion (US$2.3 billion) have been budgeted for that of the MS-21 (Komarov, 2011, p. 61).

Clearly unwilling to let market forces shape the structure of the national aircraft industry, government control is of paramount importance to Russian authorities as they try to achieve the right balance between indigenous production and international collaboration.

Ukraine

Over-reliance on government intervention is something that the Russian and Ukrainian aircraft industries have in common. However, unlike UAC, Antonov remains 100 per cent government-owned, with approximately 70 per cent of components used by Ukrainian aircraft industry being sourced from Russia (Stockholm International Peace Research Institute, 2004, p. 443). Ukraine is highly dependent on the performance of Russian manufacturers. Furthermore, contrary to Russia's focus on positioning itself in the international commercial market, Ukraine has focused on providing support services to military aircraft already in operation. Nevertheless, because only 5–10 per cent of Ukraine's total aircraft output is destined for the domestic market (Aerospace Industries Association of Canada, 2009), Ukrainian industry remains dependent on exports and therefore it is imperative for Antonov's long-term sustainability to also compete in the commercial market with its own designs, namely the An-140, An-148 and An-158. As shown in Table 9.2, the numbers of aircraft built are rather low.

In recognition of this and attempting to emulate the Russian strategy, in 2009 the Ukrainian manufacturing plant Aviant was integrated into Antonov. But, even with this integration, Antonov is still unable to undertake final assembly of all produced platforms and therefore continues to outsource systems integration to foreign, particularly Russian, contractors. In this context, a concern of Ukrainian industry is that, as Russia strengthens its collaboration with Western companies, ties with Ukrainian manufacturers might be reduced, potentially resulting in the erosion of local industrial capabilities (Bilousova, 2013). The fact, however, is that the two parties are in a situation of mutual dependence, as

Table 9.2 Ukraine commercial aircraft produced from the 1990s onwards

Jet Airliner	*Development started*	*Service entry*	*End of production*	*Engines*	*Maximum number of passengers*	*Number built*
Antonov An-148/158 regional jet airliner	1990s	Aerosvit 2009	In production	Two turbofans	85 (148) 99 (158)	34 by October 2014
Propeller aircraft						
Antonov An-38	1990; the aircraft is basically a stretched An-28	2000?	Officially not ended, but no aircraft seems to have been built since 2004	Two turboprops	27	11; built in Novosibirsk Aircraft Production Association, Russia
Antonov An-140 regional airliner	1993	Early 2000s	In production	Two turboprops	52	30+

Russia also requires constant supplies from Antonov, Aviant and Motor Sich, the Ukrainian engine design bureau.

In effect, the situation of mutual dependence is such that in 2010 Antonov and UAC established a partnership to undertake collaborative investment projects aimed at strengthening design and serial manufacturing of civil and military aircraft, accelerating technological modernisation, enhancing post-sale services and increasing exports (Oreanda News Agency, 2010). A year later, UAC and Antonov established a 50/50 joint venture, UAC-Antonov, whose main objective is to facilitate collaboration in the development, production, marketing and after-sales services of An-series aircraft, potentially serving as a platform for further integration between the Russian and Ukrainian industries.

Yet, although both the Russian and Ukrainian governments have expressed an interest in integrating the two industries, negotiations have been severely hindered by national security considerations and multiple diplomatic disputes. With both industries likely to remain as autonomous entities in the foreseeable future, Antonov is following Russian steps in employing international collaboration and partnerships to modernise capabilities and develop internationally competitive products. However, unlike Russia, Ukraine's major partners are not Western countries, but Russia, China and India, in that order. This might soon change as commercial pressures force Antonov to go beyond its comfort zone by acquiring advanced Western technologies and developing commercial relations with foreign partners, particularly in Latin America and Southeast Asia, regions targeted as key markets for the An-148 and An-158.

To date, the major challenge that Antonov faces is its ownership structure. Being a 100 per cent state-owned company prevents efficient management, as Kiev exercises total control over the company's operations and every strategic decision has to be approved by the government in line with complex legislation. Having a bureaucracy instead of corporate mechanisms is an obstacle to the company's development that delays programmes and inevitably diminishes its international competitiveness. Russia has managed to merge state control with a corporate rationale driven by commercial incentives by implementing a strategy based on partial privatisation, consolidation and collaboration with Western partners.

In contrast, Ukraine, having Russia as a strategic partner and Kiev and Russian banks as the only sources of funds, is lagging behind. Convergence will likely require more than bilateral collaboration. In fact, privatising part of Antonov in order to allow for the incorporation of economic incentives might prove to be necessary. Private ownership, even if tightly controlled by Kiev, would also enable the company to access private sources of funding, thereby overcoming its inability to offer low-interest credit to potential purchasers, which has resulted in Russian companies having to be used as intermediaries in international transactions.

Since the prohibitively high costs of self-sufficiency make it unviable, the need to combine state-ownership and national design and manufacturing with international partnerships has resulted in a hybrid 'model' that is as unique to

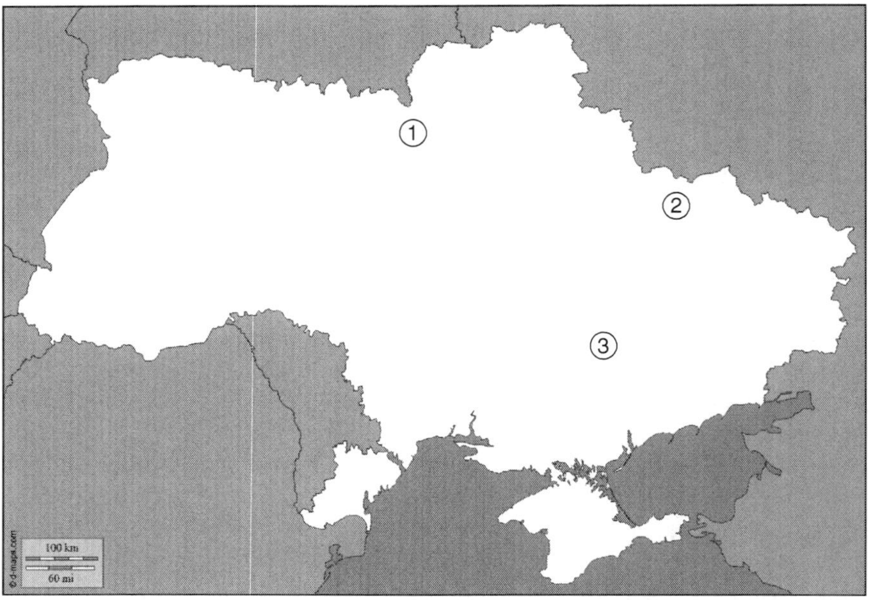

Figure 9.2 Manufacturing locations (main assembly) of current Ukrainian commercial aircraft in production. (1) Antonov Serial Production Plant, Kiev – production of the An-148/158; (2) KHDABP, Kharkiv/Kharkov – production of the An-140. This aircraft is also produced in Samara, Russia, by Aviakor. It is also assembled under licence by HESA in Iran (see Chapter 8); (3) The large aero-engine company Motor Sich – main plant in Zaporozhye.

Russia and Ukraine as their historical experience and bureaucratic regimes. The extent to which this model will be successful in achieving international competitiveness will depend as much on government policy and corporate strategies as on international market dynamics and strategies implemented by US and European competitors.

Politics and future prospects

The aerospace industry is characterised by volatile markets, with orders affected by a variety of financial and political factors (Eriksson, 2010). It is closely and heavily linked to politics, domestic as well as international, and few other industries have so intimately interacted with political systems of many nation states, not least Russia and its predecessor, the Soviet Union. The Ukrainian 'revolution' in 2014 and its aftermath have had a big influence on the economic and political relations with other countries, especially Russia. The 'revolution' implied increasing tensions with Russia, followed by protests in the south-eastern regions of Ukraine and Russia's military intervention and annexation of the Crimean peninsula. The conflict between Ukraine and Russian separatists also directly affected the international aviation industry and resulted in the probable shooting down of Malaysian Airlines flight MH17 from Amsterdam to Kuala Lumpur when travelling over the conflict-hit area.

As a result of Russia's actions and behaviour, relations have continued to deteriorate with the United States and European Union. For instance, the UK 'failed' to issue visas for half of Russia's 350-member delegation in time for the large aerospace exhibition at Farnborough, UK, July 2014 (DiMascio *et al.*, 2014) and various economic and industrial sanctions have been imposed on Russia.

Still, more than two decades after the break-up of the Soviet Union the ties are very close between Ukraine's and Russia's aerospace and defence industries. These ties may be an additional reason contributing to President Putin's opposition to letting Ukraine develop closer economic and political ties with the European Union. As previously mentioned, the Ukrainian aircraft industry is highly dependent on Russian manufacturers as suppliers of components, but the opposite is true for engines. Nowhere is there such interdependency as at the Motor Sich factory, which produces nearly all of the engines used in Russian military and transport helicopters (Birnbaum, 2014).[9]

The political tensions between the two countries started well ahead of the 2014 'outbreak', also mirrored in the aerospace industry. President Putin ordered Prime Minister Medvedev to consider no later than 1 August 2013 initiating modernizing foreign-developed aircraft (i.e. Ukraine) types without asking for the foreign developers' (type certificate holders) consent. Director of the Center for Army, Conversion and Disarmament Studies, Valentyn Badrak, sees this document as a direct attack on the Ukrainian aircraft producers (*The Day*, 2013). After the development in 2014, Ukraine has suspended a number of agreements with Russia, as well as exports of defence equipment.

Thus, there are clear signs that the close industrial linkages and cooperation between the two countries will become weakened for the foreseeable future and will create a number of problems: management, economic, technological, etc. Except for the 'internal' Russia–Ukraine problems, the outward linkages, i.e. connections to international markets, will also be affected in various ways.

Neither Russia nor Ukraine are currently competitive in the commercial aircraft and engine markets. Although Russia in recent decades has developed a few commercial airliners, they have not experienced any success. They have either been produced in rather few numbers or the projects have been terminated. Even the latest Sukhoi Superjet 100, claimed by some to be a success, is only bought by a few foreign carriers, and the number of deliveries is still rather low.[10] Ukraine currently has a few aircraft to offer: the An-140 (sold within Ukraine, Russia and Iran) and the A-148/158 (sold to Russia, Ukraine, Cuba and North Korea), produced in small numbers.

Even if Russia and Ukraine were able to manufacture aircraft and engines of the same performance and quality as the best Western products, they have limited experience with commercial business outside the previous communist sphere. The pace of technology change and fierce competition poses great dilemmas for those who have ambitions to enter global markets and no sector is immune from the technology standards of quality and price that are set by world-class firms. Another hurdle is the fact that Russian and Ukrainian companies have not yet developed any efficient, or large enough, global service network (after-sales service) for airlines using their aircraft and engines. It is a necessity that takes years to develop and is associated with huge costs. Another very import factor in the whole aerospace sector is the role of trust, which applies to companies, delivery and reliability, service levels, but also a wider political context.[11] The current economic-political situation will probably have a long-term effect on the possibilities to make any main inroads on the main global commercial markets.

What, then, are the options and strategies for Russia and Ukraine? Russia still has huge ambitions in this industry and seems to have a strategic goal to return to its Soviet-era position. In 2014 Russia's government decided to funnel US$28 billion into Russia's aircraft industry in order to haul Russia up into the world's top-three aircraft manufacturers (*Moscow Times*, 2014). Under the programme, designed by the Industry and Trade Ministry and approved by the cabinet, the government will invest just over US$20 billion, while the rest will come from private sources. According to the plan, over 3,000 aeroplanes and 5,500 helicopters (military and civil) should be produced up to 2025. The goal is to increase the global market share of Russian-manufactured aircraft, helicopters and engines.

To succeed, it is not enough to make huge economic investments and very good aerospace and technical skills. There are so many other dimensions needed to be successful in the long term; in addition to the factors previously mentioned, there is also access to top-level management and marketing skills.

Both Russia and Ukraine became independent republics inheriting the USSR's technological and industrial assets, but infrastructure and policy asymmetries have shaped the two industries differently. Russia inherited the major part of the USSR's design and production assets and has identified the need for international cooperation and openness. The Russian policy has to some extent embarked on a strategic process of industrial transformation for commercial viability, while Kiev has yet to do so. What is clear is that the two countries have struggled to overcome their Soviet past and neither of them is ready to allow market mechanisms to determine the performance of the aircraft industry, as evidenced by the strong levels of government control and intervention that shape industrial developments in both countries.

Both Ukraine and Russia will probably need to further increase international cooperation and industrial connectedness to modernize capabilities (technology, management, etc.) and develop internationally competitive products, but this is also linked to the future economic and political development in the two countries. It seems that Ukraine will move towards closer economic and political cooperation towards the Western world. Such a development can also imply a closer cooperation in industrial sectors such as aerospace. In spite of the current differences and tensions between Russia and the West, the situation can change, implying increased cooperation also in the aerospace sector. The various economic and technology sanctions applied to Russia could lead to a closer cooperation with China, a country with huge ambitions in the whole aerospace sector. Recently it has been disclosed in various journals that there is an increased interest from the

Russian aerospace industry in cooperating with China. Russia needs to advance its ability to develop and manufacture electronic components, while China has needs in many areas, not least engines.

In spite of their impressive aviation/aircraft industry heritage, Russia and Ukraine have another challenge to face – namely the global industrial changes that have taken place during the last decades. Many emerging economies have invested heavily in the aviation/aircraft industries and have built up an advanced manufacturing capability focusing on becoming subcontractors to the main Western companies or, in the case of Brazil, developed into a major player as an aircraft manufacturer. Russia and Ukraine have to take these changes into consideration. From a strategic view the new emerging nations could be looked upon as either competitors or cooperating partners.

Notes

1 Airbus began as a consortium, Airbus Industrie, in the late 1960s with the aim to develop and manufacture commercial airliners. The first aircraft, A300, was then followed by a whole family of airliners. Airbus Industrie was formally established in December 1970.

2 Chapter 10 deals with effects of the Cold War and its aftermath.

3 See Chapter 4 for a wider discussion about the loss of aircraft markets, also affecting the engine industry.

4 An aircraft platform is a structural or technological form that enables the development of present or future aircraft. It includes common design, engineering and production efforts, as well as major components sharing. Platform sharing is to reduce the cost and have a more efficient product development process. For instance, the Tu-334 was based on the Tu-204 fuselage/platform, but unlike the Tu-204 the Tu-334 had a T-tail and had rear-mounted engines; the latter programme was cancelled after only two aircraft had been built.

5 The aircraft is still in production and Aermacchi developed a modified version, the M-346, that uses equipment exclusively from Western manufacturers.

6 This was the first time a Russian airliner was supplied with Western engines.

7 In comparison, Boeing delivered 290 commercial jet aircraft and Airbus 378 during the same year.

8 See Chapter 2 for an overview of the SSJ: background, development, aircraft characteristics, etc.

9 The Zaporozhye Motor Sich Public Joint Stock Company is the only company in Ukraine manufacturing engines for aeroplanes and helicopters. Except engines for Ukrainian aircraft and helicopters, the company has built engines for a number of Russian civil and military aircraft and helicopters. Due to the dramatic decline of the number of Russian airliners and transport aircraft manufactured since the 1990s, Russia's dependence on Ukraine has diminished in this part of the industry. Motor Sich also built the engines for the late Tu-334 airliner, a programme that was cancelled in 2009, after only two had been built. The few Russian airliners currently in production use Russian, Western or joint-manufactured engines. See the engine chapter.

10 On 10 November 2014, 75 aircraft had been built and 48 delivered (Sukhoi Superjet 100 – Production list and backlog, 2014). Of the 48 delivered, only three foreign airlines operate the SSJ100: Lao Central Airlines (one aircraft), Interjet (Mexico, 11 aircraft) and Sky Aviation (Indonesia, three aircraft).

11 This can also be attributed to safety issues. The crash of a Sukhoi Superjet 100 on a demonstration flight in Indonesia (Mount Salak) in May 2012, had probably no positive impact on reputation and trust.

References

Aerospace Industries Association of Canada (2009) 'Ukrainian Aerospace and Aviation Market Overview', www.aiac.ca/uploadedFiles/News_and_Events/Calendar_of_Events/Ukrainian%20Aerospace%20Market%20Overview%20June%2010_eng.pdf, accessed 3 September 2013.

Antonova, M. (2010) 'New Orders but No Lift for Superjet', *Moscow Times*, 22 July, www.themoscowtimes.com/news/article/new-orders-but-no-lift-for-superjet/411118.html, accessed 2 September 2013.

ATO.RU (2010) 'Regional Aircraft for International Market', www.ato.ru/content/regional-aircraft-international-market, accessed 2 September 2013.

Bek, M. and Bek, N. (1998) 'Strategic Planning and Management of Russia's Aerospace Industry Enterprises Development: State, Tendencies, and Problems', *Acta Astronautica*, Vol. 43, No. 1, pp. 47–49.

Bilousova, N. (2013) 'Russia has Gone on the Offensive Against Ukrainian Aircraft Industry', 11 April, www.day.kiev.ua/en/article/day-after-day/russia-has-gone-offensive-against-ukrainian-aircraft-industry, accessed 2 September 2013.

Birnbaum, M. (2014) 'Ukraine Factories Equip Russian Military Despite Support for Rebels', www.washingtonpost.com/world/europe/ukraine-factories-equip-russian-military-despite-support-for-rebels/2014/08/15/9c32cde7-a57c-4d7b-856a-e74b8307ef9d_story.html, accessed 2 October 2014.

Daniels, J. and Perez, R. (2007) 'Environmental Dynamics and Collaboration: Case Studies of U.S.–Russian Aerospace Joint Ventures', *The Journal of High Technology Management Research*, Vol. 17, pp. 175–185.

De Kort, J. and Kluiters, S. (2003) 'Reforming the Russian Aviation Industry', *European Business Review*, Vol. 15, No. 6, pp. 381–389.

DiMascio, J., Buyck, C. and Pyadushkin, M. (2014) 'For Russia, No Love', *Aviation Week & Space Technology*, 21 July, p. 26.

Dominese, G. (2005) 'Ukraine Economy and Finance in the Reform Process and the European Partnership: A Focus on Aerospace Industry', *Transition Studies Review*, Vol. 12, No. 2, pp. 257–292.

Ecorys Research and Consulting (2009) 'FWC Sector Competitiveness Studies: Competitiveness of the EU Aerospace Industry with a Focus on: Aeronautics Industry', Final Report for European Commission, Munich, 15 December.

Elenkov, D. (1995) 'Russian Aerospace MNCs in Global Competition: Their Origin, Competitive Strengths and Forms of Multinational Expansion', *The Columbia Journal of World Business*, Vol. 30, No. 2, pp. 66–78.

Eriksson, S. (2010) 'China's Aircraft Industry: Collaboration and Technology Transfer – The Case of Airbus', *International Journal of Technology Transfer and Commercialisation* (IJTTC), Vol. 9, No. 4, pp. 306–325.

Gansler, J. (2011) *Democracy's Arsenal: Creating a Twenty-First-Century Defense Industry*, Cambridge, MA: MIT Press.

Giles, R. (ed.) (1999) *Russia's Aerospace Industry*, Surrey: Jane's Information Group.

Harned, D. (1995) 'Can Russian Aerospace Rise Again?', *The McKinsey Quarterly*, Vol. 3.

ITAR-TASS World Service (2010) 'Sukhoi Supports Further Localising Superjet-100 Production – CEO', 23 November.

ITAR-TASS World Service (2013) 'United Aircraft Corporation to be Seriously Changed over Next 15 Years – OAC President', 28 August.

Karnozov, V. (2004) 'State of Change', *Flight International*, 14–20 September, p. 40.

Komarov, A. (2008) 'Russia Lays Out Grand Strategy for Aerospace: The Issue Will be its Delivery', *Aviation Week & Space Technology*, Vol. 168, No. 9, p. 41.

Komarov, A. (2009) 'Russia's United Aircraft Corp. Reconsiders Commercial Aviation Plans', *Aviation Week & Space Technology*, 23 February, p. 26.

Komarov, A. (2011) 'The Russian Aerospace Industry has Big Plans for its Commercial Aircraft Sector, But Bringing Them to Fruition is Proving Difficult', *Aviation Week & Space Technology*, Vol. 173, No. 28.

Kuznetsov, E. (1997) 'Ukraine: Space Management for Industry Success', *Acta Astronautica*, Vol. 41, No. 4, pp. 551–558.

Matthews, R. and Lozano, A. (2012) 'The Mercurial Development of Russia's United Aircraft Corporation', *Defense & Security Analysis*, Vol. 28, No. 2, pp. 152–162.

Moscow Times (2014) 'Russia's Aviation Industry gets $28 Bln to Become Global Powerhouse', www.themoscowtimes.com/business/article/russia-s-aviation-industry-gets-28bln-to-become-global-powerhouse/500331.html, accessed 14 September 2014.

Murman, E., Allen, T., Bozdogan, K., Cutcher-Gerschenfeld, J., McManus, H., Nightingale, D., Rebentisch, E., Shields, T., Stahl, F., Walton, M., Warmkassel, J., Weiss, S. and Widnall, S. (2002) *Lean Enterprise Value: Insights from MIT's Lean Aerospace Initiative*, Basingstoke and New York: Palgrave.

Oreanda News Agency (2010) 'UAC, Vnesheconombank, Antonov signed Cooperation Agreement', 3 November.

RIA Novosti (2008) 'Sukhoi Wins Bid to Build Wings for New MS-21 Passenger Plane', 13 March.

Sanati, C. (2012) 'In Aerospace Wars, Don't Count Russia Out Yet', *Fortune*, 16 May.

Shaw, B. (1997) 'The Role of Marketing in Managing the Transition from a Command Economy to a Market Economy with Special Reference to the Russian Aerospace Industry', Hills, G., Giglierano, J.J. and Hultman, C.M. (eds), *Research at the Marketing/Entrepreneurship Interface*, Chicago, IL: Institute for Entrepreneurial Studies.

SKRIN Newswire (2013) 'United Aircraft Corporation Doubles Revenues in Six Years', 19 June.

Stockholm International Peace Research Institute (2004) 'The Arms Industry of Ukraine', In *SIPRI Yearbook 2004*, Oxford: Oxford University Press.

Sukhoi Civil Aircraft Company (2013) 'Sukhoi Superjet 100 in Partnership with Alenia Aermacchi', www.scac.ru/en/products/sukhoi-superjet100, accessed 2 September 2013.

Sukhoi Superjet 100 – Production list and backlog (2014) http://superjet100.info/registry-english, accessed 10 November 2014.

The Day (2013) 'Russian has Gone on the Offensive Against Ukranian Aircraft Industry', www.day.kiev.ua/en/article/day-after-day/russia-has-gone-offensive-against-ukrainian-aircraft-industry, accessed 15 September 2014.

Ullrich, W. (2008) 'Mergers and Growth', *MS&T Magazine*, Vol. 1.

United Aircraft Corporation (2013a) 'About UAC', www.uacrussia.ru/en/corporation/, accessed 2 September 2013.

United Aircraft Corporation (2013b) 'MS-21', www.uacrussia.ru/en/models/civil/ms-21/, accessed 2 September 2013.

US Department of Commerce (n.d.) 'Russia: Consolidation of the Aerospace Industry', www.trade.gov/mas/manufacturing/oaai/build/groups/public/@tg_oaai/documents/webcontent/tg_oaai_003738.pdf, accessed 3 September 2013.

Warwick, G. (1993) 'Military Meetings', *Flight International*, 30 June–6 July.

10 Transformation of the aviation industry in Central and Eastern Europe

Czech Republic and Poland

Zbigniew Bochniarz, Zbyněk Hruška, Emilia Barbara Sieńko-Kułakowska, Grzegorz Pisarczyk and Josef Zbořil

Introduction to transforming economies and the aviation industry in Central and Eastern Europe

Over the last 20 years, the region of Central and Eastern Europe (CEE) has become notable worldwide as the poster-child of historical transformation from a totalitarian communist-party-dominated system with a centrally planned economy to democracy and market economy. These political and economic reforms were accompanied by significant environmental reforms and the introduction of radical institutional changes that affected all aspects of public life. For this reason they are often called a systemic transformation with certain characteristic features of CEE (Archibald *et al.*, 2009; Dabrowski *et al.*, 2001) different than Russian or Chinese reform models (Stieglitz, 1999). The successful implementation of CEE transformation inspired many leaders outside of that region, particularly in Eastern and Southern Europe, and led those countries to join the European Union (EU) in 2004 (Czech Republic, Estonia, Hungary, Latvia, Lithuania, Poland, Slovakia, and Slovenia; adding Bulgaria and Romania in 2007). This way the major requirements of the systemic transformation were completed while being anchored to the EU democratic governance system and a mature market economy. Despite cultural, economic and ethnic differences, these ten new EU member states (EU-10) have many features common to other transforming economies, particularly those from the former Soviet Union. However, they experienced much better economic performance, significant environmental improvements and more political stability than the rest of the former Soviet republics (Archibald *et al.*, 2009; Bochniarz and Radzilowski, 2003; Gemma, 2000).

Those who were observing the successful systemic transformation of the EU-10 might ask: How successful was these countries' industrial restructuring, particularly in the aircraft industry? Which is the subject of this chapter.

In order to answer the question of the impact of this economic transformation on the aviation industry in CEE, the authors decided to focus on the two largest

CEE economies – the Czech Republic (until 1993 part of Czechoslovakia) and Poland, which together at the beginning of the transformation represented almost 50 percent of the population of the future EU-10 and over 70 percent of the combined EU-10 GDP. In this way, these two countries serve as a good representation of the entire region. In addition, these countries have some common roots as far as their territory is concerned. The entire country of Czechoslovakia and significant parts of Poland (Galicia) were under the rule of the Austro-Hungarian state until 1918, when the first examples of aviation industry emerged. The end of World War I brought dramatic changes in CEE (regaining independence after long occupation in Czechoslovakia and Poland in 1918) and gave great momentum to industrial development, including the aviation industry. Just a few years after gaining independence, these countries' aviation industries reached a level of maturity which allowed them to produce large quantities of airplanes of their own design, mainly for their own air forces – the major customer during that period. Although this book is devoted to commercial aviation, military production shaped the core of the aviation supply chain in those countries for many years. Without acknowledging the role of this basic driver of the aviation industry, it would be impossible to understand the development dynamics of the commercial aviation industry, particularly in the early period before World War II and during the first 45 years after the war.

These mid-sized countries developing 30 mature types of aircraft and manufacturing over 4,000 of them over the course of 20 years presents quite convincing testimony of the dynamics of the aviation industry in the CEE region (Mietelski, 2005). Although the threats of war were the driving force behind this production, it is worthy of note that there were over 100 different types of plane designed during that period, but only a few of these were actually ordered. Measuring innovation by the number of patents in the aviation industry (class 62) during the period of 1919–39 worldwide, Poles registered 103 of 419 patents in this class, coming second after France with 107 patents, but far ahead of Great Britain (59), Germany (55), the United States (31), Italy (20) and Czechoslovakia (13) (Chmiel, 2005: 186–187). With the outbreak of World War II, most of these creative minds left Poland, through Romania, and then headed West, finally landing in the United States. Looking back at the interwar period, it should be acknowledged that these creative engineers were an important driver of the aviation industry in CEE and when they could not find appropriate conditions to implement their inventions in their home countries, they moved to the country that offered them the best conditions to succeed.

Although many talented engineers left Poland and Czechoslovakia, the aviation manufacturing facilities there were utilized by the Nazis to boost their war machine, first by finishing incomplete native aircrafts and then converting the facilities to produce, repair and maintain German aircraft, employing over 350,000 employees. Because of this, the basic facilities of the industry were retained and in some areas even expanded before massive bombardment at the end of the war. Its reconstruction started slowly after 1945, but was accelerated by the beginning of the Cold War and rapidly growing demands from the military. Contrary to the post-World War I period (1919–1939), the post-World War II (1945–2005) period was characterized by only 12 originally designed and produced aircrafts due to the Soviet pressure to produce thousands of different types of MiGs to fulfill the needs of the Warsaw Pact (Mietelski, 2005).

Although the absolute number of aircraft produced during the post-World War II period is twice as high as the post-World War I period, the post-World War II period was three times longer (60 years), making the average annual production of 147.5 planes significantly lower than in the post-World War I period, which saw production of 247.9 planes per year. These data show how extensively the Soviet Union controlled CEE military aviation production, and how this suppressed the endogenous creativity of those countries. The situation was much better in non-military production, such as agricultural, sport and utility planes, as well as helicopters and gliders. These areas, however, did not represent the mainstream of aviation manufacturing in CEE, and until the 1990s they stayed within state-owned, largely inefficient enterprises.

Liberalization – both political and economic – was the main feature of the systemic transformation in CEE since 1989. Abolishing the oppressive Warsaw Pact and the dysfunctional CMEA in 1990, and finally dissolving the Soviet Union in 1991, symbolized significant milestones in gaining long-awaited freedom for CEE countries. For that reason, one could observe an acceleration of creativity and innovation in the entire region and across all industries after an initial shock at the beginning of transformation.

The following two sections, written with experts and enthusiasts of the aviation industry in the Czech Republic (Josef and Zbyněk) and Poland (Barbara and Grzegorz), will examine how these new opportunities emerged at the beginning of the 1990s and were utilized by business and public leaders in the CEE region. There are several questions the authors will try to answer:

First, what are the major drivers in aviation production and facility development? Did replacing Soviet-built passenger planes with Western planes create any sustainable cooperation between CEE aviation industries and their Western partners, particularly Airbus, Boeing, Bombardier and Embraer? Was there any significant shift from military-dominated production before 1990 to civilian manufacturing after the transformation?

Second, how good was the human capital, particularly the managerial part of it, at building a new competitive advantage in the market economy? How effective were foreign investors in discovering the unique capacities of the aviation industry in CEE? How forward thinking and concerned with sustainability were public leaders when privatizing their industry?

Third, how did governmental, institutional and policy changes brought on by the transformation address the specific needs of the aviation industry and how effective were they? Did they contribute to increased competitiveness and reduction of monopolistic practices? Did governmental policies encourage stronger cooperation with universities and research organizations to develop supportive industries?

Fourth, how innovative and competitive is the CEE aviation industry now? How deeply is the industry connected with the international supply chains of major producers? How strong are the aviation clusters and how far did they move in building social capital, particularly trust for cooperation? What are the prospects for the CEE aviation industry for the next five, ten or twenty years?

The fourth section will summarize the answers and conclusions from the country sections.

Transformation of the aviation industry in the Czech Republic

Roots of the aviation industry and its development until 1945

The history of the Czech aviation industry goes back even before the formation of independent Czechoslovakia, when the Kingdom of Bohemia was a part of the Austro-Hungarian Empire. At the dawn of the twentieth century, several aviation enthusiasts started to experiment with airplanes of their own design. Most significant among these were Jan Kašpar and Eugen Čihák. Kašpar designed and built an airplane and in 1911 accomplished the first long-distance flight in Bohemia, from Pardubice to Prague. He and his cousin, Čihák, built another plane according to their own design and later established a private plane production company.

Another important event for Czech aviation came in 1913, when the Český Aviatický Klub (Czech Aviator Club) was established. The club offered a platform for discussion and work, bringing together nearly all of the future Czech aviation designers, including Pavel Beneš, Miroslav Hajn and Alois Šmolík.

The effort to establish the aviation industry started immediately after the independence of Czechoslovakia in 1918. There was no aviation industry in the territory of Bohemia except for a small military airplane repair station called Al-Ma and the Breitfeld-Daněk company, which produced aviation engines; both were located in Prague. However, as the Bohemian Kingdom was one of the most industrially advanced parts of the Empire in 1918, the relatively high number of skilled workers and experienced technicians provided a good source for the new industry. The Al-Ma repair station soon became the Letecký Arsenál (Aviation Arsenal) and served as the foundation of the whole industry; the careers of several famous technicians and designers began there.

In 1919, a second company, Aero, was established as a private enterprise. In addition to their famous A-100 and A-101 bombers, they successfully entered the passenger plane market with the Aero A-35, originally designed for transatlantic flights, but ended with seven aircrafts serving the Czechoslovak Airlines (ČSA) and four aircrafts in the private fleet of the Bata Corporation.

A third firm, the Avia factory, was also established in 1919 and started production with the Avia BH-Exp (Exp for "experimental") sport monoplane. This monoplane was later developed into the more sophisticated BH-5 and military version BH-9/11 designs, which achieved great success in aviation challenges and won trophies all over Europe in the early 1920s. Avia achieved notable success with the aerobatic planes of the B-122 family, and in 1938 it designed and built the most modern fighter plane of Czech design in the pre-war period, the Avia B-35/135.

Apart from the Great Three, there were several other aviation manufacturers in Czechoslovakia, and all of them were located in Bohemia or Moravia.

To support the Czech Air Force in testing new airplanes, the Military Technical Aviation Institute (VTÚL) was established in 1922 equipped with a wind tunnel and other research equipment to support the whole industry with its theoretical research. In order to respond to the rapidly developing aviation industry's need for more designers and technicians, the Czech technical universities introduced special aeronautical studies as early as 1929.

The dynamic growth of the Czech aviation industry before World War II was characterized by its expansion eastwards, mainly to Moravia. The development of this industry was also marked by an impressive range of plane designs and prototypes, but its overall capacity was somewhat inadequate. Individual manufacturers could only meet the army's requirements by mustering all of their resources, especially in the late 1930s. The number of employees did not exceed 4,000.

After invasion on 15 March 1939, the Germans found the aviation industry to be very strong, innovative, diversified and mature. They immediately integrated the Czech industry into their own war effort. Thanks to forced labor (Totaleinsatz), the number of people working in aviation swelled to approximately 120,000.

Transformation of the industry to centrally planned economy: 1945–1990

After World War II, the aviation industry in liberated Czechoslovakia inherited a high number of personnel – more than 14,000 – but lacked a reasonable program for such a large industry. Many plants were forced to search for an alternative production program outside the aviation industry. The post-war transformation of the aviation industry can be divided into three periods: 1945–1948, 1948–1954 and after 1954.

The first period, from 1945 to 1948, was characterized by consolidation and a gradual transition to a central planned economy. As a result of a government decision in 1945, all of the most significant aviation manufacturers were nationalized, yet, at this first phase, they still existed as independent companies.

The second period started in 1948 and ended in 1954. The most significant change occurred within this period. In 1948, Czechoslovakia became part of the Soviet bloc. The national economy shifted to a centrally planned system, and aviation manufacturers (except for the Avia Company) were integrated under a single national enterprise, Let, and the engine producers consolidated under the Motorlet Company (formerly Walter).

The third period began with the easing of tension after 1954. The aviation industry returned to civilian production on a much wider scale and resumed its own design and development. From 1960 onward, the central design office was delimited back to particular manufacturing companies, but the VZLÚ retained some joint design capabilities. In addition, the transformation of the centralized management was completed. The VHJ Aero (the abbreviation for the production economic unit) was established in 1965, and the following companies came to be governed under this umbrella: Aero Vodochody, Rudý Letov, Let Kunovice, Moravan Otrokovice, Motorlet, Technometra, Mesit, Jihočeské Strojírny, Čenkovské Strojírny and Strojmetal Kamenice. This meant that particular companies governed by the VHJ Aero lost the freedom to make their own decisions regarding their production program.

At the end of the 1980s, the Czechoslovakian aircraft industry was governed by the Aero Corporation and included more than 35,000 personnel; the manufacturing program followed the CMEA strategic concept of focusing on two principal market segments: jet trainers and small passenger airplanes, including the production of agro- and sport-planes. The aircraft industry was considered a strategic industrial sector, and, as such, it was fully supported by the government. The major companies and their final products are presented in Table 10.1.

The remaining companies in the Czechoslovakian aircraft industry produced parts or equipment for the companies assembling planes. In total, the Czechoslovakian aircraft industry consisted of 19 companies:

- three dedicated to the development and serial production of airplanes;
- one dedicated to the development and serial production of turboprop engines;
- eleven dedicated to the development and production of equipment for airplane and engines;
- one dedicated to the development and serial production of jet engines;
- one that provided research and test work and developed ejection seats, avionics and flight data recorders;
- one dedicated to plane overhauls and maintenance; and
- one that provided engine overhauls and maintenance.

Almost 90 percent of this production was earmarked for foreign markets, especially the Soviet Union.

Table 10.1 Major airplanes produced, 1954–1990

Plant	*Airplane type*	*Quantity delivered*
Aero	L-29s trainer	3,500
Vodochody	L-39s	2,800
Let Kunovice	L-410s passenger	1,138
	L-610	7
Zlin Aircraft	Z-26/126/226 sport	1,400
	Z-37s agriculture	800
	Z-42/43	800
Orličan in Choceň	L-13 gliders	2,600

Restructuring of the industry after 1990

The aeronautical industry in Czechoslovakia was well developed and, in the early 1990s, still had a rather high capacity. Due to political and economic changes after 1990, however, this capacity was not fully utilized, and a gradual process of decline began.

In the autumn of 1990 the Czechoslovak government decided to transform the Aero Corporation into a joint-stock (holding) company. From the original setup, the joint-stock company incorporated 11 companies as its subsidiaries. The rest of the units established individual companies. This change disrupted relations between particular companies and cut-off their traditional cash flows, supply chains and access to markets. In 1991 Aero Holding was included in the first run of the voucher privatization. Unfortunately, the privatization process took several years, and, by 1996, it became clear that the process was far from a success. In the new ownership structure, the state owned 62 percent of shares, private investors (mainly individual shareholders) acquired 27 percent, and the remaining 7.5 percent belonged to investment funds. Despite high expectations and extensive negotiations at both the corporate and government levels, no strong foreign strategic partner was found to join the privatization process and buy the shares. Under such circumstances, and particularly with the disappearance of traditional markets, almost all aviation companies, including Aero Holding, went quickly into debt. Some of them went bankrupt, which left their shares devolved to creditors, mainly banks.

The US company Ayres bought into Let Kunovice; The Boeing Company (TBC) bought into Aero Vodochody; and the Novus Company bought into Walter (the Motorlet Company, which had returned to its original name). Unfortunately, these new owners did not bring much to the Czech industry because they failed to revive sales and plug them into their supply chains. Despite such trends, some Czech companies did seek new opportunities and new markets. They tried to modernize some older airplanes with improved avionics and other equipment according to Western standards. They also tried to incorporate Western standards into new designs. Thus, several airplanes were certified as compliant with American or European requirements. After the splitting of Czechoslovakia in 1993, the Czech Republic became a member of the Joint Aviation Authorities (JAA), which promised to facilitate sales to non-traditional markets.

Upon closer inspection, it is clear that one of the biggest troubles was a change in the funding system. While, in the past, the companies forming the Aero Corporation had been financed through the state budget, after 1990 they were forced to finance themselves from their own revenues earned on the market. This way they moved from soft (state) to hard (market) budget constraints, as J. Kornai described many years ago (Kornai, 1980). Unfortunately, the former system had not left any reserve of development funds to finance production restructuring and modernization. The Let Company failed to secure the funds needed to either finish the certification process of the L-610 plane or prepare the project for a sale. Nevertheless, the Let Company prepared a new version of the L-410 plane, converted to comply with American Federal Aviation Regulations (FAR) 23 specifications; this plane, the L-420, obtained the Federal Aviation Administration (FAA) type certificate. When Let Kunovice was purchased by the Ayres Company, the new owner declared its willingness to develop and produce a transport plane for FedEx containers, but after completing some development work the Ayres Company encountered financial troubles and soon went bankrupt. Unfortunately, as a consequence of this company failure, the promised new aircraft was not developed. Ayres did not contribute to the L-610 project either, and, by the end, it had nearly destroyed the Let factory.

On the other hand, the Aero Vodochody performed quite well until 1998. After 1990 Aero sold nearly 200 jet trainers in completely new markets (e.g. Egypt, Tunisia and Thailand). In an effort to create a civilian alternative to the military program, they developed a new utility turboprop airplane, the Ae 270, jointly with Aerospace Industrial Development Corporation (AIDC) from Taiwan. They formed a joint venture – Ibis Aerospace Ltd – for marketing and production support in 1997. Seven prototypes were built from 2000 to 2004 during the continuing redesigning process. Unfortunately, none of those prototypes met the high expectations for the high-performance, single-engine turboprop aircraft, and the project was cancelled in 2008. One of the major reasons for the prototype's underperformance was insufficient resource allocation for Ae 270 by Aero Vodochody management, who preferred development of military aircraft. The new owner, TBC, was not interested in supporting either military or civilian projects, but did help move the assembly line for the Sikorsky helicopters into the Vodochody plant, which in the end allowed the company to survive, although with some reduction in its capacities.

Since the remaining companies were part of the supply chain for manufacturers of complete airplanes, they were dependent on the overall sales as well. Thus, when production of complete planes diminished, companies from the supply chain also encountered financial problems. This was usually linked with a reduction in the number of personnel and, consequently, with a decline in capacity. For instance, the Letov Company, once the significant subcontractor for Aero Vodochody, was split into four parts. Letov Simulátory went bankrupt and perished, and Letov Nástrojárna (tools works) was transformed into several small companies. Letov Letecká Výroba has become part of the French Latécoere group and manufactures parts and sub-assemblies for other European or world aircraft manufacturers (Airbus, Embraer, etc.), and Wolfsberg–Letecká Továrna became privately owned. This last company developed and built a prototype of the Raven 257 transport plane, but after several years attempting to finish this project they cancelled all associated work and are now producing microlight (ultralight) planes. Other companies reduced their development capacities and focused on new markets, often outside the aviation industry.

In contrast to trends in the aviation industry in the United States or Europe, where capital tends to become more concentrated, in the Czech Republic this process went in reverse, fragmenting a fairly compact industry. The number of employees fell by 60 percent, while the number of companies more than doubled. In an effort to mitigate the effects of this process, the Association of the Aviation Manufacturers was established in 1996 with the intention of coordinating the activities of member companies.

Current state and opportunities for the Czech aviation industry

Today, the Czech aviation industry comprises over 40 companies with more than 10,000 employees. These companies are still able to provide variety of services (Table 10.2).

The current situation of the Czech aviation industry could be characterized as follows:

- All companies are independent, and they are driven by the interests and capabilities of their management alone. There is no central management apart from some coordination within the frameworks of certain larger projects.
- Nearly all companies have their own design teams capable of providing design and technological development and testing; nevertheless, shares of the design staff and the development budgets are generally lower than in comparable European companies.
- Development is funded almost entirely from the resources of particular companies.

The Czech aviation industry gained vast experience in the past, particularly with regard to the development and production of jet trainers, commuters, sport

Table 10.2 Allocation of major aviation services in 2013

Aviation services	*Number of companies*	*Major companies*
Development, prototyping, and serial production of airplanes	6	Aircraft Industries, Czech Sport Aircraft, Evektor, Jihlavan Airplanes, Wolfsberg–Letecká Továrna, Zlin Aircraft
Development and production of parts and assemblies	2	Aero Vodochody, Letov Letecká Výroba
Development and serial production of jet and turboprop engines	2	Walter/General Electric, PBS VB
Development and serial production of propellers	2	Avia Propeller, Woodcomp
Development and production of equipment	26	
Scientific and applied research and tests	4	VZLÚ, Technical University in Brno, SVÚM, VTÚL
Maintenance and overhauls	2	CSA Technics and LOM Prague

and utility airplanes and unmanned aircraft vehicles (UAVs). The companies became able to cooperate promptly on projects focused on the following items: landing gear, auxiliary power units (APUs), electronic devices, on-board instruments, hydraulic devices, emergency equipment and flight recorders.

To illustrate the capabilities of the Czech aviation industry, it is appropriate to mention several ongoing projects. The Aircraft Industries Corporation has been formed out of the former Let Kunovice. Let found a new owner who was able to stabilize the company and support new development. The main product, the L-410 commuter, is still in demand in many markets, especially in Russia, and development of an enhanced version under the acronym MOSTA has begun. The new aircraft, the L-410NG (i.e. New Generation) will include some more attractive features, such as higher speeds, longer flight range and better performance in hot environments, thus offering reliable and proven design in combination with more up-to-date characteristics. In the meantime, production of the original L-410UVP-E has resumed; it provides about 15 planes per year, mostly delivered to Russia.

A new private company, Evektor, was established in Moravia, taking advantage of numerous specialists laid-off from downsized companies. Evektor started manufacturing microlights/ultralights, but in the end it has made use of its experienced staff and developed the VUT 100 "Cobra," a four-seat utility plane. They also started producing the EV-55 twin-engine transport plane within the project known as MISTRAL, which is currently going through the military certification process. It is intended as a light transport aircraft for various military uses, but there are also plans for it to be certified later as a civilian commuter plane for 14 passengers.

The Walter Company went through several changes of ownership and it is now part of the General Electric Corporation. The original turboprop engine, M-601, has been developed into its latest version, the GE H-80, which has recently been certified. The engine is intended to equip the L-410NG and the L-410UVP-E aircraft; this project is currently under certification by the EASA.

Aero Vodochody is now independent of TBC, which sold its share back to the Czech government. Aero Vodochody's new owner, the Penta investment group, has been utilizing the assembly of Sikorsky helicopters to stabilize the company and has successfully entered a cooperation agreement with Alenia Aeronautica to produce a complete wing central section for Alenia's Spartan transport plane. Nowadays, Aero is also cooperating with Brazilian Embraer on the development of a new plane with the intention of producing part of its wing.

Zlin Aircraft has been transformed from the previous Moravan Company and has returned to its historical name. The Z-42/43 family of sport planes is still in production, but in more modern versions equipped with a variety of engines. The final version has recently been certified with a glass cockpit.

The First Brno Engineering Company in Velká Bíteš, near Brno (PBS VB), has developed several alternatives of an auxiliary power unit originally intended for the L-39 and has successfully offered them in various markets. The company's production program is rounded out by small jet engines suitable for

Table 10.3 Airplanes currently in production in the Czech Republic

Category	*Type*	*Producer*
Microlights	Eurostar	Evektor-Aerotechnik
	Skyleader 200/500	Jihlavan Airplanes
	TL 2000 Sting	TL-Ultralight
VLA/LSA	Harmony	Evektor-Aerotechnik
	Skyleader 600	Jihlavan Airplanes
	PS 28 Cruiser	Czech Sport Aircraft
Glider	Duo Discus	Schempp-Hirth Výroba Letadel
	Discus CS	
Normal category	Zlin Z 143 LSI	Zlin Aircraft
	Zlin Z 242 L	
	VUT 100 Cobra (prototype)	Evektor-Aerotechnik
Commuters	L-410 UVP-E20	Aircraft Industrie
	EV-55 Outback (prototype)	Evektor-Aerotechnik

Note
The table shows only serial production; for clarity, smaller producers and custom-made aircraft are not included.

powered gliders or pilotless aircraft – the TJ100 engine renders 225 lb of thrust at 19 kg of its dead weight only. The company is leading the European project ESPOSA, aimed at the development of small turbine engines suitable for utility or even sport airplanes.

The American Honeywell concern has bought into the Moravian company Mora and established a subsidiary: Honeywell Aerospace. This company produces hot parts of jet engines and cooperates with numerous companies around the world. Honeywell also established a development subdivision in Brno and a logistics and management center in Prague using highly qualified personnel from the Czech aviation industry.

It should be noted that the capacities of the aviation industry in the Czech Republic have remained fairly high. The process of engagement in development projects within Europe or even across the Atlantic is still slow. Many companies focus on manufacturing cooperation only in insignificant volumes. This approach gives the companies enough immediate cash to survive but leaves them without long-term prospects. The majority of companies still depend on final products and, because of their financial limitations, can only partially join larger development projects. Thus, the Czech aviation industry needs to either acquire a financially powerful strategic partner capable of concentrating small manufacturers around a reasonably large open project, or give serious support to domestic development, which would create an airplane able to break into new markets. Ideally, though, it should do both.

Transformation of the aviation industry in Poland

The beginnings of the Polish aviation industry

The Polish aviation industry has existed since nearly the birth of flight itself. The organization of such an industry was first attempted in 1910, when the Warsaw Flight Society, Awiata, was founded to train pilots and run flight schools. That same year, Stanisław Cywiñski and Czesław Zbierañski built the first Polish airplane in a hangar owned by Awiata in Warsaw (Babiejczuk and Grzegorzewski, 1974: 8–26).

Along its path of development, the Polish aviation industry endured much more difficult conditions than did countries such as France, Germany, the United Kingdom, the United States and Russia. Despite the fact that Poland did not even formally exist as a country at the beginning of the twentieth century, due to partitioning by its neighbors, as early as the 1910s the initial construction of a Polish aircraft factory was attempted and the first notable pilots appeared in Polish territory (Banaszczyk, 1972: 17–20).

Under German occupation during World War I, a branch of the Belgian company Albatros was founded in Warsaw. From 1916 to 1918, about 200 Albatros BII trainer planes were built there and more than 120 general repairs were completed. Those repair workshops became the first base of the Polish aviation industry after the war. An interesting development took place: while many countries started to cut back on aviation developments due to the economic effects of World War I, a newly independent Poland began to build its industry from scratch, primarily by providing aircraft for defense purposes (Konieczny, 1983: 24–27).

During the 20-year period between World War I and World War II, Poland built a relatively large and modern industry; in the late 1930s, it employed about 13,000 people. Although the industry was small compared to the German aviation sector, with 120,000 employees at that time, it was a significant achievement of the newly reborn Poland. As of September 1939, more than 4,100 planes had been built in Poland, including 1,100 constructed under foreign licenses and 1,400 gliders (Bondaryk *et al.*, 2011).

In the late 1930s, the Polish aviation industry boasted several notable achievements, including advanced designs and innovative aircraft solutions (e.g. the famous PZL-37 Łoś medium bomber and RWD-6 touring monoplane) developed by designers such as Puławski, Dabrowski, Prauss, Rudlicki and Jakimjuk. Significant manufacturing facilities were built in Warsaw and its suburbs, including the State Aviation Works (Pañstwowe Zakłady Lotnicze – PZL) in Warsaw; the Airframe Factory (Wytwórnia Płatowców) Nr 1 in Paluch; the Engine Factory (Wytwórnia Silników) Nr 1 in Okêcie; and factories in Lublin and Biała Podlaska. Further, the central industrial region (Centralny Okrêg Przemysłowy) included the Airframe Factory (Wytwórnia Płatowców) Nr 2 in Mielec and the Engine Factory (Wytwórnia Silników) in Rzeszów (Hypki, 1995: 33–34).

An important part of the Polish aviation industry during the interwar period was engine production, which began in 1927 with licensed designs and eventually gave way to domestic engines manufacturing in Warsaw and Rzeszów (Majewski, 2006: 45–57).

Looking back at the whole interwar period, one could conclude that domestically built Polish fighters, bombers and civilian planes did not cede qualitative or technical parity to the machines of leading foreign manufacturers.

By analyzing the development of the Polish aviation industry from its very beginning until the outbreak of World War II, one can conclude that its development was primarily driven by enthusiasts and ambitious people like those who realized their dreams by building the first planes in 1910. Despite insufficient financial resources, they developed highly advanced and innovative planes that were successful in international competition. A major source of the competitive advantage of the Polish aviation industry was the creativity of its designers and highly skilled engineers, who produced many innovative products and technologies documented by more than 100 patents, a figure that comprised almost 25 percent of the global patents between World War I and World War II (Chmiel, 2005). Taking into account these facts, one could say that Poland was an innovation powerhouse of the world aviation industry. The Polish aviation industry of the interwar period is a great testimony to how critical human and intellectual capital is to economic development. An important driving force behind its growth was the drive for independence and freedom.

The outbreak of World War II caught the Polish aviation industry at an unfortunate moment. The industry was transitioning from the production of bombers to advanced fighters and fighter-bombers, most of which were destroyed in the airports and warehouses by the Luftwaffe.

As a result of World War II, the aviation industry in Poland was almost completely destroyed. Operating aircraft were removed from Poland, and a huge number of workers were either killed or left the country. The most damaging losses were Poland's most qualified designers, engineers and machinists.

After the war, the whole industry had to be rebuilt from scratch, focusing on building civilian, military, agricultural and sport aircraft, as well as helicopter and glider production (Banaszczyk, 1972: 19–25).

Development of the Polish aviation industry from 1945 to 1990

A significant changed happened after World War II. The strategic direction of the aviation industry in Poland started not to be shaped by talented designers but to be dictated by politics and close cooperation within the Warsaw Pact, mainly based on licenses acquired from the USSR. From 1950 to 1966 the Polish aviation industry produced over 3,000 gliders, over 10,000 aircraft and helicopters and 21,000 aircraft engines. There was also dynamic growth in exports beyond the Warsaw Pact countries.

Unfortunately, in the next period, from 1966 to 1970, the industry experienced serious problems that adversely affected production and export dynamics and even resulted in the cancellation of some production and the closing of some plants. This was an unprecedented setback. The primary cause of this slowdown was a dramatic shortage of specialists and qualified personnel for the rapidly growing industry. In response, the government decided to significantly expand education and training of engineers in production centers such as Warsaw, Kraków, Wrocław, and Rzeszów.

In addition to those large metropolitan areas, aviation manufacturing centers were developing in smaller cities and followed similar patterns that reflected the condition of the entire industry. One such case was the PZL plant in Mielec. The first plane constructed in Mielec was a simple trainer, the PZL S-1, flown on November 15, 1945, of which only one unit was built. It was the second plane built in Poland after World War II (Hypki, 2007: 18–19). The factory grew dramatically and soon became the biggest Polish aircraft manufacturer. It license-built the MiG-15 (produced as Lim-1), MiG-15bis (Lim-2), MiG-17 (Lim-5) and their Polish-developed variants. About 1,500 Lims were built by 1964. The TS-11 Iskra jet trainer began production in 1963; it would become the basic trainer for the Polish Airforce (Mêtrak *et al.*, 1991).

The plane produced in the largest quantity at Mielec was the licensed Soviet Antonov An-2 utility biplane, manufactured since 1960 in several different variants. More than 13,000 of these aircraft were built by 1991, mostly for the Soviets, but they were also used in Poland and exported to numerous countries. In 1984, PZL Mielec became the exclusive producer of the Soviet short-takeoff-and-landing (STOL) transport plane, the Antonov An-28. Subsequently, Mielec developed a significantly modernized variant equipped with advanced Western avionics, called the PZL M-28 Skytruck, for civilian purposes (domestic and foreign customers), and the Bryza for the Polish Navy (Chojecki and Oleksiak, 2013: 120–180).

The factory also began cooperating with American firms, resulting in the M-18 Dromader, the successful agricultural aircraft, which was first flown in 1976 and is still in production. More than 740 M-18s have been produced and mostly exported to Western countries (Hypki, 2009: 4–11). The M-18 Dromader is designed for agricultural air operation for large fields and forest, bush and crop firefighting. The M-18 has been type-certificated by 15 foreign aviation authorities, including the FAA, Canadian, Australian, Brazilian, EASA and others.

In 1951 a third state-owned aerospace factory, WSK-Œwidnik, was built in the small town of Œwidnik near Lublin (in 1957 renamed WSK PZL-Œwidnik). Since its beginning in 1956, this plant has become one of the world's major helicopter manufacturers, producing helicopters under Soviet license, starting with the SM-1 (Mil Mi-1). Œwidnik was the main producer of the Mi-1 and exclusive producer of the Mil Mi-2, which was widely used abroad. Until 1985, when production ended, it produced about 7,200 Mi-2 helicopters, mainly for export, with about one-third for military customers. Polish engineers modernized the initial design of the Mi-2 by developing plastic rotor blades, and the wide-body Mi-2M carried ten passengers instead of eight. Since the late 1980s Œwidnik has produced the Polish-designed medium helicopter PZL W-3 Sokół (Sobczak, 2010: 20–21).

Analysis of that period reveals that the necessary infrastructure for the production of aircraft, helicopters, engines, spare parts, equipment and human capital was developed, but mainly for the non-competitive military markets and planned economies. The Polish aviation industry entered a transformational period with a network of specialized facilities offering final products, components and specialized services. Undoubtedly, the biggest achievements of this period were light aircraft models such as the Wilga, Orlik, Dromader and Skytruck, among others, all of which were characterized by simplicity and reliability that made their purchase and operation relatively inexpensive. The industry provided a base for aircraft repair and maintenance and allowed for modernization.

Transformation of the Polish aviation industry after 1990

The beginning of the transformation of Poland in 1990 opened new opportunities for the aviation industry, but also created new challenges that had to be met to avoid potential development slowdown or even bankruptcy. One of the most important strategic challenges was to decide how the industry should be privatized by choosing either a solid strategic investor (a company providing significant investment capital) or by considering alternative methods of ownership transfer. For the strategic investor privatization (buyout) method preferred by the Polish government it was essential to enter privatization agreements to show the strength and competitiveness of the company designated for sale. Strategic sectoral studies and market analyses existing at the time indicated that Poland could take advantage of well-established aviation industry production infrastructure, records of past achievements and potential competitive advantage mainly in the light aircraft market (Słotwiński 2002: 26).

The Polish aviation industry entered the transformation process with seven major state-owned companies (Table 10.4).

Table 10.4 Allocation of major aviation production in 1990

No.	*Name of aviation producer*	*Major products*
1	PZL WSK Mielec	M28 Skytruck transport plane Iryda advanced trainer jet Dromader agriculture plane Iskierka trainer plane
2	PZL WSK Warszawa Okęcie	Lightweight plane Wilga Turbo engine trainer plane Orlik
3	PZL WSK Świdnik	Sokół helicopter family
4	PZL WSK Rzeszów	Jet engines for Iskra Iryda planes Helicopter engines for Sokół and Mi-2, and others Engines refit
5	PZL WSK Hydral	Components for other aviation companies
6	WZL no. 1 in Łódź	Helicopter refit and modernization
7	WZL no. 2 in Bydgoszcz	Jet planes such as MiG29 and Su22 refit and modernization

Decommissioning of the Warsaw Pact and the collapse of the Soviet Union put the Polish aviation industry in a difficult position, losing almost 75 per cent of its aviation customers overnight. It led to a dramatic depreciation of the major manufacturing infrastructure facilities. This way, the privatization strategy based on strength and competitiveness lost its attractiveness and made transferring ownership a complex and time-consuming process, often with negative effects for the whole industry.

During the transformation period (1990–2010) the Polish aviation industry had many development opportunities, and its entrance to new markets with its product mix was marked by both successes and failures (Table 10.5).

Table 10.5 Analysis of the major projects' performance

No.	*Project*	*Success*	*Failure*
1	Exporting of W3 Sokół helicopters	150 units exported to 12 countries	
2	Modernizing Wilga planes to Wilga 2000 standard		Production ended after selling PZL Warszawa Okęcie to EADS
3	Modernizing Mi 2 helicopters to PZL Kania standard		Only 19 units built due to problems with certification and poor promotion in foreign markets
4	Refitting and upgrading planes produced by the Polish industry in the past (especially Mi 2, Sokół, Iskra, Wilga, An-2) and Soviet-made planes such as MiG21, MiG29 and Su22	Partial success – contract to refit and modernize Polish MiG29 and Su22 to NATO standards	
5	Developing and selling the Iryda jet trainer to domestic and foreign markets		Failure due to political and managerial mistakes
6	Arming the anti-tank version of Sokół helicopter, called W3W Huzar		Failure due to ineffective decision making while choosing anti-tank missiles
7	Manufacturing a modern close air support plane called Skorpion		Reached only prototype stage in 1993
8	Producing Iskra II modern advanced trainer jet, Iskra replacement		Achieved only prototype phase in 2003 due to lack of interest from the Polish Airforce and postponed modernization of trainer fleet

The examples shown in Table 10.5 prove that it has been extremely hard for Polish companies to find their place in the highly competitive global aviation market. A combination of poor ability to advertise their products, an ineffective decision-making process (including interference of the government representatives as owners) and dependence on the Polish Airforce as the main customer resulted in many wasted opportunities. For this reason, it was a process of learning by doing for both the government representatives – changing frequently due to instability of governments during the 1990s – and for the majority of business managers entering the uncharted waters of free markets.

Current state of and prospects for development of the aviation industry in Poland

Poland became well known not only as the initiator of radical transformation in 1989, but also as one of the most successful cases of its implementation – marked by sustaining positive and one of the highest economic growth rates in the EU even during the financial crisis (2007–2010). These undisputable achievements attracted a lot of foreign direct investments (FDI) and significantly increased international business cooperation, contributing to more sustainable development after a short period of negative growth (1990–1991). During the transformation, the Polish aviation industry moved, with the whole national economy, toward the West – to the most competitive markets worldwide. Today, Polish aviation companies offer advanced products and services and are present in all major supply chains to the extent that almost every passenger aircraft in the world is equipped with at least one part manufactured in Poland.

This positive picture, illustrated in economic terms by the total sales of all aviation companies in Poland, shows over €1.5 billion revenues in 2012. The sector has been growing dramatically, with sales first quadrupling in 2003–2008, and then doubling in 2008–2012. This unprecedented dynamic is closely tied to FDI since the majority of sales came out of companies that were privatized by large multinational corporations (MNC) (Polish Information and Foreign Investment Agency, 2012; Sienko-Kułakowska, 2014).

The main specializations of the existing aviation plants are fixed-wing aircraft (agricultural, training and executive), commercial and military helicopters, gliders, assemblies and sub-assemblies (aluminum, composite, GRFP), and a great variety of accessories. The majority of aviation production is exported to highly competitive markets such as the United States, Canada, Spain, Germany, Greece, Indonesia, Italy, South Korea, Venezuela and Vietnam.

Due to the global market structure (practically a duopoly of Airbus and Boeing in large commercial jets) and quite oligopolistic market in mid-size commercial planes, limited numbers of final products come out of the Polish aviation industry in the form of rather small planes and helicopters. These are mainly the products of large companies such as PZL Mielec, EADS PZL Warszawa-Okêcie and PZL-Swidnik. There are also small businesses that make final products by manufacturing their own designs, including technologically advanced small aircraft and gliders. Examples of such businesses include the Margański & Mysłowski aircraft plant (Zakłady Lotnicze) S.A, which produces the EM-11C Orka aircraft and MDM-1 FOX glider; the Metal-Master company, which produces ultralight FLARIS jet, and MSP Marcin Szender, builder of UAVs and the ultralight, two-seater Osa aircraft in cooperation with the Military Aviation Works (Wojskowe Zakłady Lotnicze – WZL) No. 2 and AM Technologies Polska.

In general, the Polish aviation industry is dominated by small and medium enterprises (SMEs), which are mainly owned by Poles, while a few large and medium firms belong to MNCs (Figure 10.1 and Table 10.6).

The WSK PZL-Rzeszów is the biggest manufacturer of aircraft engine components in Poland, producing sheet metal, precision metal castings and gears for the majority of Pratt & Whitney engines (part of United Technology Corporation Holding – UTC).

Another example of an MNC-owned firm, and one of the best indicators of the advanced level of processes used in the Polish aviation sector, is the participation of Avio Polska and GE EDC Poland in development of modules for the innovative jet engine GEnx, which will be used in the Boeing 747-8 and 787 Dreamliner. Avio Polska is the designer and sole producer of the GEnx2 turbine blade module, while GE EDC Poland is responsible for the engineering works (Polish Information and Foreign Investment Agency, 2012).

Goodrich Krosno is also part of a huge MNC, producing mainly landing gears for the main aviation manufacturers such as TBC (e.g., Boeing 777 and F-16), Gulfstream and Bombardier; since recently, also for the new Airbus A380.

Figure 10.1 Major aviation companies in Poland in 2014 (source: materials provided by the Aviation Valley cluster).

Table 10.6 Selected companies with foreign capital in the aviation and related industries

Company name	*City*	*Employees*	*Products*
WSK Rzeszów/Pratt & Whitney	Rzeszów	4000	Engine components
WSK "PZL – Świdnik"/Augusta Westland	Świdnik	2900	A129 cabin, A149, SW4, W3 Sokół. W3PL Głuszec (armed) helicopters
Pratt & Whitney Kalisz	Kalisz	1400	Engine components
PZL Mielec/Sikorsky	Mielec	1400	S70I Blackhawk, M28 Skytruck/Bryza. M18 Dromader
General Electric Engineering Design Centre (EDC) Poland	Warszawa	1000	Research to improve engine components
EADS-PZL "Warszawa-Okęcie"	Warszawa	533	C295 and A320 components, Orlik trainer
PZL Wrocław/Hamilton Sundstrand	Wrocław	500	Aircraft small components
Avio Polska	Bielsko-Biała	400	APU units, chopper engine components, jet engine assembly and components production,
Goodrich Krosno	Krosno	400	Aircraft components
Hispano Suiza	Sędziszów Małopolski	400	Aircraft small components
MTU Aero Engines Polska	Rzeszów	270	Aircraft components
Hamilton Sundstrand Poland	Rzeszów	250	Aircraft components
Gardner Poland	Tczew	100	Aircraft small components

Source: Polish Information and Foreign Investment Agency (2012).

It is worth mentioning that about 80 percent of the manufacturing facilities are located in the southeastern part of the country; specifically, the Podkarpackie and Lubelskie Voivodships (administrative regions). These are dominated by SMEs. For that reason, there have been many attempts to connect them in collaborative clusters. These efforts produced three currently existing aviation clusters (Table 10.7).

There are high expectations among both the business community and political leaders of clustering processes. They often link the prospects of the Polish aviation industry with operating aviation clusters. So far, the Aviation Valley (Dolina Lotnicza) cluster, one of a handful of effectively operating clusters in Poland, serves as a good model. This cluster contains innovative manufacturing businesses that are responsible for a huge number of aviation products such as parts, major assemblies and sub-assemblies for jet engines, gliders and helicopters for some of the most important aviation manufacturers in the world. Companies in the Aviation Valley are also responsible for manufacturing final products such as the Blackhawk, Sokół, and SW4 helicopters, as well as many light and ultralight aviation designs. Associated partners are worldwide leaders in their respective fields, such as Pratt & Whitney, Sikorsky, Augusta Westland, Hispano Suiza Polska, Goodrich, MTU Aero Engines and Hamilton Sundstrand.

A critical undertaking in developing the cluster was to bring SMEs to the production standards represented by the leading Polish and foreign manufacturers and connect them with potential investors and/or cooperation partners. This way, the cluster could facilitate development of new businesses and spill-over new technologies among these businesses, thus securing them a place in the large, often international supply chains. Experiences from the world's largest clusters indicate that such undertakings lead to synergetic effects measured by increased effectiveness, efficiency, innovation and improved competitiveness. So far the Aviation Valley, which has existed since 2002, has managed to attract over 100 firms, institutions and organizations, including the largest and most technologically advanced firms. Participation in cluster activities is also advantageous for larger firms, and for that reason the UTC initially supported organizing this cluster. This is the case of MTU Aero Engines, the leading German manufacturer

Table 10.7 Aviation clusters in Poland

Cluster name	*Center of operations*	*Members*	*Employees*	*Planned sales (2013)*
Aviation Valley	Rzeszów, SE Poland	112	23,000	€1.5 billion
Silesian Aviation Cluster	Bielsko-Biala, SW Poland	23	2,500	€105 million
Wielkopolska Aerospace Cluster	Kalisz, W Poland	24	2,100	Not available

Source: authors' work based on information acquired directly from cluster representatives (November 2014).

of jet engine parts for civilian and military aircraft. This company recently built an advanced production and research center in Jasionka, near Rzeszów. The other businesses in Aviation Valley, which gained recognition on international markets, include B&M OPTIK (manufacturer of optical elements) and the transport company M&M Air Sea Cargo S.A., Hispano Suiza and Creuzet – both in Sêdziszow.

There is a common understanding that research and development (R&D) play a huge role in shaping the future of the Polish aviation industry. Aviation Valley is a partner and founder of the Advanced Technology Centre – "AERONET – Aviation Valley," a consortium of six Polish universities of technology (Warsaw, Lublin, Lódÿ, Rzeszów, Czestochowa and Gliwice) and other universities and organizations such as the Rzeszów University (Uniwersytet Rzeszowski), the Aviation Institute, the Technical Division of the Air Force (Dział Techniczny Sił Powietrzynch) and two institutes from the Polish Academy of Sciences. The main goal of the consortium is conducting academic research and development, as well as establishing innovative solutions in the field of aviation engineering. Aviation Valley is also a partner and founder of the Polish Platform of Aviation Technology (Polska Platforma Technologiczna Lotnictwa), which deepens the cooperation and participation of Polish aviation companies and institutions of higher education in European research projects (European Aeronautics, 2010).

The development of the aviation sector would not be possible without well-educated labor. Over 11,000 engineers (650 of them in aviation studies) graduate from Polish technical universities every year.

Aviation is one of the most innovative sectors in the Polish economy due to companies' large expenditure on R&D, cooperation with research centers, participation in international projects, human potential, and dynamically developing clusters. Moreover, initiatives such as AERONET have led to closer cooperation between industries, local government authorities and school and university authorities, aimed at even more effective training of personnel.

Strengths of the Polish aviation industry can be summarized (Polish Information and Foreign Investment Agency, 2012):

- long-standing tradition;
- high product quality;
- competitive production costs;
- highly qualified workforce;
- constantly developing R&D, educational and training activities;
- well-developed supplier network;
- three aviation clusters; and
- a well-established network of international and domestic airports.

Opportunities for the aviation sector are:

- growth of production during the economic boom;
- increasing cooperation between small and large companies;

- further development of supply chains in Poland due to foreign companies;
- development of R&D activities;
- investment in engineering and services centers;
- development of new aircraft engines; and
- construction of new helicopters and light aircraft, including UAVs.

Summing up, the competitive edge of Polish aviation companies lies in the high quality of products (expertise in treatment of materials, casting, mechanical engineering and electronics) and competitive labor costs combined with skills. The Polish network of production and service companies supported by R&D centers creates potential for cooperation and orders for aviation spare parts and final products. Taking into account the above presented facts, the Polish aviation industry made a historic step during the last 25 years by moving successfully from predominant military and non-competitive drivers to the competitive commercial markets. For that reason, the recently announced modernization of the Polish helicopter fleet will be important, but not as crucial as it was before its transformation, for the future of this industry (Budżet MON *et al.*, 2013). This industry has been already well connected with the leading supply chains worldwide and has seasoned business leaders well prepared to compete globally. They will be able to find market niches for their companies and become world leaders in their areas of strength due to quality and technologically advanced products and services. Taking into account the recent achievements of the Polish aviation industry, its current strengthening of existing clusters, the solid position of the Polish economy and its stable government, as well as the nation's liberal access to primary markets due to its EU and NATO membership, the prospects look good.

Achievements and challenges ahead

The most impressive achievement of the aviation industry in the Czech Republic and Poland is its survival under the radical systemic changes of the 1990s, when the major driver of the industry – military procurement – disappeared almost overnight with the end of the Cold War. The industry lost 75 percent of its market in a very short period of time. The managers and business leaders of these industries had to learn very quickly how to shift from nearly full dependence on the central government with significant subsidies (soft budget constraint) – particularly in Czechoslovakia and Romania, where almost the whole aviation industry was kept under one national holding – to independent firms with hard budget constraints. They learned how to move effectively from "East to West," from the non-competitive COMECON market to a highly competitive global market. In addition, the industry's transformation was often interrupted by changes in government, which initially kept control as the owner of the majority shares of aviation companies, and by workers' protests against proposed privatization and restructuring which led to massive layoffs. Today there are no longer 70,000 aviation industry employees, as it used to be in those three countries during the Cold War, but a solid 35,000 employees that make the industry very competitive and increasingly connected within global markets and leading supply chains. The military is no longer the major patron of this industry, but by joining NATO, upgrades to the national air forces were required to meet the new standards of military equipment and many strategic import barriers were abolished, which allowed military technology to pass more freely between countries. Poland, switching from MiG-29 and SU-22 fighters and Tupolev airliners to F-16 fighters and Boeing passenger planes, gained some strategic US investors like General Electric, Pratt & Whitney (jet engines), Sikorsky (Black Hawk helicopters) and Goodrich (aviation components). Replacing Soviet-built passenger jets with Western planes in CEE brought major manufacturers such as Airbus, Boeing, Bombardier and Embraer to order products and seek maintenance there.

After the initial shock at the beginning of the transformative period, managers and business leaders in these countries started learning quickly and discovered new markets and strategic partners to upgrade their products and become more attractive to foreign investors. These changes were much more drastic in Poland than in the Czech Republic. In the Czech Republic, foreign investors made some missteps which led either to bankruptcy (the Ayres case) or to resale back to the state (the Boeing case). The governments of these countries did not have clear strategic concepts for these companies because they were usually too short-lived to ever develop sufficiently detailed plans, or did not have enough time to implement them. The best they could do was to create an attractive environment for investors and entrepreneurs to take initiatives in the industry. Based on how many investors – both domestic and foreign – were attracted to the country and to this particular industry, as well as how many small and medium enterprises were established, the Polish governments performed the best despite their frequent changes. These governments should also get credit for supporting investments in human capital, particularly in engineering, economics and management, which significantly contributed to the successful restructuring of the industry (Archibald *et al.*, 2009). In addition, governmental investments in R&D and infrastructure made significant contributions to the growth of the industry, and as a result, human capital was significantly improved –at both management and factory levels.

It is worth mentioning that the role of the central government is often overestimated in comparison to the role of regional and local governments. In the Polish case, the role of regional governments was critical in attracting investors and supporting aviation cluster development, particularly in the Podkarpackie and Silesian regions. They were also often advocates for strengthening links between the industry and local universities. The regional development agencies were also critical in delivering structural funds, particularly those from the EU Regional Development Fund, which supported clustering activities. So far, three Polish and one Moravian cluster in the Czech Republic have received such support. Particularly in the Podkarpackie region and Aviation Valley, one could find that the support from the EU was both an effective and efficient regional development policy tool.

Observing the trend toward getting CEE aviation companies involved in the global market, one might notice that they are moving step-by-step from a lower level in the supply chain to a more advanced one, which is more appropriate for the highly skilled labor in this region. There are also several instances where CEE companies are involved in the upper part of the supply chain. One such instance is Czech Aero, who are currently working with the Brazilian company Embraer to develop a new plane. The famous American defense corporation Honeywell also moved its management and logistics operations to the Czech Republic. Engineers from Avio Polska are the designers and sole producers of the turbine blades for the General Electric GEnx2 engine, and GE EDC Poland helped during the design phase of the engine. These examples show that CEE companies are moving up in the global supply chain, toward more innovative and much higher-paying jobs, thus improving their competitiveness and bringing prosperity to their communities.

In order to continue the trend set by these examples and sustain movement up the supply chain, CEE countries will have to continue public and private investment in education and training, as well as R&D. They are still lagging behind the most advanced countries in R&D expenditure, but are quite close or sometimes ahead in building human capital. This is a promising sign, but will require further investment in better infrastructure, particularly in telecommunication, in order to allow broadband internet access throughout the country.

Unfortunately, investment in human capital and infrastructure alone are not all that is necessary to build and sustain a competitive advantage. As examples in the most advanced countries indicate, an innovative and competitive economy requires rich social capital, which is usually generated in well-functioning clusters (e.g., the aerospace cluster in Washington state in the United States). The case of the Polish Aviation Valley indicates that such practices exist in CEE and their excellent performance comes from their collaborative work as a cluster. Other CEE clusters, particularly the Silesian Aviation Cluster in Poland and the Moravian Cluster in the Czech Republic, follow this practice and build capacity for high performance. It should encourage two other Czech Associations – the Confederation of the Czech Aviation Industry (CCAI) and the Association of the Aviation Manufacturers of the Czech Republic (ALV) – to follow their Moravian colleagues and establish one or two industrial clusters. Past experiences from the totalitarian system prevent many people from building a collaborative network and exchange information due to lack of trust. This is why the establishment of industrial clusters is still slow in this part of the world despite all the inherent advantages of such an institution. The main challenge is to overcome old prejudices from the past system and put the aviation industry in CEE on the fast track for development in twenty-first-century conditions. Only highly skilled human capital, advanced technology and a strong industrial network based on trust and good communication will make this industry competitive in the global market. Successful completion of their transformation will build a solid foundation for future development.

Bibliography

Introduction

Archibald S, Bochniarz Z, Gemma M, Srebotnjak T. 2009. Transition and Sustainability: Empirical Analysis of Kuznets Curve for Water Pollution in 25 Countries in Central and Eastern Europe and the Commonwealth of Independent States, *Environmental Policy and Governance*, Vol. 19, No. 2: 73–98.

Bochniarz Z, Radzilowski J. 2003. As a New EU Member, Poland has Lessons for the World, *Detroit Free Press*, October 8, 2003, p. 13A.

Chmiel M. 2005. Polskie patenty lotnicze w latach 1919–1939. Radwan, K. (ed.) *Srodkowoeuropejskie dziedzictwo lotnicze, Acta Aeronautica-Muzeum Lotnictwa Polskiego*, Krakow

Dabrowski M, Gomulka S, Rostowski J. 2001. Whence Reform? A Critique of the Stiglitz Perspective, *Journal of Policy Reform*, Vol. 4, No. 4: 291–324.

Gemma M. 2000. Industrial Development in Transition Economies: Lessons and Implications, *Waseda Studies in Social Sciences*, Vol. 1, No. 10: 19–31.

Mietelski M. 2005. Od Berga do Grippena – Czy istnieje srodkowoeuropejska szkola tworzenia samolotow mysliwskich, in: Radwan K. (ed.) *Srodkowoeuropejskie dziedzictwo lotnicze, Acta Aeronautica-Muzeum Lotnictwa Polskiego*, Krakow.

Stieglitz J. 1999. Whiter Reform? In 1999 ABCDE Conference, World Bank. http://worldbank.org/knowledge/ (accessed July 7, 2012).

The Czech aviation industry

Antras PF. 2010. Czech Aerospace Companies: The Main Players. www.czechinvest.org/en/czech-suppliers (accessed December 15, 2012).

CzechInvest. 2008. Aerospace Industry in the Czech Republic. www.czechinvest.org (accessed January 10, 2013).

CzechInvest. 2011. Czech Republic: Aerospace Industry. www.czechinvest.org (accessed January 5, 2013).

CzechInvest (n.d.) Aerospace. http://aerospace.czechinvest.org (accessed December 20, 2012).

Kornai J. 1980. *Economics of Shortage*, Amsterdam: North Holland Publishing.

Kučera P. 1999. *Aero 1919–1999*, Prague: GT Club – Motormedia.

Němeček V. 1983–1984. *Československá letadla 1 & 2*, Naše Vojsko, Prague: Naše Vojsko.

The Polish aviation industry

Babiejczuk J, Grzegorzewski J. 1974. *Polski przemysł lotniczy 1945–1973*, Warszawa: Wydawnictwo MON.

Baczko T. 2011. *Report on Innovativeness of the Aviation Sector in Poland in 2010*, Warszawa: Wydawnictwo Key Text.

Banaszczyk E. 1972. *Pierwsze skrzydła*, Warszawa: Wydawnictwo MON.

Baron Al. 2010. *Samolot szkolno-bojowy I-22"IRYDA', wymagania, realizacja, ocena*, Warszawa: Wydawnictwo Naukowe Instytutu Lotnictwa.

Bartosik S, Łaz M, Senkowski R. 2001. *Monografie Lotnicze no. 1 – TS-11 Iskra*, Warszawa: LAF.

Bochniak D. 2012. *Mielec – w PZL-u coś się kroi.* http://gazetylokalne.pl/a/mielec-w-pzl-u-cos-sie-kroi/print (accessed August 13, 2013).

Bondaryk P, Gruszczyński J, Klosowski M, Kopański TJ, Matusiak W, Ruchała P, Rusiecki M, Witkowski R. 2011. *Historia lotnictwa w Polsce,* Warszawa: Wydawnictwo Carta Blanca.

Budżet MON na 2013 rok (Budget of the Ministry of Defence). www.mon.gov.pl/pl/artykul/13368 (accessed January 4, 2013).

Chojecki J, Oleksiak J. 2013. *Mieleckie samoloty na niebie świata,* Warszawa: Wydawnictwo Naukowe Instytutu Lotnictwa.

Cumft O, Kujawa H. 1989. *Księga lotników polskich,* Warszawa: Wydawnictwo MON.

Sienko-Kułakowska E.B. 2014. Analiza motywów decyzji lokalizacyjnych na Podkarpaciu – na przykładzie dużych firm lotniczych z klastra Dolina Lotnicza. The report from the research project titled: Effective Clusters – basis for innovation and source of sustainable regional development (not published), Rzeszow.

European Aeronautics. 2010. *European Aeronautics: A Vision for 2020.* Luxembourg: EU.

FDI Report 2013. 2013. http://ftbsitessvr01.ft.com/forms/fDi/report2013/files/The_fDi_Report_2013.pdf (accessed March 12, 2014).

Glass A. 1980. *Samoloty PZL 1928–1978,* Warszawa: Wydawnictwo Komunikacji i Łączności.

Grzegorzewski J. 1979. *Śmigłowiec MI-2.T.nr 60,* Warszawa: Wydawnictwo MON.

Hypki T. 1995. Bez propagandy sukcesu, *Skrzydlata Polska,* Vol. 9.

Hypki T. 2007. Przekręt stulecia w Mielcu, *Skrzydlata Polska,* Vol. 3, No. 2329.

Hypki T. 2009. Karmienie nowotworu, *Skrzydlata Polska,* Vol. 1, No. 2351.

Jaxa-Małachowski R. 1996. 'OFFSET ważna figura na szachownicy', *Skrzydlata Polska,* Vol. 2.

Kłosiński P. 2005. Plusy z problemami, *Skrzydlata Polska,* Vol. 8, No. 2310.

Konieczny RJ. 1983. *Kronika lotnictwa polskiego 1945–1981,* Warszawa: Biblioteczka Skrzydlatej Polski.

Majewski M. 2006. *Samoloty i zakłady Lotnicze II Rzeczypospolitej,* Warszawa: ZP Poligrafia.

Malecki A. 2013. *Inwestycje zagraniczne w sektorze lotniczym.* www.paiz.gov.pl/files (accessed February 28, 2013).

Małkowski T. 1993. *Samolot dzieło człowieka,* Wrocław, Warszawa, Kraków: Wydawnictwo Zakład Narodowy im. Ossolińskich.

Mętrak P, Makowski T, Żurek K.M. 1991.. *I-22 Iryda. Seria Przegląd Konstrukcji Lotniczych 3,* Warszawa: Wydawnictwo Altair.

Polish Information and Foreign Investment Agency. 2012., *Invest in Poland, Aviation.* www.paiz.gov.pl/sectors/aviation (accessed June 23, 2013).

Słotwiński A. 2002. W obronie polskiego przemysłu lotniczego, *Skrzydlata Polska,* Vol. 6, No. 2272.

Sobczak G. 2010. Świdnik na chińskim rynku, *Skrzydlata Polska,* Vol. 4, No. 2366.

Wojnicka E. (ed.). 2006. *Perspektywy rozwoju małych i średnich przedsiębiorstw wysokich technologii w Polsce do 2020 roku. Ekspertyza dla Polskiej Agencji Rozwoju Przedsiębiorczości.* www.parp.gov.pl/files/74/75/76/perspektywy_rozwoju_msp.pdf (accessed March 25, 2013).

Zdancewicz, M. 2013. FLARIS LAR, Nie znajdziesz w nim lodówki na szampana. *Motoszybowce.pl kwartalnik lotniczy* 1 (5).

11 Governance and environmental performance

An airlines perspective

Marie-Josée Roy, Isabelle Dostaler and John Fiset

With growing sensitivity toward social issues, companies are increasingly striving to become better corporate citizens. Some leading firms have recognized that sustainability principles are important for long-term corporate profitability and are paying more attention to these issues. These companies acknowledge that many constituents have a legitimate stake in their activities and that they must integrate consideration of many stakeholder interests into day-to-day management decisions and strive to balance and maximize these interests. Accordingly, many companies have established policies and designed programs as a means to better manage the impact of their activities on society.

Often blamed for contributing significantly to the greenhouse effect, the airline industry cannot avoid looking for ways to balance economic, environmental and social performance. While the OECD estimated in 2012 that aviation was responsible for 2–3 percent of the total global carbon emissions, the organization also indicated that this percentage could become higher in a not too distant future (OECD, 2012; ICAO, 1999). Similarly, the International Civil Aviation Organization (ICAO) recently predicted a growth of 3–4 percent annually in the CO_2 emitted by air transportation (ICAO, 1999). These concerns are being taken seriously by aviation stakeholders who are not impassive in front of this worrying situation. The setting up of the Air Transport Action Group (ATAG) illustrates this. ATAG is a not-for-profit association of over 40 world members, including the International Air Transport Association (IATA), Airports Council International, Civil Air Navigation Services Organisation (CANSO), as well as aerospace players such as Boeing, Airbus, Bombardier and Embraer. The action group is particularly vocal on its Aviation Benefits Beyond Borders website and on its Twitter account created to announce the "latest news on sustainable aviation from the commercial air transport sector."[1] The Aviation Benefits Beyond Borders website claims that "the aviation industry collectively agreed in 2008 to the world's first set of sector-specific climate change targets." The association sees in a positive light the progress made in the industry, adding that airlines are "already delivering on the first target — to continue to improve fleet fuel efficiency by 1.5% per year until 2020." ATAG is also very optimistic and forecasts that the net carbon emissions of air transportation will peak in 2020, adding that "By 2050, the industry has committed to reduce its net carbon footprint to 50% below what it was in 2005" (Aviation/Benefits Beyond Borders, 2010).

While it could be argued that the Air Transport Action Group is too optimistic, there is evidence that airline companies have taken action to reduce their carbon footprint in recent years. In this chapter we will examine specific policies and programs that some airline companies have implemented to help move toward their environmental performance goals. However, because corporate boards are increasingly being asked to play a bigger role in environmental issues, we will also investigate the involvement of airlines' corporate boards in environmental performance matters. Indeed, the rising costs associated with environmental expenditures and liabilities have turned these once commonplace operational issues into highly strategic ones that may require board oversight.

This chapter is organized as follows. We will first identify some of the key trade groups and organizations which are forming the institutional environment in which airlines operate and which demonstrate a growing concern for environmental matters. We will then explore the role of corporate boards and environmental committees established by these boards in the greening process occurring in air transport. Following this we will turn our attention to some of the options airlines companies have chosen to reduce the environmental impacts of their activities in response to societal and institutional pressure. We will also look at some airline companies who have gone a step further and established environmental management systems (EMS) that they proudly publicized on their websites. Lastly, we will argue that beyond institutional pressure, strong evidence of a causal relationship between environmental and financial performance is one of the key driving forces to enjoin all aviation players to engage in reducing their respective carbon footprints. The structure of this chapter is illustrated by Figure 11.1, which shows that the institutional environment in which airlines operate influences them towards developing sustainability initiatives and an EMS. As indicated in Figure 11.1, corporate boards – also in response to the institutional

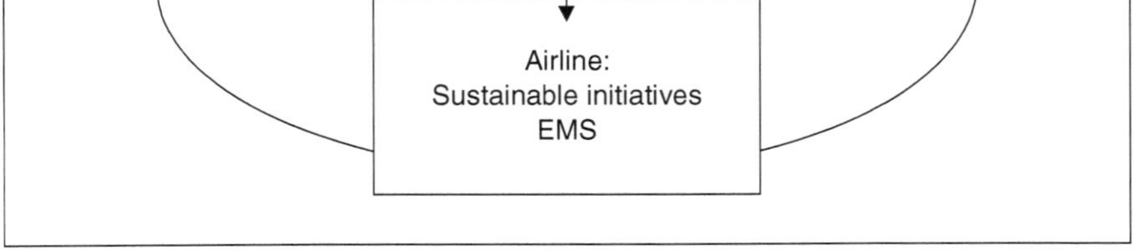

Figure 11.1 The push for greener airlines.

pressure – can play an important role as well in this greening process and influence airlines' sustainable development initiatives.

Institutional environment

Air transportation can be considered as a system encompassing numerous activities, starting with aircraft design and ending when travelers reach their final destinations. All the actors involved in this system have growing environmental and social concerns and are aware of the contribution of aviation to climate change. For example, engine manufacturers and aircraft designers are making efforts to improve the environmental efficiency of their products. The trade press has recently reported that competing aircraft makers such as Airbus, Boeing and Embraer are collaborating to develop and test alternative sources of jet fuel (McCurry, 2012). Countries are also joining forces: the United States, Australia, New Zealand and Japan participate in the Asia/Pacific Initiative to Reduce Emissions. As part of this initiative, Japanese and US aviation authorities have tried new air-traffic management procedures in the hope of increasing the efficiency of transpacific flights (Schofield, 2009). Similarly, carriers are examining every aspect of air and ground operations to find ways to make them cleaner and quieter.

As mentioned above, environmental concerns have resulted in the creation of ATAG. Other institutional stakeholders sharing the common goal of improving the overall environmental performance of the airline industry are also mobilized, as indicated in Table 11.1, where key aviation trade associations and interest groups are listed. These organizations play a prominent role in this aviation greening process and many of them have a particular interests in the development of alternative fuels, as indicated in Table 11.1. It is clear that institutional stakeholders put pressure on airlines and their corporate boards for a better environmental and social performance.

The role of corporate boards

The role of corporate boards has evolved significantly over the past decades in response to changing stakeholders' expectations (Anderson *et al.*, 2007). While they used to focus primarily on monitoring management, they are now increasingly expected to assume an advisory role as well and to participate actively in the strategic management process (Adams and Ferreira, 2007; Sundaramurthy and Lewis, 2003). This increased involvement in strategy decisions includes, in many instances, decisions regarding environmental matters.

It is through the establishment of committees on which a subset of board members sit that corporate boards play their advisory roles. The adoption of this board committee structure has been strongly recommended for large companies attempting to address some of their fundamental responsibilities more effectively (Business Roundtable, 2005; Hall *et al.*, 2005). Consistent with regulatory requirements in many countries, boards have typically established three committees:

Table 11.1 Aviation trade associations and interest groups

Air Transport Action Group (ATAG)	ATAG is a not-for-profit association that represents all sectors of the air transport industry. It describes itself as "the only global industry-wide body to bring together all aviation industry players so that they can speak with one voice – and it works to promote aviation's sustainable growth for the benefit of our global society."
Aviation Global Deal Group (AGDG)	The AGDG is an industry coalition that includes leading international airlines, aviation sector companies and The Climate Group. Its goal is to "contribute towards a pragmatic, fair and effective policy solution that incorporates international aviation CO2 emissions into a new global climate change deal."
Commercial Aviation Alternative Fuels Initiative (CAAFI)	CAAFI is a broad association that includes airlines, aircraft/ engine manufacturers, energy companies, researchers and some US government agencies. "CAAFI's goal is to promote the development of alternative jet fuel options that offer equivalent levels of safety and compare favorably on cost with petroleum based jet fuel, while also offering environmental improvement and security of energy supply for aviation."
International Air Transport Association (IATA)	"The IATA is the trade association for the world's airlines, representing some 240 airlines or 84% of total air traffic. IATA supports many areas of aviation activity and helps formulate industry policy on critical aviation issues."
International Civil Aviation Association (ICAO)	"The ICAO is a specialized agency of the UN and was created in 1944 to promote the safe and orderly development of international civil aviation throughout the world. It sets standards and regulations necessary for aviation safety, security, efficiency and regularity, as well as for aviation environmental protection. The Organization serves as the forum for cooperation in all fields of civil aviation among its 191 Member States."
Roundtable on Sustainable Biofuels (RSB)	"The RSB is an international multi-stakeholder initiative that brings together farmers, companies, non-governmental organizations, experts, governments, and inter-governmental agencies concerned with ensuring the sustainability of biofuels production and processing."
Sustainable Aviation Fuel Users Group (SAFUG)	The SAFUG was formed in September 2008 with support and advice from the world's leading environmental organizations such as the Natural Resources Defense Council and the Roundtable on Sustainable Biofuels (RSB). The group is focused on accelerating the development and commercialization of sustainable aviation biofuels."
World Green Aviation Council (WGAC)	"The WGAC is a not-for-profit Environmental Organization that offers Fly-360-Green™ Accreditation to Airlines, Airports and Corporations for their sustainability efforts around the world. Its mission is to foster the international standard for sustainable aviation through cutting-edge technological advancements while also taking into consideration aviation's absolute emissions which are constantly on the rise despite various pro-environmental actions taken by stakeholders."

audit, nominating/governance[2] and compensation committees. However, some boards have more than three committees, the most common being executive committees and finance committees, as well as committees that focus on specific areas, such as environment and risk. In the case of the airline industry, corporate boards often establish safety committees.

Committees with a focus on social and environmental issues generally oversee company programs and performance in dealing with these issues and how they may affect their reputation. These committees are often known as "corporate social responsibility" or "public affairs" committees. Ricart *et al.* (2005) have reported that Dow Jones Sustainability World Index companies are more likely to create stakeholder-oriented board-level committees. However, this is not the case for Air France-KLM, which Dow Jones Sustainability World Index ranked as the leader in the transport category in 2013 for the fifth consecutive year. Air France-KLM's board of directors has nevertheless three permanent committees: the audit committee, the appointment committee and the compensation committee. According to the internal regulations posted on Air France-KLM website, the corporate board may sometimes create "ad hoc" committees. As illustrated in Figure 11.2, environment-related issues at Air France-KLM are brought directly to the full board.

The approach is slightly different at Cathay Pacific, which was included in the Dow Jones Sustainability Index for the first time in 2013. As illustrated in Figure 11.3, Cathay Pacific's existing board committees assume these responsibilities and the board's management committee also gets involved in sustainability-related issues.

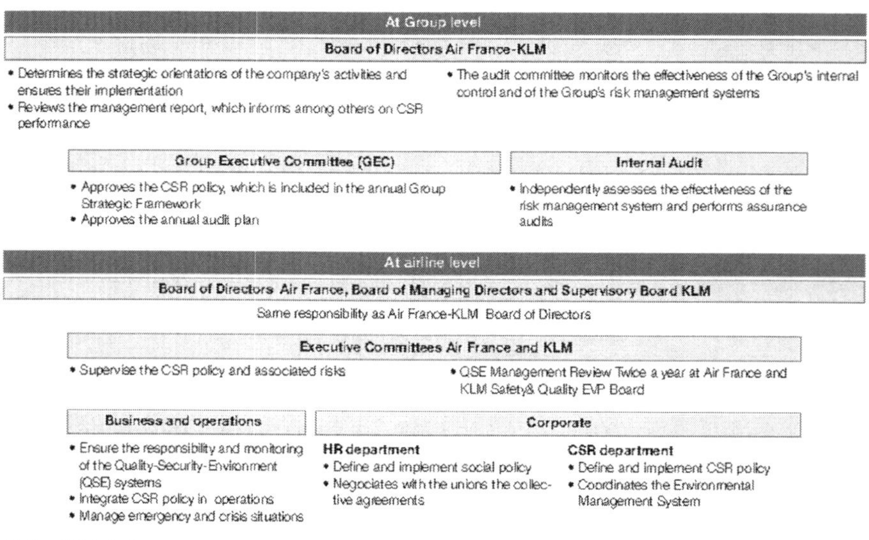

Figure 11.2 Air France-KLM.

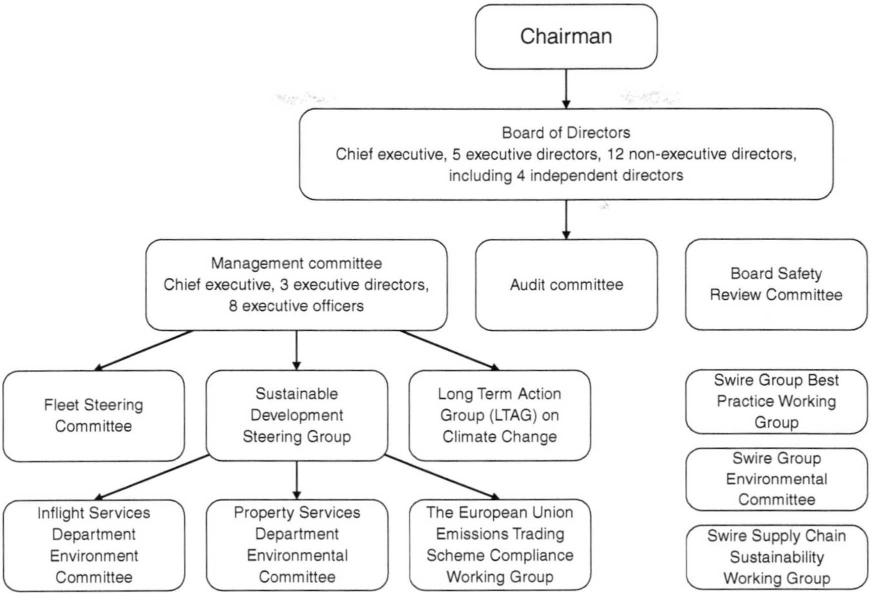

Figure 11.3 Cathay Pacific.

The board of Alaska Airlines has established a safety committee whose responsibilities include the periodical review of all aspects of airline safety, including health, safety and environmental policies. Air Canada's board has also given additional responsibilities to its audit, finance and risk committee, which is in charge of reviewing the corporate policies, procedures and reports regarding environmental matters.

There are advantages to the creation of committees with specific social responsibilities. First, committees can enhance legitimacy and corporate accountability to stakeholders (Harrison, 1987). The creation of sub-committees can also send a clear message about a firm's commitment to corporate social performance matters (Davidson and Worrell, 2001). A second advantage resides with the formalization of initiatives toward improved social performance, thus creating valuable institutional memory about these issues (Addy, 2006). However, while some studies have found a positive link between the existence of these committees and social performance (Ricart *et al.*, 2005), others have cast some doubt upon this connection. Indeed, McKendall *et al.* (1999) found that companies that created board-level committees did not reduce the occurrence of illegal corporate behavior. Carson (2002) has reported that board-level committees may indeed be formed to promote the appearance of good corporate governance without serving any useful purpose. Furthermore, these committees may impose an additional layer of bureaucracy that may lead to duplication, wasted effort and useless additional monitoring. Also, supporting board-level committees costs money, uses precious director time, takes additional effort away from other initiatives and puts demands on the limited attention of senior management (Addy, 2006; Charan, 2005). Such findings call for a thorough examination of the inner workings of social committees and potential problems that can impede a committee's efficacy.

As indicated in Table 11.2, some airlines do have committees focusing on environmental and social issues. The review of the charters of the committees listed on Table 11.2 indicates that they are involved in various activities such as

Table 11.2 Airline board committee's responsibilities

United Continental: Public Responsibility Committee Charter	The purpose of the Committee is to review the Company's policies and positioning with respect to social responsibility and public policy.
	The Committee shall oversee management's identification, evaluation and monitoring of the social, political and environmental trends, issues and concerns, domestic and international, that affect or could affect the Company's reputation, business activities and performance or to which the Company could make a meaningful contribution.
China Eastern: Aviation Safety and Environmental Committee	Major Responsibilities: include implementing laws and regulations related to national aviation safety and environment protection, inspecting and supervising aviation safety management, researching and discussing the planning of aviation safety measures, advising and supervising the implementation of safety measures, inspecting and supervising important issues concerning carbon emissions of domestic and international aviation, and advising and supervising implementation of environmental measures.
Thai Airlines: Corporate Social Responsibility Committee	The Corporate Social Responsibility Committee will provide counseling and guidance in supporting THAI CSR activities. The Committee shall establish policies and set directives to conduct social responsibility that aims to promote green environment though its Travel Green project.
Westjet: SH&E Committee	The SH&E Committee monitors compliance with the Corporation's safety, health and environmental principles (the Principles), recommends policies and programs to maximize compliance with the Principles, periodically reviews the Principles, and reviews various metrics for quantifying and evaluating compliance with the Principles, and identifying areas for improvement.
Quantas: Safety, Health, Environment & Security Committee	The Committee is responsible for the review and monitoring of safety, health, environment, security and risk management strategies, systems, policies and processes implemented, and reported on, by Qantas Management.

reviewing social issues, monitoring compliance and establishing policies and standards. These various activities reveal different types of committee involvement that can be connected with the monitoring and advisory roles of directors. As such, they are aligned with the inherent dual roles of directors: control and advisory (Adams and Ferreira, 2007; Anderson *et al.*, 2007; Sundaramurthy and Lewis, 2003). Whereas the advisory role focuses on the review and formulation of policies and programs, the monitoring role focuses on the level of compliance of these policies and programs with regulatory requirements or internal objectives.

Airline initiatives to improve environmental performance

Numerous types of initiatives are designed and implemented by airline companies in the hope of improving their environmental performance. These initiatives can be classified in five broad categories: green procurement, aircraft design and maintenance, air traffic management, scheduling (optimizing load factors) and fuel efficiency (including biofuel). They will be reviewed in what follows.

Green procurement practices

Interesting examples of green procurement practices can be found at Virgin America and Cathay Pacific. Virgin America favors local or closely located suppliers in order to reduce its transportation costs, use less fuel and, as a result, reduce its carbon footprint. In its 2009 *Climate and Sustainability Report*, the company indicated that it uses environmentally responsible office materials that are purchased in consolidated shipments to reduce procurement costs. Examples of other green practices are also listed in the 2009 report (Virgin America, 2009):

- orders for computers, equipment and software processed through a local company;
- hot and cold cups for guests are fully recyclable and made from 50 percent recycled material;
- on-board pillow weight reduced from 3.5 ounces to 3 ounces to lessen packaging and carbon footprint of shipping;
- headsets for purchase to reduce the number of free headsets that are given away and disposed of after one use;
- blanket-cleaning program allows blankets to be reused up to ten times (with cleanings) before being disposed.

Some airline companies have established codes of conduct for their suppliers. For example, Cathay Pacific expects its suppliers to have an effective system in place to measure and report on their environmental impact. As explained in Cathay's Supply Chain Sustainability Code of Conduct, suppliers should demonstrate that they are making formal efforts to limit the impact of their operations on the environment and that they are cautious with regards to environmental matters. The carrier claims to have "a strong preference for suppliers whose goods or services can make a significant difference to reducing their environmental impact."[3] Suppliers who wish to do business with Cathay Pacific need to complete a detailed questionnaire that the carrier uses to evaluate the extent to which the supplier is in compliance with its Supplier Code of Conduct. Selected suppliers will have to sign a contract requiring them to continue to conform to Cathay Pacific's social and environmental standards.

Aircraft design and maintenance

There is no doubt that the main reason why airlines harm the natural environment is because they operate aircraft. It is therefore not surprising that considerable attention is placed on aircraft design and maintenance. In a document written in preparation for the 27th Round Table on Sustainable Development held at its headquarters in 2012, the OECD argued that the technical improvements of their fleet constitute one of the main carbon abatement options for airlines. The use of lighter-weight materials for the structure and any other components, the addition of winglets to the tips of wings and the improvement of engine fuel efficiency were identified as promising avenues. The OECD also noted aircraft makers do share airlines' motivation to reduce environmental damage:

> With the rising price of jet fuel, all of the major suppliers in the aviation sector are exploring every technical option to improve aircraft performance. They have a large incentive to do so, as these technical improvements lead to lower costs for their customers and provide them with a real advantage in an extremely competitive market.
>
> (OECD, 2012: 16)

Older aircraft that were constructed before sustainability became a major concern often contribute to the poor environmental performance of air carriers. It is always possible to retrofit existing aircraft with new engines, but, as noted by the OECD, this is a "high-cost abatement option with a low total greenhouse gas abatement potential" compared to the construction of brand new aircraft because of the places where lighter material can be applied are somewhat limited (OECD, 2012: 17).

Air traffic management

While the decisions that are taken when aircraft are designed have a significant impact on their fuel efficiency and overall environmental performance, the way air traffic is managed can also favor higher environmental performance of the aircraft while they are in operation. Creating fuel-efficient flight paths with fewer changes in altitude and direction is a promising avenue. However, according to the OECD more efforts are needed in this area: "In European airspace alone there are thousands of daily flights. Airlines and air traffic controllers are not currently in a position to optimize flight paths to drive reductions in fuel use and greenhouse gas emissions" (OECD, 2012: 15). There is hope that the next generation of satellite-based air traffic management (ATM) systems will rely on high-performance computers able to process a large amount of data. Progress, however, is somewhat slow. In the United States the development of the Next Generations Air Transportation System (or NextGen), which was expected to be operational between 2012 and 2025, is slowing down due to public spending cuts. Those in charge of the NextGen programs were told to "right-size" it and review priorities.[4] Europe is also working on its own next-generation traffic control system which in known as the Single European Sky ATM Research initiative or SESAR. Illustrating the lack of integration and the fragmented nature of air traffic control, given that country sovereignty encompasses airspace, Central European countries such as Austria, Bulgaria, Lithuania, Poland and Slovenia have recently signed the "Gate One" cooperation agreement, creating a regional entity that will have a "stronger voice" with regard to air traffic control.[5] When they are implemented the next-generation satellite-based ATM systems will generate a marginal cost of carbon abatement of €109.2 per ton CO_2-eq and the total abatement will be 21.9 million ton CO_2-eq (OECD, 2012: 15). This projection from the International Centre for Trade and Sustainable Development (ICTSD) might take longer than expected to become reality, and the 2020 time horizon appears to be rather optimistic.

Table 11.3 presents examples of companies who have implemented both aircraft and ATM-related initiatives and publicized them on their websites. Although airlines take pride in green ATM initiatives, this is a domain that is largely beyond their control as it is mainly in the hands of air navigation service providers, airports, country aviation authorities and, to some extent, vocal unions protecting air controllers.

Green departures

It is well known that aircraft consume a considerable amount of fuel during take-off and landing. ATAG has reported that some airlines and airports are currently experimenting with "green departures." While traditionally aircraft climb to the cruising altitudes in several steps, green departures method enables pilots to take-off and "climb to the optimal cruising altitude in one smooth, continuous ascent." ATAG claims that this method resulted in savings of 10,000 tons of fuel and 32,000 tons of carbon dioxide in one year at Copenhagen Airport (Aviation/Benefits Beyond Borders, 2010).

In a similar vein, Virgin's Climate and Sustainability Report comments on "RNAV departures," a technique that enables jets to climb more quickly to an altitude where they are more fuel efficient (Virgin America, 2009: 12). RNAV, which is an acronym for "area navigation," is a navigation system that can greatly improve airport traffic flow and therefore contributes to reduced carbon emissions.

Table 11.3 Aircraft and ATM-related initiatives

	Aircraft design and maintenance	*ATM*
ANA	ANA's most effective measure to reduce hazardous exhaust emissions from aircraft has been to deploy the latest, most advanced aircraft equipped with state-of-the-art engines. Emissions of aircraft currently in use at the ANA Group are all within ICAO emission standards stipulated in Annex 16.	The ANA Group began official operations of RNAV in 2002. RNAV navigation is a procedure that navigates aircraft and assures the scheduled flight path by radio navigation facilities as well as by satellite and on-board equipment. Not only does RNAV achieve faster and shorter flights while reducing fuel consumption and CO_2 emissions, it also reduces noise around airports. The ANA Group aims to expand the use of RNAV in Japan and overseas.
China Eastern	The Company ensures the mechanical functionality of its fleet by eliminating and surrendering the lease of old aircraft and introducing newer aircraft on an annual basis, in addition to repair and replacement of engines and routine maintenance works. In 2011 the Company eliminated certain old aircraft models through disposal, introduction of new aircraft and replacement. A younger fleet helps to boost the efficiency of jet fuel consumption.	The Company strives to facilitate the implementation of the DOC (Direct Operation Control) system in the Company and optimize long-haul routes by implementing information management of route segments. By selecting the most economical route from several routes, the Company reduced the flying time of flights and thus effectively lowered fuel consumption. The annual saving of jet fuel was about 34,200 tonnes.
Quantas	The Group is investing in newer, more fuel efficient aircraft. This is a highly effective way of improving fuel efficiency. The fuel efficiency and lower emissions technology of newer aircraft will contribute significantly to the Group achieving the fuel efficiency target by 2020.	Implementation of advanced navigational aircraft technology, enabling procedures such as Required Navigation Performance (RNP) to find the most fuel efficient flight path
AER Lingus	On an ongoing basis, engines are monitored, maintained and overhauled to maximise fuel efficiency and minimise emissions, and environmental upgrades are added on overhaul where available. This engine conditioning monitoring aims to give advance warning of impending deterioration of parts, allowing for preventative maintenance which contributes to ensuring efficient engines and therefore has both emission control and fuel burn benefits.	Continuous Descent Approaches (CDAs) are now performed wherever possible

Scheduling and route management

Managing and scheduling routes is also an important lever airline companies can use to improve their environmental performance through higher load factors. Indeed, higher load factors means that each passenger's footprint is reduced because total emissions are divided among the number of passengers on board. Fewer occupied seats means a larger share is assigned to each person. For example, in their 2010–2011 environmental and social report, JetBlue proudly claimed that they scheduled their aircraft near capacity and, unlike many airlines, avoid using overbooking strategies: "By ensuring our aircraft are more fully loaded before adding segments to a market, we maximize the value of our assets and minimize the intensity of our GHG emissions."[6] Norwegian also addressed this issue in its 2012 annual report, mentioning that their business model based on high load factors and higher capacity per flight resulted in lower emissions per passenger, therefore more environmentally sustainable operations. The carrier even claimed, rather boldly, that their emissions per passenger kilometer were "well below the industry average and less than many forms of land and sea-based transportation."[7]

Fuel management

According to ATAG, airlines spent $140 billion on fuel in 2010, representing 26 percent of their operating cost (Aviation/Benefits Beyond Borders, 2010). Whereas labor cost was traditionally the largest expenditure for airlines, the cost breakdown of the average $506.62 Los Angeles to New York City 2010 flight fare indicated that $95.33 went to labor and $97.85 was allocated to fuel, according to IATA.[8] Needless to say, the high volatility of fuel prices in recent years was a strong motivator for airlines to reduce their fuel consumption or to look for new energy sources, such as biofuels.

The Beginner's Guide to Aviation Biofuels published by ATAG in 2009 is an indication of the growing interest for aviation biofuels. This guide explains that these fuels "are produced from renewable biological resources such as plant material (rather than traditional fossil fuels like coal, oil and natural gas)" (ATAG, 2009). The cycle of absorption and release is described as follow: biofuels "absorb carbon dioxide from the atmosphere as the plant matter (biomass) is grown, which is then released back into the atmosphere when the fuel is burnt" (ATAG 2009: 2) According to the literature, biofuel seems to be one of the most promising green activities in terms of CO_2 emission reductions. Researches are currently trying to make biofuel economically viable as costs are lowered by improvements in production technology and through economies of scale in production. ATAG reported that transport, home heating, power generation from stationary engines and cooking have used first-generation biofuels for a number of years. However, these fuels do not yet offer the necessary safety and performance attributes necessary to be used for jet engines. Some critics have also voiced their concerns about the fact that biofuels compete for resources with food supplies. Fortunately, this is not the case with second-generation biofuels that could be used for air transportation. These fuels include bio-derived oil obtained from feedstocks such as halophytes, algae, camelina and jatropha. These sources could potentially deliver considerable quantities of greener aviation fuel. Second-generation biofuels can be grown at a large scale in varied locations such as deserts and in salt water. They could therefore be available at more stable prices.

In a written document created in 2009 to outline their views and actions in favor of a low-carbon aviation industry, Virgin Airlines noted that improvements to fuel and air traffic management efficiency could result in an overall efficiency gain of 1.5 percent per annum, although significant technology challenges remains for this gain to be achieved. Furthermore, building on the Intergovernmental Panel on Climate Change (IPCC) 1999 Special Report on Aviation and the Global Atmosphere,[9] the airline added that "more dramatic initiatives like sustainable biofuels are needed because these efficiency gains will be outstripped by a projected industry growth of up to 4% per annum" (Virgin Group, 2009).

As disclosed on their websites, many airline companies are involved in research efforts regarding biofuels. For example, Cathay Pacific indicates that they are working with the Sustainable Aviation Fuel Users Group (SAFUG) "to accelerate the commercialization of sustainable jet fuel, including subscribing to a set of sustainability criteria to ensure that these biofuels do not compete with food and drinking water supplies, biodiversity and local populations." Similarly, United Airlines is working with the Commercial Aviation Alternative Fuels Initiative (CAAFI) to identify near- and longer-term alternatives to petroleum-based fuels. Another example can be found on All Nippon Airways' (ANA) website, where the company proudly announced that they conducted the world's first transpacific flight in an aircraft operating on biofuel:

> A delivery flight for a Boeing 787, the flight used conventional jet fuel containing a 15% mixture of biofuel derived mainly from used cooking oil. Through the synergy of the cutting-edge, low-environmental impact Boeing 787 and the biofuel, the flight achieved a 30% reduction in CO2 compared with the Boeing 767.

The airline also commented on its participation in a biofuel development group with Boeing and other organizations. The objective of this group is to put alternative aviation biofuels into use by 2020.

Environmental management systems

In the previous section we examined some of the initiatives airlines have been designing to reduce the environmental impacts of their activities. To help them implement their environmental strategies and to ensure that green practices are integrated into a cohesive plan, companies in various industrial sectors rely on environmental management systems (EMS). EMS provide a rigorous and systematic method to integrate environmental issues into the organization's decision-making process. The system contains appropriate data and tools to translate the company's environmental mission and policies into an action plan with objectives and procedures for evaluating progress toward them. It also serves to motivate employees to join in the effort towards the achievement of the environmental performance objectives.

Asiana Airlines, Singapore Airlines and Korean Air are using environmental management systems as illustrated in Figure 11.4. These EMS include elements related to the organizational structure, planning activities, responsibilities, practices, procedures, processes and resources for developing, implementing, achieving, reviewing and maintaining the environmental policy.

Several airlines are using EMS. These EMS include elements related to the organizational structure, planning activities, responsibilities, practices, procedures, processes and resources for developing, implementing, achieving, reviewing and maintaining the environmental policy. As illustrated in Figure 11.4, Korean Air's EMS translates as a dynamic process through which plans are formulated and regularly updated as a result of external influence and internal monitoring activities.

As highlighted in this EMS illustration, the implementation process of the airline environmental strategy relies on the airline's ability to identify an appropriate set of measures for each action undertaken. Indeed, as carriers implement new programs to improve their environmental performance, they must clearly

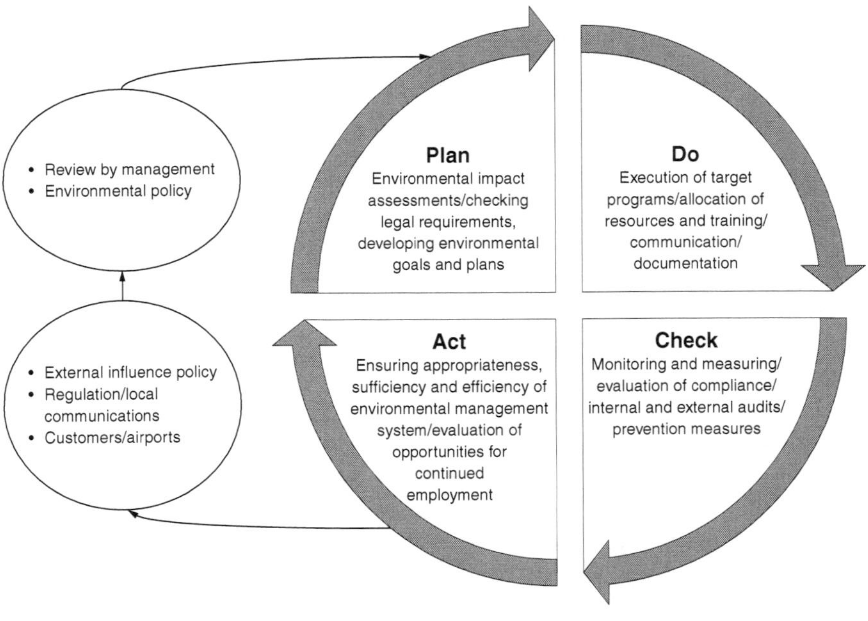

Figure 11.4 Korean Air's EMS (source: Korean Air, "2013 Sustainability Report: Sustaining Excellence").

Table 11.4 All Nippon Airlines environmental performance targets

Item		*Target*
Climate change countermeasures	Reduce CO_2 emissions from aircraft fuel	Unit target For 2021, achieve a 20 percent reduction in CO_2 emissions per revenue ton-kilometer compared with the fiscal year ended March 2006. Total target
		For the fiscal year ending March 2013 through March 2021, keep annual CO_2 emissions on domestic routes below 4.4 million tons
	Reduce ground energy	Reduce energy use at all work sites by 1 percent each year
	Introduce aircraft biofuel	Conduct a study toward the start of full-scale use of aircraft biofuel during ANA FLY ECO 2020
Air pollution countermeasures	Conform with aircraft emission standards	All aircraft, including leased aircraft, to conform to chapter 4 of ICAO emission standards
	Introduce low-pollution vehicles	Actively introduce hybrid, electric and other low-pollution vehicles, and study the use of biofuel
Noise countermeasures		All aircraft, including leased aircraft, to conform to chapter 4 of ICAO noise standards.
Resource savings		Reduce waste and promote paperless operations Promote 3R activities, including closed recycling of in-flight magazines and other items
Environmental contribution activities for local communities		Enhance environmental education activities through Team Tyura Sango coral regeneration project Conduct forestation that provides new value to communities and society

define goals and targets, compare these to actual performance, and measure progress. Examples of airlines' environmental performance targets are presented in Table 11.4 and Figure 11.5. Measurement is indeed critically important because it links performance to the strategy and allows performance to be continuously improved. Airlines can then compare these indicators to actual performance and measure success. Aviation managers must be constantly using feedback to challenge their assumptions regarding the viability of various decisions and their long-term implications for both the airline and society.

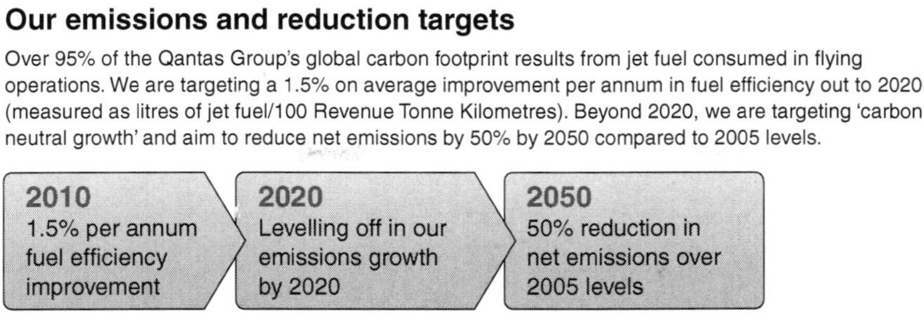
Our emissions and reduction targets

Over 95% of the Qantas Group's global carbon footprint results from jet fuel consumed in flying operations. We are targeting a 1.5% on average improvement per annum in fuel efficiency out to 2020 (measured as litres of jet fuel/100 Revenue Tonne Kilometres). Beyond 2020, we are targeting 'carbon neutral growth' and aim to reduce net emissions by 50% by 2050 compared to 2005 levels.

Figure 11.5 Qantas environmental performance targets (source: www.qantas.com.au/travel/airlines/climate-change/global/en).

Airlines' environmental commitment and financial performance

In this section we will examine what the driving factors toward better environmental management in the aviation industry are. The case study of Scandinavian Airlines has allowed Lynes and Dredge (2006), quoted by Chen (2013), to identify five followed primary drivers that shaped the airline's commitment to environmental management: (1) the financial cost–benefit of environmental management; (2) the regulatory setting; (3) the desire to be a "good corporate citizen"; (4) the airline image; and (5) relationships with the aviation community. Several sustainability researchers have indicated that, across various industrial sectors, the most prominent driving forces that influence a company's decision to adopt environmental management practices are rising environmental legislation, concern over liability and direct and indirect costs of regulatory compliance (Haddock-Fraser and Tourelle, 2010; Delmas and Montiel, 2009; Delmas and Toffel, 2008; Kassinis and Vafeas, 2006; Christmann and Taylor, 2002). These factors demonstrate that companies are still somewhat coerced to examine these environmental issues. This is far from surprising. Indeed, there is still a perception of negative financial costs associated with implementing (environmental management) policies (Coles *et al.*, 2009). Virgin, however, had been trying to encourage players in the aviation industry to "change the mindset that running a business in a responsible and sustainable way means sacrificing growth and profits" (Virgin, 2011). The company also argues that "by continuously trying to lead the debate, raising the bar, challenging our competitors and lobbying governments, we can make sustainable businesses a reality as well as being economically beneficial" (Virgin, 2010).

There is a growing literature that examines the financial payoffs of social and environmental investments. Although evidence on this relationship is not clear, leading airlines companies have nevertheless recognized that sustainability principles are important for long-term corporate profitability and are paying more attention to these issues. However, understanding how social performance relates to shareholder value and identifying which practices provide the greatest net benefits to both companies and society is certainly a major challenge in the formulation of a sustainability strategy (Hillman and Keim, 2001; King and Lenox, 2002; Martin, 2002; McWilliams and Siegel, 2001). To implement their environmental strategy, companies are faced with the enormous challenge of quantifying the link between corporate actions and social and financial performance. In their report, Cathay Pacific underscore the difficulties associated with this process:

> Whilst it has not always been a simple matter to find environmentally sound solutions that are both operationally and economically feasible, the continuing quest to do so has provided new opportunities for innovation and lateral thinking. Through the resourcefulness, creativity and dedication of our staff and with the cooperation of our business partners, we have been able to build the case for adopting many of these initiatives – some small, some more significant – and they are now adding value to the business, as well as bringing positive benefits to the community and environment.
>
> (Cathay Pacific, 2012)

Unfortunately, companies in many industrial sectors, aviation included, have not focused on quantifying the link between environmental initiatives and financial performance and have not made the business case for corporate social responsibility. Instead, they act in socially responsible ways because they believe it is "the right thing to do." However, programs put in place solely for this reason are vulnerable because they are subject to the whim of swaying public priorities, changes in senior management and financial cycles. Furthermore, airline executives certainly relate more to issues of long-term profitability and value creation than unclear and emotional discussions of social and environmental issues.

In order to present a clear business case, airline managers need to identify the drivers of social performance and how that performance impacts overall long-term corporate profitability. This increased attention to a thorough identification and measurement of the drivers of performance is echoed in popular management frameworks like balanced scorecard and value-based management. Frameworks such as these focus on a better understanding of the causal relationships and linkages within organizations and the actions managers can implement to improve both customer and corporate profitability (Epstein and Westbrook, 2001; Kaplan and Norton, 2000).

An appropriate set of measures should be developed so that managers can quantify how one element drives another until the link to ultimate corporate financial performance is clear. They need concrete metrics to evaluate and monitor performance on both the intermediate and final goals of improving corporate social, environmental and economic performance. When examining company reports, we found that many airline companies have quantified fuel savings stemming from environmental initiatives. For example:

> In 2010, [Southwest Airlines] completed the installation of winglets on the 102 eligible 737-300 aircraft. [The airline] estimates that these winglet

> installations are resulting in annual fuel savings of more than six million gallons. Southwest Airlines' fleet of 737-700 aircraft is also equipped with winglets. Overall, winglets on aircraft in the Southwest Airlines fleet are responsible for an estimated annual fuel savings of more than 42 million gallons.
>
> (Southwest Airlines, 2011)

Also, in a 2011 press release, Virgin America announced that it had selected CFM International's advanced LEAP™ engine to power 30 new Airbus A320 Neo aircraft scheduled for delivery in 2016:

> Together, the A320neo and the LEAP™ engine promise to deliver one of the world's most fuel-efficient commercial aircraft, with more than 15 percent improved fuel efficiency, corresponding improvements in carbon efficiency and double digit reductions in NOx emissions. Virgin America estimates this will deliver a fuel cost savings to the carrier of $1.9 million per aircraft per year.
>
> (Virgin America, 2011)

In order to quantify the link between environmental and financial performance, companies must map carefully and explicitly the corporate model and underlying assumptions motivating environmental performance improvements. By assigning a strategic value to environmental performance, airlines are placing a bet that improving performance will lead to increased profits. For example, senior managers might believe that a given set of explicit management actions can lead to improved environmental performance, which will enhance the company's reputation and encourage travelers to fly on this airline. This increased market share should then lead to increased long-term profitability. Alternatively, the desire for improved environmental performance may be driven by cost or liability-reduction goals, long-term responsiveness to market trends, or a variety of assumptions relating improved environmental and social performance to improved business performance.

As we suggested, airline managers need to better understand the implications of their decisions and the levers they can pull to improve both their environmental performance and long-term financial performance. Some airlines have already recognized the significant value that can be added by the identification and measurement of environmental impacts into business decisions, particularly for environmental expenditures. Though improvements toward environmental performance are admittedly often driven by regulatory requirements, an increasing number of airlines are noticing that decreased operating costs and higher revenues are frequently the result of such initiatives.

Conclusion

The pressure toward a greener air transportation system is exerted by society as a whole, but also by the institutional environment comprising various trade and interest groups such as ATAG, ICAO and IATA. In this chapter we have seen that the response to this pressure can be observed at various levels in airline companies. Airlines' corporate boards play a role in the greening of aviation, most visibly through the establishment of sustainability committees. Air carriers have put in place a number of environmental initiatives as well as environmental management systems that favor a systematic approach to achieving precise environmental performance targets. Furthermore, as discussed above, demonstrating the value of environmental initiatives in terms of increased revenues and long-term financial performance, if not survival, is a key driver of airlines' environmental commitment: "By most accounts, the core of [environmental management] rests in the assumption that environmental responsibility leads to an improved bottom-line through long-term efficiency and image-related rewards" (Uecker-Mercado and Walker, 2012: 3)

There is some evidence that the airline industry is on the right environmental path. IATA has recently argued that air transport is one of the rare industrial sectors to have committed to ambitious carbon reduction targets. The association appears confident that the four "pillars" on which its strategy is based – (1) new technology, (2) more efficient operations, (3) better infrastructure and (4) positive economic measures – will have positive results. IATA proudly insists on the fact that the key actors of the air transport supply chain, including airlines, airports, air navigation service providers and aircraft manufacturers are all involved in the coordination of this four-pillar strategy (IATA, 2013). Virgin Airlines' 2009 and 2010 sustainability reports illustrated this commitment. The airlines claimed that investment in new aircraft has resulted in a fleet considered to be 25 percent more carbon efficient than the US average. Virgin's technology and operational improvements include: "minimizing use of auxiliary power units, single engine taxiing, idle reverse landings, utilizing advanced avionics to fly more efficiently, and cost index flying – the practice of regulating cruising speed to reduce fuel burn" (Virgin America, 2009: 5) The carrier seems to play the role of the green cheerleader, enjoining all aviation stakeholders to "work together" (Virgin, 2010: 22) and specifically highlighting the important role of aircraft manufacturers on which the aviation industry mainly relies to reduce its carbon emissions.

It is important to keep in mind that although there is a considerable range of initiatives to reduce aviation greenhouse gas emissions, the expected growth in air transport demand in years to come could very well offset the positive impact of these initiatives. As noted by the OECD,

> the expected growth in Asia alone will mean efforts to improve flight paths, the addition of winglets to the tips of aircraft wings, more efficient taxiing of aircraft and ongoing improvements to the fuel efficiency of jet engines will all be overtaken by the dramatic increase in flights and passenger miles.
> (OECD, 2012: 1)

While the OECD suggested that biofuels might be the only greenhouse gas abatement opportunity available to counterbalance the negative environmental impact of air transport demand growth, it could be argued that the world population might eventually be forced to return to a more sedentary lifestyle to protect the natural environment.

Notes

1 @enviroaero on Twitter.
2 Nominating/governance committees nominate candidates when positions become available.
3 http://downloads.cathaypacific.com/cx/CSR/CSR_Code_of_Conduct.pdf.
4 www.airtrafficmanagement.net/2013/10/nextgen-executives-told-to-rightsize-and-review/.
5 www.ainonline.com/aviation-news/ain-air-transport-perspective/2013–11–25/eastern-central-european-ansps-align-stronger-voice.
6 www.jetblue.com/p/ERS-091412.pdf.
7 http://annualreport.norwegian.no/2012/board_of_director_s_report/pdf.
8 http://money.cnn.com/magazines/fortune/storysupplement/airline_costs/.
9 www.ipcc.ch/pdf/special-reports/spm/av-en.pdf.

References

Adams, R.B. and D. Ferreira. 2007. A Theory of Friendly Boards, *The Journal of Finance* 62: 217–250.

Addy, J.A. 2006. View from the Boardroom: Corporations and Public Responsibility. John F. Kennedy School of Government, Harvard University, Cambridge, MA. Available at: www.ksg.harvard.edu/m-rcbg/CSRI/publications/studentpaper_1_Addy.pdf [accessed November 14, 2013].

Air Nippon. 2013. Medium-term Targets and Results. Available at: www.anahd.co.jp/en/csr/environment/objective.html [accessed April 13, 2013].

Anderson, D.W., S.J. Melanson and J. Maly. 2007. The Evolution of Corporate Governance: Power Redistribution Brings Boards to Life, *Corporate Governance: An International Review*, 15: 780–797.

ATAG. 2009. Beginner's Guide to Aviation Biofuels. Available at: www.cphcleantech.com/media/2450696/beginnersguide.pdf [Accessed February 24, 2013].

Aviation/Benefits Beyond Borders. 2010. Environmental Efficiency: Aviation's Global Environmental Profile in 2010. Available at: http://aviationbenefitsbeyondborders. org/environmental-efficiency/overview [Accessed February 26, 2013].

Business Roundtable, 2005. Principles of Corporate Governance, 2005. Business Roundtable. Available at: www.ibm.com/ibm/governmentalprograms/pdf/BRT CorpGov-Principles2005.pdf [Accessed December 16, 2013].

Carson, E. 2002. Factors Associated with the Development of Board Sub-Committees, *Corporate Governance: An International Review*, 10: 4–18.

Cathay Pacific 2012. Cathay Pacific CSR Code of Conduct. Available at: http://downloads.cathaypacific.com/cx/CSR/CSR_Code_of_Conduct.pdf [Accessed February 26, 2013].

Charan, R. 2005. *Boards that Deliver*. San Francisco, CA: Jossey-Bass.

Chen, F.Y. 2013. Managers' Views on Environmental Management: An Examination of the Taiwanese Airline Industry. *Journal of Sustainable Development*, 6: 65–75.

Christmann, P. and G. Taylor. 2002. Globalization and the Environment: Strategies for International Voluntary Environmental Initiatives. *The Academy of Management Executive*, 16: 121–135.

Coles, T., C. Dinan and E. Fenclova. 2009. Corporate Social Responsibility: Issues for Future Development in the Low-Fares Airlines Sector. Centre for Sport, Leisure and Tourism Research, University of Exeter.

Davidson, W.N.I. and D.L. Worrell. 2001. Regulatory Pressure and Environmental Management Infrastructure and Practices. *Business and Society*, 40: 315–342.

Delmas, M. and I. Montiel. 2009. Greening the Supply Chain: When is Customer Pressure Effective? *Journal of Economics & Management Strategy*, 18: 171–201.

Delmas, M. and M.W. Toffel. 2008. Organizational Responses to Environmental Demands: Opening the Black Box. *Strategic Management Journal*, 29 (10): 1027–1055.

Epstein, M.J. and R.A. Westbrook. 2001. Linking Actions to Profits in Strategic Decision Making, *MIT Sloan Management Review* (Spring): 39–49.

Haddock-Fraser, J.E. and M. Tourelle. 2010. Corporate Motivations for Environmental Sustainable Development: Exploring the Role of Consumers in Stakeholder Engagement. *Business Strategy and the Environment*, 19: 527–542.

Hall, R.F., T.P. Keane, C. McConnell and S. Becker. 2005. The 21st Century Board: Structure, Responsibility, Assessment. *Journal of Leadership & Organizational Studies*, 11: 62–71.

Harrison, J.R. 1987. The Strategic Use of Corporate Board Committees. *California Management Review*, 30: 109–125.

Hillman, A.J. and G.D. Keim. 2001. Shareholder Value, Stakeholder Management, and Social Issues: What's the Bottom Line. *Strategic Management Journal*, 22: 125–139.

IATA. 2013. Annual Review 2012. Available at: www.iata.org/about/Documents/annual-review-2012.pdf [Accessed February 24, 2013].

ICAO. 1999. Air Transport Bureau. Environment Branch – Aircraft Engine Emissions. Available at: http://legacy.icao.int/env/aee.htm [Accessed February 26, 2013].

JetBlue 2011. Environmental and Social Report. Available at: http://annualreport.norwegian.no/2012/board_of_director_s_report/pdf [Accessed February 24, 2013].

Kaplan, R.S. and D.P. Norton. 2000. *The Strategy-Focused Organization: How Balanced Scorecard Companies Thrive in the New Business Environment*, Cambridge, MA: Harvard Business School Press.

Kassinis, G. and N. Vafeas. 2006. Stakeholder Pressures and Environmental Performance. *Academy of Management Journal*, 49: 145–159.

King, A. and M. Lenox. 2002. Exploring the Locus of Profitable Pollution Reduction, *Management Science*, 48: 289–299.

Lynes, J.K and D. Dredge. 2006. Going Green: Motivations for Environmental Commitment in the Airline Industry: A Case Study of Scandinavian Airlines. *Journal of Sustainable Tourism*, 14: 116–138.

Martin, R.L. 2002. The Virtue Matrix: Calculating the Return on Corporate Responsibility, *Harvard Business Review* (March): 68–75.

McCurry, J. 2012. Striving for a greener alternative. *Air Cargo World*, 102: 40–46.

McKendall, M., C. Sanchez and P. Sicilian. 1999. Corporate Governance and Corporate Illegality: The Effects of Board Structure on Environmental Violations. *International Journal of Organizational Analysis*, 7: 201–223.

McWilliams, A. and D. Siegel. 2001. Corporate Social Responsibility: A Theory of the Firm. *Academy of Management Review*, 26: 117–127.

Norwegian Air Shuttle. 2012. The Board of Directors' Annual Report. Available at: http://annualreport.norwegian.no/2012/board_of_director_s_report/pdf [Accessed February 24, 2013].

OECD. 2012. Green Growth and the Future of Aviation. Paper prepared for the 27th Round Table on Sustainable Development.

Qantas. 2013. Qantas Sustainability Review 2012. Available at: www.qantas.com.au/infodetail/about/investors/qantas-sustainability-review-2012.pdf [Accessed February 20, 2013].

Ricart, J.E., M.Á. Rodríguez and P. Sánchez. 2005. Sustainability in the Boardroom: An Empirical Examination of Dow Jones Sustainability World Index Leaders. *Corporate Governance*, 5: 24–41.

Schofield, A. 2009. Japan Signs on to Green Flight Program. *Aviation Daily*, 378: 5–7.

Southwest Airlines. 2011. We Conserve Jet Fuel, Ground Support Equipment Fuel, Electricity, and Water to Reduce our Impact on the Planet. Available at: www.southwestone-report.com/2011/#!/planet/energy-and-resource-use/energy-and-resource-conservation [Accessed February 17, 2013].

Sundaramurthy, C. and M. Lewis. 2003 Control and Collaboration: Paradoxes of Governance', *Academy of Management Review*, 28: 397–415.

Uecker-Mercado, H. and M. Walker. 2012. The Value of Environmental Social Responsibility to Facility Managers: Revealing the Perceptions and Motives for Adopting ESR. *Journal of Business Ethics*, 110: 269–284.

Virgin. 2009. Aviation in a Low Carbon World. Available at: www.virgin.com/unite/business-innovation/aviation-low-carbon-world [Accessed February 23, 2013].

Virgin. 2010. Virgin Group's Corporate Responsibility and Sustainable Development Report. Available at: www.virgin.com/unite/business-innovation/virgin-groups-corporate-responsibility-and-sustainable-development-report [Accessed February 23, 2013].

Virgin. 2011. People & Planet: Governance. Available at: www.virgin.com/people-and-planet/governance [Accessed February 10, 2013].

Virgin America. 2009. Climate and Sustainability Report. Available at: www.virginamerica.com/html/Virgin_America_Climate_&_Sustainability_Report_2009.pdf [Accessed December 17, 2013].

Virgin America. 2011. Virgin America Leaps into the Future as Launch Customer for New CFM Engine. Available at: www.virginamerica.com/press-release/2011/Virgin-America-Leaps-Into-the-Future-As-Launch-Customer-for-New-CFM-Engine.html [Accessed February 23, 2013].

Index

Page numbers in *italics* denote tables, those in **bold** denote figures.